THE

COMPLETE WORKS

OF

EDWARD PAYSON, D. D.

MEMOIR,

SELECT THOUGHTS

AND

SERMONS

OF THE LATE

REV. EDWARD PAYSON, D. D.

PASTOR OF THE SECOND CHURCH IN PORTLAND.

BENE ORASSE EST BENE STUDUISSE.—LUTHER.

COMPILED BY

REV. ASA CUMMINGS,

EDITOR OF THE CHRISTIAN MIRROR.

IN THREE VOLUMES.—VOL. II.

PHILADELPHIA:

PUBLISHED BY J. L. GIHON,

NO. 409 CHESTNUT STREET.

1858.

CONTENTS.

SERMON XVI.

SERMON XVII.

SERMON XVIII.

SERMON XIX.

SERMON XX.

SERMON XXI.

SERMON XXXI.

SERMON XXXII.

SERMON XXXIII.

SERMON XXXIV.

SERMON XXXV.

SERMON XXXVI.

SERMON XXXVII.

SERMON XXXVIII.

SERMON XXXIX.

SERMON XL.

SERMON XLI.

SERMON XLII.

SERMON XLIII.

SERMON XLIV.

SERMON XLV.

SERMON XLVI.

SERMON XLVII.

SERMON XLVIII.

SERMON I.

THE BIBLE ABOVE ALL PRICE.

Preached before the Bible Society of Maine, May 5, 1814.

THERE are two objects which a speaker who addresses his fellow-beings on an occasion like the present, ought ever to keep in view. Of these objects, the first, and with respect to his hearers, the most important is, to induce them to prize as it deserves a volume, which, notwithstanding its unrivalled claims to attention, is too generally neglected. The second is, to procure their assistance in gratuitously distributing this volume among their destitute fellow-creatures. These objects, though distinct, are intimately connected; for if we can be induced suitably to prize the Sacred Scriptures ourselves, there will be little difficulty in persuading us to aid in communicating them to others; and there is but too much reason for presuming that he, who is not desirous to impart this treasure to all around him, knows nothing of its real value, nor of the temper which it is designed to produce.

With respect to a part, and we trust a very considerable part, of the present assembly, the objects which we have mentioned may be considered as already attained. There are, we doubt not, many before us, who entertain a profound veneration for the Bible; and in whose breasts it has an advocate, who pleads its cause, and that of the destitute, far more powerfully and successfully than we can do. To such persons nothing need be said in favor of a book, which not only affords them support and consolation under the troubles of life, but enables them to contemplate death with pleasure, and, to borrow its own language, makes them "wise unto salvation." If all present are of this description, our object is obtained, and farther remarks are needless. But it is presumable that, in every assembly, many are to be found, who, through inattention to the subject, or from some other cause, have formed very inadequate conceptions of the worth of this volume, and who consequently do not feel the infinite importance of putting it into the hands of others. It is also notorious, that even among such as profess to venerate the scriptures, there are not a few who seem to regard them as deficient in those qualities which excite interest and attention. It may not be improper therefore, on an occasion like the present, to make a few remarks with a design to show, that while the scriptures are incalculably valuable and important, viewed as a revelation from heaven, they are also in a very high degree interesting and deserving of attention, considered merely as a human composition. As the whole volume of scripture will form the subject of these remarks, it was thought unnecessary to select any particular part of it as a text.

Were we permitted to adduce the testimony of the scriptures in their own favor, as a proof that their contents are highly interesting, our task would be short, and easily accomplished. But it is possible that, to this testimony, some might think it a sufficient reply, to apostrophize the sacred volume in the language of the captious Jews to our Savior;—"Thou bearest record of thyself; thy record is not true." No similar objection can be urged however, against our availing ourselves of the testimony which eminent uninspired men have borne in favor of the scriptures. From the almost innumerable testimonies of this nature, which might easily be adduced, we shall select only that of Sir William Jones, a Judge of the supreme court of judicature in Bengal—a man, says his learned biographer, who, by the exertion of rare intellectual talents, acquired a knowledge of arts, sciences, and languages, which has seldom been equalled, and scarcely, if ever, surpassed. "I have carefully and regularly perused the scriptures," says this truly great man, "and am of opinion, that this volume, independent of its divine origin, contains more sublimity, purer morality, more important history, and finer strains of eloquence, than can be collected from all other books, in whatever language they may have been written." How well he was qualified to make this remark, and how much it implied in his lips, may be inferred from the fact that he was acquainted with twenty-eight different languages, and with the best works which had been published in most of them. That a volume, which in the opinion of such a man, is thus superior to all other books united, cannot be so insipid and uninteresting a composition as many seem to imagine, it must be needless to remark. That his praises, though great and unqualified, are in no respect unmerited, it would be easy, were it necessary, to prove by appropriate quotations from the book which he so highly extols. But its morality will be more properly considered in a subsequent part of this discourse; and its unrivalled eloquence and sublimity are too obvious, and too generally acknowledged, to require illustration. If any imagine that he has estimated too highly, the historical information which this volume contains, we would only request them to peruse it with attention, and particularly to consider the assistance which it affords in accounting for many otherwise inexplicable phenomena, in the natural, political, and moral world. A person who has never attended to the subject, will, on recollection, be surprised to find for how large a proportion of his knowledge he is indebted to this neglected book.* It is the only book which satisfactorily accounts, or even professes to account, for the introduction of natural and moral evil into the world, and for the consequent present situation of mankind. To this book we are also indebted for all our knowledge of the progenitors of our race, and of the early ages of the world;—for our acquaintance with the manners and customs of those ages;—for the origin and explanation of many remarkable traditions, which have extensively prevailed, and for almost every thing which is known, of many once flourishing nations; especially of the Jews, the most singular and interesting people perhaps, that ever existed. It is the Bible alone, which by informing us of the deluge, enables us to account satisfactorily, for many surprising appearances in the

* It will be recollected, that we here refer to such information only as uninspired men might communicate.

internal structure of the earth, as well as for the existence of marine exuviæ on the summits of mountains, and in other places far distant from the sea. By the same volume we are assisted in accounting for the multiplicity of languages which exist in the world; for the degraded condition of the Africans; for the origin and universal prevalence of sacrifices; and many other facts of an equally interesting nature. We shall only add, that while the scriptures throw light on the facts here alluded to, the existence of these facts powerfully tends, on the other hand, to establish the truth and authenticity of the scriptures.

In addition to these intrinsic excellencies of the Bible, which give it, considered merely as a human production, powerful claims to the attention of persons of taste and learning, there are various circumstances, of an adventitious nature, which render it peculiarly interesting to a reflecting mind. Among these circumstances we may, perhaps not improperly, mention its great antiquity. Whatever may be said of its inspiration, some of the books which compose it are unquestionably the most ancient literary compositions extant, and perhaps the most ancient that ever were written; nor is it very improbable that letters were first employed in recording some parts of them, and that they were written in the language first spoken by man. It is also not only the most ancient book, but the most ancient monument of human exertion, the eldest offspring of human intellect, now in existence. Unlike the other works of man, it inherits not his frailty. All the cotemporaries of its infancy have long since perished and are forgotten. Yet this wonderful volume still survives. Like the fabled pillars of Seth, which are said to have bid defiance to the deluge, it has stood, for ages, unmoved in the midst of that flood which sweeps away men, with their labors, into oblivion. That these circumstances render it an interesting object of contemplation, it is needless to remark. Were there now in existence a tree which was planted; an edifice which was erected; or any monument of human ingenuity which was formed, at that early period, in which some parts of the Bible were written, would it not be contemplated with the keenest interest, carefully preserved as a precious relic, and considered as something little less than sacred? With what emotions then, will a thoughtful mind often open the Bible; and what a train of interesting reflections is it, in this view, calculated to excite?—While we contemplate its antiquity, exceeding that of every object around us, except the works of God, and view it, in anticipation, as continuing to exist unaltered until the end of time, must we not feel almost irresistibly impelled to venerate it, as proceeding originally from him, who is yesterday, to-day, and forever the same, and whose works, like his years, fail not?

The interest which this volume excites by its antiquity will be greatly increased, if we consider the violent and persevering opposition it has encountered, and the almost innumerable enemies it has resisted and overcome. We contemplate, with no ordinary degree of interest, a rock which has braved for centuries the ocean's rage, practically saying, "Hitherto shalt thou come, but no farther; and here shall thy proud waves be stayed." With still greater interest, though of a somewhat different kind, should we contemplate a fortress which, during thousands of years, had been constantly assaulted by successive generations of enemies;—around whose walls millions had perished;—and to overthrow which, the utmost efforts of human force and ingenuity had been excited in vain. Such a rock, such a fortress, we contemplate in the Bible. For thousands of years this volume has withstood, not only the iron tooth of time, which devours men and their works together, but all the physical and intellectual strength of man. Pretended friends have endeavored to corrupt and betray it; kings and princes have perseveringly sought to banish it from the world; the civil and military powers of the greatest empires have been leagued for its destruction; the fires of persecution have often been lighted to consume it, and its friends together; and at many seasons, death, in some horrid form, has been the almost certain consequence of affording it an asylum from the fury of its enemies. It has also been almost incessantly assailed by weapons of a different kind, which, to any other book, would be far more dangerous than fire or sword. In these assaults, wit and ridicule have wasted all their shafts; misguided reason has been compelled, though reluctantly, to lend her aid, and after repeated defeats, has again been dragged to the field; the arsenals of learning have been emptied to arm her for the contest; and in search of means to prosecute it with success, recourse has been had, not only to remote ages and distant lands, but even to the bowels of the earth, and the region of the stars. Yet still the object of all these attacks remains uninjured, while one army of its assailants after another has melted away. Though it has been ridiculed more bitterly, misrepresented more grossly, opposed more rancorously, and burnt more frequently, than any other book, and perhaps than all other books united, it is so far from sinking under the efforts of its enemies, that the probability of its surviving until the final consummation of all things is now evidently much greater than ever. The rain has descended; the floods have come; the storm has arisen, and beat upon it; but it falls not, for it is founded upon a rock. Like the burning bush, it has ever been in the flames, yet is still unconsumed; a sufficient proof, were there no other, that He who dwelt in the bush preserves the Bible.

If the opposition which this volume has successfully encountered renders it an interesting object of contemplation; the veneration which has been paid to it, the use which has been made of it, and the benefits which have been derived from it by the wise and good, in all ages, make it still more so. Who would not esteem it a most delightful privilege to see and converse with a man who had lived through as many centuries as the Bible has existed; who had conversed with all the successive generations of men, and been intimately acquainted with their motives, characters, and conduct; who had been the chosen friend and companion of the wise and good in every age—the venerated monitor, to whose example and instructions the wise had ascribed their wisdom, and the virtuous their virtues? What could be more interesting than the sight, what more pleasing and instructive than the society of such a man? Yet such society we may in effect enjoy, whenever we choose to open the Bible. In this volume, we see the chosen companion, the most intimate friend of the prophets, the apostles, the martyrs, and their pious cotemporaries; the guide, whose directions they implicitly followed; the monitor, to whose faithful warnings and instructions they ascribed their wisdom, their virtues, and their happiness. In this volume, we see the book in which the deliverer, the king, the sweet psalmist of Israel delighted to meditate, day and night; whose counsels made him wiser than all his teachers; and which he describes as sweeter than honey, and more precious than gold. This too is the book, for the sake of which our pious ancestors forsook their native land and came to this then desolate wilderness; bringing it with them, as their most valuable treasure, and at death, bequeathing it to us, as the richest bequest in their power to make. From this source, they, and millions more now in heaven, derived the strongest and purest consolation; and scarcely can we fix our attention on a single passage in this wonderful book, which has not afforded comfort or instruction to thousands, and been wet with tears of penitential sorrow or grateful joy, drawn from eyes that will weep no more. There is probably not an individual present, some of whose ancestors did not, while on earth, prize this volume more than life, and breathe many fervent prayers to heaven that all their descendants, to the latest generation, might be induced to prize it in a similar manner. Thousands, too, have sealed their belief of its truth with their blood; rejoicing to shed it in defence of a book, which, while it led them to the stake, enabled them to triumph over its tortures. Nor have its effects been confined to individuals. Nations have participated largely in its benefits. Armed with this volume, which is at once sword and shield, the first heralds of Christianity went forth conquering and to conquer. No less powerful than the wonder working rod of Moses, its touch crumbled into dust the temples of paganism, and overthrew, as in a moment, the immense fabric of superstition and idolatry which had been for ages erecting. To this volume alone it is owing that we are not now assembled in the temple of an idol; that stocks and stones are not our deities; that cruelty, intemperance and impurity do not constitute our religion; and that our children are not burnt as sacrifices at the shrine of Moloch. To this volume we are also indebted for the reformation in the days of Luther; for the consequent revival and progress of learning; and for our present freedom from papal tyranny. Nor are these benefits, great as they are, all which it has been the means of conferring on man. Wherever it comes, blessings follow in its train. Like the stream which diffuses itself, and is apparently lost among the herbage, it betrays its course by its effects. Wherever its influence is felt, temperance, industry, and contentment prevail; natural and moral evils are banished, or mitigated; and churches, hospitals, and asylums for almost every species of wretchedness, arise to adorn the landscape, and cheer the eye of benevolence. Such are the temporal benefits which even infidelity itself, if it would for once be candid, must acknowledge that the Bible has bestowed on man. Almost coeval with the sun, its fittest emblem, it has, like that luminary, from the commencement of its existence, shed an unceasing flood of light on a benighted and wretched world. Who then can doubt that He, who formed the sun, gave the Bible to be "a light to our feet, and a lamp to our path?" Who, that contemplates this fountain, still full and overflowing, notwithstanding the millions who have drank of its waters, can doubt that it has a real, though invisible connection with that river of life, which flows forever at the right hand of God?

Thus far we have considered the Bible as merely a human composition, though, as was unavoidable, some rays of divinity have from time to time burst through the cloud in which we vainly attempted to shroud it. But if it be in this view thus valuable and interesting, in what language shall we describe the importance it assumes, when viewed as a revelation from God;—as the book which has guided millions of immortal beings to heaven; as the book which must guide us there, if we ever reach those mansions of eternal day! That it is so, we shall not at present attempt to prove. In addressing such an assembly, on such an occasion, we have a right to take it for granted—to proceed on the supposition, that you believe with the apostle that "all scripture is given by inspiration of God." Viewed in this light, what finite mind can estimate its worth, or describe the reverence and attention with which it ought to be regarded? The ancient Greeks had one sentence, which they believed, though without foundation, to have descended from heaven; and to evince their gratitude and veneration for this gift, they caused it to be engraven, in letters of gold, on the front of their most sacred and magnificent temple. We, more favored, have not a sentence only, but a volume, which really descended from heaven; and which, whether we consider its contents, or its Author, ought to be indelibly engraven on the heart of every child of Adam. Its Author is the author of our being; and its contents afford us information of the most satisfactory and important kind, on subjects of infinite consequence; respecting which all other books are either silent, or speak only doubtfully and unauthoritatively. It informs us, with the greatest clearness and precision, of every thing necessary either to our present or future happiness;—of every thing, in fact, which its Author knows, the knowledge of which would be really useful to us; and thus confers those benefits, which the tempter falsely pretended would result from eating the forbidden fruit; making us as gods, knowing good and evil. In the fabulous records of pagan antiquity, we read of a mirror endowed with properties so rare, that by looking into it, its possessor could discover any object which he wished to see, however remote; and discern with equal ease, persons and things above, below, behind, and before him. Such a mirror, but infinitely more valuable than this fictitious glass, do we really possess in the Bible. By employing this mirror in a proper manner, we may discern objects and events, past, present, and to come. Here we may contemplate the all-enfolding circle of the Eternal mind, and behold a most perfect portrait of Him, whom no mortal eye hath seen, drawn by his own unerring hand. Piercing into the deepest recesses of eternity, we may behold Him existing independent and alone, previous to the first exertion of His creating energy. We may see heaven, the habitation of His holiness and glory, "dark with the excessive brightness" of his presence; and hell, the prison of his justice, with no other light than that which the fiery billows of his wrath cast, "pale and dreadful," serving only to render "darkness visible." Here too, we may witness the birth of the world which we inhabit;—stand as it were by its cradle, and see it grow up from infancy to manhood, under the forming hand of its Creator. We may see light at his summons starting into existence, and discovering a world of waters without a shore. Controlled by His word, the waters subside, and islands and continents appear, not, as now, clothed with verdure and fertility, but sterile, and naked as the sands of Arabia. Again he speaks; and a landscape appears, uniting the various beauties of spring, summer, and autumn; and extending farther than the eye can reach. Still all is silent; not even the hum of insects is heard, and the stillness of death pervades creation; till, in an instant, songs burst from every grove; and the startled spectator, raising his eyes from the carpet at his feet, sees the air, the earth, and the sea, filled with life and activity, in a thousand various forms. Here too, we may contemplate the origin and infancy of our race;—trace from its source to its termination that mighty river, of which we compose a part; and see it separating into two great branches; one of which flows back in a circle, and loses itself in the fountain whence it arose; while the other rushes on impetuously in an opposite direction, and precipitates itself into a gulf which has no bottom. In this glass, we may also discover the fountain, whence flow those torrents of vice and wretchedness which deluge the earth; trace the glorious plan of Divine providence running, like a stream of lightning, through the dark and stormy cloud of sublunary events; and see light and order breaking in upon the mighty chaos of crimes, revolutions, wars and convulsions, which have ever distracted the world; and which, to a person unacquainted with the scriptures, must ever appear to produce no beneficial effect; but to succeed each other without order, and to happen without design. Here too, we may contemplate ourselves, in every conceivable situation and point of view;—see our hearts laid open, and all their secret recesses displayed;—trace as on a map, the paths which lead to heaven and to hell; ascertain in which we are walking; and learn what we have been, what we are, and what we shall be hereafter. Above all, we may here see displayed to view, that wonderful scheme for the redemption of self-destroyed man, into which "angels desire to look;" and without which the knowledge of God, and of ourselves, would serve only to plunge us in the depths of despair. We may behold Him, whom we had previously seen creating the world, lying as a helpless infant in a manger; expiring in agonies on the cross; and imprisoned in the tomb. We may see Him rising—ascending to heaven—sitting down "at the right hand of the throne of the Majesty on high;" and there swaying the sceptre of universal empire, and ever living to make intercession for his people. Finally, we may see Him coming in the clouds of heaven, with power and great glory, to judge the world. We may see the dead, at His command, rising from their graves;—standing in awful silence and suspense before His tribunal;—and successively advancing, to receive from His lips, the sentence which will confer on each of them an eternal weight of glory, or consign them forever to the mansions of despair. Such are the scenes and objects, which the scriptures place before us;—such the information which they afford. Who will deny that this information is important; or that it is such as we might naturally expect to find in a revelation from God?

Equally important to the present, and future happiness of man, are the precepts which the scriptures inculcate. With the greatest clearness and precision; and with an authority, to which no other book can pretend, they teach us our duty to God, to our fellow-creatures, and to ourselves. That spiritual kingdom, whose laws they promulgate, consists in "righteousness, and peace, and joy in the Holy Ghost;" and were these laws universally obeyed, nothing but righteousness, peace, and holy joy, would be found on earth. Should any one deny this, after perusing them attentively, it would prove nothing, but the weakness of his understanding, or the depravity of his heart. They require us to regard God with filial, and our fellow-creatures with fraternal affection. They require rulers to "be just; ruling in the fear of God;" and subjects to "lead quiet and peaceable lives in all godliness and honesty." They require the husband to "love the wife even as himself;" and the wife "to reverence her husband." They require parents to educate their children "in the nurture and admonition of the Lord;" and children to love, honor, and obey their parents. They require masters to treat their servants with kindness; and servants to be submissive, diligent, and faithful. They require of all, temperance, contentment, and industry; and stigmatize, as worse than an infidel, him who neglects to provide for the necessities of his family. They provide for the speedy termination of animosities and dissensions, by requiring us to forgive and pray for our enemies, whenever we pray for ourselves; and to make reparation to all whom we may have injured, before we presume to appear with our offerings in the presence of God. In a word, they teach us, that "denying ungodliness, and worldly lusts, we should live soberly, righteously and godly, in this present world; looking for that blessed hope, and the glorious appearing of the great God and our Saviour, Jesus Christ." These duties they require us to perform, with constancy and perseverance, on penalty of incurring the everlasting displeasure of our Creator, and its dreadful consequences.

In addition to these instructions and precepts, the scriptures furnish us with the most instructive examples—examples, which most plainly and convincingly teach us, both what we must shun, and what we are to pursue. On every rock, where immortal souls have been wrecked;—at the entrance of every path which leads to danger, they show us some self-destroyed wretch, standing like a pillar of salt, to warn succeeding travellers not to approach it; while at the gate, and in the path of life, they place many divinely instructed and infallible guides, who lead the way, beckon us to follow, and point to the happy mansions, in which it ends. Knowing how powerfully we are influenced by the example of those with whom we associate, it introduces us to the society of the most amiable and excellent of our species; makes us perfectly acquainted with their characters and pursuits; admits us into, not only their closets, but their hearts; unveils to us all their secret springs of action; and shows us the hidden source whence they derived wisdom and strength to subdue their sinful propensities, and overcome the world. By opening this volume, we may at any time walk in the garden of Eden with Adam; sit in the ark with Noah; share the hospitality, or witness the faith of Abraham; ascend the mount of God with Moses; unite in the secret devotions of David; or listen to the eloquent and impassioned addresses of St. Paul. Nay more, we may here converse with Him, who spoke as never man spake; participate with the spirits of the just made perfect, in the employments and happiness of heaven; and enjoy sweet communion with the Father of our spirits, through his Son, Jesus Christ. Such is the society, to which the scriptures introduce us;—such the examples, which they present to our imitation; requiring us to follow them, "who through faith and patience, inherit the promises;" to walk in the steps of our divine Redeemer; and to be "followers of God, as dear children."

Nor does this precious volume contain nothing but instructions, precepts, examples, and threatenings. No, it contains also "strong consolation;"—consolation suited to every possible variety and complication of human wretchedness; and of sufficient efficacy to render the soul, not only resigned, but joyful in the lowest depths of adversity;—not only tranquil, but triumphant in the very jaws of death. It is the appointed vehicle, by which the Spirit of God, the promised Comforter, communicates not only his instructions, but his consolations to the soul. It is, if I may so express it, the body which he assumed, in order to converse with men; and he lives and speaks in every line. Hence it is said to "be quick," or living, "and powerful." Hence its words "are spirit, and they are life;"—the living, life-giving words of the living God. The consolation which it imparts, and the blessings which it offers, are such as nothing but omnipotent goodness can bestow. It finds us guilty; and freely offers us pardon. It finds us polluted with innumerable defilements; and offers us moral purity. It finds us weak and enslaved; and offers us liberty. It finds us wretched; and offers happiness. It finds us dead; and offers everlasting life. It finds us "having no hope and without God in the world," with nothing before us, "but a certain, fearful looking for of judgment and fiery indignation;" and places glory, and honor, and immortality, full in our view; and while it urges us to pursue them, by the exercise of faith in the Redeemer, and "patient continuance in well doing," it encourages and animates us in the pursuit, by the most condescending offers of assistance, and "exceedingly great and precious promises;" promises signed by the immutable God, and sealed with the blood of his eternal Son; promises which, one would think, are sufficient to render indolence active; and timidity bold. Unfailing pleasures; durable riches; immortal honors; imperishable mansions; an unfading crown; an immovable throne; an everlasting kingdom; an eternal weight of glory; perfect, uninterrupted, never-ending, perpetually increasing felicity, in the full fruition of God, are the rewards, which these promises assure to all penitent believers. But in vain do we attempt to describe these rewards; for "Eye hath not seen, nor ear heard, neither have entered into the heart of man the things, which God hath prepared for them that love him."

Such are the circumstances, which render the Bible interesting as a human composition;—such the instructions, precepts, and promises, which it communicates as a revelation from God.

And in proportion to the importance of its contents, are the evils which would result from its absence or loss. Destroy this volume, as the enemies of human happiness have vainly endeavored to do; and you render us profoundly ignorant of our Creator; of the formation of the world which we inhabit; of the origin and progenitors of our race; of our present duty, and future destination; and consign us, through life, to the dominion of fancy, doubt and conjecture. Destroy this volume; and you rob us of the consolatory expectation excited by its predictions, that the stormy cloud which has so long hung over a suffering world, will at length be scattered and a brighter day succeed;—you forbid us to hope that the hour is approaching, when nation shall no more lift up sword against nation; and righteousness, peace, and holy joy, shall universally prevail; and allow us to anticipate nothing, but a constant succession of wars, revolutions, crimes, and miseries, terminating only with the end of time. Destroy this volume; and you deprive us, at a single blow, of religion, with all the animating consolations, hopes, and prospects which it affords; and leave us nothing but the liberty of choosing,—miserable alternative!—between the cheerless gloom of infidelity, and the monstrous shadows of paganism. Destroy this volume; and you unpeople heaven; bar forever its doors against the wretched posterity of Adam; restore to the king of terrors his fatal sting; bury hope in the same grave which receives our bodies; consign all who have died before us, to eternal sleep, or endless misery; and allow us to expect nothing at death, but a similar fate. In a word, destroy this volume; and you take from us, at once, every thing, which prevents existence from becoming, of all curses, the greatest. You blot out the sun; dry up the ocean; and take away the atmosphere of the moral world; and degrade man to a situation, from which he may look up with envy to "the brutes that perish." Who then would not earnestly wish to believe the scriptures, even though they came to him, unattended with sufficient evidence of their divine origin? Who can be so much his own enemy, as to refuse to believe them, when they come attended with evidence, more than sufficient to satisfy all but the wilfully incredulous? Who, in this view of them, imperfect as it is, is prepared to say, that they are not of all books the most important; that they ought not to be prized and studied as such, by all who possess them; and put, without delay, into the hands of all who do not? Were this inestimable treasure in the exclusive possession of any individual, would you not consider him as the most malevolent of beings, if he neglected to communicate it, as soon as possible, to his fellow-creatures? And if he were a stranger to the use of the press, would not the common feelings of humanity require him to spend whole nights, as did a wealthy merchant in the East, in transcribing it for their use? What possible excuse then, can we assign, for neglecting to distribute this treasure, when the press affords us the means of doing it at so trifling an expense? Will it be said, that few, or none of our fellow-citizens are destitute? It is a fact, within the knowledge of this society, that the deficiency of Bibles in this District, to say nothing of other places, is far greater, than they are able to supply. Will it be said, that none are destitute of the sacred volume, but in consequence of their own fault; and that they are therefore unworthy to receive such a gift? Admitting this to be the case, which in many instances, however, it is not, is this an excuse for neglecting them, which it becomes *us* to assign? Had God adopted such a rule in the distribution of his favors;—had he bestowed the Bible on none but the deserving; who among ourselves should ever have been favored with it? Will it be said, that the other wants of the poor are so numerous and pressing, that nothing can be spared for the supply of this? But what other want can be so pressing, so deserving of immediate attention, as that of the Bible? In what other way can we, at an equal expense, do so much to alleviate the miseries, and promote, I will not say the eternal, but even the temporal happiness of the poor, as by putting into their hands a book, which contains such a mass of the most valuable and important information?—which is so eminently calculated to render them better, and consequently happier, in all the relations of life; which teaches them, "in whatever state they are therewith to be content;" and to look for the relief of their necessities to Him who "hears the young ravens when they cry;" and to whom they will never look in vain, while they take this precious volume for their guide. Were they experimentally acquainted with the worth of this volume, they would themselves feel the want of it to be the first, the most pressing of wants. Send us any famine, they would cry, but "a famine of the word of God." Keep your wealth; enjoy your possessions; give us but the Bible to smooth the path of life, and the bed of death; and we will envy none their possessions, but living, and dying, will bless you; though we should perish with hunger. Such *is* the language of the pious poor. Such, were it not for their vices or their ignorance, would be the language of all the poor; and who will deny, that their vices and ignorance render it still more necessary, that they should be put in immediate possession of the Bible? In requesting you to assist in supplying them with it, this Society does not so much solicit you to confer a favor, as to share in a privilege;—the privilege of uniting with the pious and benevolent in all parts of the world, in the noble design of distributing the scriptures; and the still more enviable privilege of becoming "workers together with God," in diffusing the knowledge of Himself, and His will. With what has been already done; with what is now doing for the promotion of this God-like design, you are in some measure acquainted. You are not ignorant, that societies for the gratuitous distribution of the scriptures, have been formed in all parts of the world; and that new societies, for the same purpose, are constantly forming. By the members of these various societies nearly a million of dollars was contributed during the past year; more than four hundred thousand dollars of which, were received by the British and Foreign Bible Society alone. To aid the efforts of these societies, not only have kings and princes lent their influence, and the rich opened their treasures; but the widow has cast in her two mites; the child has presented all his little hoard; servants have given a third part of their annual wages; and more than one military corps have offered a certain proportion of their pay. In consequence of these astonishing and unprecedented exertions, the sacred scriptures, or at least parts of them, have already been printed and circulated in upwards of forty different languages and dialects. Shall we then be idle, while all ranks and denominations are thus actively engaged in this glorious work? While Britons, Russians, Swedes, Polanders, Germans, Swiss, Italians, Greeks, Africans, and Indians, are employed in diffusing the scriptures, shall Americans alone do nothing? Or shall we be last and least among Americans in favoring and promoting such a design?

It is with no small reluctance we are obliged to confess, that in this rank, a very considerable part of this District may justly be placed. All that has been done here, has been done by comparatively a few. We speak with confidence, when we assert, that among all the societies which have been formed for the distribution of the scriptures, in our own or in other countries, not one can be found which has received assistance so disproportionate to what might have been reasonably expected, as this. And to what is the existence of this disgraceful fact to be ascribed? Are the inhabitants of this District less religious, —do they value the Bible less,—or their property more than others? This, we presume, you will not feel disposed to allow. Shall we not then, do all in our power, to wipe off so foul a stain from this section of our country? Shall we give our destitute countrymen regret, that they were not born in any other part of the world, where they would have been supplied with the scriptures, rather than in this Christian land? Shall the eye of Omniscience, while it surveys the globe, find here the only spot, where the water of life is not permitted to flow freely;—where the cry of the poor for Bibles is disregarded; and thus be provoked to take from us a gift, of which we seem not to know the worth? There is reason to believe, that unless we speedily and diligently exert ourselves, this will be the case. He "who cannot lie" has declared, that "the knowledge of the Lord shall fill the earth as the waters cover the seas." The period in which this prediction will be fully accomplished, is now evidently and rapidly approaching. The greatest of those obstacles, which once opposed its fulfilment, are already removed or overcome; and it is more than probable that before very many years have elapsed, there will be scarcely a human habitation on earth, unless indeed it be among ourselves, in which the Bible will not be found. Let us then engage as one man, in hastening the arrival of this glorious and long expected day. Let us give wings to the Bible. Let us guide this life-giving stream into every abode and cottage in our wilderness. And permit us to express a hope, that your assistance in promoting this design, will not be confined to the present occasion; but that you will aid our exertions, by becoming active members of this society. Above all, while engaged in conveying the Bible to others, let us beware of neglecting it ourselves. Let us bind it to our hearts as our most valuable treasure; study it with that reverence and attention which its character demands, and submit implicitly to its decisions, as to "the lively oracles of God." Thus we shall be impressed with a conviction, far more strong and abiding than any external evidence can produce, *That all scripture is given by inspiration of God, and is profitable for doctrine, for reproof, for correction, and instruction in righteousness; that the man of God may be perfect, thoroughly furnished unto all good works.* Thus shall we be enabled by our own experience, to feel and adopt the language of the Psalmist, "*The law of the Lord is perfect, converting the soul; the testimony of the Lord is sure, making wise the simple. The statutes of the Lord are right, rejoicing the heart; the commandment of the Lord is pure, enlightening the eyes. More to be desired are they than gold; yea than much fine gold; sweeter also than honey, or the honey-comb. Moreover by them is thy servant warned, and in keeping of them there is great reward.*"

SERMON II.

GOD'S WAYS ABOVE MEN'S.

For my thoughts are not your thoughts, neither are your ways my ways, saith the Lord. For as the heavens are higher than the earth, so are my ways higher than your ways, and my thoughts than your thoughts.—Isa. lv. 8, 9.

In the preceding verses God commands and invites sinners to repent and embrace his offers of mercy. "Ho, every one that thirsteth, come ye to the waters, and he that hath no money; come ye, buy and eat; yea, come, buy wine and milk, without money and without price. Let the wicked forsake his way, and the unrighteous man his thoughts; and let him return unto the Lord, and he will have mercy upon him; and to our God, for he will abundantly pardon." He was however aware, that the natural unbelief, the guilty fears and narrow views of sinners, would lead them to distrust these promises, and to turn the unspeakable good which they offer into an argument against their truth. He therefore proceeds in our text, to caution them against judging of him by themselves, and measuring his thoughts and ways by their own dark, confused and limited conceptions. "My thoughts are not your thoughts, neither are your ways my ways. For as the heavens are higher than the earth, so are my ways higher than your ways, and my thoughts than your thoughts." To illustrate the truth of this declaration, and to notice some particular instances in which it is strikingly manifest, is my present design.

1. God's ways and thoughts must be far above ours, because in situation and office he is exalted far above us. God is in

heaven, and we upon earth. We occupy the footstool, and he the throne. As the Creator and Preserver, he is of course, the rightful Governor of the universe. All worlds, creatures and events are subject to his control, and he is under a blessed necessity of overruling and conducting all things in such a manner, as to promote, in the highest possible degree, his own glory and the universal good. In forming and executing his purposes therefore, he must take into view not only the present, but past and future circumstances and events; not the concerns of a single individual only, but those of the whole race of beings in heaven, earth, and all the worlds around us. Now consider a moment, the extent and duration of Jehovah's kingdom. Think of the innumerable armies of heaven; the perhaps scarcely less numerous hosts of hell; the multitudes of the human race, who have existed, who now exist, and will hereafter exist on earth before the end of time. Then raise your eyes to the numerous suns and worlds around us. Borrow the telescope of the astronomer, and penetrating far into unfathomable recesses of the etherial regions, see new suns, new worlds still rising into view. Consider that all we can discover is perhaps but a speck, a single sand on the shore, in comparison with what remains undiscovered; that all these innumerable worlds are probably inhabited by immortal beings, and that God's plan of government for this boundless empire must embrace eternity; —consider these things, and then say whether God's purposes, thoughts, and ways, must not necessarily be high above ours, as the heavens are above the earth, or as his sphere of action exceeds ours. Must not the thoughts and ways of a powerful earthly monarch be far above those of one of his subjects, who is employed in manufacturing a pin, or cultivating a few acres of ground? Can such a subject be competent to judge of his sovereign's designs, or even to comprehend them? How far then must the thoughts and ways of the eternal monarch of heaven, the King of kings, and Lord of lords, exceed ours; and how little able are we to judge of them, farther than the revelation which he has been pleased to give, enables us.

2. God's thoughts and ways must be infinitely above ours, because his nature and perfections raise him infinitely above us. He is a self-existent, independent, all-sufficient, infinite, eternal, pure, and perfect intelligence. We are dependent, finite, imper-

fect, frail, dying creatures, fettered by gross, heavy bodies, and exposed to the influence of innumerable infirmities, temptations and prejudices, which bias and blind our reason. But more particularly, God is infinitely superior to us in wisdom. He is the all-wise God. Even the foolishness of God, says the apostle, is wiser than men; and the angels, who are far above us in wisdom, are in comparison with him, chargeable with folly. He must therefore, be able to devise a thousand plans and expedients, and to bring good out of evil in numberless ways, of which we never could have conceived, and of which we are by no means competent to judge, even after they are revealed to us. If the ways and thoughts of a wise man are above those of a fool, how much more must the ways and thoughts of the all-wise God exceed ours.

Again. God is infinitely superior to us in knowledge. We are of yesterday and know nothing; our foundation is in the dust. We have little real knowledge of present objects and events; and of the future we are entirely ignorant, except so far as God has been pleased to reveal it. But God perfectly knows all things. He has a perfect knowledge of the properties and qualities of all creatures; for he made them what they are, and upholds them. He knows everything that is now taking place in the universe; for he is everywhere present. He knows every thing that ever has occurred, or that ever will occur; for we are told that he sees the end from the beginning; that he calls things that are not as though they were; and that known unto God are all his works from the beginning. At a single glance he looks through eternity and immensity, and takes into view at once, the whole circle of existence. That this perfect knowledge must cause his thoughts and ways to be infinitely above ours, it is needless to remark. Are not the thoughts and ways of man above those of the brute? Are not the thoughts and ways of the parent above the comprehension of his new born infant? Do not our own change, as we increase in wisdom and knowledge? How far then, must the thoughts and ways of the omniscient, infallible God, exceed those of ignorant, short-sighted and fallible men.

Farther. God is infinitely above us in power. We are weak and frail to a proverb; and our plans, ways, enterprizes, must conform to the weakness of our powers. But God is all-powerful; with him nothing is impossible. He can do numberless things, of which we can form no conception; and he can do what he does in an inconceivable variety of ways. This consideration alone, were there nothing else, would prove that his thoughts and ways are far above ours.

Again. God is eternal and unchangeable, while we are but of yesterday, and die perhaps to-morrow, and are continually changing, as our situation and circumstances change. Surely the thoughts and ways of such creatures cannot be suitable or proper for a being, who had no beginning, who cannot change, but is yesterday, to-day, and forever, the same.

Once more. God is perfectly benevolent and holy; but we are entirely selfish and sinful. We love sin, that abominable thing which his soul hates. We care for nothing but our own private interest; while his concern is for the interest of the universe. Hence his thoughts, his affections, his maxims and pursuits, must be entirely different from ours. Do not the thoughts and ways of angels differ from those of devils? Do not even the thoughts and ways of good men differ widely from those of the wicked? How infinitely then must a perfectly holy God differ from us, polluted worms, who are dead in trespasses and sins! If man at his best estate, and even angels themselves, are incompetent to comprehend God's thoughts and ways, because he is infinitely superior to them in wisdom, and knowledge, and power; how unable must we be, since sin has blinded our understanding, hardened our hearts, defiled the whole man, debased all our faculties, and exposed us to innumerable temptations, prejudices and mistakes, which lead us to hate and shun the pure light of divine truth; to delude and deceive ourselves, and to form erroneous opinions respecting almost every thing around us; to call evil good, and good evil; to put sweet for bitter, and bitter for sweet; shadows for realities, and realities for shadows; darkness for light, and light for darkness. The pleasures, ways and pursuits of an oyster, enclosed in its shell, at the bottom of the sea, do not by any means differ so widely from those of the eagle that soars to the clouds and basks in the beams of the sun, as do the thoughts and ways of sinners from those of the infinitely benevolent and holy Monarch of the universe.

Having thus shown that the thoughts and ways of God must far surpass ours, I proceed, as was proposed,

II. To exhibit particularly, some instances in which this difference most strikingly appears.

1. In permitting the introduction and continued existence of natural and moral evil, God's ways and thoughts are very different from ours. Why he should permit angels or men to fall, we cannot tell. That he did permit them to fall, is certain; because had he thought proper, he could doubtless have prevented their apostacy. It is also certain that he still permits the existence of natural and moral evil; because if he chose, all things considered, to banish it from the universe, he could easily do it. But if we had been consulted, we should have decided that it was best that sin and its consequences should never enter the world; or if they must enter, that they should be immediately banished. In this particular therefore, God's thoughts and ways are evidently not like ours.

2. In appointing Adam to be the covenant head and representative of the human race, so that if he stood his posterity should stand, and if he fell, his posterity should fall, God did not act as we probably should have done. That he has done this, is evident from fact; for we find that sin and its consequences do descend to every individual of the species; and we are told, that in Adam all die. But we should have thought it best to have no such constitution; but to have had the condition of every individual independent of that of every other. This method God did adopt with angels; and why he thought fit to adopt a different method with respect to us, he has not seen fit to inform us, and we cannot tell. It is however evident that in this particular, God's thoughts and ways are above ours. The same may be said,

3. Of the difference he has made between our race and the fallen angels. For them no way of salvation was provided. To them no space for repentance, no day of grace, no offers of mercy were given; but their punishment immediately followed their offence. We, on the contrary, have space for repentance, and are favored with the offers of salvation, and the means of grace. Christ *took not hold of angels*, says the apostle; but he *took hold of the seed of Abraham.* But we should have thought no difference ought to be made; or, if either angels or men were to be left, that they should be saved rather than we; because they are of a higher rank in the scale of being. But God

thought otherwise; and the only reason we can assign is, that so it seemed good in his sight.

4. In devising a way of salvation, and in providing a Savior, God's thoughts and ways are very different from ours, and far, very far, above them. We should have thought, that if God intended to save sinners, he would bring them to repentance and save them at once; or at least, after suffering them to endure for a season, the bitter consequences of their own folly and disobedience. We never should have thought of providing for them a Redeemer; still less should we have thought of proposing, that God's only Son, the Creator and Preserver of all things, should undertake this office; and least of all should we have expected, that he would for this purpose think it necessary to become man. If we had been informed that this was necessary, and it had been left for us to fix the time and manner of his appearing, we should have concluded that he ought to come soon after the fall; to be born of illustrious parents; to make his appearance on earth in all the splendor, pomp and glory imaginable; to overcome all opposition by a display of irresistible power; to ride through the world in triumph, conquering and to conquer. Such were the expectations of the Jews; and such most probably would have been ours. But never should we have thought of his being born of a virgin in abject circumstances; born in a stable, cradled in a manger, living for many years as a humble artificer; wandering, despised and rejected of men, without a place to lay his head, and finally arraigned, tried, condemned and crucified as a vile malefactor, that he might thus expiate our sins, and by his death, give life to the world. Had we been forewarned of these things, we should have considered them as too foolish, incredible and absurd to obtain the smallest credit; and instead of thinking them cunningly devised, should have thought them very clumsily contrived fables, unworthy of the least notice or regard. And thus in fact they have appeared, and do still appear, to the wise men of this world; for says the apostle, the cross of Christ is foolishness to them that perish. When the self-righteous Jews and vain-glorious Gentiles were told that one who had been crucified as a malefactor, was the Son of God, the Creator of the world, the only Savior of men, that his blood cleanses from all sin, and that without an interest in his merits they must perish

forever — they could find no language sufficiently strong to express their contempt and indignation; and the aid of the stake, the rack, and the cross, was called in to express what language could not. Yet this was the way which God thought proper to choose, and all things which appear in the view of men so ridiculous, irrational and absurd, are in his view, infinitely proper, wise and amiable; and display far more wisdom than all the works of creation, wonderful as they are. Surely then, as the heavens are higher than the earth, so are his ways and thoughts higher than ours.

5. God's thoughts and ways differ widely from ours in his choice of means and instruments for propagating the religion of Christ. We should have thought that a religion, whose author had been crucified as a malefactor; a religion, which instead of favoring and flattering the ruling passions, prejudices and propensities of men, directly opposed them all, and which was therefore exceedingly hateful to them, — would have needed the assistance of angels, or at least, of the most powerful monarchs, the most enlightened sages, the most splendid natural and acquired abilities, to procure it success. But instead of such instruments, which we should have chosen, God saw fit to employ a handful of ignorant fishermen to effect this purpose, and even forbade them to use any human artifices to procure them success; but charged them to rely entirely on the effect of a faithful, simple, unadorned statement of the great truths of Christianity. Hence the language of the apostle, "God hath chosen the foolish things of the world to confound the wise; and the weak things of the world to confound the mighty; and base things of the world, and things that are despised hath God chosen; yea, and things that are not to bring to nought things which are, that no flesh should glory in his presence. For when, in the wisdom of God, the world by wisdom knew not God, it pleased God by the foolishness of preaching to save them that believe."

6. A wide difference between God's thoughts and ways, and our own, appears, when we consider the manner in which he dispenses the benefits which Christ has purchased, and the character and situation of those whom he chooses to make wise unto salvation. We should expect that if such a Savior were provided, all would be saved; and that if for any reasons, this

were impossible, the most noble, wise, rich and learned, or at least, the most moral and amiable would always be called. But this we see is not the case. It is evident from scripture, if any thing can be, that all will not be saved, and it is also evident from observation, so far as we can see; for we find that multitudes appear to live and die without any spiritual knowledge of the Savior, or preparation for heaven. We also find, both from scripture and observation, that it is not always the most wealthy, wise, or learned, nor even the most moral and amiable, who are called to embrace the gospel. Christ told the moral, but self-righteous pharisees, that the publicans and harlots would go into the kingdom of God before them. Hath not God, says St. James, chosen the poor of this world to be rich in faith and heirs of the kingdom? Ministers and private Christians very often find reason to acknowledge that God's thoughts and ways are not like theirs; for he rarely converts such, as they think the most probable subjects of conversion; and while they are watching such persons, and daily hoping and expecting to see them embrace the truth, others, of whom perhaps they never thought, start up and seize the prize.

7. God's thoughts respecting the way in which men become partakers of the salvation of the Gospel, differ widely from ours. We all naturally suppose, that men are to be saved by their good works; by obeying the law; by subduing their sins; by alms and prayers. But the gospel teaches us, that men are to be saved, not by working, but by believing; that we are saved by grace, through faith; and that to him that worketh not, but believeth on him who justifieth the ungodly, his faith is counted to him for righteousness. This truth men neither love nor understand, and even after they are awakened and convinced of sin, it is one of the most difficult things imaginable to convince them that their pretended good works are no better than sins; and that if they ever obtain salvation, it must be by simply believing in the Son of God. In scarcely any thing do God's thoughts and ways differ so widely from ours, as in this great doctrine of salvation through grace—of justification by faith in the righteousness of Christ.

Lastly. God's thoughts and ways are not as ours respecting the best methods of dealing with his people, and carrying on the work of grace in their souls after it is begun. When God delivered his people from Egyptian bondage, if he had led them by the nearest and most direct way to Canaan, they might have reached it in a very few days; and had they been consulted, they would probably have thought the nearest way the best. But God thought otherwise. So when God converts his people from sin to holiness, he could, if he pleased, render them perfectly holy at once; and they are often ready to imagine, that this would be much the better way, both for his glory and their own good. But instead of adopting this method, he grants them, at first, but small degrees of grace, and increases it in a very slow and gradual manner. He leads them round for many years, through a wilderness beset with temptations, trials and sufferings, with a view to humble them, prove them, and show them all that is in their hearts. By the discoveries which they make of their own weakness, ignorance and propensity to sin, their pride is humbled; their self-confidence destroyed; their patience, meekness and candor are increased; the Savior, and his method of salvation rendered more precious, and all ground for boasting forever excluded.

All these happy effects, however, are produced in a way which they would never have thought of; and it is a long time before they can be made to understand God's method of proceeding, so that they are often ready to say with Jacob, "All these things are against me!" when in fact, every thing is working together for their good. Even when God answers their prayers, he very often does it in ways and by means, which they did not expect; and as often as they attempt to mark out a path for him in their own minds, so often they find themselves disappointed, and are constrained to confess, that his ways are not like theirs. Often too, when they contemplate their own unworthiness, their stupidity, their obstinacy, their inconsistencies, their propensity to backslide, to grieve their Savior and requite him evil for good, notwithstanding the innumerable pardons and mercies they have received, — are they constrained to use the same language, and to cry, Lord, why am I saved? why are such favors heaped on a wretch so unworthy? Surely, this is not the manner of men — to adopt rebels and traitors, as children, and heap such honors and blessings upon them. What manner of love is this that we should be called the sons of God! Who is a God like unto thee, that forgivest iniquity, transgression and sin, and overcomest evil with good? If thy ways were not high above ours, as the heavens are higher than the earth, we must have perished forever!

INFERENCES.—1. If God's ways and thoughts differ thus widely from ours, then it is no reasonable objection against the truth of any doctrine, or the propriety of any dispensation, that it is above our comprehension, and appears strange and mysterious to us. On the contrary we should have reason to doubt the truth of the scriptures, and to suspect that they are not the word of God, if they did not contain many things which appear mysterious, and which we cannot fully comprehend. In this case they would want one great proof of having proceeded from him, whose thoughts and ways must be infinitely above ours. Yet, my friends, all the objections which men make against the truth of revelation, or against any of its doctrines, are founded on the supposition, that God's ways and thoughts must be precisely like ours; and that if any thing appears unreasonable or mysterious to us, it certainly is so, and therefore cannot proceed from God.

2. If God's thoughts and ways are thus high above ours, it must be abominable pride, impiety, folly and presumption in us to censure them even in thought. Yet how often men do this! How often do they, at least in their hearts, find fault with God's word, murmur at his dispensations, repine under afflictions, feel dissatisfied with his manner of governing the world, quarrel with his sovereignty in the bestowing of favors, and thus in effect say, that God is either unwise, unkind, or unjust, and that they could conduct things in a better manner! My friends, if this is not horribly impious and presumptuous, if it does not discover the most abominable pride, what does? For an illiterate peasant to censure the conduct of his prince, with the reasons of which he is utterly unacquainted; for a child of a week old to condemn the proceedings of his parent, would be nothing to this. We are told, that if any man judgeth a matter before he heareth it, it is folly and shame unto him. What folly and shame is it then to us to attempt to judge of God's conduct, when we know only so small a part of his ways, and know even this part but very imperfectly. An ancient writer

tells us of a man, who having a house for sale, carried a brick to market to exhibit as a specimen. You may perhaps smile at his folly in supposing that any purchaser would or could judge of a whole house, which he never saw, by so small a part of it. But are not we guilty of much greater folly in attempting to form an opinion of God's conduct from that little part of it, which we are able to discover? In order to form a correct opinion of it we ought to have a correct view of the whole; we ought to see the whole extent and duration of God's kingdom; to be equal to him in wisdom, knowledge, power, and goodness; in one word, we ought to be God ourselves; for none but God is capable of judging accurately of the conduct of God. Hence, whenever we attempt to judge of it, we do in effect, set ourselves up as Gods, knowing good and evil. Well therefore may God reply to our vain, proud and impious objections, Who is this, that darkeneth counsel by words without knowledge? Gird up now thy loins like a man, and I will demand of thee, and answer thou me. Where wast thou, when I laid the foundations of the earth? declare, if thou hast understanding. Hast thou an arm like God? or canst thou thunder with a voice like him? Wilt thou disannul my judgment? wilt thou condemn me, that thou mayest be righteous? And while God may thus with propriety address each of us, it becomes us to reply with Job, Behold, I am vile; what shall I answer thee? I will lay my hand upon my mouth. Once have I spoken, but I will not answer; yea, twice, but I will proceed no farther. I have uttered that I understood not; things too wonderful for me, which I knew not.

3. From this subject we infer the reasonableness of faith. The very essence of faith consists in a humble, docile, childlike temper, which disposes us to embrace without objecting or disputing, every thing which God reveals; and to believe that all his words and dispensations are, even though we cannot see how, perfectly right. Christians are often ridiculed for exercising this implicit faith in God, and believing what they cannot fully comprehend. But we appeal to every one present, whether in so doing, they do not act reasonably. If God's ways and thoughts are thus high above ours, ought we not implicitly to believe all his declarations; to believe that all he says and does is perfectly right? Is it not reasonable for children thus to

believe their parents? for a sick man to trust in a skilful physician? for a passenger unacquainted with navigation, to trust to the master of the vessel? for a blind man to follow his guide? If so, then it is certainly much more reasonable for such ignorant, short-sighted, fallible creatures, as we are, to submit and trust implicitly to an infinitely wise, good, and infallible Being; and when any of his words or works appear wrong, to ascribe it to our own ignorance, blindness, or prejudice, rather than to suppose that there is any thing wrong in him. Is it not more likely that we should be wrong or mistaken, than that God should be? If so, we ought to praise him, when his conduct appears wise and right, and to impute it to ourselves when it does not, and to believe and to submit to him implicitly in all things. This is not only reasonable, but absolutely necessary to our happiness; for if God's thoughts and ways differ thus widely from ours, we must either believe that he is right and we wrong, or else feel unreconciled and dissatisfied. But if we feel unreconciled and dissatisfied we must be unhappy; for we cannot help ourselves. God will do as he pleases, whether we are pleased or not. On the contrary, if we exercise faith and submission to his will, and believe that all is right; that even when clouds and darkness are round about him, justice and judgment are the habitation of his throne, then we shall be peaceful and happy. He will guide us by his counsel, and afterwards receive us to glory. Then the cloud will be scattered; we shall see all things clearly, and understand the meaning of those truths, and the reason of those dispensations, which have appeared most mysterious and perplexing; for God's language to every sincere believer is, What I do, thou knowest not now; but thou shalt know hereafter.

SERMON III.

ALL THINGS CREATED FOR CHRIST.

All things were created by him and for him.—COLOSSIANS I. 4.

BY whom were all these worlds and beings made? is probably the first question, which a view of the created universe would excite in a seriously inquisitive mind. For what purpose and with what view were they created? would no less probably be the second. There are two inspired passages, one in the Old Testament and the other in the New, which contain a direct answer to both these questions. In the Old Testament we are told, that Jehovah hath made all things for himself, yea, even the wicked for the day of evil: and in the New, that all things were created by Christ and for Christ. At first view these passages appear to differ, not only in language, but in sentiment. The former asserts that Jehovah made all things. The latter declares that all things were created by Christ. The former assures us that Jehovah made all things for *himself;* the latter that all things were created *for Christ.* To those however who believe that the Jehovah of the Old Testament is the Jesus of the New, these apparently different assertions will appear perfectly consistent. They will recollect and readily assent to the declaration of our Lord, He that hath seen me hath seen the Father; I and my Father are one; and will feel that the expression, Jehovah hath made all things for himself, is synonymous with the declaration in our text, All things were created by Christ and for him.

In discoursing on this passage we shall endeavor to illustrate particularly the general assertion, that all things were created for Christ. That none may suspect us of asserting more than our text will warrant, it may be proper to quote the remaining part of the verse which contains it. "By him," says the apostle speaking of Christ, "were all things created that are in heaven and that are in earth, visible and invisible, whether thrones, or dominions, or principalities, or powers; all things were created by him, and for him." From this passage it appears that there are invisible as well as visible creatures; things in heaven, as well as things on earth. But whether visible or invisible, whether in heaven or on earth, they were all created for Christ; all created to promote his glory and subserve his purposes. This I shall now attempt to illustrate in several particulars.

I. Heaven was created for Christ. That there is a place called heaven, where the presence of God is specially manifested, and which is in a peculiar sense, the habitation of his holiness and glory, is abundantly taught by the inspired writers. Some, it is true, have supposed that heaven is only a state of happiness, and not a place; but the supposition may be easily shown to be groundless; for though God is every where, and though his presence would render any place a heaven to holy beings; yet the glorified body of Christ cannot be every where. A body, however purified and refined, must be in some place; and the place, where now exists the glorified body of our Redeemer, is heaven. Agreeably St. Paul informs us, that Christ has entered into heaven itself; that he is seated at the right hand of God in the heavenly places; and he elsewhere speaks of desiring to depart and be with Christ. Our Saviour himself, in his last prayer says, Father, I will that those whom thou hast given me be with me, where I am, that they may behold my glory. In addition to these proofs we may observe, that the bodies of Enoch and Elijah must have been in some place, since their removal from this world, and that the glorified bodies of the saints, which are to be raised at the last day, must be in some place after their resurrection. Heaven is therefore not only a state, but a place, as really a place as this world. And the same arguments which prove that there is such a place as heaven, prove that heaven was created on purpose for Christ. God, considered as a pure spirit, cannot be said to be in one place, any more than in another. "Do not I fill heaven and earth? saith the Lord." Nay more, the Psalmist says, "If I make my bed in hell, thou art there.' God therefore, considered as a spirit, had no occasion for a material heaven. Nor was there any need of such a place for the angels; for they also are spirits, and wherever they are, they behold the face of God, so that to them every place is heaven. But when God became incarnate in the person of Christ; when he became God manifest in the flesh, then a material heaven became necessary for the place of his residence; a place, to which his redeemed people might be brought, and where they might dwell with him and behold his glory. Agreeably Christ speaks of heaven as a kingdom prepared for them from the foundation of the world; and elsewhere he says to his disciples, I go to prepare a place for you; and if I go to prepare a place for you, I will come again, and receive you to myself, that where I am there ye may be also. It appears then, that if God had not taken our nature into union with himself in the person of Christ; and if Christ had not redeemed the bodies of his people from the grave by his own death, there would have been no occasion for a material heaven; and of course, none would have been created. It is not then for God simply considered, but for God manifest in the flesh, or in other words, for Jesus Christ, that heaven was originally formed. It was designed to be the royal city, the court, the palace, in which the King of Zion should dwell and reign with his redeemed people forever.

II. The angels were all created for Christ. When forming the great scheme of redemption, God was pleased to determine that he would employ the agency of created, but highly exalted spirits in carrying it on. With this view the angels were created. They were employed in worshipping Christ. When he brought the first begotten into the world he saith, let all the angels of God worship him. They are also employed by Christ in executing his purposes of love to his people. "Are they not all ministering spirits, sent forth to minister unto them who shall be heirs of salvation?" It would perhaps be impossible, to point out a single work ever performed by them, which was not in some way connected with the work of redemption by Christ. Hence they are called his angels. Jesus Christ, says St. John, sent his angel. The Lord Jesus shall be revealed from heaven with his mighty angels. Among these exalted spirits thus created to be the worshippers and servants of Christ, some were found who fell from their first estate. Of what particular sin they were guilty, we are not informed; but in some way or other, they refused to perform the duties required of them, and were in consequence cast down from heaven to hell. But though from angels they are transformed to devils, they are still subject to Christ; he holds them in a chain which they cannot break, and overrules for the advancement of his kingdom all their endeavors to destroy it. For instance, were it not for their temptations, Judas had probably never betrayed his master, nor the Jews crucified him. How much this event, which they designed should overthrow his kingdom, tended to advance it, or rather, how absolutely necessary it was to its advancement, you need not be told.

III. Hell was created for Christ. That hell is a place, as well as a state, is evident from the fact, that the bodies of the wicked, as well as their souls, are doomed to inhabit it. It will be apparent, in what respects this place was created for Christ, if we consider, that when he was appointed in the counsels of eternity to reign over his mediatorial kingdom, and to be the Judge of the world, it was foreseen that he would have rebellious, as well as loyal subjects; and that for the restraint and punishment of the rebellious, a prison would be necessary. Hell was therefore created for a prison, in which the enemies of Christ and of the peace and happiness of the universe should be confined. Hence its fires are said to be prepared for the wicked. In a word, it was designed, that in Christ and in the scheme of redemption by him, a full exhibition should be made of all the glorious perfections of the divine character. And as heaven was created to serve as a theatre for the display of the glories of divine mercy, love and grace, so hell was created for the display of divine justice and wrath.

IV. This world was created for Christ. It was created, in the first place, for the display of his natural perfections; for the display of creative wisdom and power to angelic minds. Accordingly we are told, that when he laid the foundation of the earth, these sons of God sung his praises together and shouted for joy. It was created, in the second place, to serve as a stage on which he might display to all intelligent creatures his moral perfections, and especially on which he might display the glories of an incarnate God, and act the wonders of the great scheme of redemption. It was also created to be a province of his dominions, the place where his mediatorial kingdom should be set up, and where his chosen people should be prepared by his grace for admission into his kingdom above. When it shall have served for all these purposes, when Christ shall have done with it, the end of its creation will be accomplished, and then the earth will of course be destroyed. Then the visible heavens, being on fire, will be dissolved, and the elements shall melt with fervent heat, and earth with the works thereof shall be burnt up, and its destruction, no less than its creation, will display the perfection of its Creator.

V. The human race, and all the inferior inhabitants of the world, were created for Christ. They were created, in the first place, to show his ability to form different kinds and orders of beings. By forming the inferior animals he displayed his power to create material beings, while his manifold wisdom appeared in the various qualities bestowed on them, and in their fitness for the various uses and elements for which they were designed. In the creation of man he farther showed his power to create beings who were both material and spiritual. The union of a material body with a spiritual, immortal soul, is a work in some respects more wonderful than any of his previous works of creation, and displays in a new and striking manner, that power by which he was enabled to subdue all things to himself. To form such a being as man of such materials as the dust of the earth, and to endue him with a living soul, which should bear the image and likeness of God, must have appeared to angels impossible; and when they saw such a work accomplished, it must have given them new and enlarged views of the unlimited power and wisdom of its Author.

In the second place, the inhabitants of this world were created to be the subjects of Christ. It was intended that he should have a kingdom embracing all conceivable kinds or orders of created beings, from the highest archangel to the meanest insect, that he might have an opportunity of displaying his perfections in governing such a kingdom, in dispensing happiness suited to the capacities of the individuals of every kind, in adapting them all to their various uses and relations, and in causing all the parts of this complicated machine to work together for the accomplishment of his purposes, and in making them all the objects of his providential care.

In the third place, the human race was created, that Christ might display his infinite condescension in assuming their nature. In order to display this condescension in the most clear and striking manner, it was necessary that he should assume the nature of the lowest class of rational beings,—a nature subject to many evils and infirmities,—a nature, in which he might become visible, and act and speak in a visible manner. Had he taken the nature of angels into union with his own, it would have been a less wonderful act of condescension, nor could the act have been made equally apparent; for angels are spiritual beings, and the divine nature of Christ is spiritual, and the union of two beings purely spiritual could not be made to appear so evidently, as the union of a spiritual being with our nature which is partly material. We can conceive of God manifest in the flesh, much more clearly than of God manifest in an angel. We may farther observe, that a part of the designed display of Christ's condescension consisted in his becoming subject to hunger, thirst, weariness and pain, and in his dying, in the nature which he assumed. He was to appear in the likeness of frail, sinful flesh. But angels are subject to none of these infirmities. They can neither hunger, nor thirst, nor be weary, nor die. Christ could not therefore appear in the nature of a sinful angel as he could in the likeness of sinful flesh. Hence, in order to the full display of his condescension, it was necessary that rational beings should be created inferior to angels, or in other words, such beings as those who compose the human race.

In the fourth place, the human race was created that Christ might display all his perfections in their redemption. In this work is made the brightest and most wonderful display of those perfections which men or angels have ever seen. The glory of God appears most resplendent and full orbed in the face of Jesus Christ. Power, wisdom, goodness, justice, truth, love, mercy, grace and faithfulness, here shine with united lustre in full brilliancy, nor can we determine which appears most glorious or lovely. In God's other works, some drops of that overflowing fountain, some rays from that infinite sun, are seen; but in the work of redemption, in the glorious gospel of the blessed God, the whole Deity, the whole fulness of the Godhead, flows out in one boundless tide; a tide which will forever fill to the brim every holy mind, and in which all holy beings will bathe with rapturous delight through eternity. Accordingly we are told, that by the church is made known to principalities in heavenly places, the manifold wisdom of God; that in the work of redemption he made known the riches of his grace; that at the last day Christ shall be glorified in his saints, and admired in all them that believe. Even the wicked, who refuse to submit to Christ, shall be made unwillingly to honor him; that the Lord hath made all things for himself, yea, even the wicked for the day of evil. He now causes their wrath to praise him, and restrains the remainder. At the judgment day, they will all be compelled to bow to Jesus, and confess that he is Lord; and he will show his wrath and make his power known in their everlasting destruction.

Reflections. 1. What exalted ideas is this subject suited to give us of the dignity and glory of Christ. The assertion, that all things were created by him, is sufficient to prove his divinity; for he who built all things, must be God. But when in addition to this, we are assured that all things were created *for* him, we have a proof of his divinity, which is if possible still more convincing; for supposing for a moment that God could and would employ a creature to perform the work of creation, can we suppose that he would permit that creature to create all things for himself, for his own pleasure and glory? Surely not. God has said, I am Jehovah, that is my name, and my glory I will not give to another. But if Christ be not God, all the divine glory is given to another. The glory of creating all things, of upholding all things, of governing all things, of redeeming and judging the world, is all given to Christ. Nay more, all things were created on purpose that the glory resulting from all might be given to Christ. If then Christ be not Jehovah, Jehovah's glory is all given to another, and nothing remains to himself. But view Christ as God manifest in the flesh and the difficulty vanishes. Then in honoring the Son, we honor the Father. Then we shall understand why all the inhabitants of heaven are represented as ascribing joint glories to Him that sitteth on the throne, and to the Lamb. By him that sitteth on the throne, is meant the divine, and by the Lamb slain, the human nature of Christ. Both are inseparably united, and Christ's human nature is the temple in which Jehovah will dwell, and in which he will be worshipped by saints and angels through eternity.

2. From this subject we may learn, that, if we would view every object in its true light, and rightly estimate its nature and design, we must consider it with reference to Christ and his cross. To the cross of Christ all eternity has looked forward: to the cross of Christ all eternity will look back. The cross of Christ was, if I may so express it, the first object which existed in the divine mind; and with reference to this great object all other objects were created. With reference to the same object they are still preserved. With reference to the same object every event that takes place in heaven, earth and hell, is directed and overruled. Surely then, this object ought to engage our undivided attention. We ought to regard this world merely as a stage, on which the cross of Christ was to be erected, and the great drama of the crucifixion acted. We ought to regard all that it contains as only the scenes and draperies necessary for its exhibition. We ought to regard the celestial luminaries merely as lamps, by the light of which this stupendous spectacle may be beheld. We ought to view angels, men and devils as subordinate actors on the stage, and all the commotions and revolutions of the world as subservient to this one grand design. Separate any part of this creation, or any event that has ever taken place, from its relation to Christ, and it dwindles into insignificancy. No sufficient reason can be assigned for its existence, and it appears to have been formed in vain. But when viewed as connected with him, every thing becomes important; every thing then appears to be a part of one grand, systematic, harmonious whole; a whole worthy of Him that formed it. It was such a view of things, which led the apostle to exclaim, God forbid that I should glory, save in the cross of our Lord Jesus Christ. My friends, if we view the cross of Christ in the same light in which it was viewed by the apostle, we shall soon find it producing similar effects upon ourselves, and shall experience the emotions and adopt the language of that distinguished saint.

3. From this subject, my Christian friends, you may learn what reason you have for gratitude and joy. You, as well as all other objects and beings, were created for Christ. You were created on purpose to promote his glory and execute his will. Nay more, you were created on purpose to be his servants, his friends, his members; you were created that he might redeem you by his blood, sanctify you by his grace, dwell in you by his spirit, form in you his image, raise you to heaven by his power, and show forth the unsearchable riches of his glory in you as vessels of mercy, through eternity. You were created that at the last day, Christ, your exalted Redeemer and Lord may be glorified in you as his work, and admired, as he will be, in all them that believe. You were created, that like so many planets, you may revolve around Christ the Sun of Righteousness, drink in light, and love, and glory, from his beams, and reflect those beams to the admiring eyes of fellow saints and angels forever and ever. Yes, these are the great and benevolent purposes for which you were created and destined; you were beloved with an everlasting love; and with loving kindness you were drawn to Christ, that these purposes might be fulfilled. And they shall be all fulfilled. They are the purposes of him with whom designs and actions are the same; who never changes, and who will not, cannot, be disappointed. O then, what a gift is the gift of existence, endless existence, given for such purposes as these! What reason have you to rejoice in such a gift, and to bless the free, great and glorious Giver! Can you find love for any thing else? Can you find affections for any other object? Can you waste admiration on any thing besides? If you were thus created for Christ, ought not all your powers and faculties to be devoted to him? Ought not your whole soul to be engrossed and swallowed up by this infinitely worthy object? Ought you not always to remember that you are not your own, that you are bought with a price, that you are bound by every tie to glorify Christ in your bodies and in your spirits which are his? This indeed you have covenanted and vowed to do. Come then, with willing minds, and hearts broken with contrition, bursting with admiration, and glowing with love and zeal, and renew your covenant engagements afresh, at Christ's table. Come and see him, by whom and for whom all things were created, dying and dead

for you. See his flesh freely offered as your food. See his blood no less freely presented to wash away your stains. Hear him, who is Lord and heir of all things, addressing you in the tenderest expressions of infinite, consolatory love, saying, "Come my sister, my spouse, to my table: eat, O friends; drink, yea, drink abundantly, O beloved." Drink, and remember your sorrows no more. Drink, and remember the man of sorrows, who sorrowed and died that your sorrows might cease. Drink, and remember him, who is now preparing a mansion for you in heaven; who will soon come again and receive you to himself, and drink the fruit of the vine new with you in the kingdom of my Father forever. And while you remember this inestimable Friend, and listen to him thus addressing you, reply, "Even so, Lord Jesus, come quickly." And until he shall come, exclaim with united voices, "Now unto him, who hath loved, and created, and redeemed us, and washed us from our sins in his own blood, to him be glory, and honor, and dominion, forever and ever."

SERMON IV.

THE WAY WHICH WICKED MEN HAVE TRODDEN.

Hast thou marked the old way, which wicked men have trodden? Which were cut down out of time, whose foundation was overthrown with a flood: Which said unto God, depart from us; and what can the Almighty do for them?—Job xxii. 15, 16, 17.

WIDE, says our Divine Teacher, is the gate, and broad is the way, which leadeth to destruction; and many there be who go in thereat. Of this broad way Eliphaz here speaks. Infering from the unprecedented afflictions of Job, that he must be a wicked man, he asks him whether he had duly considered the old way which had been trodden by other wicked men of former ages, who were cut down out of time, whose foundation was overthrown with a flood.

My hearers, this is an important question, a question which may be very properly addressed to all, and from which the most salutary consequences may result. If any of you have not suitably considered the way which wicked men have trodden, you may even now be ignorantly pursuing it; nor can any be sure, that he has forsaken this way, unless he knows what it is. Permit me then to address this question to you,—Have you marked, have you duly considered the way of wicked men, and the end to which it leads? If you have not, let me request your attention while I endeavor, by the light of revelation, to *trace this way*, to show *in what it consists*, and *what is its termination.*

I. Let us consider the way itself. In tracing it, it will be proper to begin at its commencement. It was, you will observe, even in the time of Eliphaz, an old way, a way which had long been trodden. Indeed, it is almost as old as the human race, or as the world which they inhabit; for it was formed in the days of our first parents, at the time when they ate of the forbidden fruit. Then the wide gate, which leads into the broad way, was opened; and alas, it has never since been closed. By carefully attending to the conduct of those, who first formed the way, and first walked in it, we may learn in what it consists. It is thus described by the inspired historian: "And when the woman saw that the tree was good for food; and that it was pleasant to the eyes, and a tree to be desired to make one wise; she took of the fruit thereof, and did eat, and gave also unto her husband with her, and he did eat."

In this account of the conduct of the first sinner we see, in the first place, *selfishness*, or a preference of herself to God; for had she loved him supremely, she would have chosen to obey his commands, rather than to gratify herself. This must ever be the first sin; for so long as any creature prefers God to himself, he will choose to please God rather than to gratify himself; of course, he will avoid every sin, and no temptation will induce him to offend his Maker, while he loves him with all his heart. But so soon as any creature begins to prefer himself to God, he will choose to gratify himself, rather than please his Maker; and will of course commit any sin, which promises him self-gratification or self-aggrandizement.

The second thing to be noticed in the conduct of the first sinner, is *pride*. She saw that it was a tree to be desired to make one wise; that is, she fancied, as the tempter had asserted, that it would cause her to become as a god, knowing good and evil. Now this wish was the effect of pride; and it was accompanied by the inseparable attendant of pride, discontent; discontent with the situation in which God had placed her.—This sin is the natural consequence of selfishness; for as soon as we begin to prefer ourselves to God, we shall wish to put ourselves in the place of God, and to rise above the sphere of action which he has assigned us, and to grasp at those things which he has not thought proper to bestow.

The third thing in her conduct, the third step in the way of sin, was *sensuality*, or a disposition to be governed and guided by her senses, and to seek their gratification in an unlawful manner. She saw that the fruit of the tree was good for food and pleasant to the eyes. Here was something to gratify two of the senses, those of tasting and seeing; and this gratification, though forbidden, she was determined to enjoy. The influence of sin, which had hitherto existed only in the passions of the mind, began to extend itself to the appetites of the body, and by this influence they were inflamed to such a degree, that they prompted her to disregard the dictates of reason and conscience, and the commands of God.

The next step in the fatal way, was *unbelief;* a distrust of God's word, and a consequent belief of the tempter's suggestions. God had said, "In the day thou eatest, thou shalt surely die." This threatening she now disbelieved. The tempter said, "God doth know that ye shall not surely die; but in the day that ye eat of it, your eyes shall be opened, and ye shall be as gods, knowing good and evil." This falsehood she did believe. This disbelief of God's word, and belief of Satan's suggestions, were the natural consequence of sins already mentioned; for when the passions and appetites are inflamed by the influence of sin, they immediately blind the understanding in such a manner, that it can no longer discover the evidence which attends divine truth, nor the force of those arguments and motives, which should induce us to obey it. Every thing which is urged against a compliance with our sinful inclinations then appears weak and groundless; while those sophistical reasonings, which favor their gratification, seem powerful and conclusive. In this state therefore, the mind is completely prepared to disbelieve the God of truth, whose word opposes and forbids its sinful inclinations, and to believe the father of lies, who urges us to gratify them. And this in fact is the source of all the unbelief which prevails in the world; for the evidence attending God's word, is so convincing, that men never would, never could disbelieve, did they not first wish to disbelieve it.—But to proceed, God's threatenings being thus disbelieved, and the lies of the tempter embraced as truth, every barrier, which opposed her progress, was removed; and the sinful propensities that have been mentioned, broke out into open, actual disobedience. She took of the fruit of the tree and did eat. Thus she made a full entrance into that way, which wicked men have ever since trodden. The first step was selfishness; the second, pride; the third, sensuality; the fourth, unbelief; and the last, actual, open, wilful disobedience. To the same result every one will come, who begins to tread in her steps. Selfishness, pride, and sensuality, will lead them in pursuit of forbidden objects up to the gate which opposes their progress in the broad way; a gate, which is secured by God's awful threatenings. Unbelief, by disregarding these threatenings, will draw back the bolts, and then actual disobedience will burst open the gate, and hurry them onward without restraint, in the broad way. And as the first sinner was unwilling to walk in this way alone, and became a tempter, by presenting the fatal fruit to her husband, and persuading him to eat; so all, who have since walked in it, have wished for companions, and enticed their relatives, friends, and acquaintances to follow them.

But without insisting on this, let us trace the farther progress of the first sinners in their fatal career. Though they had disbelieved God's threatenings, they soon found, as sooner or later all sinners will find, that their unbelief did not render them false, or prevent their fulfilment, Before the close of the day, which they had stained by their disobedience, their offended Maker came to call them to an account; and from their conduct on that occasion, we may obtain a further acquaintance with the way in which sinners walk.

They exhibited sullen hardness of heart, impenitence, and despair of forgiveness. They expressed no sorrow, or penitence, nothing like brokenness of heart. They made no confession of sin; they uttered no cries for mercy; they expressed no wish to be restored to the favor of their offended Judge.

They displayed a self-justifying temper. Adam attempted to throw the blame upon his wife; and she, in turn, endeavored to transfer it to the serpent.

They showed a disposition to reflect upon God, as the cause of their disobedience. "The woman whom *thou* gavest to be with me, she gave me of the fruit of the tree, and I did eat."

In a manner precisely similar have sinners ever since conducted. They will not confess their sins; they will not repent of them; they will not cry for mercy; they will not seek the favor of their offended God. On the contrary, they excuse and justify themselves, and indirectly cast the blame of their sinful conduct upon Jehovah, by saying, the passions, appetites, and inclinations, which *thou* gavest us, have led us to act as we have done. This hard, impenitent, self-justifying temper, taken in connection with those things which were previously mentioned, constitute the old way, which wicked men have trodden. Of this we shall be convinced by examining the temper and conduct of successive generations of sinners; and making proper allowance for the different circumstances in which they were placed. Such, for instance, was the way trodden by that generation of mankind, which was destroyed by the flood. I mention this generation, partly because there is an evident allusion to it in our text; partly because their situation resembled our own, more nearly than did the situation of our first parents; and partly, because we have in the writings of Moses, and in the discourses of our Savior, a more particular account of their temper and conduct, than is given of any other generation in those early ages of the world. Now from this account we find that they were guilty of the same sins, that they walked in the same path, which has already been described.

In the first place, they were guilty of selfishness and pride. Their sinful passions they displayed in their disregard of the rights of their neighbors, in their contests for superiority; in consequence of which the earth was filled with violence, as we have abundant reason to believe it would now be, did not human laws restrain, in some degree, the passions of men.

In the second place, the persons who composed this generation, were sensual and earthly minded, governed by appetites and passions, rather than by reason, conscience and the law of God. This appears from the account given us of their alliances and connections, in forming which they seem to have regarded nothing but external appearances, choosing for their partners in life the irreligious, immoral and profane. That this was a distinguishing trait in their character, as well as that of the Sodomites, who lived some ages after them, appears from the account given of them by our Savior. As it was in the days of Noah, says he, so shall it be in the day when the Son of Man is revealed. They ate, they drank, they bought, they sold, they planted, they builded, they married and were given in marriage, and knew, or considered not, till Noah entered into the ark, and the flood came and destroyed them all. This, my hearers, is a most accurate description of worldly minded, wicked men; of men completely under the control of their appetites and passions, and regardless of every thing but the present life, with its transitory objects and pursuits. From this account it also appears, that they were guilty of unbelief, impenitence, hardness of heart, and a consequent neglect of the day and means of grace, and the offers of salvation. To this unbelief and hardness of heart alone can it be ascribed, that they did not know, or as the word signifies, did not consider, till the flood came and destroyed them; for they were most clearly, and for a long time, warned of its approach. God allowed them a reprieve of one hundred and twenty years, during which Noah, as a preacher of righteousness, reproved them for their sin, and warned them of the approaching deluge, and pointed out the only possible way of escape. In addition to their neglect of his warnings, they resisted the strivings, the influences of the divine Spirit; for we are told that Christ, by his Spirit, went and preached to them, and that God said respecting them, My Spirit shall not always strive with man; nevertheless his days shall be a hundred and twenty years—thus plainly intimating, that during that time, his Spirit should continue to strive with them. And to what cause is it to be ascribed, that though thus favored, thus warned, they did not consider, till it was too late? To their unbelief and hardness of heart—the two great causes to which it is still owing, that notwithstanding the preaching of the gospel, the offers of salvation, and the strivings of God's Spirit, men will not consider their latter end, nor fly to the Savior for refuge from the wrath to come. This account of the way in which antediluvian sinners walked, is the more deserving our attention, because our Savior informs us, that in the same way sinners will be found walking, when he comes to judge the world. Now if sinners trod this way four thousand years ago; and if they will be still found pursuing it at the end of time; we may fairly infer, that they have walked in it ever since the days of Noah, and that they are following it at the present day; an inference, which is abundantly verified by the history of the Jews and their heathen neighbors, by the writings of the prophets, and by the preaching of Christ and his apostles, and by the present character and conduct of sinners.

There is however a way, which many wicked men have trodden, that appears to differ very widely from this, though it is in reality the same—a modification of it produced by the influence of a religious education, or of an awakened conscience operating upon a selfish, sinful heart. This way it is necessary to describe particularly, lest those who are following it should be deceived, and fancy that they are walking, not in the old way which wicked men have trodden, but in the narrow path of life. To understand in what the way of which I am speaking consists, it should be recollected, that immediately after the fall of man, God was pleased to reveal a way, in which sinners might be reconciled, return to him, escape the punishment which they deserve, and regain his forfeited favor. This way consists in repentance towards God, and faith in a Mediator of God's providing, and reliance upon an atonement for sin made by that Mediator. This way of salvation was at first revealed to mankind in an imperfect manner, under a veil of types and shadows. The atonement, which Christ, the Lamb of God, intended to make in the fulness of time, was typically represented by the sacrifice of a lamb without spot or blemish. His human nature, in which, as in a temple, dwelt all the fulness of the Godhead bodily, was represented by a tabernacle, and afterwards by a temple, in which God manifested his presence in a sensible manner, and in which his worshippers might approach, while the mediatorial or priestly office of Christ was shadowed forth in the appointment of an order of men, who acted as mediators between God and man, presenting the sacrifices of men to God, and pronouncing the blessing of God upon men. Now that modification of the way trodden by wicked men, which we are at present considering, consists in rejecting the Mediator, and the atonement which God has provided, and substituting something else in their place. In other words, it consists in presumptuously attempting to approach God in a way of our own devising, instead of that way which he has provided. The first wicked man who walked in this way, was Cain. While his righteous brother Abel, agreeably to God's appointment, offered a lamb in sacrifice as an atonement for his sin, Cain presented nothing but a gift of the fruits of the earth, disbelieving the great truth, that without the shedding of blood, there is no remission of sin; and showing, that he did not regard himself as a sinner, who needed an atonement. The consequence was such as might have been expected. The sacrifice of Abel, offered in faith and in obedience to the requisitions of God, was accepted; while the offering of the self-righteous Cain was rejected—a circumstance, which led him to murmur against God, to envy, hate, and at length murder his brother. In the way thus marked out and trodden by Cain, we find the wicked Jews in all ages of their history exceedingly prone to walk. Neglecting the temple where God dwelt, and the priests or mediators whom he had appointed, they erected high places and planted groves, in which they pretended to worship Jehovah, though in a way directly contrary to his commands; and like Cain, they hated and persecuted those who approached God in his own appointed way, and endeavored to convince them of the folly and sinfulness of their conduct. In the same way their descendants were found walking in our Savior's time. Instead of embracing him as the only Savior, approaching God through him as the Mediator, and relying on his atonement and intercession for acceptance, they depended on their own works, their religious ceremonies, their alms, fastings, prayers and moral duties. Being ignorant of God's righteousness, they went about to establish their own, and refused to submit to the righteousness of God. And because our Savior and his apostles assured them, that in this way they could never be justified or saved, they hated, persecuted, and put them to death. Soon after the death of the apostles, the Christian church began to apostatize from the faith, to forsake the way of life, and to walk in the way we are describing. They lost the power of Godliness, but multiplied its forms, and substituted ceremonies, as a ground of dependence for salvation. Hence the Christian church gradually degenerated into the Church of Rome. Neglecting Jesus Christ, the one Mediator between God and man, they prayed to angels, to the virgin Mary, and to departed saints, as mediators; and instead of relying on his merits and atonement, they substituted in their room penances, bodily austerities, superstitious observances, and the endowment of churches and monasteries, by which they vainly hoped to atone for their sin, and obtain the favor of God. In a way which is essentially the same, many walk at the present day. They depend for salvation on their religious services, their moral duties, their liberality to the poor, their orthodox sentiments, or on a profession of religion; while they neglect the atonement and intercession of Christ, the only sure foundation, the only way of access to the Father, and like their predecessors, hate, though they cannot persecute, those who warn them that their way is false, and their confidence vain.

From what has been said, it appears that this way, though apparently different from that in which openly wicked men walk, is essentially the same; and that it conducts of course to the same end. Its principal characteristics are self-righteousness and pride, flowing from ignorance of God and of ourselves, attended by a disbelief of the gospel, impenitence, and a substitution of something else in the place of Christ, as a ground of dependence. Wicked men then, may be ranked in two classes; the one having no religion, the other a false religion. The first follow the tempter in his own proper shape, as an angel of darkness; the second are deceived, and led to him in the garb of an angel of light. The first walk openly in the broad road to destruction, without fear or remorse; the second follow the same road, but are so blinded by ignorance and unbelief, that they mistake it for the path of life.

Having thus marked the old way which wicked men have trodden, let us consider,

II. Its termination. Our Savior informs us, that it leads to destruction. That it does so, we might infer from what has taken place in this world. It led our first parents out of paradise, out of a state of holiness and happiness into a state of sin and misery; out of the clear light of the knowledge and favor of God into a land of darkness and the shadow of death. It led Cain into the guilt of murder, the murder of a brother, and banished him from the presence of God, and constrained him to cry, My punishment is greater than I can bear! For walking in this way the antediluvian sinners were cut down out of time, prematurely, being overwhelmed by a flood; the men of Sodom were destroyed by a fiery storm from heaven; Jews were scourged by a long series of calamities, terminating with their complete destruction by the Romans. What calamities have since befallen the Romish church, and successive generations of sinners, I need not inform you. But if we would see the final termination of this old way, we must go into the sanctuary of God, and look through the glass of revelation into eternity. There we shall see that this way leads directly down to the gates of hell. We are there taught, that the souls of those who were destroyed by the flood, are now spirits in prison, the prison of God's wrath; and may therefore fairly infer, that the souls of other wicked men, who have since been cut down out of time, are in the same situation. We are there told, that there is no peace to the wicked; that destruction and misery are in their paths; that they are driven away in their wickedness; that they shall go away into everlasting punishment. In a word, all the inspired writers cry with one voice, Wo unto the wicked! it shall be ill with them; for the reward of his hands shall be given him. Indeed, it is evident from the very nature of things, that these declarations must be true; that such a way as we have described can lead to nothing but endless misery.

Application. — Having endeavored to trace the old way in which wicked men have trodden, to show in what it consists, and what is its termination; permit me, in applying the subject, to inquire,

1. Whether some of you are not walking in this way? Are none of you guilty of selfishness in preferring your own gratification to the glory of God and the happiness of your fellow creatures? Are none of you influenced by pride and discontent to murmur at the situation in which God has placed you, and to attempt to rise above it, by recurring to means which he has forbidden? Are none of you controlled by your sinful appetites, and passions, and inclinations, rather than by reason, conscience, and the fear of God? Have these evil counsellors led none of you to desire, and to eat forbidden fruit; to gratify them in a way, or to a degree, which the law of God forbids? Do none of you disbelieve God's solemn declarations, that the soul who sinneth shall die; that the wicked shall be turned into hell, with all who forget him? Are none of you worldly minded, living a careless, irreligious life; acting as if your sole business was to obtain and enjoy what it affords? Are none of you excusing and justifying your conduct at your Creator's expense, saying in your hearts, the appetites, passions, and inclinations,

which *thou* gavest me, cause me to conduct as I do? If you avoid open sins, are none of you neglecting repentance towards God, and faith in our Lord Jesus Christ; substituting your own works or merits in the place of his atonement; trusting to your own prayers rather than to his intercession, and thus, like the Jews, going about to establish your own righteousness? These things, you will recollect, constitute the old way, which wicked men in all ages have trodden; and if they are found in your temper and conduct, then you are walking in that way.

If you feel unable to determine with certainty what path you are pursuing, permit me to mention three things, which may assist you in determining where you are. In the first place, remember there are but two ways mentioned in scripture, in one or the other of which every man is walking. One is that which has now been described, the old and broad way which wicked men have trodden, and which leads to destruction; the other is the narrow, good old way, marked out by the Son of God, in which patriarchs, prophets, apostles and martyrs have walked, which leads to life. Now since there are only these two ways, it is evident that all who are not walking in the latter are pursuing the former. Inquire then whether you are in the latter, the narrow path. It is totally, and in every respect, unlike the former. Those who walk in it are supremely influenced, not by selfishness, but by that love which seeketh not her own; not by pride, but by humility; not by discontent, but by constant acquiescence in the will of God. Instead of indulging and seeking to gratify their appetites and passions, they deny, mortify, crucify them; instead of disbelieving God's threatenings, they believe them, as well as his promises; they are heavenly and not earthly minded; they condemn, instead of justifying themselves; they rely for acceptance and salvation, not on any work or merits of their own, but on the atonement and intercession of Christ alone; and in dependence on his grace live a life of self-denial, watchfulness and prayer, endeavoring to walk even as he walked. If this, my hearers, is not your character; if you are not walking in this path; then you are most certainly in the old way which wicked men have trodden; for there is no middle path. He that is not with Christ is against him.

Again. Remember that in the way of the wicked, all men naturally walk. This the scriptures abundantly assert. Says the prophet, All we like sheep have gone astray; we have turned every one to his own way. And again, The Lord looked down from heaven upon the children of men, and behold they are all gone out of the way. Since then all are naturally out of the way of life, and in the broad road to death, it is evident that if you have never forsaken this road, if a great change has not taken place in your feelings, views, character and conduct, you are in the broad road still. I do not say that it is necessary to know precisely the time and the manner, in which this change, this passing from one road to the other, took place. But I say that it is absolutely necessary that it should take place. And if you have never been convinced that you are in the broad road, convinced that it is a sinful and dangerous road, then you have not forsaken it. Says our Savior, Strive to enter in at the straight gate; for many, I say unto you, shall seek to enter in, and shall not be able. Now is it possible that a man should strive to enter in at the straight gate and still know nothing of it? Yet if you have not striven to enter it, you are yet in your sins.

Once more. We are taught, that the old way trodden by wicked men, is the way of the world, and a crowded way. Many there be, says Christ, who go in thereat. Says the apostle to the Ephesians, In time past ye walked according to the course of this world, according to the prince of the power of the air, the spirit that now worketh in the children of disobedience; among whom we all had our conversation, and were by nature the children of wrath even as others. The narrow path, on the contrary, is trodden by a comparatively small number; "few there be," says our Savior, "that find it." If then you would know in which path you are walking, inquire whether you have many or few companions; whether you are walking with the world or contrary to it. If you find yourselves in a crowded road, then you are in the broad road. If you are walking with the majority of mankind, then you are most certainly walking in the old way, which wicked men have trodden.

2. Should any of you be convinced by these remarks that you are in this dangerous way, permit me to apply the subject further, by urging you to forsake it without delay. Consider, O consider, whither it leads, and whither it has led those who fol-

lowed it in former ages. Consider too, what God has done to turn you from it. He has clearly described it in his word. He has there traced it, as on a map, from its commencement to its fatal termination. All along the path he has set up way-marks with the inscription, *This road conducts to hell;* while a hand, pointing to a narrow path, which opens to the right, has written over it, *This path leads to heaven.* Lest you should be so occupied by the cares and business of the world, as to pass these way-marks without noticing them, he has placed at each of them a watchman to warn thoughtless travellers, and to call their attention to these inscriptions; and lest any should rush on without stopping to hear their warnings, he has placed the Sabbath, like a gate, across their path to compel them to stop till it be opened, and to hear the warning voice. To one of these gates, my impenitent hearers, you have now come. It has compelled you to pause a few moments, in your sinful career; and to pass away the time till the Sabbath is gone, you have come to the house of prayer. Here is a watchman appointed by your Creator. I stand to call your attention to the inscriptions which he has recorded; to the marks which he has drawn of the various paths in which men walk. Sinner, stop! I have a message to thee from God. See it written with his own finger, *This broad road leads to destruction!* Look at the map which he has drawn. See here a way opening out of the gates of paradise, leading on, broad and crooked, through the mazes of the world, and terminating at the iron gate of the bottomless abyss. See written on its margin, *Destruction and misery are in this path; it leads down to the chambers of eternal death.* This is the path of the openly irreligious. See close by its side another path, opened by the first murderer. See written on it, *There is a way which seemeth right unto a man, but the end thereof is death.* This is the path of the self-righteous, the formalist, the hypocrite, and like the other, leads to death. Sinners, you have seen this path; it is yours; it is the path in which you are now walking. You have also seen its end. Let it be yours then no longer. This day, this hour, forsake it, and enter that path which opens to the right hand. Here you may see it; and the straight gate, which leads into it, opens to every one who knocks. Close by its side stands a cross; rays of light darting from it, illuminate and mark out the path. Just within the gate stands an invisible guide, with extended hand offering to lead, to assist, to support you; while at the termination are the wide open gates of heaven, from which issue a flood of glory, which you will discover more and more clearly, as you approach them. O then, enter this path. Strive, strive to enter in at the straight gate. Will you reply, I know not what to do. I am in utter darkness. I see not the gate, nor the way, nor the cross. Then cry earnestly for light. Let your heart be toward the king's highway, and light will soon shine upon your steps. Above all, take not another step in the fatal road, which you have hitherto pursued. Pass not this Sabbath, this warning way-mark, lest you never see another.

SERMON V.

SINS ESTIMATED BY THE LIGHT OF HEAVEN.

Thou hast set our iniquities before thee, our secret sins in the light of thy countenance.—Psalm xc. 8.

It is a well known fact that the appearance of objects, and the ideas which we form of them, are very much affected by the situation in which they are placed in respect to us, and by the light in which they are seen. Objects seen at a distance, for example, appear much smaller than they really are. The same object, viewed through different mediums, will often exhibit very different appearances. A lighted candle, or a star, appears bright during the absence of the sun; but when that luminary returns, their brightness is eclipsed. Since the appearance of objects, and the ideas which we form of them, are thus affected by extraneous circumstances, it follows, that no two persons will form precisely the same ideas of any object, unless they view it in the same light, or are placed with respect to it in the same situation.

These remarks have a direct and important bearing upon the intended subject of the present discourse. No person can read the scriptures candidly and attentively, without perceiving, that God and men differ very widely in the opinion which they entertain respecting almost every object. And in nothing do they differ more widely, than in the estimate which they form of man's moral character, and of the malignity and desert of sin Nothing can be more evident than the fact, that in the sight of God our sins are incomparably more numerous, aggravated, and criminal, than they appear to us. He regards us as deserving of an endless punishment, while we scarcely perceive that we deserve any punishment at all. Now whence arises this difference? The remarks which have just been made will inform us. God and men view objects through a very different medium, and are placed with respect to them in very different situations. God is present with every object; he views it as near, and therefore sees its real magnitude. But many objects, especially those of a religious nature, are seen by us at a distance, and of course appear to us smaller than they really are. God sees every object in a perfectly clear light; but we see most objects dimly and indistinctly. In fine, God sees all objects just as they are; but we see them through a deceitful medium, which ignorance, prejudice and self-love place between them and us.

Apply these remarks to the case before us. The Psalmist, addressing God, says, "Thou hast set our iniquities before thee, our secret sins in the light of thy countenance." That is, our iniquities or open transgressions, and our secret sins, the sins of our hearts, are placed, as it were, full before God's face, immediately under his eye; and he sees them in the pure, clear, all-disclosing light of his own holiness and glory. Now if we would see our sins as they appear to him, that is, as they really are, if we would see their number, blackness and criminality, and the malignity and desert of every sin, we must place ourselves, as nearly as is possible, in his situation, and look at sin, as it were, through his eyes. We must place ourselves and our sins in the centre of that circle, which is irradiated by the light of his countenance, where all his infinite perfections are clearly displayed, where his awful majesty is seen, where his concentrated glories blaze, and burn, and dazzle, with insufferable brightness. And in order to this, we must, in thought, leave our dark and sinful world, where God is unseen and almost forgotten, and where consequently, the evil of sinning against him cannot be fully perceived,—and mount up to heaven, the peculiar habitation of his holiness and glory, where he does not, as here, conceal himself behind the veil of his works, and of second causes, but shines forth the unveiled God, and is seen as he is.

Let us then, my hearers, attempt this adventurous flight.

Let us follow the path by which our blessed Savior ascended to heaven, and soar upward to the great capital of the universe, to the palace, and the throne of its greater King. As we rise, the earth fades away from our view ; now we leave worlds, and suns, and systems behind us. Now we reach the utmost limits of creation ; now the last star disappears, and no ray of created light is seen. But a new light now begins to dawn and brighten upon us. It is the light of heaven, which pours in a flood of glory from its wide open gates, spreading continual meridian day, far and wide through the regions of etherial space. Passing swiftly onward through this flood of day, the songs of heaven begin to burst upon your ears, and voices of celestial sweetness, yet loud as the sound of many waters, and of mighty thunderings, are heard, exclaiming, "Alleluia ! for the Lord God omnipotent reigneth. Blessing, and glory, and honor, and power, be unto Him that sitteth on the throne, and to the Lamb, forever." A moment more, and you have passed the gates ; you are in the midst of the city, you are before the eternal throne, you are in the immediate presence of God and all his glories are blazing around you like a consuming fire. Flesh and blood cannot support it ; your bodies dissolve into their original dust, but your immortal souls remain, and stand naked spirits before the great Father of spirits. Nor in losing their tenements of clay, have they last the powers of perception. No ; they are now all eye, all ear, nor can you close the eyelids of the soul, to shut out for a moment, the dazzling, overpowering splendors which surround you, and which appear like light condensed, like glory which may be felt. You see indeed, no form or shape ; and yet your whole souls perceive, with intuitive clearness and certainty, the immediate, awe-inspiring presence of Jehovah. You see no countenance ; and yet you feel as if a countenance of awful majesty, in which all the perfections of divinity shone forth, were beaming upon you wherever you turn. You see no eye ; and yet a piercing, heart-searching eye, an eye of omniscient purity, every glance of which goes through your souls like a flash of lightning, seems to look upon you from every point of surrounding space. You feel as if enveloped in an atmosphere, or plunged in an ocean of existence, intelligence, perfection and glory ; an ocean, of which your laboring minds can take in only a drop ; an ocean, the depth of which you cannot fathom, and the breadth of which you can never fully explore. But while you feel utterly unable to comprehend this infinite Being, your views of him, so far as they extend, are perfectly clear and distinct. You have the most vivid perceptions, the most deeply graven impressions, of an infinite, eternal, spotless mind, in which the images of all things, past, present, and to come, are most harmoniously seen, arranged in the most perfect order, and defined with the nicest accuracy: of a mind, which wills with infinite ease, but whose volitions are attended by a power omnipotent and irresistible, and which sows worlds, suns and systems through the fields of space with far more facility, than the husbandman scatters his seed upon the earth;—of a mind, whence have flowed all the streams, which ever watered any part of the universe with life, intelligence, holiness, or happiness, and which is still full, overflowing and inexhaustible. You perceive also, with equal clearness and certainty, that this infinite, eternal, omnipotent, omniscient, all-wise, all-creating mind is perfectly and essentially holy, a pure flame of holiness, and that as such, he regards sin with unutterable, irreconcilable detestation and abhorrence. With a voice which reverberates through the wide expanse of his dominions, you hear him saying, as the Sovereign and Legislator of the universe, Be ye holy; for I, the Lord your God, am holy. And you see his throne surrounded, you see heaven filled by those only, who perfectly obey this command. You see thousands of thousands, and ten thousand times ten thousand of angels and archangels, pure, exalted, glorious intelligences, who reflect his perfect image, burn like flames of fire with zeal for his glory, and seem to be so many concentrations of wisdom, knowledge, holiness and love; a fit retinue for the thrice holy Lord of hosts, whose holiness and all-filling glory they unceasingly proclaim.

And now, my hearers, if you are willing to see your sins in their true colors; if you would rightly estimate their number, magnitude and criminality, bring them into the hallowed place, where nothing is seen but the whiteness of unsullied purity, and the splendors of uncreated glory; where the sun itself would appear only as a dark spot, and there, in the midst of this circle of seraphic intelligences, with the infinite God pouring all the light of his countenance round you, review your lives, contemplate your offences, and see how they appear. Recollect that the God, in whose presence you are, is the Being who forbids sin, the Being of whose eternal law sin is the transgression, and against whom every sin is committed. Keeping this in mind, let us,

I. Bring forward what the Psalmist, in our text, calls *our iniquities*, that is, our more gross and open sins, and see how they appear in the light of God's countenance. Have any of you been guilty of impious, profane, passionate, or indecent, corrupting language? How does such language sound in heaven? in the ears of angels, in the ears of that God, who gave us our tongues for noble purposes? Bring forward all the language of this kind which you have ever uttered; see it written as in a book; and while you read it, remember that the eye of God is reading it at the same time. Then say, Is this fit language for an immortal being to utter? Is this fit language for God to hear? Especially, let every one inquire, whether he has ever violated the third commandment, by using the name of God in a profane or irreverent manner. If he has, let him bring forward his transgressions of this kind, and see how they appear in the light of God's presence. Sinner, this is the Being, whose adorable name thou hast profaned, and who, bending upon thee a look of awful displeasure, says, I will not hold him guiltless, that taketh my name in vain. O, what an aspect of shocking, heaven-daring impiety, does this assume, when viewed in this situation! Have any of you been guilty of uttering what is untrue? If so, bring forward all the falsehoods, all the deceitful expressions, which you have ever uttered, and see how they appear in the presence of the God of truth; of that God, who has declared, that he abhors a lying tongue, and that all liars shall have their portion in the burning lake. O, what is it to stand convicted of falsehood before such a God as this! Have any of you been guilty, either at home or in foreign countries, of perjury or false swearing? If so, you may here see the awful Being, whom you mocked, by calling him to witness the truth of a known, deliberate lie. And how, think you, such conduct appears in his eyes? How does it now appear in your own? When you took that false oath; when you said, so may God help me as I speak the truth, you did, in effect, utter a prayer that his vengeance might fall upon you, if what you swore was untrue. And will not God take you at your word? Will not that vengeance, which you imprecated, fall upon you? O, be assured that it will, unless deep, timely repentance and faith in Christ prevent. Nor is the guilt of those, who share in the gain of perjury, and permit such as are employed by them to make use of it, much less black and aggravated in the estimation of him, whose judgment is according to truth.

Have any of you transgressed the command which says, Remember the Sabbath day to keep it holy? Such transgressions, I am aware, appear very trivial on earth; but do they appear so to him who gave this command? Do they appear so in heaven, where an everlasting Sabbath is observed? Let those, who have been guilty of such transgressions, hear a voice from the glory around them, saying, I, to whom you are indebted for all your time, allowed you six days for the performance of your necessary labors, and reserved but one for myself, but one to be employed exclusively in worshipping me, and in working out your own salvation. But even this one day you denied me; when spent in my service, you considered it as a weariness, and therefore employed it, either wholly or in part, in serving yourselves; thus proving yourselves to be wholly unqualified and unfit to enjoy an endless Sabbath in my presence.

Have any of you—we must propose the unpleasant question—been guilty of violating the command which forbids adultery and its kindred vices? If so, bring forward these abominations, and see how they look in heaven, in the presence of the holy angels, in the sight of that thrice Holy God, who has said, I will come near and be a swift witness against the adulterers, and they shall have their portion in the lake of fire.

Have any of you been guilty of fraud, injustice, or dishonesty? Have you in your possession any portion of another's property, without the owner's consent fairly obtained? If so, bring forward your dishonest gains; hold out the hands which are polluted by them, and see how they look in heaven, in the presence of that God, who has said, Let no man overreach or defraud his brother in any matter; for the Lord is the avenger of all such.

Have any of you been guilty of intemperance? If so, let such look at themselves, and see how a drunkard, a rational being, self-degraded to a level with the beasts and wallowing in the mire of his own pollution, appears in heaven, in the society of pure angelic spirits, in the sight of that God, who endued him with intellectual powers, and thus capacitated him for being raised to an equality with the angels.

While attending to the preceding remarks, probably many, perhaps most of my hearers may have felt as if they were not personally concerned in them, as if they were guilty of none of these gross iniquities. I would indeed hope, that of some of them at least, none of you are guilty. But these are by no means the only iniquities, of which God takes notice; for our text further informs us, that he has set *secret* sins, the *sins of our hearts*, in the light of his countenance. Let us then,

II. Bring our hearts into heaven, and there, laying them open to view, see how they will appear in that world of unclouded light, and unsullied purity.

And, O, how do they appear! What a disclosure is made, when, with the dissecting knife of a spiritual anatomist, we lay open the human heart, with all its dark recesses, and intricate windings, and expose the lurking abominations, which it conceals, not to the light of day, but to the light of heaven! My hearers, even in this sinful world the spectacle which such a disclosure would exhibit could not be borne. The man, whose heart should thus be laid open to public view, would be banished from society; nay, he would himself fly from it, overwhelmed with shame and confusion. Of this every man is sensible, and therefore conceals his heart from all eyes with jealous care. Every man is conscious of many thoughts and feelings, which he would be ashamed to express to his most intimate friend. Even those profligate, abandoned wretches, who glory in foaming out their own shame, and whose mouths, like an open sepulchre, breathe out moral contagion, putrefaction, and death, scarcely dare utter to their own equally abandoned associates every thought and feeling, which rises within them. And if this is the fact, if the heart, laid open to view, would appear thus black in this dark, sinful world; who can describe, or conceive of the blackness which it must exhibit, when surrounded by the dazzling whiteness of heaven, and seen in the light of God's presence, the light of his holiness and glory? How do proud, self-exalting thoughts appear, when viewed in the presence of him, before whom all the nations of the earth are less than nothing and vanity? How do self-will, impatience, and discontent with the allotments of Providence appear, when viewed as exercised before the throne of the infinite, eternal, universal Sovereign? How do angry, envious, revengeful feelings appear in the eyes of the God of love, and in those regions of love, where, since the expulsion of the rebel angels, not one such feeling has ever been exercised? How do wanton, impure thoughts appear—but we cannot pursue the loathsome, sickening enumeration. Surely, if all the evil thoughts and wrong feelings which have passed in countless numbers through either of our hearts, were poured out in heaven, angels would stand aghast at the sight, and all their benevolence would scarcely prevent them from exclaiming in holy indignation, Away with him to the abode of his kindred spirits in the abyss! To the omniscient God alone would the sight not be surprising. He knows, and he alone knows, what is in the heart of man; and what he knows of it he has described in brief, but terribly expressive terms. The heart of the sons of men is full of evil, and madness is in their hearts. The heart is deceitful above all things, and desperately wicked! Thus our own hearts appear even to us, if we view them in the light of God's countenance, and recollect that in his sight, thoughts and feelings are actions, that a wanton look is adultery, and hatred murder.

III. Having thus viewed our actual sins of heart and life, as they appear in the light of heaven, let us take a similar view of our sins of omission. Should we neglect to do this, we should see but a small part of our sinfulness; for our sins of omission are by far the most numerous, and by no means the least criminal offences, of which we are guilty. But before we proceed to take this view, allow me to remind you once more, where you are, and in whose presence you stand. Recollect all which you have heard and seen of God's infinite perfections; of his unapproachable glory, of the offices which he sustains, of the works which he has performed, of the blessings which he has bestowed upon us, upon our fellow creatures. Look at him once more, as he appears when seen in the light of heaven; as he appears in the eyes of the angels and archangels around you, and then say what he deserves from his creatures. Does he not deserve, can you avoid perceiving that he deserves, all their admiration, love, reverence, confidence, gratitude and obedience? Does he not, O does he not, deserve to be loved, and feared, and served with all the heart and soul and mind and strength? This, you are sensible, is what his law requires of us; and can any requisition be more just and reasonable? Can we refuse to comply with it; can we withhold our affections and services from such a being as this, without incuring great and aggravated guilt? Yet this, my fellow sinners, is the being, from whom we have all withheld our affections and services. Our whole lives present one unbroken series of duties neglected, of favors not acknowledged. And, O, how do they appear, when we review them in the light of God's countenance! When we see before us our Creator, our Preserver, our Benefactor, our Sovereign, and our heavenly Father; when we see in him, to whom all these titles belong, infinite excellence, perfection, glory and beauty; when we see with what profound veneration, with what raptures of holy, grateful affection, he is regarded and served by all the bright armies of heaven; and then turn and contemplate our past lives, and reflect how they must appear in his sight, can we refrain from exclaiming with Job, We have heard of thee by the hearing of the ear, but now our eyes see thee; wherefore we abhor ourselves, and repent in dust and ashes? I have sinned; what shall I say unto thee, O thou Preserver of men? Must not each of us say with the Psalmist, Innumerable evils have compassed me about; my iniquities have taken hold upon me, so that I am not able to look up; they are more in number than the hairs of my head; therefore my heart faileth me? Nay more, when you see what God is, and how he is worshipped in heaven, and then look at the coldness, the formality, the want of reverence, with which you have often approached him in prayer, and listened to his word, must you not feel conscious, that should he call you into judgment, you could not answer for one in a thousand of the iniquities, which have stained your holy things, your religious duties?

But the duties which we owe to God, are not the only duties which we are required, and which we have neglected, to perform. While his law requires us to love him with all the heart, it also requires us to love our neighbor as ourselves. And this general command virtually includes a great number of subordinate precepts; precepts, which prescribe the duties of the various relations, that subsist between us and our fellow creatures. And how far have we obeyed these precepts? How far have we performed the duties, which God requires of us, as husbands, as wives, as parents, as children, as masters, as servants, as citizens, and as members of the human family? When we spread our lives before God, and look at them as they appear in the light of his countenance, can we fail to perceive, that we have in all these respects been grossly deficient, that we have left undone many, very many things, which we ought to have done, and that we are far from having discharged the duties of a single relation which we sustain? O, how much more might we have done, than we actually have done, to promote the temporal and eternal happiness of all, with whom we are connected!

Nor do our sins of omission end here. There is another being, whom we are under infinite obligations to love, and praise, and serve with supreme affection. This being is the Lord Jesus Christ, considered as our Redeemer and Savior, who has bought us with his own blood. We are required, and sacredly bound to feel, that we are not our own, but his; to prefer him to every earthly object, to rely upon him with implicit confidence, to live, not to ourselves, but to him, and to honor him even as we honor the Father. Every moment then, in which we neglected to obey these commands, we were guilty of a new sin of omission. Nor have we the smallest excuse for neglecting to obey these commands; for he is most worthy of all which they require. Even the angels, for whom he never died, regard him as worthy to receive every thing, which creatures can give. Much more then may it be expected, that we, for whom he has done and suffered so much, should regard and treat him as worthy. But how grossly have we failed in performing this part of our duty? How must the manner, in which we have treated his beloved Son, appear in the sight of God? How does it appear to us, when we contemplate him as he appears in heaven; when we see the place which he there fills; when we recollect, that in him all the fulness of the Godhead dwells, and that to him are unceasingly ascribed wisdom, and strength, and blessing, and honor, and glory, and power?

The subject before us is far from being exhausted, and very far from having had justice done to it; but we must leave it, and hasten to a conclusion. Before we close however, permit me to ask, whether you cannot now perceive the reason, why your sins appear more numerous and criminal in the sight of God, than they do in your own? Have you seen or heard nothing, which convinces you, that they are far more numerous and aggravated than you had supposed? If so, you have seen nothing of what has been exhibited; you have, properly speaking, heard nothing, which has been said; you have not seen your sins in the light of God's countenance; for had you seen them in that light, they would have appeared, in some measure, to you, as they appear to God himself. Witness, for instance, the effect which a view of God's glory produced upon the prophet Isaiah. Though he was an eminently good man, and had probably fewer sins to answer for than either of us, yet when in vision he saw Jehovah seated upon his eternal throne, and heard the surrounding seraphim exclaiming, Holy, holy, holy is the Lord of hosts; the whole earth is full of his glory, —he cried out in amazement and consternation, Woe is me; for I am undone; I am a man of unclean lips. In a similar manner, my hearers, would you have been affected, had you seen even but a glimpse of those glories, which we have vainly attempted to exhibit. Can you not easily conceive, that this would have been the case? Can you not conceive, that were you really placed in heaven, before the throne of God, with all the light of his glory shining around you, all the majesty of his countenance beaming upon you, every glance of his omniscient eye piercing your hearts,—your sins would appear to you far more black and numerous, than they now do? If so, allow me to remind you that a day is approaching, in which you will be constrained to see your sins, as they appear in the light of God's countenance. When that day arrives, his eternal Son, the appointed Judge, will be seen coming in the clouds of heaven, with all his Father's glories blazing around him, and all the bright armies of heaven following in his train. Seated on a throne of resplendent whiteness, with a countenance from the terrors of which the heavens and the earth will flee affrighted, he will summon the whole race of men before him, and there cause their lives to pass in review, expose all their secret sins, lay open the inmost recesses of our hearts; while the flood of pure, celestial light which pours itself around him, will by contrast cause their blackness to appear seven fold more black. Then all disputes respecting the depravity of mankind, and the demerit of sin, will be ended forever. Then no more complaint of the strictness of God's laws, or of the severity of the punishment, which it denounces upon transgressors, will be heard; for every mouth shall be stopped, and all the world stand guilty before God. But a conviction of sinfulness and guilt will then come too late; for there is no available repentance beyond the grave. He that is found a sinner at the judgment day, will continue a sinner, and be treated as a sinner forever. O, then, my hearers, be persuaded now to come to the light, that your deeds may be reproved, and set in order before you; exercise such feelings respecting them, and so judge yourselves, that you may not be condemned of the Lord in that day.

SERMON VI.

MEN TRIED AND FOUND DEFECTIVE.

Thou art weighed in the balances, and art found wanting.—Daniel v. 27.

In the preceding part of this chapter we are informed, that Belshazzar, king of Babylon, made a great feast to a thousand of his lords and drank wine before the thousand. And while he tasted the wine, he commanded his servants to bring forth the golden vessels, which were taken out of the house of God at Jerusalem; and he, with his guests, drank wine in them, and praised the gods of gold and silver, of brass and iron, of wood and of stone. But while they were thus insulting the Majesty of heaven and earth, by consuming his bounty upon their lusts, and profaning the vessels of his sanctuary, in the same hour there came forth the fingers of a man's hand, and wrote over against the candlestick upon the plaster of the wall of the palace, and the king saw the part of the hand, which wrote. Though he knew not the awful import of the mysterious words thus written, his guilty conscience soon told him, that he had no reason to expect messages of mercy from the invisible world; and therefore his countenance was changed and his thoughts troubled him, so that the joints of his loins were loosed and his knees smote one against another. Nor were his terrors without foundation; for after the hand was withdrawn, the words, mene, tekel, upharsin, were found written; words, which were thus interpreted by Daniel the prophet; mene, God hath numbered thy kingdom and finished it· tekel, thou art weighed in the balances, and art found wanting; UPHARSIN, thy kingdom is ivided, and given to the Medes and Persians. The justness of this interpretation was confirmed by the event, for that same night was Belshazzar slain.

My fr ends, this story affords an instructive, admonitory lesson to us all; for though we have not, like Belshazzar, profaned the consecrated vessels of the Lord, or praised the gods of the heathen, who are vanity and a lie, yet we have in various ways insulted our Creator and provoked him to jealousy. We have often consumed his bounty upon our lusts; we have perverted those faculties, which ought to have been consecrated to his service; we have loved and served and idolized the world, and the God, in whose hand our breath is, and whose are all our ways we have not glorified; and though the displeasure of offended heaven is not now suddenly and openly displayed, as it was in the days of Daniel; though no hand is now sent to write the sentence of condemnation on the walls of our houses, yet there is still an invisible witness, which continually records our actions; there is still a just and omniscient God, by whom these actions are weighed; it is still true that we shall receive of him a just recompense of reward, according to our works. Our days are already numbered and will soon be finished; for God has set bounds to our lives which we cannot pass. Soon shall we be weighed in the balance of eternal truth and justice, and if we are found wanting, we shall be cut in sunder, and have a portion appointed us with hypocrites and unbelievers. And say, my friends, are you all prepared to pass this solemn test? Should the same hand, which wrote the doom of impious Belshazzar on the plaster of the wall of his palace, be now commissioned to write our names, our characters and our doom on the plaster of the walls of this house, are there none here present, whose thoughts would trouble them; none, whose countenances would be changed by conscious guilt; none, over against whose names the damning sentence, *tekel*, would be seen inscribed?

This is a most interesting and important question to all of us; a question, which ought by no means to remain doubtful; a question, which it is perhaps as much as our immortal souls are worth, to leave for a single day undecided. And why should it remain undecided? Have we not, in our own hands, the balance in which our actions and characters will one day be weighed? Has not the Judge himself informed us, in the clearest manner, of the rules and maxims by which he will be guided in determining our irrevocable doom? Let us then avail ourselves of the information, which he has given us, and resolve, before we leave this house, to know the worst of our situation, and ascertain what sentence we have reason to expect from the mouth of God. Let us this evening, anticipate the proceedings of the judgment day, and impartially weigh our characters, hopes and pretensions in the balance of the sanctuary, that we may discover, before discovery will be too late, whether we are prepared to meet our Judge in peace.

I. Let us place in this balance the pretensions and characters of those, who hope for heaven because they were born in a Christian country, are descended from pious parents; and were by them in their infancy given up to God in the ordinance of baptism, and have enjoyed the advantages of a religious education. That there are persons, who build their eternal hopes on this foundation, daily experience but too plainly evinces; and perhaps there may be some such in this assembly. If so, we must assure them, that they are building upon the sand, and that they will be found wanting, when weighed at the bar of God. For though the privileges, with which such persons are favored, afford them peculiar advantages for becoming religious; yet they do not render them so, but on the contrary, unless suitably improved, greatly aggravate their guilt and punishment. To whom much is given, of them will much be required; and those who are thus early taught their Lord's will, unless they perform it, will be beaten with many stripes. Think not, says John the Baptist to the Jews, who trusted in their religious privileges—think not to say within yourselves, we have Abraham to our father; that is, trust not in your descent from that pious patriarch, nor to your covenant relation to God; for I say unto you, that God is able, of these stones, to raise up children unto Abraham. To the same purpose St. Paul writes to the Philippian Christians. If any man, says he, thinketh that he hath whereof he might trust in the flesh, I have more: Circumcised the eighth day, of the stock of Israel, of the tribe of Benjamin, a Hebrew of the Hebrews; as touching the law, a Pharisee. But, he adds, what things were gain to me, those I counted loss for Christ.

II. Let us bring to the test of the law and the testimony, the characters and hopes of those, who are trusting for salvation to a good natural disposition, and a harmless, inoffensive life. It is possible, that some of you, my friends, may be trusting to these things. You can plead that your tempers are gentle, conciliating, mild and amiable; that your conduct and deportment are winning and prepossessing; that you are admired and beloved by your friends and acquaintance, and are not conscious of having, in a single instance, wilfully injured your fellow creatures or offended your Creator. But if you can plead nothing more than this, you will most certainly be found wanting in the sight of that God, by whom actions are weighed. He will not be satisfied with a bare negative goodness, if we may be allowed the expression. He will not think it sufficient, that you have abstained from outward offences, or avoided overt acts of sin, while you have failed to perform what he has commanded. Those who leave undone what they ought to do, will be as certainly, if not as severely punished, as those who do what they ought not to have done. Not only those vines which produce the grapes of Sodom, and the clusters of Gomorrha, but those also which do not produce the fruits of holiness, will be cast into the fire; and though you are covered with leaves, and adorned with flowers; though you make a fair flourishing appearance in the sight of men, yet he must and will consider you as barren and unprofitable, because you are destitute of these fruits; he must condemn you as slothful and unfaithful servants, because you have neglected to improve the talents with which you were entrusted. It was part of the heavy charge brought against the king of Babylon, that he had not glorified the God, in whose hands his life was, and whose were all his ways. To the same charge you must plead guilty, since you have never glorified, nor even sincerely aimed to glorify God. The amiable dispositions in which you trust, do not lead you to seek his glory, or to obey his commands. In fact, they have nothing in them of the nature of true religion; but are merely corporeal instincts, and are often found in perfection among irrational animals. You are therefore found wanting. You want the one thing needful; and were our blessed Saviour now on earth, he would say to each of you, as he did to the amiable young ruler, One thing thou lackest. Go, and sell all that thou hast, and give to the poor, and come, take up thy cross and follow me.

III. Another class, perhaps, will boldly come forward and say, though these characters are justly considered as deficient, yet we do not fear that we shall be found wanting; for we have something more than mere negative goodness to plead. Instead of misimproving, or abusing our time and talents, we have improved them with diligence and faithfulness. Instead of injuring our fellow creatures, we have endeavored to promote their happiness by every means in our power. We have been sober, temperate, honest, and industrious; have carefully fulfilled all the social and relative duties of life; have provided for the support of our own families, and been kind and liberal to the poor and afflicted. In short, we have been useful members of society, and have faithfully discharged the various duties, which we owed to our parents, our children, our friends, and our country. We do not, indeed, pretend to be perfect, and confess that in the course of our lives, we have sometimes been induced by strong and sudden temptations to say or do things, which were perhaps improper and sinful. But we have always been sorry for these offences, and they are but few and trifling compared with our good actions. We therefore trust that a merciful God has forgiven them, and are ready to appear cheerfully at his tribunal, whenever he shall think proper to summon us away. Such ever has been and ever will be the language of those, who are ignorant of their own hearts, and of the requirements of God's law; and such we have reason to fear, is the secret language of some in this assembly. But we must assure you, my friends, that if you can plead nothing more than this, you will certainly be found wanting at the bar of God, however safe and confident you may feel; nor can you possibly escape, unless the Judge should break his word, and act contrary to his own solemn declarations. He has summed up the law, by which you will be tried, in the two great commands which enjoin it upon us to love God with all our hearts, and our neighbor as ourselves. Now even though we should allow what we presume none of you will pretend, that you have through life perfectly obeyed this latter command, and loved your neighbor as yourselves; yet you would still be condemned for neglecting to love God with all your hearts. The performance of all the duties, which you owe your fellow creatures, can make no atonement for neglecting the far more important duties, which you owe to your God; for as our Savior has said, in a similar case, these ought ye to have done, and not to have left the other undone. If therefore, we should even allow the truth of all your pleas, you would still be found guilty, when weighed in the balance of the sanctuary, of wanting that perfect love to God, which the divine law inflexibly requires of all, who seek to be justified by its works.

But we cannot allow the truth of these pleas. We cannot allow that any of you have perfectly discharged the duties, which you owe your fellow creatures. You know, you must know, that you have not loved your neighbors as yourselves, and that therefore in this respect also, you will be found wanting. But you will perhaps object, that it is impossible for any to love his neighbor as himself; it is contrary to nature; it is morally impossible; and since God is a merciful being, he certainly will not judge us by this severe law, but will make some allowance for the imperfections and infirmities of his creatures. If such are your hopes, listen to our Savior and his apostle, and they will vanish at once. Says the apostle, As many as have sinned without law, shall also perish without law; and as many as have sinned in, or under the law, shall be judged by the law. But will not the rigor of this law be mitigated? No; for, says theJudge, though heaven and earth should pass away, yet one jot or one tittle shall in no wise pass from the law, till all be fulfilled. Whosoever therefore shall break one of the least of these commandments and shall teach men so; the same shall be called least in the kingdom of heaven; that is, shall never enter it; for I say unto you, that except your righteousness exceed the righteousness of the scribes and pharisees, ye shall, in no wise, enter into the kingdom of heaven. Yet the pharisees had at least as much righteousness, as any moralist at the present day. Some of them could say, we are not as other men are, unjust, extortioners, or adulterers. We fast twice in a week, and give tithes of all we possess. But it is evident from our Savior's own declarations, that those who can say nothing more than this, will be found wanting, and never be admitted into the kingdom of God.

IV. Perhaps another class will come forward and say, we

allow that those who trust to their own moral duties for salvation, will be justly condemned; but we have carefully obeyed the commands of the first table; we do not trust to our moral duties, and therefore hope to escape. We have never worshipped false gods; we have made no graven images; we have never taken God's name in vain, nor do we profane his holy sabbath. On the contrary we entertain a great degree of veneration and love for God, we worship him daily in our families and closets; we study his word, honor his institutions, and diligently attend to the preaching of the gospel, in season, and out of season.

But permit me to ask,—are you equally careful to perform all the duties, which you owe to your fellow creatures? Does not your whole religion consist in the observances of external forms, prayer, reading and hearing the word? Are you not among the number of forgetful hearers, rather than the doers of the word; and do you not hope, by your religious duties, to atone for your moral deficiencies? Are you not hard and unmerciful in your dealings; peevish, fretful and morose in your families, or indolent in performing the proper duties of the station in which you are placed? Are you not harsh and severe in censuring the conduct, or condemning the character of your neighbors? Above all, are you not deficient in the great duty of liberality to the poor, and of doing to others, as you would wish that they should do to you? If so, vain are all your religious duties; vain your pretensions of love to God. In vain do you pretend to obey the commands of the first table, while you neglect those of the second; for piety, without morality, is even worse than morality without piety. You will be found guilty of wanting love to man; and consequently, of being destitute of all true love to God, whatever you may pretend; for, says the apostle, he that loveth not his brother, whom he hath seen, how can he love God, whom he hath not seen? And again, whoso hath this world's goods, and seeth his brother have need, and shutteth up his bowels of compassion from him, how dwelleth the love of God in him? And again, if any man among you seem to be religious, and bridleth not his tongue, but deceiveth his own heart, that man's religion is vain.

V. Perhaps some may be found, who will say notwithstanding these observations, still our hope remains unshaken; for we have both piety and morality. We not only deal justly and love mercy, as it respects our fellow creatures, but also walk humbly with our God. We do not make the performance of our duties to men an excuse for neglecting our duties to God; nor, on the other hand, do we consider the discharging of our duty to God as an excuse for neglecting our duties to men; but we carefully attend to both. We keep up the worship of God in our families and closets; we bring up our children in the nurture and admonition of the Lord; we reverence the sabbath and other institutions of religion, and diligently attend to the word read and preached. In addition to this, we are sober, moral and exemplary in our conduct; careful to promote the welfare and happiness of our families, and kind to the poor, the sick and distressed. In what respect then, can we be said to be wanting?

I answer, if you have nothing more than this, you want many things.

You want that new heart, without which no man can see the kingdom of God. You want that faith without which you must be condemned. You want that repentance, without which you must inevitably perish. You want that holiness, without which no man shall see the Lord. All these things are every where represented as indispensably necessary to salvation; and yet persons may do every thing which you profess to have done, without either regeneration, faith, repentance or holiness. You can plead nothing more than the pharisee, who went up to the temple, could plead. He discharged his duties to men no less faithfully than you profess to have done; for he was not unjust, nor an extortioner, nor an adulterer; and he gave the tenth part of his goods to the poor. In addition to this, he also attended to the duties, which he owed to God. He went to the temple, he prayed, he thanked God, and fasted twice in a week. Yet he was found wanting, and sent away empty. So the young ruler could say respecting the commandments, all these have I kept from my youth up; and St. Paul tells us, that before his conversion, as touching the righteousness of the law, he was blameless. Yet he afterwards counted all his imaginary righteousness as loss for Christ. But you will perhaps ask, if an unregenerate impenitent sinner can do all these things, what need is there of regeneration and repentance? As well may you ask, if an enemy can perform all the outward acts and services of a friend, what need is there of any real friendship? Would you be satisfied with your children, if they served and obeyed you merely from a selfish fear of punishment, or hope of reward? Would you be pleased with any of their attempts to promote your happiness, if you knew that a wish to obtain a portion of your estates was the only motive and governing principle of their conduct? But the slightest self-examination must convince those of you, whom we are now addressing, that you are actuated merely by selfish motives in all the religious and moral duties which you perform. You are not sweetly drawn by the gentle, but powerful influences of love, to obey your Father in heaven. You do not serve him merely for the pleasure of serving him. You serve him as a master, and not as a father. You are actuated either by fear of his displeasure, by a desire of obtaining a share of the heavenly inheritance, or a wish to be freed from a burden of guilt which oppresses you. Self-interest therefore, is really the god, whom you worship; you serve yourselves and not God, in all that you do; and therefore, your services are all sins; they are an abomination in his sight; because you want that principle of supreme love to God, which is found only in the renewed soul, and without which it is impossible to please him in the smallest degree. They who want this, want every thing.

But though we should not insist upon this, though we should allow that all your duties were performed with proper views and motives; yet still you would be found wanting. You would be found wanting with respect to the improvement of your time; for how much of this is misspent. How much is daily wasted in unnecessary sleep, in idle conversation, in foolish or useless pursuits, and in unproductive idleness. You would be found wanting in the government of your thoughts; for what an innumerable multitude of vain, trifling and sinful imaginations pass through your minds in the course of a single day? If your fellow creatures were acquainted with every thing that passes in your breasts, would they not consider you as wanting wisdom and goodness? How then must you appear in the sight of God? You would be found wanting in the government of your tongues; for how many foolish, vain, unprofitable words escape from your lips in the course of a day. Yet says our Savior, for every idle word that men speak, they shall give account in the day of judgment. In a word, you would be found wanting in every respect; for the law of God requires perfect obedience, in thought, word and deed, and pronounces a curse on every one, who does not thus obey it. It requires that all your time, all your talents, all your possessions, all your thoughts and all your affections should be sincerely consecrated and devoted to God; that whether you eat, or drink, or whatever you do, should be done to his glory. It is in vain to pretend, that you obey this law more frequently than you transgress it; that your good actions are more numerous than your sins. As well might a thief or a murderer say, I have obeyed the laws of my country for many years, and have only broken them in a few instances, and therefore I ought to be forgiven, since my good actions are more numerous than my crimes. Every one must, at once, be sensible of the folly of this plea. Every one must be sensible, that all laws, human and divine, do, and ought to, require perfect obedience, and to punish every wilful transgression; and that it would be the height of absurdity to make a law which allowed persons to disobey its precepts. If the law of God allows men to sin in the smallest degree, then God has become the patron and protector of sin, and is no longer perfectly holy, just and true. But the law of God does not allow men to sin in the smallest degree. It considers him who offends in one point as guilty of all, and condemns him accordingly. It considers imperfect obedience as no obedience; and therefore every one who has at any time transgressed in thought, word or deed, every one who cannot produce a perfect righteousness, will be found wanting, when weighed in this impartial balance.

But you will say, if this be the case then all will be found wanting; for the scriptures assure us, that there is not a just man on earth, who doeth good and sinneth not. True, my friends, by the law of God we are all found wanting. We have all sinned, and the whole world has become guilty before God. We are all children of wrath, and are already under condemnation. Do you ask, who then will be saved? who will not be found wanting? I answer, those, and those only, who can bring and place in the balance the righteousness of the Lord Jesus Christ. This is a perfect righteousness, without spot or blemish. He perfectly obeyed the whole law. He loved God with all his heart and his neighbor as himself; and he is declared to be the end of the law for righteousness to every one that believeth. That is, he fulfils, or obeys the law in their behalf. Believers are united to Christ by faith in such a manner, that they are one with him in the sight of God, and what he has done is considered as having been done by them; and hence they are said to be complete, or perfect in him, and he is made of God unto them, wisdom, righteousness, sanctification and redemption. Hence believers, though they have neither wisdom, strength, nor righteousness of their own, are wise in Christ's wisdom, strong in his strength, and righteous in his righteousness; and therefore, when weighed in the balance they shall not be found wanting. There is no condemnation to them that are in Christ Jesus. But all, who are not united to Christ by faith, will be found wanting; all their righteousness will be proved light as nothing and vanity, and they will share in the doom of impious Belshazzar.

But here an important question arises: How may an interest in the righteousness of Christ be obtained? I answer—it cannot be purchased, for it is infinitely above all price, nor will he sell his favors. It cannot be merited; for the best, merit nothing but destruction. It must come as a free gift. But to whom will it be given? I answer, it is freely and unconditionally offered to all who will accept it by faith. None however, will ever accept it but those, who see that they have no righteousness of their own to plead. None will accept it but those who are truly convinced, that they have never performed a good action, uttered a good word, or exercised one good affection. Hence our Savior informs us, that publicans and harlots, the very refuse of society, will sooner enter the kingdom of heaven, than those, who like the pharisees, trust in themselves that they are righteous. Hence also we find that the promises of the gospel are ever made to the poor in spirit, to the self-condemned sinner, to the mourners for sin, and to the penitent and contrite heart. Such characters see and feel that they have nothing of their own to plead; nothing which they dare place in the balance. They see, as did the apostle, that in them there dwells no good thing; they see that they are wholly unworthy of God's favor, and deserve nothing but death at his hands; they see that if they ever are saved, they must be saved by free, sovereign grace. Hence they are willing to throw themselves at Christ's feet, and resign themselves entirely to his disposal. They are willing to receive him by faith, as he is freely offered in the gospel, and to depend on his righteousness, and intercession alone for salvation. But never will the self-righteous sinner do this; never will he submit to be saved in this humbling way. He may indeed be willing that Christ should supply the deficiencies of his own imaginary righteousness, and atone for the few trifling sins which he has committed; but he is resolved to have at least part of the glory of his salvation; he will not depend on Christ alone; and therefore in reality does not depend upon him at all, nor will he receive any benefit from him; for our Savior will have no partners in this work. He will save us alone, or leave us to perish. He will have all the glory, or we never shall join in the song of the redeemed.

Thus have I endeavored, in a plain, simple, unadorned manner, to set before you the sentence which you have reason to expect at the judgment day, and the manner in which you may escape the fate of those who will be weighed in the balance and be found wanting. I have avoided every thing which might tend only to amuse, or to render the subject obscure, and have only sought to render it intelligible to persons of every description. And now permit me to ask, what is the result? Will you go to the judgment seat in your own righteousness, or in that of Christ? If you are still determined to depend on yourselves, or on the mercy of God out of Christ, I cannot help it. I would only remind you of what God has said, Cursed be the man, that trusteth in man, and maketh flesh his arm, whose heart departeth from the Lord. Behold, all ye that kindle a fire, that compass yourselves about with sparks, walk in the light of your fire, and in the sparks that ye have kindled; this shall ye have at my hand; ye shall lie down in sorrow. But if there are any of you, who begin to fear that you shall be found wanting on that awful occasion; any, who feel that they are poor, and miserable, and wretched, and blind, and naked, let them comply with the gracious counsel and invitation of Christ, and receive of him, a complete and perfect righteousness, without money and without price. He requires of you no other worthiness than a heartfelt conviction that you are utterly unworthy. He requires no other goodness, than a sincere acknowledgment, that you have in you no good thing. He requires nothing else of you, in order to salvation, but a readiness to be saved in his own way and upon his own terms. Be not then discouraged to find that you are the chief of sinners; that you have no goodness, no worthiness, no righteousness of your own to plead. Did you possess any of these, he would not receive you; for he came to save, not the worthy, but the unworthy; not the righteous, but the sinful; not those who feel able to save themselves, but those, who feel utterly lost and undone without him. So long as you imagine, that you have any good qualities to recommend you to his favor, you are separated from him by an impassable gulf; for sooner may a camel pass through the eye of a needle, than one who is rich in his own opinion enter the kingdom of God.

SERMON VII.

OUR SINS INFINITE IN NUMBER AND ENORMITY.

Is not thy wickedness great? and thine iniquities infinite? Job. xxii. 5.

This question was addressed by Eliphaz to Job. He was led to ask it by a suspicion, that Job was a hypocrite. He had imbibed the erroneous opinion, that great temporal calamities are inflicted on none, except the wicked. Hence he inferred from the unprecedented afflictions of Job, that notwithstanding all his professions and fair appearances of piety, he was a wicked man. He therefore endeavored to convince him that this was his character, and that he had been deceived respecting himself? With this view he addressed him in the language of our text: Is not thy wickedness great? and thine iniquities infinite? Had Job really been what Eliphaz erroneously supposed him to be, this would have been a very proper question, and the charge which it implies, would have been strictly just. It is, therefore, still a proper question to be proposed to all who are ignorant of themselves. Indeed, it may without impropriety be addressed to every child of Adam; since there is not an individual among them, who, if he answer it truly, must not answer it in the affirmative. To establish the truth—that the sins of men are infinite in number and enormity—is my present design.

In prosecuting this design it becomes necessary to show, as clearly as possible, what meaning is attached to the terms, sin, and wickedness, in the Word of God; I say, in the Word of

God; for it is too evident to require proof, that by these terms, men usually mean something very different from what is meant by the inspired writers. The word, sin, for instance, is considered by many as synonymous with crime; and by crime they mean the violation of some human law, or of the common rules of morality and honesty. Hence they conclude, that if a man obeys the laws of his country, and lives a sober, moral life, he has few, if any, sins to answer for. A similar meaning they attach to the term, wicked. By a wicked man, they suppose, is intended, a man openly and grossly immoral, impious, or profane; one who treats religion with avowed disrespect, or who denies the divine authority of revelation. But very different is the meaning, which the inspired writers attach to these terms. By wicked men, they mean all who are not righteous; all who do not repent and believe the gospel, however correct their external conduct may be; and by sin, they mean a violation of the divine law, which requires us to love God with all our hearts, and our neighbor as ourselves; for, says the apostle, sin is a transgression of, or a deviation from, the law. This law branches out into various and numerous precepts, prescribing, with great minuteness, our duties towards all the beings, with whom we are connected, and the dispositions, which are to be exercised in every situation and relation of life; and the violation and disregard of any of these precepts is a sin. The gospel, also, has its precepts, as well as the law. It requires repentance, faith and obedience; and neglecting to obey these precepts, is represented as sinful in the highest degree. In a word, when we do not perfectly obey all God's commands, in feeling, thought, word, and action, we sin. When we do not feel, and think, and speak, and act, as he requires, we are guilty of what are denominated sins of omission. When we feel, think, or speak, or act, in such a manner as he forbids, we are guilty of the sin of commission. These general remarks will be sufficient to convince every one who knows any thing of God, of himself, or of the divine law, that his sins are exceedingly numerous. But since most men are unacquainted with all these subjects, and especially, with the nature, strictness and extent of God's law, it will be necessary, in order to produce conviction, to be more particular. And since the heart is represented as the fountain, whence all evil flows; the tree which gives its own character to all the fruit produced by it, let us begin with that, and consider,

1. The sin of our hearts; or in other words, of our dispositions and feelings. The sins of this class alone, of which the best man on earth is guilty, are innumerable. They form by far the heaviest part of the charge, which will be brought against every impenitent sinner at the judgment day. Yet most men think nothing of them. They seem to imagine, that if the outside be clean, the feelings and dispositions of the heart are of little consequence. But God thinks very differently; and a moment's reflection will convince us, that a being, who commits no outward sins, may, notwithstanding, be the chief of sinners. Such, for instance, are the evil spirits. None will deny, that they are sinful in the highest degree. But they have no hands, to act; no tongue, to speak. All their sins are inward sins; sins of the heart. It is obvious then, that persons may be the greatest sinners in the universe, without being guilty of one outward sin. The law of God, and the gospel of Christ, teach the same truth. What they principally require, is right feelings and dispositions. What they chiefly forbid and condemn is, feelings and dispositions that are wrong. For instance, love is an affection; repentance is an affection; faith is a feeling; humility a feeling; hope, patience, resignation, and contentment, are feelings. Yet all these are required of us as indispensable duties. On the other hand, unbelief is a feeling; selfishness, impenitence, pride, love of the world, covetousness, envy, anger, hatred, and revenge are feelings. Yet all these things are forbidden as the worst of sins; sins, for which those, who indulge them, will be condemned. It is evident then, that if we wish to know the number of our sins, we must look first, and chiefly, at the feelings and dispositions of our hearts. And if we do thus look at them, we shall be convinced, in a moment, that our sins are numberless. Every moment of our waking existence, in which we do not love God with all our hearts, we sin; for this constant and perfect love to God his law requires. Every moment in which we do not love our neighbor as ourselves, we sin; for this also we are commanded to do. Every moment, in which we do not exercise repentance, we sin; for repentance is one of the first duties required of us. Every moment, in which we do not exercise faith in Christ, we sin; for

the constant exercise of faith the gospel every where requires. When we do not set our affections on things above, we sin; for on these we are required to place them. When we are not constantly influenced by the fear of God, we sin; for we are commanded to be in the fear of the Lord all the day long. When we do not rejoice in God, we sin; for the precept is, Rejoice in the Lord always. When we are not properly affected by the contents of God's word, we sin; for this want of feeling indicates hardness of heart, one of the worst of sins. When we do not forgive and love our enemies, we sin; for this Christ requires of us. In a word, whenever our hearts are not in a perfectly holy frame, we are sinning; for God's language is, Be ye holy, for I am holy; be perfect, as your Father in heaven is perfect. And if we thus sin, when we do not exercise right feelings, much more do we sin, when we exercise those that are wrong. When we are dissatisfied with any part of God's word, or with any of his providential dispensations; when we feel a disposition to murmur at our situation, at our disappointments and afflictions, at the weather, or the seasons, we sin; for these are heart-risings of rebellion against God, and they render it impossible for us to say, sincerely, Thy will be done. When we hate any one, we sin; for he that hateth his brother, is a murderer. When we feel a revengful, or unforgiving temper, we sin; for if we forgive not our enemies, God will not forgive us. When we secretly rejoice in the calamities of others, we sin; for he that is glad at calamities, shall not go unpunished; and God is said to be displeased with those, who rejoice when their enemy falls. When we envy such as are above us, we sin; for envyings are mentioned among the sinful works of the flesh. When we covet any thing, that is our neighbor's, we sin; for this is expressly forbidden by the tenth commandment. When we love the world, we sin; for if any man love the world, the love of the Father is not in him. But I forbear to enlarge; for who, that knows any thing of himself, will deny, that the wickedness of his heart is great, and its iniquities numberless?

2. Let us, in the next place, consider the sinfulness of our thoughts. The thoughts are the offspring of the mind, as the feelings are of the heart; and that they may be sinful, the scriptures plainly teach. The wise man declares foolish thoughts to be sinful. Our Savior classes evil thoughts with thefts, mur-

ders, and adulteries. O Jerusalem, says Jehovah, wash thy heart from wickedness, that thou mayest be saved. How long shall vain thoughts lodge within thee? Let the unrighteous man forsake his thoughts. The thoughts of the wicked are an abomination. Hear, O earth, I will bring evil upon this people, even the fruit of their thoughts. Even men's characters are determined by their thoughts and purposes; for as a man thinketh in his heart, so is he. These passages are more than sufficient to prove that there may be much sin committed in thought. And if vain, foolish thoughts are sinful, who, who, my hearers, can enumerate his sins? Who can even number the sins of this kind of which he is guilty in a single day? And many of these thoughts are rendered peculiarly sinful by being indulged in the house of God, during the hours set apart for devotion, when, if ever, the mind ought to be solemn and collected. But it is here impossible to descend to particulars. We must leave every one to reflect, as he pleases, on the atheistical thoughts, the impi[illegible]s and profane thoughts, the impure, covetous, vain, foolish, and absurd thoughts, which have passed through his mind, and been entertained there. And while you reflect on this, remember, that thoughts are the language of disembodied spirits; that thoughts are words in the ear of God; and that our guilt in his sight, is no less great than if we had actually given utterance to every thought, which has lodged in our minds. Agreeably, we find our Savior answering the *thoughts* of those around him, just as he would if they had expressed them in words; and in many passages, God charges sinners with saying, what, it appears, they only thought. In the ear of Jehovah then, our thoughts have a tongue; and what he hears them say, we may learn from the inspired declaration. Every imagination of the thoughts of man's heart is evil continually. And surely no man who believes this declaration, none who believes that thoughts are words in the ear of Jehovah, can doubt that his wickedness is great, and his iniquities numberless.

3. From sins of thought let us next proceed to those of the tongue. From what has been said of our feelings and thoughts, it is evident that this class of sins also must be exceedingly numerous; for it is out of the abundance of the heart, that the mouth speaketh. If then, sin prevails in the heart, it will flow out through the lips. That it does so, is but too obvious. Not to

insist on the falsehoods, the slanders, the profane, impious, and indecent expressions, which are daily uttered by many persons, it may be sufficient to remind you, that of every *idle* word which men speak, they shall give account in the day of judgment. Every idle word then is a sin. But what are idle words? I answer, all that are not necessary, and which do not tend to produce good effects. God's precepts are, Let no corrupt communication proceed out of your mouth; but that which is good to the use of edifying. Let your speech be always with grace, that it may minister grace unto the hearers. Let not foolish talking or jesting, which are not becoming, be once named among you; but rather giving of thanks. These rules, perhaps, will be considered by some as too strict; but, my friends, they are the rules, which God prescribes in his word; they are the rules, by which we must be tried hereafter. And every word, which does not comport with them is an idle word; and consequently, sinful. How innumerable then, are the sins of the tongue! How large a portion of all the words, which we utter, are at best, but idle words, to say nothing of those which are obviously sinful! Well might the wise man say, that in the multitude of words there wanteth not sin. I shall only add, that whenever we speak of others as we should not wish them to speak of us, we sin against the law of love, and violate our Savior's golden rule, Whatsoever ye would that men should do unto you, do ye even the same to them. Happy is the man, who can truly say, that in this respect alone, his transgressions are not numberless.

4. Let us now consider our sinful actions. And here, my friends, we shall not speak of what the world call sins. We shall say nothing of thefts, frauds, injuries, intemperance, and debauchery. If there are any among my hearers, who are not free from these gross enormities, I must leave the task of reproving them to their own consciences. Our concern is principally with those sinful actions, which are by most men thought innocent; and for which therefore, conscience seldom, if ever, reproves them. To begin with what have been called sins of omission: Withhold not good from him to whom it is due, when it is in the power of thine hand to do it. For to him that knoweth to do good, and doeth it not, to him it is sin. From these passages it appears, that whenever men have an opportunity to

do good, either to the bodies or souls of men, or of doing any good work for the glory of God, and neglect to improve it, they sin. Of how many sins, then, are we guilty! How many thousands of opportunities for doing good have we suffered to pass unimproved! How much good has been done by many of our fellow creatures, with no greater means, than we have enjoyed! Is not the charge, which was brought against the proud king of Babylon, applicable to many of us? We have failed to glorify the God, in whose hand our breath is. Prayer and praise glorify God. But these duties we have all neglected during a considerable part of our lives; and many of us are still neglecting them. We are commanded, whether we eat, or drink, or whatever we do, to do all to the glory of God. These precepts apply to our words as well as to our actions; and they prove, that every word which we have not spoken, every action which we have not performed, with a view to promote the glory of God, and, in the name of the Lord Jesus Christ, is a sin. Hence it follows, that all the words and actions of unrenewed men are sinful; for they never do any thing, either to the glory of God, or in the name of Christ. Agreeably, we are told, that the ploughing of the wicked is sin; that the prayer, and the sacrifice of the wicked, are an abomination; and that they who are in the flesh, that is, in an impenitent, unconverted state, cannot please God; for without faith it is impossible to please him. We do not mean, that all the words and actions of unrenewed men are outwardly wrong, or sinful; but they all proceed from wrong motives, and are not accompanied by right feelings; they are not performed with that temper and disposition, which God requires, and are therefore, sinful by defect. They are like a body without a soul; the heart, at which God principally looks, and which he requires, is unholy; and therefore, the actions are the same. This is the import of our Savior's comparison; the tree is corrupt, and therefore, the fruit is not good; for a corrupt tree cannot bring forth good fruit. To bring all that need be said on this subject to a point;—every feeling, thought, word, and action, which is not, in all respects, as it ought to be, or as God requires it to be, is sinful: but no feeling, thought, word, or action of an impenitent sinner, is in all respects, what God requires it to be; therefore, every feeling, thought, word, and action of a sinner is sinful. If then men's feelings, thoughts, words, actions, are numberless, so are their sins.

I am aware, my hearers, that this conclusion will startle, and perhaps, offend some of you; but if we follow the scriptures, I see not that we can come to a different conclusion. I only ask to be judged, or rather ask you to judge yourselves, by this rule. If you can prove, by fair appeal to scripture, that any part of your temper and conduct has been perfectly right, perfectly agreeable to God's law, I will acknowledge, that my conclusion is wrong. I will only add, that the scriptures assert, in plain terms, that the thoughts of the wicked are an abomination to the Lord, that the way of the wicked is an abomination to him; that every work of their hands, and all they offer, is unclean. If we believe these assertions, we must acknowledge that our wickedness is great, and our iniquities infinite,—absolutely numberless.

II. It is further necessary to show, that our sins are infinite, not only in number, but in criminality; that every sin is, in fact, infinitely evil, and deserving of infinite punishment. It is so,

1. Because it is committed against an infinite being, against God, a being infinitely powerful, wise, holy, just and good. The criminality of any offence is in proportion to the excellence and greatness of the person, against whom it is committed. For instance, it is wrong for a child to strike his brother. Should the same child strike his father, it would be incomparably more so. Were his father a king, possessed of every good quality, the act would be still more criminal. But God is our heavenly Father, the universal King, infinitely exalted above every human parent, above every earthly monarch; possessed, in an infinite degree, of every perfection, which can entitle him to the perfect love, confidence, and obedience of his creatures. He is also the author and preserver of the very powers and faculties, which we employ in sinning against him, and he has conferred on us innumerable favors. Of course we are under infinite obligations to love and obey him; and therefore, to violate these obligations, and sin against such a being, must be an infinite evil.

Again—that every sin is infinitely evil and criminal, is evident from the fact, that it is a violation of an infinitely perfect law. It will readily be allowed, that to violate a good law, is a greater evil than to violate a law, the goodness of which is doubtful. It will also be allowed, that if there were any law made by human governments, on obedience to which the honor, the welfare, and even the existence of a nation depended,—to violate that law, would be the greatest crime, which a subject could commit. Now the law of God is perfectly holy, just, and good. If it were universally obeyed, universal and endless happiness would be the consequence. But disobedience to this law tends to produce universal and endless misery. Take away the law and the authority of God; there would be no right, but that of the strongest; violence, discord, and confusion would fill the universe; sin and misery would overspread the earth, would ascend to heaven, subvert the throne of Jehovah, and compel him to live in the midst of a mad, infuriated mob, the members of which were continually insulting him, and injuring each other. Now every violation of God's law tends to produce this effect.

Farther—every sin is an infinite evil, because it tends to produce infinite mischief. Let us trace this tendency. Suppose all the universe to be holy and happy. A thought or feeling tending to produce sin, rises in the breast of some one creature. This thought or feeling is indulged. It gains strength by indulgence; gradually it extends its influence over the faculties of the mind, enslaves the whole man, and prompts him to disobey God Now did it proceed no further, it would still be an infinite evil, for it has depraved and ruined an immortal being, a being, who, but for sin, would have been eternally happy: but who must, in consequence of sin, be forever miserable. But it will not stop there. The being thus ruined by sin, will become a tempter, and seduce his fellow beings, and they, in turn, will tempt others; and unless God prevent, the infection will spread through the created universe, transforming holy beings into devils, and all worlds into hell! Such, my hearers, is the tendency of sin. Do any deny it? We appeal to facts. The whole universe was once holy and happy. A thought or feeling tending to produce sin, rose in the breast of Satan. He indulged it, and it ruined him. It transformed him from an archangel into a devil. He tempted other angels, and they became devils. He tempted our first parents; they complied sinned, and became the parents of a sinful race.

Thus all the sin and all the misery in the universe, all on earth and all in hell, may be traced back to one sinful thought or feeling entertained, at first, in a single breast; and this sin and misery would be far greater than they are, were it not for the restraining power and grace of God. Such then, is the tendency of sin, of every sin; and such effects it would produce, did not God prevent. A sinful thought, or feeling, is like a spark of fire. It seems but a little thing, and is easily extinguished; but it has a tendency to consume and destroy; and let it have room and opportunity to exert itself; let it be fed by combustible materials, and fanned by the winds, and it would destroy every thing destructible in the universe. Similar is the tendency of sin; and who then, will say, that it is not an infinite evil?

Sins derive an infinite malignity from being committed in defiance of motives and obligations infinitely strong. It is evident, that the criminality of any sin is in proportion to the motives and obligations, which opposed its commission. To sin against many and powerful motives, indicates greater depravity, and is, of course, more criminal than to sin against few and feeble motives. Suppose a person is informed, that if he commits a certain crime, he shall be imprisoned. If, notwithstanding the threatening, he perpetrates the crime, he shows that he loves the crime more than he loves liberty. Again, suppose him to be assured, that if he commits the crime, he shall be put to death. Should he, after that, commit the crime, it would indicate greater depravity than before. It would show, that he loved the crime more than life. But the word of God threatens sinners with everlasting misery, if they persist in sin; and promises them everlasting happiness, if they will renounce it. I need not tell you that what is everlasting, is in one respect infinite, viz. in duration. Here then, are two infinitely powerful motives presented to the sinner, to deter him from sin—infinite happiness, and infinite misery. Every one then, who persists in sin, notwithstanding these motives, shows that he loves sin more than everlasting happiness; that he hates holiness more than he dreads everlasting misery. His attachment to sin, and of course, his depravity and criminality, are therefore boundless, or infinite. From all that has been said, it appears that our sins are numberless, and that every one of our sins is infinitely evil or criminal. Every one then, who answers the question in our text with truth, must answer it in the affirmative.

INFERENCES. 1. If our sins are thus infinite in number and criminality, then of course, they deserve an infinite, or everlasting punishment; such a punishment, as God threatens in his word. There is scarcely any truth, which men are more disposed to deny, than this. They contend, that it cannot be just for God to punish sins committed during the short period of our residence on earth, with everlasting misery. But let us examine this objection. Do you not all acknowledge, that a murderer may justly be put to death? Yet he might not have been employed more than a single moment in committing that murder. The fact is, in other cases we never think of inquiring how much time was spent in the commission of any crime. We consider only the nature and magnitude of the crime, and its effects upon society. If the crime is great, and its effects highly pernicious, we conclude at once, that it deserves a severe punishment. Now we have shown, that sin is an infinite evil; that the effects, which it tends to produce, are infinitely mischievous. Of course, it deserves an infinite punishment. And permit me to add, that complaints of the severity of this punishment come with a very ill grace from impenitent sinners; for they will persist in sin, notwithstanding this punishment. It seems then, that instead of being too severe, it is not sufficiently severe to deter them from sin. If men will now violate God's laws, what would they do, had he annexed to their violation only a temporary punishment?

2. If sin deserves an infinite punishment, then it is perfectly right, that God should inflict such a punishment upon sinners. It is no impeachment of his character, no reflection upon his goodness, to say, that he will inflict it. This evidently follows as a necessary consequence from what has been said; for justice consists in treating every one as he deserves to be treated; and if sinners deserve an endless punishment, then it is perfectly just and right for God to inflict such a punishment upon them.

3. If it is just that God should inflict such a punishment upon impenitent sinners, then he must inflict it; he is bound by the strongest obligation to inflict it, for he must do what is

just and right. And if it is just and right thus to punish impenitent sinners, then it cannot be just and right not to do it. To spare them, would not be treating them as they deserve, and justice consists in treating them according to their deserts. In a word, it is as much an act of injustice to spare the guilty, as it would be to condemn the innocent. This God himself teaches us in his word. He that justifieth the wicked, and he that condemneth the just, even they both are an abomination to the Lord. And will the just God do that, which he declares to be an abomination in his sight? The Judge of all the earth must do right.

4. Hence we see why the atonement made by Christ was necessary. Men had all sinned. Their wickedness was great, and their transgressions infinite. Hence they deserved an infinite punishment; and God was obliged, in justice, to inflict on them such a punishment, unless some sufficient atonement could be made. As sin, and the punishment due to sin, were infinite; no atonement, which was not infinite in value, could suffice. And where could such an atonement be found? Men could not make it; for they were already under sentence of death, and forfeited every thing which they possessed. Yet the atonement must be made by a man; because it was for the benefit of men. The language of the law was, man has sinned, and man must die. In this exigency, the Eternal Word, the Son of God, interposed. He consented to become man, to bear the sins of men, or, in other words, the punishment, which their sins deserved; to stand as the representative of sinners, and suffer the curse of the law in their stead. This he has done. He has thus magnified the law and made it honorable. He deserves some reward for this wonderful act of benevolence and obedience. A just God is as much bound to reward him, as he is to punish the wicked. But what reward shall he give him? He needs nothing for himself. But there is a reward infinitely valuable in his estimation, infinitely dear to his benevolent heart. It is the pardon and salvation of his people, of every sinner, who confides in his merits and intercession, and submits to be reconciled, through him, to God. This reward was promised him. This reward is given him. God can now be just, and yet the justifier of him that believeth in Jesus. None, however, will believe in Jesus, none will

apply to him for salvation, but those who see and feel, that their wickedness is great, and their iniquities infinite. You may see therefore, my friends, why it is, that I have led your attention to this subject. It is not because I love to dwell upon it. It is not because I, a miserable sinner, take pleasure in accusing and condemning my fellow sinners. But it is because I, a pardoned sinner, a sinner washed from numberless and infinite offences in the atoning blood of Jesus, wish to bring my fellow sinners to that precious fountain, of which I know the efficacy. It is because, as a messenger of the Lord of hosts, I am commanded to cry aloud, and show to the people their transgressions and their sins: and because I am also directed to preach to you the unsearchable riches of Christ. You may easily conceive how precious the Savior would appear to you, did you feel burdened with the weight of all the sins, with which you are here charged. My friends—penitent sinners, true Christians, do feel thus burdened; they feel that their wickedness is great, and their iniquities numberless. This it is, which leads them to adopt such expressions, as you hear them use in prayer; expressions, which have been used by all the pious before. It is this which leads them to complain, that they are the chief of sinners, and to cry out with the apostle, O, wretched man, that I am! Who shall deliver me from the body of this death? Could you feel thus, how would you rejoice to hear of a Savior! How eagerly fly to his atoning blood! And are there none, who feel thus? none, whose sins God has set in order before their eyes? none, who are ready to cry out, My sins have gone over me as a heavy burden; mine iniquities have taken hold upon me, so that I am not able to look up; they are more in number than the hairs of my head; therefore my heart faileth me! Fly, then, to the cross of Christ, in whom we have redemption, through his blood, even the forgiveness of our sins, according to the riches of his grace.

SERMON VIII.

THE WICKED, FROM PRIDE, REFUSE TO SEEK GOD.

The wicked, through the pride of his countenance, will not seek after God.—PSALM x. 4.

IN this psalm we have a full length portrait of a careless, unawakened sinner, drawn by the unerring pencil of truth; and so perfect is the resemblance, that were it not for the blinding influence of sin, every such sinner would discover in it, as in a glass, his own image. Two of the features, which compose this portrait, are delineated in our text. The first is an unwillingness to seek after God. The second is pride, which causes that unwillingness. The wicked, through the pride of his countenance, will not seek after God. In discoursing on this passage, we shall endeavor to show—that the wicked will not seek after God—and that it is the pride of their hearts, which prevents them from seeking him. It will be understood, that by the wicked, we here intend careless, unawakened sinners.

I. The wicked will not seek after God. The expression implies, not only that they do not seek after him, but that they will not. It is the settled, determined purpose of their hearts, not to seek him; and to this purpose they will obstinately and unalterably adhere, unless their wills are subdued by divine grace. With a view to illustrate and establish this truth, we observe

1. That the wicked will not seek after the knowledge of God. This the scriptures plainly assert. The wicked say unto

God, Depart from us; for we desire not the knowledge of thy ways. It is also evident from the experience of all ages, that no careless, unawakened sinner, ever used any means, or made the smallest endeavors to acquire a knowledge of God. Our Savior explicitly declares, that all who seek, shall find. But the wicked do not find the knowledge of God; therefore they never seek it. They will not study the scriptures with a view to become acquainted with God. It is true, they sometimes read the scriptures; but they read them either in a formal, careless manner, or to quiet the remonstrances of conscience, or to find arguments in favor of some false system of religion, which may encourage them in sinful pursuits, and enable them to indulge delusive hopes of future happiness. They never look into the Bible with a sincere desire to find God there; nor study it with that humble, docile, childlike temper, without which it will ever be studied in vain. And while many thus read the scriptures with improper views, or wrong feelings, many also, there is reason to fear, scarcely read them at all. From week to week, and from year to year, their Bibles lie on the shelf unopened, while they know little more of their contents than of the Koran of Mahomet.

The wicked will not pray for the knowledge of God. It can never be said with truth of a wicked man, behold he prayeth. On the contrary, he invariably casts off fear, and restrains prayer before God. He may indeed, and, as we have already seen, often does, request God to depart from him, and like the evil spirits in our Savior's time, he may cry, I beseech thee, torment me not. But never does he sincerely ask for divine instruction. Never does he cry after knowledge, or lift up his voice for understanding. If he did, he would infallibly obtain it; for every one that asketh, receiveth. Ye have not, says the apostle, because ye ask not.

The wicked will not improve those opportunities for acquiring the knowledge of God, which our public and private religious institutions afford. It is true that many of them attend frequently, perhaps constantly, on the instructions of the sanctuary; but it is equally true, that custom, curiosity, a regard to reputation, or a wish to pass away the time, and not a desire for divine knowledge, induces their attendance. That this is not an uncharitable supposition is apparent from their conduct.

Often, while the most solemn and important truths are proclaimed in their hearing, their thoughts, like the fool's eyes, are in the ends of the earth; and they literally hear as though they heard not. If at any time they listen more attentively to the preached word, it is not with a wish to understand, believe and obey it. Their whole aim in listening often appears to be, to find some real, or apparent contradiction; some plausible excuse for disbelieving or neglecting what they hear. They watch, as the prophet observes of the Jews, to find some iniquity in the speaker. Their minds are full of cavils and objections against the truths delivered; and, no sooner do they leave the house of God, than they forget or banish all that has been said; or remember it only, that they may pervert, misrepresent, and deny it, and thus harden themselves and others in ignorance and sin. Nor is this all. Private religious conversation, and meetings for this purpose, afford opportunities for acquiring the knowledge of God, as favorable, and in some respects, perhaps, more so, than the public instructions of the sanctuary. But these opportunities the wicked will by no means improve. Seldom, if ever, is the instance known of a careless, unawakened sinner visiting a minister of Christ for the purpose of religious conversation, or attending a private religious meeting, unless it were with some improper motive. They can readily and cheerfully attend meetings of a different kind, and engage in conversation on subjects of a different nature, but they avoid places and circles in which religion will probably be introduced, as they would shun a place infected by the plague. We have no fear, that these assertions can, with truth, be contradicted. Scripture, observation, and experience unequivocally testify, that careless, unawakened sinners will not seek after the knowledge of God.

2. The wicked will not seek after the favor of God. Indeed, it is perfectly natural, that those, who think the knowledge of God not worth pursuing, should scarcely consider his favor as worth seeking. Knowing nothing experimentally of his excellence and perfections, and ignorant of their entire dependence on him for happiness, they cannot, of course, realize, that the favor of God is life, and his loving kindness better than life. Hence they will not seek to obtain it, but prefer almost every thing else to the divine favor; and love the praise of men more

than the praise of God. The way to obtain and secure the favor of God is as plainly marked out, and, at least, as easy to be followed by those who are so disposed, as the way to acquire any temporal blessing whatever. God has stated in his word, with the greatest possible clearness, both what will secure and what will forfeit his favor; both what will incur and what will avert his displeasure. Yet all the wicked daily practice those things which are displeasing to God, and entirely incompatible with the enjoyment of his favor; while, on the contrary, they totally neglect to cultivate those dispositions and perform those actions, which will secure his approbation. In fact, they think, they care, nothing about it. How he shall avert God's displeasure, or obtain his favor, is no part of an unawakened sinner's inquiry or concern. He asks innumerable other questions, many of which are in the highest degree frivolous and useless; but never is he heard to ask, What must I do to be saved? He pursues other objects, the most trifling objects too; but never is he seen engaged in the ardent pursuit of this. He is exceedingly jealous of his own reputation, and solicitous to acquire the good opinion of his fellow creatures, even of the meanest and most worthless among them, while he proportionably dreads their censures. But the wrath of him, in whom he lives, and moves, and exists, who can in a moment cut short his life, and destroy both soul and body in hell, he does not fear; nor does he consider his highest approbation as a worthy object of desire or pursuit. In the language of inspiration, the wicked cry out by reason of the arm of the mighty; but none saith, where is God, my Maker, who giveth songs in the night?

3. The wicked will not seek after the likeness of God. That they do not at all resemble him, is certain, if the scriptures are true. That they do not wish or endeavor to resemble him, is equally evident. There is, indeed, in their view, no reason, why they should. There are but two motives, which can induce any being to imitate another, or to wish to resemble him. The first is a wish to obtain the approbation of the person imitated. The second is admiration of something in his character, and a consequent desire to inscribe it into our own. But the wicked can be influenced by neither of these motives to seek after conformity to God. They cannot be led to imitate him by a wish to obtain his favor; for this, as we have already seen,

they have no desire to obtain. Nor do they discover any thing in his character, which they wish to transcribe into their own; for they have no knowledge of God, no desire to know him, no taste for the beauties of holiness. Christ, we are told, is the image of the invisible God, the brightness of the Father's glory, and the express image of his person. Yet they evidently, as the prophet observes, discover in Christ no form or comeliness; and when they see him, he has in their eyes no beauty, that they should desire to resemble him. And as it is with Christ, the image of God, so of course, it must be with respect to God himself. Since they have no wish to imitate the former; they cannot, they will not seek after conformity with the latter. The truth of this conclusion is evident from their conduct. Though man is naturally an imitative being; and though the wicked imitate many things in the conduct of their fellow creatures; things too, which are, in many respects, foolish, ridiculous, and sinful, yet they never evince the least desire, or make the smallest exertion to imitate the inimitable perfections of God. On the contrary, they refuse to be reconciled to him, follow a course directly opposite to his, and daily become, if possible, more and more unlike him.

4. The wicked will not seek after communion with God. That there is such a thing, as the enjoyment of fellowship or communion with God, the inspired writers most unequivocally assert; and one of them, St. John, informs us, that to bring those, whom he addressed, to the enjoyment of this privilege, was the principal design of his epistle. That which we have seen and heard declare we unto you, that ye also may have fellowship with us; and truly our fellowship is with the Father, and with his Son Jesus Christ. That this fellowship with God and his Son is a blessed reality, and that it is productive of the purest and most exalted pleasures, all true Christians well know; for they often taste its sweetness, and rejoice with joy unspeakable and full of glory. But for this joy in God, and the fellowship which produces it, the wicked will not seek; for they do not desire it; they have no conception of it, and while they continue wicked, it is morally impossible that they should have.

Communion, or even a desire for communion with any being, always presupposes some degree of resemblance to that being, and a participation of the same nature, views and feelings. Irrational animals evidently cannot enjoy communion with men in rational pleasures, because they have no capacity for such pleasures; nor can they even desire to enjoy communion with us, because they have no conception of such a quality as reason, nor of the pleasures which it qualifies us to enjoy. But cause them to resemble us, endue them with reason, and they will, at once, desire and enjoy communion with us in rational pleasures and pursuits. For similar reasons wicked men cannot enjoy, or even wish to enjoy, communion with a holy God; for they resemble him as little, as the irrational animals do us; and, as we have already seen, they will not seek to resemble him. As they cannot know spiritual things, because they are spiritually discerned; so they cannot enjoy spiritual pleasures, because they are spiritually enjoyed. Not only have they no relish or capacity for such pleasures; they do not even know that such pleasures exist, nor can they form a conception of them, any more than an irrational animal can conceive of intellectual enjoyments. Of course, they will not seek after communion with God; and while the Christian, who has been made partaker of a divine nature, enjoys the most exquisite felicity in communion with his Maker and Redeemer, praying, Lord, lift thou up the light of thy countenance upon me, they roam unsatisfied from creature to creature, still vainly crying, who will show us any good?

Thus have I endeavored to illustrate and establish the assertion of the Psalmist. I proceed now, as was proposed,

II. To the reason why the wicked will not seek after God, viz. their pride. In illustration of this, I observe,

1. That the pride of the wicked is the principal reason, why they will not seek after the knowledge of God. This knowledge it prevents them from seeking in various ways. In the first place, it renders God a disagreeable object of contemplation to the wicked, and a knowledge of him as undesirable. Pride consists in an unduly exalted opinion of one's self. It is therefore impatient of a rival, hates a superior, and cannot endure a master. In proportion as it prevails in the heart, it makes us wish to see nothing above us, to acknowledge no law but our own wills, to follow no rule but our own inclinations. Thus it led Satan to rebel against his Creator, and our first

parents to desire to be as Gods. Since such are the effects of pride, it is evident that nothing can be more painful to a proud heart, than the thoughts of such a being as God; one, who is infinitely powerful, just, and holy; who can neither be resisted, deceived, nor deluded; who disposes, according to his own sovereign pleasure, of all creatures and events; and who, in an especial manner, hates pride, and is determined to abase and punish it. Such a being pride can contemplate only with feelings of dread, aversion and abhorrence. It must look upon him as its natural enemy; the great enemy whom it has to fear. But the knowledge of God directly tends to bring this infinite, irresistible, irreconcilable enemy full to the view of the proud man. It teaches him, that he has a superior, a master, from whose authority he cannot escape, whose power he cannot resist, and whose will he must obey, or be crushed before him and rendered miserable forever. It shows him what he hates to see, that in despite of his opposition, God's counsel shall stand, that he will do all his pleasure, and that in all things, wherein men deal proudly, God is above them. These truths torture the proud, unhumbled hearts of the wicked; and hence they hate that knowledge of God, which teaches these truths, and will not seek it. On the contrary, they wish to remain ignorant of such a being, and to banish all thoughts of him from their minds. With this view they neglect, pervert, or explain away those passages of revelation, which describe God's true character, and endeavor to believe, that he is altogether such an one as themselves.

In the second place, the pride of the wicked prevents them from seeking after the knowledge of God, by rendering them unwilling to be taught. Pride is almost as impatient of a teacher, as it is of a master. The proud man is ever vain of his knowledge, and is unwilling to confess, or even to think, that there is any thing of importance, of which he is ignorant, or that any person is capable of giving him instruction. But if he consents to seek after the knowledge of God, he must acknowledge his ignorance, he must submit to be taught, he must, as it were, put himself to school and become as a little child. This his proud heart cannot brook; and therefore he will not seek the knowledge of God.

In the third place, pride renders the wicked unwilling to use the means, by which alone the knowledge of God can be acquired. For instance, it renders them unwilling to study the scriptures in a proper manner. Every thing, which the Bible reveals, is suited to mortify pride; for in dictating it God had purposed in his heart to stain the pride of all human glory. The description, which it gives, of the desperately sinful, guilty, and ruined condition of mankind; of our entire dependence on the sovereign grace of God; the mysterious, humbling doctrines and self-denying precepts, which it inculcates; the self-condemning spirit, which it requires, and the self-abasing way of salvation which it reveals, render it exceedingly disagreeable to the taste of the proud, wicked man. In addition to this, it commands him to renounce his proud dependence on his own understanding, to sit with a teachable, childlike temper at the feet of Jesus, and learn of him, who was meek and lowly in heart; to believe truths which he cannot fully comprehend, and which, perhaps, appear unreasonable to his prejudiced, blinded, unhumbled mind. These things the proud man cannot endure, and therefore will not study the scriptures.

Pride also renders the wicked man unwilling to pray. Prayer is an expression of wants and dependence, and a direct acknowledgment of a superior; and in addition to this, prayer for the knowledge of God includes a confession of ignorance, and a request to be taught. But this the proud man abhors. No wonder then that he will not pray for divine knowledge. No wonder, that even when he attempts this duty, he forgets its design, and, like the self-righteous pharisee, instead of soliciting pardon, grace and instruction, proudly thanks God, that he is better than others.

In an equally powerful manner does the pride of the wicked operate in preventing them from improving public and private opportunities for acquiring religious instruction. If the public instructions of the sanctuary coincide, as they ever ought to do, with the contents of God's word, the same pride, which leads the wicked to dislike and neglect the one, will prevent them from believing and obeying the other. And with respect to more private meetings for religious conversation and instruction, an attendance on them is still more offensive to the pride of their hearts. Indeed, since they are too proud to request divine illumination from God, it could scarcely be expected, that they will stoop to receive instruction from man. Even after the wicked man begins to be convinced of his ignorance of God, and of the importance of divine knowledge, he is unwilling to have it known, and is ashamed to confess to his Christian friends, or to the minister of Christ, that he is ignorant of religious truth. Such are the principal ways, in which the pride of the wicked operates to prevent them from seeking the knowledge of God.

2. The pride of the wicked will not allow them to seek after the favor of God. The proud always aim at independence. They wish to believe themselves, and to persuade others, that they are able to render themselves happy, without the assistance of any one. But to seek the favor of God, implies dependence on him for happiness; it implies imperfection, inferiority. Hence it is easy to see how the pride of the wicked prevents them from seeking the divine favor. The way in which alone God's favor can be obtained, is, if possible, still more offensive to pride. The very entrance upon the way, is a death-blow to it; for the Gospel casts down imaginations and every high thing, that exalteth itself against the knowledge of God, and requires us, if we would enjoy his favor, to bow our stubborn wills to his authority, to mortify our pride, and renounce our vain-glorious, self-righteous thoughts and feelings. It tells us, that God resisteth the proud; that every one, who exalteth himself, shall be abased; and that the proud in heart are an abomination to the Lord, while he gives his grace to the lowly, and will dwell in none but the humble and contrite heart. We can, therefore, be at no loss to know why the pride of the wicked will not suffer them to seek the favor of God.

3. Pride renders the wicked unwilling to seek after the likeness of God. Those, who have an exalted opinion of themselves, will not easily be persuaded to imitate others. They will rather expect others to imitate them. Besides, an attempt to imitate others, involves a confession, that they are our superiors; at least, that they excel us in those respects, in which we endeavor to imitate them. But pride hates a superior, and is unwilling to allow that it is excelled by any one.

4. The pride of the wicked renders them unwilling to seek after communion with God. The proud man never wishes to associate with those, who are above him. If he must have

superiors, he wishes to be as far from them as possible, that the sight of their superiority may not mortify his pride. Hence the remark of proud Cæsar, when passing through an insignificant village—"I would rather be the first man in this village, than the second in Rome;" a speech, which, though admired by the proud and ambitious, nearly resembles that, which Milton has put into the mouth of Satan, after his fall:

Better to reign in hell than serve in heaven.

This is the genuine language of pride; and therefore the proud man shuns the society of his superiors, and prefers that of his inferiors. He chooses to look down, rather than to look up, because, when he looks down, his pride is flattered by seeing others below him; but when he looks up, it is mortified. Hence he will not look up to God. He chooses rather to hold communion with irrational animals in the gratifications of sense, than to seek for fellowship with the greatest and best of beings, in the pure, exalted, and exquisite pleasures of religion. Thus clearly does it appear, that it is the pride of the wicked, which renders them unwilling to seek after God.

Reflections. 1. How evident it is from what has been said, that salvation is wholly of grace; and that all the wicked, if left to themselves, will certainly perish! They do not seek after God; they will not seek after him; they are fully determined not to do it; the pride of their hearts supports the resolution, and they will infallibly adhere to it unless divine grace prevents. But if they do not seek God, they will not find him; and if they do not find him, they are undone forever. Their eternal destruction is therefore inevitable, unless God, of his mere sovereign, self-moved grace, seeks those, who will not seek him, subdues the pride of their hearts, and makes them willing. This he has done for all, who are saved. This he must do for all, who ever will be saved. Need any thing more be said to prove, that salvation is wholly of grace?

2. How depraved, how infatuated, how unreasonable do the wicked appear! and how evident it is, that if they perish, they will be the sole authors of their own destruction! God has given them all the powers and faculties necessary to enable them to seek and pursue any object. This is evident, because

they do, in fact, seek and obtain many objects. God also commands them to seek his face; assures them, that none shall seek in vain; and at the same time warns them, that all, who seek him not, will be miserable forever. But the wicked neglect his warnings, disbelieve his promises, and pay no attention to his commands. When they hear him saying, Seek ye my face: instead of replying with the Psalmist, Thy face, Lord, will we seek—their proud hearts obstinately refuse to obey. They pursue the perishing vanities of time and sense through labors, dangers, and death itself; and wandering far from the way of peace, and neglecting the infinite beauty, the supreme good, the fountain of life and happiness, they madly rush on, with blind impetuosity, into the yawning gulf of destruction. They are therefore, evidently and incontestably, their own destroyers, and when they shall hereafter be sentenced to depart accursed from him whom they now refuse to seek, should the whole intelligent universe be summoned to inquire what occasioned their fate, they would unite in a verdict of self-murder.

3. How foolish, how absurd, how ruinous, how blindly destructive of its own object, does pride appear! By attempting to soar, it only plunges itself in the mire; and, while endeavoring to erect for itself a throne, it undermines the ground on which it stands, and digs its own grave. It plunged satan from heaven into hell; it banished our first parents from paradise, and it will, in a similar manner, ruin all, who indulge it. It keeps us in ignorance of God, shuts us out from his favor, prevents us from resembling him, deprives us, in this world, of all the honor and happiness, which communion with him would confer; and in the next, unless previously hated, repented of, and renounced, will bar forever against us the door of heaven, and close upon us the gates of hell. O, then, my friends, beware, above all things, beware of pride. Beware, lest you indulge it imperceptibly; for it is, perhaps, of all sins, the most secret, subtle, and insinuating. That you may detect it, remember, that he only, who seeks after God in his appointed way, is humble; and that all who neglect thus to seek him, are most certainly proud in heart, and, consequently, an abomination unto the Lord.

Lastly—This subject may be applied for the purpose of self-examination. Say, then, my friends, are there none present, who do not seek after God? Are you all seeking after the knowledge of God, by diligently and humbly studying the scriptures, by fervent prayer, and by a conscientious improvement of the public and private opportunities, with which God has favored you? Are you all seeking the favor of God as the one thing needful, avoiding every thing which will tend to displease him, and practising every thing that tends to secure his approbation? Are you seeking conformity with God, aiming to be followers of him as dear children, and desiring to be perfect, as your Father in heaven is perfect? Is communion with God the grand object of your desires, the principal source of your pleasures, the reward at which you aim, in the performance of religious duties? If this be the case with all present, you are indeed happy, and the preceding observations have no application to you. But if there be one person present, who is not thus seeking God, that person is a wicked person, one who is entirely under the influence of pride, and against whom all the dreadful curses, denounced by inspired writers upon the wicked are levelled. If there be one such person in this assembly, may God, by his Spirit, single him out, convince him of his wickedness, his pride, his guilt and danger, and bring him as a trembling inquirer after God, to the feet of Jesus, and as a humble suppliant for mercy, to the foot of the cross.

SERMON IX.

RECOLLECTIONS OF GOD PAINFUL TO THE WICKED.

I remembered God, and was troubled.—Psalm lxxvii. 3.

God is a being, whom it is impossible to contemplate with indifference. His character is so interesting, our dependence on him is so complete, and his favor is so indispensably necessary to our happiness, that a distinct recollection of him must always excite either pleasing or painful emotions. We must view him with dread and anxiety, or with confidence and joy. Agreeably we find, that the recollection of God always produced one or the other of these effects upon the mind of the Psalmist. It was usually productive of delight. My soul, says he, shall be satisfied as with marrow and fatness, and my mouth shall praise thee with joyful lips; when I remember thee upon my bed, and meditate on thee in the night watches. But sometimes the remembrance of God produced on his mind very different effects. An instance of this we have in the psalm before us. My soul refused to be comforted; I remembered God and was troubled; I complained, and my spirit was overwhelmed; I am so troubled, that I cannot speak.

The account, which the Psalmist here gives of his experience, naturally leads to some very interesting inquiries and remarks; remarks, which will probably come home to the bosoms and feelings of almost every person present. There is, I presume scarcely an individual of mature age in this assembly, who cannot say, with reference to some seasons of his life, I remembered God and was troubled. And there are, I trust, not a few present, who can say, my meditations on God in the night watches have been sweet. Now whence arises this difference? Why is the remembrance of God pleasant to some of us, and painful to others? Why is it sometimes pleasant, and at others painful, to the same individual? These are inquiries intimately connected with our happiness; for since it is impossible for any one to banish all recollection of God, and since the period is approaching, when he will be always present to our minds, it is highly necessary for our happiness, that we should be able, at all seasons, to remember him with pleasure.

I. In pursuing these inquiries, it may be necessary, in the first place, briefly to state what we mean by remembering God. We certainly mean something more than a transient recollection of the word, God, or of any other name, by which he is known. A person may hear or mention any of the names of God, many times in a day, without forming any distinct conceptions of his character, or of any part of it. He cannot, in this case, be said to remember God; for, properly speaking, it is only a word, which he remembers. But by remembering God, I mean, as the psalmist undoubtedly meant, recollecting those ideas, which the term God is used by the inspired writers to signify. When they use the word, they use it to denote an eternal, self-existent, infinitely wise, just, and good Being, who is the Creator and Upholder of all things, who is our Sovereign Lawgiver, and who worketh all things according to the counsel of his own will; who is always present with us, who searches our hearts, who approves or disapproves our conduct, who loves holiness and cannot look on sin but with abhorrence, who has power to make us eternally happy or miserable, and who will hereafter exert that power in bestowing endless happiness on some persons, and dooming others to endless wo, according to their respective characters. Whenever a person has these ideas of God in his mind, when he feels convinced for the time, that there is such a being, and that he is what the Scriptures represent him to be, then he remembers God in the sense of the text.

II. The way is now prepared to inquire, why the recollection of such a being should ever be painful; or in other words, why any of God's creatures should be troubled at the remembrance of him. It may easily be shown, that there is nothing in the divine character or government, which necessarily renders the remembrance of God productive of painful emotions. If there were, the remembrance of God would be painful to all his creatures, upon all occasions. But this is not the case. On the contrary, the remembrance of God is always delightful to holy angels, and to the spirits of just men made perfect. In fact, the constant presence of God constitutes their heaven. The recollection also of his existence, character, and government, is usually, though not always, highly pleasing to all good men. Nor is it strange that it should be so. It is always pleasing to an affectionate child, to reflect on the character, wealth, honor and influence of his father. The power, grandeur, and riches of their sovereign, are a source of heart-felt exultation and delight to all loyal subjects. They would consider their habitations as highly honored by his presence, and themselves as still more honored by an admission to his palace. For similar reasons, the affectionate children and loyal subjects of the King of kings cannot but exult and rejoice in contemplating the existence, the glories, the favor and the constant presence of their heavenly Father and King. It is and must be pleasing to them to reflect, that they are the creatures, the subjects of such an infinitely great, wise, and powerful being. The thought that Jehovah exists and reigns God over all, blessed forever; that he brings good out of evil, causes the wrath of man to praise him, and makes all things work together for the accomplishment of his wise and just designs, cannot but be exceedingly gratifying and consoling to persons of this description, while they contemplate the dreadful prevalence of natural and moral evil in this ruined world.

But if there be nothing in the character or government of God, which renders the remembrance of him necessarily painful to his creatures; and especially if the recollection of him be in itself suited to console, delight and animate them, then it follows, that if any are troubled by the remembrance of God, the cause must exist solely in themselves. My friends, it does so. Nor is it difficult to discover and point out the cause. In one word, it is sin. Nothing but sin can ever render the remembrance of God painful to any of his creatures. None but such as are conscious of sin indulged and guilt contracted, can have reason to say, I remembered God and was troubled. This is evident from facts. The once holy, but now fallen angels, rejoiced in God, till they sinned. Our first parents in paradise contemplated his character and government with unmixed delight, till they transgressed his commands. Good men find a similar pleasure in meditating upon these subjects, when they can view themselves as justified from the guilt of sin by the blood of Christ, and when they are conscious of no allowed deviation from the divine law. If our hearts condemn us not, says the apostle, then have we confidence towards God; and the man, who has confidence towards God, cannot be troubled at the remembrance of him. But on the other hand, if our hearts or consciences condemn us, it is impossible to remember him without being troubled. It will then be painful to remember, that he is our Creator and Benefactor; for the remembrance will be attended with a consciousness of base ingratitude. It will be painful to think of him as Lawgiver; for such thoughts will remind us, that we have broken his law. It will be painful to think of his holiness; for if he is holy, he must hate our sins, and be angry with us, as sinners:—of his justice and truth; for these perfections make it necessary that he should fulfil his threatenings and punish us for our sins. It will be painful to think of his omniscience; for this perfection makes him acquainted with our most secret offences, and renders it impossible to conceal them from his view:—of his omnipresence; for the constant presence of an invisible witness must be disagreeable to those, who wish to indulge their sinful propensities. It will be painful to think of his power; for it enables him to restrain or destroy, as he pleases:—of his sovereignty; for sinners always hate to see themselves in the hands of a sovereign God:—of his eternity and immutability; for from his possessing these perfections it follows, that he will never alter the threatenings which he has denounced against sinners, and that he will always live to execute them. It will be painful to think of him as Judge; for we shall feel, that as sinners, we have no reason to expect a favorable sentence from his lips. It will even be painful to think of the perfect goodness and excellence of his character; for his goodness leaves us without excuse in rebelling against him, and makes our sins appear exceedingly sinful. Thus it is evident, that the consciousness of sin committed and guilt contracted must render the government, and all the perfections of God, objects of terror and anxiety to the sinner; and of course, the recollection of them must to him be painful.

Nor is this all. Every sinner loves sin. He places his whole delight in it. The only happiness, with which he is acquainted, consists in gratifying either the desires of the flesh, the desires of the eye, or the pride of life. But all these things are contrary to the will of God. He forbids the sinner to pursue them; he forbids him to indulge or gratify his sinful propensities; he commands him to mortify and destroy them, to deny himself, to take up his cross, follow Christ, and live a religious life, in which sinners can find no pleasure. He not only requires all this, but threatens all, who do not comply, with everlasting punishment. Whenever, therefore, the sinner thinks of God, he thinks of a being, who crosses all his darling inclinations, thwarts all his schemes of happiness, and treads down self, that idol which he loves to worship, and to which he wishes every thing to give way. The sinner, therefore, cannot but look upon God, when he views him in his true character, as his greatest and most irreconcilable enemy. Agreeably, he is represented by the inspired writers as saying in his heart, No God; that is, would there were no God, or that I could escape from or resist his power. But this, reason and revelation assure him, is impossible. They tell him, that he can neither deceive God, nor fly from him, nor resist him; that he is completely in his power, and that God will dispose of him just as he pleases. This being the case, it is evident, that whenever he remembers God in the sense of the text, he cannot but be troubled.

It is further evident, that the more clearly they perceive God's character and their own; the more light is thrown into their consciences, the more mercies, privileges, and opportunities they have enjoyed and abused,—so much the more they will be troubled by a remembrance of God. Whenever they contemplate him, they will be thrown into a state of intestine war, of war with themselves. Conscience will rise up in their breasts, and take God's part, and reproach them for disobeying his commands, and abusing his favors. Their understandings will side with conscience, and render its reproaches doubly terrible. On the other hand, all their sinful feelings and propensities will array themselves in opposition to reason and conscience, and attempt to defend and justify themselves. Hence inward struggles and conflicts will arise; the sinner's mind will become like the troubled sea, which cannot rest, whose waters cast up mire and dirt; and he can have no rest, until he either becomes cordially reconciled to God, or succeeds in banishing all serious thoughts of him from his breast. As well then may an imprisoned rebel think of his sovereign, or a condemned criminal of his judge, with pleasure, as an impenitent sinner remember his offended God, without being troubled.

But it may, perhaps, be objected, that many impenitent sinners appear to remember God, not only without pain, but even with pleasing emotions. I answer, it is not the true God, whom they remember, but an imaginary god, a god of their own creation. Sinners soon find, that it is impossible to think of such a God, as the scriptures describe, without anxiety and alarm. Their carnal minds are full of enmity against such a being. They, therefore, proceed to form a god of their own, one who will not interrupt, oppose, or alarm them in their sinful pursuits; and such a god they can contemplate without pain, and even with pleasure. Hence we are told, that they think God to be altogether such an one as themselves, and say in their hearts respecting sin, God will not requite it.

It will, perhaps, be further objected, that there are some things in the character and government of God, which are adapted to allay the apprehensions of sinners, and prevent them from being troubled at the remembrance of him; his forbearance, long-suffering, and mercy, for instance, and especially the display which he has made, of his love in the Gospel of Christ. I answer, it is readily allowed, that these things are suited to encourage and comfort those, who, in the exercise of repentance and faith in Christ, become reconciled to God, and embrace the offers of mercy. Indeed, were it not for these things, not one of our apostate race could ever contemplate God with any other feelings, than those of terror, remorse, and despair; for we have all sinned, and exposed ourselves to everlasting condemnation. But while the mercy and grace of God, as displayed in the Gospel, are well adapted to comfort the penitent believer, they can evidently afford no rational ground of consolation to impenitent sinners, nor enable them to contemplate him without being troubled. Promises of pardon to the penitent, the believer, the reconciled, are nothing to the impenitent, the unbeliever, the unreconciled rebel, whose heart is still at enmity against God. To such persons the divine character and government still remain no less terrible, than if Christ had not died, and mercy were not offered. Nay, they are, in some respects, more so; for the Gospel has threatenings, as well as the Law, and it denounces on those, who neglect it, a much sorer punishment, than does the Law itself. Those, therefore, who neglect the Gospel, and refuse to repent and be reconciled to God, cannot remember him without being troubled. The same may be said of hypocritical professors, at least, of those, who know or suspect themselves to be such; for to them the thoughts of an all-seeing, heart-searching Judge, who cannot be deceived, and who will bring every secret thing into judgment, cannot but be exceedingly painful. The presence of a penetrating master is ever disagreeable to an unfaithful servant.

Application. 1. This subject, my friends, affords a rule, by which we may try ourselves, and which will assist us much in discovering our real characters; for the moral character of every intelligent creature, corresponds with his habitual views and feelings respecting God. If we never remember him in the sense of the text, or if we think of him unfrequently and with indifference, it is an infallible proof, that our characters are wholly sinful, and our situation most dangerous; for we are expressly told, that all who forget God, shall be turned into hell. If we do not habitually contemplate God's true character and government with heartfelt satisfaction; if we do not rejoice, that the Lord reigns, and that he is just such a being as the scriptures represent him, and that we and all other creatures are in his hands,—it is certain, that we are not reconciled to him, that we still remain under the power of that carnal mind, which is enmity against God. If, though we can usually contemplate these objects with delight, we sometimes find the thoughts of them painful, it is a proof, that at such times, we are in a state of backsliding, from which we ought immediately to return. But whenever we can remember the true character of God, and the truths connected with it, without being troubled, when we can think of appearing in his presence at the judgment day with a humble, solemn joy; and especially, when we feel that to be with him, to see and praise him, forever and ever, is the very heaven which we desire, then we may be sure, that we are his real children, and that we are in a state of actual preparation for death.

2. From this subject we may learn how wretched is the situation of impenitent sinners; of those, who cannot remember God, without being troubled. That such persons cannot enjoy real happiness even in this life, is too evident to require proof; for the world cannot afford it, and they dare not look up for it to heaven, the only source whence it can be derived. Nay more, that great and glorious being, who alone can communicate happiness, is to them an object of dread, and a cause of anxious apprehension. The waters of life, which convey refreshment and felicity to all holy beings, are to them waters of bitterness; and what ought to be their happiness, constitutes their misery. Hence, what ever calamities and afflictions may overwhelm them, however deeply they may be distressed, and however greatly they may need consolation, they cannot look for it to the God of all consolation; for the remembrance of him would only increase their troubles. Indeed, the remembrance of him is usually most painful to sinners, when they are most severely afflicted; because they justly consider their afflictions as proofs of his displeasure. And if the situation of such persons is wretched in life, how much more so must it be at death, and in eternity! You will, I presume, allow, that if there be any such thing as consolation, it must be drawn from the contemplation of God, and of a future state; for it is most certain, that neither this world nor its inhabitants can afford it. But from the contemplation of these objects the dying sinner can derive no consolation. On the contrary, he must, if he thinks of them at all, think of them only with anxiety and dread. If he thinks of God, he can think of him only as a being, whom he has neglected and offended, whose mercies he has abused, and who can view his conduct with no feelings but those of indignation and abhorrence. Every remembrance of him must be accompanied with a recollection of duties neglected, and sins committed, and with fearful apprehensions of his just and eternal displeasure. Which way soever the expiring sinner turns his eye, he can, therefore, discover nothing, which does not add to his wretchedness and despair. If he looks forward, he sees nothing but the dark and gloomy valley of death, through which no friend

will accompany him; the burning throne of judgment, to which he is hastening, and eternity, shrouded in blackness and darkness, spreading in boundless extent beyond it. If he looks back, he sees numberless sins following him as accusers to the judgment seat, and threatening there to find him out. If he looks upward, he sees nothing but the frowning eye of a just and angry God, the glories of which search his inmost soul, and wither all his hopes. If he looks downwards, it is to that bottomless abyss, which he cannot but fear awaits him. He "turns, and turns, and finds no ray of hope."

My friends, if such be the death of those, who forget God, what must be their eternity? No sooner do they leave the body than that holy, just, eternal being, whose every remembrance troubled them, bursts, at once, in all his burning glories, upon their aching sight! And if merely to remember him were painful, what must the sight of him be? Think of a wretch deprived of his eyelids, and condemned to gaze unremittingly at a scorching sun, till the balls of sight were withered and dried up,—and you will have some faint conception of the feelings of a sinful creature doomed to gaze, through eternity, at the, to him, heart-withering perfections of that God, who is a consuming fire to all the workers of iniquity.

My sinful hearers, you, to whom the remembrance of God is painful, will you not hear and be convinced? I do not so much ask you to believe the scriptures, as to believe the testimony of your own experience. You cannot but be sensible, that the light of divine truth is painful to you; that the thoughts of God, of death, and judgment, trouble you. Nor can you deny, that you are mortal,that you must soon exchange this world for another. Now if the remembrance of God be painful to you while in health, must it not be far more painful to to you, when sickness and death come upon you. If the mere recollection of God troubles you, must not the sight of him be incomparably more productive of distress? Why, then, will you put away thoughts, which must return, at a dying hour, to overwhelm you? which must be your eternal companions! Why will you put off that preparation for death, which alone can prevent the recollection, and the sight of God from being productive of anguish? and will convert what is now painful into a source of the purest, of everlasting felicity? Why will you continue in the wretched state of those, who are rendered unhappy by the remembrance of their Creator, of a being, in whose world they live, of whom every thing tends to remind them; a being, who is not far from every one of them, and in whose presence they must dwell forever? How wretched would be the situation of the inhabitants of the ocean, if the element, which surrounds them, and out of which they cannot exist, should become to them a source of misery! And how much more wretched, then, must be the situation of those, who are made miserable by the remembrance, or by the sight of him, in whom they live, and move, and from whom they can never fly! Why then, will you not be persuaded to renounce those sins, which are the only cause, that renders the recollection of God painful, and to embrace those terms of reconciliation, which will render the thoughts, and the presence of God consoling in life, delightful in death, and productive of ineffable happiness through eternity? This leads us to remark,

3. How great are our obligations to God for the gospel of Christ, the gospel of reconciliation! Were it not for this, the remembrance, and still more the presence of God would have occasioned nothing but pure unmingled wretchedness to any human being. Were it not for this, no child of Adam could ever have contemplated God in any other light, than that of an inflexibly holy, just, and offended Judge, all whose perfections demanded his destruction. Were it not for this, there could have been nothing before us, but a certain, fearful looking for of judgment, and fiery indignation. It is only when viewed through that Mediator, whom the gospel reveals, that God can be contemplated by sinful creatures, without dismay and despair. But in and through him God is reconciled. In and through him peace is offered to rebellious men; through him we may all have access by one Spirit unto the Father. O, then, be thankful for the gospel of reconciliation, and show your gratitude, by eagerly embracing the terms of peace, which it proposes. Now, then, we are ambassadors for Christ, as though God did beseech you by us: we pray you in Christ's stead, be ye reconciled to God.

4. Is sin alone the cause, which renders the remembrance of God painful? Then let all, who have embraced the terms of reconciliation offered by the gospel, all who desire to remember

God without being troubled, beware, above all things, beware of sin. It is sin, my Christian friends, which is the cause of all your sorrows. It is sin alone which spreads a frown over the smiling face of God; sin which hides from you the light of his countenance, which prevents you from always contemplating him with pure, unmingled delight and confidence. Swear, then, an eternal war with sin; not only swear, but maintain it. Oppose sin resolutely, crucify it, mortify it in every way, and under all the forms, in which it appears, and it shall not have dominion over you. You shall not have the spirit of bondage again to fear; but the spirit of adoption, whereby ye will cry, Abba, Father.

SERMON X.

SINNERS WILFUL AND PERVERSE.

And the Lord said, whereunto then shall I liken the men of this generation? and to what are they like? They are like unto children sitting in the market-place, and calling one to another, and saying, we have piped unto you, and ye have not danced; we have mourned to you, and ye have not wept. For John the Baptist came neither eating bread nor drinking wine; and ye say, he hath a devil. The son of man is come eating and drinking; and ye say, behold a gluttonous man, and a wine-bibber, a friend of publicans and sinners! But wisdom is justified of all her children. — Luke vii. 31 — 35.

If we ever find infinite wisdom apparently at a loss, it is when she would describe the unreasonableness and perverseness of sinners, or devise proper means to reclaim them. Thus we find her saying to God's ancient people, O Ephraim, what shall I do unto thee? O Judah, what shall I do unto thee? for thy goodness is as a morning cloud, and as the early dew it goeth away. In a similar manner Christ here represents himself as at a loss how to describe the perverseness and obstinacy of his hearers. Whereunto, says he, shall I liken the men of this generation? and to what are they like? As it is, however, impossible, that the infinitely wise Savior should ever be really at a loss, he immediately fixes upon a similitude, which strikingly illustrated their character and conduct. They are, says he, like children sitting in the market-place, and saying to their fellows, We have piped unto you, and ye have not danced; we have mourned unto you, and ye have not wept. To see the force and appositeness of this comparison, it is necessary to recollect the manner, in which weddings and funerals were solemnized among the Jews. At their weddings, a procession was formed, preceded by musicians, playing cheerful tunes, and dancers, who accompanied and kept time to their music. At their funerals also they had mourners, who performed solemn and mournful airs, or uttered cries, lamentations and other expressions of grief. These various ceremonies the Jewish children were accustomed to imitate in their amusements. Sometimes they played cheerful tunes, and rejoiced as at a marriage feast; at others, they uttered mournful sounds, and affected to weep, as at a funeral procession. Sometimes however, children who wished to amuse themselves in this manner, found their companions peevish and unwilling to join them. If they piped and rejoiced, as at a wedding, these ill humored companions would not dance; if, to please them, they changed their strain, and mourned, as at a funeral, they would not weep and lament. Hence they complained, as in our text, that it was impossible to please them, they would neither do one thing nor another. Similar to the temper and conduct of these perverse children was that of the Jews in the Savior's time, and similar has been the conduct of sinners ever since. To trace this similarity, is my present design.

I. The companions of these perverse children employed various means to conquer their obstinacy and persuade them to join in their amusements. So God has employed a great variety of means to persuade sinners to embrace the Gospel. He has sent judgments to subdue, and mercies to melt them; arguments to convince, and motives to persuade them; threatenings to terrify, and invitations to allure them. In different parts of his word he has exhibited divine truth in every possible variety of form. In one place it is presented plainly to the mind in the form of doctrines; in another, it is couched under the veil of some instructive and striking parable; in a third, it is presented to us in a garb of types and shadows; in a fourth, it is illustrated by the most beautiful figures; and, in a fifth, exemplified in some well drawn character, or interesting portion of history. In a word, he addresses us, by turns, in language the most plain and simple, the most grand and commanding, the most pointed and energetic, the most sublime and beautiful, the most impressive and affecting, the most pathetic and melting. God and men, this world and the next, time and eternity, death and judgment, heaven and hell, — these rise successively to our view, portrayed in the most vivid colors, and exhibited in various forms, while the whole created universe is put in requisition to furnish images for the illustration of these awful realities; and the infinite wisdom of God himself is exerted, if I may so express it, to the utmost, in devising and employing the most suitable means to impress them upon our minds, and cause them to affect our hearts. Thus he has addressed himself, by turns, to our eyes and to our ears, to our understandings and consciences, to our imaginations and to our affections, to our hopes and to our fears; and caused divine truth to seek admission to our minds by every avenue, to try every possible way of access.

Corresponding to these various means, and to the different modes of instruction adopted in his word, are the various gifts and qualifications, with which he furnishes those, who are sent as his ambassadors to men. As he knows the different tastes and dispositions of men, and the modes of address best adapted to convince and persuade them, he endues his messengers with a great diversity of gifts, so that by one or another of them, every class of hearers may be gratified. He sends some ministers, who are sons of thunder, well qualified to awaken, rouse, and convince the careless; while others, like Barnabas, are sons of consolation, and fitted to comfort the feeble minded and support the weak. Some he furnishes with clear, penetrating minds, and strong reasoning powers, that they may perspicuously state, and ably defend the doctrines of revelation, answer objections, and by sound arguments, convince the gainsayers. To others he gives warm feelings and lively imaginations, that they may urge divine truth upon the hearts and consciences of their hearers, in a more forcible, impassioned and impressive manner. On a third class he bestows the faculty of presenting truth to the mind in a mild, insinuating, persuasive way, by which it steals into and melts the heart, descending upon it like the dews of heaven, or silent showers, which water the earth. Thus, how diversified soever are the tastes and dispositions of men, all may, in turn, be gratified, in consequence of the variety of ministerial gifts, which God employs for the conversion of sinners and the edification of his church. Thus the healing medicine of divine truth is presented to the vitiated palates of sinners in every possible variety of form; or to allude to the comparison of our text, thus do different ministers address their hearers in different strains, sometimes endeavoring to allure them to embrace the gospel, by comparing it to a marriage feast; and, at others, attempting to terrify them to fly to it, by bringing into view the solemnities of death, and the awful scenes which follow it.

II. Notwithstanding the different means employed with these perverse children, they would not be prevailed upon to comply with the wishes of their companions. We have piped unto you, say they, but ye have not danced; we have mourned unto you, but ye have not lamented. Precisely similar is the conduct of impenitent sinners. Notwithstanding the great variety of means, which God employs to persuade them to embrace the Gospel; and though, as our Saviour teaches us, these means are no less adapted to produce the effect than a message from the dead, yet still they perversely refuse to comply. Reason with them—they will not be convinced; set motives before them—they will not be persuaded; address their hearts—they will not be affected; appeal to they consciences—they will not feel guilty; attempt to excite their fears—they will not be alarmed; endeavor to allure them to Christ by promises and invitations—they will not come. Beseech them, weep over them, expostulate with them in the most affectionate and pathetic manner; set good and evil, life and death, hell and heaven, judgment and eternity before them in every form—they make light of all, and go their ways, one to his farm, and another to his merchandize. In vain have prophets prophesied; in vain have apostles preached; in vain have angels descended from heaven; in vain has the Son of God appeared on earth, and spoken as never man spake; in vain has the Eternal Father proclaimed from heaven, This is my beloved Son, hear ye him:—still sinners will not hear, they will not come to Christ for life, they will neglect the great salvation of the Gospel. Thus it always has been, thus it still is, and thus it always will be, while the heart remains what it is, and almighty grace is not exerted to subdue it.

III. The reason why these perverse children could not be persuaded to comply with the wishes of their companion, was, that they were out of humor, or for some other reason, felt indisposed to gratify them. Similar is the reason, why sinners will not be persuaded to embrace the Gospel, by all the means which God employs for this purpose. They do not come to Christ for life, because they will not. Their proud, selfish hearts, are full of enmity and opposition to God, and therefore they will not be reconciled. It is the gospel itself, which they dislike; and, therefore, how various soever may be the forms, in which it is presented, how clear soever the light, in which it is displayed, they will still reject it. It is because I speak the truth, says our Savior, that ye believe me not. This, however, sinners are by no means willing to acknowledge. They are afraid to confess, even to themselves, that it is hatred of the truth alone, which prevents them from embracing it. They therefore attempt to excuse themselves by imputing their rejection of the gospel to some other cause; and to no cause do they impute it more frequently, than to the faults of its professors, or to something in the manner or conduct of those, who preach it. Thus, we learn from our text, did the Jews. John Baptist came neither eating nor drinking; that is, he lived in the most frugal, abstemious manner, and, as a preacher of repentance, was reserved in his deportment, and severe in his rebukes. Hence they said, he hath a devil; that is, he is a morose, visionary, melancholy man, little better than one distracted, who knows not what he says. Our Savior, on the contrary, came eating and drinking; he associated with men in an affable, familiar manner, with a view to instruct them, and for the same benevolent purpose visited and conversed with the most abandoned characters. His perverse hearers then changed their tone, and cried, Behold a man gluttonous, and a wine bibber, a friend of publicans and sinners. In a similar manner do sinners at the present day, attempt to conceal and excuse their opposition to the gospel. If professors of religion and its ministers live as they ought, soberly, righteously, and godly, they are said to be too rigid, superstitious, righteous overmuch. If, on the contrary, they are of a more cheerful, social turn, the world immediately exclaims, These are your professors, your saints; but in what respect do they differ from others? If they are punctual in attending public and private meetings for religious worship, spend much time in prayer, and devote a considerable portion of their property to charitable and religious purposes, it is immediately said, that religion makes men idle and negligent of their families. If, on the other hand, they are industrious, frugal, and attentive to business, they are no less quickly accused of loving the world, as well as their neighbors, who make no pretensions to religion. If a minister reasons with his hearers in a cool, dispassionate manner, and labors to convince their understandings, he is accused of being dry and formal in his preaching, or of not believing what he says. If another preaches in a more lively, animated strain, clearly proclaims the terrors of the Lord, and warns his hearers to fly from the wrath to come, he is charged with endeavoring to work on men's passions, and to frighten them into religion. If he insists much on the doctrines of Christianity, the necessity of faith, and the impossibility of being justified by our own works, he is accused of undervaluing morality, and representing the practice of good works as needless. If, on the other hand, he clearly exhibits the pure morality of the gospel, inculcates holiness of heart and life, and states the dreadful consequences of neglecting it, he is charged with driving men to despair by unreasonable strictness and severity. Thus in almost innumerable ways men ascribe their neglect of the gospel to the faults of its professors, or to something in the manner in which it is preached, and thus harden themselves and others in unbelief.

But though they may thus deceive themselves, they cannot deceive God. He knows and has said, that the true reason of their rejecting it is, that they love darkness rather than light, because their deeds are evil. For every one, that doeth evil, hateth the light, neither cometh to the light, lest his deeds should be reproved. That this is the case, is evident from men's conduct in other respects. Think not, however, my friends, that in mentioning these things, we are indulging in a spirit of recrimination or complaint. It is not for our own sakes, that we make these remarks—for it is of very little consequence what men may say of us—but for your sakes. It is necessary to your conversion, that you should know what are the true causes of your rejecting the gospel; for until you know these, you will never embrace it. It is also necessary for God's glory, that the cause should evidently appear to be the obstinacy of sinners, and not any deficiency in the means employed by him for their conversion. Whether you will believe this or not, it is most certainly the truth, and you will one day be convinced that it is. Menn while, God has not left himself without witnesses to clear his character, and the honor of his gospel, from the groundless aspersions of sinners,—witnesses, which justify him before an ungodly world; for our Savior assures us in the conclusion of this parable, that, however sinners may reject the gospel, and condemn the manner, in which it is preached, still, wisdom is justified of all her children. By wisdom, is here meant, either God himself, or the gospel, with the means which he employs for its promulgation. He is the only wise God, and the gospel is styled his hidden wisdom, or the wisdom of God in a mystery; while by the means, which he employs to render it successful in building up his church, his manifold wisdom, we are told, is displayed. By the children of wisdom, are intended the children of God, or in other words, those who yield to the force of his appointed means and cordially embrace the gospel. By all such, God, and his ways, are justified, and the wisdom of all his proceedings is readily acknowledged. They admire, love, and adore him, for the infinite wisdom, as well as goodness, which appears in the gospel plan of salvation; and, while they contemplate it, exclaim with the apostle, O the depth of the riches, both of the wisdom and knowledge of God!

Little less do they admire the wisdom and goodness of God, as displayed in the means, which he employs to promote the success of the gospel; and in the fulness, richness, and variety of the scriptures, and in the diversity of gifts bestowed on his ministering servants. And while they acknowledge, that nothing but his all-conquering grace could have rendered these means efficacious to conquer their own stubborn hearts, and humbly cry, Not unto us, O Lord, not unto us, but to thy name be the glory,—they clearly see and unanimously testify, that the only reason, why sinners do not embrace the gospel, is their hatred of the truth, and their opposition to God. Thus wisdom is justified of all her children; and this is the only encouragement, which ministers have to preach the gospel. They know, that it always has been, and that it always will be, foolishness to them that perish; and that by all such they shall themselves be considered as little better than fools and babblers, for if men have called the master of the house Beelzebub, how much more will they thus call those of his household. But they also know, that there are some, though, alas, too few, who are the children of wisdom; and that to them the preaching of the cross will always be the wisdom of God, and the power of God unto salvation. Some such, I desire to bless God, there are in this assembly; some, who receive the truth in the love of it; some, who have felt its transforming, life-giving power; some, who, like all the children of wisdom, justify their heavenly Father and condemn themselves. It is, my Christian friends, indeed a delightful employment to preach to you the unsearchable riches of Christ; for you can, in some measure, feel their worth. It is pleasant to expatiate to you on his glories and beauties; for you have eyes to discern, and hearts to feel them. It is pleasant to invite you to the gospel feast; for you have a disposition to comply. When we display the sufferings of your crucified Lord, and the sins which occasioned them, you are ready to *mourn with us* in godly sorrow and contrition of heart. And when in more cheerful strains we proclaim the happy consequences of his sufferings, and blow the trumpet, whose silver sounds are pardon, peace, and salvation, for dying men, you are equally ready to rejoice. In a word, your hearts are in unison with the gospel harp; when we strike its golden strings, your feelings vibrate to every touch; and you can accompany us, through its whole compass of sound, from the low notes of pious grief and penitential sorrow, up to the high thrilling tones of enraptured gratitude, love and praise, which almost accord with the harps of the redeemed before the throne. Yes, you have learned that new song, which none can learn, but those who are redeemed from the earth; that song, which is sung in heaven, which will be new to all eternity; and most happy and highly honored do I think myself, in being permitted to lead your choir on earth, and to hope that we shall sing it together in the full choir of the redeemed above. It is the greatest of my present supports and consolations, to see in you a proof, that my labors are not altogether in vain. O, then, my brethren, my fellow travellers to heaven, my fellow heirs of its glories! strive to obtain hearts more and more perfectly attuned to the gospel harp; more habitually disposed to vibrate to its celestial sounds. Daily practice the song of the redeemed, and cause the notes of heaven to be heard on earth. Strive, by adorning the doctrine of God, your Savior, to justify the wisdom, which reveals it, and to put to silence the ignorance of foolish men. And if any word I have ever spoken has been blessed to excite godly sorrow or religious feelings in your breasts, let me beseech you, in return, to pray for me, that I may be better furnished with the necessary qualifications for the ministry; that I may never utter an uncertain sound, and that, when I call sinners *to mourn* for their sins, or *to rejoice* in a Savior, God's grace may render the call effectual.

Would to God, my friends, we could believe, that the class now addressed included all this assembly. But melancholy experience constrains us to believe, that the comparison in our text applies to many present, no less exactly than it did to the Jews. As promising means, as God employed to effect their conversion, have been employed with you. Indeed you enjoy far greater advantages than they did. They had only the Old Testament. You, in addition to that, enjoy the New. They were stumbled and perplexed by the mean circumstances, in which Christ appeared, so different from what they expected. To you the reasons of his appearing in this manner, are fully explained. They rejected the Sun of Righteousness, when he first rose, and when his beams were comparatively feeble; you reject him, while shining in meridian splendor, and after his beams have blessed the nations for more than eighteen hundred years, diffusing light and happiness, wherever they come. They only *heard* the predictions of Christ; you have witnessed their exact fulfilment. They refused to hear Christ, while he spake on earth; you turn away your ears now he speaks from heaven. They refused to believe the testimony of prophets and apostles; you reject, not only their testimony, but that of all the multitudes of Christ's ministers, who have preached ever since. It is not surprising therefore, that you should refuse to believe my testimony. I have exerted, to the utmost, the abilities God has given me; in his name, I have, by turns, reasoned and persuaded, exhorted and entreated, invited and threatened, warned and promised, prayed and wept,—but to no purpose. I have set before you, all that is awful and all that is amiable, all that is alarming and all that is alluring, but without effect. I have sounded the brazen trumpet of the law, but you have not mourned. I have blown the silver trumpet of the gospel, but you have not rejoiced. Other and more able ministers have also addressed you. You have, from this pulpit, heard, at different times, cogent reasoners, eloquent speakers, and impressive, persuasive preachers, endeavoring to prevail with you to embrace the gospel. But all has been vain, and with respect to many of you, I fear, worse than in vain. My labors have now apparently less effect upon many of you than ever. Where they once made some impression, they now pass like water over a rock; where they once convinced, they now only irritate; where I was once received with affection, I am now considered as an enemy, because I tell you the truth. My friends—if, to labor, and watch, and pray for your salvation, with a heart broken with apprehension and tortured with anxiety, lest you should fail of it; if, to goad on a worn out body and jaded mind to exertions in your behalf, under which nature sinks, and life becomes a burden; if, to desire your conversion more than riches, more than reputation, more than health, more than life,—if these things are marks of an enemy, then I am your enemy, and such an enemy, I trust, I shall continue to be to my last breath. In fact, if I except the tempter and the world, you have no enemies but yourselves. God, and Christ, and his servants, are your friends, or would be, if you would permit them; but, alas, you will not. Often would they have gathered you, but ye would not. A deep rooted, unconquerable aversion to what you think the strictness of Christ's regulations, frustrates all the endeavors of your friends to save you. You know that religion is important, you are convinced that it should be attended to; but you have no heart to it, you have no love for it, and therefore, as you sometimes confess, you cannot give your minds to it. My friends, what will be the end of this? You have seen its end in the Jews. You know how terribly they were destroyed for neglecting Christ; and if they escaped not, who refused him, when he spake on earth, much more shall not ye escape, if ye turn from him who addresses you from heaven. Once more, then, we conjure you by every thing sacred and every thing dear, by every thing dreadful and every thing desirable, to renounce your unreasonable opposition, and yield yourselves the willing servants of Christ.

But there is also a third class of persons in this assembly, who must be addressed, though we hardly know in what manner to address them. It is composed of such as resemble the son in the parable, who, when his father said, Son, go work to-day in my vineyard, immediately replied, I go sir, but went not. When we speak to these persons in an affecting, mournful manner, and bring to their view the solemnities of death, judgment, and eternity, they seem ready to weep. And when we tell them of the goodness of God, the love of Christ, and the happiness of those, who come to his marriage feast, they are equally ready to rejoice, and seem to desire nothing so much as religion. But in a week, or perhaps in a day, they are the same as before. That there are many such among us, is evident from recent circumstances. We, a short time since, as you probably recollect, invited all, who considered religion as the one thing needful, and who meant to pursue it as such, to meet us at a certain place. We particularly requested, that none would attend, who had not made up their minds on the subject, who were not fully determined to persevere. In consequence of this invitation nearly one hundred persons assembled. I rejoiced at the sight, and immediately wrote to a society, that wished me to make a missionary tour, that in consequence of the serious attention, that existed among my people, I could not leave them. But where now are those, who thus pledged themselves to God, and to each other, and to me, that they would pursue religion? Alas! I fear that their goodness has been as the morning cloud and early dew, that soon pass away. That *I* should not know what to say to such persons, is not surprising, since, as I observed at the commencement of this discourse, God himself seems as if at a loss what to do with them. As an ancient writer observes, they are, by turns, a minister's comforters and tormentors. They excite his expectations to-day, but they disappoint him most painfully to-morrow. Let them not think however, that their temporary convictions will prevent them from being numbered among the characters described in our text. Let them not flatter themselves, that their conversion is rendered more probable by these transitory impressions. Every resistance of conviction renders such an event more hopeless.

SERMON XI.

AMIABLE INSTINCTS NOT HOLINESS.

And the very God of peace sanctify you wholly; and I pray God your whole spirit and soul and body be preserved blameless unto the coming of our Lord Jesus Christ.—1 THESSALONIANS v. 23.

THIS prayer of the apostle for the universal sanctification of the Thessalonian Christians, leads us to notice a distinction in the natural constitution of man, which is not, perhaps, sufficiently attended to. He speaks, you will observe, not only of their body, and their spirit, but of their *soul.* The question is, what does he mean by this? The word soul, usually signifies the intellectual, immortal part of man, by which he is distinguished from the brutes. But this cannot be its meaning here, because he expressly mentions the spirit, or immortal part, in distinction from the soul, or as something different from it. What then does he mean by this term? If we turn our attention, for a moment, to irrational animals, we shall find a satisfactory answer to the question. We have no reason to believe, that these animals possess an immortal soul, or what the apostle in our text calls a spirit. On the contrary, we have reason to believe, that they do not possess such a soul; for an inspired writer speaks of a difference between the spirit of a man, which goeth upward, and the spirit of a beast, which goeth downward to the earth. Yet animals have something, which may be called a soul, that is, something besides a body; for they can love and hate, they can be pleased or made angry; they have various wonderful instincts, and they evidently possess memory. Now take away the intellectual, immortal part of man, or what is called in the text, his spirit, and he would be like one of these animals. He would still possess not only a body, but what may be called an animal soul; and it is, I conceive, this animal soul, which the apostle means in our text, and which he prays might be sanctified and preserved blameless. By praying that this might be the case, he evidently intimates, that it ought to be the case, that the animal soul of man, as well as his body and immortal part, ought to be sanctified or made holy.

I have often explained the nature of sanctification, and its effects upon the appetites and members of the body. I propose, in the present discourse, to consider more particularly the sanctification of the animal soul of man, or that part of human nature, which does not, properly speaking, belong either to the body or to the mind, but which is distinct from both.

In the prosecution of this design I shall naturally be led to show more fully, *what belongs to the animal soul of man*, and in what respects the animal feelings of those, who are sanctified, *differ* from the same feelings in those, who are not.

The *first* thing, which I shall mention as belonging to the animal soul, is that mutual affection, which subsists between parents and their children. I consider this affection as belonging to the animal soul, because irrational animals evidently possess it. While their offspring are in a dependent state, and need their care, they display an affection for them, at least as strong, as was ever exhibited by human parents. They not only hazard, but often lose their own lives in defending their young. And their offspring no less evidently return their affection. We may add, that the sorrow which animals feel when deprived of their young, appears to be as deep, though by no means so lasting, as that which parents feel for the loss of their children. We have, therefore, I conceive, sufficient reason to conclude that parental and filial love, as it naturally exists in mankind, is an affection, not of the immortal part or spirit, but of the animal soul, though it is doubtless, in some measure, modified and often regulated by our rational soul. And hence we farther conclude, that these affections, while they remain unsanctified by the Spirit of God, or as they exist in men void of religion, have nothing in them of a religious nature, nothing of moral goodness or true holiness, nothing, which God is under any obligation to accept or reward. No one supposes, that there is any moral goodness in the affection, which animals feel for their young. And the affection, which parents and children feel for each other, appears to be of the same nature. We do not naturally love our children, because God requires it; we do not love them with a view to please him; we do not love them because it is a duty; our affection for them seems to be a mere natural animal instinct, which is, in itself, neither holy nor sinful. But as it now exists in fallen man, it partakes largely of that universal depravity, which infects his whole nature. In various ways it becomes sinful itself, and leads us into other sins.

It becomes sinful, for instance, when it is inordinate. Our affection for any creature is inordinate and sinful, when we love that creature more than we love God; for he requires the first place in our affections, and forbids us to prefer any object to him. Agreeably, we find most awful punishments denounced upon Eli, because he preferred his sons to God. But all parents naturally love their children far more than they love God. Hence they take more pains to gratify them than they do to please God. Hence they are unwilling to part with them, when he calls, and often feel unreconciled and murmur, when he takes them away. Hence too, they are often so much engaged in acquiring wealth for their children, and in promoting their temporal advancement, that they neglect many of the most important duties which God requires them to perform. Now, when such are the effects of parental love, that love is evidently inordinate and sinful.

Again. Affection for our children becomes sinful, when it takes a wrong direction. Such a direction it takes, when it leads us to prefer their bodies to their souls; to seek their present, rather than their future happiness; to indulge their sinful propensities, rather than give them pain by restraining and correcting them. Yet such, in a considerable degree at least, are the invariable effects of parental love in those parents, who are not influenced by religion. Such parents show no more concern for the souls and eternal happiness of their offspring, than irrational animals. They neither pray for them, nor give them religious instruction, nor set before them a religious example. Surely no one, who believes the Bible, need be told, that such conduct is both highly irrational and exceedingly sinful.

Lastly. Parental affection is sinful, when it is not prompted by right motives. It ought to proceed from a regard to the appointment and will of God. We ought to look upon them from their birth, not as mere play things—to love them, not as irrational animals do, but as rational and accountable creatures. We ought to love them for God's sake, because they are his creatures, because he gave them to us to be educated for him, and trained up for heaven. In a word, we ought to love them with a holy love, and because he requires it. But after what has been said, it is almost needless to remark, that no parents naturally love their children in this manner. Of course, there is nothing morally good, and there is much that is morally wrong, in their parental affection. Hence it is evident, that the affection of the animal soul needs to be sanctified, or brought under the controlling influence of religion. It must be sanctified, or we cannot be universally holy. And from the preceding remarks it will be easy to learn in what this sanctification consists, and what will be its effects. It is sanctified, when it is prompted by right motives, when it takes a right direction, and when it is kept in due subordination to the will of God. When this is done, we shall love our children as God's gifts, and for his sake. We shall prefer him to them. We shall feel ready to resign them, when he calls; and if he takes them away, our sorrow for their loss will have no mixture of repining or discontent. While they are spared to us, we shall make it our chief concern to educate them for God and heaven; their souls will receive a much greater share of our attention than their bodies; we shall be far more anxious for their eternal, than their temporal welfare; and to secure it, will be the principal object of all our exertions respecting them. Those, whose affection for their children is not thus regulated and directed, may be certain, that it is not yet sanctified, that it is sinful in the sight of God, and that they are very far from being such parents, as he approves. And yet they may feel very well satisfied with themselves; they may regard themselves as patterns of parental goodness, and even hope that God will reward them as such. Such is the blindness and deceitfulness of the human heart.

The *second* affection of the animal soul, which I shall mention, is that pain, which is excited by seeing our fellow creatures in distress, and that instinctive desire, which we feel, to relieve them. This affection is called sympathy, pity, and compassion. I infer, that it belongs to the animal part of our nature, from the fact, that many species of irrational animals often appear to feel it in a very high degree; and from the equally well known fact, that it is usually felt most strongly by children at a very early age, before the developement of their intellectual powers, and while they can scarcely be considered as rational beings. And in persons farther advanced, it seems to be a merely animal instinct; for it is not guided by reason, and often operates partially and capriciously. Many persons, for instance, who are painfully affected by the sight of bodily suffering, seem to feel no compassion for the mental sufferings of their fellow creatures; and in others, who boast much of their sensibility, it seems to defeat the very end for which it was given, by rendering them unable to support the sight of keen distress, and impelling them to fly from their suffering friends, when they most need their assistance. Indeed, many plead this as an excuse for neglecting to visit the sick and necessitous, and for leaving their friends, when any painful surgical operation is to be performed. They urge that their sensibility is too exquisite, that their feelings are too easily affected, to allow them to witness such scenes, or to perform such duties. We may add, that the same persons, when provoked, are often cruel, and feel no pity for the sufferings of those, who have offended them. What is still worse, they feel no compassion for the souls of men; no grief, in view of the future miseries, to which sinners are exposed; nor will they make the smallest exertion to save them from these miseries. If a friend or relative is sick of a mortal disease, and, unconscious of his danger, is flattering himself with hopes of a speedy recovery, they will not speak a word to undeceive him, and perhaps will not even allow others to do it, lest it should give him pain. Supremely selfish, even in their sensibility, they leave him to discover his danger, when too late, to die unprepared, rather than perform the painful duty of warning him, that death is approaching. How widely this pity or compassion, if it deserves the name, differs from that which glowed in the bosom of our Savior, no one, who has read the New Testament with attention, needs be informed. It is true, he pitied the corporeal sufferings which he witnessed, and was ever ready to relieve them; but it is equally true, that he felt and displayed incomparably more compassion for their perishing souls. It was to save *them*, that he came from heaven. It was to save *them*, that he shed, not tears only, but blood. He bore their sins in his own body on the tree, and freely consented to be wounded for their transgressions, to be bruised for their iniquities, and to pour out his soul unto death, that they might live. His compassion evidently differed very widely from that blind instinct, that animal affection, which we dignify with the name. It was benevolence viewing misery, and willing to make that misery its own, not merely by sympathising with it, but by actually bearing it, that the miserable might escape.

Nor was his sensibility blunted, as ours often is, by familiarity with scenes of suffering, or by the criminality of the sufferers. It is evident then, that our natural sympathy, amiable as it appears, necessary as it is, needs to be sanctified, and that until it is sanctified, it has nothing in it of moral goodness, or true benevolence. Before it can lay any just claim to these titles, it must be made to resemble the compassion of our Savior. It must cease to be capricious, partial, and selfish in its operations. It must make us willing to deny ourselves, and to suffer pain, inconvenience, and provocation, for the sake of alleviating the distresses of others. It must be excited by the sufferings of our enemies, as well as those of other men. Above all, it must be excited chiefly by the miseries, to which the souls of men are exposed; and enable us, when viewing our unconverted relatives, to say with Paul, I have great heaviness and continual sorrow in my heart, for my brethren, my kinsmen according to the flesh. So far only, as we can truly say this, are our natural sensibility and sympathy sanctified. And if they are not thus sanctified, in some degree, at least, in vain shall we pretend to belong to the merciful, who shall obtain mercy of God, or claim any relation to our Savior; for if any man have not the spirit of Christ, he is none of his. And if there is any thing in the spirit of Christ, by which he was peculiarly distinguished, it was compassion for the souls of men.

There are two other marks, by which we may be assisted in ascertaining how far our natural sympathies are sanctified. Merely natural sympathy usually declines, as men advance in years; so that, if they live to old age, it becomes almost extinct. But when it is sanctified, it not only continues, but increases in proportion to the christian's religious advancement. In this case it is truly beautiful to see the affectionate sensibility of youth united with the experience, firmness, and mature wisdom of age; to see the veteran disciple, who has learned to endure hardness as a good soldier of Christ, putting on bowels of mercies, tenderness and gentleness of mind, to see the same tree adorned at once with the blossoms of spring and the fruits of autumn. The second mark of sanctified sympathy, is a disposition to participate in the joys, as well as sorrows, of our fellow creatures. This the scriptures require. They command not only to weep with those who weep, but to rejoice with those who rejoice. This command we shall obey, so far as our natural affections are sanctified. We shall make the happiness of others our own. But merely natural affection will not lead to this. On the contrary, it will often lead us to envy those, who are more prosperous than ourselves, to repine at their prosperity, especially if they are our rivals, and to wish that some calamity may befall them. He, in whom this disposition is subdued; he, that can truly rejoice in the happiness of those who do not love him, may safely conclude that he has made advances in the work of sanctification.

Thirdly. What is commonly called the natural temper, or disposition, seems to belong chiefly to the animal soul. I say, *chiefly*, for some of the passions, which affect the temper, such as pride, ambition, avarice, envy, malice, and revenge, evidently belong to the spirit, or immortal part; for we are taught, that evil spirits, who have no animal soul, are subject to these passions. But setting these passions aside, there is something in the natural temper or disposition of men, which may be, and which indeed often is, called constitutional. In this respect different persons differ very widely, even from their birth. Some appear to be constitutionally timid, mild, gentle, quiet, affectionate, and yielding; while others are bold, boisterous, restless, irritable, and obstinate. In a word, some have naturally an amiable, and others an unamiable temper. Now that this difference of temper depends upon the animal soul, appears, to say the least, highly probable from the fact, that we find a similar difference among irrational animals, even among those of the same species. For instance, among the domestic animals, which are employed by man, there seems to be as great a diversity of natural temper, as is found among human beings. Some are quiet, mild, gentle, and tractable. Others, of the same species, are irritable, quarrelsome, and perverse. What renders it still more probable that the temper belongs to the animal soul, is the well known fact, that it seems to be much affected by the state of the health. Persons, who, while in good health, appear to be mild, affectionate, and contented, will often, when assailed by disease, become peevish, fretful, irritable and querulous. This is especially the case with children, who are less careful, than older persons, to conceal their feelings. Now every one will probably acknowledge, that when the temper is naturally unamiable and bad, it needs to be sanctified. When persons of such a temper profess to have become christians, an amelioration of their temper is always expected. This is, perhaps, one of the first proofs of their sincerity, for which their acquaintance look; and if it is not found, their professions are naturally supposed to be insincere. On the contrary, when a great and obvious change for the better is witnessed in the temper of such persons, their sincerity is usually acknowledged, and religion is honored. This being the case, it is evidently of very great importance, that those professing christians, whose temper is naturally bad, should pay the strictest attention to this subject, and make it their chief concern to have their temper sanctified by divine grace. Until this is done, they can neither possess themselves, nor exhibit to others, satisfactory evidence of their sincerity, nor can they adorn the religion, which they profess. Indeed, they will not fail to dishonor it, and cannot be either useful, consistent, or happy. As persons, who have such a temper, are not unfrequently bold, resolute, and unyielding, it is easy for them to be firm, zealous, and courageous in the cause of Christ, and they may easily mistake their constitutional courage for holy boldness and christian zeal. But let them beware of this mistake. Let them not conclude they have made much progress in the work of sanctification, until their zeal and boldness are guided by knowledge, tempered with gentleness and prompted by love; nor until they habitually possess and exercise a kind, affectionate, meek, humble, contented and quiet spirit. When this is done, they will resemble their Master, who united in himself the apparently inconsistent qualities of the lion and the lamb, the serpent and the dove,—and will be of all christians the most amiable, exemplary, and useful.

But while all will allow, that a naturally bad temper needs to be thus sanctified, there are many who by no means suppose, that tempers naturally amiable equally need sanctification. But if we take the scriptures for our guide, a little reflection will convince us, that this is actually the case. The scripture teaches, that without holiness, no man shall see the Lord. But there is nothing of the nature of holiness in a naturally amiable temper. Holiness consists in a conformity to the law of God. But persons, who possess the temper of which we are speaking, naturally pay no more regard to the law of God than others do. They are not gentle, kind, and affectionate, because God requires them to be, or because they wish to please him; for they often live without God in the world. They do not naturally love prayer, or the Bible, or the Savior, or any part of religion; but it is as difficult to draw their attention and affections to these subjects, as it would be if their tempers were unamiable. The young ruler, who asked our Savior what he should do to inherit eternal life, evidently possessed a naturally amiable disposition. Yet when Christ said to him, Take up thy cross and follow me, he was no more willing to obey, than were the scribes and pharisees. Hence we find that when our Savior asserted the necessity of regeneration, repentance, and faith, he represented them as alike necessary to all, and made no exception in favor of amiable characters. It is therefore evident, that in his view, such characters need sanctification no less than other men. Their natural affections must be *christianized*, if I may so express it, or baptized by the Holy Spirit, before they can possess any thing of the nature of true religion. Until this is done, they are no more christians, merely for possessing such affections, than an animal of a mild and tractable disposition is a christian. And besides this general radical defect of such characters, which consists in an entire want of true holiness, they are subject to many particular defects; defects which often attend them even after they become christians. They are often constitutionally timid, irresolute, and easily prevailed upon by solicitations, to do what they know, or at least suspect to be wrong.

To these solicitations, they find it very difficult to say, NO, with firmness, and to obey the precept, which says, My son, if sinners entice thee, consent thou not. Nor do they usually display much zeal and courage, in doing good, or in maintaining their Master's cause. Many of them also are constitutionally indolent: hence, if they become christians, they are often slothful christians. Like the sluggard mentioned by Solomon, they are too ready to say, There is a lion in the way; and the fear of man, a fear of giving offence, often entangles them in a snare. Often too, they forget or neglect the rule of being just before they are generous; and, prompted by natural temper, give away what is not theirs to give. If they *do not* become christians, these defects prevail in their character in a still greater degree, and often prove their ruin, both for this world and the next. A large proportion of those, who fall a prey to dissipation, gaming, intemperance, and debauchery, are of this class. They are, at first, led into these vices by the example and solicitations of their companions, which they have not sufficient strength of mind to resist; and afterwards continue to practice them through habit. If they escape this snare, and maintain a correct moral character, they are in danger of falling into other errors, hardly less fatal. As they are commonly much beloved and esteemed, their company is sought after, and they find themselves so pleasantly situated in this world, that they have little leisure or inclination to think of another. Besides, the good opinion of their fellow creatures, tempts them to think too highly of themselves, and to trust in their amiable temper and correct morals, while they neglect the Savior of sinners, the only name under heaven, by which any can be saved. Surely then, no one, who regards the scriptures, can doubt, whether such characters need to be sanctified by divine grace. And those of them, in whom this work is begun, need to go on unto perfection. They must judge of their progress towards perfection by the degree, in which they conquer those sins and errors, to which they have a constitutional propensity. If they are enabled to overcome indolence and timidity, and to be zealous, bold, and diligent in the cause of Christ; if they can resolutely resist temptation; if their natural mildness and gentleness are exalted into true benevolence; if they become as unwilling to offend God, as they naturally are to offend their fellow creatures; and if they become more and more sensible of their constitutional failings, and more solicitous to correct them—they have reason to hope, that the work of sanctification is rapidly advancing.

I have now mentioned the principal affections of the animal soul, and attempted to show, that they need to be sanctified. It remains to make some improvement of the subject.

1. What has been said, may throw some light upon the doctrine of man's entire depravity, and remove some plausible objections, which are often urged against its truth. When we say, that men are entirely depraved, we mean, as I have often stated to you, that they are entirely destitute of holiness. They are as destitute of holiness, as a dead man is of life; and hence they are said by the inspired writers to be dead in trespasses and sins. In reply, the adversaries of the doctrine refer us to parental and filial affection, to that sympathy or compassion, which seem natural to man; to the amiable tempers, which many seem to possess, and to the moral actions, which flow from these several sources. They suppose the existence of these things proves conclusively, that men are not entirely depraved. But it has been clearly shown, if I mistake not, that there is no holiness in any of these things; that we possess them in common with irrational animals; that they are, in many respects, imperfect and sinful, and that they lead us into many sins. Now if this has been proved, it evidently follows, that the existence of these animal affections is no proof at all, that men are not entirely depraved. It has also been proved, indeed our text clearly proves, that these affections of the animal soul need to be sanctified, or made holy. But if they need to be made holy, is is evident, that they are not originally holy, but that they are, on the contrary, depraved, or sinful; for nothing, which is not sinful, needs to be made holy.

2. From this subject it appears, that those who are sanctified, and those who are not, differ very widely, even in those respects, in which they seem to be alike. For instance, both classes eat and drink; but he who is sanctified, eats and drinks to the glory of God, while the unconverted sinner eats and drinks to gratify himself. Both classes love their children. But in unsanctified persons, parental love is a merely animal affection, inordinate, wrongly directed, and not subordinate to the love of God. In those, who are sanctified, on the contrary, it is

a holy affection rightly directed, regulated by God's law, and in subordination to his love. Both classes may pity and relieve the distressed. But the former are led to do this by a blind animal instinct, which is capricious, irregular, and partial in its operations; while the compassion of the latter is elevated and ennobled by divine grace, and resembles that, which glowed in the bosom of our Savior. Both classes may possess amiable tempers, and live correct moral lives. But the amiable tempers of the former, and the morality, which they sometimes produce, do not spring from religion; they are not influenced by religion; nor have they any reference either to God and his law, or to Christ and his gospel. The temper and morals of the latter, on the contrary, spring from religion in the heart; they are the effects of God's law written in the heart; their love to men flows wholly from love to God; their morality is true christian morality, and they are constrained by the love of Christ to imitate his example. In short the governing motives, the main-springs of action, in the sanctified and un-sanctified man are totally different; and since God looks at motives, since, in his view, the character of every action is determined by its motive, it is evident, that the same actions which are good when performed by a good man, may be altogether wrong when performed by a sinner. The sanctified, and the unsanctified may apparently resemble each other in temper and conduct, and yet the latter may be justly punished, while the former are rewarded. Hence we see,

3. How greatly and fatally those are deceived, who found a hope of heaven on their naturally amiable tempers and moral lives. We have seen that these need to be sanctified, and that till they are so, they are imperfect and sinful. Those then, who found their hope on these things, found it on their sins and imperfections. They found it on something, which needs pardon, and which cannot therefore merit reward. St. Paul tells us, that if any supposed they had something of this kind, in which they might safely trust, he had more. But, he adds, what things were gain to me, those I counted loss for Christ; and he proceeds to inform us that he counted all his supposed goodness and morality as mere filth, that he might win Christ. O then, let all, who share in Paul's salvation, imitate in this respect the example of Paul.

4. This subject may assist us to understand that memorable declaration of Christ, From him that hath not shall be taken away even that, which he seemeth to have. We have seen that every thing, which appears to be naturally good and amiable in sinners, such as parental and filial affection, sympathy or compassion, and a sweet natural temper, belongs to the animal soul. Now this dies with the body. Nothing survives death, but the immortal spirit. Of course, at death, sinners, who have no grace, no real goodness, will lose all this apparent goodness, all those natural affections, which made them appear amiable here; and nothing will remain, but a spirit wholly given up to the power and rage of malignant passions. Thus from those, who have no grace, no real goodness or holiness, will be taken away all which they now appear to have. O then, be persuaded, ye, who now appear amiable, to seek, most earnestly to seek the sanctifying grace of God. This alone can render your apparent goodness real, and cause it to be permanent. This alone can stamp on your souls that image of God, which consisteth in knowledge, righteousness, and true holiness, and without which no man shall ever see the Lord.

To conclude. Let me urge all, who profess to be the disciples of Christ, to aim at universal and complete sanctification, even to be sanctified throughout in spirit, in soul, and in body. Remember, that to aim at this, is your indispensable duty. Regard it to as your privilege. O, how desirable it is, to be thus universally holy; to have the immortal spirit clean and white, the animal soul without spot, and the body rendered worthy of such an inhabitant. This you are taught to believe, will, at length, be your happy state in heaven. Will you not, then, strive to make as near approaches to it, as possible, on earth? But the present subject leads me to press upon you, more particularly, the sanctification of the animal soul, with its affections. This is one of the principal seats of depravity. Let it then be one of your chief objects to have it sanctified. Think it not sufficient to love your children, unless your affection for them be such as has been described. Think it not sufficient to be compassionate and sympathising, unless your compassion resembles that of your Saviour. And be not satisfied with your temper, until you feel in full strength, that heaven-born charity which seeketh not her own.

SERMON XII.

THE PROMISED FRUIT OF CHRIST'S SUFFERINGS.

He shall see of the travail of his soul, and shall be satisfied.—ISAIAH, LIII, 11

COULD any of us have seen what angels saw, when the Son of God left the bosom of his Father, and exchanged a throne in heaven for a manger on earth; could we have seen him divesting himself of his glory, laying aside the form of God, assuming the form of a servant, and appearing on earth, in the likeness of sinful flesh, with the avowed purpose of living in poverty, and dying an ignominious, agonizing, and accursed death—we should naturally have been led to exclaim, What adequate object can he have in view? What motive can be sufficiently powerful to induce such a being to make sacrifices so great, to encounter sufferings so exquisite! This question an apostle has partially answered. He has informed us, that Jesus Christ endured the cross and despised the shame for the sake of the joy set before him. In what this joy consisted, we may learn from the chapter before us, and especially from our text. It is here predicted, that he shall see of the travail of his soul, that is, of the fruits or effects of his sufferings, and be satisfied. In the context we are informed what these fruits will be. He shall justify many, he shall see his seed, and the pleasure of the Lord shall prosper in his hand. The joy set before him, for the sake of which he endured the cross, and despised the shame, was then the joy, which would result from seeing his Father glorified and sinners saved, in consequence of his incarnation, sufferings, and death. This, our text declares, he shall see, and the sight will satisfy him. While contemplating it, he will feel that he is amply rewarded for all his sacrifices, toils, and sufferings.

My hearers, the prediction in our text has already been partially fulfilled; it will be fulfilled in a still greater degree, before time shall end; and its complete fulfilment will be witnessed in eternity. These three assertions we propose to illustrate, establish, and improve.

I. The prediction before us has already been partially fulfilled. Already has our Redeemer seen much of the fruit of his sufferings. Our once barren world, watered by his tears and his blood, has already produced a large harvest of righteousness and salvation. His cross, like Aaron's rod, has budded and blossomed, and begun to bear precious incorruptible fruit. From his cross sprang all the religious knowledge, all the real goodness, all the true happiness which has existed among mortals since the fall. On his cross, which, like the ladder seen by Jacob in vision, unites heaven and earth, myriads of immortal beings, who were sinking into the bottomless abyss, have ascended to the celestial mansions;—other myriads, now alive, are following them in the ascent. In the patriarchs, prophets, and pious Israelites; in the apostles, and other primitive preachers of christianity; in the numerous converts, who, by their instrumentality, were turned from darkness to light; in all the truly pious individuals, who have since existed among men; in all the real Christians who are now on earth, our Redeemer has seen the fruits of his sufferings. In every real Christian now present he sees one of these fruits, sees a soul, which has been redeemed by his blood from endless wretchedness and despair, and made an heir of glory and honor and immortality. O then, how much, how very much, has he already seen effected, in fulfilment of the promise before us! How many immortal souls have been plucked as brands from everlasting burnings! How many individuals have been instructed, sanctified, pardoned, comforted, and made more than conquerors, through him that loved them! How many pious families have rejoiced together in his goodness; how many churches have been planted, watered, and made to flourish! How much happiness have the members of all these churches enjoyed in life, in death, and in heaven! What an exceedingly great, and almost innumerable multitude of happy spirits, redeemed from among men, are now surrounding the throne of God and the Lamb! And even while I speak, the number of these happy spirits, and the harvest, which springs from a Savior's sufferings, is increasing. Even while I speak, sinners in different parts of the world are flocking into the kingdom of God. Even while I speak, immortal souls, washed in a Savior's blood, sanctified by his spirit, and just made victorious over the last enemy, death, are entering heaven from the four quarters of the globe, and commencing their everlasting song, Now unto him that loved us, and washed us from our sins in his own blood, be glory and dominion forever and ever.

And while our thrice blessed Redeemer has thus seen, and still sees the happiness of human beings increased by his sufferings, he has also seen, and still sees the glory of God augmented in an equal degree. He has seen millions, who were once enemies to his Father, transformed to friends; he has seen millions, who once blindly worshipped false gods, and ascribed to them the glory of creating, preserving, and governing the world, turning from their worthless idols to worship the only living and true God, who made heaven and earth. He has seen his Father's law obeyed and honored by multitudes, who, but for him, would have continued to trample it under foot. He has seen ten thousand times ten thousand of prayers and ascriptions of praise, ascending from a world, which, but for his interposition, would never have offered one of these acceptable, spiritual sacrifices to his Father. He has seen the eternal throne surrounded, and him who sits upon it adored by almost countless multitudes, who were once dishonoring God on earth, and preparing to blaspheme him in hell. In fine, he has seen his religion flying through the world as on angels' wings, scattering blessings wherever she comes, and loudly proclaiming peace on earth, good will to men, and glory to God in the highest. Surely then, the prediction before us has already been partially fulfilled.

II. During the period which must elapse before time shall end, this prediction shall receive a much more ample accomplishment. That this will be the case, we might almost venture to predict from present appearances, even were the scriptures silent respecting it. Never since the days of the apostles have such exertions, as are now witnessed, been made to extend the triumphs of the cross; never has such a grand and powerful combination of means been employed for this purpose; never has the blessing of heaven more evidently attended human efforts; never have been seen such clear and striking indications that a great moral revolution in the world is approaching. If we turn to the scriptures, we shall find the hopes and expectations thus excited abundantly confirmed. We there find the most explicit predictions, the most animating assurances of the future universal prevalence of pure christianity. All that has been seen, is but the first fruits of that rich harvest, which our Redeemer will yet gather in. He who cannot lie has not only promised, but sworn by himself, that the Jews and Gentiles shall be brought into the fold of Christ, that the knowledge of the Lord shall fill the earth, even as the waters cover the seas; that the kingdoms of this world shall become the kingdoms of our Lord and Savior, and that for many successive ages, he shall reign triumphantly over every nation, and kindred, and people. While predicting this extension of the Messiah's kingdom, and describing the future glories of his reign on earth, the sacred writers exhaust all the powers of language, and burst forth into such poetic, enraptured strains, as the Spirit of God could alone inspire. And O, how will our Redeemer see the effects of his sufferings, when all these glowing descriptions shall be realized; when, with benevolent delight, he shall glance his eye over this once ruined, polluted, wretched world, and see all his enemies baffled; ignorance, error, superstition, vice, and misery banished, his religion every where enthroned in the hearts of men, the earth filled with holiness, and happiness, and peace; while from fertile plains, smiling villages, flourishing towns, and populous cities, one universal cloud of incense ascends before God, and the voice of the whole human family, as the voice of one man, pours forth the language of prayer, and praise, and thanksgiving to the Father of all; and the wide open gates of heaven are continually thronged by those, who pour into it from the east and the west, from the north and the south, to swell the number of its happy inhabitants, and add new voices to its everlasting songs! What countless myriads will then be saved! How gloriously will salvation triumph! How will God be glorified, how will the fruits of holiness abound, when all those parts of the world, which are now a moral wilderness, shall become as Eden, and the whole earth be made as the garden of God. And how will human happiness be increased, when generation after generation shall taste the felicity of heaven, during a long life on earth; and then, by an easy and peaceful death, be removed to the mansions of eternal rest.

III. But it is to the final consummation of all things, it is to eternity, that we must look for the complete fulfilment of this animating prediction. Not till then will the great work of redemption be finished; not till then will our Redeemer see so much of the fruit of his suffering, as is necessary to satisfy him. But then he will see all, that is here promised; all, that he ever expected to see; all, that is wanting to render him perfectly satisfied. He will then see the bodies of all his people raised from the grave, glorious, incorruptible, immortal, and perfectly resembling his own; for, says an apostle, addressing Christians, he shall change our vile bodies, and fashion them like unto his own glorious body, according to the working of that mighty power, by which he is able to subdue even all things to himself.

Then will his triumph over death and the grave be complete. Then, as inspiration expresses it, death will be swallowed up of victory. Then, too, our Redeemer will see all his chosen people assembled around him, perfect in holiness, and perfectly happy in the contemplation of his glory and the enjoyment of his presence. For this he prayed just before his crucifixion. Father, said he, I will that those whom thou hast given me, be with me where I am, that they may behold my glory. He cannot then be entirely satisfied, till this prayer is answered in its full extent, till every one whom the Father has given him is brought home to glory. At the period to which we refer, and not till then, will this be done. The last redeemed sinner will then have exchanged earth for heaven, and have begun to gaze with rapture on the unveiled glories of his Redeemer.

Finally. Our Savior will then see the great work, for the accomplishment of which he died, completed. He will see that spiritual edifice, the foundation of which was laid in his blood, which has been so long erecting, standing before him finished, resplendent in glory, and perfect in beauty. Says an apostle,

Christ loved the church, and gave himself for it, that he might sanctify and cleanse it with the washing of water by the word, that he might present it to himself a glorious church, not having spot, or wrinkle, or any such thing; but that it should be holy, and without blemish. The church which Christ thus loved, and for which he gave himself, is called his body. All who compose it are styled his members. Now until the last member of this mystical body is raised to heaven, and fixed in its destined place, the body itself will not be perfect and complete, and of course, Christ its head will not be satisfied. But when that is done, his satisfaction will be complete. Then all his members will be fixed forever in the place, which he is now preparing for them, in a state of absolute perfection—perfection in knowledge, and holiness, and happiness. And O, what tongue of man can describe, what finite mind can conceive, the enrapturing sight, on which the eye of our Redeemer will then rest! He will see an innumerable multitude of immortal beings, with capacities like those of angels, reflecting in body and in mind, his own spotless, glorious image, no less perfectly than the polished mirror reflects the dazzling image of the noon day sun. He will see them all filled to overflowing, with unutterable felicity, and glowing, like the seraphs around them, with burning love and melting gratitude to him, who redeemed them by his blood. He will see them casting their eyes downward to contemplate the lake of fire, the everlasting burnings, from which they have been thus redeemed, and then raising them to gaze on their Deliverer, with emotions which even the language of heaven cannot express, but which he can read in their swelling, and almost bursting hearts. He will see them, in holy transports of affection and humility, casting themselves and their crowns at his feet; hear them cry, with a voice like that of many waters, and of mighty thunderings, Alleluia, for the Lord God omnipotent reigneth! Blessing, and glory, and honor, and power, be unto him that sitteth on the throne, and to the Lamb forever and ever. Stretching his omniscient eye through eternity, he will see them enjoying all this happiness, and ascribing all this glory to God, during its endless ages; their minds continually expanding, their faculties enlarging, and their souls drinking in more and more of that fulness of the Godhead, the whole of which they can never contain.

And while he sees all this, he will see, that but for his sufferings and death, all these immortal beings, now so holy, so glorious, so happy, would have been sinners, demons, fiends, doomed to drink forever of the fierceness of the wrath of Almighty God, which is poured out without mixture into the cup of his indignation. All this, and much more than this, much more than man or angel can describe, he will see, and while he sees it, will exclaim, Father, it is enough; thy promise is fulfilled; I am satisfied.

Permit me now, my hearers, to lead your attention to some reflections, which our subject naturally suggests, and which will, I trust, be found to have an intimate connection with the object* for which we are now assembled.

1. How great, how glorious, how worthy of its Author, does the work of redemption appear, when viewed in the light of this subject. If it was a work worthy of God, to create the world; if it is a work worthy of God, to preserve and govern the world, much more was it a work worthy of him to redeem the world. If his infinite perfections were ever called into action by an adequate motive, it was when they were called to exert themselves in effecting the salvation of a self-destroyed race of immortal intelligences, and to promote the glory of his great name in effecting it. The accomplishment of such a work as this was a motive, which might well bring down the Son of God from heaven, and carry him through all his toils, and support him under all his sufferings. His toils and sufferings were indeed inconceivably great; but so was the object which he had in view; and so was his promised reward, the joy set before him.

2. What conceptions is this subject suited to give us of the happiness, which is now enjoyed, and which, through eternity, will be enjoyed by our divine Redeemer! You have all, my friends, heard much of the happiness of heaven. Those of you, who are christians, know something of it experimentally; for you have tasted the first fruits of the heavenly inheritance. Your conceptions of it are, indeed, exceedingly inadequate, but

* This Sermon was preached at the first meeting of the Foreign Missionary Society of the County of Cumberland, Auxiliary to the American Board.

you know it to be great. Estimate, then, as far as you are able, the amount of happiness which a single individual will enjoy in heaven, during a whole eternity. Proceed to multiply this amount of happiness by the almost countless number of the redeemed. Then recollect, that Jesus Christ has said, it is more blessed to give than to receive; that is, there is more blessedness, or happiness, in giving, than in receiving. Now Jesus Christ gives, and saints and angels receive, all the happiness, which creatures will ever enjoy in heaven. Of course, as the giver of this happiness, is more blessed, more happy, than all the receivers, could we then concentrate in one bosom all the happiness, which is enjoyed by all the saints and angels in heaven, it would still be inferior, far inferior to that, which is enjoyed by Jesus Christ alone. Christian, does not your heart exult to hear of the happiness which your Savior enjoys? Does it not labor, and swell almost to bursting, while vainly attempting to fathom that bottomless tide of felicity, which every moment pours, and through eternity will continue to pour, all its fulness into his infinite mind!

3. In the light of this subject how great, how lovely does our Savior's benevolence appear? It is to his benevolence alone, that his happiness is to be ascribed. It is the benevolent mind only, which finds more happiness in giving than in receiving. Of course, if our Savior were not benevolent, he would never place his happiness in making others happy. He would be far from being satisfied, far from feeling that he is amply rewarded for all his toils and sufferings, by seeing others enjoy the fruits of them. But this it appears, does satisfy him. All the reward which he expected, all which he desires is, the satisfaction of seeing God glorified, and sinners saved. Here then is perfect disinterested benevolence, benevolence worthy of him whose name is love.

And now, my hearers, permit me to apply these remarks to the object for which we are now assembled. This object is, as you are all aware, to unite our efforts, and afford our assistance, in extending the benefits of redemption, in carrying on the great work of man's salvation. We have seen that this is the noblest of God's works, a work, which is every way worthy of himself. To be employed as a willing instrument in carrying on this work, is then the greatest honor, which God can confer on man. Would you not think it an honor to be employed by him in preserving and governing a world? But greater, far greater is the honor of being employed as a co-worker with God in saving a world. This honor have all his saints. This honor we are invited to share.

Again. We have seen, that with the promotion of this work, our Savior's enjoyment of his promised reward is connected. In proportion as this work advances, his satisfaction increases. And does not this fact furnish all who love him with a powerful motive to exertion? Professed disciple of Jesus Christ, do you love, do you wish to gratify your Master, your Redeemer? Is it the language of your heart, what shall I render to my Lord for all his benefits? If so, this is the answer, Labor to promote that cause, which lies so near his heart; that cause, for which he shed his blood; Labor and pray, that the Savior may see more and more of the fruit of his sufferings. While doing this, you will, in effect, be employed by God as a hand, to convey to him a part of his promised reward. And what employment can be more honorable, more delightful, more congenial with the best and strongest feelings of every Christian's heart!

Farther, we have seen that this subject exhibits, in the clearest light, our Savior's disinterested benevolence. We have seen, that the joy set before him, for the sake of which he endured the cross and despised the shame, was the joy, not of exalting or of enriching himself, but of communicating happiness to others. This, this, was all the reward, which his benevolent heart desired, for labors and sufferings unexampled. In this, as in other respects, his example is proposed to us for our imitation. And imitate it we must, if we would prove that we are his disciples; for if any man have not the Spirit of Christ he is none of his. I repeat it, if any man have not the Spirit of Christ, he is none of his. No, the man who does not possess and exhibit some portion of the Savior's disinterested, self-denying benevolence, of his compassion for immortal souls, of his readiness to labor and suffer for their salvation, is not, cannot be, a Christian. He may be any thing else, but he cannot be a Christian. Nor can *he* be a disciple of Christ, who would not feel himself amply rewarded for all his exertions by the pleasure of seeing them crowned with success. This reward will, as we have seen, satisfy our Savior. Surely then, it ought to satisfy us. And this reward, all, who cordially engage in promoting his cause, shall receive. For the Savior must be satisfied. God has said it, and it must be done. He must have the heathen for his inheritance, and the uttermost parts of the earth for his possession. As sin has reigned unto death, so must grace reign through righteousness unto eternal life by Jesus Christ our Lord. Talk not of difficulties. What are difficulties to omnipotence; to him, who speaks and it is done; who commands, and it stands fast; and who can cause a nation to be born in a day? All then, who cordially engage in this work, may engage in it with the certainty, that they shall not labor in vain. As certain as it is that the Savior shall not lose his reward, so certain it is, that they shall not lose theirs. His interest and theirs are inseparably united; when he is satisfied, they will be satisfied. Nor will his faithful servants be required to wait long for their promised reward. Not very far distant probably, is the period, when our Redeemer shall see the promise before us fulfilled in its utmost extent. Already do we witness no equivocal indications, that its complete fulfilment is approaching. Already has the day of millennial glory begun to dawn. Already has the day star been seen from mountains of the East. Already are "blest voices" heard exclaiming from heaven, Now is come salvation, and strength, and the kingdom of our God, and the power of his Christ; and we have no small reason for hoping, that, before the conclusion of the present century, the same blest voices will be heard to cry, Alleluia, the kingdoms of this world are become the kingdoms of our Lord and of his Christ, and he shall reign forever and ever! My hearers, when this period shall arrive, will it not be in the highest degree painful and mortifying to be constrained to say, the long predicted, long expected hour is at length come, but I have done nothing to hasten its arrival. My Savior has gathered in his promised harvest, but none of the seed, which produced it, was sown by my hand, or watered by my tears! If you would not be the subjects of reflections so mortifying, seize the precious opportunity which is afforded you, of committing your seed to the earth, so that hereafter, when he who soweth, and he who reapeth shall rejoice together, you may participate in the joy of your Lord.

Let no one attempt to excuse himself by saying, My services are not wanted. Let no one say, Since God has promised, that his Son shall see of the travail of his soul and be satisfied, we may safely sit still, and leave him to fulfil this promise. He will indeed fulfil it, but he will fulfil it by human agency. And before it can be fulfilled, before every enemy can be put under our Savior's feet, many exertions must be made, much treasure expended, and many battles fought. Satan, the prince and god of this world, will not resign his usurped dominion without a struggle. The more clearly he perceives, that his time is short, the greater will be his wrath, and the more violent his efforts. During that portion of time, which yet remains, the war which he has long waged with the Captain of our Salvation, will be carried on with unexampled fury. If you would survey the progress and result of this war, cast your eyes over the world, which is to be at once the field of battle, and the prize of victory. See the earth filled with strong holds and high places, in which the prince of darkness has fortified and made himself strong against the Almighty. See all the hosts of hell, and a large proportion of the inhabitants, the power, the wealth, the talents, and influence of the world ranged under his infernal standard. See his whole artillery of falsehoods, sophistries, objections, temptations, and persecution, brought into the field, to be employed against the cause of truth. See ten thousand pens, and ten times ten thousand tongues, hurling his poisoned darts among its friends. On the other hand, see the comparatively small band of our Savior's faithful soldiers drawn up in opposing ranks, and advancing to the assault, clothed in panoply divine, the banner waving over their heads, while in their hands they wield unsheathed the sword of the Spirit, the word of God, the only weapon, which they are allowed, or wish, to employ. The charge is sounded, the assault is made, the battle is joined,—far and wide its fury rages; over mountains and plains, over islands and continents, extends the long line of conflict; for a time, alternate victory and defeat wait on either side. Now, exulting acclamations from the christian army proclaim the fall of some strong hold of Satan. Anon, infuriated shouts from the opposing ranks announce to the world, that the cause of Christ is losing ground, or that some christian standard bearer is fallen.—

Meanwhile, far above the noise and tumult of the battle, the Captain of our salvation sits serene, issuing his commands, directing the motions of his followers, sending seasonable aid to such, as are ready to faint, and occasionally causing to be seen the lighting down of his own glorious arm, before which whole squadrons fall, or fly, or yield themselves willing captives. Feeble, and yet more feeble still, gradually becomes the opposition of his foes. Loud, and yet louder still, rise the triumphant acclamations of his friends, till at length, the cry of Victory! Victory! resounds from earth to heaven; and, Victory! Victory! is echoed back from heaven to earth. The warfare ceases,—the prize is won,—all enemies are put under the conquering Savior's feet; the whole earth, with joy, receives her king; and his kingdom, which consists in righteousness, and peace and holy joy, becomes co-extensive with the world. Such, my hearers, is the nature, and such will be the termination and result of the contest, which is now carrying on in the world. In this contest we are now all engaged on the one part or the other; for in this warfare there are no neutrals, he that is not with Christ is against him. Let us all, then, if we have not already done it, enlist under his banner, and make a common cause with him against a rebellious world; and when he shall appear to judge the universe, he will say to us, Come and sit down with me on my throne, even as I overcame, and am seated with my Father on his throne.

SERMON XIII.

MESSIAH'S VICTORY PREDICTED AND DESIRED.

Gird thy sword upon thy thigh, O most Mighty, with thy Glory and thy Majesty; And in thy Majesty ride prosperously because of truth and meekness and righteousness; And thy right hand shall teach thee terrible things. Thine arrows are sharp in the heart of the king's enemies whereby the people fall under thee. — Psalm xlv. 3, 4, 5.

In these words the psalmist, led by the Spirit of truth, addresses Jesus Christ, the great Captain of our salvation, to whom, as we learn from St. Paul, this psalm refers. In the first verse, the inspired author describes the state of his mind, when he began to pen it. My heart, said he, is inditing a good matter; I speak of the things, which I have made touching the king; my tongue is the pen of a ready writer. But before he could proceed farther, the illustrious personage, who was the subject of his meditations, seems to have revealed himself to his enraptured mind, resplendent in glory, and pre-eminent in beauty; so that, instead of speaking of him, as he had intended, he felt constrained to address him as present; and cries out in an ecstacy of admiration and love, Thou art fairer than the children of men; grace is poured into thy lips; therefore God hath blessed thee forever. The exquisite pleasure which he felt while contemplating this delightful vision, and speaking the praises of his Redeemer, naturally excited in his heart the most fervent desires, that Christ's kingdom might be extended; and that others might be conquered by his grace, and brought to know one whose presence produced such fulness of joy. Hence he cries out in the language of our text, Gird thy sword upon thy thigh, O Most Mighty, with thy glory and thy majesty; and in thy majesty ride prosperously, because of meekness and truth and righteousness, and thy right hand shall teach thee terrible things. His benevolent prayer was no sooner uttered, than with the prophetic eye of faith he saw it answered. He saw this Lord of his affections, this object of his admiration, this subject of his praises, riding forth through the world in the chariot of his salvation, conquering and to conquer; and exultingly cries, Thine arrows are sharp in the hearts of thine enemies, whereby the people fall under thee.

My professing friends, no man was ever favored with a view of the glory and beauty of Christ, without feeling emotions and desires similar to those here expressed by the psalmist, without being constrained to pray, as he does, in our text, for the exertion and the triumph of his all conquering grace. For it is impossible to contemplate such a being, and to know the joy, which his presence gives, without ardently desiring, that others, and especially our acquaintance and friends, may share in our joys. And should he be pleased to favor any of us with such views of himself, now we are assembled professedly to pray for the effusions of his grace, and to commemorate his dying love, we shall find no language better suited to express our feelings and desires, than that which is employed by the psalmist in our text. Let us then consider the *import* of the language, the *reasons*, why he employed it, and the *happy effects*, which are witnessed, when the petitions contained in it are answered.

I. The first thing which deserves our attention in this prayer of the psalmist, is the *appellation*, by which he addresses Christ, O thou Most Mighty. He had, in the preceding verse, celebrated the preeminent beauty and loveliness of his person; Thou art fairer than the children of men. He had also noticed his grace and mercy, as a mediator, displayed in the invitations and promises, which he uttered; Grace is poured into thy lips. But as he was now about to pray for an exertion of his power, he addresses him by a corresponding appellation, and calls him Most Mighty.

The propriety of this appellation will not be questioned, when we consider that with respect to his divine nature, Christ is the Mighty God; the Lord Jehovah, in whose arm dwells everlasting strength. Nor is it less applicable to him considered as mediator. In this character he is Immanuel, God with us; and as such is mighty to conquer, and mighty to save. He is mighty to conquer; for he has led captivity captive; he has conquered sin, and death, and hell—the three most formidable enemies, that ever assailed the happiness of men, or the throne of God; enemies, who have repeatedly foiled, and who laugh to scorn all power short of Omnipotence. Nor is he less mighty to save; for he has saved millions from the most awful fate, in the most desperate circumstances. He says of himself, I am he that speaketh in righteousness, mighty to save. So say all the inspired writers. In a word, all power in heaven and earth, is his; and he is able to save, even to the uttermost.

Let us next consider the import of the *petition*, which the psalmist presents to this Most Mighty of beings. It is, in brief, that he would exert his might, or the power of his grace, for the conversion and salvation of sinners. For this purpose, he prays,

1. That he would arm himself with the necessary weapons; Gird on thy sword. Christ has a sword of justice, and a sword of grace; a sword of justice, to cut off incorrigible offenders; and a sword of grace, to subdue his chosen people, and make them willing in the day of his power. It is the latter, which the psalmist here wishes him to gird on; and this is his word; for, says the apostle, the sword of the Spirit is the word of God. Agreeably, when St. John beheld him in vision in the midst of his churches, he saw a sharp two edged sword proceeding out of his mouth. It is with propriety, that this word is compared to such a weapon; for the apostle informs us, that it is quick, or living, and powerful, and sharper than any two edged sword, piercing even to the dividing asunder of the soul and spirit, and of the joints and marrow, and laying open the thoughts and intents of the heart.

It must be observed, however, that this description of the word of God, is applicable to it, only when Christ girds it on, and employs it as his sword. Of what use is a sword, even though it be the sword of Goliath while it lies still in its scabbard, or is grasped by the powerless hand of an infant? In those circumstances it can neither conquer, nor defend, however well suited it might be to do both, in the hand of a warrior. It is the same with the sword of the Spirit. While it lies still in its scabbard, or is wielded only by the infantile hand of Christ's ministers, it is a powerless and useless weapon; a weapon, at which the weakest sinner can laugh, and against which he can defend himself with the utmost ease. But not so when he, who is Most Mighty, girds it on. Then it becomes a weapon of tremendous power, a weapon resistless as the bolt of heaven. Is not my word like a fire, and a hammer, saith the Lord, which breaketh the rock in pieces? It is indeed; for what can be more efficacious and irresistible, than a weapon sharper than a two edged sword, wielded by the arm of omnipotence? What must his sword be whose glance is the lightning? Armed with this weapon, the Captain of our salvation cuts his way to the sinner with infinite ease, though surrounded by rocks and mountains, scatters his strong holds and refuges of lies, and with a mighty blow, cleaves asunder his heart of adamant, and lays him prostrate and trembling at his feet. Since such are the effects of this weapon in the hand of Christ, it is with the utmost propriety, that the psalmist begins by requesting him to gird it on, and not suffer it to be inactive in its scabbard, or powerless in the feeble grasp of his ministers.

2. The psalmist petitions Christ to go arrayed in his glory and majesty; that glory and majesty, with which he then saw him to be clothed. Feeling himself deeply impressed and affected by the view of this glory and majesty, he could not but hope, that the displays of it would produce similar effects upon others. As if he had said, Lord, thy glorious perfections and awful majesty subdue, overwhelm, dazzle, and delight me, and fill my soul with admiration, reverence and love; go then, I beseech thee, and display them to others; and they will feel constrained to submit to thee, as I have been, and to acknowledge that thou art fairer than the children of men, the chief among ten thousand, and altogether lovely.

But in what do the glory and majesty of Christ consist? I answer,—glory is the display, or manifestation of excellency. Now Christ is possessed of excellencies or perfections of various kinds; he has some excellencies, which belong to him as God; some, which belong to him as man, and some, which are peculiar to him as God and man united in one person. Of course, he has a threefold glory: This glory, as God, consists in a display of the infinite perfections and excellencies of his nature. This glory he possessed with his Father before the world was. His glory as man, consists in the perfect holiness of his heart and life. His glory as God and man united in one person, the mediator, consists in his perfect fitness, or suitableness to perform all those works, which the office of mediator requires of him. This is the glory of which St. John speaks, We beheld his glory, the glory as of the only begotten of the Father, full of grace and truth. This is the glory in which Christ appears, when he goes forth to subdue sinners to himself; and this, therefore, is the glory which is meant in our text. If it be asked, in what this glory more particularly consists, I answer,—it consists in a fulness or sufficiency of every excellence and perfection necessary to qualify him for the all important office of mediator between God and man; every thing, which is necessary, either to satisfy the justice and honor of God, or to excite and justify the utmost love, admiration, and confidence of man. Now all this Christ possesses in perfection. He possesses every thing necessary to satisfy the justice and secure the honor of God; for he has once and again declared, by a voice from heaven, that in him, or with him, he is ever well pleased. He also possesses every thing necessary to excite, encourage, and justify the highest love, admiration, and confidence of sinful men; for in him all fulness dwells, even all the fulness of the Godhead. There is in him a fulness of truth, to enlighten sinners, and lead them to believe in him; for in him are hidden all the treasures of divine wisdom and knowledge. He has also a fulness of grace, to pardon, sanctify, and save them; for the riches of his grace are unsearchable. Now the display or manifestation of this infinite fulness of grace and truth constitutes the glory, in which the psalmist wished Christ to appear. He wished him also to appear in his majesty. The difference between majesty and glory consists in this; glory is something, which belongs either to the person or the character of a being; but majesty is more properly an attribute of office, especially of regal office. This office Christ sustains. He is exalted to be a Prince as well as a Savior; he is King of kings and Lord of lords; and it is principally in his character of a king, that he subdues his enemies, and dispenses pardon. The psalmist, therefore, wished him to appear in this character, arrayed in his awful majesty, that while his glory excited admiration, and delight, and love, his majesty might produce reverential awe, and lead sinners to submission and obedience.

In the next place, the psalmist prays, that being thus armed with his powerful sword, and arrayed in his glory and majesty, Christ would ride forth through the world, conquering and to conquer. In thy majesty ride prosperously. There is in these words an evident allusion to the manner, in which monarchs were, in those days, accustomed to go forth to battle. Arrayed in dazzling armor, and adorned with all the ensigns of royal dignity, they ascended a splendid chariot and rode forth at the head of their armies, to assist friendly, or subdue hostile nations. In a similar manner the psalmist wishes Christ, the Captain of our salvation, to go forth, to deliver his people and destroy his enemies; and in the same word prays for and predicts his success.

A most striking description of him, as going forth in this manner, we have in the revelation of St. John. I saw heaven opened, said he, and behold a white horse, and he that sat upon him was called faithful and true; and in righteousness doth he judge, and make war. His eyes were as a flame of fire, and on his head were many crowns: and he had a name written, which no one knew but himself. And he was clothed with a vesture dipped in blood, and his name is called the Word of God. And the armies of heaven followed him, clothed in fine linen, white and clean. And out of his mouth goeth a sharp sword, that with it he should smite the nations; and he shall rule them with a rod of iron; and he treadeth the winepress of the fierceness and wrath of Almighty God. And he hath on his vesture and thigh a name written, King of kings and Lord of lords. With a similar view of our Redeemer the prophet Isaiah was favored, when he cried, Who is this that cometh from Edom, with dyed garments from Bozrah; this that is glorious in his apparel travelling in the greatness of his strength? It is I, the Savior answers, I, that speak in righteousness, mighty to save. Such is the glorious personage, whom the psalmist here addresses, such the manner, in which he wished him to go forth to war.

II. We proceed now to consider the *reasons*, why the psalmist wished the Savior to go forth prosperously, and the cause, in which he wished him to engage. Do this because of truth, and meekness, and righteousness. This passage may be taken in two different senses, and it is rather doubtful which was in the mind of the psalmist. He might perhaps intend the truth, meekness, and righteousness of Christ himself; for all these qualities belong to him in the highest degree. He is the Amen, the Faithful and True Witness, the way, the truth, and the life; and when he goes forth to battle, righteousness is the girdle of his loins, and faithfulness, or truth, the girdle of his reins.

Meekness is also an eminent characteristic of Christ. Learn of me, says he, for I am meek and lowly in heart. Nor is he less distinguished for righteousness. We have seen in the passage already quoted, that he is one, who speaks in righteousness; and that in righteousness he doth judge and make war; and the prophet Isaiah informs us, that as a king, he shall rule in righteousness, and with righteousness judge the poor. If we suppose this to be the meaning of the psalmist, we must understand him as assigning, in these words, the reason why he wished and prayed for the success of the Savior in his glorious expedition. Mayest thou ride prosperously, because thou art true, and meek, and righteous; and therefore, deservest the victory. Or,

2. By meekness, truth, and righteousness, the Psalmist might mean these qualities in the abstract; and if this be his meaning, we must understand him as specifying the cause in which he wished Immanuel to engage. He saw that meekness, truth, and righteousness, were in a great measure banished from the world; that the few, who loved and exercised these virtues, were despised and oppressed, and that error, falsehood, violence, and injustice almost universally prevailed. In a word, he saw what the prophet so feelingly describes and laments. Men, says he, sin in transgressing and lying against the Lord; speaking oppression and revolt, conceiving and uttering from the heart words of falsehood. And judgment is turned away backward, and justice standeth afar off; for truth is fallen in the street, and equity cannot enter. Yea, truth faileth, and he that forsaketh evil maketh himself a prey. For this wretched state of things the psalmist saw there was no remedy but in the

success of his arms, whose kingdom consists in righteousness, and peace, and joy in the Holy Ghost, and whose design it is, to save all the meek of the earth. Hence, as a lover of goodness, and a friend to mankind, he wished and prayed that the great Deliverer might ride forth prosperously, diffusing truth, and meekness, and righteousness through the land.

III. To enforce his petition, the psalmist predicts the certain success, which would attend Messiah, if he thus rode forth to battle. Thy right hand shall teach thee terrible things; that is, thou shalt know experimentally what terrible things thy power can perform. Hence the church is represented as saying, By terrible things in righteousness shalt thou answer us, O God of our salvation. By these terrible things are intended,

1. The destruction, with which he shall overwhelm his incorrigible enemies. This destruction the prophet Isaiah described, when he saw him in vision returning from battle and victory. Why, he exclaims, art thou red in thine apparel, and why are thy garments like his, that treadeth the wine vat? Because, he answers, because I have trodden the wine press alone, and of the people there was none with me; for I have trodden them down in mine anger, and trampled them in my fury, and their blood is sprinkled upon my garments, and I have stained all my raiment. This was fulfilled, when he so terribly destroyed his incorrigible enemies, the Jews, agreeably to his own predictions. It was fulfilled when he no less terribly overthrew pagan, persecuting Rome, and other nations, that conspired against his church. It is still fulfilled in the destruction of all, who obstinately reject his offered grace, and refuse to submit to his authority; and it will be still more signally fulfilled in the awful day, when he shall say, Those mine enemies, that would not have me to reign over them, bring hither and slay them before me.

2. There are also many terrible things which attend, or rather precede, the conquest of those, whom he makes willing to be his people in the day of his power. He sends his spirit to convince them of sin, of righteousness, and judgment; sets his terrors in dreadful array round about them; causes the flaming curse of his broken law to pursue them, pierces the conscience, and cleaves asunder their hearts with his sharp two edged sword, beats down their fancied strength to the earth, and often brings

them to the very verge of despair, before they submit, and cry for mercy. That these are terrible things indeed to the awakened sinner, none who have suffered thus need be told; and such are the terrible things, which the right hand or power of Christ performs, when he rides forth to battle, as the Captain of salvation.

Lastly. While thus beseeching the Redeemer to ride forth prosperously, and predicting his success, he seems suddenly to have seen his prayers answered, and his predictions fulfilled. He saw his all conquering Prince gird on his resistless sword; array himself in glory and majesty; ascend the chariot of his gospel, display the banner of his cross, and ride forth, as on the wings of the wind, while the tremendous voice of a herald proclaimed before him, Prepare ye the way of the Lord; exalt the valleys, and level the hills; make the crooked ways straight, and the rough places plain; for, behold, the Lord God comes; he comes with a strong hand; his reward is with him, and his work before him. From the bright and fiery cloud which enveloped his chariot, and concealed it from mortal eyes, he saw sharp arrows of conviction, shot forth on every side, deeply wounding the obdurate hearts of sinners, and prostrating them in crowds around his path, while his right hand extended raised them again, and healed the wounds which his arrows had made; and his omnipotent voice spoke peace to their despairing souls, and bade them follow in his train, and witness and share in his triumph. From the same bright cloud he saw the vengeful lightnings, flashing thick and dreadful, to blast and consume every thing that opposed his progress; he saw sin, and death, and hell with all its legions, baffled, defeated, and flying in trembling consternation before him; he saw them overtaken, bound, and chained to his triumphant chariot wheels; while enraptured voices were heard from heaven exclaiming, Now is come salvation, and strength, and the kingdom of God, and the power of his Christ. Such was the scene, which seems to have burst upon the ravished sight of the entranced prophet; transported with the view, he exclaims, Thine arrows are sharp in the hearts of thine enemies, whereby the people fall under thee

And, my friends, permit me to add, that similar scenes, though on a smaller scale, are witnessed by the eye of faith in every place, through which Christ now rides invisibly in the chariot of his salvation. Then the sword of the Spirit, the word of God, which, in the feeble hands of his ministers, had long seemed like a sword rusting in its scabbard, or grasped by an infant, becomes a weapon of resistless energy. Then the arrows of conviction, which had been vainly aimed, and feebly sent, are guided between the joints of the harness, and sinners feel them quivering in their hearts. Then the obdurate and incorrigible enemies of Christ are either laid low by the stroke of death, or blasted and seared by the lightnings of his vengeance, and left like a withered oak, on which the bolt of heaven has fallen, to stand naked and barren, till the appointed time for cutting them down and casting them into the fire! Then truth, and meekness, and righteousness, which had long seemed dead, revive, and ignorance, falsehood, and unrighteousness, are compelled to fly. Then the bonds of sin are burst; Satan is unable to retain his captives; death and the grave lose their terrors; joyful acclamations are heard in heaven, celebrating the return of penitent sinners; and crowds of those, whom Christ's arrows have wounded, and his right hand healed again, are seen flocking around his chariot, shouting the praises, and extolling the triumphs of their great Deliverer; while those, who, like the psalmist, have been praying and waiting for his appearance join in the song, and exultingly cry, Thine arrows are sharp in the hearts of thine enemies, whereby the people fall under thee.

And now, if such are the blessed effects of Christ's presence, when he rides forth prosperously, who, that ever saw his glory, can forbear exclaiming with the psalmist, Gird on thy sword, O Most Mighty, and in thy majesty ride prosperously! And are there not now special reasons to hope, that this prayer will be answered? nay, that Christ has already begun to answer it? Has he not begun, in more than one heart, to give power and energy to his long inactive sword? Has he not begun to show himself in his glory and majesty to some of his mourning, waiting people among us? Has not the voice of his herald been heard exclaiming, Prepare ye the way of the Lord, make straight in this desert a high way for our God? Do not some parts of this town begin to shake under the weight of his thundering chariot wheels, and do not his arrows of conviction begin to fly thick around, causing some of the people, who have hitherto been his enemies, to fall before him? Do not some of you, my hearers, already feel these arrows sharp in your hearts, and does not his word, which has long assailed you in vain, like a sword that had lost its edge, now begin to cut deep, to wound your consciences and lay open your hearts? Yes, my friends, we know, and you know, that these tokens of the approach of his presence begin to be seen and felt. Yes, let his church hear and be glad; let his enemies hear and tremble; he comes, our Prince, our Savior, our Deliverer comes, riding gloriously in the chariot of salvation; comes to bless his people with peace; comes to do terrible things, and make bare his omnipotent arm. And how do you intend to meet this majestic Prince, the King of glory, this illustrious conqueror, should he visit you? Will you meet him as an enemy or as a friend? Will you fall under his arrows of conviction, or be blasted by the lightnings of his vengeance? Alas, at present many of you can meet him only as enemies. His mark is not instamped on your foreheads; his protecting blood is not sprinkled upon the door posts of your houses, to prevent the entrance of the destroying angel. There is no altar for prayer erected in your families, to distinguish you from the heathen, who call not upon his name, and upon whom, we are told, his fury will be poured out. Nay, you have not even a seat at his table, to serve as a visible token that you acknowledge him for your friend. Soon will many of you crowd away from him, though one would think you should tremble lest he meet you at the door and ask, why you thus fly from the table of your Maker and Redeemer. But though now his enemies, it is not too late to become his friends. One great object, on which he goes forth in his chariot of salvation, is to convert his enemies into friends. O, then, seek to be found in this happy number. Cry to him in all the anxiety of alarm, Lord, bend thy course towards me, plant one of thy sharp, but salutary arrows in my flinty heart, that I may fall under thee, and become one of thy people in this day of thy power. And let those, who already feel his arrows in their hearts, beware how they endeavor to extract them, or permit any hand to do it but his own. To those, who will apply to no other physician, he will in due time return to heal their wounds, and speak peace to their consciences. But remember the time is short. Soon will the Savior be gone, and then he that is unjust, must remain unjust still, and he that is filthy, must be filthy still. Now, in a peculiar manner, is the accepted time, and day of salvation. And we, my christian friends, how shall we receive our Prince and Savior, should he visit this place? What shall we, what can we render to him, who has remembered us in our low estate, and returned to visit us with his salvation? What indeed, but that offering, which he prizes above all others, a broken and contrite heart? Bring to him such a heart. Show him the scars, which his arrows of love formerly made in it. Remind him and yourselves of the memorable time, when he came to heal the wound, and speak peace to your consciences. Let every heart which he has thus wounded and healed, prepare him room. Let every voice, which he has tuned to join in the hallelujahs of heaven, be now heard celebrating his perfections, and praying for his speedy and universal triumph.

SERMON XIV.

SINNERS ENTREATED TO HEAR GOD'S VOICE.

The Holy Ghost saith, to-day if ye will hear his voice, harden not your hearts. — HEBREWS III. 7, 8.

MY brethren, I can think of no introduction to a discourse on this awakening passage more suitable, than that often repeated command of our Savior, He that hath an ear, let him hear what the Spirit saith. You are here told what the Spirit saith. The Holy Ghost saith, To-day, if ye will hear his voice, harden not your hearts. To sinners of all ages, in all situations, of all descriptions, to every one who hath an ear to hear, or a heart to be hardened, the Holy Ghost saith, To-day, if ye will hear his voice, harden not your hearts.

The import of this language is so obvious as to need little explanation. It requires us to hear God's voice; to hear it, not merely with the external ear, but with appropriate feelings of heart, with faith, love and obedience. It commands us to do this to-day, immediately, without the smallest delay. The import of the language is, if you ever mean to hear God's voice, if you do not intend to die without obeying it, you must hear it now. And what is the voice of God, which we are thus commanded to hear immediately? It is that voice, which says respecting Jesus Christ, This is my beloved Son, hear him; that voice, which now commandeth all men, every where, to repent; that voice which says to every child of Adam, My son give me thine heart; come ye out from an unbelieving world, and be ye separate and touch not the unclean thing, and I will receive you, and be a Father to you, and ye shall be my sons and my daughters, saith the Lord Almighty. The import of all these passages is, be truly religious, and if you intend ever to be so, become so to-day; while yet it is called to-day, repent and believe the gospel.

This, then, is the great duty enjoined in our text, the command which we are now to enforce. But when God speaks to men; when the Creator speaks to his creatures; when the King eternal speaks to his lawful subjects, and the Holy Ghost saith, hear his voice and harden not your hearts against him, can it be necessary to urge upon you the duty of immediately obeying his commands? Alas, my friends, that it should be necessary. But necessary as it is, it will be in vain to attempt it unless divine grace incline you to obey. O, then, that the God, whose voice you are commanded to hear, and the Holy Spirit, who now commands you to hear it, may be present in his powerful influence, while I attempt to enforce upon you an immediate compliance with his commands, to press home upon your consciences the reasons, the motives, which should induce you to become religious to-day.

Before I proceed to do this let me state, particularly, whom I mean to address. It is not the fool, who says in his heart, there is no God. It is not the profane scoffer, who, disbelieving the scriptures, sneeringly asks, Where is the promise of his coming? It is not he, who, having already presumptuously hardened his heart against the truth, has been given over by the righteous judgment of God to strong delusions, to believe a lie. Such characters, if any such are present, I must leave, where they have wilfully thrown themselves, in the hands of that God who is a consuming fire, who has declared, that he will deal with incorrigible offenders. It is the young, who are not hardened through the deceitfulness of sin; it is those, who, rationally convinced of the truth and importance of religion intend at some future period to embrace it; those, whose consciences, not yet seared as with an hot iron, sometimes cause them to tremble, as did Felix, when they hear of righteousness, temperance, and the judgment to come; but who, like the same Felix, are postponing a compliance with their convictions to some more convenient season. Such are the characters, whom I now address, and upon whom I would press the importance, the necessity, of immediately becoming religious.

The *first* motive, which I shall set before you with this view, is the shortness and uncertainty of life. I urge you to become religious to-day, because you are not sure of to-morrow; because to-day is, perhaps, the only opportunity, with which you will ever be favored. Need I enter upon a labored proof of this truth? Need I remind you, that you are mortal, that it is appointed to all men once to die? Does not the tolling bell almost daily remind you of this? Do you not see your fellow mortals borne, in rapid succession, to their long home, while the mourners go about your streets? Need I tell you, that you are frail, as well as mortal; that you must not only die, but may die soon and suddenly; that the time allotted you, when longest, is short, and may prove much shorter than you are aware; that many are swept into eternity, as in a moment, by unexpected casualties? and that those who fall victims to diseases, are in perfect health the day, nay, the hour, before it assails them; and that of course, the full possession of health, to-day, is no proof that you will not be assailed by fatal disease to-morrow? Who, let me ask, are the persons, that die suddenly and unexpectedly? Are they the feeble, the infirm? No, my hearers; observation will tell you, that they are the youthful, the vigorous, the strong. She will tell you that while the former, like a reed, bend before the blast and escape, the latter, like the stubborn oak, brave its fury, and are prostrated. She will tell you, and the physician will confirm her remark, that those, who enjoy the most vigorous health, are most exposed to many of those diseases, which arrest their victims by surprise, and cut short the thread of life, as in a moment. Such is the wise appointment of him, in whose hands is our breath, that none may be tempted to abuse their health and vigor, by drawing from them encouragement to postpone preparation for death. Will you then frustrate the design of this appointment? Will you boast of to-morrow, as if it were your own, when you know not what a day may bring forth? You would pity and condemn the madness of a man, who should stake his whole fortune on the turn of a die, without the smallest prospect of gain. But, my delaying hearers, you are playing a far more dreadful and desperate game than this. You are staking your souls, your salvation on the continuance of life; on an event as uncertain as the turn of the die. You stake them without any equivalent; for if life should be spared, you gain nothing; but should it be cut short, you lose all, you are ruined for eternity. You run the risk of losing every thing dear, and of incuring everlasting misery — for what? For the sake of living a little longer without religion, of spending a few more days or years in disobeying and offending your Creator, of committing sins, which you know must be repented of. And is it wise, rather is it not madness, to incur such a risk? Let the following case furnish the reply. I will suppose that you intend to defer the commencement of a religious life for one year only. Select, then, the most healthy, vigorous person of your acquaintance; the man, whose prospects are fairest for long life, and say, whether you would be willing to stake your soul on the chance of that man's life continuing for a year? Would you be willing to say, I consent to forfeit salvation, to be miserable forever, if that man dies before the expiration of a year? There is not, I presume, a single person present, who would not shudder at the thought of entering into such an engagement, if he supposed it would be binding. My delaying hearers, if you would not stake your salvation on the continuance of any other person's life, why will you stake it on the continuance of your own? Yet this you evidently do, when you resolve to defer repentance to a future period; for if you die before that period arrives you die impenitent, unprepared, and perish forever. O, then, play no longer this desperate game; a game, in which millions have staked and lost their souls; but if you intend ever to become religious, begin to-day, for to-morrow is not.

Permit me to enforce these remarks by an instance in point. A person, who formerly met with you in this house, while in the full enjoyment of youth and health, became convinced of the importance of religion; and expressed a determination to attend the next weekly meeting for religious inquiry. When the day of meeting arrived, she however concluded to defer her attendance till the following week. But before the close of that week, she was in her grave. It is not for us to limit the divine mercy, or to say what was her fate; but, for aught we can tell, the delay of a week proved fatal. Permit me to remind you of another circumstance, which many of you will recollect. I observed to you on the Sabbath, I think the first Sabbath of a year, that perhaps some person might then be present in God's house for the last time. The event verified the peradventure. On the following Wednesday, one, who had been present on the Sabbath, was dead. At the ensuing Thursday evening lecture, I noticed the circumstance, and repeated the remark. Again was it verified. Before the next Sabbath, a person, who had been present at that lecture, was a corpse. On the next Sabbath, I mentioned this also, and repeated the remark a third time; and the following day, a third person, who on the Sabbath, was in perfect health, expired. My hearers, what has occurred, may occur again. No person now before me can be sure that he will be permitted to re-visit this house of prayer. If, then, you intend ever to become religious, begin to-day, for to-morrow is not.

This remark suggests a *second* reason, why you should not postpone religion to another day. You cannot properly, or even lawfully, promise to give what is not your own. Now to-morrow is not yours; and it is yet uncertain whether it ever will be. To-day is the only time which you can, with the least shadow of propriety, call your own. To-day, then, is the only time, which you can properly or lawfully give to God. To promise that you will give him to-morrow, or which is the same thing, to resolve that you will become religious to-morrow, is to promise what is not yours, and what may never be yours to give. If then, God deserves any thing at your hands, if you mean to give him any thing, give him what is your own, and do not mock him and deceive yourselves, by promising to give him what you do not possess. If you adopt a different course, and postpone the commencement of a religious life till to-morrow, you will, in effect, say, all the time, that is mine to give, I will give to sin and the world; but that time, which is not mine, and which I have no right or power to give, I will give to God.

A *third* reason why you should commence a religious life to-day, is, that if you defer it, though but till to-morrow, you must harden your hearts against the voice of God. This our text plainly intimates. It excludes the idea of any middle course between obeying God's voice to-day, and hardening our hearts; and affirms of course, that all, who neglect to do the former, will do the latter. Every sinner present then, who does not become religious to-day, will harden his own heart. This is evident also from the very nature of things. God commands and exhorts you to commence immediately, a religious life. Now if you do not comply, you must refuse, for there is no medium. Here then is a direct, wilful act of disobedience to God's commands; and this act tends most powerfully to harden the heart; for after we have once disobeyed, it becomes more easy to repeat the disobedience. But this is not all. If you disobey, you must assign some excuse to justify your disobedience, or your consciences will reproach you, and render you uneasy; if no plausible excuse occurs, you will seek one. If none can readily be found, you will invent one. And when God proceeds to enforce his commands by frowns and threatenings, and to press you with motives and arguments, you must fortify your minds against their influence, and seek other arguments to assist you in doing it. This also tends most powerfully to harden the heart. A man, who is frequently employed in seeking arguments and excuses to justify his neglect of religion, soon becomes expert in the work of self-justification. He is, if I may so express it, armed at all points against the truth; so that in a little time, nothing affects him, no arrow from the quiver of revelation can reach his conscience. Urge him to what duty you will, he has some plausible excuse in readiness to justify himself for neglecting to perform it. But if, as is sometimes the case, his excuses prove insufficient, and his understanding and conscience become convinced, that he ought to hear God's voice to-day he can avoid compliance only by taking refuge in an obstinate refusal, or by resolutely diverting his attention to some other object, till God's commands are forgotten, or by a vague kind of promise that he will become religious at some future period. Whichsoever of these methods he adopts, the present impression is effaced, and his heart is hardened. He has engaged in a warfare with his reason and conscience, and has gained a victory over them. He has resisted the force of truth, and thus rendered it more easy for him to resist it again. In a word, he has less religious sensibility; he has become more inaccessible to conviction, and less disposed to yield to it, than before. Now this is precisely what the scriptures mean by hardening the heart. And this, my delaying hearers, is what you must do, what you will do, unless you become religious to-day. God now commands and exhorts you to repent, and places before you many powerful motives and arguments to induce you to obey. If you do not yield to him, you must resist him. You must, if I may so express it, brace up your minds and hearts against the force of the means which he employs to persuade you. Your spirits must resist and strive against his. Of course, you will leave this house more hardened than you entered it; salvation will be placed farther from you, and your conversion will be rendered more improbable than ever. O, then, if you intend ever to hear God's voice, hear it to-day, and do not, by hardening yourselves against it, render it a source of death unto death to your souls. As a farther inducement to this, permit me to remark,

First, That if you do not commence a religious life to-day, there is great reason to fear that you will never commence it. This is a most important, as well as a most alarming truth; and could I persuade you to believe it, I should feel strong hopes, that you would comply with the exhortation in our text; for I venture to assert, that there is no one thing, which encourages you to neglect religion to-day, so much as a secret hope, that you shall become religious at some future time. Could this delusive hope be destroyed, could you be made to feel, that your eternal salvation depends on your becoming religious to-day, you would scarcely postpone it till to-morrow. Permit me then to attempt the destruction of this hope, by showing you how groundless it is, and how many circumstances combine to render it probable, that if you do not hear God's voice to-day, you never will hear it. With this view I remark, that the very causes which induce you to defer the commencement of a religious life, render it highly improbable, that you will ever become religious. When this duty is urged upon you, you allege, perhaps, that you are not able to become religious, or that you cannot give your minds to it; or that you have not sufficient time for it, or you know not how to begin. Now all these causes will operate with equal force another day. You will then feel just as unable, or, to speak more properly, just as unwilling to become religious, as you do now. When to-morrow arrives you will, therefore, probably defer repentance to some future time; when that time arrives, you will again defer it; and will continue to pursue this course till life is spent. Would the work be rendered more easy by delay, there might be some appearance of a reason for defering it. But it will not. On the contrary, every day's delay will render it more difficult. Your hearts, as you have already been reminded, will to-morrow be more hard and insensible than they are now; your sinful habits also will be more confirmed; your consciences will be less tender; you will be less susceptible of religious impressions; in a word, you will have greater difficulties to overcome, and less disposition to contend with them, than you have today. It is, therefore, exceedingly improbable, that those who neglect religion to-day, will attend to it to-morrow.

There is another circumstance, which renders this improbability still greater. The inspired writers teach us, very explicitly, that after a time, God ceases to strive with sinners, and to afford them the assistance of his grace. He gives them up to a blinded mind, a seared conscience, and a hard heart. Thus he dealt with the inhabitants of the old world. Thus he dealt with the wicked sons of Eli. They hearkened not to the voice of their father, says the inspired historian, because the Lord would slay them. That is, God had determined, in consequence of their wickedness, to destroy them, and, therefore, he did not accompany the warnings of their father with his blessing. Thus he dealt with the Jews in the time of the prophet Isaiah, Make the heart of this people fat, and make their ears heavy, and shut their eyes; lest they see with their eyes, and hear with their ears, and understand with their heart, and convert, and be healed. The same terrible punishment was inflicted on the inhabitants of Jerusalem in our Savior's time. He beheld the city, we are told, and wept over it, saying, O, that thou hadst known, even thou, at least in this thy day, the things which belong to thy peace; but now they are hid from thine eyes! This passage very clearly intimates, that there is a time, when sinners may know the things of their peace; but that, if they suffer that time to pass without improving it, the things of their peace will then be hidden from them, and their destruction will be sure. Hence the apostle exhorts us, in the context, to take warning from the fate of the Jews, who hardened their hearts against God's voice, and thus provoked him to swear in his wrath, that they should not enter his rest. Hence, also, he informs us, that now is the accepted time, now is the day of salvation; thus plainly intimating, that to-morrow the day of salvation may be past. If then you, my delaying hearers, harden your hearts to-day, God may seal them up in impenetrable hardness to-morrow. If you say, I will not embrace the offers of salvation to-day, God will say, No offers of salvation shall be made you to-morrow. Nor is there small reason to fear this; for of all the sins which men can commit, perhaps no one is more provoking to God, than that of refusing immediately to hear his voice. It is a direct and wilful act of rebellion against his authority; it is a sin committed against light and conviction; it is resisting and grieving the Holy Spirit; it is crucifying Jesus Christ afresh; it is practically saying, I know that I must, at some period of life, become religious. It is true death may surprise me, or God may deny his grace, and leave me to perish, if I delay; but I choose to encounter this danger, to incur the risk of losing everlasting happiness and of suffering eternal misery, rather than hear God's voice to-day. I will therefore, once more, harden myself against it; I will again trifle with his commands, again make light of my Savior's invitations and walk a little longer in the broad road, sit awhile longer on the crumbling brink of perdition. This, O delaying sinner, is the plain language of thy conduct. Thus strong is the aversion which it expresses to religion, to the service of God. That he must be exceedingly displeased with such a course, must be obvious to your own mind. You have then great reason to fear, that your day of grace has almost expired, that God will soon swear in his wrath you shall never enter his rest. How groundless must be your hopes of a future conversion; how small the probability, that if you refuse to hear God's voice to-day, you will ever become religious. You ought to feel as if this were the only accepted time, as if your day of grace would end with the setting sun, as if all eternity depended on the present hour, on your immediate obedience to the voice of God.

But once more, setting aside for a moment all that has been said, suppose that you could be sure of long life, sure of repenting at some future period, it would still be the dictate of wisdom, as it is of revelation, to become religious to-day. You expect, if you ever do become religious, to repent of all your past sins; for you well know, that without repentance there is no pardon, no true religion; of course, if by postponing religion to-day you resolve to commit a few more sins, you expect to repent of those sins. You are then, while you delay, constantly making work for repentance; you are doing what you mean to be sorry for; you are building up to-day, what you mean to throw down to-morrow. How irrational and absurd is this! How foolish, how ridiculous, does a rational, immortal being appear, when he says, I mean to omit some duty, or commit some sin to-day, but I will be very sorry for it to-morrow. I will not now hear God's voice, but I mean to mourn, to be grieved for it hereafter. My hearers, could you say this to your fellow creatures without blushing? How then can you, without shame, say it to God by your actions? What sincerity can there be in such promises? How can a man sincerely resolve that he will to-morrow repent of conduct which he loves and chooses to-day! It cannot be. There is not, therefore, the smallest sincerity in the delaying sinner's resolutions of future repentance and amendment. He has no real intention to become religious at any future period of his life; and all his promises are designed merely to quiet his conscience, and prevent her from disturbing him in his sinful pursuits. In every point of view then, it clearly appears to be your duty, your wisdom, your interest, to become religious to-day.

Thus have I stated some of the reasons, which should induce you to commence, immediately, a religious life. To crown all, permit me to remind you, that it is the express command of God. God now commandeth all men, every where, to repent; and the Holy Ghost saith, obey God's command, hear his voice to-day, and do not harden your hearts against it. This command, O sinner, I lay as a terror across thy path. You cannot proceed one step farther in an irreligious course, without trampling it under foot; without practically saying, God now commands me to repent, but I will not repent; the Holy Ghost saith, hear his voice to-day, but to-day I will not hear it. If to-morrow's rising sun finds you out of the narrow way of life, it will find you where God expressly forbids you to be, on pain of incuring his severest displeasure. He has said, rebellion is as the sin ot witchcraft, and stubbornness is as idolatry; and if you disobey his voice to-day, you will be guilty both of rebellion and of stubbornness. We might almost venture to say, it would scarcely be more sinful to go away and commit murder, than to go away and defer repentance; for why is murder a sin? Because, you will reply, God has said, Thou shalt not kill. And has not the same God said, with equal clearness, Repent now, and believe the gospel? To violate this command, then, is no less a direct act of rebellion against God, than it would be to take the life of a fellow creature. And will you, can you, dare you, then, be guilty of it? Have any of you already reached such a pitch of impiety and wickedness, as to dare trample on a known command of God, to commit known, wilful, deliberate sin, when he has assured us that, if we sin wilfully, after we have received a knowledge of the truth, there remaineth no more sacrifice for sin; but a certain fearful looking for of judgment and fiery indignation? My friends, if any of you dare do this, it is too late to exhort you not to harden your hearts; for they are hardened to the utmost already. I am, however, aware, that you will not see, or at least will not acknowledge this to be the case. I am aware, that you always have many excuses in readiness, to prove that you are not guilty of wilful disobedience. But what will these excuses avail at the last day? They may serve to quiet your consciences, to harden your hearts and buoy you up with deceitful hopes now; but they will answer no purpose then; nay, you will not then dare to offer them; for God has declared that every mouth shall be stopped. Besides, you cannot find a single instance in the Bible, in which God has ever paid the smallest regard to the excuses of sinners. We read of some, who, when they were invited, as you now are, to the gospel feast, began with one consent to make excuse. And what was the consequence? God declared that not one of them should taste it. We read of another who attempted to excuse himself by pretending that he was not able to do what his Lord required. And what was his Lord's reply to this excuse? Out of thine own mouth will I judge thee, thou wicked servant. This, I presume, is the excuse which most of you are now secretly making. You are saying, I do not become religious to-day, because I am not able; and I must wait till God assists me. Of all the excuses, that sinners can make, this is the most foolish, the most groundless, the most provoking to God. If you can make no better excuse than this, you had much better make none, and say at once, I will not obey God. Groundless and impious, however, as this excuse is, I would pay it some attention, did you really believe it yourselves. But you do not believe it. The resolutions and promises, which you often secretly make, that you will repent to-morrow, or on your dying bed, prove that you do not believe it; for none ever resolves or promises to do what he knows he cannot do. These promises and resolutions then, show that you suppose yourselves able to repent.

There is another fact, which shows still more clearly, that you do not really believe this excuse. When any important event, an event which nearly concerns your present interests, is in suspense, you always feel anxious. If you have no control over the event, you feel more anxious. You cannot rest till it is decided. Suppose, for instance, that your property, your reputation, or your lives, depended on the verdict of a jury, over which you had no control. You would not say, while they were deliberating, it will avail nothing for me to be anxious; I will therefore feel easy and unconcerned. You could not feel unconcerned; you would be anxious till the decision was known. To apply these remarks to the case before us: You know that God now commands you to repent, and threatens you with everlasting punishment, unless you obey. You profess to believe, that you cannot obey without the assistance of his grace. At the same time you must be sensible that it is altogether uncertain whether you will ever receive this assistance; that is, altogether uncertain whether you shall not perish in your sins, as thousands do, while few find the way of life. Now if you really believe this, you would be in a state of constant anxiety, until your destiny was decided; until you knew whether you should obtain divine assistance or not. Shall I be saved, or shall I perish? is a question, which you would be constantly and anxiously asking. But you do not ask this question. You do not feel this anxiety. You are habitually easy and unconcerned, a demonstrative proof that you do not believe this excuse, that you suppose salvation to be in your own power. Deceive not yourselves then, and insult not God with an excuse, which you do not really believe, and which, if it were true, would transfer all blame from sinners to God, and prove that he alone is guilty of all the wickedness which is perpetrated by his creatures. He knows what you can do, and he does command you to become religious to-day, and you must obey, or take the consequences. It is painful, my friends, to address you in this language; but when I deliver God's message, I must deliver it plainly: I must, to the utmost of my power, apply it to your consciences, in all its unbending, unaccomodating strictness; turn it which way we please, it will say nothing but this,—repent, or you perish. And what, after all, is there so very irksome, or disagreeable, in a religious life, that you should wish to defer its commencement? If you must begin some time, why not begin to-day? Will you reply, I know not how to begin? God's voice, if you listen to it, will inform you. It tells us, that there is a veil upon our hearts; a veil, which prevents us from discerning the path of duty; and it also tells us, that when our hearts turn to the Lord, that veil shall be taken away. Turn then to God Go to him, as his servants, for direction, and he will teach you what you must do. If I mistake not, many of you are like Agrippa, and for a long time have been almost persuaded to be christians; but you hesitate, you linger, you dread to take the first step. Perhaps when you are just on the point of yielding to conviction, the question, what will the world, what will my companions say, occurs to you and causes you to fear. You fear to be thought serious; you dread the remarks, the ridicule, which it would draw upon you, and therefore do violence to your convictions, or lock them up in your own breast, till they die away. In this manner thousands gradually and insensibly harden their hearts, till the truth ceases to effect them. Let such remember, that the fear of man bringeth a snare, that Jesus Christ has said, Whosoever is ashamed of me, of him will I be ashamed at the last day. If you cannot bear the reproach of men, how will you bear his condemning sentence; and the everlasting shame and contempt which will follow it? It will then be known that you had serious thoughts, but that you banished them through fear of men; and sinners themselves will despise you as a coward, who did not dare do what he knew to be right. Dare then to do your duty, to obey your conscience and your God, to be religious; for you cannot be a christian in disguise. You must come out and be separate, or God will not receive you. Take then, at once, some decided step, and let it be known what you mean to be; and you will find that this, and all the other objects of your fear, are mere shadows, and will feel ashamed that they should ever have influenced you for a moment. If your heart still lingers, press it with the command of God; press it with the dreadful consequence of offending and provoking him to forsake you; press it with the terrors of the last day and all the awful realities of eternity. Above all, press it with the consideration, that if you ever turn to God, it must be to-day; that your soul, your salvation, your everlasting happiness, depends on your becoming religious to-day. My friends, are you not convinced that this is the case? Do you not perceive, that if you disobey, or trifle with this solemn command, it will, it must harden your hearts; and render your conversion exceedingly improbable? Do you not perceive that if with this command before you, and with all these motives to obey it, you cannot resolve to obey, you will feel still less disposed to obedience to-morrow, when the subject is forgotten and the world, with all its cares and allurements, again rushes upon you? Be persuaded then to listen and obey, while God, and Christ, and the Holy Spirit—while death, and judgment, and eternity, and heaven and hell, continually cry, to-day, to-day, hear God's voice, and harden not your hearts!

SERMON XV.

THE DIFFICULTY OF ESCAPING THE DAMNATION OF HELL.

My hearers, I am not without apprehensions, that the passage, which I have chosen for the subject of this discourse, will sound harshly in your ears; and that its first effect will be to excite, in many breasts, feelings by no means favorable to the reception of truth. But it is a passage, which was uttered by the compassionate Savior of sinners, and I cannot, I dare not, pretend to be more merciful than he; I dare not suffer either a false tenderness, or a fear of giving offence, to prevent me from calling your attention to his words; words, which, if properly regarded, cannot fail to produce the most salutary effects. The words, to which I refer, are recorded in Matthew XXIII. 33. *How can ye escape the damnation of hell?*

This appalling question was addressed by our Lord to the scribes and pharisees. It evidently intimates that their situation was exceedingly dangerous, if not desperate;—that it was almost, if not quite, impossible for them to escape final condemnation. My impenitent hearers, I will not assert that your situation is equally dangerous, or that your escape from the dreadful retributions of eternity is equally improbable. But the word of God will justify the assertion, and a regard to your eternal interest constrains me to assert, that your situation is exceedingly dangerous; that the obstacles which oppose your salvation are very great and numerous; and that the improbability of your escaping the wrath to come, is by no means small. To produce in your minds a conviction of this truth, is my object in the present discourse. Could you be thoroughly convinced of it, one great obstacle, which now opposes your salvation, would be removed. So far as I have observed, nothing more effectually prevents men from flying from the wrath to come, than a groundless persuasion, that to escape it is easy. Nothing so much encourages men to neglect religion, as a false belief, that they can easily become religious at any time. Nothing prevents more persons from obtaining a well founded hope of salvation, than a delusive hope that they shall, some how or other, be saved. Could this delusive hope, this groundless persuasion, be destroyed; could they be made to see their real situation, and the obstacles, which oppose their escape, they would, at once, be alarmed; their false peace would be effectually disturbed, and they would begin to cry, with earnestness, what shall we do to be saved? How shall we escape the wrath to come?

It is for these reasons, my careless hearers, and not to gratify myself, that I call your attention to this subject. It is much more for your interest, than it can be for mine, that you should entertain just views respecting it. Let me then hope for your attention, while I endeavor to show you, from the word of God, *what your situation actually is:* what are the *obstacles* which oppose your escape and which render it highly improbable that you *will escape* final condemnation.

In the *first* place, permit me to remind you, that you are, even now, under sentence of condemnation. You are already doomed to eternal death by the righteous law of God. This is a truth, which persons of your character are ever apt to forget. Many who assent to the fact, that sinners will be condemned at the judgment day, do not seem to be aware, that they are condemned already. Yet nothing can be more certain. On this point the declarations of scripture are explicit and full. They assure us, that all have sinned, that the wages of sin is death, that the soul that sinneth shall die, that sinners are under the curse, or condemnatory sentence of God's violated law, that he who believeth not is condemned already, and that the wrath of God abideth on him. This being the case, it is evident, unless the execution of this sentence can be averted, unless you can obtain pardon of your offended God, you must perish forever. But the inspired writers assure us, with one voice, that the execution of this sentence cannot be averted, that pardon cannot be obtained, without the exercise of repentance and faith in Christ. On these terms alone salvation is offered, and if we neglect them there is no escape. Now that you may exercise repentance and faith, or become truly religious, several things are necessary, each of which is attended with great difficulties.

It is necessary that you should be roused from that careless, secure state, in which all men naturally live; that you should see religion to be all-important, and thus be led to attend to it with earnestness. To use the language of inspiration, you must be awakened; for with respect to your spiritual and eternal interests, you are asleep. Now it is evident, that no man will attend seriously to religion, unless he sees it to be an object of importance. No man will exert himself to escape a danger, which he does not perceive; no man will think seriously of flying from the wrath to come, until he sees that he is exposed to this wrath. And it is equally evident, that no man, who, in a spiritual sense, is asleep, will see that he is exposed to this wrath, until he is roused from his slumbers, until he becomes awake to eternal realities.

Of this, your own experience and observation must convince you. You cannot but know, that religion does not appear in your view to be all important; that you do not perceive yourselves to be exposed to the wrath of God; and you know also, that so long as this continues to be the case you will make no exertions to escape it. You cannot but be sensible, that should you live a hundred years in your present state of religious indifference and insensibility, you would not advance a single step towards preparation for death, nor make one effort to become truly religious. It is then evidently necessary, that you should be roused from this spiritual lethargy to a sense of your danger; your slumbers must be disturbed; your dreams of security and of worldly happiness must be banished, and you must awake to the realities of the eternal world; awake to a conviction that religion is the one thing needful, and that without it you must perish forever. Until this is done, nothing can be done. Until this is done you will no more take one step towards heaven, than a man buried in sleep will commence a journey. But to rouse you from this slumbering, careless state, to fix your attention on religious subjects, is exceedingly difficult. Of this, too, your own experience may convince you. The speaker has been laboring for many years to effect this object by every means in his power; but with how little success, you well know. Nay more, God has long been using means to rouse you. He has called you, Awake thou that sleepest; rise up, ye that are at ease; be troubled, ye careless ones; woe to them that are at ease in Zion! He has enforced attention to these calls by the dispensations of his providence. He has sent mercies and afflictions. Many of you he has visited with sickness, and thus brought you near to the eternal world; and he has caused all of you to witness, in repeated instances, the death of friends and acquaintance. But all in vain. You still slumber on, and dream of worldly objects, while death is daily approaching to hurry you to the bar of God. You still feel a strong unwillingness to have your false peace disturbed, and to commence a religious life. To every messenger of God, to every friendly monitor you reply, I pray thee have me excused. A little more sleep, a little more slumber, a little more folding of the hands to sleep. Here then is one great difficulty, which opposes your conversion. And is there not great reason to fear, that it will prove insuperable? Does it not render your conversion, and consequently your escape from final condemnation, highly improbable? Since you have already lived so many years without becoming religious, and even without being persuaded to make it an object of earnest attention, is it not probable that you will continue to live in the same manner till death arrives, especially since all means have been tried in vain, and no new means remain to be employed?

But this is not all. That you may escape final condemnation it is necessary, not only that you should be roused to think seriously of religion, but that you should be induced to pursue it with constancy and perseverance. You must be awakened, and you must be kept awake; and the latter is the more difficult thing. For though it is by no means easy to rouse you to a sense of your situation, it is far more difficult to prevent you from relapsing into a state of spiritual slumber. The very air of this world, has a drowsy effect; and there is a strong and constant propensity in the human heart to lose all serious impressions, and to become careless and indifferent respecting its eternal interests. Besides, religion is always disagreeable to men, when they first make it a subject of attention. They cannot then embrace its promises; they know nothing of its divine consolations; they see nothing in the Bible, but a system of restrictions, and threatenings, and penalties; it requires them to renounce the objects which they love, and gives them nothing in return; every page seems to impose on them some duty which they are unwilling to perform, or requires of them some sacrifice which they are unwilling to make, or denounces against them some threatening which they are unwilling to believe. Hence they are strongly tempted to withdraw from it their attention, and return to their former careless state. Hence scarcely one in five of those who are roused from their slumbers, can be prevented from again falling asleep, though to sleep is to perish.

Here again, we may appeal to your own observation and experience. Many of you have, at different times, been roused from your natural state of careless security. You have been made to see that religion is important. You have felt something of the powers of the world to come, and resolved to attend to your eternal interests. But no sooner were these impressions made, than they began to be effaced; in a few days, or at most in a few weeks, they were entirely gone, and your slumbers became more profound than before. Similar effects of this propensity to lose serious impressions you have often witnessed in others. How many in this assembly have you seen attending to religion for a while with earnestness, and then again treating it with entire neglect. Now this propensity remains in your breasts in its full force, and it will forever oppose all persevering attempts to become religious. Here, then, is another great obstacle which opposes your conversion. And when you consider how great it is; when you reflect on the instability of your religious views; on the proneness of your thoughts to wander from religious subjects, even while in the house of God, does it not appear highly improbable, even to yourselves, that you shall ever be the subjects of permanent religious impressions; that you shall ever be induced to pursue religion with that fixedness of purpose, that intensity of feeling, and that persevering diligence, which alone can secure success? Does it not appear exceedingly probable, that you will continue to live as you have done, making resolutions, but delaying their accomplishment, until your day of grace comes to an end, and the sentence of final condemnation is executed upon you?

Should you however be enabled to overcome these obstacles, others still greater will oppose your progress. With whatever diligence and perseverance you may attend to religious subjects, it will avail nothing, unless you obtain proper views of your own characters, or, to use the language of scripture, unless you are convinced of sin; for no man will seek to escape the condemning sentence of God's law, unless he fears it; no man will fear it, unless he sees that he deserves it, and no man will see that he deserves it, unless he sees himself to be, not only a sinner, but a great sinner; such a sinner as the Bible asserts him to be. Besides, no man can repent of his sins, until he is convinced of them; and we have already seen, that without repentance there is no pardon. A deep and thorough conviction of your own sinfulness then, is indispensably necessary to your salvation. But to produce such a conviction in your minds, is one of the most difficult things imaginable. It is always exceedingly difficult to convince a man against his will, to convince him of any unwelcome or disagreeable truth; and the more disagreeable any truth is, so much the more difficult it becomes to produce a conviction of it. How difficult it is for instance, to convince a consumptive man of his danger. How difficult to make men sensible of their own faults, or to make fond and injudicious parents see the faults of their children. But there is no truth more disagreeable to men, no one, therefore of which they are so unwilling to be convinced, as that which asserts their exceeding sinfulness. To see their sins is mortifying, is painful, is alarming. They will therefore shut their eyes against the sight as long as possible. Many sins they will deny themselves to be guilty of; what they cannot deny they will extenuate, and for those which they cannot extenuate, they will make a thousand excuses. If the fallacy of one excuse is shown, they will fly to another, and from that to a third, and fourth; and when all their pleas and excuses are answered, they will return and urge them all a second time with as much confidence as at first.

But this is not all. The scriptures teach, and observation proves, that one effect of men's sinfulness is to make them blind to their own sins. It prevents men from forming clear conceptions of the rule of duty, that is, the law of God. Sin consists in a transgression of this law, and so long as men have indistinct conceptions of it, they will, of course, have very imperfect views of their transgressions. Sin too renders men in a great degree insensible to the perfections, the authority, and even to the existence of God; and therefore, they see little of the criminality of offending him. Besides, sin impairs, and almost destroys the sensibility of conscience, and thus prevents her from perceiving and reproving what is wrong in our temper and conduct. These remarks we see daily verified in our intercourse with the world. We often see the most abandoned characters entirely blind to their own views. We see, that the longer men persist in vicious courses, the more insensible they become to the voice of conscience. It is the same with respect to those sins of the heart, of which you are all, my careless hearers, guilty; and of which you must be convinced, or perish. It is even more difficult to see these sins in ourselves, than it is to perceive those which are open and gross. Hence the exclamation of the psalmist, Who can understand his errors! Hence too, we find multitudes of sinners mentioned by the inspired writers, who when reproved by God's messengers for their sins boldly replied, What is our iniquity, and what is our sin, that we have transgressed against the Lord? When he said, Ye have despised my name, they replied, Wherein have we despised it? When he said, Ye have robbed God, they did not fear to reply, Wherein have we robbed thee? And when he charged them with uttering impious language, they asked, What have we spoken against thee? Now since human nature is the same in every age, and since it can thus impudently repel the charges of God himself, how exceedingly difficult, or rather how impossible, must it be for us to convince you, that you are sinful in that degree which the Bible describes! Here, as before, we may appeal to your own experience. You know the scriptures assert, in the most unequivocal terms, that the hearts of men are full of evil, that they are desperately wicked, that they are enmity against God; yet these assertions do not convince you that your hearts are thus sinful. What then will ever convince you of it? God will give you no new revelation of the fact, and his ministers can say nothing more than you have already heard, hundreds of times. And yet you must be convinced of it, or your condemnation is certain. Here then is another and apparently an insuperable obstacle which opposes your escape, and which renders it exceedingly improbable, that you ever will escape final condemnation.

But suppose all these difficulties removed; suppose, though there is little ground for the supposition, that by some means or other you should be made sensible of your sins; still, new obstacles no less insurmountable remain to oppose your salvation. Every sinner, when convinced of his sinfulness and danger, invariably asks deliverance in a way in which it cannot be obtained. He relies upon his own watchfulness, strength and exertions to subdue his sinful propensities, and upon his own prayers, tears and merits, to obtain the pardon of his sins. In the language of an apostle, he goes about to establish his own righteousness, and does not submit to the righteousness of God. Disregarding our Savior's assertion, without me ye can do nothing, he attempts to do every thing without obtaining by faith the assistance of Christ. He says, I am the way, the truth and the life. No man cometh to the Father, but by me. Yet still the convicted, but misguided sinner will endeavor to come to God and to obtain his favor without Christ. And though he is assured, that without the teaching of God's good Spirit he never will be able to understand the scriptures, he will not humbly pray for this teaching, but endeavor to ascertain their meaning by his own unassisted researches. These errors, if persisted in, prove fatal. The man is soon bewildered and lost, and never finds the way to heaven; for we are taught, that the scriptures make men wise to salvation, only through faith in Christ Jesus. Agreeably, the apostle, speaking of such characters, says, they followed after righteousness, but they have not attained to righteousness. Wherefore? Because they sought it not by faith, but by the works of the law; for they stumbled at that stumbling stone. At the same stumbling stone multitudes have ever since continued to stumble and fall to rise no more. After laboring a while to establish their own righteousness, as the apostle expresses it, they begin to fancy that they have succeeded. They become pleased and satisfied with themselves, and imagine that all is safe; their alarm subsides, their religious zeal declines, and they settle down upon a false foundation, never to be disturbed till the day, in which God shall come to sweep away their refuges of lies, and overflow, as with a flood, their hiding-place. Others fall into a mistake of a different nature, but no less fatal. Eager to obtain relief from their guilty fears and apprehensions, and yet unwilling to obtain it by the exercise of repentance and faith in Christ, they daily seek for the application of some promise, or for some change in their own feelings, which shall encourage a hope, that their sins are forgiven. What they thus earnestly seek, they are almost sure to find. They are powerfully, but transiently, affected by some promise or encouraging portion of scripture; like the stony ground hearers, they receive it with joy; they consider this joy as a proof of their conversion, and sit down satisfied, that now they are safe. But they are deceived, fatally deceived. They have no root in themselves, and therefore endure but for a time, and in a season of temptation fall away. My careless hearers, if you would know how many are thus deceived and perish, look at this church, or at any other church of Christ. See how many there are, who, after professing to be converted, and appearing joyful and zealous for a time, lose every thing of religion, except the name, and a little of the outward form. Yet all these persons had surmounted the first two great difficulties mentioned above. They had been roused from their slumbers, and they had been convinced of their sins; but in consequence of that strong propensity which is natural to all men, to neglect the guide provided by God, they only escaped one snare, to be entangled in another equally fatal. The same propensity exists with equal force in your breasts. Should you then be roused to think seriously of religion; nay, should you be convinced of your sins, still it is exceedingly probable, that like them you would go about to establish your own righteousness, or be fatally deceived by a false conversion. If you think this improbable, if you say within yourselves, we would be more wise and more cautious, it only proves, that you are under the influence of a self-confident spirit, which would infallibly plunge you into these very snares.

But suppose you should be preserved from these snares, that you should be enabled to surmount all the difficulties which have been mentioned, there would still remain another obstacle, which would alone be sufficient to render your conversion altogether improbable. This is a sinful, hard, unbelieving heart, which is full of enmity against God, and of opposition to his truth; and which will never believe, or submit to God, until its enmity and opposition are taken away. This you do not at present perceive. No sinner perceives it, until he has been convinced of his sinfulness and danger; till he sees, that his own exertions cannot save him, and till the true character of God and of his law is clearly brought to his view. Until this is done, he always fancies that he has some love to God, and that he sincerely desires to please him. But when he sees what God is, and what he requires, then this long concealed opposition never fails to burst forth, and the sinner finds his heart, instead of submitting to God, filled with dislike of his character and of his law. It will not repent, it will not believe in Christ, for we are assured, that every sinner hates the light, and will not come to it. Finding the light then unpleasant, the convinced sinner, if left to himself, makes a desperate effort, shuts his eyes against it, returns to his former state, and probably plunges into infidelity or some other error equally fatal. Thus it was with many during our Savior's residence on earth. They followed him so long and so constantly, that they considered themselves as his disciples, and are so called by an inspired writer. But on a certain occasion our Savior brought clearly to their view some of those truths, which are peculiarly disagreeable to a sinful heart. The consequence was, that they forsook him forever. In a similar manner, I have known many go back and perish, after they seem to have almost reached the entrance of the way of life. I have seen them sensible, that they were the chief of sinners, fully convinced, that everlasting misery would be their portion, unless they repented and embraced the Savior, and assenting to the truth that he was able and willing to save them. I have seen them in this state for several days, unutterably distressed by a sense of guilt and fear of God's wrath, while their understandings and consciences waged an ineffectual war with their obdurate hearts, and made vain attempts to subdue them. At length their hearts gained a fatal victory; their conviction of the truth was banished, the voice of conscience was silenced, and they returned to their former courses, and their last state became seven-fold worse than the first. The same obstacle, my careless hearers, will oppose your salvation with a strength and violence, of which you can, at present, form no conception. Terrible proofs of its power I have often witnessed, when attending the sinner's dying bed. I have seen them, when they knew that their disease was mortal, and that they had but a few days to live, fully convinced that hell would be their portion unless they repented—agonizing in view of their approaching fate—expressing no doubt, that the Savior was ready to receive them, if they would apply to him with sincerity, and yet refusing to apply to him, and at last dying in despair, rather than accept, on these terms, his offered grace. While I have been holding up to their view the power, the compassion, and love of the Savior, his precious promises, and his readiness to receive all who come to him, they have replied, yes, it is all true, but my hard, wicked, unbelieving heart will not repent, will not believe, will not pray. I can repeat prayers with my lips, but my heart feels them not. My hearers, how great, how insuperable, must be the obstacle, which, in such circumstances as these, can prevent a sinner from accepting salvation on the terms of the gospel! Whether you now believe it or not, O sinner, the same obstacle opposes your salvation, and you will one day be convinced of it.

I might easily proceed to mention other obstacles, which render your escape from final condemnation improbable, for it would require a volume to enumerate them all. I have said nothing of the fascinating power of worldly objects; nothing of the contagious influence of evil example; nothing of the strong current of prevailing customs and prejudices, which must be stemmed; nothing of the chain, which long continued habits of sinning have thrown over you; nothing of the many deceivers, who will spread snares for your feet, and cry peace, when there is no peace; nothing of the sophistical arguments, which will be employed to overthrow your conviction of the truth; nothing of the temptations to neglect religion, which will daily assail you on the right hand and on the left; nothing of that great adversary, who, as inspiration informs us, keeps your hearts like a strong man armed, and is not to be cast out of them, but by a stronger than he. But the obstacles, which I have mentioned, are surely sufficient to render it exceedingly improbable, that you will escape final condemnation. And remember that all these obstacles are of such a nature as to furnish you with no excuse. They all originate in your own sinful carelessness, presumption and opposition to the truth. There are no obstacles on the part of God, or of the Savior. It is your hearts, it is yourselves, which place all these mountains in the path to heaven.

And now, my careless hearers, would it answer any purpose, I could sit down and weep in anguish over the picture I have drawn, or rather, which the pencil of inspired truth has drawn of your situation. To see immortal souls thus situated, to see their way to life thus blocked up by their own folly and sinfulness, to see so many powerful causes combining to thrust them down to endless, remediless ruin,—is a sight, over which even angels might weep; nay more, it is a sight, over which the Lord of angels has wept with unavailing compassion.

Do any of you reply, It cannot be, that our situation is so terrible, so dangerous, so nearly desperate, as has now been represented? Why then do the scriptures of truth describe it as such? Why were all the inspired messengers whom God has ever sent to men so much alarmed and distressed by the situation of their hearers? Why did one cry, O that my head were waters, and mine eyes a fountain of tears, that I might weep day and night on their account? Why did another exclaim, I have great heaviness, and continual sorrow in my heart; for I could wish that I myself were accursed from Christ for my brethren my kinsmen according to the flesh? Nay more, why is there joy in heaven, why do angels rejoice over every sinner who repents? They must be perfectly acquainted with his situation; and did they not see it to be dangerous, awfully dangerous, they never would think his escape from it, by repentance, an occasion of such joy. O then, believe not your own deceitful hearts; but believe the angels, believe the scriptures, believe God, believe the Savior, when he tells you, that strait is the gate, and narrow the way, which leadeth unto life, and that few there be who find it. If you will not believe all these witnesses, if you refuse to pay any attention to this warning it will furnish another proof of the greatness of those obstacles, which oppose your salvation, and of the improbability of your escape. I have no hope of ever being able to set before you truths more alarming, more adapted to rouse you from your slumbers than those, which have now been exhibited. The word of God contains nothing more alarming, and did you really believe it, the archangel's trump would not rouse you more effectually than these truths. And shall they not rouse you? Will you still sit unconcerned on the verge of the abyss, with the wrath of God abiding on you, while you are so far from safety, while so long and difficult a journey is before you, while precipitous mountains rise, and deep gulfs sink, and powerful enemies lie in ambush, and numberless snares are spread between you and heaven? Will you sit thus, and lose the precious hours, while the night of death is approaching, while the shadows of evening are already stealing upon some of you, and while none of you is sure of a week or a day? O ye gay, thoughtless triflers! is this a situation for carelessness and gaiety? O ye, who are laboring to be rich! is this the place, in which you would lay up treasure? O ye immortal spirits! condemned already, and hastening to hear the confirmation of your sentence at the tribunal of God, can you find nothing more important than the trifles, which now engross your attention? If you have not cast off all regard to God's word, if you are not infidels in theory, as well as in practice, you cannot, methinks, contemplate with perfect indifference the view, which has been given of your situation. You cannot feel perfectly at ease, while you hear it clearly proved from the scriptures, that there is very little probability of your escaping final condemnation. If you are, in any degree, roused from your slumbers, one great obstacle is removed. But remember, that it may easily return. Consider how easily the present impression may be effaced, how soon it may be lost, and how much more dangerous your situation will then be. Welcome every serious thought then, as you would welcome an angel from heaven. Cherish it as the apple of your eye, nay, as your own soul. Avoid every thing which tends to banish it. Dread more than death its departure. Repair to every place, in which your serious impressions may be strengthened, and use, with earnest diligence and solicitude, every means which may increase them. Remember, that your soul, your eternal all, is at stake; that the question to be decided, is, whether you shall spend your eternity in heaven, or in hell, and that at present, it is exceedingly probable the latter will be your portion.

Do any reply, the difficulties to be surmounted are so great, and the probability of our surmounting them so small, that we have no courage to make the attempt. It will therefore be best to give ourselves no concern respecting it, but to enjoy life while we can. And do you thus talk of enjoyment in such a situation, and while exposed to such a fate as this? Well may we say of such enjoyment, it is madness. It is far more irrational and preposterous than the mirth of criminals confined in a dungeon, and doomed to die, who attempt to drown their fears by noise and intoxication. There is no necessity for your adopting this desperate resolution. Though your destruction is probable, it is not yet certain, and nothing but your own folly can make it so. It would indeed be certain, the obstacles before you would be insurmountable, were there not an Almighty, Sovereign Helper, who can assist you to overcome them, and who is ready to afford you assistance. While, therefore, you justly despair of saving yourselves, go to him, and implore his help. Go, and tell him, that you have ruined yourselves by disobeying him; that you have raised impassable mountains between yourselves and heaven; that you do not deserve his assistance; that you are justly condemned already, and merit nothing but eternal condemnation. This, however, which is the only safe course, I fear your sinful hearts will not consent to pursue. I fear, that however you may now feel, you will dismiss your serious thoughts, and banish the subject from your minds, almost as soon as you leave this house. This I cannot prevent. My arm is too weak to draw you out of that fatal current, which is rapidly sweeping you away to destruction. I can only sit on the bank and weep as I contemplate the increasing strength of the current, and breathe out in agony, cries to that God, who can alone rescue you from its power, and prevent it from hurrying you into that bottomless gulf, in which it terminates. And come, you my Christian hearers—come all, who have been rescued from this fatal current; all, who can feel compassion for perishing immortals, come, and assist in crying to him for help. That you may be excited to this, look at the scene before you. Look around, and see how many of your children, acquaintances and friends, are swept away towards perdition, while they sleep and know it not, and no voice, but that of God, can rouse them. Do you know whither they are hastening? Do you know what hell is? Do you consider how improbable it is, that they will escape its condemnation? Do you consider, that unless grace prevents, they will, in a few years, be lifting up their eyes in torment and despair? Surely, if you know and consider these things, one universal cry of, God have mercy upon them! will burst from every Christian heart.

SERMON XVI.

THE DEAD IN SIN MADE ALIVE.

And you hath he quickened, who were dead in trespasses and sins; wherein in time past, ye walked according to the course of this world, according to the prince of the power of the air, the spirit that now worketh in the children of disobedience; among whom also we all had our conversation in times past, in the lusts of the flesh, fulfilling the desires of our flesh and of the mind; and were by nature the children of wrath, even as others. But God, who is rich in mercy, for his great love wherewith he loved us, even when we were dead in sins, hath quickened us together with Christ; (by grace are ye saved;) and hath raised us up together, and made us sit together in heavenly places in Christ Jesus; that in the ages to come he might show the exceeding riches of his grace, in his kindness towards us, through Christ Jesus.—Ephesians ii. 1—7.

Nothing, my friends, is more profitable to Christians, than frequent meditations on what they once were, and what has been done for them by divine grace. Meditations on these subjects are exceedingly well suited to increase, at once, their gratitude, love and humility. To such meditations our text naturally invites us. The apostle here reminds the Ephesian Christians of their former state and character, and contrasts it with their then happy situation, and mentions the Author of the great change, in consequence of which they had passed from death unto life. And lest any should suppose that such a change was necessary for none but those, who like the Ephesians had been heathen and idolaters, he intimates, that he and his fellow apostles, who were Jews, had been by nature in a similar state, and had experienced a similar change. To all the true disciples of Christ, then, whether Jews or Gentiles, and to you, my Christian friends, among the rest, the language of our text may, with propriety, be addressed. You know, that once you were dead in trespasses and sins; you know, that you once walked according to the course of this world, as children of disobedience, fulfilling the desires of the flesh and of the mind; you know that you were by nature children of wrath, even as others; and you hope that God has quickened, or made you alive, and raised you up to sit together in heavenly places with Christ Jesus. This passage, then, contains your religious history. It describes what you once were, and shows what you are now, and what God has done for you. To illustrate more largely these several particulars, is my present design. To you the subject cannot but be interesting, and it will be little less so to you, my impenitent hearers, if you recollect, that in describing what Christians once were, we are describing what you are still.

I. Once, my Christian friends, you were dead in trespasses and sins. In the figurative language of scripture, a man is said to be dead to any object, or class of objects, when he is wholly insensible to it, or unaffected by it, or unsusceptible of impressions from it. Thus Paul speaks of himself, as dying, or becoming dead to the world; meaning that he was less and less affected by worldly objects, and more and more insensible to their influence. So you were once dead with respect to your Creator, your Redeemer, to religious, to divine things, and to all the concerns of your everlasting peace. In other words, you were entirely insensible to these things; they did not affect you, they made no impression upon your minds, any more than if they did not exist, and, in fact, you did not at all realize their existence. You were alive to other objects. You possessed an animal life, which enabled you to have communion with the irrational animals in the pleasures of sense. You possessed what may be called rational, or intellectual life, by which you were qualified to maintain intercourse and communion with your rational fellow creatures in the pursuit and enjoyment of worldly objects. But of that spiritual life, which renders the soul susceptible of impressions from spiritual objects, and prepares it for the enjoyment of intercourse with God and holy beings, you were entirely destitute. Being thus spiritually dead, you were, of course, devoid of spiritual sense. You could neither hear, nor see, nor feel. You could not hear God's voice, either in his word, or in the dispensations of his providence. He spoke once, yea, twice, but you perceived it not; nor did you ever truly hear a single sermon, though you might, perhaps, listen to many. You were also spiritually blind. You saw no glory in God, no beauty in Christ, no hatefulness in sin, no excellency in the plan of salvation revealed in the gospel. Like all men in their natural state, you received not the things of the Spirit of God, but they were foolishness to you; neither could you know them, because they are spiritually discerned, and you had no spiritual sight. Nor were you less destitute of feeling. You felt nothing of the load of guilt, which pressed you down; nothing of the wickedness and hardness of your own hearts; nothing of the goodness of God and the dying love of Jesus Christ. You did not even feel, that you were dead, but lay buried in a grave of trespasses, and wrapped up in a winding sheet of sins, as insensible of your situation as a corpse, and as completely cut off from all intercourse or communion with God and holy beings, as a corpse is from intercourse with the living; nor did you any more desire to rise from this state, than a corpse desires to rise from the slumbers of the grave. Many attempts, indeed, were made by the beings around you, to rouse you from this state, and sometimes they seemed, for a moment, to be attended with partial success. Like a corpse operated upon by the power of electricity, or galvanism, you exhibited some faint symptoms of returning animation, or at least of irritability; your eyes were perhaps half unclosed, and you cast an anxious glance around; but the bands of death were too strong to be thus broken, and you soon relapsed into a state of complete moral insensibility. But,

2. While you thus lay, in a spiritual sense, dead in trespasses and sins, you were in another sense, alive, awake and active. Though dead to your Creator, you were alive to your fellow creatures; though dead to the future world, you were alive to this; though destitute of that life which the holy Spirit communicates, you were vehemently actuated by that evil spirit, which, as our text informs us, works in all the children of disobedience. Hence, you walked according to his will, or which is the same thing, according to the common course of this sinful and apos-

tate world. The tempter, as a strong man armed, kept possession of your hearts, as his castle, and by a constant succession of temptations suited to your depraved taste, he excited your appetites, inflamed your passions, and thus hurried you forward with blind eagerness and impetuosity in a course of self-gratifications and disobedience to God. As the world around you lived, so you lived. Like them, you cast off fear, and restrained prayer before God; like them, you neglected your Creator, your Redeemer, your souls and eternity; and like theirs, your whole employment and happiness consisted in fulfilling the desires of the flesh and of the mind. Some of you, especially during the season of youth, were most intent on gratifying the desires and appetites of the body. You drank deep of the intoxicating cup of pleasures, rejoicing in youth, and walking in the way of your own hearts, and the sight of your eyes. Others were more devoted to the service of those passions, which are seated in the mind; and to gratify them by the acquisition of wealth, or honor, or applause, was the grand object of your lives. In a word, you lived, just as hundreds around you, whose madness and depravity you contemplate with mingled surprise, pity and abhorrence, are living now. Meanwhile, God hearkened and heard, but you spake not aright. None of you repented of his wickedness, saying, What have I done? but every one turned to his course, as the horse rusheth into the battle.

3. Being then dead in sin, and children of disobedience, you were of course children of wrath; or in other words, objects of the just indignation and wrath of God. He was angry with you every day; and once and again insulted justice cried, Cut them down—why cumber they the ground? But mercy interposed, and you were spared. Meanwhile, you thought nothing of the justice, which threatened, or the mercy, which spared you, but were wholly occupied by your worldly pursuits; and with scarcely a thought of an hereafter, remained insensible as a corpse, over which the thunders were rolling, and round which the lightnings of heaven were spending all their fury. You went on with the tempter enthroned, and strongly fortified in your hearts; sin spreading its deadly influence through all the powers of your soul, and all the members of your body; a frowning and angry God looking down upon you from above, his curse resting upon your persons, your possessions, and all

the works of your hands; the world spreading all her allurements, to draw you on in the broad road to destruction, and hell opening wide in the path before you; while death, with his envenomed dart, stood waiting a commission to transfix and hurl you down to quenchless flames below. Such, my christian friends, was once your character and situation. Such, my impenitent hearers, is still yours. Having thus shown what you were, we proceed,

II. To show what God has done for you. And,

1. When you were thus dead in trespasses and sins, he quickened, or made you alive. You lay, some of you a longer, and some a shorter time in the wretched state, which has been described, like the dry bones which the Prophet saw in the valley of vision, and there you had lain till now, had not sovereign grace interposed. But he, who had from the beginning chosen you to salvation, through sanctification of the Spirit, and belief of the truth, in his own appointed time, began to manifest towards you his eternal purposes of love. The season approached, in which he determined, that the dead should hear the voice of the Son of man; and that they who heard should live. In preparing you for the great change, God dealt with you, not as machines, but as rational beings. He sent some one to call to you, saying, O ye dry bones, hear ye the word of the Lord. Awake thou that sleepest and arise from the dead. By the influences of his Spirit, the call was rendered in some measure effectual. These influences were, however, as yet exerted only in operating upon your rational powers and faculties. Your attention was roused, and turned to religious objects. Your slumbering consciences were awakened, and began to review your past lives and present characters; to compare them with the divine requirements, and to upbraid you with your numerous deficiencies. Your understandings were convinced, that something must be done, and done speedily. The new objects thus presented to your mind, and the new interest which they excited, weakened the influence of worldly objects, and rendered you less eager in their pursuit. You began to read the scriptures, and other religious books, with something of a desire to understand them. You felt disposed, you could scarcely tell why, to associate with pious persons, to hear religious conversation, and to frequent religious meetings.

You listened with more interest, than formerly, to the preached word; you felt yourselves personally addressed, and the truths which you heard, sometimes pleased, sometimes offended, and sometimes condemned and distressed you. Thus your attention was more and more strongly fixed on religious subjects; and the interest which they had excited increased. But still you were far from being sensible of your true character and situation. You did not know, or even suspect, that you were dead in trespasses and sins; that your minds were enmity against God, or that it was impossible for you, in your situation at that time, to please him. Ignorant of God's righteousness, you went about to establish your own, and refused to submit to the righteousness of God. While engaged in this fruitless attempt, your minds were agitated and perplexed by various and conflicting emotions. Sometimes you imagined that you were almost a Christian, and not far from the kingdom of heaven. Then some new discovery of the wickedness of your hearts seemed to put you farther from it than ever. In consequence of repeated disappointments of this kind, you were often strongly tempted to entertain hard thoughts of God. You falsely imagined, that you were willing to come to Christ, but could not; and that God refused you the necessary assistance. Hence you were often tempted to go back, and give up your religious pursuits in despair. But this you found impossible. The burden of guilt, and the deep anxiety which you now felt, would not allow you to rest, though you felt more and more at a loss what to do, or to conjecture the cause of your ill success. By slow degrees, however, you begin to discover the cause. The commandment, as the apostle expresses it, came to you more clearly and powerfully; and as its light increased, sin revived and you died. You began to perceive something of that spiritual death, of which you had not been aware. You found, that in you there dwelt no good thing, that your hearts were impenetrably hard and insensible; that all your religious duties had proceeded from selfish principles, and were of course abominable in the sight of God. Then you felt, more than ever, your need of a Savior; but, at the same time, more unable, or more unwilling than ever, to come to him. But at length you were made to see clearly, that the fault was your own; that you would not come to Christ for life; and that you were dead, utterly dead, in trespasses and sins, and that unless God interposed to save you, you should remain dead forever. This led you to submit, unconditionally, to sovereign mercy, and prepared you to feel, that if ever you were saved, you must be saved by grace,and to give all the glory of your salvation to him to whom it is due. Thus the preparatory work was accomplished, and he, whose work it was, saw that all obstacles to the display of his grace were removed; and then, as the apostle expresses it, by the working of that mighty power which wrought in Christ, when he raised him from the dead, he breathed into you the spirit of life, and you became a living soul. At first, however, you were perhaps scarcely conscious of the wonderful change, or at least, were conscious of it only by its happy effects. But these effects were such, as could result from nothing but the communication of spiritual life.

You found yourselves as it were, in a new world. A new and interesting class of beings and objects, which had always surrounded you, but which you had hitherto never perceived, now presented themselves to your view; and the scriptures, which had heretofore seemed like the earth, at its first creation, a mighty chaos, without form and void, now appeared to you full of beauty, order and harmony. This was the consequence of your possessing those spiritual senses, which ever accompany spiritual life; and which enable the possessor to discern both good and evil. You now began, for instance, to possess and to exercise spiritual sight. The eyes of your understanding were opened to see wondrous things out of God's law. Among these wondrous things, one object appeared preeminently glorious, beautiful and lovely. This was Christ, the Sun of Righteousness. The light, which flowed from him, rendered both himself and other spiritual objects visible. The wondrous plan of salvation by him, now opened to you: you began to know God, and Jesus Christ, whom he hath sent, a knowledge of whom is eternal life, and to understand something of the various offices, which Christ sustains with respect to his people. At the same time, you began to hear God's voice in his word and in the dispensations of his providence. You could now hear him speaking peace to his people and to his servants, and the sound was music to your ears. You were also endued with spiritual feeling. Your hearts of stone were transformed to flesh, you became susceptible of deep and lasting impressions from religious objects, and felt a quick sensibility when they were presented to your minds. Nor were you devoid of spiritual taste. You could now taste and see that the Lord is good; you hungered and thirsted after righteousness; and as new-born babes, desired the sincere milk of the word. And while you were thus endued with new senses, adapted to perceive spiritual objects, the new life, which God had given you, began to spread through all the powers and faculties of your nature, rendering them instruments of righteousnesss unto holiness. Having thus restored you to life, God next proceeded,

2. To raise you from the grave of sin, and cause you to sit together in heavenly places with Christ Jesus. The situation, which had suited and pleased you while in a state of spiritual death, became disagreeable and irksome to you, when restored to life. The spirit of disobedience, which had wrought in you, was banished, and succeeded by the Holy Spirit, the author of life and peace. You could no longer walk according to the course of this world, nor were you any longer children of wrath. God, therefore, by freely pardoning all your sins, removed the load of guilt and wrath, which, like the great stone at the door of Christ's sepulchre, had confined you to the tomb; called you out from among the dead, who had hitherto been your associates; added you to his church, as members of the great body of Christ; conferred on you the name and privileges of sons and heirs of God, and thus gave you a title to the heavenly inheritance, and did, in effect, make you sit together in heavenly places in Christ Jesus. Believing in him, you were sealed with that Holy Spirit of promise, which is the earnest of the heavenly inheritance. By the influences of the same Spirit you were taught, as are all who have risen with Christ, to set your affections on things above, to look at things unseen and eternal; and to seek for that heavenly city, into which Christ as the forerunner of his people, has entered to take possession in their name, and to prepare a mansion, which shall receive them at death; when you shall actually sit down with him on his throne in the heavenly places, and live and reign with him forever and ever.

3. We are told what prompted God to raise you from the

dead, and confer on you these unmerited favors, namely, his own sovereign, self-moved goodness. God, says the apostle, who is rich in mercy, for the great love wherewith he loved us, even when we were dead in sins, hath quickened us together with Christ; for by grace are ye saved, not of works, lest any man should boast. That nothing but sovereign grace thus saved you; and that nothing but God's self-moved goodness or love prompted him to bestow on you that grace, is evident from the description already given of your natural character and situation. You were by nature dead in trespasses and sins. Of course, you did not raise yourselves from the dead. You did not even know, that you were dead, nor had you one desire to be raised from death, till God gave it you, much less did you, while in that state, perform any good works, to merit God's favor. On the contrary, you were children of wrath, and deserved nothing but the wrath of God forever. Nothing but God's grace then, or in other words, nothing but his unmerited favor, raised you from this state, and nothing but his love led him to grant you that grace. But how could he love those who were dead in trespasses and sins, and consequently more hateful in his sight, than a putrefying corpse is in ours? I answer,—he loved you as in Christ, and merely for the sake of Christ, whom he had from eternity appointed to be your covenant head. Our Savior, you recollect, often speaks of a people, who were given to him by his Father. All that the Father giveth me, says he, shall come to me; and this is the will of my Father, that of all that he has given me I should lose none. Now of all who were thus given to Christ, he was from eternity appointed to be the covenant head. Hence we find the apostle, in the preceding chapter, saying of himself and all other Christians, Blessed be the God and Father of our Lord Jesus Christ, who hath blessed us with all spiritual blessings in Christ Jesus, according as he hath chosen us in him, before the foundation of the world, that we should be holy and without blame before him in love. Of this people, thus chosen in Christ as their head, and given to him, you, my Christian friends, were a part, and as such God loved you. As he says to his ancient people, I have loved you with an everlasting love, therefore with loving kindness have I drawn you; so we may consider him as saying to us, I have loved you in Christ, and for his sake, with an everlasting love, therefore I have raised you from the death of sin.

Hence the apostle, speaking of Christians, says, God hath saved us, and called us with an holy calling, not according to our works, but according to his own purpose and grace which was given us in Christ Jesus before the world began. Here then, my Christian friends, you may trace up the streams of your happiness to the fountain, and see them all flowing from the great abyss of God's eternal, sovereign, distinguishing love. And his design, in thus loving and saving you, was, as the apostle informs us in the verse succeeding our text, that in the ages to come, he might show the exceeding riches of his grace in his kindness toward us through Christ Jesus. Not for your sakes, then may he say, do I this, be it known to you, but for my great name's sake, that it may be glorified thereby. Not unto us, then may we in turn reply, not unto us, but unto thy great name alone, O Lord, be all the glory and all the praise.

Application.—1. My Christian friends, has God done all this for you? Has he loved you with an everlasting love? Has he quickened you, when you were dead in trespasses and sins; has he raised you up together and made you sit together in heavenly places in Christ Jesus? Has he done all this for children of wrath, done it for you of mere grace or mercy, without any desert of such favors on your part? Need any thing, then, be said to convince you, that you ought to love him, to praise him, to live to him and him only? If it is a sin not to be grateful for life, is it not a much greater sin to feel no gratitude for the gift of spiritual and eternal life? If sinners ought to love him, who created them, because he is the former of their bodies, and the father of their spirits, ought not you much more to love him for creating you anew in Christ Jesus unto good works? What sum would induce you to be again thrown back into the awful situation from which his grace has raised you? What would tempt you to consent to be again dead in trespasses and sins, under the power of Satan, and children of wrath, and in a state of awful uncertainty, whether you ever awake? For what would you sell the gifts, which you hope a benevolent God has given you? Would you exchange them for all the worlds he ever created? If not, you ought to be as grateful, as if he had actually given you all these worlds; for, in fact, he has given you more. O then, bless the Lord and forget not all his benefits. Let the love of Christ constrain us. Let me urge and entreat you, by the tender mercies of God, by all that he has done for you, by all that you hope for, to present your bodies and your souls a living sacrifice holy and acceptable unto God, which is your reasonable service.

2. Has God done all this for you? then he will do more. Has he loved you from eternity? then he will love you to eternity. Has he raised you from spiritual death? then he will never suffer you to fall under the power of death a second time. Has he given you spiritual life? then he will give it more abundantly. Has he made you sit together in heavenly places in Christ Jesus? Then, as surely as Christ ascended to heaven after his resurrection, so surely shall you ascend to heaven, and sit down together with him there forever and ever. This is evident from the design, which God had in view in raising you from spiritual death. He did it, as our text informs us, that in the ages to come, he might display the exceeding riches of his grace in his kindness toward us in Christ Jesus. But should he cease to carry on the work he has begun, the riches of his grace could not be displayed; all the glory of his grace would be obscured, and all that he has done for you, would be worse than thrown away. For his name's sake, for his glory's sake therefore, he will continue to carry on the work he has begun in you, and render it perfect in the day of Christ Jesus. Be not then discouraged by the difficulties and obstacles you meet with; work out your salvation with fear and trembling, knowing that God worketh in you to will and to do. He will give more grace. He will perfect that which concerneth you; he will not forsake the work of his own hands. Plead with him, then, what he has done, as a reason why he should do more. Cry to him, with the Psalmist, thou hast delivered my soul from death; wilt thou not deliver my feet from falling, and my eyes from tears?

To conclude. We have already observed, my impenitent hearers, that what Christians once were, you are still. You are dead in trespasses and sins; you are walking according to the course of this world, according to the prince of the power of the air, and are, of course, children of wrath. Whether God will ever raise you from this state, is altogether uncertain. He has no where promised that he will. You are altogether unworthy of such a favor. You are condemned already, and he may justly leave you to perish. If you ask what you shall do; God's answer is, Awake thou that sleepest, and arise from the dead, and Christ shall give thee light. If you reply, We cannot do this,—I can only say, I have no commission to notice such an excuse; my business is to bring you God's messages. This I have done in his own words. Consider how you will treat them.

SERMON XVII.

UNIVERSAL LAW OF FORGIVENESS.

If thy brother trespass against thee, rebuke him; and if he repent, forgive him. And if he trespass against thee seven times in a day, and seven times in a day turn again to thee, saying, I repent; thou shalt forgive him. LUKE XVII. 3, 4.

ON hearing this passage read, you will probably conclude, that the duty of forgiving those who injure us, is to be the subject of discussion. That is, indeed, an important subject, and a subject, to the consideration of which our text would naturally lead us. I do not, however, at present propose to discuss it. I wish to make a somewhat different use of this passage. I wish to set before you the proof, which it indirectly exhibits, of our Savior's readiness to forgive, again and again, those who trespass against him. It may, I conceive, be very satisfactorily shown, that he regulates his own conduct by the rule, which he here gives to us, that he is quite as ready to forgive, as he requires us to be, and that however frequently we may have trespassed against him, he will, if we repent of our trespasses, forgive us. And it is highly important, that his people should entertain a deep, heartfelt conviction of this truth; for many of the evils under which they groan, result from the want of such a conviction, or from their not having just and adequate views of the boundless extent of his pardoning mercy They believe that it is great, but are far from seeing how great it really is. They believe that he can forgive them once, twice, thrice, and they find that he does so. But when, after being often forgiven, they are betrayed into new offences, they not unfrequently begin to think that he must be weary of forgiving them, and that it will be little better than an insult to ask him to forgive them again. Hence they dare not implore his forgiveness, dare not approach him with confidence, but remain at a distance, unpardoned, oppressed with conscious guilt, and a prey to gloomy, desponding, apprehensions. They have no courage to attempt the performance of difficult duties, no strength to resist temptations; their comfort is gone, their religious progress is interrupted. Thus a sin, which, had it been immediately repented of and confessed, would have been pardoned, becomes the occasion of many sins, and perhaps of a long course of declension. Now all these evils would be prevented by adequate views of our Savior's readiness to forgive. Of course, it is highly important, that all his people should possess such views. I shall therefore, endeavor to show, that if we trespass against Christ seven times, or any number of times, in a day, and as often turn unto him in the exercise of unfeigned repentance, he will freely forgive us, and restore us to favor. But before we proceed to establish this truth, it will be necessary to make some remarks with a view to illustrate its import, and prevent dangerous mistakes. And,

1. It must be carefully kept in mind, that the rule, which our Savior here gives us, relates not to what men would call crimes, not to those gross public offences, which transgress the laws and disturb the peace of society; nor even to gross injuries, but to trespasses only. We cannot suppose him to mean, that if a man should attempt seven times in a day to murder, or rob us, or to steal our property, and when detected, should say, I repent,—we must forgive him, and suffer him to go at large unpunished. It would be perfectly evident in such a case, that the offender did not repent, and that his professed repentance was all a pretence. The word, trespass, seems to mean offences of a different kind, and of a more private nature; such offences as a man may be led into repeatedly by misapprehension, or sudden passion, or an unhappy temper. These causes may, it is evident, lead men to offend, and to offend often, those whom they really love. They may lead a relative, a friend, a christian brother, or one, on whom we have conferred favors, to speak reproachfully, to treat us unkindly, to withhold such acts

and expressions of kindness, as we had a right to expect, and in various other ways to wound our feelings. Now offences of this nature, are what our Savior means by trespasses, and such trespasses, however often they may be repeated, we are to forgive, if the offender expresses sorrow and asks forgiveness. It is to offences of a similar nature, committed against Christ by his disciples, that we refer in the present discourse. He, it will be recollected, sustains with respect to his people various offices and various relations. He is their master, their teacher, their shepherd, their guide, their advocate, their benefactor, their brother, their friend. He has therefore, a right to be regarded and treated as such. He has a right to expect their obedience, their confidence, their gratitude and love; in a word, their supreme affection and regard. He has also a right to expect, that they will follow him wherever he leads the way; that they will be contented and satisfied with all his dispensations, and that his honor and interest shall lie near their hearts. Whenever his people forget and overlook these rights, when they cease to regard and treat him as he deserves; when their love and gratitude grow cold; when their confidence in him declines, and they indulge doubts and suspicions respecting his faithfulness; when they murmur, repine, or become discontented with his allotments; when they feel little concern for his cause; in short, when they neglect to do what will please him, or indulge in any thing, which they know will grieve or offend him, then they are guilty of trespassing against Christ; for all offences of this nature are directly against him. They are not, strictly and literally speaking, direct violations of the moral law; nor are they committed directly against God the Father, though he is, of course, offended whenever he sees his Son treated unworthily; but they are, in the strictest sense, trespasses against Christ, considered as sustaining all those offices and relations, which were mentioned above. They are trespasses against one, who has condescended to become our brother, benefactor and friend; and he might justly be provoked by them to withdraw and hide himself from the offenders, and to suspend all further bestowal of his favor, all his kind interpositions on their behalf. Now these trespasses against Christ include *all* the sins, into which his people are most liable to fall, and *almost* the *only* sins, into which they are liable to fall *fre-*

quently; for Christians will not sin wilfully, nor will any Christian be frequently guilty of gross and open offences. But any Christian may trespass against Christ, we cannot say how frequently, in some of the ways, which have just been mentioned. He may daily, and many times in a day, grieve his Savior, by the want of right feelings towards him, or by the exercise of those which are wrong. Many times in a day he may forget him, or think of him without gratitude, confidence and love; at all times his affection for his Savior falls very far short of what he deserves. Now these are the trespasses which, however often repeated, Christ will always forgive, as soon as we turn to him in the exercise of repentance: and should we grieve and offend him by such trespasses seven times, or seventy times seven in a day, and continue thus to multiply our trespasses for years, still, every new exercise of repentance on our part, would be followed by a new act of forgiveness on his. But let no bold presumptuous offender infer from this truth, that Christ will, in like manner, forgive known, wilful, deliberate sins. Let no one suppose, that he may be daily or frequently guilty of fraud, or intoxication, or profaneness, or of any wilful transgression, and yet escape punishment by saying at night, I repent. It is most evident, that such a man does not repent, that he is not a disciple of Christ, that he has no part nor lot in the matter. This leads me to remark,

2. That in the rule which our Savior here gives, he requires us to forgive an offending brother on his professing repentance, or on his exhibiting external evidence that he repents. As we cannot search the heart, this external evidence is all which we can justly require or expect; and where this evidence is given, we must charitably hope that the repentance is sincere. But our Savior, it must be recollected, can search the heart. He therefore cannot, and ought not, to be satisfied with any professions or external evidences of repentance, or with any thing indeed but repentance itself. In this respect therefore, the rule before us, considered as adopted by our Savior for the regulation of his conduct, must be slightly varied. We must forgive, when offenders seem to repent. He will forgive, when they really do repent. We remark,

3. That the word, forgiveness, may be used in two senses somewhat different. It may be used to signify either an official

act, or the act of a private individual. Considered as an official act, forgiveness is the remission of deserved punishment, or of that punishment, to which transgressors are legally doomed. In this sense, forgiveness can be granted only by one, who has authority to do it. It cannot be granted by a private individual. No private individual, for instance, can forgive or pardon a murderer. No such individual has any right to say, that a murderer shall not be punished. But forgiveness, considered as the act of a private individual, is something different. It consists in laying aside all feelings of revenge, and ill will, and displeasure, towards the offender, and in restoring him to the same place in our favor and friendship, which he held previous to his trespass. Now it is more especially, though not exclusively, in the latter sense, that we use the word forgiveness in the present discourse. What we mean to assert is, that Jesus Christ, not in his judicial character, but in his private capacity as an individual, will forgive every penitent, however frequently he may have trespassed against him. In other words, he will entertain no feelings of displeasure towards the penitent offender, will regard him with no coldness, but will restore him to his favor, and receive him with as much affection as if he had never offended him. Not only so, but he will continue to act as his Savior and Advocate, and intercede for him, that he may be forgiven by his Father. This view of the subject will be found to meet exactly the case and the wants of one, who feels conscious that he needs forgiveness, but who is ashamed or afraid to ask it. Ask such a man the cause of his guilty fears and apprehensions, and he will reply, I have sinned against God, I have transgressed his law, and am justly condemned to die. Remind him, that God is ready to forgive every sinner, for whom Christ intercedes, and that Christ is equally ready to intercede for all who trust in him, and he will reply, I am ashamed to ask Christ to intercede for me; I have trespassed against him so often, have so often been forgiven, and abused his kindness afresh, and my whole treatment of him has been such a series of distrust, ingratitude, and want of affection, that it seems as if it must be impossible for him to pardon me again, and as if I ought not to ask it. But let such a man be convinced that his much injured Savior has adopted his own rule with respect to forgiveness, and that he will receive with unabated kindness every penitent, however numerous his trespasses may be, or however frequently he may have been previously forgiven; I say, let him be convinced of these truths, and his difficulties will vanish; he will again repent, and again be forgiven. And when he has thus obtained his injured Savior's forgiveness, he will through his intercession obtain forgiveness of God.

Having thus shown what is meant by the assertion, that our Savior regulates his conduct towards his offending people by the rule, which he has given us in the text, and that he is therefore as ready to forgive, as he requires them to be,—we proceed,

II. To show what reason we have for believing this assertion. We have reason to believe it,

1. Because the relations, which Jesus Christ has taken upon himself, require that he should regulate his conduct by this rule. By assuming our nature, he has become, in the sense of the text, our brother. Agreeably, we are informed, that he is not ashamed to call us brethren. He taught the same truth, when he said to his disciples, I ascend unto my Father and to your Father; for they who have the same father are brethren. He is also said to be the first-born among many brethren. Now if Jesus Christ has condescended to take upon himself the relation of a brother to his people, we may be assured, that he will faithfully perform all the duties of that relation. He has thus in effect bound himself to do it. And since he has taught us, that one duty of a brother is to forgive the trespasses of a penitent brother, however numerous they may be, or however frequently he may repent, we may be sure, that if we are penitent, he will forgive our trespasses, though they should be as numberless as the sands of the sea, and though they may have been repeated after frequent pardons.

Again. By assuming our nature, Jesus Christ is become a man. Of course, he has brought himself under obligations to obey all the laws and precepts, which God has given to man. Agreeably we are informed, that being made of a woman, he was made under the law; that is, was made subject to its authority, and placed under obligations to obey it. That it was incumbent on him to obey all other divine precepts, as well as those of the moral law, appears from the reply which he made u John the Baptist previous to his baptism. John had said to him on this occasion, I have need to be baptized of thee, and comest thou to me? Jesus answered, Suffer it to be so now, for thus it becometh us to fulfil all righteousness. As if he had said, It is incumbent on me to obey every divine precept, and observe every divine institution, and since baptism is a divine institution, I must be baptized. Now if it was incumbent on Jesus Christ, considered as a man, to obey every divine precept, it was of course incumbent on him to obey those precepts, which require us to forgive the trespasses of a penitent brother. And if it was incumbent on him to regulate his conduct by these precepts, we may be perfectly sure, that he has done it, and will do it, since he invariably does what is right.

Once more. When Christ came into this world, as the Savior of lost men, he undertook to be their teacher and guide. As such, it was evidently proper that he should teach them, not only by precept, but by example. Accordingly we are told, that he has left us an example, and that we should walk in his steps. But if he has set us an example, it must be in every respect perfect. It must be a perfect example of forgiveness, as well as of other duties. And that it may be so, it is necessary, that he should exhibit the same readiness to forgive, and to repeat forgiveness, which he requires of us. If he requires us to forgive a penitent brother, though he should trespass against us seven times, or even seventy times seven, he will forgive as frequently those, who trespass against him; for it is impossible to suppose, that in this, or in any other respect, he will suffer himself to be excelled by any of his disciples.

2. We have reason to believe that our Savior has adopted the rule before us, for the regulation of his conduct, because he has, in fact, always acted in conformity with this rule. However frequently any of his disciples may have trespassed against him, they have invariably found him more ready to forgive, than they were to repent. As it respects yourselves, those of you who are his disciples know, that this has been the case. You know, that after you have spent years in grieving and offending him and wearying his patience in ten thousand ways, after you have been a thousand times forgiven, and have then trespassed again; after you had treated him with such unkindness, ingratitude and neglect, as no human friend or relation

could have borne, he has still been just as ready to forgive you, when penitent, as if you had never offended him before. And those of you, who have been his disciples for many years, know that he has forgiven you more than seventy thousand times seven trespasses. You have therefore ample reason to believe, and all his disciples have similar reasons for believing, that he regulates his conduct, in this respect, by the rule under consideration.

In passing to a practical improvement of what has been said, permit me to remark, that I am well aware of the manner, in which those who are disposed to convert the bread of life into poison, may abuse this subject. I am aware, that from the Savior's readiness to forgive those who trespass against him, they may draw encouragement to repeat their trespasses. Such men there were in the days of the apostles; men, who turned the grace of God into wantonness, and continued in sin, because grace abounded. But the apostles did not therefore conceal the grace of God, neither should we. We are not to conceal truths, which will be beneficial to Christ's real disciples, because his enemies may abuse them. And none but his enemies will abuse the truth which has now been exhibited. To all his real friends it will, if believed, prove most salutary. Nothing tends more powerfully to melt their hearts, to make them ashamed of their sins, to bring them to deep repentance, and to increase their confidence in the Savior, than just views of his readiness to forgive, and to renew his forgiveness, as often as they renew their trespasses. Such views I have now endeavored, my christian friends, to give you.

In improving what has been said, allow me to place before you the Savior as he appears in the light of this subject. See him adorned with every possible excellence and perfection, uttering the kindest invitations, and bestowing freely the richest blessings; blessings, which cost him labors, privations, and sufferings, the greatness of which we can never estimate. See him, in return for these blessings, treated with the most cruel unkindness, ingratitude and neglect; wounded in the house of his friends by those, who have eaten at his table, and trespased against, on every side, by multitudes in ten thousand ways. See him still forgiving all these trespasses, repeating his forgiveness a thousand and ten thousand times, maintaining, as it were, a contest with his people, which shall exceed, they in trespassing, or he in pardoning. See him invariably gaining the victory in this strange contest, and constraining each of his disciples in turn to exclaim, O who is equal, or like to thee, in forgiving iniquity, transgression and sin! Christian, can you contemplate the spectacle without emotion? Does it excite no shame or sorrow in your bosom? Does it not cause your heart to glow with admiration, and gratitude, and love to your Savior, and with indignation against yourself? And does it not, at the same time, inspire you with confidence to come and seek forgiveness afresh? You expect soon to approach your Master's table. And you will surely wish to meet with a kind reception. You surely will not wish to come borne down with guilty fears, and harassed by jealousies, doubts and suspicions. Believe what you have now heard, and your wishes will be gratified. Believe what you have heard, and you will repent, you will be forgiven, there will be peace between you and your Savior, and you will approach his table with confidence. Let no one say, I have already been forgiven so often, that I dare not, cannot ask forgiveness again. Let no one offend his Savior by suspecting that he is less ready to forgive than he requires us to be. It is a false humility, or rather it is concealed pride and unbelief, which prevents us from asking forgiveness and leads us to say, I am too unworthy to be forgiven. O then, my brethren, indulge not these feelings, but rather turn at once to Christ, receive his forgiveness, and love much, because much is forgiven. And while you receive your pardon, remember what it cost him to procure it. Remember, that it is wet with his own blood, and let it be wet with your tears, tears of deep contrition and repentance.

2. If Christ is so ready to forgive every penitent offender, then nothing can prevent any offender from obtaining forgiveness, but his own refusal to repent. And O, how great will be the guilt, how terrible, and yet how just, the punishment of every one who fails to obtain forgiveness. The guilt of such a man will be in exact proportion to the greatness of the mercy, against which he has sinned. But there can be no mercy greater than that which Christ displays. Consequently, there can be no guilt greater than that of those, who sin against this mercy. My impenitent hearers, cease, O cease, I beseech you, to incur this aggravated guilt. If you repent, you will find the

Savior no less ready to forgive you, than he is to forgive his penitent disciples. His language to you is, though you may have not only trespassed, but sinned wilfully against me a thousand and ten thousand times ; though you may have spent many years in neglecting and offending me, yet I am still ready to forgive you; I wish to forgive you, but I must not, I cannot forgive any, who refuse to repent. My hearers, how is it possible that any man can retain a good opinion of himself, or refrain from despising himself, while conscious that he is insensible to such goodness; that he is not affected by the invitations of a Savior so ready to forgive; that he is refusing to accept of forgiveness and salvation on terms so reasonable, so easy? How is it possible, that he should not say to himself, surely I must be devoid of all sensibility; I must be a stranger to every ingenuous feeling; I must be incapable of gratitude; I must have a heart of stone, or I could not hear, without emotion, of goodness so unbounded, or refuse to seek forgiveness, when it is offered on terms like these. My hearers, will any of you, can any of you, persist in refusing to comply with these terms! Will you leave this house unpardoned, when the Savior is present and ready to forgive, in a moment, every one who will return to him, saying from the heart, Lord, I repent. It should seem impossible, that any one can choose to go away unpardoned, rather than comply with these terms; and yet it is but too probable, that many will do it. What is still worse, it is but too probable, that some will take encouragement from the Savior's mercy to delay repentance, and repeat their trespasses with hopes of impunity. But if any are tempted to do this, let them recollect, that our Savior cannot regulate his conduct by the rule before us, at his second coming. At his first appearing, he came, not as a judge, but as a Savior; and it was proper that, in this character, he should display unbounded readiness to forgive. But at his second appearing, he will come, not as a Savior, but as a judge; and in that character, he will be constrained to proceed according to the strict rules of justice. Those therefore, who now refuse mercy, will then have judgment without mercy. O, then, seek the Lord, while he may be found; call ye upon him, while he is near. Kiss the Son, lest he be angry, and ye perish from the way, and sink to that world, where the sound of pardon will never break in upon the wailings of despair.

SERMON XVIII.

FRAUD EXPOSED AND CONDEMNED

It is naught, it is naught, saith the buyer; but when he is gone his way, then he boasteth. — PROVERBS. XX. 14.

It is impossible to peruse the scriptures attentively, without finding in almost every page, the most convincing proofs, that since the fall human nature has ever been the same; that the men of former ages strikingly resembled, in character and conduct, the present inhabitants of the world. How exactly, for instance, does the remark of the wise man in our text correspond with what is still daily witnessed in the commercial intercourse between man and man. He is here describing the means which were in his day employed by a dishonest buyer to procure the articles which he wished to purchase, for less than their real worth. He represents him as with this view, exaggerating their defects, and pretending that they are worthless. It is naught, it is naught, saith the buyer; the article you would sell me is of an inferior quality; the price you put upon it is too high; even if it is worth so much to others, it is not worth so much to me, as I have no particular use for it, and do not care to purchase it. But when he has gone his way, when he has by these means obtained an article for less than its value, then he boasteth; boasts of his skill and success in making a bargain; or at least secretly exults in it, if he dares not speak of it openly; and perhaps despises the man, of whom he has thus gained an advantage.

My hearers, I need not inform you, that the man who would be really religious, must be influenced by religion in every part of his conduct; and on all occasions, during the week, as well as on the Sabbath; in his intercourse with man, as well as in his approaches to God. Nor need I remind you, that no man can be a disciple of Christ, who does not yield to the authority of Christ; whose heart, and hand, and tongue, are not governed by the laws of Christ. Now, if you consider a moment, how many of this congregation are constantly employed in pecuniary transactions; how frequently almost every man is called to engage in them; how large a portion of your time they occupy; how many opportunities you have of doing wrong, and how constantly, how powerfully, you are tempted by your own self-love, the selfishness of others, and the example of the world, to deviate from the path of rectitude, you will feel convinced, that to conduct your worldly business in a perfectly fair and upright manner, in such a manner as God prescribes, is a most important and difficult part of true religion; and that it is indispensably necessary to turn your attention frequently and seriously to this subject. It is a conviction of this truth, which has induced me to address you on the passage before us. And I wish it to be distinctly understood, that I am preaching not to one, nor to a few, but to all. It is nothing, which I have seen, nothing which I have heard respecting the conduct of individuals, that has induced me to address you on this subject; but it is a conviction, that it is a most important subject, a subject in which all are interested, and which is intimately connected with the honor of religion, with your own salvation.

In discoursing upon this subject, I shall not confine my remarks to the particular case mentioned in the text, the case of a buyer, but shall extend them to pecuniary transactions of every kind; whether they are carried on between buyers and sellers, or masters and servants, or employers and those whom they employ. It will not, however, be expected, that I should discuss every difficult question which may be asked, or give particular directions respecting every perplexing case which may occur; since to do this in a single discourse would be impossible. I shall therefore, pursue the method which God has adopted in his word. He there gives us general rules, which may be applied to every particular case that can occur; rules sufficient for the direction of every one, who sincerely wishes to know and perform his duty. I shall, in the first place, mention some of these general rules which God has given us for this purpose; and then show more particularly, what these rules require, and when we are guilty of violating, or neglecting them.

The *first* general rule which I shall mention, is that which requires us to love our neighbor as ourselves. This rule is indeed applicable, not only to all our pecuniary transactions, but to all our intercourse with our fellow creatures; so that a man who should observe it, would need no other rule to direct him on all occasions. As our whole duty, with respect to God, is virtually included in loving him with all our hearts, so our whole duty with respect to men, may be summed up in loving them as we love ourselves. Agreeably, the apostle observes, that love worketh no ill to our neighbor, therefore love is the fulfilling of the law; for the commands, thou shalt not kill, thou shalt not steal, thou shalt not bear false witness, thou shalt not covet, are all contained in this one word, thou shalt love thy neighbor as thyself. Nearly of same import, and equally applicable to every case which can occur, is our Savior's rule, whatsoever ye would that men should do to you, do ye even so to them. This rule is the more deserving of our attention, because it is one of the sayings, which Christ had just uttered, when he said, whosoever heareth these sayings of mine and doeth them not, is like a foolish man, who built his house upon the sand: and the rain descended, and the floods came, and the winds blew, and beat upon that house, and it fell; and great was the fall of it.

Another general rule, connected with this subject, is that which forbids us to covet any part of our neighbor's possessions. The command is express and comprehensive. Thou shalt not covet any thing that is thy neighbor's. To covet, literally signifies, to desire. This command does not, however, forbid us to desire the property of another on fair and equitable terms. It does not forbid us to desire what our neighbor wishes to part with, provided we are willing to give him a suitable equivalent in return. But it forbids every desire to increase our property at our neighbor's expense. It forbids us to wish, that any thing should be taken from his possessions and added to our own. Of course, it forbids the employment of any means to increase our property by diminishing the property of our neighbor.

Again. We are frequently and expressly commanded strictly to observe in all our transactions, the rules of justice, truth, and sincerity; to deal justly; to defraud no one, to deceive no one, to speak every man truth to his neighbor. God's language is, Ye shall not deal falsely or deceitfully. Just balances, just weights, and just measures, shall ye have. If ye sell aught to your neighbor, or buy aught at your neighbor's hand, ye shall not injure one another. Ye shall not oppress the hireling in his wages. Give to your servants that which is just and equal. Render to all their dues; tribute to whom tribute is due; custom to whom custom. To sum up all in a word, we are informed that this is the will of God, that no man should overreach or defraud another in any matter; for, said the apostle, the Lord is the avenger of all such. This leads me to observe,

Lastly. That we are directed, in all our transactions, to remember, that the eye of God is upon us, and that he is a witness between us and our fellow creatures, when no other witness is present. Such are the principal rules, which God has given us for the regulation of our conduct in all our pecuniary transactions; rules, which are amply sufficient for our direction, in every case which can possibly occur.

II. Let us now proceed, as was proposed, to apply these rules more particularly, and show what they require, what they forbid, and when they are violated. And,

1. Let us consider what these rules require of us as subjects, or members of civil society. And here we may observe, that they evidently require us strictly to observe the laws of our country with respect to the public revenue, to contribute that proportion of our property to the general and state governments, which those laws require; and to use no artifices or evasions, with a view to avoid paying that proportion. Our Savior, when asked by the Jews whether it were right to pay tribute to Cæsar, the Roman Emperor, replied, Render to Cæsar the things that are Cæsar's. Now if he required them to pay tribute to a foreign power, by whom they had been conquered, so long as they remained the subjects of that power, much more would he enjoin it upon us to pay tribute to a government of our own forming, to rulers of our own choosing. Agreeably we are expressly commanded to pay tribute and custom to those, to whom tribute and custom are due; to submit to every ordinance of

man for the Lord's sake. The justice, and propriety of these commands, is obvious. There is an implied contract, or agreement between a government and its subjects, by which the subjects engage to give a portion of their property in exchange for the blessings of protection, security, and social order. So long as they enjoy these blessings, they receive a valuable consideration for the sums which they contribute, or in other words, for the taxes which they pay for the support of government. It is also evident, that the man who possesses a large share of wealth, derives greater advantages from the laws of the land, and from the protection afforded by civil authority, than the man who possesses little or nothing. Or, to place the subject in a little different light,—civil governments insure to their subjects the protection of their rights and property from injustice and violence; of course, they have a right to demand a premium for this insurance. This premium ought to be greater or less, in proportion to the property thus insured; in other words, every man is bound in justice to contribute to the support of law and government, in proportion to his property. This is as just a debt as any other which can be named. The man who by artifice or deceit avoids contributing in proportion to his property, is guilty of injustice and dishonesty. He not only defrauds the government, but does in effect defraud his fellow citizens; for if he contributes less than his proportion, others must contribute more to make up the deficiency. These remarks apply with equal force to those who introduce foreign goods into the country, without paying those duties which the laws require. This practice is contrary to the plain, express commands of God; it is contrary to the rules of justice and honesty; it involves deceit and artifice, and it is well if perjury be not added to the list, if the name of God and the solemnities of an oath are not impiously employed to conceal the fraud.

I am constrained to add, that it is little less criminal knowingly to purchase from the wharf, any merchandise, thus illegally introduced; for we thus become partakers in other men's sins, and we tempt them to repeat those sins, since it is evident that none would import merchandise in this unlawful manner, if none could be found to purchase it. It is vain to plead, as an excuse for these things, that government may waste, or misemploy the sums, which are put into their hands. We might as well refuse to pay a just debt, on pretence that our creditor would make an improper use of the money if it were paid. Equally vain is every other excuse, which can be assigned. No man, who means to do to others, as he wishes that others should do to him; no man, who means to obey God; no man, who is influenced by the fear of God, or who feels that the eye of God is upon him, can be guilty of the practices here mentioned. Permit me, before I dismiss this part of my subject, to express a hope, that no one will endeavor to give these remarks a political bearing, or suspect that they are aimed particularly at any individual. They are made merely with a view to discharge an important official duty. It is my duty, as a minister of Christ, to warn you, to guard you against every thing which God forbids, against every thing which may endanger your immortal interests. Hence, though fully aware that this is a delicate subject, I did not dare to waive it.

In the second place, let us consider the application of the rules above mentioned to the common pecuniary transactions of life. It is evident, that with respect to these transactions, they forbid every wish, much more, every attempt to defraud, or deceive our neighbor. They render it highly criminal for the seller to take the smallest advantage of the ignorance, inexperience, or simplicity of his customers; or to conceal any defect, which he may have discovered in the articles, of which he wishes to dispose. They render it equally criminal for the buyer to wish, or attempt to take any advantage of the seller, either by exaggerating the defects of his merchandise, or by falsely pretending that he does not wish to purchase. They render it highly criminal for any one to contract debts, when he has no sufficient reason to believe that he shall be able to discharge them; nor to persuade another to become responsible for his debts, when he has reason to suspect that his sponsor will in consequence suffer loss. In a word, they require us to put ourselves in the place of our neighbor, to be as unwilling to defraud him, as to be defrauded ourselves; to be as careful of his property and interest, as of our own; to think no more of enriching ourselves at his expense, than we should think of robbing our left hand with our right. They require us in all our transactions, to conduct as we should do, if our fellow creatures could see our hearts; for though they cannot see them, yet God can, and does see them; he is both witness and judge between us and our neighbor in every transaction, and surely his eye ought to be as effectual in regulating our conduct, as would the eye of our fellow creatures, could they, like him, search the heart. With every man, who is governed by the rule above mentioned, this will be the case. In his most secret transactions, he will conduct as if all his views, feelings, and conduct, were to be laid before the public eye. Indeed, he will be more afraid of injuring his neighbor, than of being injured himself; for in the latter case, he only suffers wrong, but in the former case he would do wrong, and he dreads sin more than suffering.

We might now proceed to show what these rules require of us, with respect to those who are employed in our service; but after the remarks which have been already made, this is perhaps needless. I would only observe, that these rules evidently forbid us to take any advantage of the necessities, or imprudence of those whom we employ, and require us to give them a prompt and adequate compensation for their services, and that on the other hand, they make it the duty of all who are employed, to be as faithful to the interests of their employers as to their own, and to avoid defrauding them of any portion of their time, by idleness, or of their property by negligence, as they would avoid theft or robbery.

Having thus shown what the rules of God's word require of us, with respect to our pecuniary transactions, let us, in the next place, apply these rules to our past conduct, that we may ascertain how far we have observed, and in what instances we have disregarded them. With this view, permit me to ask each of you, whether in conducting the business of life, you have been invariably governed by these rules? Have you, in every instance, dealt with others, as you wish that others should deal with you? Have you always acted as under the eye of God, acted as you would have done, had your hearts been laid open to your neighbor's view? Have you never practised any deception, artifice, or evasion, in buying or selling, never taken any advantage of the ignorance, the inexperience or the necessities of others? Have you always contributed to the support of government that proportion of your property, which the laws required? Have your servants, or those whom you employed, never had any reason to complain of you? Have those of you who have been employed by others, always been strictly faithful to the interests of your employers? Is there no pecuniary transaction of your lives, which you would feel unwilling to have publicly known with all its circumstances; no one, which men would condemn were it known to them? In a word, are you prepared to go to the bar of the all-seeing and heart-searching God, and there be tried by the rules mentioned above? My friends, to that bar you must shortly go, and by these rules you must be tried. To this test every transaction of your lives must be brought; for God will bring every secret thing into judgment. And my friends, if your own hearts condemn you, much more will God condemn you; for he is greater than our hearts, and knoweth all things. He will judge without partiality, favor, or affection. He will make none of those allowances and excuses for us, which self-love leads us to make for ourselves; nor will he allow the validity of any excuse which we can offer. Then, we are told, every one who hath done wrong, shall receive punishment for the wrong done, without any respect of person.

Indeed, we are taught that God takes special cognizance of those wrongs, which are done by artifice, fraud and deceit, and which human laws cannot prevent or discover. We are told, that the Lord is the avenger of all who are overreached, or defrauded in any matter, and that he will plead their cause and spoil those who oppress them. And he forbids us to take revenge of those, who have injured us, for this very reason, that he will himself execute vengeance. Recompense to no man evil for evil; for vengeance is mine, I will repay, saith the Lord. This vengeance he often begins to execute in the present life, by depriving the guilty of that property, which they have iniquitously obtained. This he often threatens to do in his word, this he often actually does in his providences. This being the case, it surely becomes every one, who is conscious of having violated the rules of God, in his pecuniary transactions, to inquire seriously what he must do. This inquiry the scriptures will readily answer. They inform such a man, that his first step must be, to repent, to repent unfeignedly before God, for repentance must always precede forgiveness. No sin can be pardoned until it is repented of. The blood of Christ can wash out no stain of guilt, on which the tear of penitence has not fallen.

In the next place, he must bring forth fruits meet for repentance. In other words, he must make restitution to every one whom he has injured, or defrauded, so far as he can recollect who they are — this is indispensable. There is no repentance, and of course no forgiveness, without it. How can a man repent of iniquity, who still retains the wages of iniquity? It is impossible. If he feels any sorrow, it is occasioned, not by hatred of his sin, but by fear of the consequences. Restitution then must be made, or the offender must perish. If thou bring thy gift to the altar, says our Savior, and there rememberest that thy brother hath aught against thee, that is, any reason to complain of thee, go thy way, first be reconciled to thy brother, and then come and offer thy gift. The altar was then the place, to which the worshippers of God brought their thank-offerings, gifts, and sacrifices for sin. Christ, we are told, is now our altar, and to this altar we must bring our prayers, our praises, our services. But he plainly intimates, that he will accept no gift of us, receive no thanks from us, listen to none of our prayers, so long as we neglect to make satisfaction to those whom we have injured. And in vain shall we attempt to atone for neglecting this duty, by performing others, by contributing to the promotion of religious objects, or by liberality to the poor; for God has said, I hate robbery for burnt offering; that is, I hate, I will not receive an offering, which was unjustly acquired. There is then, no way but to make restitution, and this every real christian will make to the utmost of his ability. Agreeably, we hear Zaccheus, the publican, saying, as soon as he became a christian, if I have wronged any man, I will restore him four-fold. I am aware that this is a most disagreeable duty. Nothing can be harder, or more painful to our proud hearts. But it will be far easier to perform it, than to suffer the consequences of neglecting it. If it is not performed, our souls must perish, as sure as the word of God is true; and in consequence of indulging a false shame, we shall be overwhelmed with shame and everlasting contempt. Even as it respects our interest in this world only, we had better, far better, put a blazing fire-brand into the midst of our possessions, than retain among them the smallest particle of gain, which was not fairly obtained; for it will bring the curse of God upon us and upon all the works of our hands.

And now, my hearers, I have discharged a most disagreeable, but as I view it, a most necessary part of ministerial duty. I have led your attention to a subject which it is exceedingly difficult to discuss in the pulpit, and which, for that reason, is seldom brought to view. I have shown you, in what manner God requires you to regulate your pecuniary transactions. I have shown you what is the duty of those, who have disregarded these requirements. And now I request you not to apply these remarks to others, but to take them home to yourselves. It is well for him who can say with truth, I have always obeyed in this respect the rules of God's word. Such an one, if he can be found, may cast the first stone at his offending neighbor.

To conclude. While we apply these rules to our past conduct, let us not forget that they must regulate our future transactions, if we mean to be the real subjects of Christ. They are, my professing friends, the laws of his kingdom, the laws which you have covenanted to obey. And I dare pledge ourselves to the world in your name, that no breach of these laws shall be tolerated in this church, and that no one, who can be proved to be guilty of disregarding them, shall remain a member of it.

SERMON XIX.

THE MARK OF DELIVERANCE.

And the Lord said unto him, go through the midst of the city, and set a mark upon the foreheads of the men that sigh and cry for all the abominations, that be done in the midst thereof. And to the others he said in my hearing, go ye after him through the city, and smite; let not your eye spare, neither have ye pity; slay utterly old and young; but come not near any man upon whom is the mark.—EZEKIEL ix. 4, 5, 6.

IN the preceding chapter we have an account of a discovery, made by Jehovah to the prophet Ezekiel, of the many idolatrous, impious and iniquitous practices, which secretly prevailed among the Jews. Being brought in vision to Jerusalem, the prophet was successively conducted to different places in the city, and introduced into the most secret recesses of its inhabitants, that he might see the hidden wickedness, of which they were guilty, and be convinced, by his own observation, that they were ripe for ruin. After giving him this view of the sins of his people, God proceeded to threaten them with the most tremendous judgments, and appealed to the prophet, whether these judgments were not richly deserved. Hast thou seen all this, says he, O son of man? Is it a light thing that the house of Judah commit the abominations that are committed here? for they say the Lord seeth not; the Lord hath forsaken the earth; therefore will I also deal in fury: mine eye shall not spare, neither will I have pity, and though they cry with a loud voice, I will not hear. The fulfilment of these threatenings was immediately witnessed by the prophet in vision, but in their execution mercy was mingled with justice. He cried in mine ears, says the prophet, Cause them that have charge over the city to draw near. And behold six men came from the way of the higher gate, every man with a slaughter weapon in his hand; and one man among them was clothed with linen, with a writer's inkhorn by his side. And the Lord said unto him, Go through the midst of the city, and set a mark upon the foreheads of the men that sigh and cry for all the abominations, that are done in the midst thereof. And to the others he said, Go ye after him through the city and smite. Let not your eye spare, neither have pity. Slay utterly young and old, but come not near any man, upon whom is the mark.

My hearers, St. Paul informs us, that all the calamities which were experienced by the Jews, happened unto them for ensamples to others, and that they were written for our admonition, upon whom the ends of the world are come. It therefore becomes us to study their history with the greatest attention, and to compare their character and conduct with our own; that we may derive from it that instruction, which it is intended to afford; and especially that we may learn what we have reason to expect at the hands of God. In this point of view, perhaps no part of their history is more interesting or instructive, than that of which a representation is given in our text. We there see, that when God commissioned the messengers of vengeance, who had charge over Jerusalem, to exterminate its guilty inhabitants, he took care to set a mark of deliverance upon all who sighed and cried for the abominations that were perpetrated among them; and since God's rules of government and methods of proceeding with mankind are in all ages essentially the same, we may, from this particular instance, fairly deduce the following general proposition;—When God visits the world, or any part of it, with his desolating judgments, he usually sets a mark of deliverance on such as are suitably affected with the sins of their fellow creatures. To illustrate and establish this proposition, is my present design; and with this view I shall endeavor to show what is implied in being suitably affected with the sins of our fellow creatures; and that on such as are thus affected, God will set a mark of deliverance, when others are destroyed by his righteous judgments.

I. What is implied in being suitably affected with the sins of our fellow creatures?

That we are naturally disposed to be little or not at all affected with the sins of others, unless they tend, either directly or indirectly, to injure ourselves, it is almost needless to remark. If our fellow creatures infringe none of our real or supposed rights, and abstain from such gross vices as evidently disturb the peace of society, we usually feel little concern respecting their sins against God; but can see them following the broad road to destruction with great coolness and indifference, and without making any exertion, or feeling much desire to turn their feet into a safer path. Our nearest neighbor may be an atheist, a deist, a profane swearer, a Sabbath breaker, a neglecter of God and religion, an intemperate man, or any other character equally remote from that of a christian, without exciting in our breasts any concern for the dishonor which he casts upon God, any uneasiness respecting his awfully dangerous situation, or any anxiety to convince him of the error of his ways. Nay more, we are naturally but too much disposed to contemplate the sins of our fellow creatures with pleasure, either because the contrast between their vices and our own virtues gratifies our pride, or because their wicked practices seem to justify ours, and encourage us to hope for impunity in sin. In short, the language of our feelings and of our actions naturally is, what have I to do with my neighbor's conduct or belief? or what is it to me how he lives? Let him, if he pleases, disobey and dishonor God, and ruin his own soul, provided he will not injure me. It is no concern of mine: he must look to himself; am I my brother's keeper? Nor is it at all surprising that this should be our language, for we naturally think as little of our own souls, or of our own sins, as of those of our neighbors; and it can scarcely be expected, that he who takes no care to save himself, should feel much concern for the salvation of others. This being the case, it is evident that a very great and radical change must take place in our views and feelings, before we can be suitably affected with the sins of our fellow creatures, if the conduct of the persons mentioned in our text is the standard of what is suitable. They are represented as sighing, and even crying, on account of the abominations which were practised by their fellow citizens; expressions, which plainly intimate that they were not only affected, but very deeply affected with a consideration of the vices which prevailed around them. Though they lived in an evil day, a day of peculiar calamity and distress, when the judgments of God were falling heavily upon their nation; yet they not only found time to mourn for the prevailing sins of the age, but they appear to have felt more poignant grief for those sins, than for the desolating judgments which they occasioned. They sighed and cried, not so much because their rulers were incorrigibly wicked and infatuated, their country laid waste, their capital destroyed, and many of their fellow citizens carried into captivity, as because of the abominations which were committed by the remnant that had escaped.

An imitation of their example in this respect, is the *first* proof we shall mention of being rightly affected with the sins of others; for we may be affected, and even deeply affected, with the sins of our fellow creatures, as well as with our own, without being rightly affected. We may mourn for them merely on account of the punishments which they bring upon ourselves, or upon the community of which we are members. But if we fear sin more than the punishment of sin; if we mourn rather for the iniquities, than for the calamities which we witness; if we are more grieved to see God dishonored, his Son neglected, and immortal souls ruined, than we are to see our commerce interrupted, our fellow citizens divided, and our country invaded, it is one proof that we resemble the characters mentioned in our text. In the sight of God however, no feelings or affections are genuine, but such as produce corresponding practical effects. He will not consider our grief for the prevalence of any evil as sincere, unless it excites habitual and earnest endeavors for its suppression. We therefore observe,

2. That being suitably affected with the sins of our fellow creatures, implies the diligent exertion, by every means in our power, to reform them. It is, perhaps, in this respect, that we are most liable to fail. There are many, who will readily allow that vice and infidelity prevail among us, in a most alarming manner; that the Sabbath is most shamefully dishonored; that God's name is impiously profaned in our streets; that multitudes of our fellow creatures are evidently in the way to eternal ruin; and that in consequence of our national sins, we have every

reason to expect national judgments still heavier than those which we have already experienced. That it should be so, they will also confess is a very melancholy thing, and for a moment they will, perhaps, appear to be deeply affected by it; but still they use no means and make no exertions to counteract, or repress the evils, which they profess to lament. But as it is not sufficient to confess and lament our own sins, without renouncing them, so neither is it sufficient to mourn for the sins of others, without attempting their reformation. This attempt must be made,

First, by our example. That men are imitative beings; that the force of example is almost inconceivably great, and that there is, perhaps, no man so poor or insignificant, as not to have some friend or dependant who may be influenced by his example, are truths so obvious, that it is scarcely necessary to mention them. This being the case, every person is most sacredly bound, in times of prevailing degeneracy, to act an open, firm, and decided part in favor of virtue and religion; and resolutely endeavor, by his example to discountenance vice and impiety in every shape. In an especial manner should he avoid the very appearance of those evils, which are most prevalent around him, and practise with double care and diligence those virtues, which are most generally neglected and despised. In vain will he pretend to mourn over the sins of the times, who by his example encourages, or at least, does not discountenance them.

In the second place, if we would prove the justice of our claim to the character described in our text, we must attempt to suppress vice and impiety by our exertions. We must endeavor ourselves, and exert all our influence to induce others to banish from among us intemperance, profanity, violations of the Sabbath, neglect of religious institutions, and other prevailing sins of the age and country in which we live. Thanks to the kind providence of him, by whom kings reign and princes decree justice, we enjoy peculiar advantages for attempting this arduous, but glorious work with success. In our highly favored land, the interests of virtue and religion are fenced around by wholesome laws; and in consequence of the nature of our government, the care of seeing that these laws are faithfully executed, is in a greater or less degree, committed to almost every individual among us. But it becomes us to remember, that where much is given, much will be required. It has been justly remarked, that when God confers on us the power to do good or repress evil, he lays us under an obligation to exert that power. Agreeably the apostle informs us, that to him who knoweth to do good, and doeth it not, to him it is sin. Hence it follows, that we are accountable for all the good which we might but have not done; and for all the evil which we might but have not prevented. By conniving at the sins of others therefore, we make them our own. If the name of God be profaned, if his holy day be dishonored, if a fellow creature by intemperance render his family wretched, spread a snare in the path of his children, destroy his health, and finally plunge himself into eternal ruin, when we by proper exertions might have prevented it, a righteous God will not hold us guiltless, nor will rivers of tears, shed in secret over these sins, wash out the guilt thus contracted. If thou forbear to deliver them that are drawn unto death, and those that are ready to be slain; if thou sayest, behold we knew it not, doth not he that pondereth the heart consider it? and he that keepeth thy soul, doth he not know it? and shall he not render to every man according to his works? If then we would avoid his displeasure; if we wish him to set upon us a mark of deliverance, we must exert all the power and influence with which we are entrusted, to repress the outbreakings of irreligion and vice. Those who will, if permitted, trample alike on divine and human laws, and thus show that they neither fear God nor regard man, must be taught by their apprehensions, if they can be taught by no other means, to hide their vicious propensities in their own breasts; or at least, not to suffer them to stalk abroad with unblushing front in open day. And I am aware, that to attempt this, is a most disagreeable and ungrateful task, a task which very few are willing to perform. Many will mourn over the prevalence of sin in their closets, who dare not, or at least will not exert themselves to oppose it in public. When God asks, Who will stand up for me against the evil doers? who will rise up for me against the workers of iniquity? too many are to be found, even among his professed friends, who instead of immediately answering to the call, and boldly appearing like the children of Levi on the Lord's side, pusillanimously shrink back from the honorable service, pretending that others may more properly engage in it than themselves. In fact, though we are willing to enjoy the consolations and rewards of religion, we are all too much afraid of its difficulties and duties; too unwilling to deny ourselves and take up the cross. We are sufficiently willing, that God should take care of our honor, interest, happiness; but when any thing is to be done or suffered for him, we are too prone to begin with one consent to make excuse. We are exceedingly jealous of our own rights and privileges, and ever ready to execute those laws, which secure our persons, our property and reputation. But we discover little jealousy for the honor of the Lord of Hosts; and too often suffer those laws, which are made to secure his name and his day from profanation, to be violated with impunity. But however natural or general such conduct may be, it is altogether inexcusable; nor can we be guilty of it without forfeiting all claims to the character mentioned in our text. In vain shall we pretend to love God; in vain shall we profess to be concerned for the happiness of man; in vain shall we express sorrow for the prevalence of vice and irreligion, if we will not expose ourselves to some inconveniences, submit to some sacrifices, and make some vigorous exertions to preserve God's name from profanation, his institutions from dishonor, and the souls of our fellow creatures from everlasting perdition. God will set no mark of deliverance upon us in the day of vengeance, unless we prove the sincerity of our attachment to his cause, of our hatred of sin, and of our grief for its prevalence by appearing openly and decidedly against it. On the contrary, he will, nay he has already set on such pusillanimous friends a mark of reprobation. Whosoever shall be ashamed of me and of my words, in this evil and adulterous generation, of him shall the Son of man be ashamed, when he shall come in the glory of his Father with the holy angels.

In the third place, to our exertions we must add our prayers. Exertion without prayer, and prayer without exertion, are alike presumptuous, and can be considered as only tempting God—and if we neglect either, we have no claim to be numbered among the characters described in our text. My hearers, permit me to request your particular attention to this remark. There is but too much reason to fear, that a regard to order, or some similar principle induces many to exert themselves for the suppression of vice, who prove by their total neglect of prayer for divine influence, that they are strangers to the first principles of the oracles of God.

Lastly. Those who are suitably affected with the sins of their fellow creatures, will certainly be much more deeply affected with their own. While they smart under the rod of national calamities, they will cordially acknowledge the justice of God, and feel that their own sins have assisted in forming the mighty mass of national guilt. While they contemplate him whom their sins have pierced, they will mourn and be in bitterness, as one that mourneth for an only son. While they feel constrained to repress the vices of others with a decided and vigorous hand, they will feel, that if they are not themselves guilty of the same vices, it is wholly owing to sovereign, unmerited grace: and the cordial conviction of this truth, will temper their firmness with meekness and tenderness, and lead them to pity the offender, while they abhor the offence. If this temper be wanting, all other proofs that we are suitably affected with the prevalence of vice, will avail nothing. It is this, which distinguishes the real mourner from the proud, censorious, self-righteous hypocrite, who condemns others that he may exalt himself, who censures the mote in his brother's eye, but knows nothing of the beam in his own; whose language to God is, I thank thee, that I am not like other men; and to his fellow creatures, stand by thyself, come not near me, for I am holier than thou. Such are, of all persons, most hateful to God, and the most unlike the characters mentioned in our text. In fact, it will ever be found, that he who is most affected by the sins of others, will mourn most sincerely and feelingly for his own; and that he who is most solicitous for his own salvation, will exhibit the greatest concern for the salvation of the souls of his fellow creatures.

Thus have we endeavored to show what is implied in being suitably affected with the vices, that prevail among us. Should any one feel disposed to question the truth of the observations, which have been made, it would be easy to confirm them, did time permit, by appealing to the history of Noah, of Lot, of Moses, of David, of Hezekiah, of Ezra, of Nehemiah, of the prophets, of the apostles, nay, of our blessed Lord himself; nor would it be difficult to prove, that there is scarcely a good man mentioned in the scriptures, who was not thus affected with the sins of the age, and country in which he lived. But it is necessary that we hasten to show, as was proposed,

II. That on such as are thus affected, God will set a mark of deliverance, when those around them are destroyed by his desolating judgments. The truth of this proposition may be inferred,

1. From the justice of God. It will be recollected, that national judgments are always the consequence of national sins. But in the guilt of these sins the characters we are describing do not share. On the contrary, they mourn for them, hate them, and oppose them by every means in their power. If their endeavors to promote national reformation are unsuccessful, the guilt does not lie at their door. Justice therefore, forbids that they should share in the punishment, which this guilt brings down. As they have separated themselves from others by their conduct, it requires that a mark of separation and deliverance should be set upon them by the hand of a righteous God. Hence the plea of Abraham with regard to Sodom, a plea of which God tacitly allowed the force. Far be it from thee to destroy the righteous with the wicked; and that the righteous should be as the wicked, that be far from thee: shall not the Judge of all the earth do right? It is true, that the characters of whom we are speaking, have like others, violated the law of God, and are by nature children of wrath, and exposed to its awful curse. But however guilty they may be as individuals in the sight of a heart-searching God, they are blameless, considered merely as members of a community, and it is in this light only that they are here considered. Justice itself therefore, requires that they should be spared, and there is no doubt that God often suspends the punishment merited by guilty nations, lest the righteous should be involved in their destruction. Witness the preservation of guilty Zoar for the sake of Lot, and the declaration of the destroying angel, I cannot do anything till thou be come thither.

The truth of the proposition we are considering, may be inferred,

2. From God's holiness. As a holy God he cannot but love holiness; he cannot but love his own image; he cannot but love those who love him. But the characters of whom we are speak-

ing, evince by their conduct, that they do love God. They bear his image. His name is written in their foreheads. Like the righteous God they love righteousness and hate and oppose iniquity. It is their love to God and their holy jealousy for the honor of his great name, which causes them to mourn when he is disobeyed and dishonored. His cause, his interest, his honor, they consider as their own. A holy God therefore, will, nay, he must display his approbation of holiness by placing upon them a mark of distinction. While he loves holiness, while he loves himself, he cannot but love them, and cause all things to work together for their good.

The truth of this assertion we infer,

3. From his faithfulness. God has said, Them that honor me I will honor. But none honor him more highly than those who appear openly and resolutely on his side, in opposition to sin. His truth, his faithfulness then requires, that he should honor them by placing upon them some mark of distinction. Besides, those who are affected with the sins of mankind in the manner described above, exhibit the most infallible proof, that they are the genuine disciples of Christ, and the real children of God. Like their heavenly Father and their divine Redeemer, they are grieved with the sins of rebellious man. They have complied with the command which says, Come ye out from among them, and be ye separate; and I will be a father unto you, and ye shall be my sons and daughters. But if they are children, then heirs; heirs of God, of all the exceeding great and precious promises, which are given us in Christ Jesus; promises, which the eternal purpose and solemn oath of God bind him to fulfil. He has provided for them chambers of protection. His name is a strong tower, into which they flee, and are safe; and to this place of refuge he invites them. Come, my people, enter into thy chambers, and hide thyself for a little moment, till the indignation be overpast.

Thus it appears, that the justice, the holiness, and the faithfulness of God, unitedly bind him to set a mark of deliverance on those who are suitably affected with the sins of their fellow creatures. But these are the perfections, which as sinners, we have the greatest reason to fear. If then they secure our safety, how safe must we be.

Lastly. That God actually does set a mark of deliverance

on such characters, is evident from various facts recorded in scripture. See, for instance, Noah, that preacher of righteousness, saved in the midst of a drowning world. See Lot, whose righteous soul was grieved and vexed with the wickedness of the Sodomites, snatched as a brand from the burning storm, which overthrew the cities of the plain. See Elijah, who was jealous for the honor of the Lord of Hosts, fed by ravens, when all his countrymen were suffering the miseries of drought and famine. See Jeremiah, Baruch, and Ebedmelech, escaping unhurt from the perils of fire and sword, when Jerusalem was taken by storm; and the disciples of our Lord, many years after, saved by his warnings from the Roman sword, while their countrymen were destroyed. And though the age of miracles has passed away, yet had we an inspired history of the world from the days of the apostles, we should doubtless find recorded many equally striking proofs of God's care of his people; for it is still true, to adopt the language of St. Peter, that the Lord knoweth how to deliver the godly and to reserve the unjust to the day of judgment to be punished. Will it be objected to this statement, that facts equally strong may be adduced on the other side; facts, which prove that God does not always thus deliver his people? We allow it. We allow that the real friends of God often drink deeply of the cup of affliction, which is put into the hands of sinful nations? But why is it so? It is because they first partake of their sins. It is because they do not bear a public testimony for God, and oppose as they ought the progress of vice and infidelity. They suffer themselves to be entangled by that fear of man, which bringeth a snare, and to be guided by the heaven-distrusting counsels and temporizing policy of that earthly, sensual wisdom, which is too often miscalled prudence. They conduct in such a manner as to leave it doubtful whether they are the real children of God; and therefore, he treats them in such a manner, as often causes them and others to doubt whether he is their Father. Were they always suitably affected with the sins which prevail around them, they would much less frequently share in the calamities which those sins occasion. But it will perhaps be said, that many of the most bold and faithful servants of God and opposers of vice, have suffered even unto blood striving against sin. We grant it, but still it is true, that the mark of God was upon them. It appeared in those divine consolations, which raised them far above suffering, and the fear of death, and enabled them to rejoice and glory in tribulation. Did not Stephen exhibit this mark, when his murderers saw his face, as it had been the face of an angel? Did not Paul and Silas display it, when at midnight their joy broke forth, in the hearing of their fellow prisoners, in rapturous ascriptions, and songs of praise? Did not some of the martyrs display it, when they exclaimed in the flames, We feel no more pain, than if reposing on a bed of roses? If we now seldom see this mark of God set upon his children, it is only because the fires of persecution are extinguished, and because such christians as Stephen, and Paul, and the martyrs, are no longer to be found in the church.

But however God may sometimes see fit to expose such as truly mourn for the prevalence of sin, to sufferings in this world, he will most certainly set a mark of deliverance upon them in the world to come. The Son of God, clothed in the linen garments of his priestly office, has sprinkled them with his blood, which, like the blood of the passover, is a signal for the destroying angel to pass them by. He has set upon them a mark, not with pen and ink, but by the Spirit of the living God, by whom they are sealed to the day of eternal redemption. Thus they bear the mark of the Lamb, and have their Father's name written in their foreheads, while their great Intercessor bears their names engraven in his book of life, and upon the palms of his hands; and neither life, nor death, nor angels, nor principalities, nor powers, nor things present, nor things to come, shall erase them.

Improvement. My hearers, the subject we have been considering, at all times interesting, is rendered peculiarly so to us by the circumstances in which we are placed. We live in a day, when the judgments of God are abroad in the earth, and the desolating flood, after laying waste many nations and kingdoms in its progress, has at length reached our shores, and where it will stop God only knows. We have however, but too much reason to expect the worst. The same sins which have ruined other nations, and which, wherever they exist, provoke the vengeance of offended heaven, evidently prevail among us in an alarming degree, and give us just occasion to fear, that since we resemble the old world in its vices, we shall share in its plagues. And even if God in mercy should avert merited ruin, it is certain that we must all appear at the judgment seat of Christ, to receive the things done in the body. It is therefore, infinitely important for us, both in a temporal and in a religious view, to ascertain whether we are in the number of those, upon whom God has set a mark of deliverance, that his destroying angel may not touch them. From our subject we may learn this. If we are in the number of those who sigh and cry for all the abominations that are committed among us, God has certainly set upon us a mark of deliverance and salvation; but if not, if we contemplate them with indifference, or while we profess to lament, make no exertions to repress them; we have reason to expect nothing but a mark of reprobation. Permit me then, my hearers, to ask, how are you affected with the sins which prevail amongst us? That there are many such sins, sins sufficient to excite and justify our most pungent grief, you need not be told. You cannot but be aware, that throughout our country, vice and impiety are awfully prevalent; that God's name is most daringly profaned; that his day is by multitudes dishonored and neglected; that his friends and institutions are ridiculed and despised; that the whirlpool of intemperance is engulfing its thousands and tens of thousands, and that the soul is almost universally neglected and undone. The cry of our sins, like that of Sodom and Nineveh, has long since ascended up before God. My hearers, how are you affected with these things? Are you more disposed to weep for our national sins, than for the miseries which we feel, and the dangers which we fear? Are you endeavoring, by your example, your exertions, and your prayers, to repress the progress of vice and impiety within your sphere of action; and do you appear openly on the Lord's side, as the bold, unwavering, determined friends of religion and morality? These are questions of infinite importance, but they are questions which conscience alone can answer. To every man's conscience then, we appeal, and ask, should God, preparatory to our destruction as a people, send a messenger into this house, to set a mark on all who are suitably affected with the prevailing sins of the age, on whose foreheads would the delivering mark appear? Would it, I address the question to every hearer, would it appear on thine? We are happy to have it in our power to remark, that a partial answer to these questions is afforded by the occasion which has called us together. The existence of the society which I now address, affords, at least presumptive evidence, that there are some present, who do not contemplate with indifference, the progress of vice and impiety; and its members exhibit, at least one of the characteristic features of the persons described in our text. We would hope that the other features necessary to complete the character, are not wanting; and that while they are unitedly endeavoring to check the progress of vice by their exertions, they are individually aiming to advance the same object by their example and their prayers. My brethren, if this hope be well founded, our subject affords you encouragement, ample as your most enlarged desires. It assures you, that he, who humbles himself to behold what is done in heaven, notices and approves the sorrow, with which you contemplate sin, either in yourselves or others, and the exertions which you are making to repress its progress. The mark of the eternal God is upon you. The destroying angel is forbidden to touch you; whatever may befal our country or the world, you are safe as omnipotence can render you. The new heaven and the new earth, wherein dwelleth righteousness, is your destined habitation, where those sins, which you now hate and oppose, shall no longer molest you, and where you shall reap the glorious rewards, which the Captain of our salvation has prepared for them that overcome. Nor is this all. The cause in which you are engaged is as honorable, and its success as certain, as the rewards of victory are glorious. It is the cause of truth, of religion, of God; the cause in which all holy beings are engaged; the cause in which the Son of God laid down his life. It will be finally victorious. Will it be descending too low, if I add, it is also the cause of our common country. It is on the exertions of the friends of morality and religion alone, that its deliverance from present calamities, and its future welfare depend. It is in the field of conflict between virtue and vice, between religion and impiety, that our enemies are to be repelled; that peace is to be conquered for us. One victory gained here, will do more for us than many on the ocean or the land; and the most encouraging circumstance attending our present situation, is, that a faithful few are to be found in different parts of our land, who are willing to fight the battles of the Lord, and come up to his help against the mighty.

Go on then, my brethren, and prosper; secure of the good wishes and co-operation of all the real friends of God, and of man, and of our country; nay more, secure of the blessing and assistance of him, who has promised, that when the enemy comes in as a flood, his Spirit shall lift up a standard against him. We will only add the address of the prophet to Asa and his people, while engaged in the work of national reformation with its happy effect. The Lord is with you, while ye be with him. Be strong therefore, and let not your hands be weak, for your work shall be rewarded. When Asa heard these words, he took courage, and put away all abominations out of the land. May God grant that you feel encouraged in a similar manner to repress, with a prudent and vigorous hand, every abomination which shall attempt to raise its baleful head among you.

And are there any present, who cannot cordially unite in this prayer; any, who contemplate the formation and the exertions of this society with an unfriendly eye; any, who instead of feeling disposed to sigh and cry on account of the prevalence of vice and irreligion, are disposed to consider it as a proof of weakness or superstition to be thus affected? If any such there are, permit me to ask, ought not the creatures, the subjects, the children of God to mourn, when their Creator, their Sovereign, their Father, is dishonored? Ought not the friends of our Redeemer to feel grieved, when he is neglected and crucified afresh? Ought not all, who love their country, to lament, when they see the same sins prevailing among us, which have already drawn down the vengeance of heaven on so many once flourishing kingdoms! * * * * * * * *

SERMON XX.

THE CHRISTIAN MANNER OF EXPRESSING GRATITUDE

The Lord give mercy unto the house of Onesiphorus; for he oft refreshed me, and was not ashamed of my chain. But when he was in Rome, he sought me out very diligently, and found me. The Lord grant unto him, that he may find mercy of the Lord in that day.—2 TIMOTHY I. 16, 17, 18.

THE enemies of Christianity, while stating its supposed defects, have asserted that it recognizes neither patriotism nor friendship as virtues; that it discountenances, or at least does not encourage, the exercise of gratitude to human benefactors; and that its spirit is unfriendly to many of the finer feelings and sensibilities of our nature. But these assertions prove only that those who make them are unacquainted with the religion, which they blindly assail. Nothing more is necessary to show that they are groundless, than a reference to the character of St. Paul. This distinguished apostle of Jesus Christ was, in a degree which has seldom, if ever, been equalled, imbued with the spirit, and controlled by the influence of that religion, which he at once inculcated and exemplified. Yet we find in his writings the most touching expressions, and in his life the most striking exhibitions, of love to his countrymen, friendship, gratitude, and indeed of every sentiment and feeling, which gives either nobleness or loveliness to human character. We readily admit however, or rather we assert it as an important truth, that his religion, though it extinguished none of these feelings, modified them all. It infused into them its own spirit, regulated their exercises and expressions by its own views, and thus stamped upon them a new and distinctive character. It baptized them, if I may be allowed the expression, with the Holy Ghost, in the name of Jesus Christ. Hence, the apostle expressed neither his patriotism, nor his friendship, nor his gratitude, precisely as he would have done, before his conversion to christianity.

These remarks, so far at least as they relate to gratitude, are llustrated and verified by the passage before us, in which he expresses his sense of obligation to a human benefactor. This benefactor was Onesiphorus, who appears to have been an Ephesian of wealth and distinction, and who had in various ways, and on different occasions, manifested a generous concern for the apostle's welfare. Especially had he manifested such a concern, when St. Paul, oppressed by powerful enemies, forsaken by those who ought to have assisted him, and struggling without success to regain his liberty, lay bound in fetters at Rome. While he was in this destitute and friendless condition, borne down by a power which it seemed impossible for him to resist, Onesiphorus generously espoused his cause, sought him out very diligently and found him, supplied his wants from his own stores, and was not ashamed to be known as the friend and patron of a poor despised prisoner in chains. This unexpected kindness from a stranger, a foreigner, on whom he had no natural claims,—kindness, too, displayed at a time when cool friends prudently kept at a distance, and many of his own countrymen were among his bitterest enemies, made a deep impression upon the grateful heart of St. Paul. The gratitude which he felt, it was natural that he should express; nor was there any thing in his religion, which forbade him to express it. But though his religion forbade neither the exercise nor the expression of gratitude, it taught him to express it in such a manner, as became a christian, an apostle, a servant of that Master, whose kingdom is not of this world. He did not therefore idolize his benefactor; he did not load him with flattering applauses: but from the fulness of his heart he poured out a prayer for him to that God, who alone could reward him, as the apostle wished him to be rewarded. In this prayer he asked for him and his family the same favor, which, as we learn from his life and writings, he supremely desired and sought for himself. This was an interest in God's pardoning mercy. The

Lord, he cries, give mercy unto his house. The Lord grant unto him, that he may find mercy of the Lord in that day.

It is more than possible, that to some persons this mode of expressing gratitude will appear frigid, unmeaning, and unsatisfactory. They will regard it as a very cheap and easy method of requiting a benefactor; and were the case their own, they would probably prefer a small pecuniary recompence, or an honorary reward, to all the prayers which even an apostle could offer on their behalf. It is certain however, that such persons estimate the value of objects very erroneously, and that their religious views and feelings differ very widely from those which were entertained by St. Paul. But so far as any man's religious views differ from those which he entertained, they must differ from truth; for the apostle, it will be recollected, was guided by inspiration; his religious views were imparted to him by the unerring Spirit of God; they must therefore, have been in perfect accordance with truth. It is surely then most important, that we should ascertain what they were, in order that we may make them our own. What they were respecting some most interesting subjects, we may learn from the passage before us. From this passage we may also learn, in what manner it becomes the disciples and ministers of Christ to express their gratitude to human benefactors. And no one, who shall adopt the religious views by which St. Paul was influenced, can fail to perceive that the method which he employed for this purpose, was most worthy of himself, and most wisely adapted to promote the best interests of the friend, to whom he felt himself indebted. What these views were let us now endeavor to ascertain.

In the petition which was offered by the apostle for his benefactor, mention is made of a day to which that petition has reference. The Lord grant unto him, that he may find mercy of the Lord in *that day*. The mode of expression here employed is in some respects peculiar, and worthy of remark. It is a mode of expression which men never adopt, except when they speak of some subject, of which their hearts are full. While it seems intended to designate a particular day, it furnishes no mark or description, by which the day referred to can be ascertained. The same expression is, however, frequently used in other parts of the inspired volume, and from the connection in which it is invariably found we may infer with certainty what day is intended by it. It is the great day, for which all other days were made, the last day of time and the first day of eternity, the day of general judgment and retribution, in which the mighty Maker, and Sovereign, and Judge of the universe, will summon all intelligent creatures before his tribunal, and subject them to a trial, on the result of which, their eternal destiny will depend. This day is elsewhere styled, the day of the Lord, the great day of his wrath, and the great day of God Almighty. It is the day of the Lord, says an apostle, in which the heavens being on fire shall be dissolved, and pass away with a great noise, and the elements shall melt with fervent heat, and the earth with all the works that are therein shall be burnt up. When that day shall arrive, the Lord himself will descend from heaven with a shout, with the voice of the archangel, and with the trump of God, and every eye shall see him coming in the clouds with power and great glory; and all that are in their graves shall hear his voice, and come forth; they that have done good to the resurrection of life, and they that have done evil, to the resurrection of damnation. Then shall be realized what St. John saw in vision. I saw, he says, a great white throne, and him who sat upon it, before whose face the heavens and the earth fled away, and there was found no place for them. And I saw the dead, small and great, stand before God, and the books were opened, and the dead were judged out of those things that were written in the books, according to their works. Such, my hearers, is the day here intended, and such are some of its attending circumstances and events. To the mind of St. Paul, who possessed that faith, which is the evidence of things not seen, this day, with all its infinitely glorious and tremendous realities, was in effect ever present and visible. His mental eye, aided by the light, and strengthened by the energies of inspiration, even then saw its dawn in the distant horizon. To that day his thoughts and affections were chained. With reference to that day he was constantly acting. To secure mercy for himself and for his fellow sinners in that day, was the great object for which he lived, and labored, and suffered, and for the sake of which he counted not even his life dear. No wonder then, that when he had occasion to mention such a day as this, a day which thus occupied and engrossed his whole soul, he should style it simply, that day, and take it for granted that every hearer would perceive at once, what day he intended. No wonder, that the transcendent brightness of such a day, should in his view, eclipse the light of other days, and that he should speak of it as if it were the only day which deserved the name. And no wonder, that with such a day in his eye, he did not pray that his benefactor might be recompensed by the enjoyment of wealth, and honor, and prosperity, in the present world. To his mind, engrossed as it was by far nobler objects, all these things, and indeed all which this world can afford, must have appeared worthless and empty indeed. And how could he ask for his friend a portion, with which he would not have satisfied himself; how could he ask for him a portion in this world only, when his inspired eye saw the flames, in which it is destined to be consumed, just ready to kindle around it, and wrap it in the blaze of a general conflagration! Might it not rather be expected, that he would ask for him a favor connected with the great day, which he saw approaching; a favor, the bestowal of which would secure his safety amidst all its perils, and his happiness forever? Such a favor he did ask. And that he should ask it, was a natural consequence of the religious views, which he entertained. He knew that his friend was an accountable creature, in a state of probation for eternity, that he, in common with the rest of mankind, must appear at the bar of God in the judgment day; and that the sentence, which he should then receive, would either raise him to the enjoyment of happiness inconceivable, or plunge him into wretchedness inexpressible. Knowing these things, how could he do otherwise than breathe out a fervent prayer, that his benefactor might be prepared to receive a favorable sentence, and find mercy of the Lord, his judge, at that day.

But what is the precise import of the petition, that he might then find mercy, and what did it imply? An answer to these questions will throw much additional light on the views which were entertained by the apostle, when he uttered the prayer before us. Mercy, as exercised by a judge, or a sovereign, is the opposite of justice. It is shown only, when the guilty are spared, or when they are treated more favorably than they deserved. Its brightest display is made, when a criminal, justly condemned to die, is pardoned. God, the universal Sovereign and Judge, shows mercy, when he pardons those who were justly doomed by his righteous law to the second death; that death, from which there is no resurrection. To pray that any one may find mercy of him at the judgment day, is to pray that he may then be pardoned, or saved from deserved punishment, and accepted and treated as if he were righteous. St. Paul, when he prayed that Onesiphorus might find mercy of his Judge at that day, must then have believed, that he would at that day need mercy or pardon. And if so, he must have believed, that in the sight of God, he was guilty; for by the guilty alone can pardoning mercy be needed. The innocent need nothing but justice. They may stand boldly and safely on the ground of their own merits. But the apostle well knew, that on this ground, not a single individual of the human race can stand before God in judgment. He knew, for he often declared, that all, without a single exception, have sinned, and come short of the glory of God; and that in his sight no man living can be justified by any performances or merits of his own. He knew, that however blameless or excellent any man's character may appear in the view of men, he has sinned against the statute book of heaven, against the Supreme Legislator's great law of love, that law which binds him to love the Lord his God with all his heart, and soul, and mind, and strength, and his neighbor as himself. He knew, that when tried by this law before an omniscient, heart-searching Judge, he must inevitably be found guilty, and receive a sentence of condemnation, and that mercy alone could then save him. Indeed these are among the fundamental truths of that gospel, which the apostle made it the great business of his life to proclaim. To these truths every fact and doctrine of that gospel bears testimony. Why was a Savior provided for all men, if all men are not sinners? Why did that Savior command his gospel to be preached to all men, if all men do not need salvation? Why is mercy offered to all men, why are all men exhorted to seek it, if all do not need mercy? And these truths, which had been revealed to him and engraven upon his heart by the Spirit of God, the apostle could neither disbelieve nor forget; nor could he suffer himself to be so far blinded by admiration, or friendship, or gratitude, as to except even his benefactor from their universal application. No; kind, and generous, and noble, as was the disposition which that benefactor had manifested, and disposed as the apostle must have been to view his character in the most favorable light, he knew it could not meet the demands of God's perfect law. He could not conceal from himself the unpleasant truth, that his friend was, like other men, a sinner, and that as such he would need mercy of the Lord at that day. And had Onesiphorus distinguished himself as a benefactor, not to himself only, but to his counted; had he sacrificed much, and hazarded every thing to secure her liberty, the apostle would still have entertained the same views respecting his character and situation in the sight of God. He entertained, and often expressed, the same views respecting himself. He knew, that notwithstanding the blamelessness of his external conduct, his zeal and fidelity in preaching the gospel, and all his unexampled sacrifices, labors and sufferings in the service of Christ, he should still need mercy at that day; that justice would condemn, and that mercy alone could save him. And were he now alive, were he a native of our country, and were he standing in the midst of us with all the feelings and partialities of his countrymen glowing in his bosom, he would believe, and would not hesitate to declare, that our own Washington, beloved, admired, and revered as he justly was, and is, will need the mercy of his Judge at that day.

Are there any present, whose feelings revolt at this assertion? Let them then select the most illustrious individual of our race; let that individual be, if they please, Washington himself; let them suppose him to approach, with a fearless air, the judgment seat of the Eternal, and say to him who sits upon it,—I demand to be exempted from every expression of thy displeasure, and to have everlasting life conferred on me as my due. I have earned it, I deserve it, justice awards it to me; give me but justice, and I ask no more. Reserve thy mercy for such as need it. Would you not strongly reprobate language like this? Then must you acknowledge, that no man can claim any thing on the ground of justice; that all, without exception, will need mercy at that day.

A distinguished modern philosopher, Adam Smith, well known by his celebrated treatise on the Wealth of Nations, has some remarks relative to this subject, which are so just and apposite, that you will readily excuse me for quoting them. "Man," says this writer, "when about to appear before a being of infinite perfection, can feel but little confidence in his own merit, or in the imperfect propriety of his own conduct. To such a being, he can scarce imagine, that his littleness and weakness should ever seem to be the proper object either of esteem or regard. But he can easily conceive how the numberless violations of duty of which he has been guilty, should render him the object of aversion and punishment; nor can he see any reason why the divine indignation should not be let loose without any restraint, upon so vile an insect as he is sensible that he himself must appear to be. If he would still hope for happiness he is conscious that he cannot *demand* it from the *justice*, but that he must entreat it from the *mercy* of God. Repentance, sorrow, humiliation, contrition at the thought of his past conduct, are, upon this account, the sentiments which become him, and seem to be the only means, which he has left, of appeasing that wrath which he has justly provoked. He even distrusts the efficacy of all these, and naturally fears, lest the wisdom of God should not, like the weakness of man, be prevailed upon to spare the crime, by the most importunate lamentations of the criminal. Some other intercession, some other sacrifice, some other atonement, he imagines, must be made for him, beyond what he himself is capable of making, before the purity of the divine justice can be reconciled to his manifold offences." Such, my hearers, is the language of a writer, whom no one, that is acquainted with his character, can suspect of superstition, or weakness, or of entertaining too favorable views of christianity.

But to return. It may perhaps be said, if the apostle's views were such as have now been described, if he believed that justice must pronounce a sentence of condemnation on all without exception, on what could he found a hope, that either himself, or his benefactor, or any other man, will find mercy of the Lord at that day? Indeed, how could he, while he entertained such views, ask mercy either for himself or for others, without being guilty of irreverent presumption? How could he, a sinful worm of the dust, dare request the inflexibly just and holy Sovereign of the universe, to pronounce from his judgment seat, a sentence more favorable than impartial justice required, or than it would seem to allow? And when he presented such a request, did he not appear to ask, in effect, that the Judge of all the earth would cease to do right; that he would deviate from the path of equity, sacrifice his justice, and sully his yet unspotted character, for the sake of sparing guilty creatures, whom law and justice condemned? These questions are perfectly reasonable and proper, and it would be impossible to answer them in such a manner as to justify the apostle, were not a satisfactory answer furnished by the gospel of Jesus Christ. That gospel reveals to us a glorious plan, devised by infinite wisdom, in which the apparently conflicting claims of justice and mercy are perfectly reconciled. It informs us that God was in Christ, reconciling the world unto himself, not imputing their trespasses unto them; that God so loved the world, as to give his only begotten Son, that whosoever believeth in him should not perish, but have everlasting life. It informs us, that in consequence of the atonement, which this Son of his love has made, he can be just, and yet justify, or show mercy to him, that believeth in Jesus. And it assures us, that to every one, who truly believes in him, abundant mercy shall be shown. On this ground alone the apostle rested all his own hopes of finding mercy at that day. On this ground alone did he found a hope, that his benefactor might then find mercy. On this ground alone, did he dare ask that mercy might be granted him. And his petition, that he might find mercy, involves a request, that he might be induced to become, if he were not already such, a sincere disciple of Jesus Christ, and be found among his faithful followers at that day; for well did the apostle know, that unless he were so he must inevitably perish without mercy. He knew, that as all the light and warmth which we receive from the sun, come to us through the medium of its beams, so all the mercy which God will ever dispense to men, must come to them through the medium of his Son Jesus Christ, who is the brightness, the effulgence, or shining forth of his glory. Take away the beams of the sun, and you cut us off from all the benefits which we derive from that luminary. Take away Jesus Christ the Savior, and you cut us off from all participation of God's mercy, and from all the benefits which that mercy bestows upon a guilty world. And the man, who shuts out Jesus Christ from his heart, shuts out the sunshine of God's mercy from himself, and, to use the language of an apostle, has neither part nor lot in the matter.

This leads us to remark farther, that though the apostle believed all men will need mercy of the Lord at that day, he did not believe that all will then find mercy. This is evidently and strongly implied in the petition, which we are considering. Would he have thought it necessary to pray that Onesiphorus might find mercy, had he believed that all will find mercy? Would he have asked for his friend, his benefactor, a favor which he believed will be conferred indiscriminately upon all? This would have been worse than idle. It would have been unworthy of himself, and a mockery of his friend. It would have been like praying that he might have a portion of the air, and the light, which are common to all. When he prayed that his benefactor might find mercy, he intimated that it was at least possible, that he might fail of finding it. And when he prayed that the Lord would grant unto him that he might find mercy, he evidently prayed for a favor, which he did not suppose would be granted to all. Indeed he knew, for he asserts, that all do not believe. And he knew that those who do not believe, shall not see life, but the wrath of God abideth on them.

My hearers, I have given you a brief sketch of the apostle's religious views, so far as they are expressed or implied in the passage under consideration. And now let me ask, could he, with such views, have expressed his gratitude in a manner more worthy of himself, or more indicative of a wise and affectionate concern for the welfare of his benefactor, than by offering for him this petition? Would not the favor which it requests, have been cheaply purchased by Onesiphorus at the expense of all his earthly possessions? And can any man whose religious views resemble those of St. Paul, express affection for his children, or concern for his friends, or gratitude to his benefactors, more clearly and consistently, than by beseeching God to grant unto them that they might find mercy of the Lord in the great day?

It would be improper to conclude this discourse without reminding you, that if Onesiphorus, notwithstanding all his generous disposition and beneficent actions, will need mercy of the Lord at that day, then each of you my hearers will certainly need it. Yes, mortal, accountable, sinful creature,

That awful day will surely come,
The appointed hour makes haste,
When thou must stand before thy Judge,
And pass the solemn test.

And O, how greatly wilt thou then need mercy, when, stripped of all thy possessions, of all thy friends, thou shalt stand a naked, trembling, helpless creature, before the tribunal of thy God! How wilt thou need mercy at that great and terrible day, in which, as inspiration declares, the sun shall be turned into darkness, and the moon into blood, and the stars shall fall from heaven; and the heaven shall depart as a scroll, and every mountain be moved out of its place; and the kings of the earth, and the great men, and the rich men, and the chief captains, and the mighty men, and the bond and the free, shall attempt to hide themselves in the dens and rocks of the mountains, and shall say unto the mountains and to the rocks, fall on us and hide us from the face of him that sitteth upon the throne, and from the wrath of the Lamb: for the great day of his wrath is come, and who shall be able to stand? He, he alone, who finds mercy. And he alone will find mercy then, who seeks it now, and who seeks it in the only way, in which it can ever be found—by believing in the Lord Jesus Christ. If you are not then found to have believed in him, you will find no mercy; and unless you find mercy, it were far better for you, that you had never been born. Do you ask, for what shall we need mercy? I answer, if for nothing else, yet for the neglect with which you have treated the Savior, to whom you are so deeply indebted. In former ages, God found reason to say to his creatures, A son honoreth his father, and a servant his master: if then I be a Father, where is mine honor? and if I be a Master, where is my fear? saith the Lord of Hosts. With at least equal force and propriety may our Savior now say, Men are grateful to their benefactors and deliverers; but if I am such, where are the proofs of that gratitude which they owe to me? I see triumphal arches raised, and costly preparations made, and loud acclamations poured forth, to welcome a human benefactor.* But where are the grateful returns which I had reason to expect from those, for whom I descended from heaven, and suffered and died? My hearers, contrast your obligations to the Savior with those which you owe the man who has recently visited us; compare the proofs of gratitude, which the latter has received,

* La Fayette — this sermon was preached on the occasion of his visit to Portland.

with those which have been shown to Jesus Christ, and then say, whether our Savior has not reason to complain; whether we have not reason to feel guilty and ashamed. Is it not, O is it not but too evident that our God and Redeemer hold at most, but the second place in our estimation, and that we honor the creature more than the Creator? If you think, that we have not rewarded our earthly benefactor more than he deserves—and that we have, I am not disposed to assert—you must surely allow, that we reward our heavenly Benefactor infinitely less than he deserves. There is not, probably, a habitation or a heart in our country, which would not be thrown open to welcome the former. But, O, how many hearts are shut against the latter, even when he comes and knocks for admission. Thousands, and tens of thousands flock to see the former; but how few, comparatively, wish for an acquaintance with the latter. To sit at table with the former, is regarded as an honor and a privilege, for which men are willing to pay dear; while the table of Jesus Christ, though spread with a banquet of God's own providing is comparatively forsaken.

My hearers, can these things be otherwise than highly displeasing to God? Can he see the son of his love treated with such neglect and ingratitude by creatures whom he died to save, and not be greatly offended? And will not such conduct appear even to us, to need pardoning mercy, when he whom we have thus requited, shall be seen coming in the clouds of heaven with power and great glory? Then our triumphal arches, our expensive preparations, and all our expressions of gratitude to a human benefactor, will rise up in judgment against us, to condemn us, if we shall be found to have neglected the infinitely great, and generous, and condescending Benefactor of our race. My hearers, in this respect we are all in a greater or less degree guilty, and have all cause for repentance. Who can say, with truth, in this respect I have made my heart clean? Who can impartially review the manner, in which he has requited his Savior, and then dare to say that he shall not need mercy?

My hearers, let me entreat you to seek that mercy now. Let me charge you, by all that is glorious and terrible, and awful in the solemnities of that day, to seek that mercy now; for he who neglects to seek it now, will not find it then. To him who rejects it now, it will not be offered then: for him who refuses to ask it now, even an apostle might then plead in vain. Let us then send many humble and urgent invitations to our Savior to bless us with a gracious visit. And should he deign to favor us with his presence, let every heart be ready to receive him; let every voice be prepared to greet him; and let old age, and manhood, and youth emulate each other in shouting him welcome, and bringing to him the tribute, which is due to our greatest and best Benefactor. * * * * *

SERMON XXI.

THE TIMELY PRESENCE AND SALUTATION OF JESUS.

And as they thus spake, Jesus himself stood in the midst of them, and saith unto them, peace be unto you. LUKE XXIV. 36.

WHEN we are studying the character of a person of whom we know little, but whom we have particular reasons for wishing to know thoroughly, every part of his past and present conduct becomes, in our view, highly interesting. We wish to be acquainted with his whole history, even with the incidents of his childhood and early youth, that from what he was then, we may infer what he probably is now. And yet, to infer what any one is, from what he has been in former years, may often lead to very erroneous conclusions, respecting his character; for man is a changeable being, and there are comparatively few persons, whose lives are all of a piece. The promising child, the amiable youth, does not always prove a valuable man; and, on the other hand, sometimes, though much less frequently, the man renounces the vices and follies of youth, and becomes, unexpectedly, an estimable character. To our Savior, however, these remarks are in no degree applicable. It is safe to infer what he is, from what he once was. If we can ascertain what he was at any former period, we shall ascertain what he is now; for inspiration assures us, that he is, yesterday, to-day, and forever, the same. And blessed be God, we may easily ascertain what he was during his residence in our world; for the inspired records of his life are before us, and they are sufficiently particular to give us a clear view of his sentiments, feelings and character. This fact renders these records particularly interesting to every one, who counts all things but loss, for the excellency of the knowledge of Christ Jesus, his Lord; who wishes to be thoroughly acquainted with the Savior, to whose care he commits his soul, and on whom he founds all his hopes. Of this Savior, and of the manner in which he treats his disciples, we may learn something from the passage before us. It describes the first manifestation, which he made of himself to his church, after his resurrection. He had indeed previously appeared to individuals among them; but not until this occasion was he seen by them all. Now he stood at once, unexpectedly, in the midst of them, and said, Peace be unto you.

In meditating on this passage, let us consider,

I. The character of the visit, which Christ here made to his church; and,

II. The time, when the visit was made.

With reference to the character of the visit we may remark, that the visits which Christ makes to his churches, are of two kinds. He sometimes comes in anger, to chastise them. In this manner he threatened to visit some of the Asiatic churches. To the church at Ephesus he says, I will come unto thee quickly, and remove thy candlestick out of its place, unless thou repent. And to the church of Sardis, If thou shalt not watch, I will come on thee as a thief, that is, suddenly, and unexpectedly; and thou shalt not know at what hour I will come upon thee. At other times, he visits his churches in a gracious manner, to comfort, animate, and bless them. The visit mentioned in our text was of this kind. He came, not in anger, but in love; came in his own beloved and appropriate characters of Savior, Friend and Brother. This is evident, in the first place, from the language in which he addressed them; Peace be with you. This was the customary form of friendly salutation among the Jews, and the use of it by a visiter, was equivalent to an assurance that he came as a friend. Indeed it probably conveyed far more meaning to their ears, than it does to ours; for the word peace as used by the Jews, was a term of very extensive signification. It was considered as including all blessings of every kind. Hence, when they said to any one, Peace be with you,—it was the same as saying, may every blessing be yours; or, may happiness attend you. And though the salutation was doubtless used by many, as our customary expressions of friendship and civility too often are, in an insincere and unmeaning manner, yet we may be sure, that in such a manner it would never be used by our Savior. And while this language, as used by him, meant all which it seemed to mean; it was, in his lips, something more than the expression of a wish, something more than even a prayer, that peace might be with them. He had just returned from the invisible world; that world, which men naturally regard with dread. In these circumstances, by saying, Peace be with you, he did in effect assure them, that there was peace between them and the invisible world; between them and the God, who governs that world. Nor was this all. He had it in his own power to give the peace which he wished them to enjoy; for all power, in heaven and on earth, was now committed to him. In these circumstances the salutation, Peace be with you, was equivalent to an authoritative declaration, that Peace should be with them. He had said to them, just before his crucifixion, Peace I leave with you; my peace I give unto you; and this dying bequest he now renewed and confirmed. We may remark further, that the three blessings, which the apostles usually asked for the churches, were grace, mercy, and peace. But the last of these blessings includes, or implies the two former; for to sinful creatures such as we are, there can be no peace, without grace to sanctify them, and mercy to pardon them. This our Savior well knew. Hence, when he said, Peace be unto you, he did in effect assure them of an interest in his grace and mercy. If farther proof that this was a gracious visit were wanting, we might find it in the context. We there learn, that at this visit, he enlightened the understandings of his disciples, increased their religious knowledge, banished their doubts, fears and anxieties, strengthened their faith, revived their fainting hopes, and filled them with wonder and joy. These surely were works of grace, and these, we may add, are precisely the works which he still performs when he makes any of his churches a gracious visit.

Let us now consider,

II. The time when this gracious visit was made.

1. We may remark, that it was made at a time when the

disciples were exceedingly unworthy of such a favor, and when they rather deserved to have been visited in anger. Since their last interview with their Master and Savior, which took place at his table, and in the garden of Gethsemane, they had treated him in a very unkind and ungrateful manner. Though repeatedly warned by him to watch and pray, lest they should enter into temptation, they had neglected the warning, they had yielded to temptation, they had proved unfaithful to their engagements, and in a most pusillanimous manner, had forsaken him, nay, fled from him in his greatest extremity. Nay more, one of them had, with oaths and imprecations, denied that he knew him. In addition to these sins, they had all been guilty of criminal and inexcusable unbelief. Though he had repeatedly forewarned them of his approaching crucifixion, referred them to predictions of it in the Old Testament, and at the same time assured them, that on the third day, he would rise again, yet they forgot his warnings, disbelieved his assurances, and were in consequence, plunged into the depths of despondency by his death. So obstinate was their incredulity, that they even refused to believe the testimony of those, to whom he has revealed himself on the morning of his resurrection. These were surely great sins; they must have been exceedingly painful and offensive to their Master; they rendered them most undeserving, not only of this gracious visit, but of ever being again numbered among his disciples. Yet instead of renouncing them, instead of treating them as they had treated him, he comes to visit them, and the first sentence which he utters is, Peace be unto you. O, if they had any feeling, how must this unmerited kindness from their injured Master have shamed them, and cut them to the heart! No reproaches or threatenings would have been one half so overwhelming, or so hard to hear. While contemplating his conduct, we may well exclaim with David, Is this the manner of men, O Lord? No; it is the manner of Christ alone.

2. This visit was made at a time, when the church was very imperfectly prepared for it, and when very few among them expected it, or had any hope of such a favor. It is true indeed, that a few individuals among them were in some good measure prepared for it. Peter had repented of his fall, and wept over it in bitterness of soul, and to him Christ had previously appeared.

as he had also to two others of the brethren, and to several of the female disciples. And some, who had not yet seen him, were so far convinced by their testimony, that their unbelief and despondency began to give way. But the great body of them appear to have been still incredulous, and by no means prepared for such a visit, or disposed to expect it. That they were so, is evident from the fact, that even after their Master had appeared among them, and spoken to them, they would scarcely believe the testimony of their own senses. He was obliged to expostulate with them, to show them his hands and his feet, bearing the scars of the cross, and to partake of food in their presence, before they would be convinced that it was indeed he himself. It is however possible, and perhaps not improbable, that this backwardness to believe, was occasioned in part, by a conviction of their own great unworthiness. They could not but recollect how they had forsaken him when he was in the hands of his enemies, though they had but just before promised never to forsake him. And this recollection, with the feelings of conscious guilt, which it must have occasioned, might perhaps lead them to suppose, that even if their injured master were risen from the dead, he would not so soon favor them with a gracious visit, but would rather consider and treat them as persons unworthy to be his disciples. If they really entertained these feelings of conscious unworthiness, they were in some measure prepared for their master's return to them; for he ever regards those who feel most unworthy of his favors, as best prepared to receive them. Indeed he confers them on none, except such as are sensible of their own unworthiness; for such persons only will receive them with thankful humility, and duly appreciate the goodness which leads him to bestow them.

3. The time when Christ made this gracious visit to his church was a time in which it was very much needed. The faith, and hope, and courage of its members were reduced to the lowest point of depression, and unless revived by his presence, must soon have expired. One member after another would have returned to his original occupation, and the church would have been scattered and become extinct. In these circumstances, it seemed indispensably necessary to the continued existence of the church, that something should be done, and done speedily, to revive it. And this gracious visit from Christ,

was precisely what it needed for its revival. The sight of their beloved Master, raised from the dead, standing among them, and addressing them in language which implied forgiveness, and expressed affection, revived their drooping spirits, banished their doubts and anxieties, rendered their faith stronger than it had ever been, and filled them with joy, and gratitude, and love. Nothing then could be more necessary or more seasonable, than this gracious visit.

4. This visit was made at a time when the church was employed in exerting the little life, which yet remained among them, and in using proper means to increase it. Though assembling at this time was dangerous, so that they did not dare to meet openly, yet they did assemble, and they assembled in the character of Christ's disciples. This proved the existence of a bond of union among them, which drew them together. This bond of union consisted in sympathy of feeling. They all felt the same affections, the same apprehensions and anxieties, and the same sorrows, and all their thoughts centered in one object. This object was their crucified Master. Though they had forsaken him in a moment of temptation, yet they could not utterly renounce him. They could not give up all the hopes which he had excited, nor cease to feel the affection with which they had regarded him. His dead body, his grave, had still more charms for them than any other object, and they found a melancholy pleasure in thinking of him, in recollecting his actions and discourses, and in speaking of these subjects to those who could sympathise with them. These feelings had prevented them from leaving Jerusalem and returning to Galilee, and the same feelings now drew them together. And while they were together, those few to whom their master had appeared, and whose faith had in consequence revived were endeavoring to revive the faith and animate the hopes of their fellow disciples. They were assuring them, that they had seen him, and spoken with him, that they had not been deceived; and were also calling their attention to the promises and predictions, which he had uttered respecting his resurrection. Thus those who had any faith in exercise, were doing all in their power to encourage those who had none; and those who had none, or who then seemed to have none, were listening to their brethren, half willing to be convinced, but still fluctuating between hope and fear.

And it was at the very moment, while they were thus employed, that their Master stood in the midst of them and said, Peace be unto you. Yes, when they who feared the Lord, thus spoke one to another, the Lord hearkened and heard it, and not only heard it, but appeared to bless them.

5. The gracious visit appears to have been made the very first time that the church met after Christ's resurrection. This circumstance is highly indicative of his affection for them, of his unwillingness to leave them mourning one moment longer than was necessary, and of his strong desire to be again in the midst of them. Since he had died for them, he loved them better, if possible, than before. They were endeared to him by the price which he had paid for them, by the agonies which they had cost him. Hence he longed to see them, to speak to them, to assure them of his forgiving, unchanging love, and turn their sorrow into joy. Should any father present, voluntarily encounter great hardships, sufferings, and dangers for the sake of saving his children from death or slavery, would he not earnestly wish, after their deliverance was effected and his own sufferings were ended, to see them again, that he might congratulate and rejoice with them; would they not now be dearer to him than ever; and would he not, when he met them, feel compensated for all that he had suffered? Similar, we may without presumption suppose, were the feelings of the man Christ Jesus, on this occasion.

We remark lastly, that this gracious visit was made on the Lord's day, or Christian Sabbath. And the next visit which he made to his church, was made on the next Lord's day. Thus early did he begin to put honor on the Christian Sabbath, and to intimate that it was designed to come in place of the seventh day, or Sabbath of the Jews. In a similar manner he has ever since continued to honor it. There has not, probably, a single Christian Sabbath passed, from that day to this, in which our Savior has not graciously manifested himself, if not to whole churches, yet to individual disciples. Nor will this day pass without similar honors. In the midst of some little band of his disciples, our Master will to-day stand invisible and say, Peace be unto you. My brethren, I doubt not that every real Christian present will unite in saying, Would to God, that we might be thus favored. Would to God, that when this church shall approach his table he would come into the midst of it, and say, Peace be unto you. For those of you who are Christ's real disciples, know experimentally, that though our Savior is no longer visibly present on earth, he still favors his church with his real presence, and manifests himself to them, as he does not to the world; and that where two or three only assemble in his name, there he is in the midst of them. You also know, that without using an audible voice he can effectually speak peace to a guilty conscience, and a trembling, doubting heart; and make fainting love revive, and faith and hope grow strong. But the great question is, Will he thus favor us? Have we any reason to hope that he will thus favor us, on the present occasion? It may be remarked, in reply to this question, that in several particulars the present situation of this church strikingly resembles that of the disciples, at the time when they were favored with this gracious manifestation of their Master's presence.

In the first place, we are, as they were, exceedingly unworthy of such a favor. This, I trust, you are all ready to acknowledge. There cannot surely be an individual present who will say, I am not unworthy of a gracious visit from Christ. To say nothing of our former sins, which were great, and numerous, and aggravated beyond all computation, have not the sins, which Christ has seen in us since our last approach to his table, been sufficient to render us forever unworthy of his presence? Have we not been unfaithful to our covenant engagements? have we not practically denied him? have we not, though often warned, neglected to watch and pray against temptation? have we not suffered worldly-mindednesss and unbelief to prevail in our hearts?

In the second place, are we not, like the disciples, far from being suitably prepared for such a visit? We are accustomed to suppose, and with truth, that thorough repentance, and deep humiliation for sin, are proper and necessary preparations for the gracious presence of Christ. But have we not reason to fear, that there is little of thorough repentance, or of deep humiliation among us? And does not unbelief prevail extensively? Do not many of you as little expect to see the Savior coming to revive his work among us, as the disciples expected to see him among them, when they assembled on that evening?

In the third place, it is certain that we greatly need such a favor. The disciples scarcely needed it more than we do. It seems as if nothing but our Master's returning presence can save us from the power of spiritual death. Unless he shall ere long thus favor us, the evils which now prevail will prevail more extensively and more fatally; iniquity will abound more and more; love will become more and more cold, and scandals and divisions will soon be seen. But on this point of resemblance we need not enlarge. No disciple of Christ among us need be told, how greatly we need his gracious presence. To these remarks it is scarcely worth while to add, that we are now assembled in the character of Christ's disciples, and on the day which he delights to honor. Thus far then, we may trace a manifest resemblance between our situation and that of the disciples. But we can, I fear, trace it no farther. I fear that we do not lament the loss of Christ's presence, and lay it seriously to heart, as they did. We are ready indeed to acknowledge, that it is an evil, and that it ought to be lamented. But do we suitably lament it? Do not many of us rather seek to console ourselves for his absence, by engaging more eagerly in worldly pursuits? And are those who have any life, using all the means in their power to revive and animate those who have none? In fine, is there among us any thing like that ardent, unappeasable desire for the presence of Christ; that preference of it to every other blessing, which we have reason to think the disciples felt? I fear not; and I cannot but suspect, that if he does not on this occasion favor us with his presence, it will be, not on account of our unworthiness, nor on account of our unpreparedness in other respects; but because he sees that we are not suitably desirous of his presence, and that we are not exciting ourselves and each other to seek for it. If we are really deficient in this respect, it is indeed a great obstacle to the coming of Christ among us; for seldom indeed does he visit any church, until he sees that his presence is earnestly desired and sought for, and that he shall meet with a joyful reception. My brethren, should he not favor us with his presence on this occasion, let us consider this evil as the cause of his absence, and set ourselves to remove it without delay. Let all, who have any religious feeling, use all the means in their power to excite similar feelings in the hearts of their brethren. Let all beware, how they forsake the assembling of themselves together, as the manner of some is. Remember that it was a private meeting of the church, at which our Savior thus appeared to them. Remember too, what Thomas lost by being absent from this one meeting. While all his fellow disciples were filled with faith, and hope, and love, and joy; he was left for a time under the power of unbelief and despondency.

But should our Master, notwithstanding our unworthiness, condescend to favor us at this time with his gracious presence; should he come and stand in the midst of us, and say, Peace be unto you; what shall we do? My brethren, we need not tell you what to do. Your own hearts will inform you. Every one, to whom the Savior shall manifest himself, will feel ready to cast himself at his feet, to admire, and wonder at, and thank him for his goodness; he will feel more than ever sensible of his own unworthiness of such a favor; he will repent in dust and ashes, and his future life, like that of the disciples, will evince his sincerity and be spent in self-denying, and persevering labors in his Master's service.

SERMON XXII.

A FESTIVAL KEPT TO THE LORD.

When ye have gathered in the fruit of the land, ye shall keep a feast unto the Lord. — LEVITICUS XXIII. 39.

IF we review attentively the religious ordinances which God has appointed, we can scarcely fail to perceive, that he has usually passed by all the inventions of men, and adopted institutions which were exclusively his own; institutions which human wisdom would never have devised, and which, in her view, are too often little better than foolishness. In this, as in many other cases, his ways have not been like our ways, nor his thoughts like our thoughts. These remarks we may see verified in the appointment of circumcision, of sacrifices, of baptism, and of the Lord's supper. In some few instances however, God has condescended to pursue a different course. He has selected some significant action, or ceremony, by which men had been previously accustomed to express strong emotion; and by commanding them to make use of it as an expression of religious feeling, has invested it with the dignity and sacredness of a religious ordinance. An instance of this kind may be found in the appointment of religious fasting. Fasting is a natural expression, because it is a natural effect, of extreme sorrow; for the emotion, when felt in a very high degree, takes away the appetite for food, and renders the reception of it not only disagreeable, but almost impracticable. Hence, God prescribed religious fasting as a proper expression of godly sorrow for sin; and were we affected by our sins as we ought to be, we should feel constrained to fast much more frequently, and should fast much more acceptably, than we do. Another instance of the same kind may be found in the institution of religious feasts, or, to use a more proper term, festivals. From the earliest ages, of which any records remain, mankind have been accustomed to commemorate joyful events, and to express the joy and gratitude which such events excited, by the observance of anniversary festivals. As the all wise God well knew how difficult it would be to wean men from the observance of such festivals, and as they were capable of being rendered subservient to his own gracious designs, he saw fit under the ancient dispensation to give them a religious character, by directing his people to observe them in commemoration of the favors, which they had received from his hand, and as an expression of their gratitude for those favors. Of these divinely appointed festivals, several are mentioned in the Levitical law, but our only concern at present is with that which is prescribed in our text; When ye have gathered in the fruit of the land, ye shall keep a feast unto the Lord.

We do not lead your attention to this command because we suppose it is still in force. It was a part not of the moral, but of the ceremonial law, which was designed to continue only till the coming of Christ, and it has long since been annulled, with the other precepts of that law, by the same authority which imposed it. There can scarcely be a doubt however, that it was this command which led the fathers of New England to establish the custom of annually observing, at the close of harvest, a day of thanksgiving and praise. But though they established this custom without any express command or warrant from God, the propriety of continuing it cannot well be questioned. To offer praise and thanksgiving to God, is a duty which we find frequently enjoined, not in the Old Testament only, but in the New. It is highly desirable that whole communities should sometimes unite in the performance of this duty, and no season seems so proper for this purpose, as that which succeeds the gathering in of the fruits of the earth, the gifts of our heavenly benefactor. In support of this custom we may remark farther, that besides the festivals which God had established, the Jews were accustomed to observe several festivals of human appointment, such as the feast of dedication, and the feast of Purim; and that our Savior while on earth, sanctioned this custom by uniting with them in the observance of these festivals. We cannot doubt therefore, that were he now residing among us he would unite with us in observing this day, though it is a festival of human appointment.

But whatever opinions any may entertain with respect to the propriety of observing this day, we presume all will agree, that if it be observed at all it ought to be observed in a proper manner; which we have reason to believe will be acceptable to God. If it is not observed in such a manner, the day will be much worse than lost. It will serve no other purpose than to increase our guilt, excite God's displeasure, and provoke him to express it by sending judgments upon us. He will regard it as he regarded the festivals of the Jews when they ceased to observe them in the manner which he had prescribed; and will in effect, say to us, as he did to them, Your appointed feasts my soul hateth; they are a trouble to me, I am weary to bear them. What then, we may and ought to inquire, what is it to observe this day in a right and acceptable manner? The best answer, which I can give to this question, is furnished by our text. It is to keep or observe it, *as a festival unto the Lord.* The necessity of thus observing it may be inferred from the answer which God gave his ancient people, when they inquired whether they should continue to fast on certain days which had long been set apart for that purpose. When ye fasted, says he, did ye fast at all unto me, even unto me? And when ye ate and drank, did ye not eat for yourselves, and drink for yourselves? As if he had said, Whether you have fasted, or feasted, ye have done it not unto me, but to please yourselves. Why then do you inquire of me whether you shall continue to observe days for these purposes? So long as you observe them for yourselves and not unto me, what is it to me, whether you do, or do not observe them? It is then most evident, that if we mean to observe this day in a manner which shall be acceptable to God, we must keep it as a festival unto him. But still the question returns, What is it to keep, or what is implied in keeping a festival unto God? To this question we may reply, in general terms, that to keep a festival unto God is to observe it with a view, not to please ourselves, but to please and honor him; to regard it as a day sacred to his special service; and to spend it in contemplating and praising his perfections, recollecting and thanking him for his favors, rejoicing before him in his existence, his character, his government, and his works, and thus giving him the glory which is due to his name. But the question before us demands on this occasion, a more particular and expanded answer; and such an answer we shall attempt to give it, not however altogether in a dry didactic form, nor by a long enumeration of particulars, but by exhibiting two views of the subject, from which we may learn every thing that it is necessary for us to know respecting it. We shall attempt,

I. To give you a view of the manner in which this festival should be observed by us, considered simply as God's intelligent creatures; and

II. Of the manner in which we should observe it, considered as sinful, guilty creatures, to whom his grace and mercy are offered through a Redeemer.

That the first of these proposed views, may be placed before you in the clearest and most interesting light, let me request you to suppose, that our first parents, instead of falling as they did, almost immediately, from their holy and happy state, had continued in it, until they were surrounded by a numerous family like themselves, and that in these circumstances they had set apart a day to be observed as a festival to their Creator and Benefactor. It is evident, that if we can conceive of the manner in which they would have observed such a day, we shall learn in what manner this day ought to be observed by us, considered simply as God's intelligent creatures; for as such our rule of duty is the same which was given to them; we are commanded, as they were, to love God with all our hearts, and as they were perfectly holy, they would render perfect obedience to this command, and spend the day in a perfectly holy manner, as we should aim to spend this, and indeed every other day. Let us then endeavor to conceive of it. Let us suppose the morning of their appointed festival to have just dawned, and before they wake from their peaceful slumbers let us draw near and take a position favorable for observing their conduct, and becoming acquainted with their views and feelings. No sooner do they wake to a returning consciousness of existence, than a recollection of the Author, Preserver, and Sustainer of that existence, and of their numberless obligations to his goodness, rushes upon, and fully possesses their minds. No sooner do their eyes open, than they are raised to heaven with a look expressive, in the highest degree, of every holy, affectionate emotion. Each one perceives, with clear intuitive certainty, that he is indebted to God for every thing—that God is his life, his happiness, his all. These views fill his heart with adoring gratitude; gratitude, not like ours, a comparatively cold and half selfish emotion, but a gratitude pure, fervent and operative, which carries out the whole soul in a rapturous burst of thankfulness, and renewed self dedication to God. At the same time, his various perfections, displayed in his works, are reflected to their view from every thing around them. Or, as the apostle expresses it, the invisible things of God, even his eternal power and godhead, are clearly seen by the things which he has made. The whole creation is to them like one vast mirror, which reflects the glory of God, as an unruffled lake reflects the image of the noon-day sun. Not more instantaneously, not more powerfully, nor with such a cheering, animating influence, does the light of the sun pour itself upon their opening eyes, as the light of God's glory, shining in all his works, pours itself upon the eye of their mind, illuminating and warming, with its vivid celestial beams, every recess of the soul, and filling that little interior world with unclouded day.

And while all the works of God thus reflect his glories to the eye, they seem to proclaim his praises to the ear of their mind. To them every object has a voice, and every voice, in language which they well understand, tells them something of the perfections of their Creator. The heavens declare to them his glory, and every leaf, and every flower whispers his praise. In fine, to them every place is full of God, every object speaks of God; every thing shines with the glory of God; and as a recollection of his favors awakened their gratitude, so a view of his glories excites their reverence, their admiration, their love, and joy, and gradually raises their affections to such a height, that it becomes impossible not to express them. Their eyes, their countenances, have indeed already expressed them, and rendered even their silence eloquent, for while they were musing the fire of devotion burned within. But they can be silent no longer, and in strains no less pure, and little less sweet and powerful, than those of the angelic choirs, they begin to pour forth the emotions of their swelling, almost bursting hearts, and with humble, but rapturous thanksgivings and praises, acknowledge the favors and celebrate the perfections of their adorable Creator. And while they thus address to him their thanks, and their praises, they feel that they are addressing not an absent, but a present God. Though invisible to their bodily eyes, he is not so to the eye of their minds; they perceive, they feel his presence; they feel that his all-pervading, all-enfolding Spirit pervades and embraces their souls, breathing into them love, and joy, and peace, unutterable, and wrapping them up, as it were, in himself. Thus each individual apart, commences the observance of their festal day, and enjoys intimate, and sweet, and ennobling communion with the Father of spirits in solitary devotion.

But man is a social being, and the social principle which God has implanted in his nature prompts him to wish for associates in his religious pleasures and pursuits. It is proper that he should wish for them, and if possible obtain them; for when a festival is to be kept unto the Lord, when thanksgiving and praise are to be offered, two are better than one. United flames rise higher towards heaven, impart more heat, and shine with brighter lustre, than while they remained separated. If private, solitary devotion be the melody of religion, united devotions constitute its harmony; and without harmony the music is not perfect and complete. What, comparatively, would the songs of heaven be, were they sung by a single voice, even though it were the voice of an archangel? Let us then now contemplate the scattered members of this holy and happy community assembling from their solitary walks, and places of retirement, to rejoice, and praise, and give thanks together, and thus unite the flames and the incense of individual devotion in the blaze of one grand, combined sacrifice. Mark the feelings with which they approach and meet. Every eye sparkles with delight; every countenance beams with affection; there is but one heart, and one soul among them all, and that heart, and that soul is filled with holy gratitude and love, tempered by adoring admiration, reverence, and awe. Fresh excitements to the increase of these emotions are furnished by their meeting. Each one sees in his rational, immortal fellow creatures, a nobler work of God, a brighter exhibition of his moral perfections, than the whole inanimate creation could afford. In each of them he sees that image of God, which consists in knowledge, and righteousness, and holiness; for in this image man was created, and we are supposing him not as yet to have lost it. And while each one contemplates this image of God in his fellow creatures, he is ready to exclaim, If these miniature images of God are so lovely, how infinitely worthy of love must the great original be? If there is so much to admire in the streams, what admiration does the fountain deserve? Nor is this all. In the various relations and ties, which bind them together, they see new proofs of all-wise benevolence, new reasons why they should love and thank him, who established these relations, and formed these ties. The husband and the wife meet with that perfect mutual affection which God enjoins, and a recollection of the happiness which has resulted from their union, leads them, with simultaneous emotion, to bless the Being who gave them to each other. Parents and children meet in the perfect exercise of holy, parental, and filial affection; and while the parents see in their children the gifts of God, and the children see in their parents those whom he appointed to be the protectors of their infancy, the instructors of their childhood, and the guide of their youth, they unite to bless him together. Thus, instead of idolizing children and friends, or putting them in the place of God, they love and enjoy God in them, and make use of them to excite their gratitude, and lead their affections to him. Under the influence of these affections, the yet stammering child is taught the name of its Creator and Benefactor; while to the attentive ear of those who are a little farther advanced in life, the history of the creation and of all that God has done for his creatures, is recounted; his commands, and their obligations to obey them, are stated; the nature and design of the festival, which they are observing, are explained; and they are taught to perform their humble part in its appropriate services. In these services all now join; and O, with what perfect union of heart! with what self annihilating humility,—with what seraphic purity and fervency of affection,—do they present their combined offering of thanksgiving and praise! Suffice it to say, that the ear of Omniscience itself can discern no shade of difference, between the language of

36

their lips and that of their hearts, unless it be this, that their hearts feel more than their lips can express.

These sacred and delightful services being ended, they prepare to feast before their Benefactor; but this preparation is made, and the feast itself is participated with the same feelings which animated their devotions; for whether they eat, or drink, or whatever they do, they do all to the glory of God. On such an occasion they may, perhaps, place upon their board a greater variety, than usual, of the fruits of Paradise; but if so, it is not so much with a view to gratify their appetites, as to exhibit more fully the various and ample provision which God has made for them; and thus, through the medium of their senses, to affect their hearts; for man has not yet begun to consume the bounty of heaven upon his lusts. He has not yet yielded himself a willing, but ignoble slave to his corporeal appetites; nor, we may add, has he yet learned, as too many of his posterity have since done, to sit down to the table of Providence, and rise from it refreshed, without acknowledging the hand that feeds him. No, the blessing of God is implored and his presence desired, as the crowning joy of their feast, without which even the fruits of Paradise would be insipid, and the society of Paradise uninteresting. And while they sit around his table, the viands which nourish their bodies, furnish their minds with new food for devotional feeling; for in every fruit before them they see the power, wisdom, and goodness of their Benefactor, embodied and made perceptible to their senses; they see that his goodness prompted him to give them that gratification, that his wisdom devised it, and that his power gave it existence. Thus while they feast upon the fruits of his bounty their souls feast upon the perfections which those fruits display. Thus God is seen and enjoyed in every thing, and every thing leads up their thoughts and affections to him, while he sits unseen in the midst of them, shedding abroad his love through all their hearts, and rejoicing with benevolent delight in the happiness which he at once imparts and witnesses. Meanwhile their conversation is such as the attending angels, who hover around, would not be ashamed to utter, nay such as God himself is well pleased to hear. The law of kindness is on all their lips, for the law of love is in all their hearts.

But we can pursue this part of our subject no farther. This

must suffice as a specimen of the manner, in which sinless creatures would keep a feast unto the Lord, indeed, of the manner in which all their days would be spent. And if so, may we not well exclaim, O sin, what hast thou done! What beauty, what glory, what happiness hast thou destroyed! How hast thou embittered our food, poisoned our cup, darkened the eye which once saw God in all his works; polluted and rendered insensible the heart, which once bore his image and was filled with his love, and by one fatal, accursed blow, murdered both the body and the soul of man! Who can wonder that God hates—who can refrain from hating—the destroyer of so much good, the cause of so much evil! Were it not for sin, we should observe this day in a manner as holy and as happy, as has now been described. We have the same powers and faculties, which were possessed by our first parents in Paradise. And if we may believe the declarations of scripture, or the testimony of good men, God's glory still shines as brightly in his works, as it did then. There is nothing but our own sinfulness to prevent us from seeing it as clearly, as it was seen by our first parents, and from being affected by the sight as they were affected.

But to return—If such is the manner, in which innocent creatures would keep a feast unto the Lord, then such is the manner in which we should aim to keep this annual festival. We should desire and aim to exercise the same feelings, to worship God with the same sincerity, fervency, and unity of affection, and to converse and partake of his bounty in the same manner. I do not say we shall perfectly succeed in such an attempt, but I do say that we ought to make it. He who does not make it, he who does not desire and aim to serve God with his whole heart, and feel dissatisfied with himself in proportion as he comes short of it, is as far from Christian sincerity, as he is from sinless perfection.

But though we all ought to be perfectly holy, it is but too evident that we are not so. We have all sinned; we still sin; we must all have perished in our sins, had not God graciously interposed to prevent it. He has revealed a new dispensation, a dispensation, in which grace and mercy are offered us through a Redeemer.

Through this Redeemer, the Lord Jesus Christ, he has also

revealed to us a new way of approaching him, of serving him acceptably, and of obtaining everlasting life. These all-important facts and truths connected with them, must by no means be forgotten or neglected by us, when keeping a feast unto the Lord. They must evidently modify, in a very great degree, the manner in which we observe it, and the views and feelings with which its services are performed. This remark we shall illustrate more fully. Having shown how we ought to keep this festival, considered simply as God's intelligent creatures, we shall now, as was proposed,

II. Attempt to show how we should keep it, considered as sinful creatures, under a dispensation of mercy.

In attempting this we shall pursue the same course, which has been pursued in the former part of the discourse. We will suppose that the holy and happy community, whose festival we have been contemplating, fall from their original state, and become sinners like ourselves. In other words, they transgress the law of God, the sanction of which is death. In consequence, sentence of death is immediately passed upon them, to be executed they know not when, but just when it shall please their offended judge. Meanwhile, they are banished from Paradise, excluded from the favor and presence of God, and from the tree of life which was the sacramental pledge of their immortality, and see a flaming sword blazing behind them, and turning every way, to prevent them from again entering their forfeited Eden. Nor is the change in their outward situation greater than that, which they find in their character and feelings. They have lost the image of God, they have lost all love to God, they no longer regard or address him with filial affection as a Father and a friend, but view him, so far as they view him at all, as an offended sovereign, whose law they have transgressed, and by whose law they are inexorably doomed to destruction. Indeed, God seems almost to have disappeared from their view. Their intellectual eyes darkened by sin, no longer see his glory in all his works; he no longer seems to sit enthroned on the universe which he had made, nor do they, in the daily gifts of Providence, see proofs of his bounty or incitements to gratitude. The immense void which his disappearance has left in the heart, is filled by self love, and an inordinate, idolatrous attachment to creatures; and to the great idol self, and other subordinate idols, is transferred that homage and those affections, which were once rendered to God alone. In fine, they are become spiritually dead, dead to God, to goodness, and to the end for which they were created, dead in trespasses and sins. Still however, conscience retains a place in their breasts, and at times it will speak; but it speaks nothing except reproach, condemnation, and terror. The only words which it has heard from the mouth of God, are, Thou shalt surely die; and these therefore are the only words which it will repeat. And when roused by these words they look forward, it is without hope of mercy, it is to death and the blackness of darkness, to judgment and fiery indignation. Then they wish in vain, that they had never existed, they curse, at once, their existence and its author, and feel all those terrible, unaccountable emotions, which agitate with more than a tempest's fury, a heart at enmity towards God, whenever it is forced to contemplate its great enemy.

Now suppose that these creatures, in this sinful, guilty, wretched, despairing state, are placed under a dispensation, in which the grace and mercy of God are offered them through a Redeemer, and that just such a revelation is made to them, as has been made to us in the New Testament. Suppose farther, that after they are placed under the new dispensation they resolve to observe a religious festival. What would be necessary, what would be implied in their keeping it as a feast unto the Lord? I answer, the first thing necessary would evidently be a cordial reconciliation to God. Until such a reconciliation took place, they could neither observe a religious festival, nor perform any other religious duty, in a right and acceptable manner. Indeed, they would have no disposition to do it, nor any of the feelings which it implies and demands. The feelings, proper to be exercised on a religious festival, are holy love, joy and gratitude. But they could exercise no love to God, unless they were previously reconciled to him, to his character, his government, and law. Nor could they exercise holy joy; for how could they rejoice in the existence, or in the perfections, or in the government of a being, whom they did not love? Nor could they sincerely offer thanksgiving and praise; for who can sincerely praise a being, or offer thanks to a being, whose character and conduct he dislikes? Can a self-justifying criminal, under sentence of death, rejoice and feast with proper feelings before the Judge who has condemned him; or a servant, under the eye of a master, whom he regards with mingled dread and aversion; or a rebel, in the presence of a sovereign, whose character and laws he dislikes, and whose power he dreads? Or could the prodigal son, had he been taken by force and placed at his father's table, while under the full influence of those feelings which led him to forsake his father's house, have enjoyed that situation, or relished the feast before him? But let the criminal be reconciled to his judge and receive pardon; let the servant love his master, and the rebel submit to his sovereign; let the prodigal come to himself, and exercise right feelings towards his father, and the difficulty would in each case be removed, and love, and joy, and gratitude be felt. Cordial reconciliation to God then, is indispensably necessary to enable sinful creatures to keep a feast unto the Lord.

But reconciliation to God necessarily involves hatred of sin, and self-condemnation, sorrow and shame on account of it. No sinner can feel cordially reconciled to God, until he sees that his character and all his proceedings are perfectly holy, and just, and good; for if they are not so, we ought not to be reconciled to them. But among God's proceedings, is the sentence of condemnation which he has pronounced upon every sinner. This therefore, the sinner must see and feel to be right, or he will not be reconciled to it. Now if a sinner sees it to be right that God should condemn him, he will of course condemn himself. He will say, God has been right, and I have been wrong; and in view of the wrong which he has done, he will feel remorse, sorrow and shame, or, in one word, he will repent. Without unfeigned repentance then, no sinner can keep a feast to the Lord; for every one who is impenitent is most certainly unreconciled to God. He justifies himself and thus condemns the Almighty.

The exercise of faith in the Redeemer, through whom grace and mercy are offered, is also indispensably necessary to the right observance of a feast unto the Lord. The sinner who has just views of God and of himself, as in some degree every penitent sinner has, is unable to see how his own salvation can be reconciled with the holiness, justice, and truth of God. He feels himself to be a sinner; he hears God's law say, The soul that sinneth shall die; and he sees that God's holiness, justice, and truth, all demand the execution of this sentence. How then dare he hope for salvation? And unless he dare hope for it, how can he keep a feast unto the Lord? How can he pour out from a happy, grateful, exulting heart, accents of thanksgiving and praise? He will rather wish to fast, to weep and lament, and scarcely will he dare ask his offended God to pardon and save him, lest it should be asking him to sacrifice his perfections for the sake of a sinful worm of the dust. But show him the Redeemer, set before him his atonement and intercession, and let him exercise faith in them, and all his difficulties, doubts and fears are removed; he sees that God can be just, and yet justify and save every sinner who believes in Jesus; and now he can hope, and rejoice, and exult; now he feels indeed prepared to keep a feast unto the Lord; now he can cry, O Lord, I will praise thee, for though thou wast angry with me, thine anger is turned away, and thou comfortest me. Now he can feel and obey the exhortation, Go thy way, eat thy bread with joy, for God now accepteth thy works.

But these are not the only reasons, why the exercise of faith in the Redeemer is necessary, in the case of sinful creatures, to the acceptable observance of a religious festival. When God prescribes a way in which sinners shall approach him and present their services, they must on all occasions approach him in that way, and in no other; or instead of finding acceptance, they will only excite his displeasure. All the Jewish sacrifices, for instance, were to be offered, all their religious services performed, and all their festivals observed, with reference to the tabernacle or temple, where God manifested his gracious presence, and through the medium of those typical mediators, or priests, whom he had appointed. If any Jew presumed to disregard these injunctions, to worship God on a high place of his own creating, or to offer his sacrifice with his own hands, instead of applying to the priests, he drew upon himself a curse, instead of a blessing. Just so under the christian dispensation. Christ is at once the true tabernacle, in whom dwells all the fulness of the Godhead bodily, and the only mediator between God and man—the only way by which sinful man can have access to God. I, says he, am the way, the truth and the life; no man cometh to the Father, but by me. And again—through him we have access by one Spirit unto the Father. Hence an apostle exhorts us, whatever we do, in word or deed, to do all in the name of the Lord Jesus, giving thanks to God and the Father by him. This being the case, we can neither keep a feast unto the Lord, nor offer thanks, nor perform any other religious duty acceptably, except in the name of Christ, or in the exercise of faith in his mediation.

And now let us suppose the community, which we have already twice contemplated, first as perfectly holy, and then as sinful, guilty, and undone, to be a third time placed before us, reconciled to God, exercising repentance and faith in Christ, and engaged in keeping a religious festival, like that which we this day observe. They still feel, though in an imperfect degree, the same affection which we saw them exercise toward God in their original state; but these affections are, in a considerable degree at least, excited by different objects, and variously modified by the change which has taken place in their situation. They still feel grateful to God for their existence, for their faculties, and for the various temporal blessings which surround them; but they now view all these things as blessings which they had forfeited and lost, and which had been re-purchased for them by their Redeemer, and freely bestowed upon them as the gifts of his dying love. Hence they seem, as it were, to see his name on every blessing, and every blessing reminds them of him. They still, as formerly, see and admire God's perfections as displayed in the works of creation; but their admiration and their praises are now principally excited by the far brighter, the eclipsing display which he has made of his moral perfections, in the cross of Christ, in the wonders of redemption. If they still adore, and praise, and thank him, as the God of nature, they adore, and praise, and thank him, with incomparably more fervency, as the God of grace, the God and Father of our Lord Jesus Christ. If they think of him with affection, as the God who made the world, they think of him with far warmer affection, as the God who so loved the world, that he gave his only begotten Son to die for its redemption. Loud above all their other praises and thanksgivings may be heard the cry, Thanks be unto God for his unspeakable gift! Thanks be unto God and the Lamb for redeeming love! This accords with God's own prediction, that under the new dispensation, his former works should be comparatively forgotten, and come no more into mind.

And while their thanksgivings and praises are thus principally called forth by the blessings which are conferred, and the divine perfections which are displayed, in the work of redemption, Jesus Christ holds that prominent place in their affections, and in all their solitary and united devotions, which he evidently held in the affections and devotions of the apostles, and to which their writings teach us he is entitled. If they come to God, it is as dwelling in Christ; if they see his glory, it is as shining in the face of Christ; if they rejoice in God it is as manifesting himself in Christ; if they trust in God, it is through the merits of Christ; if they pray to God, it is in reliance on Christ; if they enjoy God, they enjoy him in Christ; if they offer praise and thanksgiving to God, it is in the name of Christ; if they are constrained to holy obedience, it is the love of Christ which constrains them; if they hope to persevere and obtain the victory, it is in dependence on Christ; if they say, we live, they add, yet not we, but Christ liveth in us; and when they anticipate most confidently the happiness of heaven, they rejoice to borrow its language, and cry, Now unto him that loved us, and washed us from our sins in his own blood, be glory and dominion forever. In fine, Christ is their wisdom, their strength, their righteousness, their life, and they cordially unite with an apostle in saying, Christ is all in all. Without him we can do nothing; but through him we can do all things. And while their religious views and feelings and services, are all thus modified by an habitual reference to Christ, they are still farther modified by a similar recollection of the sinful, guilty, wretched state, from which he rescued them, and by a view of the sins, which still cleave to them, and defile all their duties,—the effects of these views and recollections, are penitence, contrition, and deep humiliation of soul, and by them all their religious feelings are pervaded and characterised. When they love their God and Redeemer, it is with a penitent love; when they rejoice in him, it is with a penitent joy; when they believe in him, it is with a penitent faith; when they obey him, it is with a penitent obedience; when they offer him thanksgivings and praises, penitence mingles with them her humble confessions and contrite sighs; and the place on earth, which they most covet, in which they most delight, is that of the woman who stood weeping at the feet of Christ, washing them with her tears, and wiping them with the hairs of her head. Even while observing a joyful festival, tears, the fountain of which is supplied by godly sorrow for sin, and gratitude to the Redeemer; tears, which it is delightful to shed, are seen on the same countenances which glow with love and hope, and beam with holy, humble joy in God.

And when they sit down to the table of Providence, to feast upon his bounty, the exercise of these emotions is not suspended. They feel there as pardoned sinners ought to feel, and as they would wish to feel at the table of Christ, for the table of Providence is become to them his table; they remember him there; they remember, that whenever their daily food was forfeited by sin, and the curse of heaven rested upon their basket and store, he redeemed the forfeiture, and turned the curse into a blessing. Hence they feast upon his bounty with feelings resembling those which we may suppose to have filled the bosoms of Joseph's brethren, when they ate and rejoiced before him. They had, you recollect, hated him, persecuted him, conspired his death, and sold him for a slave. But by the providence of God he was exalted to power, and had the satisfaction, not only of seeing them humbled at his feet, but of saving them and their families from death. After he had made himself known to them, assured them of his forgiveness, and showed them, that though they meant evil against him, God had overruled it for good, he invited them to a feast, and richly loaded their table with provisions from his own. We may, in some measure, conceive what their feelings must have been on such an occasion. Though they feasted and rejoiced before their highly exalted, but generous, forgiving, and affectionate brother, yet feelings of sorrow and shame could not but mingle with their joy, and they must often have felt as if they wished to rise from their table, throw themselves at his feet, and once more ask his forgiveness. Well then may the redeemed sinner feel thus, while he feasts and rejoices before that much injured, exalted, and compassionate Savior, who is not ashamed to call him brother, and who has not only redeemed and forgiven him, but called him to share in all his possessions and glories. And while such emotions toward the Savior fill the heart, his name cannot be absent from the tongue. Husbands and wives will speak of him to each other; parents will speak of him to their children; his person, his character, his offices, and his works, will furnish the subject of their conversations, and instructions; and a realizing apprehension of his unseen presence, far from damping their joy, will only chastise and purify and exalt it.

Such then, my hearers, are the views and feelings, with which, considered as sinful creatures under the christian dispensation, we ought to observe this sacred festival. And now allow me to ask, is this requiring anything unreasonable? Is it requiring one emotion for which the gospel of Christ does not furnish ample cause? Is it requiring any thing more than may be justly expected from creatures situated as we are, enjoying such distinguished blessings, and privileges, and indebted for them all to a Savior's dying love? Indeed, is it requiring any thing, which would not be, in the highest degree, conducive to your own happiness? Would not this day, if spent in such a manner, be the happiest day which you ever enjoyed; a day like one of the days of heaven, and affording a rich foretaste of its happiness? Why then should we not all spend what remains of it in this manner? why not thus keep it as a feast to the Lord? Ah, my hearers, this question cannot be answered, at least not in a manner which will be satisfactory to God, nor even to an enlightened conscience. And why should any seek for an answer? Why should any one seek an excuse for deferring his own happiness? Suppose two persons, who have been long at variance, should happen to meet to-day at one of your tables. Might they not become immediately reconciled, if they chose, and feast together in mutual love; and would not the happiness of the feast be heightened to each of them by the pleasure of reconciliation? Why then may you not all become immediately reconciled to your God, and begin to love that Savior who says, I love them that love me? Why may you not all repair to your respective habitations, and there feast before God with feelings resembling these? How can you find it in your hearts to leave his house, where he entreats you to be reconciled, return to the habitation which he has prepared for you, feast upon the provision which he has made for you, which a Savior purchased for you with his blood, look upon the children and friends whom he has given you, consider the ties with which he has bound them to you, and yet refuse to love him, and still persist in employing the powers and faculties, with which he has entrusted you, in opposing him! O do not, I entreat you, be so ungrateful to him, so cruel to yourselves. As though God did beseech you by us, we pray you in Christ's stead, be ye reconciled to God.

SERMON XXIII.

THE SECOND COMING OF CHRIST.

Behold, he cometh with clouds; and every eye shall see him, and they also which pierced him; and all kindreds of the earth shall wail because of him: even so. Amen. REVELATION I. 7.

AN apostle, speaking of the Lord's supper, intimates that the church will continue to partake of it, and by partaking of it to show forth his death until he shall come again. This ordinance then may be considered as a chain, which connects the first and the second coming of Christ. Of this chain, as of the gospel, he is at once the beginning and the end. If we look back to the time of its institution, we see Christ at his table, surrounded by a little band of disciples. If we look forward to the period of its completion, we see him on the judgment-seat, surrounded by all the glories and hosts of the celestial world. If we look at its commencement, we see him expiring on the cross; if we look at its termination, we see him coming in the clouds of heaven. It is this coming, of which the beloved disciple speaks in our text. Behold he cometh with clouds; and every eye shall see him, and they also which pierced him; and all kindreds of the earth shall wail because of him: even so. Amen.

In this passage there are three things which deserve our attention;—the *coming* of Christ; his being *seen by all*, and the *manner in which different characters will be affected by the sight.* A few remarks on each of these particulars will comprise the present discourse.

I. Let me lead your attention to the coming of Christ itself.

Behold he cometh with clouds. Of the greatness, the importance of this event I shall say nothing. To endeavor to enlarge your conceptions of it, by surrounding it with the pomp of language, would be like attempting to gild the noon-day sun. Every one must perceive at once, that if we except the first coming of Christ to die for the world, inspiration has revealed no fact more momentous and interesting than that of his second coming to judge the world. But respecting the certainty of this event, it may be proper to say something more. I need not inform you, that for evidence of its certainty we must look to the scriptures alone: for it is a fact which lies far beyond the ken of human reason; a fact, which God alone could reveal. Reason might however, perhaps, venture to expect, that if God thought proper to reveal a fact of such momentous interest he would reveal it clearly, and with a frequency of repetition proportionate to its importance. In this expectation she would not be disappointed. There is perhaps no event yet future, which is revealed so clearly, or in so many different passages as this. And in revealing it, the Spirit of God seems to have avoided with unusual care, all metaphorical and figurative expressions, and to have chosen only the plainest and most simple language; language, which cannot be misunderstood, nor, without the utmost violence, perverted. A few out of the many passages in which it is thus revealed, you will permit me to mention. Christ was once offered to bear the sins of many; and unto them that look for him he shall appear a second time without sin unto salvation. The Lord himself shall descend from heaven with a shout, with the voice of the archangel, and with the trump of God. The Lord Jesus shall be revealed from heaven, with his mighty angels, in flaming fire taking vengeance on them that know not God and obey not the gospel; who shall be punished with everlasting destruction from the presence of the Lord, and from the glory of his power; when he shall come to be glorified in his saints, and to be admired in all them that believe. Such is the language of inspired men. Equally explicit is the testimony of angels. This same Jesus, which is taken up from you into heaven, shall so come in like manner as ye have seen him go into heaven. Still more explicit, if possible, is the language of our Savior himself. The Son of man, says he, shall come in his glory, and all the holy angels with him; then shall he sit upon the throne of his glory: and before him shall be gathered all nations. And again, Ye shall see the Son of man coming in the clouds of heaven, with power and great glory. I shall mention but one declaration more, a declaration uttered in circumstances of peculiar solemnity. After he had been apprehended by the Jews, the High Priest, finding that he made no reply to their false accusations, said to him, I adjure thee by the living God, that thou tell us whether thou be the Christ, the Son of God. This, according to the customs of the Jews, was equivalent to the administration of an oath. And our Savior's answer was equivalent to an answer given upon oath. And what was that answer? I am: and hereafter ye shall see the Son of man sitting on the right hand of power, and coming in the clouds of heaven. On hearing this testimony from his lips, we may reply with the High Priest, though in a different sense, what need have we of any further witness? we have heard from his own mouth. If the solemn declaration, the oath of the Son of God is true, then it is certain that he will come a second time in the clouds of heaven. He, who does not believe this, believes nothing which the scriptures assert.

II. The next particular in our text which claims attention, is the fact, that Jesus Christ, at his second coming, shall be seen by all mankind. Every eye shall see him. This assertion teaches us, that he will come in a visible form; for though the word see, when used alone, often signifies merely to perceive, yet it never, so far as I recollect, has this signification when used, as it is here, in connection with the eye. The mind may be said, figuratively speaking, to see or perceive truth, and many other things, which are in their very nature invisible; but the eye can see nothing which is not visible. And as Jesus Christ will come in a visible form, so he will come, doubtless, in a human form. He will come arrayed with that glorious body which, as another inspired passage informs us, he now wears in heaven. Should this appear doubtful to any, we would refer them to the passages already mentioned, in which our Savior says, Ye shall see the Son of man coming in the clouds of heaven; an expression which must mean, if it mean any thing, that he will come in his human nature. The declaration of the angels is of the same import. Ye shall see this same Jesus come in like manner as ye have seen him go into heaven. But they saw him ascend to heaven in a human form; they will therefore, see him coming in a human form. The language of St. Paul is, if possible, still more decisive. God, says he, hath appointed a day, in which he will judge the world in righteousness by that man, whom he hath ordained, of which he hath given assurance to all men, by raising him from the dead. At the same time we are assured in other places, that God is Judge himself, that our God shall come and not keep silence; a fire shall devour before him, and it shall be very tempestuous round about him. And St. John, describing a view which he had in vision of the proceedings of the judgment day, says, I saw the dead small and great stand before God. These otherwise contradictory passages will appear perfectly reconcilable, if we recollect that Jesus Christ is God manifest in the flesh, God and man united in one person. His glorified body will be the temple, the vehicle, in which God will come to judgment, and this vehicle will be visible. Of its appearance we may, perhaps, form some idea from the description given by Daniel and St. John. I beheld, says the former, till the thrones were cast down, and the Ancient of days did sit, whose garment was white as snow;—his throne was like the fiery flame, and his wheels as burning fire. A fiery stream issued and came forth from before him; thousand thousands ministered unto him, and ten thousand times ten thousand stood before him. Similar are the expressions of St. John. I saw one, says he, like unto the Son of man, clothed with a garment down to the foot, and girt about the breast with a golden girdle. His head and his hairs were white as snow; and his eyes were as a flame of fire; and his feet were like unto fine brass, as if they burned in a furnace; and his voice was as the sound of many waters, and his countenance as the sun shineth in his strength. I need not remind you, that similar was his appearance on the mount of transfiguration, when his human form assumed, for a time, some of that glory which it was destined to wear after his exaltation to heaven; a glory, however, which will be, doubtless, increased in a degree that is inconceivable, when he shall come, not in his own glory only, but in that of his Father. Of this glory the sublime language of St. John is suited to give the most exalted conception. I saw, says he, a great white throne, and him that sat upon it, from whose face heaven and earth fled away. But the assertion in our text teaches us, not only that Jesus Christ will come in a visible form, but that all mankind shall behold him in this form. Every eye shall see him. The same truth is taught elswhere. He assured his disciples that they should see him. He assured his enemies, that they should see him. He declared, that when he comes, he will gather before him all nations. And an apostle says, we must all appear before the judgment-seat of Christ. And if he comes in a visible form, and all are assembled before him, all must, of course, see him. My hearers, meditate, a moment, upon this interesting truth. Let every one say to himself, *I* shall see this great sight. *I* shall see the Lord Jesus Christ, the God-man, the Savior, the Judge, of whom I have heard so much. *My* body, when slumbering in the grave, will hear his omnipotent voice and come forth. *My* long closed eyes will open, and the descending Judge, and the judgment-seat, with all its splendors, will burst upon them. Such was Job's expectation. Though worms destroy this body, yet in my flesh shall I see God; whom mine eyes shall behold, and I shall see for myself, and not another. Let us attend,

III. To the manner, in which different characters will be affected by this sight. Were the scriptures silent respecting this part of our subject, we might still be sure, that all will not contemplate this spectacle with similar feelings, nor be affected by it in the same manner. The feelings, with which men regard any object, will ever correspond with their own character. Different characters will regard the same object with different feelings; opposite characters with opposite feelings. Now we know, that among mankind there are characters not only widely different, but diametrically opposite. We know, that even now these opposite characters regard Jesus Christ, his word, his institutions, his friends, with opposite feelings. We know, that the thoughts of his second coming affect different persons in a very different manner. Some desire it, others dread it; some think of it with pleasure, others with pain. Hence we might naturally conclude, that when the event shall arrive different characters will be differently affected by it. But we are not left to our own inferences and reasonings on this point. Our text plainly intimates, and other passages clearly teach us, that the sight of Christ's coming in the clouds of heaven will produce widely different effects upon different characters. They teach us, first, that all good men desire this event, and will contemplate it with the most joyful emotions. This is intimated in our text, where the inspired writer, after predicting Christ's coming, and his being seen by every eye, adds, Even so: amen,—that is, so let it be; let the event take place, as soon as God pleases. In thus expressing his own feelings, he expressed the feelings of all, who, like himself, are faithful servants of the Lord Jesus Christ. Agreeably, Christians are described as those, who look for him; that is, who expect and desire his second coming. And St. Paul informs us, that the righteous Judge will, at the last day, give a crown of righteousness to all who *love* his appearing. In another passage, after predicting the second coming of Christ, he adds, wherefore beloved, comfort ye one another with these words. Now if good men expect and desire Christ's coming, if they love to think of it, if it comforts them to speak of it, then surely they will rejoice when they see it. Indeed, they cannot but rejoice to see him, whom they have followed by faith, whom they have loved with supreme affection; who comes to complete their salvation, to give them a crown of righteousness. Nor will this joy be checked by any guilty fears or anxieties; for in their Judge they will see their Savior, their Friend, their Head, whose love for them passeth knowledge, and who has said, whosoever shall confess me before men, him will I also confess before my Father and the holy angels. But,

2. While all the faithful servants of Christ will contemplate him with joy unspeakable and full of glory, all of a different character will witness his coming with unutterable horror, anguish, and despair. All kindreds of the earth shall wail because of him. These effects of his coming are still more forcibly described in a succeeding chapter. I beheld, says the apostle, and the kings of the earth, and the great men, and the rich men, and the chief captains, and the mighty men, and every bondman, and every freeman, hid themselves in the dens, and in the rocks of the mountains, and said to the mountains and rocks, Fall on us, and hide us from the wrath of the Lamb; for the great day of his wrath is come, and who shall be able to stand! It seems to be clearly intimated, both in this

passage and in our text, that the sight of Christ, at his second coming, will be terrible to all, or nearly all, who are then found alive in the world. We learn from other inspired passages the reason of this. It is because all, or nearly all, who are then found alive, will be wicked men. When the Son of man cometh, says our Savior, will he find faith on the earth? That is, will he find many, who believe in him, and expect his coming? a mode of expression, which forcibly intimates, that he will not. In another passage, he teaches us, that, at his second coming, he will find the world in the same situation, in which it was found by the flood, in the days of Noah, and in which Sodom was in the days of Lot. As it was, says he, in the days of Noah, and of Lot, so shall it be in the day, when the Son of man is revealed, or appears. They ate, they drank, they bought, they sold, they planted, they builded, and knew not, till the day in which Noah entered into the ark, and the flood came and destroyed them all.

From these and other passages it is evident, that at the second coming of Christ, there will be very little religion, very few pious men found in the world. But it may be asked, how does this representation agree with the many predictions, which assure us that religion is yet to prevail, in a far greater degree than it ever has done, and that the knowledge of God shall fill the earth, even as the waters cover the sea? We shall find an answer to this question in the twentieth chapter of Revelation. We are there taught, that the great tempter and deceiver of mankind, who deceiveth the whole world, shall be bound for a thousand years; that is, during that period he shall not be permitted to tempt or deceive mankind, and in consequence religion will almost universally prevail. To this period, all the passages, which speak of the great extension of Christ's kingdom, refer. But after the expiration of this period, the great adversary, will be released for a season; in other words, he will be suffered to renew his temptations, the consequence will be a great and almost universal apostacy. Religion will be ridiculed and opposed, and its friends persecuted with peculiar rancor; the church will be compassed about with enemies, and on the very point of being swallowed up, and then, in that critical moment, will be seen the signs of the Son of man coming in the clouds of heaven. The sight will strike them suddenly and unexpectedly. It will come, as our Savior informs us, as a flash of lightning; or, as an apostle expresses it, the day of the Lord will so come, as a thief in the night. For when they shall say, Peace and safety; then sudden destruction cometh upon them. And who can doubt that such a sight, bursting in such a manner upon men immersed in worldly cares and pleasures, or engaged in opposing the cause of Christ, will throw them into an agony of consternation and distress?

Suppose, for a moment, that this event should take place now; that while I speak the trumpet should sound, and the fiery brightness, which will surround the Judge, should begin to shine through these windows. Can you doubt, that many of this congregation would be distracted with guilty fear and remorse; and that all sinners, in all parts of the world, would be affected in a similar manner? Some of you have seen into what wild alarm, what temporary distraction, an assembly may be thrown in a moment by an alarm of fire, or a cry, that the house is falling. What then would be the effects produced by the sight of the final Judge, of the heaven's departing, of the world on fire! Less terrible was the sight of the flood to the guilty inhabitants of the old world; less loud, less agonizing was the cry which they uttered, than that which will burst from the lips of guilty mortals, when every eye sees the Judge coming in the clouds of heaven, with power and great glory.

It is not, however, to those only who are found alive in the world, that this sight will prove terrible. All the sinful dead, whose bodies are in the grave, will then be roused; for all that are in their graves shall hear the voice of the Son of man, and shall come forth; they that have done good, to the resurrection of life, and they that have done evil, to the resurrection of damnation. And O, how different will be the appearance of these two classes! The former, with glorious bodies, resembling that of their Savior, will shine forth like the sun; the holiness, and the love, and the happiness of heaven, beaming in their countenances and sparkling in their eyes; while the latter, dark and gloomy as night, will express nothing but fear and rage, envy and despair. Then will the prediction be fulfilled which says, Ye shall see a difference made between the righteous and the wicked. Then the whole intelligent universe will see, that verily there is a reward for the righteous, verily there is a God that judgeth in the earth.

Permit me now, my hearers, to improve the view we have taken of this subject, by endeavoring to bring it home to your bosoms, your consciences.

1. Consider the certainty of this event. The passages, which have been quoted in this discourse, will, I doubt not, convince you all, that if the Bible is true this event is certain, as certain as if it had already taken place. It is the same in the sight of God, as if it had taken place. He sees it as plainly, as if it were already past; and this fact renders it not only certain, that it will take place, but impossible that it should not take place. So certainly then as the Bible is the word of God, so certainly will *your* eyes see the Lord Jesus Christ coming in the clouds of heaven. Are any of *you* then prepared to rely on the assumption, that the Bible is a forgery? Remember, that if you rely upon this you stake every thing dear upon it, and that should you be deceived you lose every thing, lose your souls, lose salvation, and render your perdition sure. My hearers, if there is even a probability, nay, if there is a possibility, that the Bible is true, it is madness to incur this risk. But why do we talk of possibilities, or probabilities? We *know* that the Bible is the word of God. We *know* that the Son of God has already come once, and we *know* that he will come again. Heaven and earth shall pass away, but his word shall not pass away.

2. Let us improve the subject, by making use of it to obscure the glare of worldly objects, and extinguish the fires which they are continually kindling within us. Let all, who are dazzled or fascinated by the pomp and splendor of the world, come and contemplate a scene, which stains the pride of all human glory, and throws far back into the deepest shade every thing, which men call great, or splendid, or sublime. What are the pompous triumphs, the gaudy pageants, the long processions, on which men gaze with eager delight, compared with the descent of the Creator, the Judge from heaven, surrounded by all the seraphic hosts, and bearing with him the final sentence, the eternal, unchangeable destiny of every child of Adam? Pause, then, for a moment, and contemplate, with the eye of faith, or, if you have no faith, with the eye of imagination, this tremendous scene.

Look at that point, far away in the ethereal regions, where the gradually lessening form of our Savior disappeared from the gaze of his disciples, when he ascended to heaven. In that point see an uncommon, but faint and undefined brightness just beginning to appear. It has caught the roving eye of yon careless gazer, and excited his curiosity. He points it out to a second, and a third. A little circle soon collects, and various are the conjectures which they form respecting it. Similar circles are formed, and similar conjectures made, in a thousand different parts of the world. But conjecture is soon to give place to certainty—awful, appalling, overwhelming certainty. While they gaze, the appearance, which had excited their curiosity, rapidly approaches, and still more rapidly brightens. Some begin to suspect what it may prove; but no one dares to give utterance to his suspicions. Meanwhile, the light of the sun begins to fade before a brightness superior to his own. Thousands see their shadows cast in a new direction, and thousands of hitherto careless eyes look up, at once, to discover the cause. Full clearly they see it; and now new hopes and fears begin to agitate their breasts. The afflicted and persecuted servants of Christ begin to hope, that the predicted, long expected day of their deliverance is arrived. The wicked, the careless, the unbelieving, begin to fear, that the Bible is about to prove no idle tale. And now fiery shapes, moving like streams of lightning, begin to appear indistinctly amidst the bright dazzling cloud, which comes rushing down as on the wings of a whirlwind. At length it reaches its destined place. It pauses; then, suddenly unfolding, discloses at once a great white throne, where sits, starry resplendent, in all the glories of the Godhead, the man Christ Jesus. Every eye sees him, every heart knows him. Too well do the wretched, unprepared inhabitants of earth now know what to expect; and one universal shrick of anguish and despair rises to heaven, and is echoed back to earth. But louder, far louder than the universal cry, now sounds the last trumpet; and, far above all, is heard the voice of the Omnipotent, summoning the dead to arise, and come to judgment. New terrors now assail the living. On every side, nay under their very feet, the earth heaves, as in convulsions; graves open, and the dead come forth, while at the same moment, a change equivalent to that occasioned by death, is effected by Almighty power on the bodies of the living. Their mortal bodies put on immortality, and are thus prepared to sustain a weight of glory, or of wretchedness, which flesh and blood could not endure. Meanwhile, legions of angels are seen, darting from pole to pole, gathering together the faithful servants of Christ from the four winds of heaven, and bearing them aloft to meet the Lord in the air, where he causes them to be placed at his own right hand, preparatory to the sentence, which is to award to them everlasting life. Such, my brethren, is the scene which you will one day witness. And where now are the pomps, the honors, the riches, and pleasures, of this world, which yesterday appeared so dazzling? Has not all their brightness faded, even in your estimation? Ought they not to appear, must they not appear, as less than nothing and vanity to him, who looks for, who firmly believes, that he shall see such a spectacle as this? Can you wonder that faith in such truths, the faith of the Christian, should overcome the world? Christian, if you would gain more and greater victories over the world, than you ever have done, bring this scene often before the eye of your mind, and gaze upon it till you become blind to all earthly glory. He who gazes long at the sun becomes unsusceptible of impression from inferior luminaries; and he who looks much at the Sun of Righteousness will be little affected by any alluring object, which the world can exhibit.

3. Shall we all see this great sight? and will it affect us according to our characters? Let us then inquire how it would affect us, should it now appear? You cannot but be sensible, that if you have lived a careless, irreligious life, if your sins are not pardoned, if you are conscious, that you have not faithfully served Christ, his coming would fill you with guilty apprehension, remorse, and despair. You would, you must feel just as a dishonest or unfaithful servant would feel, when summoned into the presence of a long absent master, to whom all his unfaithfulness was known. On the contrary, if you are the faithful servants of Christ; if you are looking and longing for his appearing; if you have the testimony of your own consciences, that in simplicity and godly sincerity, not with fleshly wisdom, but by the grace of God, you have had your conversation in the world; then you could witness his approach with joy, and lift up your heads triumphantly, knowing that your redemption

was drawing nigh. O, then, if any of you are not prepared to meet the Judge in peace, let it be your great care to become prepared. If any of you are prepared for this event, live as becometh those who expect it. Remember, that your Master's words are, Watch ye therefore, and pray always, that ye may be accounted worthy to escape all these things that shall come to pass, and to stand before the Son of man.

SERMON XXIV.

EQUALITY OF MEN WITH ANGELS.

For they are equal unto the angels.—Luke xx. 36.

Eye, says an apostle, hath not seen, nor ear heard, neither have entered into the heart of man, the things, which God hath prepared for them that love him. With this assertion the language of many other inspired passages well corresponds. They inform us, that the faithful servants of God shall shine as the stars, and as the brightness of the firmament, forever and ever; that they shall shine forth as the sun, in the kingdom of their Father; that, when Christ shall appear, they shall be like him, and that they shall not only live with him, but reign with him, through endless ages. To mention but one passage more—our Savior informs us that those, who are counted worthy to inherit the future eternal world, shall be equal to the angels. If we consider what is elsewhere revealed respecting these celestial spirits, and how much is implied in being equal to them, we shall probably be of opinion that this assertion is as well suited to give us exalted conceptions of the future state of the righteous, as any passage in the inspired volume. Nor is it less suited to give us just views of the worth of the soul, and of the importance of every thing which is connected with its salvation . especially of the importance of the ministerial office, the design of which is to prepare men for that state. It is however supposed by some expositors, that the word here rendered equal, rather signifies likeness, and that the import of the passage is, they shall be like the angels. But perhaps this alteration would not, if adopted, materially affect the import of the passage. At least, it will not materially affect the remarks which I propose to make upon it. In making these remarks, it will be my object to show,

I. That men are capable of being made equal to the angels; and,

II. That, in the future world, good men will be made equal to them.

1. Men are capable of being made equal to the angels. This is an assertion, which it may, at first view, seem needless to prove. Who, it may be asked, can doubt, that he who gave angels their existence and all their powers, can, if he pleases, transform men into angels? But no one will ask this question, who duly considers the import of the proposition before us. This proposition relates, not to God's ability, but to man's capacity. There cannot be the smallest doubt, that God is able to transform, not only men, but even insects, into angels. But a man, thus transformed, would, it is obvious, cease to be a man, and become one of a totally distinct order of beings. But the question before us is, whether men can be made equal to the angels, without ceasing to be men; whether they possess faculties which if expanded to the utmost extent of which their nature is capable, would render them equal to the angels. What we assert is, that men do possess such faculties; and this assertion we shall now attempt to prove.

That man is capable of equalling the angels in the duration of their existence, may be very easily shown. Originally, he was, like them, immortal. And he would still have possessed immortality had he not become a sinner; for by sin death entered into the world. But what man once possessed, he must still be capable of possessing. If he was originally immortal, he may again become so.

These remarks relate, it is obvious, to the whole man, considered as composed of body and soul; for the soul, separately considered, has never ceased to be immortal. Like the angels, it is of a nature purely spiritual; and though it may, if God pleases, be annihilated, it cannot, properly speaking, die; for death implies a dissolution of parts; but a spirit has no parts, and is therefore incapable of dissolution.

Equally easy is it to show, that man is capable of being made equal to the angels in moral excellence. The moral excellence of creatures, whether human or angelic, consists in their conformity to the law of God. In other words, it consists in holiness. Every being, who is perfectly holy, possesses the perfection of moral excellence. But man is capable of being made perfectly holy, as holy as an angel. God requires him to be perfectly holy; and he would require of him nothing of which his nature is incapable. Originally he was perfectly holy; for God made man upright, in his own image, and this image consisted, as inspiration informs us, in righteousness and true holiness. Man is then capable of being made equal to the angels in moral excellence.

Man is also capable of being raised to an intellectual equality with the angels, or being made equal to them in wisdom and knowledge. The image of God in which he was created, included knowledge, as well as righteousness and true holiness. And while he retained this image, while he stood crowned by his Maker's hand with glory and honor, and invested with the dominion of the world, in which he dwelt, he was, as inspiration informs us, but little lower than the angels. The inferiority here intended, must, it is acknowledged, have been an intellectual inferiority; for we have already seen, that with respect to the duration of his existence, and in moral excellence, man was originally not even a little lower than the angels. But this small intellectual inferiority, on the part of man, may be satisfactorily accounted for, without supposing that his intellectual faculties are essentially inferior to those of angels; or that his mind is incapable of expanding to the full dimensions of angelic intelligence. It may be accounted for by difference of situation, and of advantages for intellectual improvement. Man was placed on the earth, which is God's footstool. But angels were placed in heaven which is his throne, his palace, and the peculiar habitation of his holiness and glory. They were thus enabled to approach much nearer, than could earth-born man, to the great Father of lights; and their minds were, in consequence, illuminated with far more than a double portion of that divine, all-disclosing radiance, which diffuses itself around him. While man was compelled to drink from the streams, they could repair at once to the fountain. Nor must it be forgotten, that man was encumbered with a body, which demanded daily supplies of food; while angels, free from all these incumbrances, and upborne on wings which never tire, were able to maintain an uninterrupted and unceasing flight. Who then will wonder, that man, thus situated, thus encumbered, should be a little lower than the angels in the intellectual scale? But free him, as he will hereafter be freed, from all the weights and fetters with which a gross material body encumbers his immortal mind; place him, as the good will hereafter be placed, in heaven, fast by the throne of an irradiating God; let him, instead of seeing all things as through a glass darkly, behold his Creator face to face; and who will undertake to prove, who will venture to assert, that he will remain even a little lower than the angels; that he will not, in wisdom and intelligence, soar to an equal height with them? Such an assertion, if made, must be entirely without support; for we know, we can conceive of no intellectual faculties possessed by angels, which are not possessed by man; we neither know, nor can conceive of any assignable limits, either to the advancement of the human mind in knowledge, or to the possible expansion of its faculties. So far as we know, or can conceive, it is capable of every thing, of which any created mind can be capable. If the mind of an infant can expand, during the lapse of a few years, to the dimensions of a Newton's mind, notwithstanding all the unfavorable circumstances in which it is here placed, why may it not, during an eternal residence in heaven, with the omniscient, all wise God for its teacher, expand so far as to embrace any finite circle whatever? Who can place his finger on any assignable spot, and say, Thus far can it go and no farther? We seem, then, to have sufficient reason for believing, that man is capable of being raised to an intellectual equality with the angels.

Little, if any, less reason have we to believe, that he is capable of being made equal to them in power. It has been often remarked, that knowledge is power; and observation must convince every one that it is so. Man's advances in knowledge have ever been accompanied by a proportionate increase of power. A knowledge of metals gave him power to subdue the earth. A knowledge of astronomy, and of the properties of the magnet, gave him power to traverse the ocean, and convert it from a separating barrier, into a connecting link between distant parts of the world. Another step in the progress of knowledge gave birth to the balloon, and thus furnished man with the power to ascend into the air. A multitude of equally well known facts might be mentioned, to show, that human knowledge and human power advance with corresponding and equal pace. But we have already seen, that man is capable of being made equal to the angels in knowledge. It should seem then to follow, that he is capable of being made their equal in power; and that, when he shall know every thing which angels know, he will be able to do every thing which angels can do.

Again, man is capable of being raised to an equality with the angels in glory, honor, and felicity. The glory of a creature must consist principally in the intellectual and moral excellencies, with which he is endued; and we have already seen, that in these respects man is capable of being made equal to the angels. The dignity and honor of any creature must consist in the station which he is appointed to fill, in the offices which he is employed to sustain, and in the services which he is commissioned to perform. And since man is capable of being made equal to the angels in wisdom, and knowledge, and power, he may be rendered capable of filling any station, which angels ever filled; of performing any service which angels ever performed; of coming as near the eternal throne, as angels ever came. Hence too, it follows, that every source of happiness, which is opened to angels, may be opened to man; that his capacity for receiving and containing may be made equal to theirs, and that his opportunity for enjoying happiness, or, in other words, the duration of his existence, may be, like that of angels, without end.

Having thus attempted to show that man is capable of being made equal to the angels in immortality, in moral excellence, in intellectual qualities, and in power, honor, glory, and felicity, we proceed to show,

II. That in the future world, good men shall be made equal to them in each of these particulars.

The fact, that men are capable of being made equal to the angels, goes far to prove the truth of this proposition; for it is not the manner of the all wise Creator to endow his creatures with capacities, that are never to be filled; or with faculties, that are never to be called into action. And since he has formed man with a capacity of being made equal to the angels, it is, to say the least, highly probable, that the good will hereafter be raised to this equality. This conclusion the scriptures abundantly confirm. That good men will be made equal to the angels in the duration of their existence, is proved by the numerous passages in which eternal life is promised to the righteous. Equally full and satisfactory is the proof, which the scriptures afford, that they shall be made equal to the angels in moral excellence; that the process of sanctification which is already begun in their hearts shall be carried to completeness and perfection. The souls of the righteous, which have already entered into the eternal world, are called the spirits of just men made perfect; and the perfection, to which they have attained, must include perfection in holiness. We are also assured, that Jesus Christ will finally present his whole church to himself, a glorious church, not having spot, or wrinkle, or any such thing; but holy, and without blemish. Little, if any, less satisfactory are the proofs, with which the scriptures furnish us, that the righteous shall be made equal to angels in wisdom and knowledge. They assure us, that they shall see God as he is; that they shall see him face to face; that they shall see as they are seen, and know even as they are known. Language cannot furnish expressions stronger than these. What more can be said of angel, or archangel, than that he knows, even as he is known?

And if the righteous are to be made equal to angels in wisdom and knowledge, it will follow, from remarks which have already been made, that they must equal them in power. We are informed, that their bodies, though sown in weakness, will be raised in power; and this fact seems to furnish some reason for believing, that the powers of their minds will be proportionably increased. From the appearance of Moses and Elijah on the mount of transfiguration, it seems evident, that they possessed power of various kinds, of which we are destitute. They had power to descend from the mansions of the blessed, and to return, and also, as it should seem, to render themselves visible or invisible, at their pleasure. Indeed it is certain, that in some respects at least, the powers of the righteous must be greatly increased, or they would be unable to sustain that far more exceeding and eternal weight of glory, and honor, and felicity, which is reserved for them in the future world. The scriptures fully warrant the assertion, that in each of these particulars they will be made equal, if not superior, to the angels. In the vision of the heavenly world, with which St. John was favored, he saw the representatives of the church placed immediately before the eternal throne, while the angels, placed at a greater distance, formed a circle around them. Should it be contended, that we can infer nothing from a vision, we will waive this passage, and remark, that they inform us, that Christ's faithful servants shall sit and reign with him upon his throne,—an honor, in which it is no where intimated that any of the angels shall share. Indeed, the disciples of Christ are in a peculiar sense his members, and as such they will largely share in all the honors, and dignities, and glories, of their exalted Head. It is, doubtless, in virtue of this free, intimate, and peculiar relation to him, that they will, as an apostle assures us, judge the world, and even judge angels. Speaking of the righteous as vessels of mercy, whom God is preparing for glory, the same apostle remarks, that in them God designs to show forth the riches of his glory. But has he not, it may be asked, already done this? Did he not show forth the riches of his glory, when he formed the angels? It should seem from the apostle's remark, that he did not. This however he means to do, and men are the objects which he has chosen for that purpose. Yes, in adorning, and honoring, and blessing redeemed sinners of the human race, Jehovah means to put forth his strength, to show what he can do, what glorious beings he can form, when he chooses to display all the riches of his glory. Who then can doubt, that in glory, honor, and felicity, good men will be made, at least, equal to the angels?

There is a dreadful counterpart to this truth, which, though not mentioned in our text, must be briefly noticed. Every argument, which proves that good men are capable of being made equal to the holy angels, may justly be considered as proving, with equal clearness, that wicked men are capable of equalling the fallen angels, who kept not their first estate. The same powers, which, if exerted in one direction, will raise an object high, will, if exerted in an opposite direction, sink it proportionably low. And the terribly expressive language, in which inspiration describes the final doom of the wicked,—the assertion, that they shall share the punishment prepared for the devil and his angels, fully warrants the belief, that in the future world sinners, who die impenitent, will, in moral depravity, guilt and wretchedness, sink to a dreadful equality with apostate spirits.

The subject, to which we have led your attention is connected with so many interesting truths, that it is by no means easy to select those, which are most deserving of particular notice. Indeed, every religious truth, and every thing which is connected with man, assumes, when viewed in the light of this subject, an aspect of overwhelming interest and importance. Can any religious truth be seen, as it is, unless it be viewed in this light? How inestimable, for instance, does the worth of the human soul appear; how clearly is it seen to exceed that of the whole world, when we view it as endued with a capacity of being made equal to the angels! How momentous an event occurs, when such a soul is born into the world! When an immortal being commences a flight through endless duration; a flight, which will raise him high to an equality with angels, or plunge him low among malignant demons and fiends! Think of this, ye parents! ye, to whom is committed the care of giving to this flight its earliest direction, and on whom it much depends, under God, what its termination shall be. How grand, let me farther remark, how Godlike, how every way worthy of himself, does the object of our Savior's interposition in behalf of ruined man appear, when viewed in the light of this subject! In this light, how clearly is his gospel seen to be glad tidings. What moral glory and sublimity surround his cross, when we contemplate him as voluntarily suspended there for the purpose of raising such a creature as man, from the depravity, degradation, and wretchedness of apostate spirits, to an equality with the angels in God's presence! And how evident does it appear, that the reward which raised them to such a height, must be conferred on them, from respect rather to their Savior's merits, than to their own? We know, that the holy angels have served God with perfect love, and zeal, and fidelity, for at least five thousand years. But all, which the best indvidual of our race has done, is to serve God, in a very imperfect manner, during part of a comparatively short life. Some, who have already entered heaven, spent a large portion of their lives in sinning against him, became his servants but a short time before death. And can it be made to appear fit, or proper, or even just, that men should receive, in return for such scanty and imperfect services, not only the pardon of their sins, but a reward equal, or superior to that, which will be conferred on the angels? Certainly not, if the rewards, which the righteous will receive, are bestowed from regard to their own merits alone. But when we recollect, what revelation teaches, that the righteous are the members of Jesus Christ, and that, as such, he is made unto them righteousness; that they are appointed to share the rewards which he has merited, all difficulty vanishes. We perceive, at once, that no reward can equal the merits of the Son of God, and that it may be perfectly fit and proper to raise even the most unworthy of his members, for his sake, to an angel's seat in heaven.

But it becomes necessary to waive a further consideration of this, as well as of many other important topics connected with our subject, and proceed to such an application of it as the occasion demands.

To the pastor elect* this subject, viewed in its connection with the transactions of the day, can scarcely fail to be deeply interesting. The care of your own soul, my dear brother, of working out your own salvation, of preparing yourself for an angel's seat, has hitherto constituted the principal part of your duty. This alone is a work so great, that no man ever yet accomplished it without Almighty aid. But you are now to have a still more difficult task assigned you, to engage in a still greater and more important work. In addition to the care of your own soul, the care of many other souls is to be laid upon you. For each of them our Divine Master has shed blood of inestimable price. Each of them is of more value than the world which it inhabits. Each of them is capable of being made equal to an angel. Whether they shall be raised to this equality, will depend in a very considerable degree, upon the manner in which you shall perform the work assigned you. If it be true, that the minister, who suitably takes heed to himself, and to his doctrine, shall both save himself and them that hear him, it must also be true, that he, who neglects this duty, will destroy, not himself only, but his hearers. The thought is

*Preached in Bangor at the ordination of Rev. S. L. Pomroy.

appalling, overwhelming. Indeed, the ministerial office, if seen in all its effects, and consequences, and responsibilities, would crush an angel. But if the work is great, so is the assistance which our Master offers; and so is the reward which he promises to all who obtain mercy to be faithful. This reward not a few of our race have secured already. From this very spot, where you will take the vows of God upon you, and where you will stand to fulfil those vows, the soul of your predecessor ascended,* as we have reason to hope, to an angel's seat. From this very spot, a band of those celestial beings, who minister to the heirs of salvation, and convey them home to heaven when Jesus commands, exultingly bore away the disembodied spirit to be their companion and their equal above. From this place then, my brother, look up, and contemplate the throne which he now fills, and the crown which he now wears. Such a throne, such a crown, awaits every faithful servant of Jesus Christ. May you, my dear brother, be enabled to maintain this character, and secure this reward. May you be enabled, as successive years roll away, to take a higher and higher flight toward heaven, and find your beloved people accompanying you in your flight; and may you and they together learn, in the regions above, all that is implied in being made equal to the angels.

This church and religious society, while they accept our cordial and thankful congratulation on the pleasing prospect before them, and on the healing of that wound which was so suddenly inflicted, and so powerfully felt, will permit us to applaud the concern, which they have manifested, for the resettlement of the gospel ministry among them, and for the zeal and unanimity which have so speedily led to a result so desirable. The concern, which you have felt for the attainment of this object, is, by no means, a causeless or unreasonable concern. If we have souls which render us capable of being made equal to the angels, and if these souls are liable to be lost, the care of them should evidently be the grand business of life; and every thing, which tends to promote their salvation, should be ranked among the most indispensable necessaries of life. That the stated preach-

* Rev. Harvey Loomis, to whom reference is here made, died suddenly in his pulpit.

ing of the gospel does tend to promote their salvation, that in ordinary cases, they will not be saved without it, will be denied by none, who believe the contents of that volume which assures us, that faith cometh by hearing. More necessary then, than food, or raiment, or shelter, is the stated preaching of the gospel of Christ. Allow me, however, to remind you, that the enjoyment of this means of grace, though ordinarily necessary to man's salvation, will by no means secure his salvation. Nay more, if it be not properly improved, it will but accelerate and aggravate his ruin. If it prove not a savor of life unto life, it must prove a savor of death unto death. Those, whom it does not raise to an equality with the angels, it will sink to an abyss proportionably deep. You stand then, my brethren, midway on an eminence, the summit of which is wrapped in the dazzling glories of heaven, while its base lies deep in the regions of despair, shrouded in the darkness of eternal night. The great object of your minister, the work for which God has sent him among you, is, to persuade you to ascend this eminence. Your own hearts, and numberless temptations, will, on the other hand, endeavor to draw you down, and plunge you in the gulf which lies at its base. O, then, listen not to these evil counsellors, but listen to your pastor, to your consciences, and to your God. Waiting on him you shall renew your strength, mount up as on eagles' wings, and at length sit down with angels in the kingdom of heaven.

Though fearful of wearying the patience of my auditors, I must beg them to indulge me in addressing, at greater length than is usual on such occasions, an assembly, which I cannot hope ever to address again. To those of them who are the disciples of Jesus Christ, our subject is full, not only of consolation, but of warning, of reproof, and of the most powerful motives to zeal and diligence, and untiring perseverance in performing the duties, to which their profession calls them. That you may feel the force of these motives, my brethren, consider what is the language of your profession, what you say to the world, when you approach the table of your Lord, or perform any other act which indicates that you consider yourselves as the disciples of Jesus Christ. On every such occasion, you do in effect say, I profess to be one of those, to whom all the promises of the gospel are made; one of those, who are styled children and heirs of God.

As one of this number, I expect soon to be called to mingle with the angels, and to be made, in every respect, their equal. When I shall be exalted to this state, is uncertain. It may be to-morrow. It may be the next hour, for there is but a step between me and death, and, consequently, but a step between me and an angel's seat. Such, O professed disciples of Christ, is the lofty, and, as it must appear to the world, assuming language of your profession. And can you utter such language, will shame allow you to utter it, without attempting to live in a corresponding manner! If you do indeed look for such things, what manner of persons ought you to be, in all holy conversation and godliness! How far ought you to live above the world! How dead should you be to all earthly objects and pursuits! What spirituality of temper, what heavenly mindedness, should you feel and exhibit! What can be more obvious, more undeniable, than the conclusion, that if you hope to be made equal to the angels hereafter you ought to imitate, so far as is practicable, angels now. That you may be induced to imitate them, and to climb with greater diligence and alacrity the steep ascent before you, let me persuade you to fix your eyes upon its summit. A dense impenetrable cloud appears, indeed, to conceal it from mortal eyes; but inspiration speaks, and the cloud is dissipated; faith presents her glass, and the sun-bright summit is seen. On him who sits enthroned upon it, you cannot indeed gaze. His glories, though you shall see them unveiled hereafter, are too insufferably dazzling for mortal eyes to sustain. But contemplate the resplendant forms, which float around him in an atmosphere of pure celestial light. See their bodies, resembling sunbeams seven times refined. See their countenances beaming with intelligence, purity, benevolence and felicity. Through their transparent bodies look in, and contemplate the souls which inhabit them, expanded to the full dimensions of angelic minds, bearing the perfect image of their God, and reflecting his glories, as the polished mirror reflects the glories of the noon-day sun. This, O Christian, is what thou shalt hereafter be. These dazzling forms were once sinful dust and ashes, like thyself. But grace, free, rich, sovereign, almighty grace, has made them what they now are. It has washed and justified, and sanctified, and brought them to glory. And to the same glory, O Christian, it is bringing thee. And canst thou then sleep, canst thou slumber, canst thou be slothful, canst thou complain of the difficulties which attend, of the obstacles which oppose, thy ascent to such glory and felicity as this? O let gratitude, let duty, let shame, if nothing else, forbid. Lift up, ye embryo angels, lift up the heads which hang down, and let the drooping spirit revive. Read, hear, meditate with prayer, deny yourselves, mortify sin but a little longer, and you shall mount up, not on eagles', but on angels' wings, and know what is meant by being made equal to resplendent intelligences.

To impenitent sinners this subject, taken in connection with other parts of revelation, is a subject of most solemn and awful import. They too possess faculties, which render them capable of being made equal to the angels; but these faculties will only serve, if they remain impenitent and unholy, to sink them down to a dreadful equality with the fallen angels, the spirits of disobedience, for whom the fires of hell are prepared, and to whom is reserved the blackness of darkness and eternal despair. They, indeed, are destined, like the righteous, to immortality; but not, if they remain as they now are, to a happy immortality. No, the language of our Judge is, They that have done good, shall come forth to the resurrection of life, but they that have done evil, to the resurrection of damnation. The wicked shall go away into everlasting punishment. My careless, irreligious hearers, think a moment, I beseech you, upon the terribleness of their fate. O, think how terrible it will be, to have the vast capacity of your immortal souls filled, to the very brim, with wretchedness; to see, that when you might have been raised to an equality with the holy angels you have sunk yourselves, by your own folly, to a dreadful equality with evil spirits, in character, in malignity, misery, and despair. Yet this must be your fate, unless you repent, and work the works of God, by believing on him whom he hath sent. God himself has said it, who cannot lie, and who will never change. And are these things so? Is it true, that before a century shall have passed away all the souls, who now fill this house, will be angels or demons, and fixed forever in heaven or hell? Yes, my hearers, it is true. It is as certain, as that there is a God; as certain, as that we are here. O, then, in what language can we describe, how can we adequately conceive of, the folly, the madness, of sinners, of those who neglect the great salvation.

In less than a century, and, with respect to most of them, in much less than half that time, the question, which of the two opposite states shall be theirs, is to be decided. Yes, my immortal hearers, in a few years will be forever decided the question, whether your vast and almost boundless capacities, shall be filled with happiness, or with misery; whether the noble faculties, which God has given you, shall blossom and expand in heaven, or be scorched and withered in hell; in a word, whether you shall brighten into angels, or blacken into fiends. And while this question is in suspense; a question, which might convulse the thrones of heaven, and throw the universe into agonies of anxiety, how are you, who are most nearly concerned in it, employed? In some childish, worldly scheme of temporal aggrandizement; or in laboring to amass wealth, which you can possess but for an hour, or, perhaps, in a round of frivolous amusements and dissipation. Yes,—let earth blush, let heaven weep to hear it,—these, these, are the employments, in which immortal beings choose to spend their hours of salvation, to pass away the time, till the great question is decided. Well may inspiration declare, as it does, that the heart of the sons of men is full of evil, and that madness is in their hearts while they live. And well may we exclaim, in the language of inspiration, O, that they were wise, that they understood their latter end. My dying, yet immortal hearers! will none of you be wise? Will none of you suffer me, or rather suffer the guiding Spirit of God, to take you by the hand, and lead you to that mount, on the summit of which an angel's crown, and a Savior's throne, await all who overcome the difficulties of the ascent? O, look once more, before you turn away and renounce them forever,—look once more at these inestimable rewards. Look too at Him, who dispenses them. Hear him offering you the aid of his own wisdom to guide you, and of his own power to strengthen you, while contending for the prize. Hear him repeating all the gracious melting invitations, which he addresses to sinners in the volume of his word. Hear him saying, Sinner, trust in me, and I will raise thee to an equality with angels; but neglect me, and thou wilt plunge thyself down to a level with despairing fiends.

SERMON XXV.

THE PUNISHMENT OF THE WICKED DREADFUL AND INTERMINABLE.

Where their worm dieth not, and the fire is not quenched. MARK IX. 44.

A MINISTER, my hearers, who would be faithful, must frequently compare his preaching with the scriptures, and inquire, not only whether he preached the truth, the whole truth, and nothing but the truth, but whether he gives to every particular doctrine and precept just that place in his sermons, which its importance deserves, or which is given to it in the word of God. On instituting such an inquiry, I find, that it is long since I called your attention, particularly, to the punishment, which awaits impenitent sinners in a future state. I have, indeed, frequently alluded to it, and mentioned it incidentally, as was unavoidable; but I have not, I believe, for some years, made it the subject of a discourse. In a word, the doctrine of future punishment has not, of late, filled such a place in my sermons, as it fills in the Bible, as it fills in the discourses of our great Teacher, Jesus Christ. I, therefore, feel bound in duty to call your attention to the subject, painful as it is. Some of you may, perhaps, say, or at least think, that it will do no good. I know not, that it will; for, so far as I can learn, nothing that I have said of late has done any good. Tell me what subject will do you good, and I will preach upon it.

But come will, perhaps, go farther, and say, this doctrine has no tendency to do good; it is altogether idle, to think of frightening men into religion. With such remarks I have nothing to do. It is my duty, not to decide what doctrines are likely to do good, but to preach such doctrines as I find in the scriptures; not to determine what means will prove effectual, but to use those means which God has appointed. Of these means this doctrine is one; and whether it does good to any of you, or not, I know that it has done good to thousands; that thousands have been moved by fear to fly from the wrath to come. I know also, that if you believe it, it will do good to you; and no truth can be of service, which is not believed. In fine, I dare not pretend to be either more wise, or more compassionate than our Savior; and he thought it consistent both with wisdom and with compassion, to utter the words of our text. And he evidently uttered them with a view to alarm his hearers. He addressed himself to their fears, with a view to produce obedience to his commands. The command, which he thus enforced, was this; If thine eye offend thee, pluck it out, and cast it from thee; for, he adds, it is better for thee to enter into life with but one eye, than having two eyes, to be cast into hell, where their worm dieth not, and the fire is not quenched.

There can, I think, be no doubt, that in these expressions our Savior alludes to the manner, in which the Jews disposed of the bodies of the dead. Sometimes, as is the custom with us, they placed them in tombs, where they were, of course, consumed by worms. At others, they prepared a funeral pile, on which the body was placed, in order to be consumed by fire. After the fire had been suffered to rage, till nothing remained but cinders and ashes, they quenched the glowing mass, and carefully deposited it in an urn. If we suppose that our Savior alluded to these customs, his expressions may be thus paraphrased: You have seen what is done with the body after death. You have sometimes seen it consumed by worms, which, after they had devoured it, died for want of nourishment. And you have sometimes seen it consumed by a fire, which, after a while, was quenched: But there is another death, which is followed by consequences far more terrible, which affect not the body only, but the soul. Those who die this death, shall be preyed upon by worms, which will never die, and become the fuel of a fire, that will never be quenched. They will be forever dying, forever suffering the pangs of the second death, but will never die, never cease to exist. It will be as if the bodies, which you have seen entombed or burnt, could feel the worms, which bevour, or the fires, which consume them. Such must have been the import of these expressions, if our Savior alluded, as we have every reason to believe he did, to the funeral ceremonies of the Jews. But whether he did, or not, allude to them, the import of his language is substantially the same. It is indeed figurative; but not, on that account, less full of meaning, or less terrible. Let us then, with feelings similar to those which prompted him to utter this language, lift the veil of figurative expression, and contemplate the awful truths, which it partly discloses, and partly conceals.

I. In dilating upon these truths, I shall say little of the corporeal sufferings, which await impenitent sinners beyond the grave. Such sufferings will certainly compose a part of their punishment; for we are assured, that their bodies shall come forth to the resurrection of damnation; and our Savior's language respecting the rich man, who in hell lifted up his eyes, being in torments, more than intimates, that anguish of body was an ingredient in his wretchedness. Indeed, as the body is the servant of the soul, and at once its tempter to many sins, and its instrument in committing them, there seems to be a manifest propriety, in making them companions in punishment. We shall only add, that as after the resurrection the bodies of the wicked will be immortal, they will be capable of enduring suffering, which in this world would cause instant death. But though we know little, because the scriptures say little, of the nature of their bodies, or of the miseries which await them, it is otherwise with respect to the sufferings of the soul. To these sufferings the declarations of scripture seem principally to refer; and these declarations our knowledge of the soul, and of the causes which will hereafter operate to render it miserable, enable us, in some measure, to understand. Especially, will it assist us in understanding the first clause in our text—where their worm dieth not. This expression evidently intimates, that the soul will suffer miseries, analogous to those which would be inflicted on a living body, by a multitude of reptiles constantly preying upon it. And it may be understood to intimate further, that as a dead body appears to produce the worms which consume it, so the soul, dead in trespasses and sins, really produces the causes of its own misery. What are those causes? or, in the language of our text, what is the gnawing worm, which is to prey upon the soul hereafter? I answer,

1. Its own passions and desires. That these are capable of preying upon the soul, and occasioning, even in this life, most acute suffering, those of you, whose passions are naturally strong, need not be informed. And those of you, whose passions are less violent, whose tempers are comparatively mild, may be convinced of the same truth, by seeing the effects of passion upon others. Look, for instance, at a man who is habitually peevish, fretful, and discontented. Has he not gnawing worms already at his heart? Look at the envious man, whose cheek turns pale, and who feels a secret pang, when he hears a rival commended, or sees him successful. Is there no gnawing worm in his bosom? Look at the covetous man, who wears himself out in the pursuit of wealth, and who is daily harassed by craving desires, cares and anxieties. Can any worm gnaw worse than these? Look at the votary of ambition, whose success depends on the favor of the great, or of the multitude; who pants to rise, but is kept down by a rival, or by adverse circumstances; and whose mind is full of contrivances, jealousies, and rivalships. Is there no corroding tooth at work in his breast? Look at the proud man, whose blood boils at every real or fancied neglect; at the passionate or revengeful man, who has always some quarrel upon his hands; at the drunkard, whose passions are inflamed by intoxicating potions, and you will find fresh proofs of this truth. It is true, indeed, that none of these passions make men completely wretched in this world, and the reasons why they do not, are obvious. In the first place, there are, in this world, many things, which are calculated to soothe, or, at least, to divert men's passions. Sometimes they meet with success, and this produces, at least, a transient calm. At another time, the objects, which excite their passions, are absent, and this allows them a little quietness. And there are so many things to be attended to, that men have not always leisure to indulge their passions, or attend to the uneasiness which they produce. Above all, they are from their infancy under the operation of causes, which tend to restrain their passions, and weaken, or at least confine, their rage.

Besides, every man must sleep, at intervals, and while he sleeps his passions are at rest. But suppose all these things to be removed, suppose a man to be deprived of sleep, and chained down with nothing to do, but to feel his passions rage continually; suppose him to meet with no success, nothing to soothe his ruffled feelings; suppose the objects, which excite his strongest passions, to be constantly before him; and, finally, suppose all outward and inward restraints to be taken off. Would not such a man be, even in this life, inconceivably wretched? And yet even his wretchedness would be nothing, compared with that, which the sinner's passions and desires will occasion him in a future state. There his passions, which are now in their infancy, will start up into giant strength; there, all outward and inward restraints will be taken off; there he will have nothing to divert his attention, nothing to assist him in forgetting, even for a moment, his tormenting feelings; there every object, which he ever desired, will be removed from him forever, while the desire will remain in equal, in vastly increased force; there he will be surrounded with malicious, cruel, raging companions, who will continually blow up his passions to the highest pitch of fury. There not even the respite, which sleep now affords, will be found. Nor is this all. Nothing inflames the passions of men more than suffering. Even men, who are at other times good tempered, often become impatient, discontented, and even angry, when harassed by severe pain, long sickness, or repeated disappointments. How terribly, then, will the passions of sinners be enraged by the exquisite, hopeless sufferings of a future state! How will they curse themselves, and all around them, and as the scriptures declare, blaspheme God because of their plagues. Against him and against all good beings, they will feel the most furious, implacable hostility; for they will be entirely under the dominion of that carnal mind, which is enmity against Jehovah.

In addition, the scriptures teach us, that they will see, though afar off, and with an impassable gulf between them, the happiness of the righteous; and this sight will occasion envy, compared with which, all the envious feelings ever entertained on earth are nothing. Every sinner too will find in the regions of despair some, whom his arguments, his solicitations, or at least his example, helped to bring there; and they will overwhelm him, and enrage his passions, with the bitterest reproaches. Nor will sinners there retain the least shadow of those natural affections, or amiable dispositions, which some of them possess here; for our Savior declares, that from him, that hath not, shall be taken away even that which he seemeth to have. Now consider all these things, and say, who can describe, or conceive of, the misery which sinners will suffer from their own gnawing passions, or of the blasphemies, the execrations, the wild uproar, the raging madness, which will be witnessed, when all the wicked, from all ages and parts of the world, are imprisoned together in the blackness of darkness, like ravenous lions in their dens. To this God refers, when he says of sinners, They have sown the wind, and they shall reap the whirlwind; that is, they have indulged sinful passions in this life, and those passions, blown up, as from a wind to a whirlwind, shall be their future companions and tormentors.

2. The gnawing worm, of which our Savior speaks, includes the consciences of sinners. The sufferings inflicted by conscience will be even more painful, than those which are occasioned by the sinner's passions; for terrible as are the gnawings of passion, those of conscience are still more so. Her scourge draws blood at every stroke. Even in this world she has drawn many, as she did Judas, to despair, madness, and suicide. But her loudest rebukes, her keenest reproaches here, are mere whispers, compared with the thundering voice, in which she will speak hereafter. Here she speaks only at intervals. There she will speak without intermission. Here the sinner has various ways of stifling her reproaches, or diverting his attention from them. He may rush into scenes of business or amusement; he may silence her with sophistical arguments and excuses, or with promises of future amendment; and, when all other means fail, he may drown her for a season in the intoxicating bowl, as too many, alas, madly do. But there, he will have no means of silencing, or escaping from her reproaches, for a moment. Here she knows comparatively little of God, of duty, or of sin; and therefore, often suffers the sinner to escape, when she ought to scourge him. But there she will see every thing in the clear light of eternity, and in consequence, instead of a whip of small cords, will chastise the sinner as with a scourge of scorpions. There the sinner will clearly see

what a God he has offended, what a Savior he has neglected, what a heaven he has lost, and into what a hell he has plunged himself. All the sins which he has committed, with all their aggravations and consequences; all the sabbaths he enjoyed, the sermons which he heard, the warnings and invitations which he slighted, the opportunities which he misimproved, the serious impressions which he banished, will be set in order before him and overwhelm him with mountains of conscious guilt. And O, the keen unutterable pangs of remorse, the bitter self-reproaches, the unavailing regrets, the fruitless wishes, that he had pursued a different course, which will be thus excited in his breast! The word remorse, is derived from a Latin word, which signifies, *to gnaw again*, or *to gnaw repeatedly;* and surely, no term can more properly describe the sufferings which are inflicted by an accusing conscience. Well then may such a conscience, when its now sleeping energies shall be wakened by the light of eternity, be compared to a gnawing worm. The heathen made use of a similar figure to describe it. They represented a wicked man as chained to a rock in hell, where an immortal vulture constantly preyed upon his vitals, which grew again as fast as they were devoured. Nor is this representation at all too strong. Even in this world, where conscience is comparatively weak, I have often seen the bed, and the whole chamber of the sick man, shake under the almost convulsive agonies, which her lash inflicted. I have been told by persons, suffering under most painful diseases, that their bodily sufferings were nothing to the anguish of mind which they endured. I have seen a man of robust constitution, vigorous health, strong mind, and liberal education, tremble, like an aspen leaf, and scarcely able to sustain himself, under the pressure of conscious guilt, and pungent remorse. A man in similar circumstances has been known to rise in winter, at midnight, and run for miles, with naked feet over the rough and frozen ground, in order that the bodily pain, thus occasioned, might, if possible, divert his attention, for a time, from the far more intolerable anguish of his mind. And a dying infidel has been known to exclaim, Surely there is a God, for nothing less than omnipotence could inflict the pangs which I now feel! What then must be the pangs inflicted by a gnawing conscience in eternity?

II. Our Savior speaks not only of a gnawing worm, but of

an unquenchable fire. What reference this may have to the corporeal sufferings of the wicked, I shall not pretend to decide; but it appears evident, from other passages, that so far as the soul is concerned it refers to a keen and constant sense of God's presence and righteous displeasure. He says of himself, I am a consuming fire; and a fire is kindled in mine anger, which shall burn even to the lowest hell. These expressions evidently intimate, that a view of his perfections, and constant presence, combined with a sense of his displeasure, will affect the soul, as fire does the body, withering its strength, and drying up its spirits. Some of you have formerly known a little of this; and you know, or, at least, will easily conceive, that no fire can torture the body more keenly, than a sense of God's displeasure does the soul. But to those of you, who know nothing of this experimentally, it will be more difficult to convey any clear apprehension of this subject. The following supposition may perhaps assist in doing it. Suppose, that when Washington was the commander of our armies, you had been a soldier under him, and had been detected in a plot to betray your country. Suppose yourself to be brought before him, surrounded by the whole army, and compelled by some means to fix your eyes steadily, several hours, on his,—encountering, during the whole time, his stern, indignant, and withering glances. Would you not soon have found your situation intolerably painful? Would not his glance seem to thrill through your soul, and almost scorch it like fire, or blast it like lightning? What then must it be to see yourselves surrounded by a just and holy God, to meet his heart-searching, heart-withering eye, wherever you turn, fixed full upon you; to see the Author of your being, the Sovereign of the universe, the great, the glorious, the majestic, the omnipotent, the infinite Jehovah, regarding you with severe displeasure; to see his anger burning against you like fire! O, this will be indeed a fire to the soul! a fire which will be felt in all its faculties, and fill them to the brim with anguish,—anguish, as much greater than any which could be occasioned by material fire, as the Creator is superior to his creatures. It is then, O, it is a fearful thing, to fall into the hands of the living God, that God, who is a consuming fire to the workers of iniquity!

III. We learn from the passage before us, that these sufferings will be endless. Their worm dieth not, and the fire is not quenched. And three times successively, our Savior declares, in the context, that the fire shall never be quenched. In the original language of the New Testament, the language which our Savior used, there are no expressions which more fully and unequivocally signify eternity, or endless duration, than those which are here employed. In another passage, the very same expressions are applied to the punishment of the wicked, which are used to describe the duration of God's existence. He liveth, we are told, forever and ever; and we are assured, that the wicked shall be tormented forever and ever. If any further proof of this truth is wanting, it may be found in the nature of the punishment itself. We have seen, that the gnawing worm, of which our Savior speaks, is the passions and consciences of sinners. Now these belong to the soul; they are as it were a part of it, they are some of its essential faculties. Of course, they must live as long as the soul lives; and as the soul is immortal, they must be immortal. We have also seen, that the fire, which will scorch the souls of the wicked, is a sense of God's presence and anger. Now as he lives forever, and is unchangeably the same, he must forever be displeased with sinners, and be constantly present with them. In other words, the fire of his anger must burn forever. It is a fire, which cannot be quenched, unless God should change or cease to exist. It is this, which constitutes the most terrible ingredient of that cup, which impenitent sinners must drink. Dreadful as will be their sufferings, they would be comparatively light, were there any hope of their termination. But of this there will be no hope. Every thing will conspire to force upon the sinner's mind, a full conviction, that his existence and his sufferings must continue forever; that they will be without mitigation and without end. And this conviction will above all things, wither his courage, and his strength. It will banish all thought of summoning up patience and fortitude to endure his wretchedness, and cause him to sink down under it in the faintness of despair. My hearers, if any of you think I exaggerate, or color too highly, listen to the plain, unadulterated language of God himself. The wicked shall be turned into hell, even all that forget God. They that know not God and obey not the gospel of our Lord Jesus Christ shall be punished with everlasting destruction from the presence of the Lord, and from the glory of his power. In the hand of Jehovah is a cup, and the wine is red, and he poureth out the same. But the dregs thereof, all the wicked of the earth shall wring them out, and drink them. They shall drink of the wine of the wrath of God, which is poured out without mixture into the cup of his indignation; and shall be tormented with fire, in the presence of the holy angels, and in the presence of the Lamb; and the smoke of their torment ascendeth up forever and ever. Will any one, on hearing these passages, reply, My feelings revolt at such statements; I will not, cannot believe them? Then you must reject the Bible; for it is full of such statements, and every fact, every doctrine, confirms them. The incarnation of the Son of God, the tears which he shed for sinners, the blood which he poured out for sinners, the joy which angels feel when one sinner repents, and the unutterable anxiety which inspired men felt for the conversion of sinners,—all conspire to prove, that the fate of those, who die without repentance, without conversion, must be inconceivably dreadful. Will you then say, such a punishment cannot be just? It is impossible that I should deserve it? But remember, that you know nothing of your sins, or of what sin deserves. Were you properly acquainted with your own sinfulness, you would feel convinced, that it is just. All true penitents feel and acknowledge, that it would have been perfectly just to inflict this punishment upon them. Were not you impenitent, you would feel the same. Besides, this punishment, dreadful as it is, is nothing more than the natural, necessary consequence of persisting in sin. The corroding passions, the remorse of conscience, and the displeasure of God, which will constitute the misery of sinners, are all the results of sin. Every sinner has the seeds of hell already sown in his breast. The sparks, which are to kindle the flames of hell, are already glowing within him. Christ now offers to extinguish these sparks. He shed his blood to quench them. He offers to pour out his Spirit, as water, to quench them. But sinners will not accept his offer. They rather fan the sparks, and add fuel to the fire. How then can they justly complain, when the fire shall break out into an unquenchable conflagration, and burn forever! As well might a man, who should put vipers into his bosom, complain of God, because they stung him. As well might a man, who has kindled a fire and thrown himself into it, complain of God, because the flames scorched him. But I can spend no more time in answering objections, or in defending the justice of God, against the complaints of his creatures. I cannot stand here coolly arguing and reasoning, while I see the pit of destruction, as it were, open before me, and more than half my hearers apparently rushing into it. I feel impelled rather to fly, and throw myself before you in the fatal path, to grasp your hands, to cling to your feet, to make even convulsive efforts to arrest your progress, and pluck you as brands out of the burning. My careless hearers, my people, my flock! death, perdition, the never dying worm, the unquenchable fire, are before you! Your path leads directly into them. Will you not then hear your friend, your shepherd? Will you not stop, and listen at least for a moment? Will you, O, will you refuse to believe that there is a hell, till you find yourselves in the midst of it? O, be convinced, I conjure you, be convinced by some less fatal proof than this. Yet how can I convince you? How can I stop you? My arm is powerless; yet I cannot let you go. I could shed tears of blood over you, would it avail. Gladly, most gladly, would I die here on the spot, without leaving this sacred desk, could my death be the means of turning you from this fatal course. But what folly is this! to talk of laying down my worthless life to save you. Why, my friends, the Son of God died to save you,—died in agonies,—died on the cross; and surely, that doom cannot but be terrible, to open a way of escape from which he did all this. And it is dreadful. The abyss, into which you are falling, is as deep, as the heaven, from which he descended, is high. And will you then rush into it, while he stands ready to save you? Shall he, as it respects you, die in vain? Will you receive the grace of God in vain? Shall those eyes, which now see the light of the Sabbath, glare and wither in eternal burning? Shall those souls, which might be filled with the happiness of heaven, writhe and agonize forever, under the gnawings of the immortal worm? Shall I, must I hereafter see some who are dear to me, for whom I have labored and prayed and wept, weltering in the billows of despair, and learning, by experience, how far the description comes short of the terrible reality? But I cannot proceed. The thought unmans me. I can only point to the cross of Christ, and say, There is salvation, there is blood, which, if applied, will quench the fires that are already kindling in your breasts. There is deliverance from the wrath which is to come.

I cannot, must not, however, conclude, without addressing a word, my professing friends, to you. And I hope you will bear with me, if, in view of such a subject as this, I address you with apparent severity. An apostle teaches ministers, that they must sometimes rebuke professing Christians sharply; but I trust my sharpness will be the sharpness of love; and I know that I shall say nothing to you, half so severe as the reproaches which I have directed against myself, while preparing this discourse. We all deserve perdition, a thousand times, for our stupid insensibility to the situation of those, who are perishing around us. We profess to believe the word of God; but can you all prove that you believe it? Do you all act, as if you believed it? What, believe that many of your acquaintances, your children, are in danger of the fate, which has now been described! Dare you go to God, and say, Lord, I believe thy word, I believe that all thy threatenings will be fulfilled, and then turn away, and coolly pursue your worldly business, without uttering one agonizing cry for those, who are exposed to these threatnings? Dare you go and claim relationship to Christ, and profess to have his Spirit, without which you are none of his, and then make no effort, or only a few faint efforts, to save those, for whom he shed not tears only, but blood? O, if you can do this, where are the bowels, I will not say of a Christian, but a man? Go, I may say to such, go, inconsistent, cruel, hard-hearted professors; go, slumber over the ruin of immortal souls; wrap yourself up in your selfish temporal interests, and say, I have no time to spare for rescuing others from everlasting burnings. Go, wear out your life in acquiring property for your children, and leave their souls to perish in the fire that never shall be quenched. Go, adorn their bodies, and banish from them, if possible, the seeds of disease; but leave in their bosoms that immortal worm, which will gnaw them forever. And when God asks, where is thy child? thy brother? thy friend? reply, with impious Cain, I know not, I care not: am I his keeper?

But I cannot proceed further in this strain. I would rather beseech, and melt, and win you by tenderness. Say, then, Christian, dost thou believe that Christ died to save thee from the misery, which has been imperfectly described? Dost thou believe, that if he had not loved thee and given himself for thee, the gnawing worm and the unquenchable fire would have been thy portion forever? O then, where is thy gratitude, thy love? Where are the returns, which he has a right to expect? Hast thou already made him a sufficient return for such inestimable benefits? Has he not reason to say, at least to some of you, Did I die for thee; redeem thee from sin, and death, and hell, that thou mightest crucify me afresh, by thy unkindness and unbelief? Did I watch and pray whole nights, that thou mightest neglect watchfulness and prayer? Did I purchase for thee divine grace, precious promises, and strong consolation, that thou mightest make light of them, or turn them into wantonness? And do I prolong thy forfeited life, that thou mayest live carelessly, unprofitably, or like the world around thee? No, I redeemed thee, that thou mightest be mine, wholly mine. I purchased for thee grace, that thou mightest grow. And I preserve thy life, that thou mayest live, not to thyself, but to him who died for thee. I have revealed the knowledge of thy Maker, and taught thee the way of redemption, that thou mightest adorn the doctrine of God thy Savior in all things. And wilt thou frustrate these purposes by thy sloth and negligence? Thou wilt do it, then, to thine own eternal injury; for the fearful and the unbelieving shall have their part, with the abominable, in the lake, which burneth with fire, that never shall be quenched

SERMON XXVI.

JEHOVAH, A KING.

I am a great King, saith the Lord of Hosts.—MALACHI I. 14.

WHEN God would inform his creatures what he is, he must employ language suited to their capacities; language, which they can understand. What he is himself indeed, or what constitutes his essence, no language can describe; and therefore even he cannot inform us. He can only say, I am what I am. But what he is to his creatures, and what relations he sustains with respect to them, may without difficulty be stated in language sufficiently intelligible. We all understand the import of the titles, father, master, and sovereign or king; and know something of the relations which these titles involve. With a view to inform us what he is to his creatures, God assumes by turns each of these titles, and represents himself as sustaining each of these relations. Sometimes he styles himself a father, sometimes a master, and sometimes, as in the passage before us, a king. I am a great king, saith the Lord of hosts.

Jehovah is a great king. This is evidently the truth taught in our text. And it is a most important truth, a truth richly fraught with instruction. My design is to illustrate briefly this truth, and then to state, at considerable length, some of the important consequences which result from it.

I. Jehovah is a king. A king, you are sensible, is the political head, or supreme ruler of a kingdom. Of kings, writers on the subject of royalty usually mention two kinds,—kings by right, and kings in fact. A king by right, is one who has a right to the throne, though he may not possess it. A king in fact, is one who actually possesses the throne, though he may have no right to it. But he alone, in whom both the right and the possession are united, can justly be considered as, in all respects, a king. Such a king, in the fullest and most extensive sense of the term, is Jehovah. In the first place, he is a king in fact. His kingdom is the whole created universe, and of this kingdom he is in actual and full possession. He is its sole and absolute sovereign; he has no partners, no counsellors, but governs every thing according to the counsel of his own will; doing his pleasure in the armies of heaven and among the inhabitants of the earth; nor can any one stay his hand, or say unto him, what doest thou? In passages far too numerous to mention particularly, the inspired writers represent him as exercising the most complete and uncontrollable authority over all his creatures, and ruling, with the same unlimited power, the kingdoms of nature, of providence, and of grace. If any deny that Jehovah thus governs the universe, they must suppose that it is governed by chance, that is, by nothing; for chance is only another word for nothing. But to suppose that the universe is governed by nothing is no less absurd than to suppose that it was created by nothing; and none but the fool, who says in his heart there is no God, will suppose either the one or the other.

In the second place, Jehovah is a king by right. He is not only the actual, but the rightful sovereign of the universe. He has the best of all possible titles to his kingdom; for he formed it of nothing, and constantly upholds every part of it. Nor can a single individual of the human race deny, with the least shadow of truth or propriety, that Jehovah is his rightful sovereign. It has ever been allowed, that, with some few immaterial exceptions, all who are born in the dominions of any monarch, are his rightful subjects, at least so long as they continue to reside in them. But all men were born in the dominions of Jehovah, for the earth is the Lord's and the fulness thereof. And they all reside in his dominions; nor can they possibly leave them; for his empire is, in the most unqualified sense, universal. Ascend into heaven, or make your bed in hell; fly to the East or to the West, to the planets, or to the fixed stars; still you are in the dominions of Jehovah no less than while you remain on the earth. Men cannot then cease to be his subjects, without ceasing to exist. It appears therefore, that he is, in every sense of the word, a king. And besides a kingdom and subjects, he possesses all the insignia of royalty. He has a throne; for heaven is his throne, and earth his footstool. He has a crown; for he is crowned with glory and honor and immortality. He has royal robes; for he is clothed with light and majesty as with a garment. Properly speaking indeed, he alone is a king, for earthly monarchs are no less accountable to him than are their meanest subjects. By him kings reign and princes decree justice; he is King of kings and Lord of lords. Even the thrones and dominions, the principalities and powers, in heavenly places, are but his ministering servants, who with humble reference and alacrity execute his will.

But this leads us to remark,

II. That Jehovah is a great King. He is so indeed in every conceivable, every possible respect; for, great is the Lord, and his greatness is unsearchable. Every thing that can with propriety be considered as constituting regal greatness, he possesses in a degree which places him at an immeasurable distance from all comparison, all competition. Do men, for instance, take the measure of a monarch's greatness from the extent of his dominions, and the number of his subjects? And what monarch can in this respect be compared with Jehovah? The extent of his dominions has never yet been measured, except by his own infinite mind; nor by any other mind have his subjects been numbered. We talk of great and mighty kingdoms on earth; but the whole earth is a mere speck in his empire, and all its inhabitants as nothing before him. Are the duration and stability of his empire considered as entering into the composition of a monarch's greatness? God is the King eternal. His kingdom is an everlasting kingdom. Earthly kingdoms rise and fall, as bubbles rise and burst on the surface of the troubled ocean; but his kingdom is a kingdom which cannot be moved, and like himself it has no end. He not only lives, but reigns, forever and ever. Do magnificent works and splendid enterprises render a monarch great? Among the gods, O Lord, there is none like thee, neither are there any works like thy works. Or, in fine, does the true greatness of a monarch consist in his intellectual and moral qualifications for the station which he fills? It is needless to remark that Jehovah possesses, in an infinite degree, all the intellectual and moral qualities which are necessary for a sovereign; for the sovereign of an empire immeasurable in extent and duration. Unlike earthly princes, he is constantly present in all parts of his dominions, extensive as they are; the past, the present and the future are alike under his eye, and he is as accessible to the least as to the greatest of his subjects. Indeed all the wisdom, goodness, justice and fortitude which either rulers or their subjects ever possessed, were derived from him; for he is the father of lights, from whom cometh down every good and perfect gift. All the intellectual and moral excellence in the universe is but a drop from this ocean; but a ray from this sun.

And now let mortals bring forward their monarchs, their conquerors, their heroes, their great ones, in whom they boast, and whose praises they are proud to sing; and compare them, if they dare, with the King mentioned in our text. Compare them, did I say? I recall the word. It is an insult to Jehovah to speak of comparing anything with him. But what are they in his presence? Mere puppets, shadows, nothings. Well might an apostle say, He that glorieth let him glory in the Lord. Well might the psalmist exclaim, It is better to trust in Jehovah than to put confidence in princes.

Having thus attempted to illustrate the assertion that Jehovah is a great King, I shall proceed to state some of the important consequences which result from the fact that he is so.

1. If God is a king, he is under obligations to make laws for his subjects. It will not, I presume, be denied that when he assumes any office he binds himself to perform all the duties of that office. Now it is the first and most indispensable duty of an absolute sovereign to make laws for his subjects. It is as much his duty to make laws, as it is their duty to obey them when made. Justice, benevolence, regard to the welfare of his kingdom, all require of him the performance of this duty. Indeed it seems impossible that an absolute sovereign should not make laws in some form or other; for as an intelligent being he must have a will; if he has a will he cannot but express it, and the expressions of an absolute sovereign's will are laws. We are therefore, I conceive, warranted to assert, that God could not avoid making laws for his creatures without ceasing to be their king. But he could not cease to be their king without re-

nouncing all connection with them; and he could not renounce all connection with them, without their ceasing to exist. So long therefore, as creatures continue to exist, it seems absolutely necessary in the very nature of things, that God, as their Creator and Sovereign should make laws for the regulation of their conduct. In no intelligible sense can he be a king; no intelligible meaning can we assign to the assertion in our text, unless he has actually made such laws.

2. If Jehovah is a king, he is under obligations, not only to make laws for his subjects, but to make the wisest and best laws possible. This, I presume, will not be denied. All will allow that a legislator ought to make the best laws in his power; not such laws as will please the violent or the fraudulent, but such as will most effectually secure the rights and promote the welfare of his obedient subjects. Such laws then, Jehovah, as the Sovereign and supreme Legislator of the universe, was bound to make for his rational creatures. It was incumbent on him to consult, not the private wishes and inclinations of individuals but the great interests of his whole kingdom. If he saw that these interests would be best secured by a law, commanding all his intelligent subjects to be perfectly holy; to love their Creator with all their hearts, and their fellow creatures as themselves, it was incumbent on him to make such a law. Such a law he has made, a law which all his obedient subjects declare to be holy and just and good; and with which none but the rebellious and wicked are dissatisfied.

3. If Jehovah is the great Sovereign of the universe, he was under obligations, not only to make such a law, but to annex some penalty to every violation of it. A law without a penalty annexed, is not a law; or, at least, it can in no respect answer the purpose of a law. Of this every person may be convinced in a moment, by endeavoring to conceive of a law without a penalty. I make a law, says a legislator, to this effect. But what, his subjects ask, will be the consequence if we transgress this law? Will any punishment be inflicted on us? None at all, is the reply. It must be obvious to every one that this would be a law in name only. It would be no more than counsel or advice. If then it was incumbent on God to make laws for his creatures, it was no less incumbent on him to annex a punishment to every violation of those laws. Hence also it became

necessary that he should provide a proper place for the infliction of this punishment, a prison in which the transgressors of this law might be confined, and thus prevented from doing further mischief. Such a prison, we are informed he has provided; its name is hell; no one who believes that God is a king can, consistently, entertain doubts of its existence; for who ever heard of a king that had no prison in his dominions?

4. If Jehovah, as the Sovereign of the universe, was bound to make laws for his creatures, and to annex a punishment to their violation, he is also bound to enforce those laws, and to inflict the threatened punishment on all who transgress them. Every consideration which proves that it is incumbent on him to make laws, equally proves that it is incumbent on him to enforce them, and of course to punish transgressors; for it is obvious that a law not enforced becomes a mere nullity, and that a threatened punishment not inflicted is an empty sound. But it is the duty of a sovereign not to suffer salutary laws to become a nullity. It is as much his duty to enforce them, as it was to make them. He must not bear the sword in vain, but be a terror to evil doers. Inspiration declares, He who justifieth the wicked and he who condemneth the just are both an abomination to the Lord. Hence it appears that to justify the wicked, or to exempt them from merited punishment, is in the sight of God, no less an act of injustice than to condemn the innocent. That it ought to be thus considered is obvious. Justice in a sovereign ruler consists in treating his subjects according to their deserts. He may therefore be guilty of injustice by treating them better than they deserve, as well as by treating them worse than they deserve. But God cannot act unjustly.—He cannot do that himself which he would regard as an abomination if done by an earthly monarch. He must then, as the sovereign of the universe, punish those who transgress his great law of love, and shut them up in the prison which he has prepared for that purpose; nor would he be either a just or a good king should he act otherwise. A proper attention to this truth will show us the fallacy of the most plausible objections which are urged by sinners against the scriptural doctrine of future punishment. They profess to regard God as a father only, and hence infer that since men are his children he will suffer none of them to be finally miserable. But it must be remembered

that if he is a father, he is also a king; and that as such he is under obligations to enforce the laws of his kingdom; and to punish, even though he may do it with reluctance, all who transgress them. When the king and father meet in one person, the feelings of the father must give way to the duties of the king. The page of history records at least one instance in which a father was called to sit in judgment on his own sons accused of conspiring against the state. The charge was fully proved. It became the duty of their father, as judge, to pronounce the sentence of the law. It was death, a painful and shameful death. He pronounced the sentence. He saw it executed; and all succeeding ages have applauded the inflexible regard to justice which enabled him to sacrifice parental affection to the public good. And shall man be more just than God? Shall that justice which was applauded in a human magistrate be stigmatized as cruelty, when displayed by the eternal sovereign of the universe?

5. From the fact that God is a king, taken in connection with the preceding remarks, we may learn the necessity of an atonement for sin. By an atonement we mean something which shall maintain the authority of God's law, secure the great interests of his kingdom and answer all the ends of government, no less effectually than the infliction of merited punishment upon transgressors. If there is any truth in the remarks which have been made, it undeniably follows, that without such an atonement God cannot consistently with justice or with his obligations as a sovereign, pardon a single offender. Agreeably an apostle informs us that God hath set forth Jesus Christ to be a propitiation through faith in his blood, that he might be just, and the justifier of him that believeth in Jesus; language, which most evidently intimates that were it not for this merciful provision, God could not be just in justifying or pardoning transgressors. And we may add, language which intimates with equal clearness, that notwithstanding this merciful provision he can justly pardon none who do not believe.

6. If Jehovah is a king, sin is treason and rebellion, and every impenitent sinner is a traitor and a rebel. These epithets have, I am aware, a harsh and unpleasant sound; and I should think it improper, or at least inexpedient to employ them, did not the language of inspiration warrant their use. But in many

passages of the inspired volume, sin is styled rebellion, and the words sinner and rebel are used as convertible terms. A moment's reflection will satisfy us that this language is perfectly just and proper. A rebel is one who disobeys and resists the authority of his rightful sovereign. Of this every impenitent sinner is guilty. He disobeys the great Sovereign of the universe. He neither loves God with all his heart, nor his neighbor as himself. By refusing to repent he practically justifies his disobedience, and in effect denies that Jehovah is his sovereign. He must then be regarded as guilty of rebellion. Equally obvious is it that he incurs the guilt of treason. Every subject is guilty of this offence who entertains and cherishes the known enemies of his prince. Now sin is the great enemy of Jehovah considered as a king. It directly tends to subvert his government. It strikes at the very foundations of his throne. Could it universally prevail, it would not leave him one loyal subject in the universe. This enemy to the King of kings every impenitent sinner entertains and cherishes in his heart. He is then guilty of treason against his sovereign. And it must be remembered that the criminality of treason and rebellion against God as far exceeds that of the same offences against earthly rulers, as he is superior to them. If these crimes when committed against earthly rulers, are justly punishable with death, the same crimes committed against the great Sovereign of the universe must surely deserve eternal death, the punishment denounced by his law upon transgressors. We may here add, that if every impenitent sinner is a rebel, every Christian is a pardoned rebel. He was once a sinner, an impenitent sinner, deeply involved in the guilt of rebellion against Jehovah. But repentance and remission of sins have been freely given him through that Savior in whom he believes. He ought then ever to feel and act in a corresponding manner. You can easily conceive how a rebel ought to feel, who, after his head was laid upon the block, had received a free pardon from his injured sovereign. You can conceive how penitent, how humble, how grateful, how entirely devoted to his prince's service he ever after ought to be. Much more then may such a temper and such conduct be expected of those whom God has pardoned. While they rejoice in what they are, they should never forget what they were. They should never forget that they were once rebels against the greatest and best of sovereigns, and that by his rich mercy and grace alone they have been rescued from everlasting burnings. Hence they should walk softly before God all their days in deep humility of soul; and while they approach him with confidence as a father, remember that he is also a great and glorious king, who must be worshipped with reverence and godly fear. It was for the purpose of enforcing this duty that he revealed himself as a king in the passage before us. The impious and covetous Jews, though expressly commanded to offer in sacrifice such animals only as were free from blemish, insulted him by bringing to his altar the lame and the blind. This insult he deeply resented, and he assigns his regal character as a reason why he would punish those who opposed it. Cursed be the deceiver who voweth and offereth to the Lord a corrupt thing; for I am a great king, and my name is dreadful, saith the Lord of Hosts. My Christian friends, how often do we, in consequence of the coldness, irreverence, and formality with which we approach the altar of God, offer him a corrupt thing! When he looks upon his worshipping assemblies, how often does he find reason to say as he said formerly, It is iniquity, even the solemn meeting. Permit me to express a hope that he will never find reason to say this of the solemn meetings which may be held in this house of prayer. Permit me to charge you, by his awful majesty, and to beseech you, by his tender mercies, never to forget what he is, and what you are, when you approach his throne of grace, and to remember that God is greatly to be feared in the assemblies of his saints; and to be had in reverence by all that are about him. A practical remembrance of his truth is indispensable to your religious interests; for it cannot be expected that God will visit a temple where he is treated with irreverence, and unless he favors you with his gracious visits, it will be in vain that his word is sent to you.

Omitting many other important inferences which might be drawn from this fruitful subject, I remark,

Lastly, If Jehovah is a king it seems requisite that he should have ambassadors. It is necessary that his will should be communicated to his subjects. It is necessary that his revolted subjects should be called upon to return to their allegiance. If a way has been opened in which they may escape the punishment which his law denounces upon transgressors, and regain his forfeited favor, it is necessary that way should be pointed out. For these purposes it seems desirable and proper that ambassadors should be employed. Agreeably, we are informed that God has seen fit to employ them. His inspired messengers the prophets and apostles, were ambassadors extraordinary. They had a commission and instructions with the broad seal of heaven affixed to them. Now then, said one of them, we are ambassadors for Christ. In an inferior sense, the ordinary ministers of the gospel are also his ambassadors, for the same passage which informs us that he gave prophets and apostles for the work of the ministry, informs us also that he gave pastors and teachers for the same important work. It is not indeed usual for earthly monarchs to send ambassadors to rebellious subjects, except when they are unable to reduce them to subjection by force. This however, the King of kings condescends to do. Though he is able with infinite ease to tread all his rebellious subjects in the dust, and even to dash them in pieces as a potter's vessel, he chooses rather to send them messages of mercy, to propose to them terms of peace. Nay, more, he beseeches them to accept of those terms. As though God did beseech you by us, says an apostle, we pray you in Christ's stead, be ye reconciled to God.

Application. You have heard, my fellow mortals, that God is a King. You have heard his own awful voice announcing the fact. You have listened to an imperfect description of his greatness. You have been reminded that you are all his subjects. Turn then, subjects of Jehovah, and contemplate your Sovereign. See him coming forth from that unapproachable light, in which he dwells, and disclosing his ineffable glories to your view, embodied in his works of creation, of providence, and of grace. See him seated on a throne of glory high and lifted up, while celestial thrones and dominions, principalities and powers veil their faces and bow in humble adoration before the thrice holy Lord of hosts. See his almighty arm, in which dwells everlasting strength, swaying the sceptre of uncontrolled dominion over all creatures and all worlds; while from his lips goes forth his eternal, immutable law, demanding perfect obedience from the whole intelligent universe. But hark! he speaks, he proclaims his name. O earth, earth, earth, listen to the voice of thy Creator and thy King. Let the universe keep silence, while he says, I am what I am. I am Jehovah; Jehovah God, merciful and gracious, long suffering and abundant in goodness and truth, keeping mercy for thousands, forgiving iniquity, transgression and sin; but will by no means clear the guilty. Mortals, you have seen, you have heard. Say then, is this your king? In fact and by right he most certainly is so. Whether you acknowledge him or not, he is so. But is he the sovereign of your choice, the monarch of your affection? This, this, my hearers, is the question; your answer to which determines your character and your destiny; for most sinful is the man, and most miserable is the man, who, while necessitated to be forever a subject of Jehovah, says in his heart, I will not have this being to reign over me; who cannot comply with the command which says, The Lord reigneth, let the earth rejoice. In order to answer the great question, you must ascertain whether you yield a cheerful obedience to his commands; for they only are his loyal, his willing subjects who cheerfully obey him. Know ye not, says an apostle, that to whom ye yield yourselves servants to obey, his servants ye are to whom ye obey? Say then, my hearers, do you thus obey him? Do you love him supremely? Have you repented of all your past transgressions of his law, and cordially embraced the gospel of his Son? Are you seeking first his kingdom and righteousness, and living a life of devotedness to his service, of self-denial, watchfulness and prayer? If so, you are his loyal subjects; nay more, his children, the children of a king, of the King of heaven; and if children, then heirs, heirs of God and joint heirs with Christ of his everlasting kingdom; and you shall not only live with him, but reign with him forever. Let the Christian then rejoice in his sovereign; let the children of Zion be joyful in their king. Nor let them fear that their joy will ever know a termination; for the Lord shall reign king forever, even thy God, O Zion, throughout all generations. But if Jehovah is not the chosen monarch of your affections; if his law is not written in your hearts; if you are not yielding a cordial obedience to its requirements; then you are not his loyal, willing subjects; you are still involved in the guilt of treason and rebellion against the King of kings; and unless you speedily submit and become reconciled to his government, he will be constrained to consider and to treat you as enemies. It will avail nothing to call in question his right to be your sovereign: You were all born in his dominions; you still reside in them, and in them you must forever continue to reside. It will avail nothing to think of resistance: He is almighty. It will avail nothing to think of flight or concealment: He is every where present, and he sees all things. It will avail nothing to make excuses for disobedience: He perfectly knows their fallacy. It will avail nothing to offer him pretended homage: He demands, and he reads the heart. Your only refuge, your only safety lies in submission, cordial, unreserved submission. To this, as his messengers, we now call and invite you. In his name, and as though God did beseech you by us, we pray you, in Christ's stead, be ye reconciled to God.

SERMON XXVII.

PRAYER FOR THE ADVANCEMENT OF CHRIST'S KINGDOM.

Thy kingdom come.—Matthew vi. 10.

The well known form of prayer, of which these words are a part, is in every respect worthy of its divine author. On this, as on all other occasions, he spoke as never man spake. In the compass of six short petitions, expressed in language at once simple and dignified, he has included every thing necessary for man to ask, or for God to bestow; and at the same time has shown us the spirit, which should animate our devotions; and indirectly, but impressively, taught us our duty to our Creator, to our fellow creatures, and to ourselves. Even the order, in which the several parts of this inimitable prayer are arranged, is full of meaning and instruction. By assigning the first place to those petitions, which relate to the honor of God's name, the advancement of his kingdom, and the accomplishment of his will, our Savior probably intended to teach us to prefer these objects to our own private interest; and to give them, as he invariably did, the first place in our exertions and desires. To this place indeed, they are pre-eminently entitled. They embrace at once the best interests of heaven and of earth—of God and of his creatures. So inseparably is their promotion connected with the highest happiness of our fallen race, that love to man and to ourselves as well as concern for the divine glory, must induce us to prefer it to every other object. Never do we display a temper more worthy of men and of Christians; never do we ask for such a profusion of blessings on ourselves and others, as when we sincerely pray that God's name may be hallowed, that his kingdom may come, and that his will may be done on earth as it is in heaven. These few words express or imply all that boundless benevolence can desire; and were it possible to personify benevolence, these are the words which she should be represented as uttering.

The kingdom, for the advancement of which we are here taught to pray, is that spiritual kingdom which Christ came to establish. It is styled the kingdom of God, and the kingdom of heaven, in allusion to a prediction of the prophet Daniel. In the days of these kings, says he, the God of heaven shall set up a kingdom, which shall never be destroyed; and the kingdom shall not be left to other people, but it shall break in pieces and consume all these kingdoms, and it shall stand forever. The nature and design of this kingdom, as well as its future extent, are largely and particularly described by the inspired writers. Our Savior has informed us, that it is not an external kingdom. The kingdom of God, says he, cometh not with observation; neither shall they say, Lo, here! or, lo, there! for behold, the kingdom of God is within you. He has also assured us, that his kingdom is not of this world; and we farther learn from one of his apostles that it consists in righteousness, peace and joy in the Holy Ghost. It is, therefore, a spiritual kingdom; its throne is erected in the souls of men; its laws are the benevolent precepts and doctrines of the gospel; and its subjects consist of those on whose hearts these laws are indelibly inscribed by the finger of God. When therefore we pray that this kingdom may come, we pray for the universal prevalence of Christianity; and for the removal, renovation, or destruction of every thing which tends to retard or limit its progress. We pray that the gospel of Christ may be known, believed, and obeyed throughout the world; that his religion may soon become the only religion of man; and that its glorious effects, righteousness, peace, and holy joy, may universally prevail.

The brief sketch which has been given of the nature of Christ's kingdom is intended to prepare the way for a consideration of the motives which should induce us to pray for its advancement. Some of these motives, as was unavoidable, have already been indirectly brought into view. They, however, deserve to be more fully and particularly stated.

The first motive, to which I request your attention, is the divine command. We ought to pray for the advancement of this kingdom, because God, our rightful Sovereign, requires it of us. He commands us to pray for the peace or prosperity of his church; to keep not silence and to give him no rest till he establish and make it a praise in the earth. Even that first and great command, Thou shalt love the Lord thy God with all thy heart, implicitly inculcates the same duty; and love to God will necessarily lead us to pray fervently and perseveringly for the advancement of his kingdom. I may add, that the form of prayer, a part of which we are considering, has all the force of a positive divine command; and that we violate both the letter and the spirit of this command, whenever we presume to address our Maker without praying that his kingdom may come. With the real subjects of his kingdom these commands will ever be the first and most prevailing motive; and did we all belong to the happy number, we should need no other motive to induce us to pray for its advancement. A plain thus saith the Lord, would influence us more powerfully than volumes of reasoning, or than all the motives which human ingenuity could devise.

A second motive, which should induce us to pray for the coming of God's kingdom is, that by this desirable event the divine glory will be greatly promoted. Though God's essential glory is ever the same, and incapable alike of diminution or increase, yet his declarative glory, or, in other words, his glory as displayed to his creatures, is intimately connected with the prosperity of his kingdom, and shines with a greater or less degree of lustre in proportion as that is increased or diminished. The sun is ever bright and luminous, yet its beams may by various causes be obscured or eclipsed, so as to render it apparently dark. So the glory of God, the Father of lights, the Sun of the universe, is often, as it were, shrouded in a veil, and his name is dishonored, rather than glorified, in the view of his intelligent creatures. While the world remains in its present state, this must inevitably continue to be the case. The glory of God is principally displayed in his word and in his works, especially in the great work of man's redemption. But of his word millions know nothing. Of the work of redemption they are equally ignorant; and even the glory of creating and preserving the world, is by them taken from Jehovah, and ascribed to some worthless idol, the work of their own hands. Thus as the apostle expresses it, men have changed the glory of the incorruptible God into an image made like to corruptible man, and to birds, and four footed beasts, and creeping things, and have worshipped and served the creature more than the Creator. How many myriads of intelligent, immortal beings are at this moment bowing to stocks and stones, in humble adoration, and giving that worship and glory to some impure or cruel idol, which is due to God alone—while he is comparatively left almost without a worshipper in his own world; a world which he has made, which he preserves and fills with his goodness. The apostle informs us, that when the heathen sacrifice to their idols, they in reality sacrifice to devils. Behold, then, millions of the human race robbing that God whom they ought to love and adore, of his glory, to give it to the prince of darkness, the great foe of God and man. Behold his kingdom extensive, and his subjects almost innumerable, while the kingdom of God is circumscribed within narrow limits, and his subjects are comparatively few. But this is not all, nor even the worst. Would to God that it were. But even in lands called Christian, what contempt is cast upon the ever blessed God! How openly and impiously is his sacred name profaned and blasphemed! How are his holy Sabbaths dishonored! How is his law of love trodden under foot! How is his word neglected and abused, and the gospel of his Son despised! How little do men thank God for his unspeakable gift! With what profane contempt do multitudes treat the ordinances and institutions of his religion! How little are the dispensations of his providence regarded! How much is ascribed to second causes, while the Great First Cause is overlooked and neglected! And to say no more, how many infidels, politely styled philosophers, have even attempted to rob him of the glory of creating the world, by ascribing its existence to fate or chance, while thousands wish them success in their impious endeavor! Now, my friends, who that feels as a creature of God ought to feel, who has the smallest portion of reverence or love for his Creator, can, without the utmost grief and indignation, see him thus dishonored, insulted, and robbed of his glory? Can a loyal subject hear, without emotion, his sovereign dishonored? Can an affectionate child see his father insulted without being moved? If then we are the subjects, and the children of God, how can we behold our Almighty Sovereign, our heavenly Father, thus insulted, dishonored, without feeling the strongest emotion of indignant sorrow, and fervently praying that his kingdom may come, and that the knowledge of his glory may fill the earth, even as the waters fill the seas? The psalmist informs us that, when the Lord shall build up Zion, that is, extend and establish his kingdom, the spiritual Zion, he shall appear in his glory; he will then appear peculiarly great and glorious in the view of all his creatures. Pray then, ye, who, like David, are grieved when men keep not God's law; ye, who, like Elijah, are jealous for the honor of the Lord of hosts, ye, who, like Moses, desire to see God's glory; pray and beseech him to come quickly, and build up his kingdom on earth.

The benefits which will result to mankind from the coming of God's kingdom, furnish another powerful motive to induce us to pray for its advancement. The number and value of these benefits, as they respect the present life, may in some measure be inferred from a consideration of the nature and tendency of Christ's kingdom. It essentially consists, as has already been observed, in righteousness, peace, and holy joy. That all these are much needed in our world, you need not be told. Wherever we turn our eyes, we find little but melancholy proofs of their absence, and of the dreadful prevalence of the opposite evils. Injustice, discord, and wretchedness everywhere abound. The whole earth is filled with violence. Mankind have long been at war with God; they can therefore have little peace either in themselves or with each other. If we contemplate them individually, we find them destitute of benevolence, actuated by base or malignant passions, a prey to care, anxiety and discontent, and often harassed by guilty fears and the reproaches of a guilty conscience. If we turn our attention to families and societies, we see the effects of these evil principles in the neglect of family religion, and of the education of youth; in frequent difficulties and dissensions; in the invention or circulation of false and scandalous reports; and in innumerable petty frauds and acts of injustice. If we extend our views to the nations of the earth we see the same evils operating on a larger scale. We see nation rising up against nation, and kingdom against kingdom; whole countries desolated; extensive cities wrapt in flames; millions of human beings dragged from their families and led forth as sheep appointed for the slaughter, and millions more fainting and dying under the calamities of war, or groaning in hopeless anguish under the iron rod of oppression, or the merciless scourge of slavery. Could we hope that the myriads of immortal souls, who are hurried out of time by these complicated evils, found an end to their miseries at death; could we hope that, after a life embittered by so many sufferings and sorrows, they entered into eternal rest, we might contemplate these scenes with emotions comparatively pleasing. But we cannot hope thus. The scriptures forbid it. They uniformly teach us that a life spent in sin unrepented of, is a prelude to an eternity of wretchedness and despair; and those who live without God in the world, are expressly said to have no hope. With respect to those, therefore, who die in this situation, we are compelled to believe, unless we renounce our belief in Christianity, that they lie down in everlasting sorrow.

From this imperfect sketch of the temporal evils which mankind are suffering, and of the far more to be dreaded evils to which they are exposed beyond the grave, it must, we conceive, be apparent that a remedy for these evils is the one thing needful. But this remedy is only to be found in the universal spread of the kingdom of Christ. Reason and philosophy have long been endeavoring to discover such a remedy, and their votaries have often boasted of their success. But their boasts have proved false, and their endeavors fruitless. They have not even succeeded in finding a remedy for the evils of time; much less for those of eternity. The world is still as full of vice and wretchedness as ever; and it still is and ever will be true, that there is salvation for sinful man in none but Christ; for there is no other name given under heaven among men whereby we must be saved. But while no other remedy can possibly be found, the universal extension of Christ's kingdom will prove a certain and effectual remedy for all the present and future evils, to which the race are exposed. This is undeniably evident from its very nature. Let righteousness, peace and joy in the Holy Ghost universally prevail, and sin and misery will be banished from the world. By righteousness is here intended a temper and conduct conformable to our Savior's rule of equity; whatsoever ye would that men should do to you, do ye even so to them. By peace is intended peace with God, peace of conscience, and peace with our fellow creatures. By joy in the Holy Ghost is intended those divine consolations which God imparts to his people, and which often cause them to rejoice, as the apostle expresses it, with a joy unspeakable and full of glory.

Now were these things universally prevalent, what evil could remain to infest the world. Universal righteousness would banish all those evils which spring from fraud, injustice, and oppression; all the crimes which now disturb the peace of society; all causes of contention between nations and individuals. Peace with God would deliver mankind from the heavy judgments and calamities with which he is now constrained to afflict them on account of their opposition to his authority; and from all the unhappiness occasioned by want of resignation, by anxiety, and discontent. Peace of conscience would entirely free them from that guilty fear, remorse, and dread of death, which now often embitter their choicest comforts. Peace with each other would destroy at once the innumerable evils which arise from public and private wars, disputes, and dissensions, while the consolations of the Holy Spirit would fill them with that peace which passeth all understanding, and give them, while on earth, a continual foretaste of the joys of heaven; toward which they will be constantly advancing, and at which they would at length arrive, there to live and reign throughout eternity with him in whose presence is fulness of joy, and at whose right hand are pleasures forevermore. Such, my friends, are the benefits which would result to mankind from the universal spread of Christ's kingdom, such the glorious effects which it naturally tends to produce. That the description here given of them is not exaggerated, is evident from the language of the inspired writers when speaking on the same subject. In his days, say they, referring to Christ, in his days shall the righteous flourish and abundance of peace so long as the sun and the moon endure. Men shall be blessed in him, and all nations shall call him blessed. The desert and the solitary place shall be glad, and the wilderness shall rejoice and blossom as the rose. Then shall the eyes of the blind be opened, and the ears of the deaf unstopped; the lame man shall leap as an hart, and the tongue of the dumb shall sing. Nation shall no more lift up sword against nation, but they shall beat their swords into ploughshares and their spears into pruning hooks, neither shall they learn war any more. The wolf also shall dwell with the lamb, and the leopard lie down with the kid, and the calf and the young lion together, and a little child shall lead them; and the lion shall eat straw like the ox, and the cow and the bear shall feed, and their young shall lie down together; and the sucking child shall play on the hole of the asp, and the weaned child shall put his hand on the serpent's den. Thus that paradisaical state, which was lost by the first Adam, shall be restored by the second; and love, peace, and happiness universally prevail under the mild reign of him who is emphatically the Prince of peace. Who then, that is not totally destitute of benevolence, can refrain from praying, most fervently praying, that Christ's kingdom may come? He who will not thus pray, and still more he, who opposes the spread of this kingdom, ought to be banished from it forever, and to be considered as the common enemy, fit only to be a subject of the prince of darkness.

But it will perhaps be asked, by some, is not this universal spread of Christ's kingdom a mere chimera; one of those delightful visions which a benevolent mind loves to form, but which will never be realized? No, my friends, it is no chimera; if it be a vision, it is one of the visions of the Almighty; and it shall be realized, more than realized; for he has said it and sworn it, who cannot lie.

We may therefore add, as another motive which should induce us to pray for the universal spread of Christ's kingdom, that he has promised, and even sworn by himself, that this event shall infallibly take place. All the prophetic writings abound with the most full, explicit, animating predictions of the approach of a glorious period when the stone that was cut out of the mountain without hands, shall fill the earth; and when all the kingdoms of this world shall become the kingdom of our Lord and Savior. The fulfilment of these predictions was in vision beheld by the prophet Daniel. I saw in the night visions, says he, and behold, one like unto the Son of man came with the clouds of heaven, and came near to the Ancient of days, and there was given unto him dominion, and glory, and a kingdom, that all people and nations and languages should serve him. We are further assured, that the Lord shall be King over all the earth; that there shall be one Lord and his name one; that all flesh shall see his glory, and that the knowledge of him shall fill the whole earth, even as the waters fill the seas, and that Christ shall reign till all enemies are put under his feet.

We have therefore all the encouragement to pray for the universal spread of Christ's kingdom, which the most positive divine assurances of an answer to our prayers can give. If it be said, since the event is certain, why should we pray for it? We answer, God has said that for all these blessings, he will be inquired of. Prayer is still no less necessary, than if no promises had been made; for the grand design of these promises is, not to supersede, but encourage prayer, and to afford a firm foundation on which faith may stand, and wrestle with God for their accomplishment. Shall we then despise the riches of his goodness? Shall we lose these invaluable benefits, by neglecting to pray for them? Shall we see God's arm extended, and his hand filled with blessings inestimable and innumerable, and yet neglect to employ the means which he prescribes, to bring them down in copious showers on ourselves, our posterity, and our fallen race? No: let us not thus imitate the fool into whose hands a price is put to get wisdom, but who has no heart to it. Rather let us firmly grasp the divine promises, and pray unceasingly that they may speedily be fulfilled in their fullest extent.

As a farther inducement to do this, permit me to remind you that the time allotted for their fulfilment is rapidly advancing, and that the present appearance of the world and the dispensations of providence plainly indicate that God is about to finish his work and cut it short in righteousness, and that the latter day of Christ's kingdom is beginning to dawn. God is now, agreeably to the predictions of the prophets, overturning the nations; and he will continue to overturn, and overturn, till he shall come whose right it is to reign. In almost all parts of the Christian world, he is exciting desires and producing exertions for the extension of his kingdom, which have never been equalled since the days of the apostles. So long since as the commencement of the last year [1812] translations of the scriptures had been begun, and in many instances completed, into upwards of fifty different languages and dialects; and from that time to the present the blessed work has been prosecuted with unabated, with constantly increasing zeal. At the same period forty-seven societies had been formed in England, Scotland, and Ireland, and seventeen more in this country, for the sole purpose of disseminating the sacred scriptures throughout the world. Since that period, the number of societies for this purpose in England has been nearly doubled, and by their exertions the word of life has been sent, and is still going to almost every part of the habitable globe. In aid of the same glorious cause, more than a hundred missionary societies, and societies for the diffusion of religious knowledge, and for the conversion of the Jews, have been formed, within a few years, in different parts of the Christian world; and they are now with united efforts endeavoring to diffuse the knowledge of God and extend the bounds of the Redeemer's kingdom. Notwithstanding the disappointments they have met with, and the various difficulties which they have been called to encounter, their endeavors have in very many instances been crowned with success, so that from the farthest parts of the earth we have heard songs of praise, ascribing glory to the righteous God. For all these unusual and unparalleled exertions it is impossible satisfactorily to account, without ascribing them to their true cause, the agency of God. He it is, and he alone, who has excited in the Christian world these strong desires and extraordinary endeavors to promote the extension of his kingdom. And since he has begun to work, we may confidently expect that he will finish what he has begun, and that the long expected time for the universal spread of his kingdom will soon arrive. Soon will the Jews be brought in with the fulness of the Gentiles; soon will Ethiopia stretch out her hands to God, and the isles of the southern ocean wait for his law. Soon will the enrapturing cry be heard, Alleluia! for the Lord God omnipotent reigneth; and the kingdoms of the world have become the kingdoms of our Lord and of his Christ. Even now the angel with the everlasting gospel is flying through the world, saying to every nation and people, Fear God, worship him who made heaven, and earth, and sea; for the hour of his judgment is come. He who sits on the throne is exclaiming Behold, I create all things new. I create new heavens, and a new earth wherein dwelleth righteousness. Prepare ye then the way of the Lord; make straight in the desert a high way for our God. Exalt the valleys, and level the hills, make the crooked ways straight, and the rough places plain, that the glory of the Lord may be revealed, and all flesh see it together. Since then the kingdom of Christ is thus comparatively nigh even at the door, let us seize the golden opportunity and improve the precious moments which yet remain, in fervently praying for its arrival.

As a farther motive to induce you to this, consider the happy effects which it will have upon yourselves. Nothing can more directly or more powerfully tend to destroy every baleful, malignant passion in your breasts, or promote in them the growth of divine benevolence, than frequently praying for the advancement of Christ's kingdom. When you leave your closets, after supplicating the Father of mercies with strong cries and tears to send the blessings attending his kingdom to all mankind, and to forgive all, not excepting your bitterest enemies, you will breathe the very spirit and temper of heaven; you will be transformed for a time into the image of Christ; you will feel that his kingdom is set up in your hearts, and that they are filled with righteousness, peace and joy in the Holy Ghost; an earnest of that heaven, at which you will then be sure of coming. On the other hand, nothing can more certainly prove that you are destitute of love to God, that you are not subjects of his kingdom, that you are not the disciples of Christ, than a habitual neglect of praying that his kingdom may come; nor can you, while guilty of this neglect, offer up a single acceptable petition for yourselves. If then you would not be considered and treated as the enemies of God; if you would possess a heavenly temper and obtain a full assurance of your title to heaven; if you would have your hearts filled with holy peace and joy, and taste the happiness of heaven before you arrive there, pray sincerely, fervently, and perseveringly, that God's kingdom may come.

Let us now, my friends, on the wings of faith, fly forward a few years, and contemplate the world under the mild reign of the Prince of Peace. Let us escape from the wars, the vices and miseries, which surround us, and visit the earth restored to its original state. See it no longer groaning under its Creator's curse; but rejoicing in his smiles. See it no longer producing briars and thorns, but bringing forth fruit in abundance for its almost innumerable inhabitants. See volcanoes forever extinguished, storms hushed to peace, the bolt of heaven deprived of its terrors, the earth no longer trembling and threatening to ingulph its inhabitants, and the air no longer wafting the seeds of pestilence and death. Walk through the villages, and behold the lion, the leopard and bear, grazing with domestic animals around the habitations of man. See children sporting near them, fearless of danger, or twining around their bodies the serpent now deprived of his sting. Walk through the cities, and behold every countenance bearing the traces of happiness and benevolence, and clothed with smiles indicative of the peace which reigns within.

That our prayers for this event may be acceptable to God, two things are indispensably necessary. The first is, that they be accompanied by corresponding exertions. If it is our duty to pray for the advancement of Christ's kingdom, it is no less our duty to do all in our power to promote it, to use all our influence in supporting its laws, and in bringing others to obey them, especially our families and friends; and when occasion requires, to contribute cheerfully to its propagation and support. He who refuses or neglects to do this, cannot sincerely pray that Christ's kingdom may come; nor can he even repeat our Lord's prayer, without incurring the guilt of formality and hypocrisy.

The second thing necessary to render our prayers for the advancement of Christ's kingdom sincere and acceptable is, that we become willing subjects of his kingdom ourselves. It is too evident to require proof, that none can sincerely desire others to submit to the sceptre of Christ, so long as they themselves refuse or neglect to obey him; nor can any present to him an acceptable petition, who do not unreservedly comply with his requisitions. Why call ye me Lord, Lord; and do not the things which I say? Are we, then, my friends, the willing subjects of Christ? This question may be easily answered: If any man, says the Apostle, be in Christ, he is a new creature. Verily, verily, says our Savior, except a man be born again, he cannot see the kingdom of God. If then, we are not new creatures, if we have not been born again, we are not, we cannot be, the subjects of Christ's kingdom. And it becomes us to remember that, if we are not his subjects, we must be his enemies; for he has himself said, He that is not with me is against me. But he is willing, he waits to be reconciled. He died for the express purpose of reconciling offending man to his offended God. Come then, my friends, if you have not already done it, come, and touch the golden sceptre of mercy, which he now holds out to you. Open wide your hearts, that the King of glory may come in, and write upon them his law of love, and set up his throne in your affections. Like the Philipians, first give your own selves to the Lord, and then your prayers and offerings will indeed be acceptable. You will find by experience, that Christ's kingdom is righteousness, peace, and joy; and as a reward for obeying and promoting his kingdom on earth, he will finally advance you to share his throne and kingdom in heaven, there to live and reign with him forever and ever.

SERMON XXVIII.

THE FULNESS OF GOD DWELLING IN CHRIST.

In him dwelleth all the fulness of the Godhead bodily.—COLOSSIANS II. 9.

THIS is asserted of Jesus Christ. It appears, at the first glance, to contain most important truth; truth which cannot but be interesting to all who wish to form just conceptions of our God and our Redeemer. Indeed, there are few passages in the inspired volume which would sooner arrest the attention and excite the inquiries of one who was reading it for the first time.

I. Let us endeavor to ascertain its import, that we may learn what it is designed to teach us.

In attempting this it is necessary to inquire what is meant by all the fulness of the Godhead. The original word, here rendered fulness, signifies that by which any thing is filled, completed, or made perfect. Thus when it is said, the earth is the Lord's and the fulness thereof; by the fulness of the earth is evidently meant, all those things with which the earth is filled or every thing which it contains. So by the fulness of the Godhead is meant, all that the Godhead contains, all the natural and moral attributes of Deity; every thing, in short, which renders the divine nature perfect and complete. This phrase then includes in its import the whole deity or divinity, with its attributes of infinity, eternity, immutability, omnipotence, omniscience, omnipresence, holiness, justice, goodness, mercy, faithfulness and truth. Should it be thought that the word fulness does not necessarily mean so much as this, yet it must, I think, be allowed, that all the fulness of the Godhead cannot mean any thing less; for if any one perfection or attribute of divinity be taken away, all the fulness of the Godhead would not remain. There would be something wanting. The divine nature would not be full; or in other words, perfect and complete. Wherever then all the fulness of the Godhead dwells, there every natural and moral attribute of divinity will be found.

Let us next inquire what is meant by the assertion, that all this fulness dwells in Christ. There are, in the original, two words which, in our translation, are rendered *to dwell.* The first literally signifies, to reside, as in a tent or tabernacle, and is used to denote a temporary residence. This word is used by St. John when he says, The word was made flesh, and dwelt among us; literally, resided among us, as in a tabernacle or temporary habitation. The other word signifies, to dwell as in a house, or fixed habitation, and is always used to signify a more permanent residence; because a house is permanent, compared with a tent. Now it is the latter word, the word that signifies a permanent residence, which is used in our text. The import of the assertion which it contains, then, is this: All the fulness of the Godhead resides in Jesus Christ, as in its permanent or fixed habitation.

It is further asserted that all the fulness of the Godhead dwells in him bodily. The word body is not unfrequently used by the inspired writers to signify what is real and substantial, in distinction from that which is shadowy, figurative, or typical. Thus an apostle, speaking of the rites and ceremonies of the Mosaic law, says, They are a shadow of good things to come, but the body, that is, the real substance, of which they are only shadows or types, is Christ. In a similar sense the word *bodily* appears to be used in our text. It signifies really or substantially, and teaches us that all the fulness of the Godhead dwells in Jesus Christ, not in a figurative or apparent, but in a real sense.

From the preceding examination of the several parts of our text, the import of the whole appears to be this: The whole Deity, with all its natural and moral attributes, actually resides in Jesus Christ, as a fixed or permanent habitation.

II. Let us inquire, whether this statement of the import of

our text corresponds with other parts of the inspired volume. A very slight examination will convince us that it does.

In the first place, we are taught in many passages that the Father and the Spirit dwell in Jesus Christ. Our Savior frequently declared that the Father dwelt in him, and added, He that hath seen me hath seen the Father. And the Spirit of God, the Spirit which inspired the Jewish prophets, is repeatedly said to be the Spirit of Christ. He is also represented as having the Spirit without measure, and as communicating the Spirit to others. Now the whole Godhead is included in the Father, the Son or Word, and the Holy Spirit. Wherever all these dwell, all the fulness of the Godhead must dwell. But we have seen that the Father and the Spirit dwell in Jesus Christ. And all allow that the Son or Word dwells in him. In him, therefore, the whole Godhead dwells.

In the second place, Jesus Christ is represented in many parts of the inspired volume as possessing and exercising all the perfections of Deity. We are informed that all things were made by him, that without him was not anything made that was made; that he upholds all things by the word of his power, and that all power in heaven and on earth is his. He must then be Almighty. We are informed that in him are hidden all the treasures of wisdom and knowledge, that he knows the Father, even as the Father knows him, and that he knows what is in man. Speaking of himself he says, all the churches shall know that I am he who searcheth the heart. He must then be omniscient. We are informed that he is with his ministers always to the end of the world, and that wherever two or three are assembled in his name he is in the midst of them. While residing on earth, he spoke of himself as being in heaven, and after he ascended to heaven he was represented as still being on earth. He must then be omnipresent. In fine, we are informed that he fills all things, that he filleth all in all, and that he is all in all. In him, of whom this is said, all the fulness of the Godhead or every natural and moral attribute of the Deity must surely dwell.

Having thus given a brief statement of the import of our text, and confirmed the truth of that statement by an appeal to other parts of revelation, I request your attention to some important inferences which naturally result from it.

1. If all the fulness of the Godhead dwells in Jesus Christ,

then in Jesus Christ alone can God be found. The scriptures inform us that mankind have, without a single exception, forsaken God, that they have all gone out of the way, have all gone astray like sheep, and turned every one to his own way, and that the way of peace they have not known. Having thus wandered from God, they have lost him, lost a knowledge of him, lost his image, lost his favor, so that they naturally live without God in the world. But they must return to him, they must find him again, or be lost forever; for he is the Father of lights, the Fountain of holiness and felicity. Agreeably, an apostle declares it to be the will of God that the sons of men should seek after him, if peradventure they may find him. Now if we wish to find a man who is always in one place, we must go to that place, go to his residence. It is vain to seek him or to expect to find him anywhere else. So, since the whole Godhead resides in Jesus Christ, as in a permanent habitation, we must repair to Jesus Christ, if we would find God. We shall in vain attempt to find him, to acquire a knowledge of him, or to gain his forfeited favor, if we seek him anywhere else. Thus the scripture, speaking of spiritual wisdom and understanding, or, in other words, of the knowledge of God says, Where shall it be found, and where is the place thereof? Man knoweth not its place, neither is it found in the land of the living. The depth saith, it is not in me; the sea saith, it is not with me. Where then is its place, seeing it is hid from the eyes of all living? God understandeth the why thereof, and he knoweth the place thereof. What he knows he has revealed to us. He has informed us, that it is all placed in Jesus Christ, that all the treasures of wisdom and knowledge are laid up in him. In him alone then can we find God. Accordingly he says, I am the way and the truth and the life. No man cometh to the Father but by me. No one knoweth the Father save the Son, and he to whom the Son will reveal him. Whosoever denieth the Son, the same hath not the Father. Let every man then, who would find a lost God, come without delay to Jesus Christ, in whom he dwells. In him, God is, if I may so express it, always at home. In him he will always be found. No where else will any find him. They may seek him in the works of creation; they may search for him in the dispensations of his providence; they may look for him in his word; but never will they find him, till they come to Jesus Christ; for even the scriptures, we are informed, make men wise unto salvation only through faith in Christ Jesus. But if we come to him, we shall be enabled to say with the primitive christians, God, who commanded the light to shine out of darkness, hath shined in our hearts, to give us the light of the knowledge of the glory of God in the face of Jesus Christ.

On hearing these remarks some will perhaps say, we do not understand what is meant by finding God. It is not easy to make an impenitent sinner understand what is meant by this expression, though it is perfectly understood by every real disciple of Christ. So far as it can be explained to others, I will, however, endeavor to explain it. To a careless, thoughtless sinner, God does not appear to be a present reality. He may assent to the fact that God is every where present, but he does not feel his presence, it does not appear real to him ; it does not affect him, it does not influence his conduct. He comes, perhaps, to the house of God on the Sabbath. He is told that God is here; but he does not perceive his presence. There is no weighty impression upon his spirits of a present God, none of that awe or reverence or godly fear which the presence of God ought to produce. He hears hymns sung in which strong emotions of admiration, gratitude and love to God are expressed; but he does neither feel such emotions himself, nor perceive any thing to excite them in others. He stands up to pray, but he perceives no being present to whom his prayers may be addressed. If he has been taught that prayer is a duty, he may perhaps enter his closet and attempt to pray. But he does not feel that God is present there to hear him. He speaks, as it were into the air, and his prayers, as such a person once expressed it, do not seem to rise above his head, do not appear to ascend to heaven. Should his conscience be awakened, and should he in consequence begin to feel that there is a God, and to cry for mercy, God appears to be at a great distance from him, and he cannot come near, cannot find any way in which to approach him. He cannot understand what the apostle meant when he said to christians, ye who were formerly afar off are now brought near by the blood of Christ. But let such a man come to Christ, in whom all the fulness of the Godhead dwells, and a great change will take place in his views and feelings. God will then be come to him a present and most interesting reality. Then he will perceive his presence every where, especially in his closet, and in places of public worship. His heart will glow with those emotions which are expressed in the songs of praise; his affections and desires will ascend to heaven with the public prayers, and in private devotion he will be able to say with the Psalmist, It is good for me to draw near to God; and instead of living as he once did, without God in the world, he will like the primitive saints walk with God.

2. If all the fulness of the Godhead dwelleth in Christ, then no man can obtain a portion of that fulness, except by applying to Christ. The truth of the inference is so obvious as scarcely to require either illustration or proof. Did all the light in the universe dwell in the sun, no man, it is evident, could obtain light except from the sun. Were all the water which exists in the world collected into one reservoir, no man, it is obvious, could obtain water without applying to that reservoir. Equally evident is it that since all the fulness of the Godhead dwells in Christ, no man can obtain a portion of that fulness without applying to Christ. This truth will appear exceedingly important and interesting to all who are aware of the fact, that unless we can obtain a portion of the fulness of God, we must pine in eternal want. The mercy which pardons sin, the divine light which illuminates the understanding, the grace which purifies the heart, the strength which resists temptation, overcomes the world, and endures to the end; the consolation which supports the soul under trials and afflictions; the triumphant faith, and the hope full of immortality, which are requisite to give victory over death, and all the everlasting joys and glories of heaven flow from the fulness of God, and no man can partake of them without partaking of that fulness. A participation of that fulness is then the one thing needful to every child of Adam; and better, infinitely better would it be for any one to be destitute of every thing else than to want this. Better would it be for us to be deprived of possessions, friends, reputation, health, sense and reason, than to lose forever this one thing needful. If any think that this is too strong language, I answer, it is not stronger language than the scriptures warrant us to use. They represent it as the greatest of all blessings to partake of this fulness; and the want of it as of all evils the most terrible. Addres-

sing those who were destitute of it, our Savior declares that they were poor, and miserable, and wretched, and blind, and naked. At the same time, he counsels them to come to him for a supply; thus intimating that from him alone they could obtain it. All his invitations speak the same language. When he stood and cried, If any man thirst, let him come unto me and drink; that is, if any man feels a want, let him come unto me and receive a supply, he plainly intimated that in him alone the water of life could be found, that by him alone human wants could be supplied. Well then, might an apostle exclaim respecting him, Neither is there salvation in any other.

3. From the fact that all the fulness of the Godhead resides in Jesus Christ, we may infer the necessity and the worth of that faith in him, on which the inspired writers lay so much stress. That you may have just views of this subject, look first at him. See in him an infinite, inexhaustible fulness of all spiritual blessings; a fulness of light sufficient to illuminate all minds; of mercy to pardon all sins; of grace to sanctify all hearts; of happiness to make all human beings forever blessed. Then turn and look at mankind. See them as they are described in the word of God, spiritually blind, sinful, guilty and wretched. Now what is necessary to banish all their evils, supply all their wants, and secure to them endless felicity? Is any thing, can any thing more be necessary, than to form such a channel of communication between them and Jesus Christ, that the fulness of the Godhead which dwells in him may flow out to them? If such a channel could be formed, would not this fulness of light, mercy, grace, and felicity pour itself into their souls till, in the language of an apostle, they were filled with all the fulness of God? My hearers, faith, faith in Christ, and faith alone does form such a channel of communication as this. This is the appointment of God. He has established such a constitution, that whenever any sinner begins to exercise faith in Christ, he shall begin to partake of that fulness which dwells in Christ, and the degree in which he partakes of this fulness, will be just in proportion to the strength of his faith. We may illustrate this truth by a reference to events which took place during his residence on earth. The whole multitude, we are informed, sought to touch him; for there went virtue out of him and healed them all. On another occasion, a diseased

female said, if I may but touch the hem of his garment, I shall be whole. She did touch it, and healing virtue instantly flowed into her enfeebled frame. In both these cases, it was the touch of faith which drew virtue from Christ. They touched him, because they believed, or had faith that there was in him virtue sufficient to heal their diseases. Agreeably, our Savior said to the patient last mentioned, Thy faith hath saved thee. Just so now, when a sinner, who feels that he is sick in soul, exercises faith in Christ, though he cannot, as then, manifest his faith by touching him, yet he finds that a spiritual healing virtue is imparted to him. He finds that his understanding is enlightened, that his sins are pardoned, that his wounded conscience is healed, that his heart is sanctified, and that peace and happiness, such as he never tasted or even conceived of before, are shed abroad within him. Hence an apostle informs us, that he who believeth on the Son of God hath the witness in himself, that is, the happy effects which result to him from believing, are a witness within that there is such a person as Jesus Christ, and that to believe in him is to partake of his fulness. These effects of faith are illustrated by our Savior himself in an address to his disciples. I, says he, am the vine, ye are the branches. This comparison he pursues at considerable length, and clearly teaches them, that by faith a union was formed between him and them, analogous to that which exists between a vine and its branches, and that as life and sap flow from the vine into every branch, so his fulness flows into the souls of all who believe in him. Hence an apostle, speaking of believers, says, Of his fulness have we all received. Well then, might St. Peter call faith in Christ, precious faith; for what can be more precious than that which forms an indissoluble union, and a free communication between a lost, needy, guilty sinner, and a Savior in whom dwells all the fulness of the Godhead. He who has this faith is incalculably rich, though he should possess nothing else, and he who has it not, is miserably poor, though he should possess all which the world can give; for

4. If all the fulness of the Godhead dwells in Jesus Christ, then he who is destitute of faith in Christ, or he who has never made a believing application to Christ, has no share in that fulness. His mind is not enlightened; his sins are not pardoned; his heart is not sanctified, he has no part in the kingdom

of heaven. It is written that, though he who believeth on the Son hath everlasting life, yet he who believeth not the Son is condemned already and shall not see life, but the wrath of God abideth on him. It is true that such a man may have many qualities which appear amiable and estimable in the view of men; his moral character may be fair, and he may possess the external form of religion. But he has not a particle of that fulness which dwells in Christ, and his doom is pronounced in those words of our Savior, From him that hath not, shall be taken away even that which he seemeth to have.

5. Does all the fulness of the Godhead dwell in Jesus Christ? Then all the spiritual wisdom, knowledge, holiness, and happiness which exist in the world, and all which are possessed by the spirits of just men made perfect in heaven, proceed from him. You cannot find either on earth or in heaven, a good man who does not derive all his goodness from Christ, or who will not humbly and gratefully acknowledge that he does so; one who will not say with St. Paul, I live, yet not I, but Christ liveth in me; and the life which I now live in the flesh, I live by faith in the Son of God; that is, my spiritual life is constantly supported by supplies which faith draws from him. And how amiable, how glorious, how worthy of all love, admiration, and praise, does our Savior appear in the view of these truths. See him containing in himself all the infinite fulness of Deity. See myriads of his believing disciples in all parts of the world daily, hourly, living upon this fulness, and drawing from him those supplies which are necessary to the promotion and advancement of religion within them. Every hour virtue flows out of him, to heal them all. Some of them are poor, some of them afflicted, some of them tempted, some of them sick, some of them dying; yet to all and to each, he imparts just what their situation requires. To each he says, My grace is sufficient for thee. And while he is thus imparting grace to many thousands on earth he is pouring a flood of glory and felicity into ten thousand times ten thousand of his servants in heaven, filling them to overflowing with all the fulness of God. And who can conceive the benevolence, the tenderness, the compassion, with which he looks down on his great family, and sees them all deriving life and nourishment from him! Must not the affectionate feelings with which he regards them, far

exceed in tenderness, in intensity, those with which a mother contemplates the infant to which she gives support? Can we disbelieve him, when he says to his church, Though a mother should forget her infant son, yet will not I forget thee? And if there is happiness in doing good, in communicating happiness, how exquisitely happy must our Savior be! If we should feel exquisite gratification in feeding a hundred famished orphans, what must he feel while he feeds so many thousands of once perishing immortal souls with the bread and water of life!

6. Does all the fulness of the Godhead dwell in Jesus Christ? How safe, how happy, how enviable then is the situation of those, who believe in him? They are inseparably united to one in whom all the fulness of the Godhead permanently dwells; a way of communication is opened by which this fulness will forever flow out to them. What more can they wish for, or conceive of? Well might our Savior say to one in this situation, I know thy poverty, but thou art rich: poor in thyself, but rich in me. My professing friends, if you are what you profess to be, this enviable situation is yours. If you would enjoy all its advantages, you must pray unceasingly for increasing faith, since the supplies which you obtain from the fulness of Christ will be in exact proportion to the strength and constancy of your faith. And if you wish your faith to be strong, you must look not at your own emptiness merely, but at his fulness; not at your poverty, but at his riches. You must contemplate him as he is exhibited in our text. You must endeavor to obtain enlarged views of what is meant by all the fulness of the Godhead. You must remember that he loves to impart it, that he has promised to impart it, that he cannot but impart it to all who believe in him; and that his language to every believer is, My grace is sufficient for thee, for my strength is made perfect in thy weakness. And remember too, that when you approach his table, if you come in a proper manner, you come to Christ himself; if you receive these sacramental symbols in a proper manner, you will receive Christ himself, and of course will receive a portion of that fulness which dwells in him. If you do this, you will know experimentally the truth of his declaration, My flesh is meat indeed, and my blood is drink indeed. He that eateth my flesh and drinketh my blood, dwelleth in me and I in him; and I will raise him up at the last day.

Finally, does all the fulness of the Godhead reside in Jesus Christ? then let every one present, who has not already done it, be persuaded to apply to him for a share of this fulness. That you may be induced to take this step, let me ask, is there nothing in all this fulness which you need? Have you all the spiritual wisdom and knowledge which you need? Have you no sins to be pardoned, no sinful propensities to be subdued, no temptations to overcome? Is your preparation for death, and for heaven completed? Have you provision made sufficient to supply your wants through eternity? If not, I invite you, in Christ's name, to come to him for a supply. I invite you to a friend, a brother, in whom all the fulness of the Godhead dwells, and who will take far more pleasure in imparting to you this fulness, than you will in receiving it; for he says himself, It is more blessed to give than to receive. But why do I invite you. Let me rather set before you his own invitation. Come unto me, all ye that labor and are heavy laden, and I will give you rest. If any man thirst, let him come unto me and drink. The Spirit and the bride say, Come; and let him that heareth say, Come; and let him that is athirst come; and whosoever will, let him come and take of the water of life freely.

SERMON XXIX.

CHRIST AND HIS HARBINGER COMPARED AND DISTINGUISHED.

I indeed baptize you with water unto repentance; but he that cometh after me is mightier than I; whose shoes I am not worthy to bear; he shall baptize you with the Holy Ghost and with fire; whose fan is in his hand and he will thoroughly purge his floor, and gather his wheat into the garner; but he will burn up the chaff with unquenchable fire.—MATTHEW III. 11, 12.

THESE words were uttered by John the Baptist with reference to Christ. On many accounts they richly deserve our attention. John was raised up, commissioned, and sent to be the harbinger of the Messiah. He came, as we are told by the apostle, to bear witness of Christ the true light, that through him all men might believe. He was the morning star which preceded and indicated the approach of the Sun of righteousness. In the language of the prophet who foretold his birth, he was the voice of one crying in the wilderness, Prepare ye the way of the Lord; make straight in the desert a high way for our God. In a word, as it was in those days customary for monarchs to be preceded by a herald, who proclaimed their titles, their approach, and the object of their coming, so Christ the Prince of Peace, the King of kings, and the Lord of lords was preceded by John the Baptist, as a herald, who announced his approach, and turned the attention of them that heard him from himself to his divine Master. This being the case, the testimony which he bore in favor of Christ is fully entitled to belief, and well deserves our attention. This testimony is principally contained in the passage before us. Let us then attentively consider the import of the passage, that we may learn from it what we are to believe respecting Christ.

The great object of John the Baptist, as it will be of all who preach Christ, appears to have been, to give his hearers high and exalted conceptions of the transcendent worth and dignity of his Master. With this view he describes in the most energetic language Christ's superiority. He that cometh after me is mightier than I, whose shoes I am not worthy to bear. To unloose a person's shoes or sandals and bear them after him, was considered by the Jews as the most servile and degrading of all menial employments, and fit only for the meanest slaves. Yet John considered the performance even of this service for Christ, as an honor of which he was utterly unworthy. If we would feel the full force of this language and learn what conception it should lead us to form of Christ, we must recollect by whom it was uttered. It was the language of no common person. It was uttered by one who was by birth one of the chief priests, an order of men who sustained a high rank in the estimation of the Jews. It was uttered by one whose appearance in the world had been repeatedly predicted for some hundreds of years, whose conception was foretold by an angel and accompanied by miracles; who was born contrary to the common course of nature; who was filled with the Holy Ghost from the moment of his birth, who was favored with the gift of prophecy, after that blessing had been withheld from the world almost four hundred years; who was admired, followed, and applauded, in an unexampled degree, by all classes of men from the least to the greatest, and who by many was thought to be the promised Messiah himself. To say all in a word, it was uttered by one of whom the Son of God, the faithful and true witness has said, he is a prophet, yea I say unto you, and more than a prophet; for among them that are born of women there has not risen a greater than John the Baptist. Yet even this illustrious personage, so favored, so honored, so distinguished, publicly declared himself, in the presence of his followers and admirers, not worthy to perform the most servile and degrading office for Christ. What then must he have thought of Christ? Did he view him only as a man, as some others have done? To have used such language respecting any man, would have been the grossest flattery; and surely he who boldly dared reprove the tyrannical Herod in his own court, would never have stooped to use flattering words respecting a fellow creature. Is it not then evident, or at least highly probable, that he must have regarded Christ as divine? The prophet who foretold his birth represents him as saying, Prepare ye the way of the Lord; make straight in the desert a highway for our God. Another prophet represents him as going before the face of the Lord to prepare his way. Now if these predictions were fulfilled, it is evident that John must have considered Christ, whose harbinger he was, and whose way he came to prepare, as the Lord God who was to come as a shepherd with a strong hand, whose reward was with him and his work before him. On this supposition alone can we rationally account for the manner in which he here speaks of Christ.

With a view to convince the people still farther of his inferiority to Christ, he next proceeded to show them how far the baptism administered by Christ would exceed his own. I indeed baptize with water unto repentance, but he that cometh after me shall baptize you with the Holy Ghost and with fire. Though the church of God had been favored, from its first establishment in the world, with the influences of the divine Spirit, yet under the Old Testament dispensation these influences were communicated, comparatively speaking, but in a small degree. Even after the coming of Christ, but previous to his death, we are told that the Holy Ghost was not yet given, because Jesus was not yet glorified; and our Savior himself represents the gift of the Spirit as inseparably connected with his ascension to heaven; If I go not away, the Comforter, the Spirit of truth, will not come; but if I depart, I will send him to you. Even the Old Testament prophets were inspired to predict this truth. Addressing Christ, as if he had already come, the psalmist says, Thou hast ascended up on high, thou hast received gifts for men, yea, for the rebellious also, that the Lord God might dwell among them. This prediction the apostle expressly applies to Christ, and teaches us that it was fulfilled at his ascension. It was also foretold by the prophet Isaiah that Christ should sprinkle many nations. This must refer, chiefly at least, to his baptizing them with the Holy

Ghost, of which John speaks in our text: for Christ personally baptized none with water. All these predictions were literally fulfilled at the day of pentecost, when there came from heaven a sound as of a mighty rushing wind, which filled the place where the disciples were assembled, and there appeared unto them cloven tongues, like as of fire, which sat upon each of them; and they were all filled with the Holy Ghost. Another similar instance of the fulfilment of these predictions was witnessed by St. Peter while preaching to Cornelius and his friends. The Holy Ghost, we are told, fell on all who heard him, and he remembered the word of the Lord, how he said, John indeed baptized with water, but ye shall be baptized with the Holy Ghost.

From the account of the baptism administered by our Savior, it is easy to see how far it was superior to the baptism of John. John baptized with water those who professed repentance for sin; but the baptism of the Holy Ghost produced in those to whom it was administered, repentance and faith and all the other fruits of the Spirit. John's baptism could only put away the filth of the flesh; but Christ's baptism by purifying the conscience from dead works, produced the answer of a good conscience toward God. He was the Lamb of God who taketh away the sin of the world, and whose blood cleanses from all sin. John's baptism could be applied to the body only; it could not reach the soul nor change the character of those who received it. But the baptism of the Spirit converted and purified the soul, and they who received it were washed and justified and sanctified in the name of the Lord Jesus and by the Spirit of our God, however vile and abandoned they had been before. In a word, John could at most confer only the sign; but Christ gave the thing signified in his baptism, a baptism with which John, like all others of our fallen race, needed to be baptized, as he himself ingenuously confessed. Hence it is easy to see how much this testimony of John tended to exalt our Savior in the opinion of his hearers. It was as if he had said to them, He who comes after me can cleanse the soul as easily as I can the body, he can confer the thing signified as easily as I can confer the sign; he can pour out the Holy Spirit upon you as easily as I can apply water. This expression, like the former, intimates with sufficient clearness that the Baptist believed

Christ to be God; for who but God can pour out upon men the Spirit of God? Who but he that possesses the Spirit can baptize sinners with the Spirit? As a farther confirmation of this truth, permit me to call your attention to another passage, which has not received the attention which it deserves. We are told by St. John that Jesus after his resurrection breathed upon his disciples, saying, Receive ye the Holy Spirit. That we may perceive the full force and meaning of this significant action, it is necessary to recollect that, in both the Hebrew and Greek languages, the same word signifies *spirit* and *breath*. Now if Christ could breathe the Spirit of God into the souls of his disciples, or, in other words, if the breath or spirit of Christ be the breath or spirit of God, then beyond all controversy Christ must be God; and by the action and the words which accompanied it, he most forcibly intimated that he was so.

Still farther to enlarge his hearers' conception of the infinite superiority of Christ above himself, the Baptist proceeds to state the character which Christ should sustain, and the works which he would perform; Whose fan is in his hand and he shall thoroughly purge his floor, and gather his wheat into the garner; but he will burn up the chaff with unquenchable fire. In these words there is an evident allusion to a prediction of the prophet Malachi, which foretells the coming both of Christ and of John his harbinger. Jehovah is there represented as saying, Behold I will send my messenger, and he shall prepare the way before me, and Jehovah whom ye seek shall come suddenly into his temple; even the angel of the covenant whom ye delight in. But who may abide the day of his coming, and who shall stand when he appeareth? For he shall sit as a refiner and purifier of silver; and he shall purify the sons of Levi and purge them as gold and silver, that they may offer unto the Lord an offering in righteousness. In a similar manner the Baptist here represents him as purifying the church, which he compares to a threshing floor, the true members of which are as wheat and the false as chaff. When he calls the church Christ's floor, he plainly intimates that while he was himself only a servant in the church, Christ is the head of the church; and when he represents him as separating the wheat from the chaff, and consigning the former to the garner and the latter to the fire, he evidently teaches us that he is the Judge of quick and dead, who will reward every one according to his works, and who is able with unerring certainty to distinguish characters, and search the heart. As if he had said to his hearers, You may easily deceive me by false pretences, and by professing a repentance which you do not feel, may induce me to baptize you. But you cannot thus deceive him who comes after me. He will discern with infinite ease your true characters, and will purify the floor of his church from all the chaff which I may ignorantly bring. Think not therefore that my baptism can avail any thing, unless you are baptized by him with the Holy Ghost as with a purifying fire. Such, my friends, in brief, is the import of the testimony borne by John the Baptist in favor of Christ; and we know that this testimony is true, because he was raised up, commissioned and inspired by the Holy Ghost, on purpose that he might bear testimony. To this testimony I have drawn your attention principally for the sake of many important reflections which it suggests, some of which it is now proposed to consider.

1. From this subject we may learn who are, and who are not the real preachers of the gospel, the true ministers of Jesus Christ. You need not be told that among those who claim this title great differences prevail. Some preach one thing, and some another; and it is of infinite importance, of no less importance than your everlasting happiness, that you should be able to ascertain who are right; who are the true guides whom God hath appointed to conduct you to heaven. By attending carefully to the conduct and character of John the Baptist, you may learn how to do this. We know that he was divinely commissioned and taught; for we are told that he was a man sent from God; that he was a prophet and more than a prophet. We may therefore conclude that all, who are sent of God to preach the gospel, will resemble John in their preaching. And what did he preach? I answer, he preached repentance toward God. I, indeed, says he, baptize you with water unto repentance. In those days, says the evangelist, came John the Baptist preaching and saying, repent, for the kingdom of heaven is at hand. This he preached to all classes and characters alike. He also taught his hearers to manifest their repentance by a corresponding life: Bring forth therefore fruits meet for repentance; for the axe is laid to the root of the trees; every tree that bringeth not forth good fruit is hewn down and cast

into the fire. But while he inculcated repentance, he taught his hearers not to trust to their penitence, nor to baptism, nor to any outward privileges for salvation, but to Christ alone. To exalt Christ and turn the attention of sinners to him, seems to have been the great object which he always kept in view. Especially was he careful to teach his disciples that he could not himself save them. All who came to him he sent to Christ. He seems to have considered himself only as a *waymark*, whose business it was to stand with extended finger and point to the Savior, crying, Behold the Lamb of God, who taketh away the sin of the world. He told the people that they should believe on him who should come after him, that is, on Christ Jesus. In all his preaching still he held up Christ to view as all in all, and like St. Paul testified to all his hearers of every description, repentance toward God and faith in our Lord Jesus Christ. That they might know how repentance and faith were to be obtained, he taught them the necessity of divine influence, of being baptized with the Holy Ghost as a purifying fire; and informed them that Christ alone could baptize them in this manner; that without this they would be no better than chaff, and as such would be burnt up with unquenchable fire. Thus he made Christ the whole subject matter of his preaching, and represented him as the beginning and ending, the author and finisher of our faith. Thus then will all preach who, like John, are sent of God. They will determine to know and to make known nothing but Jesus Christ and him crucified, and will teach all men to honor the Son even as they honor the Father. They will not seek their own glory but the glory of Christ. They will strive to draw disciples not to themselves but to him, and will feel no apprehension of exalting or teaching others to exalt him too highly. Nor will they fail to insist much on the necessity of divine influences, of being baptized with the Holy Ghost, saying with our Savior, Except a man be born of water and of the Spirit he cannot see the kingdom of God. In the second place, all true ministers of the gospel will imitate John in their temper and conduct; especially in his humility. Highly honored and distinguished as he was, you see how meanly he speaks of himself in comparison with Christ. He felt his need, as a sinner, of being baptized with his baptism. He felt unworthy to stoop down and loose the lachet of his shoes, a plain intimation of his readiness to cast himself and all that he possessed at his Savior's feet. Similar will be the temper of all who truly preach the gospel. They will learn of their Master to be meek and lowly in heart; and though, in consequence of his removal from this world, they cannot perform menial services for himself in person, yet they will be ready, in imitation of him who washed his disciples' feet, to perform the meanest and most laborious offices of kindness for the lowest of his followers. Such, my friends, will be the mode of preaching, such the temper and conduct of the true ministers of Christ. When you find such you may safely follow them, for they are the followers of John, of the apostles, and of Christ; and those who refuse to follow such guides would have refused to follow Christ and his apostles, had they lived in their day.

2. From this subject you may learn, not the characters of Christ's ministers only, but your own. That you may learn this, permit me to ask, what think ye of Christ? and what are your feelings toward him? What John thought and felt respecting him, you have already heard; and that his thoughts and feelings respecting him were such as they ought to be, we cannot doubt, since he was filled with the Holy Ghost even from his birth. Say then, my hearers, do your thoughts and feelings on this subject resemble his? That you are in any respect, unless it be in religious privileges, superior to the harbinger of Christ, you surely will not pretend. If then John felt unworthy to perform the meanest offices for Christ; if he thought, that to stoop down and loosen the Savior's shoe-latchet, when he appeared in the form of a servant, was an honor which he did not deserve; much more may we think and feel the same, now he is exalted to heaven in the form of God. Do you think and feel thus? That some of you do, I doubt not. You love, like Mary, to sit at Christ's feet and hear his word; or like the woman, who had been a sinner, to lie at his feet and wash them with the tears of unfeigned repentance, and feel unworthy even of this privilege. You feel that much has been forgiven you, and therefore you love much. Happy souls! you have chosen the good part, and it shall not be taken from you. But are there not many present, who do not feel thus? Your conduct, my hearers, compels us to fear that this is the case.

It proves that you are ashamed of Christ and of his words, ashamed to confess him before men. Many of you would, I fear, be ashamed to have your acquaintance suspect that you worship him in your closets; and many are evidently afraid or ashamed to worship him in your families. But why is this? You are sufficiently fond of what you consider as honorable. If then you felt as did the Baptist, if you thought it would be an unmerited honor to perform the most servile offices for Christ, you would certainly feel it a much greater honor to be allowed to address him in prayer, to be enrolled among his followers and friends, and to commune with him at his table. God forbid, you would exclaim, that I should glory save in the cross of my Lord Jesus Christ. But since you disclaim this cause of glorying, since you refuse to accept the honors which Christ offers, we must conclude that your views and feelings respecting the Savior are dissimilar to those of John the Baptist, or in other words, that they are entirely wrong.

3. Did Christ come to baptize with the Holy Ghost and with fire? Then surely, my friends, it becomes you all to inquire whether you have ever been baptized by him in this manner. The importance of this inquiry will fully appear, if you consider our Savior's words to St. Peter, If I wash thee not, thou hast no part with me; i. e. If thou art not baptized with my baptism, the baptism of the Holy Ghost, and sprinkled with the blood of sprinkling, which cleanses from all sin, thou hast no share in the blessings which I bestow. Say then, my friends, has the Savior baptized you in this manner? Have the influences of the Holy Spirit, like a penetrating, purifying fire, melted your once stony hearts, purified them from the dross of sin, caused them to glow with love to God and man, and prepared them to receive the impress of your Savior's image? Has the Spirit of truth taught you to know the truth? Has the Spirit of adoption taught you to cry, Abba Father, with the feelings of a child? Has the Spirit of grace and supplication, who, we are told, helps the infirmities of Christ's people in prayer, taught you to pray? Are you led by the Spirit of God as, we are told, all the children of God are? Do you find in yourselves those dispositions which compose the fruits of the Spirit, such as love, joy, peace, long suffering, meekness, goodness, faith, and temperance? If so, you have indeed been baptized with the Holy

Ghost as with fire. Christ has washed you, and you have a share in all his blessings. But if not, you have no part nor lot in the matter. You have not the Spirit of Christ, and therefore, as the apostle asserts, you are none of his. You have received the grace of God in vain, and Christ has profited you nothing. Whether in the church of Christ or not, you are no better than chaff; and as such you will, unless speedy repentance and faith prevent, be burnt up with unquenchable fire.

4. From this subject, my Christian friends, we may learn how to estimate the favors which we receive from our Savior's condescending love. John, than whom a greater was never born of woman, thought it would be too great an honor for him to perform the most menial service for Christ. What then ought we to think of being admitted to his church and table; of being called, not his servants, but his friends; of enjoying communion with him as members of his body, and of sharing as fellow heirs with him in the heavenly inheritance! My friends, did we realize, like John, the infinite dignity of him who confers on us these favors, we should be continually in a transport of gratitude and praise; and the love of Christ would constrain us, as it did the apostle, to live not unto ourselves, but unto him who died for us.

To conclude, is Christ's fan in his hand, is he determined thoroughly to purge his floor, and to burn up the chaff with unquenchable fire? Alas! then, for those who are at ease in Zion; for those false professors who are empty, and light, and worthless as chaff. It is true that for a time, the chaff is of use. It serves to shelter, protect, and ripen the grain, while it remains in the field. But a separating time must come; the chaff is not for the garner, where it would be worse than useless. So wicked men and false professors may, for a time, be useful to the church in various ways, while it remains in the field of this world. But in heaven they will be of no use. To heaven, therefore, they shall never come. Their doom, their portion is unquenchable fire. My friends, I cannot without trembling think of the day, when this separation is to take place, when this church and congregation will be visited with their final reward. I tremble to think how many of you I shall miss in heaven, should I ever arrive there. How many whom I have heard singing the songs of Zion in this house, I shall

48

never hear there; how many with whom I have here sat down at Christ's table, I shall look for in vain at his table above. Then not one hypocrite, not one particle of chaff will be left in this church, or in that part of this assembly which will be blessed with a place at God's right hand. This numerous assembly now resembles a fair and flourishing field; but when death cuts us down, when the wheat and chaff are separated, when the last tempest arises to drive the latter into the fire, how much will your numbers be diminished, how many of my flock shall I lose forever!

SERMON XXX.

MAN IN HIS ORIGINAL, AND IN HIS LAPSED STATE.

Lo, this only have I found, that God hath made man upright; but they have sought out many inventions.—ECCLESIASTES VII. 29.

I NEED not inform those of you who are acquainted with the contents of scripture, that in this book Solomon has recorded the result of numerous trials and experiments which he had made in searching after happiness and inquiring after truth. His success in these pursuits does not appear to have been very flattering. After making a fair trial, whether any or all worldly objects could afford happiness, he found nothing but vanity and vexation of spirit. Nor could he boast of much greater success in his inquiries after truth; I said I will be wise, but it was far from me. I applied my heart to know, and to search, and to seek out wisdom and the reason of things, and to know the wickedness of folly, even of foolishness and madness. But, here again, he found himself entangled and perplexed by innumerable questions which he could not answer, and difficulties which he could not solve; so that at last he was obliged to sit down content with the discovery of one truth; a truth however of great importance; a truth indeed, which if rightly understood, will go far to elucidate most of the religious questions by which men are perplexed, and respecting which they are divided in opinion; Lo, this only have I found, that God made man upright; but they have sought out many inventions.

This passage, which contains the result of the wise man's inquiries, and the sum of his discoveries, includes two propositions:

I. God made man upright.

II. Men have sought out many inventions.

To illustrate and establish these two propositions, is my present design.

I. God made man upright. This assertion evidently refers to the nature of man as he was originally created. In other words, it refers to our first parents, the progenitors of mankind; for we are informed in the account given us of the creation, that God created man in his own image, after his own likeness; and that, after the work of creation was finished, God saw that all was very good. Man then, at his creation, was not only good, but very good, perfectly good. He was, as one observes, a miniature picture of his Maker; for he was made in the image, and after the likeness of the holy God. These passages evidently teach the same truth which is contained in our text, that mankind, or human nature was originally made upright.

Let us consider more particularly the import of this term. The words, upright and righteous, literally signify agreeable, or conformable to rule. Our text then teaches us that man was made in a state of perfect conformity to some rule. If it is asked what rule? I answer, the law of God, for this is the only perfect, immutable and eternal rule to which God requires his creatures to be conformed, and in conformity to which, rectitude or uprightness consists. I say that this is a perfect, eternal and immutable rule; for we are assured that the law of God is perfect; that it is holy, just and good; and that though heaven and earth pass away, one jot or one tittle shall in no wise pass from it, till all be fulfilled. Man then was created in a state of perfect conformity to the law of God. If it be asked in what this state of conformity consists, or what it implies; I answer, it implies the possession of an understanding perfectly acquainted with the law; of a memory which perfectly retains all its precepts; of a conscience which always faithfully applies it; of a heart which perfectly loves it; and a will perfectly obedient and submissive to its authority; and of an imagination which presents to the mind no images, but such as ought to be entertained. If either of these be wanting, man cannot be perfectly upright, or, in other words, perfectly conformed to the divine law. This assertion it will be necessary to illustrate and prove more particularly.

1. A state of perfect conformity to the divine law implies the possession of an understanding perfectly acquainted with that law. This, I conceive, is too evident to be denied; since no being can act in conformity to a law, or regulate his conduct by a law, with which he is not acquainted. Man then, at his creation, was endued with such an understanding. In the language of Scripture, the divine law was put in his mind. He was not like St. Paul, alive without the law, but alive with the law. He was perfectly acquainted both with the letter and the spirit of it; and saw with the greatest clearness its nature, spirituality, strictness, and extent; so that the path of duty lay, in all cases, as plainly before the eye of his mind, as the path from this house to our habitations ever lay before our bodily eyes. In a word, he so perfectly understood what was required of him, and had such a perfect knowledge of truth and falsehood, of right and wrong, that it was impossible for him, while he remained in his original state, ever to transgress ignorantly, or by mistake. Agreeably, we find knowledge expressly mentioned by the inspired writers as one thing in which the image of God, that image in which man was created, consists.

2. In the next place, a state of perfect uprightness, or conformity to the divine law, implies a memory which faithfully retains all its precepts. The necessity of such a memory is obvious. We cannot regulate our conduct by a law not remembered, any more than by a law which does not exist. Just so far as any of its precepts are forgotten, they must cease to affect us. Memory is the storehouse of the mind, in which all its treasures are laid up; and when any thing fades out of the memory, it no longer exists in the mind. Man then, was originally created with a memory, which faithfully retained every jot and tittle of the divine law, as wax retains the impression of a seal; so that every precept was ready at hand to direct his conduct, on all occasions, and in all circumstances. Of course, while he remained as God created him, it was impossible that he should ever transgress the law through forgetfulness.

3. In the third place, a state of perfect conformity to the divine law implies a conscience which always faithfully applies it,

As we have of late repeatedly reminded you, the office of conscience is to apply to our conduct the rule which is given it; and to pass sentence upon us according to that rule. The rule given to man at his creation, was the divine law, and as he perfectly understood and remembered this law, his conscience was ever guided by an infallible rule; and this rule it was always ready to apply. Memory gave her the words, in which the rule was expressed; and understanding gave the exact meaning of those words, so that she could never pronounce an erroneous sentence, never lead man to think, as St. Paul afterwards did before his conversion, that he was verily doing God service when in reality he was violating his commands. Nor did conscience ever slumber or lose any portion of her quick sensibility to right and wrong, but was ever awake, susceptible, and active; so that man always found her saying, as a voice within him, This is the way, walk thou in it. And as man, while he retained his original character, always perfectly complied with her admonitions, conscience, of course, always approved his conduct. Their constant language was, Well done, good and faithful servant; and as her voice was the voice of God, so her approving sentence was sanctioned by the power of God, and spoke peace to the soul with all his authority and energy. Man, therefore, then possessed in a perfect degree peace of conscience. He had, in the fullest sense of the words, a conscience void of offence; a conscience which was never offended, and which did not offend.

4. In the fourth place, a state of perfect conformity to the divine law implies a heart which perfectly loves that law. This is even more necessary than any thing which has yet been mentioned. Indeed, it is absolutely indispensable: for though the understanding were perfectly acquainted with the law; though the memory perfectly retained, and conscience ever faithfully applied it; yet if the heart did not love its precepts, and love to obey them, they would not be obeyed; for the heart, or in other words, the affections and inclinations, is the ruling faculty of the soul, and will sooner or later subdue and lead captive all the other faculties. Besides, as the law is fulfilled by love, as it principally requires love, it is evident that where there is no love, there can be no real obedience to any of its requirements. Man then, was created with a heart, which perfectly loved the divine law, and which was perfectly inclined

to obey. His inclinations perfectly coincided with his duty. He not only walked in the path of duty, but loved to walk in it, and proposed it to others. That he was so, is farther evident from the fact, that he was created in the image of God, for God is love, holy love; and therefore an essential part of his image, in which man was created, must consist in love. God also loves his own law; for it is a transcript of his mind, an expression of his will; and, of course, since man was made in the likeness of God, he must have loved his law. In a word, the divine law was written in his heart by the finger of God, as it afterwards was upon the tables of stone; so that, while man retained the character which God gave him, he could never transgress the law by choice or design.

5. In the fifth place, a state of perfect conformity to the law of God, implies a will perfectly obedient and submissive to that law; or, in other words, to the divine government and authority. This, I conceive, is too evident to require proof; for a rebellious, stubborn will, is utterly incompatible with conformity to the law of God. A perfectly obedient and submissive will, then, man originally possessed. His will was swallowed up in the will of God, following just as the shadow follows the body. This resulted as a necessary consequence from the holy love to God's law which reigned in his heart; for the will is the servant of the heart, and follows where the heart leads. The understanding, which is the eye of the mind, discovers objects with the consequences of pursuing or avoiding them; the heart chooses or refuses those objects; and then the will resolves either to pursue or avoid them, according to the inclination of the heart. So long then, as man's understanding was perfectly clear, and his heart perfectly right, his will could not but be perfectly obedient and submissive to the law of God.

6. There still remains one faculty possessed by man, which it is necessary to consider, viz. that which is usually called the imagination. Whether this faculty is possessed by spirits in a disembodied state, may be doubted. It seems probable that it belongs exclusively neither to the soul nor to the body, but that it results from the union of both. It is that faculty by which the images or ideas of absent sensible objects are presented to the mind. I say the images of sensible objects; for intellectual objects, such as truth, for instance, are perceived by

the understanding; and I say of absent sensible objects, for when such objects are present with us, they are perceived by our senses. Now it may be made to appear evident, that such a faculty was necessary for man in his present situation. He is an inhabitant of one world, destined after a short residence here, to be removed to another. Now the world to which he must remove, differs so widely from this, that in consequence of the imperfection of language many of its objects cannot be described or presented to our minds, except by the assistance of figures and comparisons drawn from the sensible objects around us. It was therefore necessary that we should be endued with a faculty of perceiving these figures and comparisons, and of forming by their assistance some images or conceptions of heavenly and eternal objects. It was doubtless for this reason that God gave us the faculty which we call imagination; and when man left the forming hand of his Maker, this faculty, like the others which we have mentioned, was entirely free from moral imperfection. Instead of filling the mind, as it now does, with vain thoughts, waking dreams, and worthless or sinful fancies, it presented nothing but holy images of spiritual and heavenly objects. In every object which met man's senses, his pure imagination enabled him to discover some striking illustration of important truths, some analogical resemblance to those things that eye hath not seen, nor ear heard, which God has prepared for them that love him. A striking instance of the manner in which a holy imagination operates, we have in the life of our Savior. To him the whole world was a Bible, and every object a text, from which he drew the most convincing arguments, the most instructive lessons, the most striking illustration of divine truth. Such was the imagination of man, and such its employment, while he retained his original character.

Thus have I separately considered the several faculties of the human soul, and attempted to show that they were all made at first upright, or in a state of perfect conformity to the divine law. And a little reflection will convince us that, if either of these faculties had been imperfect, man could not have been made upright, or created in the image and after the likeness of God. If he had not clearly understood the law, or had not perfectly remembered it, or faithfully applied it, or cordially loved it, or willingly obeyed it, or if his imagination had presented vain, impure, or sinful images to the mind;—in either of these cases, he would have been imperfect, or not upright, and God would have been chargable with the imperfection; nor could it have been said with truth, that all his works were very good. It may perhaps be expected that I should now proceed to say something of the human body, with its appetites and propensities; but this is needless. The body is only the habitation of the soul, and its members only the instruments by which the soul acts on surrounding sensible objects. In itself, without the soul, it is nothing but a little mass of organized dust, incapable of doing either good or evil. It is the soul, the inhabitant within, which gives a character to its motions; and if the soul be perfectly holy, its habitation must be perfectly pure. It may, however, be proper to remark, that the appetites of the body were originally, not as they now are, disorderly, craving, and excessive in their desires, but were perfectly under the guidance and control of the mind and desired nothing more than the divine law allowed, and the welfare of man required. Such then was man at his creation, sanctified throughout in spirit, soul, and body, perfect in that image of God which consists in knowledge, righteousness, and true holiness, But,

II. Though God made man thus upright, they have sought out many inventions. The disjunctive particle, with which the latter clause of our text is introduced, intimates that the royal preacher here means sinful inventions, or inventions contrary to that uprightness, that state of conformity to the divine law, in which man was created. That this must have been his meaning, is farther evident from many other inspired passages in which this truth is taught. Thus we are told, that men have all gone astray, like sheep, and turned every one to his own way; that when the Lord looked down from heaven on the children of men, to see if there were any that did understand or seek after him, he saw that they had all gone out of the way, that they had together become filthy, so that there was none righteous or upright, none that did good, no not one. These expressions teach us, not only that man is now out of the way of righteousness, but that he was originally in it; for otherwise it could not with propriety be said that he had turned or gone out of it. Similar therefore must be the meaning of the wise man, when he says, men have sought out many inventions.

That is, first, they have sought out or invented many new ways in which to walk, forsaking the good old way in which God originally placed them. Of this you may be convinced by looking a moment at the present and past situation of mankind, and considering the almost innumerable foolish, sinful ways in which men seek for happiness, and the various forms of false religion which have prevailed, and which still prevail in the world. While the way of truth and uprightness is always one and the same, the new and false ways which men have invented are numerous and continually changing.

In the next place, men have forsaken the one living and true God, in whom they live, and move, and are, and sought out or invented innumerable false gods and created idols, to which they give that homage and attention which are due to him alone. To use his own language, they have forsaken him, the Fountain of living waters, and hewn out for themselves broken cisterns which can hold no water. When they knew God, says the apostle, they glorified him not as God, neither were thankful, but became vain in their imaginations, and their foolish hearts were darkened; so that they changed the truth of God into a lie, and worshipped and served the creature more than the Creator, who is blessed forever. Of similar conduct we, my friends, are in reality guilty; for, though we do not bow down to false gods of wood and stone, we have all set up idols in our hearts; we all love and serve the creature, more than the Creator; we all take pride in some of those things, the glory of which God has resolved to stain; and are all more or less fascinated and bewitched by the innumerable inventions of luxury and art which men have sought out, and which the world places before us to draw off our hearts from God.

In the third place, men have ceased to be conformed to the divine law, and have sought out many other rules, rules more agreeable to their present sinful inclinations, by which to regulate and try their conduct. How numerous and how various are these rules, no one who is acquainted with mankind need be informed. Some adopt for this purpose the laws of their country; others the opinion of some human teacher; while a third and more numerous class govern themselves by the maxims which pass currently in the society of which they happen to be members. Thus in various ways men measure themselves by themselves, and compare themselves among themselves, and therefore are not wise; for while they follow these rules of human invention, they have lost all that uprightness, that conformity to the divine law, which has been described. For instance, their understandings are so blinded by sinful prejudices and inclinations, that they have lost the knowledge of the divine law. They are all, like St. Paul before his conversion, alive without the law; nor can they be made by mere human teaching to know any thing of its nature, spirituality and extent. Agreeably, we are told that their understandings are darkened, being alienated from the life of God, through the ignorance that is in them because of the blindness of their hearts.

And as men do not now understand, so neither do they remember the law of God. They retain indeed with care, many things which they ought to forget; but are prone to forget what they ought to remember. How many are there among us, who have heard the word of God inculcated from their childhood, who pass whole days without recollecting one of its precepts, or even without reflecting that God has given them a law for the regulation of their conduct. Hence men are represented as not liking to retain God in their knowledge and as saying to the Almighty, Depart from us, for we desire not the knowledge of thy ways. Hence too the wicked are described as those who forget God; and hence Paul exhorts the Hebrews to give the more earnest heed to the truths they had heard, lest at any time they should let them slip,—an exhortation which plainly intimates that we are exceedingly prone to suffer the truth to slip out of our minds. That we are so, and that our memories are exceedingly depraved, every one must be convinced, who will reflect how much more easily he retains an idle tale or slanderous report than the truth of God's word; and how much sooner he forgets the mercies he has received from God, than the injuries which he receives from men. The conscience also shares in these malignant effects of sin. No longer does she faithfully apply the law of God to our conduct, or pronounce sentence according to its rules. Indeed, it is impossible that she should; for if men neither understand the nature, nor remember the precepts of the divine law, how is it possible that conscience should apply it to our conduct. It is a rule of which she now knows nothing. She judges according to the rule which is put into her hands, and we have already observed that men invent or seek out false rules for her use. Besides, in consequence of sin, she has lost much of her sensibility, and is prone to slumber, so that nothing disturbs her but crimes of the first magnitude, and nothing can awaken her but the Spirit of God. Hence St. Paul, speaking of unbelievers, says, even their mind and conscience is defiled; and of others he says, that their consciences are seared as with an hot iron. Nor has the heart of man escaped the contagion of sin. Indeed, this is the first part affected by it; for while man's heart loves the law, he will always understand, remember, and apply it. It is only because men have ceased to love God's law, that they now misunderstand and forget it. It is the sinfulness of the heart alone, which darkens the understanding, renders the memory treacherous, and the conscience insensible and unfaithful. A sinful heart cannot endure an understanding which perceives, a memory which retains, and a conscience which applies the law of God; for these faculties would then be at constant war with the heart, opposing and condemning all her sinful inclinations. A sinful heart loves darkness for the same reason with the midnight thief. Agreeably, our Savior informs us that every one that doeth evil hateth the light neither cometh to the light, lest his deeds should be reproved. This then is the reason why men do not like to retain God in their knowledge. Set the heart right, let it be again reconciled to God and to his law, and all the other faculties will be rectified at once. But alas, the heart will not be set right; for it has become deceitful above all things, and desperately wicked. In this depravity of man's heart, the will also shares of course. It has become rebellious, like an iron sinew; for the carnal mind is enmity against God, and not subject to his law. Hence the language of the unsubdued will is, I will not have God to reign over me; not his will, but mine be done.

Would time permit, I might proceed to show how the imagination is depraved by the loss of its original conformity to the divine law; how, instead of raising the mind from earth to heaven, it drags down the mind from heaven to earth; fills it with vain thoughts, foolish fancies, and impure sinful images, and debases and degrades every thing great and good by its mean grovelling conceptions of them. I might also show how the infection of sin has spread from the soul to the body, inflam ing its appetites, and often reducing men by their instrumentality almost to a level with the brutes, and sometimes below them. But on this part of my subject time forbids me to enlarge. I must, however, briefly notice,

Lastly, among the inventions of sinful man the innumerable excuses, pleas, and apologies, which he has sought out to justify his conduct, and to make himself appear unfortunate, rather than criminal. These excuses are far too numerous to particularize; and in nothing have mankind displayed more ingenuity than in forming them; for though they have lost the knowledge to do good, they are wise to do evil, and to justify it when done. All these excuses, however different, agree in this: they attempt to transfer the guilt of sin from man to God. Indeed it is evident that the guilt cannot be removed from man without casting it upon God; for if man be not guilty, certainly guilty, God,—if I may venture to utter it,—is so. But our subject overthrows all these excuses at once; for if God made man upright he cannot be justly blamed for the sins of men; and if men have sought out many wicked and foolish inventions, they alone ought to bear the blame of them and suffer their consequences.

Thus, my friends, have we taken a brief view of what man was, and of what he is; of what he was as God made him, and of what he is since he has, if I may so express it, unmade or destroyed himself. And now who can forbear to weep over such a scene as this; over a world thus dreadfully marred, over a race of immortal beings once bearing the image and likeness of God, perfectly conformed in every faculty to his holy law, and in all respects but little lower than the angels; but now debased, ruined, and enslaved by sin, the image of God lost, his law effaced from their minds, and themselves dead in trespasses and sins, transformed into children of wrath, and heirs of endless perdition. O, how has the gold become dim, and the most fine gold changed! Well might such a spectacle make heaven weep, could tears be shed in heaven. And if it has not done this it has done more. It has brought down God's eternal Son from heaven to earth on an errand of mercy, to seek and to save a race thus ruined and lost. This fact alone, if rightly considered, taken in connection with the manner in which this salvation was effected, will give us more just and enlarged conceptions of the greatness of man's ruin than any thing which can be said of it beside. It will show us that the work of saving was incomparably greater and more difficult than that of creating the world. When the world was created, its Maker did not leave his celestial abode. A word, an act of his will, was sufficient. But when the world was to be saved, its Maker was constrained to descend from heaven, the Creator to take the form of a creature, and a whole life of toil and suffering closed by a most painful and ignominious death, was necessary to effect the work. From the greatness of the work of salvation, then, infer the greatness of man's ruin. Judge that if one, if such an one, died for men, then men were indeed dead.

2. From this subject we may learn the nature and necessity of that moral change which the Scriptures call a new birth, a new creation, and a resurrection from the dead. In other words, we may learn the nature and necessity of true religion. The word religion, literally signifies *to circle* or *bind again* what had been broken or separated. We have seen how the bands which bound men to God were sundered by the sin of the former. True religion consists in a reunion of these bands, in bringing man back into the state in which he was originally created, and from which he has fallen. Now in order to this, is not a great moral change necessary, if our text be true? If man was originally upright, or perfectly conformed to the divine law, must he not become again upright, before he can be restored to the favor of God? And if all his powers and faculties are depraved by sin, as above described, must not this change be so great, as to be justly styled a new creation, or a new birth? Must not the man be, as it were, made or created anew? That he must be so, the Scriptures most clearly assert: If any man be in Christ, he is a new creature. Ye are created anew in Christ Jesus unto good works. Put off the old man, which is corrupt according to the deceitful lusts, and be renewed in the spirit of your minds; and put on the new man which is renewed in knowledge, or made anew, after the image of God. Add to these and many other passages, our Savior's declaration, Except a man be born again, he cannot see the kingdom of God,—and you must, I think, be convinced that a great moral change is absolutely necessary;

that there can be no true religion, no bringing a man into his former state, no reconciling him to God without it. You will, at least, see that the Bible is a complete whole; that it contains a connected and consistent scheme of divine truth. * * *

3. From this subject, my professing friends, you may learn whether you are what you profess to be; and if so, how far you have advanced in your Christian course. * * * *

SERMON XXXI.

KNOWLEDGE OF ONE'S SINS, A DIFFICULT ACQUISITION.

Who can understand his errors?—PSALM xix. 12.

FROM the preceding part of this psalm it appears that, when David uttered this exclamation, he had been meditating on the purity and perfection of the divine law. From this subject he passed by a very natural transition, to his own transgressions of that law. The more he reflected upon them the more numerous and aggravated did they appear; and the more he felt convinced that he was still very far from discovering them all. Hence he was constrained to exclaim, Who can understand his errors? Cleanse thou me from secret faults; that is, from those faults of which I am not sensible, which are hidden even from myself. To understand our errors, is to be acquainted with our faults, or in other words, with our sins; to know how often we transgress the divine law. By asking who can do this, the psalmist evidently intimates that it is exceedingly difficult, and that the knowledge of our sins is a very rare attainment. That it is so, every one, who knows any thing of the divine law, of himself, and of mankind, will readily acknowledge. Every such person is sensible that he is very far from knowing his own sinfulness, in its full extent, and feels the necessity of beseeching God to pardon his secret faults. And my friends, it is exceedingly important that we should all be sensible of this, that we should be duly aware how very difficult it is for any person to understand his errors. I propose, therefore, in discoursing on the passage, to show,

I. That to acquire a knowledge of our sinfulness, is exceedingly difficult; and,

II. Why it is so.

I. To acquire a knowledge of our sinfulness is exceedingly difficult. That it is so, may be inferred from the fact, that very few acquire this knowledge, and that none acquire it perfectly. It may reasonably be presumed that any thing, which all men are concerned to obtain, and which very few do obtain, must be of difficult acquisition. Now it is obvious that all men are concerned to obtain a knowledge of their errors, their sins. Scarcely a person can be found, who does not profess to wish for this knowledge. But it is equally obvious, that very few obtain it in any considerable degree, and that none obtain it perfectly. So obvious is this, that the blindness of men to their own faults has been the constant theme of satirical and moral writers from the earliest ages, whose writings have come down to us. Indeed it is one of the first traits of the human character, of which young persons take notice when they begin to mix with the world; so that he must be very young, and very unobserving, who has not learned that his neighbors and acquaintances are ignorant of their own feelings. Even children, at a very early age, will often discover faults in their parents or instructors, of which these parents or instructors are wholly unconscious. But without insisting on these things, let me appeal to your own observation. Do you not, every day, meet with persons who appear to be perfectly insensible of faults and imperfections, which every man of common sagacity would discover in them on a very slight acquaintance? Do you not know many individuals, whose failings are known from one end of the town to the other, but who know nothing of them themselves? Did you ever know a covetous person, who thought himself covetous? or a vain man, who thought himself vain? or a proud man, who thought himself proud? Do you not often hear persons censure others for faults of which they are themselves guilty, and perhaps in a much greater degree? Do not persons often apply sermons to their neighbors, which all who know them, are sensible would apply much better to themselves? In a word, do you know any person who, you have reason to believe, is perfectly acquainted with his own failings? or even one who knows them as well as they are known to others? Now if mankind are thus universally blind to their own faults, even to those faults which their fellow creatures can discover in them, much more must they be blind to those secret sins of the heart, which men cannot discover, but which are exceedingly sinful in the sight of a holy, heart-searching God; for it is evidently much more difficult to acquire a knowledge of the latter than of the former. Agreeably, we learn both from observation and from the scriptures, that of those sins of the heart, in which men's errors or sinfulness principally consist in the sight of God, they are all by nature entirely ignorant. For instance, the scriptures inform us that the human heart is deceitful above all things and desperately wicked, that it is full of evil, that in it there dwells no good thing, that all its thoughts and imaginations are sinful; that it is enmity against God, and not subject to his law, and that it is hard, a heart of stone. They tell us that all men have gone out of the way; that they are dead in trespasses and sins; that there is none righteous, none that doeth good, no not one; that all have broken the divine law, and are under its curse; in a word, that all deserve everlasting misery, from which it is impossible for any to escape, but through the atonement and mediation of Christ. Now it is too evident to require proof that men naturally know nothing of all this, that they are completely blind to the sinful state of their hearts; and so blind, that it is impossible for human means to convince them of it, or to make them sensible of the justice of their condemnation.

Thus, my friends, it ever has been. Thus it was in the days of Solomon; for we read, There is a generation that are pure in their own eyes, and yet are not washed from their filthiness. Thus it was with the Jews in the days of the prophets. When God charged them with despising his name, they impudently replied, Wherein have we despised thy name? When he threatened them with the punishment which their sins deserved, they cried, Wherefore hath the Lord pronounced all this great evil against us? or, what is our iniquity? or, what is our sin that we have committed against the Lord? Thus it was with the same nation in our Savior's time. When they were crucifying the Lord of glory and persecuting his disciples, they fancied that they loved God, and flattered themselves that they were beloved by him; and at the very moment, when the measure of their iniquity was full, and they were ripe for ruin, they confided in their own supposed innocence and felt secure. The same ignorance of their own characters, the same blindness to their own sinfulness, has been exhibited by mankind ever since. Hundreds of writers have asserted, in opposition to the scriptures, that the human heart is naturally good; that mankind are naturally virtuous, and thousands and tens of thousands have believed the assertion. This is the reason why so many reject the Savior. They will not come to him, because they do not feel that they need him; and they do not feel that they need him, because they are blind to their own sinfulness. And this, my hearers, is the reason why so many of you neglect him. You do not understand your errors. There was a time, when none of you understood them; and though some of you have been convinced of your mistake, in this respect, the larger part are still insensible; and even those who are best acquainted with their own transgressions will readily acknowledge that they are very far from knowing them all. Since then all men are thus ignorant of their own failings and offences, it is evident that to acquire a knowledge of them must be exceedingly difficult.

That it is so, is farther evident from the fact, that the influences of the divine Spirit are represented as necessary to communicate this knowledge. Speaking of this divine agent, our Savior says, When he is come, he shall convince the world of sin. Now it will, I presume, be allowed, that God would not send his Spirit to perform a needless work. But it would be needless to convince men of sin, if they were not ignorant of their sins. Did they possess knowledge of them, or could men communicate to them this knowledge, the convincing influences of the divine Spirit, would be entirely needless. But they are not needless; they are indispensably necessary. It follows then that mankind are so blind to their own sinfulness, so ignorant of their true characters, that the Spirit of God alone can remove this blindness, and give them a knowledge of themselves, of their sins.

Having thus shown that it is exceedingly difficult for men to understand their errors, or to know their sins, I proceed,

II. To shew why it is so.

1. It is so, because men are ignorant of the divine law. The apostle observes that, where there is no law, there is no transgression. Of course, while men are ignorant of the law, they must be ignorant of their transgressions. Again, the apostle observes, that by the law is the knowledge of sin. Of course, those who know little or nothing of the divine law, must know little or nothing of sin. Once more; St. John observes, that sin is a deviation from the law. Of course, unless men are well acquainted with the law, they cannot discover their own deviations from its requirements. But mankind are naturally ignorant of the divine law. In the language of the apostle, they are alive without the law. They have no proper sense of the strictness and spirituality of its precepts. Hence they regard many things as innocent and even as laudable, which the law of God condemns as sinful. Agreeably, Christ informs us, that what is highly esteemed among men is abomination in the sight of God. It is evident that he who would understand his errors, must understand the divine law, which alone can tell him what his errors are. He must have this law in his mind, in his memory, in his conscience; and he must be familiarly acquainted with all the preceptive and practical parts of God's word, and have a disposition to measure his conduct daily by this rule. But men have naturally neither this acquaintance with the rule, nor this disposition to apply it. On the contrary, they measure themselves by themselves, and compare themselves among themselves. Of course, they must be very far indeed from understanding their errors.

But perhaps it will be asked, if men are thus ignorant of the law, how can they be justly condemned for transgressing it? I answer, because their ignorance is a voluntary ignorance. They have the law of God in their hands, and might become acquainted with it, if they would; and it is a maxim with the divine, as well as with human governments, that ignorance of the law excuses no one.

2. Another cause, which renders it difficult for us to acquire a knowledge of our sins, may be found in the nature of the human mind. The mind has been justly compared to the eye, which, while it perceives other objects, cannot see itself, unless it be furnished with a mirror. Hence men usually find it difficult to examine themselves, to discover their own real motives,

and the secret springs of action, and to become acquainted with the various exercises of their minds. It is true, they have, in the law and word of God, a faithful mirror, by looking into which they might see and know them; but into this mirror, unhappily, men do not love to look. They dislike it, for the same reason that the Jews hated Christ, viz., because it testifies that their deeds are evil, and threatens them with the divine displeasure. Now while men indulge this dislike, and neglect the Bible, it is as certain that they will never become acquainted with their own hearts, as it is that they will never see their own countenances without a mirror; for Jehovah declares that he alone knows the heart, that none but himself can know it; and the knowledge of it which he possesses is communicated to men only through the medium of his word.

3. Another cause, which renders it exceedingly difficult for men to discover their own faults, is the prevalence of self-love. I presume, my friends, you will not deny that every man naturally loves himself more than any other object in the universe. Of course, he will be extremely partial in judging himself, and exceedingly unwilling to discover faults in one he loves so well. You are sensible that men are seldom, if ever, so keen-sighted in discovering the faults of their children, their friends, and partizans, as they are in discerning the faults of others. You know that we can all see failings in an enemy much more easily, than in a friend. Of course, since men love themselves better than even their friends, or children, they must be still more blind to their own failings, still more slow to discern and acknowlege them. Should a man be counsellor, witness, jury, and judge, in a case where his estate or his life was concerned, would you not expect him to determine it in his own favor? But when a man sets himself to examine his own character, and to try his title to the heavenly inheritance, he is counsellor, witness, jury, and judge, all in one; and, of course, he will, if possible, pronounce a favorable sentence. He will try himself by some easy rule; he will make the best excuse in his power for every thing that can be excused; he will keep some things entirely out of sight; he will call his faults by the softest name which they can be made to bear; and if there be any thing which he can neither deny, nor overlook, he will ascribe it to the force of temptation, or the frailty of human nature, and

plead that it is nothing worse than thousands are guilty of, who pass for honest men.

Besides, to counterbalance these few failings, he can bring a multitude of good actions and qualities, so that on the whole his life and character appear very fair. Thus thousands, whom God would condemn, and who will be condemned at the judgment day, contrive, under the blinding influence of self-love and self-partiality, to make themselves appear innocent, and even praise-worthy, when tried at their own bar. To say all in a word, a bad action appears much less criminal, and a good action much more laudable, when performed by ourselves, than when performed by others: and the self-love which occasions this, would alone, without any assisting cause, render it exceedingly difficult for any man to perceive his own sins in their true colors. But this is not all. Self-love not only makes us partially or totally blind to our sins, but renders us exceedingly unwilling to see them, and of course indisposed to search for them. To see our sins, is always painful. It mortifies our pride, lowers that good opinion of ourselves which we all naturally love to entertain, disturbs our consciences, destroys our hopes of happiness after death, and perhaps excites some guilty fears of the divine displeasure. Now self-love prompts us almost instinctively to avoid every thing which gives us pain; and since the sight of our sins is thus painful, it will prevent us from desiring it, and even lead us to avoid it by every means in our power; and it is well known that what a man does not wish to see, he very seldom does see.

4. What the Scriptures call the deceitfulness of sin, is another cause which renders it extremely difficult for us to understand our errors. I need not tell you that vice can cloak itself with the garb of virtue, or that sin can assume the name and appearance of goodness. Nor need I inform you that actions derive their character from the motives which prompt us to perform them, so that the same action, which is good when prompted by a right motive, will become sinful when it proceeds from motives which are wrong. Now it is by no means easy for men to ascertain in all cases the real motives by which they are actuated. In consequence of the false names and fair disguises which sin assumes, and in which its deceitfulness consists, we may easily fancy that we are governed by right motives, when

in fact we are not so, and thus class our sins among our virtues. For instance, a man may fancy that he is actuated by true zeal for God, when in reality it is nothing but a selfish zeal for his own party, or sinful anger against those who oppose him. We may fancy that we love Christians, when in fact we feel nothing but selfish affection for those of our own denomination. We may flatter ourselves that we are truly charitable, when we give alms to the poor, and yet we may be really actuated by a desire of applause, or by a wish to do something which gratifies our pride, and makes us think more highly of ourselves. We may think that we feel a true filial fear of God, when we have nothing but that slavish fear of punishment, which makes the devils tremble before him. We may fancy that we are serving God, and aiming to glorify him, when in fact we are only serving and aiming to honor ourselves. We may fancy that we read and attend public worship with right views and feelings, when in fact we perform these duties merely from custom, or formality, or with a design to quiet our consciences. We may fancy that we are only prudent, industrious, and economical, when we are really influenced by that love of money which is the root of all evil, or that love of the world which proves us to be the enemies of God. Now in all these cases, that self-love which has been mentioned, and that partiality which results from it, will prompt us to decide in our own favor, and to conclude that our motives are good. Thus, as the Scriptures inform us, men are hardened through the deceitfulness of sin; and hence as sin communicates its own character to the sinful heart, the heart is said to be deceitful above all things. My friends, it is difficult to know thoroughly a deceitful man. How much more difficult must it be to know a heart which is deceitful above all things!

5. Another cause, which renders it exceedingly difficult for men to acquire a knowledge of their sins, is, the effects which sin produces upon their understandings and consciences. I need not tell you these faculties are the eyes of the soul, without which she can discern nothing. Now it is a most certain truth, that, just so far as sin prevails in the heart and life, so far it puts out or darkens these eyes of the mind, with respect to all spiritual objects; so that it is always the case, that the more sinful a man really is, so much the less sinful does he appear to

himself to be. The more faults he has, the fewer he can discover in himself. This may appear to some of you a paradoxical assertion, but however it may appear it is strictly true, as a moment's attention to the Scriptures will convince you. If you read the accounts there given us of different characters, you will find that the worst men ever seem to be most ignorant of their own faults, and most unwilling to confess and repent of their sins; while, on the contrary, those who were most eminently good, seem to have the worst opinion of themselves, and to be most ready to confess that they were the chief of sinners. And, my friends, is it not so still? Do not some of the worst characters, with whom you are acquainted, appear to think very highly of themselves? And are there not others, whom you can justly accuse of no particular fault, who, so far as you can judge, regard themselves as exceedingly sinful? Now this apparently unaccountable difference is owing entirely to the effects of sin. When sin prevails in the heart, it sears the conscience, and darkens the understanding, so that sin is not perceived, and the unhappy, blinded wretch feels most innocent and secure, at the very moment, when he is most in danger. To use our Savior's expression, the light that is in him becomes darkness: how great then he adds, is that darkness. When this is the case, men, as the prophet expresses it, call evil good and good evil, and put darkness for light, and light for darkness. They can no more discover their own sins, than a blind man can discern spots of blood on his garment, or than dust can be perceived in a dark room. We may add in connection with these remarks, that the effect of habit is exceedingly great in rendering men insensible to their sins. Many things which shock us when first presented to our view, cease to affect us at all, after we become familiarized to them. Now men soon become familiarized to their own thoughts, feelings and conduct. They seem like a part of themselves, and, however wrong they may at first appear, they soon cease to shock or offend, and at length pass unnoticed and unperceived. The young soldier starts at the sight of bloodshed and carnage, but after a few battles he plunges his bayonet into the body of a fellow creature with as little emotion as an artificer hews a block of wood. Or, to take another comparison: Enter the mud-walled habitatio of a savage, blackened with smoke, covered with filth of every kind, and half filled with the putrefying remains of his loathsome repasts, and endeavor to make him sensible how disgusting these things are, and to inspire him with the love of neatness and order. Could you succeed? Not at all. He sees nothing filthy, nothing disgusting, no want of neatness in his miserable and disgusting abode. Why? Because he is accustomed to it; and his blunted senses are not offended. My friends, it is the same with the sinner. Sin is the defilement, the pollution of the soul. In the sight of God and all holy beings, it is a thousand times more loathsome and disgusting, than any material filthiness can possibly be in ours. But the sinner has always lived in the midst of this moral pollution. He is therefore familiarized and accustomed to it. His spiritual senses, blunted and deadened, are not offended, and of course, he does not perceive his deformity. He sees nothing loathsome, nothing wrong in his heart, when in the sight of God, it is like an open sepulchre, full of putridity and rottenness. Hence he hears of that fountain which is set open for uncleanness, of that blood which cleanses from all sin, with the same indifference that the savage would listen to a harangue on the benefits of personal and domestic neatness. This being the case, we need not be at a loss to know why it is so difficult to convince men of their sinfulness, to make them understand their errors.

My impenitent hearers, this subject is, or ought to be, exceedingly interesting to you. It touches upon the very point, respecting which you are at issue with the Bible, upon the greatest difficulty which opposes your salvation. The point of dispute, the great question is, whether your sins are so numerous and aggravated, and whether your hearts are so entirely depraved, as the Scriptures represent them to be. I presume, if you were convinced that this representation is strictly true; if you were fully convinced that your hearts are deceitful above all things and desperately wicked; that they are opposed to God and all goodness, and unwilling to be reconciled to him, there would be no difficulty in the way of your assenting to all the doctrines of the gospel. You would then feel that it is perfectly just for God to condemn you; you would feel that your situation is dangerous and critical; you would feel your need of a Savior, and the necessity of regeneration; and you would feel the need of spiritual and divine influences to effect this change. The great, the only question then, is, are you entirely sinful, or are you not? The Scriptures, you must be sensible, seem at least to assert that you are. You, on the contrary, contend that you are not. But, my friends, methinks the remarks which have been made ought to excite at least a suspicion in your minds that you may be deceived in this respect. You have heard that it is exceedingly difficult for a man to understand his own errors; that we are extremely prone to be partial to ourselves, to judge too favorably of our own characters. You have heard, and you see that other men do this; you see many around you entirely blind to their own faults; you see that none appear to be sufficiently sensible of all their faults; you have heard how many causes combine to hide our sins from us; and you must be sensible that you are exposed to the influence of all these causes. Is it not then possible, that you may be deceived; that you may have formed too favorable an opinion of your own characters? Will any one of you undertake to say, that he is wiser than all other men; that though they are blind to their faults, he can discover and has discovered all his own? My friends, if you dare not say this, you must allow it to be, at least possible, that after all your hearts may be as sinful, as much depraved, as the Scriptures represent them to be. You must allow that, perhaps, you are hateful and abominable in the sight of the holy, heart-searching God, and exposed to his everlasting displeasure. All your good opinions of yourselves may be nothing but the effects of secret pride and self-delusion; and at the last day, when the discovery will come too late, you may find that you have deceived and destroyed yourselves. My friends, I entreat you to lay these things seriously to heart; for a mistake here will be, must be, fatal. Describing the feelings of penitent sinners, God says, Then shall ye loathe yourselves in your own sight, on account of your iniquities and abominations. But no man can loathe himself, or repent of his sins, in this manner, until he sees that his character and conduct are loathsome; and he who cannot repent, cannot be pardoned; for Christ has said, Except ye repent, ye shall perish. Let me then prevail upon you to bring your characters to a strict, impartial scrutiny, to try them by the law of God, and to remember, during the trial, that there is no danger of forming too low an opinion of yourselves; that all the danger lies on the other side; that you will be exposed to the blinding influence of self-love, and many other causes, which will combine to draw from you too favorable a sentence. And when you have done all, remember that, if your heart condemn you, God is greater than your heart, and knoweth all things.

SERMON XXXII.

SINNERS IN ZION DESCRIBED AND DOOMED.

Wo to them that are at ease in Zion. Amos vi. 1.

The inspired writers, my friends, do not scatter either blessings or curses arbitrarily and indiscriminately without informing us on whom they will fall. They never pronounce a blessing, without specifying the character to whom it belongs. And they never denounce a curse or a woe, without describing some class of sinners against whom it is directed. Thus they rightly divide the word of truth, and give every one his proper portion. An instance of this we have in our text, where God by the mouth of his prophet, denounces a woe or curse against such as are at ease in Zion.

My hearers, all who believe that the threatenings of Jehovah are not vain words, will allow that it is highly important for all to know the import of this woe, and whether it is directed against ourselves. That we may obtain this knowledge, let us consider the characters here mentioned, and the woe which is denounced against them.

I. The persons here mentioned are described, as being at ease in Zion. Zion, you are sensible, was the name of an eminence on which the Jewish temple formerly stood. Hence the temple was called Zion; and to go up to Mount Zion, was to go up to the temple for the professed purpose of worshipping Jehovah. From the place of worship, the name was gradually extended to the worshippers, so that in process of time the word Zion embraced all who professed to know and worship God, or in other words, the whole Jewish nation; the only nation at that time in the world, by which the true God was worshipped or known. To be in Zion then, taking the word in its largest sense, means to be in a land where the true God is known and worshipped; where religious privileges, similar to those of the Jews, are enjoyed; a land of gospel light and liberty, where Christ, of whom the temple on Mount Zion was a type, is publicly preached, as the only way of access to God. Taking the word in a more limited sense, to be in Zion is to have a seat in the house of God, and to be among those who statedly meet for the professed purpose of religious worship. If we confine the meaning of the term within still narrower limits, it will include only those who have made a public profession of religion. In this sense the word Zion is often used; but from the context it appears that, in this passage, the word is used in its most extensive signification, embracing all who are members of a nation or community by which the true God is professedly known or worshipped. Of course, my hearers, it applies to ourselves; for in this sense we are all in Zion. We live in a land of gospel light and liberty; we enjoy religious privileges similar to those of the Jews; and we assemble at stated seasons in the house of God ostensibly and professedly with a view to worship him. Since then we are all in Zion, let us in the next place, inquire whether we are at ease in Zion.

You will readily perceive that the ease here intended is ease, not of body, but of mind; ease relating not to our temporal but to our religious or spiritual concerns. Our bodies may be filled with pain, and our minds harassed with continual afflictions, disappointments, and anxieties, so as to be strangers to peace, and yet we may be perfectly at ease in the sense of our text. Speaking in general terms, persons are at ease in this sense; when they feel neither sorrow nor alarm on account of their sins; when they are seldom troubled by the admonitions of conscience; when they are unconcerned respecting their future destiny; in a word, when they are not engaged in working out their salvation with fear and trembling, but feel safe, quiet and secure. This unconcern respecting themselves is usually accompanied by at least equal unconcern respecting the salvation of others. Agreeably we are informed in the context, that the persons here described are not grieved for the affliction of Joseph; that is, for the evils and calamities that affect the church. They are far from being able to say with the psalmist, I beheld the transgressors and was grieved; rivers of waters run down mine eyes, because men keep not God's law. They never weep over, or pray for, a world lying in wickedness, but view with frigid indifference the prevalence of sin; and manifest no zeal to promote the religious interests of mankind. From this general description of those who are at ease in Zion, it must be evident to the most superficial observer, that they compose a very numerous body. This body may be divided into several classes, corresponding with the various causes to which their ease is to be ascribed. These causes it is necessary to notice.

Since it is impossible for a rational being to be perfectly at ease and unconcerned, while he perceives that he is exposed to endless punishment on account of his sins, it is evident that all who are at ease in Zion, must feel persuaded, either that the punishment with which sinners are threatened will never be inflicted; or that they are not themselves sinners; or that, though sinners, they shall in some way or other escape the punishment which their sins deserve. These three classes include all who are at ease in Zion. The first class deny that any punishment will be inflicted on sinners. The second class allow that sinners will be punished, but deny, or at least, do not perceive that they are sinners. The third class acknowledge that they are sinners, and that sinners will be punished; but still flatter themselves that they shall escape punishment. Let us consider each of these classes in order.

1. The first class includes infidels of every description. Such were those who denied the immortality of the soul, and said, Let us eat and drink, for to-morrow we die. Such were those who denied God's government of the world, saying, The Lord seeth not, the Lord hath forsaken the earth; he will not do good, neither will he do evil. Such were those of whom the psalmist speaks, who contemned God, and encouraged themselves by saying, He will never requite it; and whose conduct led him to conclude that there was no fear of God before their eyes. Such also were the scoffers, mentioned by St. Peter, who walked after their vain lusts, and asked, Where is the promise of his coming? Such characters, there is reason to fear, are to be

found at the present day; but it will probably be impossible to disturb their false peace by arguments drawn from a book whose contents they disbelieve. They must be left, unless other means prevent, to enjoy their fatal ease till the day, in which, like the devils, they will believe and tremble.

In this first class may also be placed those who believe that all men will be saved; for they deny that the punishment threatened in the Bible will be inflicted on any. Such were those false prophets who cried Peace, peace, when there was no peace, and of whom God said, I have seen a horrible thing in the prophets of Jerusalem; for they walk in lies, and strengthen the hands of evil doers, so that none of them doth return from his wickedness. They say still unto them that despise me, Ye shall have peace; and they say unto every one that walketh after the imagination of his own heart, No evil shall come upon you. With lies they make sad the heart of the righteous whom I have not made sad, and strengthen the hands of the wicked that he should not return from his wicked way, by promising him life. Therefore, thus saith the Lord of Hosts concerning the prophets, Hearken not unto their words, for they make you vain; they speak a vision of their own heart, and not out of the mouth of the Lord, and behold, I will feed them with wormwood, and make them drink the water of gall; for from the false prophets is profaneness gone out into all the land. Such too were the disciples of these prophets who when they heard the curse of the law blessed themselves in their hearts, and said, We shall have peace, though we walk in the imagination of our hearts, to add one sin to another; and of whom God said, The Lord will not spare them, but the anger of the Lord and his jealousy shall smoke against them, and all the curses that are written in this book shall be upon them; and the Lord shall blot out their name from under heaven. My friends, if any man, after hearing these passages, can find ease in believing the doctrine of universal salvation, I envy him not the enjoyment of that ease.

2. Let us proceed, in the next place, to the second class mentioned above; the class composed of those who allow that sinners will be punished, but who deny, or, to speak more properly, do not appear to believe that they are sinners. They will allow indeed, in words, that they have committed some sins,

though even this they do not seem to feel; but they utterly deny that they are such sinners as the Bible describes; and flatter themselves that their sins are far too few and too small to require an infinite atonement, or to merit everlasting punishment. They find, or fancy that they find none better than themselves, few so good, and very many worse. Hence they conclude that they are in no danger, that they have nothing to fear, and of course feel easy and secure. Such were the generation mentioned by Solomon who were pure in their own eyes, but who had never been cleansed from their filthiness. Such too was St. Paul before his conversion. I was alive, says he, without the law once, but when the commandment came, sin revived, and I died. Now to the persons of whom we are speaking, the commandment never came. They are without the law. They know nothing of its spirituality, strictness, and extent; and since by the law is the knowledge of sin, they being without the law, know nothing of their sins. They never tried themselves by this rule. They never considered that he who does not love God with all his heart and his neighbor as himself, tramples at once upon the law and the prophets, and violates in effect every precept of both. And as they never tried themselves by the law of God, it is evident they cannot feel condemned by this law; and since neither human laws nor human maxims condemn them, they feel free from condemnation, and fear no condemnatory sentence, when tried at the bar of God. We endeavored to show you, a few Sabbaths since, how exceedingly difficult it is to understand our errors. Now these persons do not understand their errors. They have never been convinced of sin, of righteousness and of judgment; or have never been awakened, have never complied with the apostolic exhortation, Awake thou that sleepest, and arise from the dead, and Christ shall give thee life. They are, therefore, like a man buried in sleep, totally unconscious of their true character and situation, insensible of their sins, and of the danger to which their sins expose them. Their slumbering consciences were never thoroughly awakened to perform their office. In the language of scripture, they have eyes, but they see not; ears have they, but they hear not; for the spirit of deep slumber is fallen upon them. So deep indeed, so profound are their slumbers, or rather their lethargy, that they are said to be dead in trespasses and sins; and hence, like the lifeless tenants of the tomb, they perceive not that they are dead. Hence they never felt that they are exposed to the wrath to come; and, of course, have never fled from it, never asked with anxiety, or even with seriousness, What shall we do to be saved? What may appear still more strange, though they profess to hope for heaven, they seem to regard it with indifference. At least their hopes do not appear to wean them from the world, or to support them under the evils of life, or to afford them any solid consolation, or even to excite any gratitude; nor do they manifest any desire to anticipate the happiness of heaven by engaging in its employments while here below. In short, every religious feeling is dead or asleep in their breasts; and to every religious object they are insensible. At morning, at noon, and at night, religion may knock at the door of their hearts, but there is no voice, nor any that regardeth. All within is silent, and cold, and still, as a sepulchre. They are at ease in Zion, asleep in the house of God, dreaming of worldly objects and pleasures, to which they are all awake and alive, and in the pursuit of which, all their powers are engaged. In this class too may be included those who have at some period of life been the subjects of serious impressions, but have either stifled those impressions by a violent resistance—dismissed them with excuses, or suffered them to be effaced by negligence. Such persons have not always been at ease in Zion. Their false peace has been disturbed, their consciences have been awakened, and they have trembled at her voice and smarted under her scourge. But in some one of the ways mentioned above, her voice has been silenced, or she has been lulled to sleep by opiates; and now these wretched self-destroyers slumber even more quietly and profoundly than before, except when the unwelcome light of truth or the disagreeable voice of reproof disturbs them by exciting mingled emotions of anger, contempt and fear. Such persons the apostle compares to trees, twice dead, plucked up by the roots. Their consciences are seared as with an hot iron; and because they receive not the truth in the love of it, that they may be saved, God often sends them strong delusions, so that they believe a lie. Hence they usually remain not long in this class, but after various changes seek refuge and ease in universalism or infidelity.

3. Our attention is next called to the third class mentioned

above. This class seem to be less distant from the truth than either of the others. They acknowledge that they are sinners, and that sinners will be punished; and yet they are at ease, for they contrive in various ways to persuade themselves that though other sinners will be punished, they shall themselves escape. In places where the gospel is clearly and faithfully preached, this class is usually much more numerous than either of the former, and includes a greater variety of characters. In the first place, it includes all who maintain their false peace by promises of future repentance and reformation, and by hopes founded on these promises, that they shall secure salvation before death arrives. Such persons, though habitually, are not always at ease. Their avowed belief that they are sinners, and that sinners will be punished, renders it impossible for them to be perfectly free at all times from anxiety and alarm. The attacks of disease, or the sudden death of an acquaintance, or a pungent sermon, will often disturb them for a moment; but they soon recover their peace of mind by making fresh promises and resolutions to become religious at some future period. On the fulfilment of these promises and resolutions they rely with the fullest confidence. They seem not to entertain the smallest doubt that they shall become truly pious before the close of life. At the worst, they shall repent on their dying bed; for these persons almost ever expect to die of some lingering disease, which will afford them full opportunity to fulfil their resolutions and make their peace with God. The possibility that death may surprise them suddenly and unexpectedly, or that God, provoked by their delays, may give them up, is entirely overlooked; and they rely with as much confidence on their anticipated goodness, as if they were actually possessed of it; so that perhaps the most established Christian does not feel more sure of salvation. Agreeably, they are represented in the context as putting far away the evil day. At the head of the class stands Felix. When he heard Paul reasoning of righteousness, temperance, and judgment to come, he trembled. His delusive ease was for the moment disturbed, but he soon restored it, by saying, Go thy way for this time, when I have a convenient season I will call for thee. My hearers, if all the fair promises and good resolutions which have since been made, with reference to a future convenient season, had been executed, the situation and appearance of mankind would be widely different from what they are; joy would have been much more frequently felt in heaven over repenting sinners, and the celestial city would have been thronged by millions who will never enter its gates. But alas, this convenient season very seldom arrives; and, of course, the resolutions which depend for fulfilment upon its arrival, are seldom performed. They serve only to defraud those who make them of their opportunities, and of salvation, and to maintain a delusive, fatal ease, which could be maintained by those persons in no other way, and which, if not destroyed, inevitably destroys all who indulge in it. The greater part of those who recur to this method of maintaining it, are to be found among the young, especially among those of them, who have received a religious education, or who have enjoyed from their childhood the clear light of the gospel. Such persons are usually not sufficiently hardened in unbelief to make light of God's threatenings; nor are their consciences so far seared as to render them insensible of their sins; nor can they at once reject the truths which they have been taught, and seek refuge in infidelity. They have therefore no way to render themselves easy in their sins, except that which has now been described; making good resolutions; and their youth, their health, and their expectation of long life, encourage them to adopt this method by promising them many future opportunities or convenient seasons for the performance of these resolutions. There is perhaps no class of sinners whose situation is more dangerous; certainly no one which occasions more anxiety and uneasiness to the faithful ministers of Jesus Christ, than this. It is impossible to know what course to pursue with them. To wait for the fulfilment of their resolutions, is like pursuing the termination of a rainbow, which still recedes as you advance. They assent to every thing, but they really yield to nothing. Tell them that they are sinners, they confess it; that they are objects of God's displeasure, they acknowledge it; that they are exposed to the wrath to come, they allow it; that they ought immediately to repent and secure salvation, they are sensible that this is their duty. But he, who therefore, expects to see them do this, will find himself most wretchedly disappointed. Visit them to-morrow, and you will find them just where they were before, just as far as ever from the kingdom of heaven; and all your efforts to rouse them must be again repeated, and again prove unavailing. Yet these very persons often look with contempt or indignation upon infidels and heretics, though they are far more inconsistent than either. They seem to fancy that there is some merit in holding and assenting to the truth, though they hold it in unrighteousness; nay more, even though they wrest it to their own destruction; for this many of them do. They justify their delays by pretending that they can do nothing, and by pleading that they must wait God's time; that when he shall see fit to convert them, they are willing to be converted; thus wholly casting the blame of their sins upon Jehovah, and condemning the Almighty that they may justify themselves.

In the second place, this class includes all who entertain a false and groundless persuasion that they have already become pious, obtained the pardon of their sins, and secured the favor of God. The reasons why persons feel such a persuasion are various. Some feel it because they are more sober, more moral, and more attentive to the externals of religion, than they were; others, because they have made a public profession of religion, and united themselves to the visible church of Christ; a third class, because their religious sentiments are correct and orthodox; and a fourth, because they fancy that they have experienced that great moral change, which the inspired writers call regeneration. Their consciences have, perhaps, been awakened, their understandings enlightened, their fears alarmed, and their feelings strongly excited. They have been in some measure convinced of their sins, and fancy that they have truly repented, believed in the Savior, and obtained pardon, when in fact, this is not the case. Many such instances are mentioned in the Scriptures, and daily observation proves that they are still to be found. But in whichever of these ways, or for which of these reasons soever, persons falsely persuade themselves that they are pious, the effects are the same; they immediately appropriate to themselves all the precious promises which are made to the pious; call God their Father, Christ their Savior, and heaven their portion; and leave to others the warnings and threatenings. Of course they feel perfectly secure. They flatter themselves that their souls are safe, that their salvation is secured; and now they have little or nothing to do, but reap the reward of their labors, and pursue their secular concerns without interruption or restraint.

Thus, my hearers, have we noticed particularly the several classes which together compose the great body of those who are at ease in Zion. How little reason they have to be thus at ease, will appear, if we consider, as was proposed,

II. The wo, which is denounced against them in our text. Wo to them that are at ease in Zion! The expression is remarkable. There is no particular curse or threatening denounced against them; but the doom is expressed in general terms; in terms, which may include curses and threatenings of every kind; and which are therefore the more terrible. Wo to them; that is, let curses be upon them, let misery pursue them. In the context, however, their doom is more particularly described. It is there declared that the punishment, which they did not fear, shall fall first upon them. But why, it may be asked, is this doom denounced on such characters? Why are they thought worthy of a punishment so severe? I answer,

1. Because the ease which they feel proves that they belong to the number of the wicked. If there is any truth in the Scriptures, it is certain that all who are habitually at ease in Zion know nothing of true religion. They are either careless sinners, or self-deluded hypocrites. The pious man, the true Christian, is described by the inspired writers, as one who mourns for sin, who is engaged in a spiritual warfare, who is fighting the good fight of faith, who crucifies the flesh with its affections and lusts, who is running the Christian race, who is engaged in subduing and mortifying his sinful propensities, who denies himself, takes up his cross daily, and follows Christ, who, as a pilgrim, a stranger, a traveller, is seeking another and better country, who works out his salvation with fear and trembling. Now is it possible, that a man, who is doing all this can be at ease in the sense of our text? A soldier in the field of battle at ease! a man running a race at ease! a traveller, toiling up a steep ascent, bearing the cross, at ease! a man crucifying sinful propensities, dear as a right hand or right eye, at ease! a man working out his salvation with fear and trembling, at ease! a man who hates and mourns for sin, loves God, and feels concerned for his perishing fellow creatures, at ease in a world lying in wickedness, where God is dishonored, where Christ is neg-

lected, where immortal souls are perishing by millions; where there is so much to be done, so much to be suffered, so much to be guarded against, and resisted; where death stands at the door ready every moment to summon him to his great account! My friends, it is impossible. No Christian can be habitually easy, careless, and indolent in such a situation as this? He may, perhaps, slumber for a moment, but even then he is not at ease. Agreeably, our Savior represents the enjoyment of this false peace, as the characteristic of one, who is completely subjugated, enslaved, and blinded by sin. When the strong man armed, says he, keepeth his palace, his goods are in peace; that is, when sin and Satan keep the heart, and fortify it against God; when the eyes of the mind are so blinded, that they see no danger; when the voice of conscience is stifled, so that it does not warn us of danger; when the heart is so hard, that it does not tremble at God's word; then the soul is at peace, then it is at ease in Zion. But does the Christian, it may perhaps be asked, enjoy no peace? Are we not told of a peace of God which passes all understanding? Does not Christ promise rest to his followers; and are we not told that they who believe have entered into rest? I answer, yes; the Christian does enjoy peace, but it is a peace as widely different from the careless, indolent ease, which we have been describing, as is the rest of a healthy man, from the lethargic slumber of the apoplectic, or the stupefaction of the drunkard. The rest which Christ promises is promised to those who take upon them his yoke, and learn of him. And does he inculcate indolence, or carelessness? Was he ever at ease in this world? Was it not his meat and drink, his employment, and his recreation, his labor and his rest, to do his Father's will and finish his work? Did he not teach his disciples both by precept and example, to work while the day lasts, to be up and doing, waiting for his coming, and watching unto prayer? So the peace which passes all understanding, is promised to them only who, in every thing, by prayer and supplication, with thanksgiving, make known their requests unto God. And we read when the churches of Christ enjoyed rest, they walked in the fear of God. The man then, who is habitually at ease in Zion, is not, cannot be a Christian; he has not one feature of Christ's image, one mark of the Christian character. And if he is not a Christian, he is an impenitent sinner; if he is not righteous he is wicked; for in the sight of God there are but two classes of character among men; and if he is one of the wicked, then wo unto him; for God directs all his messengers to say, Wo to the wicked, it shall be ill with him, for the reward of his hands shall be given him.—Again, Wo to them that are at ease in Zion! for they are not only sinners, but sinners of no common stamp, sinners whose guilt and sinfulness are peculiarly aggravated, and whose punishment will therefore be peculiarly severe. This will be evident if we reflect a moment on their situation and on the privileges which they abuse, on the motives which they resist, on the obligations which they violate. They are in Zion; and in Zion God is known, in Zion, is his earthly dwelling place, in Zion, he makes the clearest manifestations of himself which have ever been made to mortals; in Zion the thunders of his law are heard; in Zion the gracious invitations of the gospel are proclaimed; in Zion, Christ is set forth evidently crucified as a propitiation for sin; in Zion, life and immortality are brought to light; in Zion, the Sun of righteousness shines; on Zion, the rain of righteousness is poured out; in a word, Zion is God's vineyard, in which his servants are commanded to labor; the field of battle, in which the Captain of our salvation summons his soldiers to combat; and in which crowns, thrones, and kingdoms, immortal as their Giver, are held up to view as the reward of victory. Here then is every motive to exertion, which can be presented to rational beings; motives addressed to every power and faculty of our natures, to our understandings and to our consciences; to our wills and our affections; to our hopes and to our fears, to our love and to our gratitude; to our desires of happiness, and to our aversion to misery. These motives too are presented to us and urged upon us by God himself, by our Creator, our Father, our Preserver, our Benefactor, our Sovereign and our Judge; by the God and Father of our Lord Jesus Christ. He then who is at ease in Zion, must be deaf to God's voice, he must be blind to God's glories; he must be insensible to every spiritual object; he must be regardless of his immortal soul, and unconcerned for the salvation of others; he must sin against light and against love; he is a servant who knows his Lord's will and does it not, and shall therefore be beaten with many stripes. He is a sentinel who slumbers on his post. He then who can be indolent in Zion, would be indolent in heaven; and fall asleep while the glories of Jehovah blazed around him, and the countless myriads of the redeemed celebrated those glories with eternal songs. If the heathen are without excuse, as an apostle declares them to be, though they have nothing but the light of nature; how awfully inexcusable, must those be who are at ease in Zion!

Once more, Wo to them that are at ease in Zion! because there is little reason to hope that they will ever repent. With respect to those whose false peace is disturbed, who are awakened, alarmed, convinced of sin, and inquiring for a Savior, there is some ground to hope. But on what grounds can we hope for the salvation of them that are at ease; at ease in Zion, who scarcely realize that they have a soul; who either feel not that they need salvation, or fancy that it is already secured? If they cannot be roused, if their false peace cannot be disturbed, they must inevitably perish; and, humanly speaking, to rouse them seems impossible. Indeed, what can rouse those who sleep in Zion, where every thing calls to activity? The thunders of Sinai have roared around them; the trumpet of the gospel has loudly sounded in their ears; Christ has called, saying, Go, work to-day in my vineyard; a voice from heaven has exclaimed, Whosoever hath ears to hear, let him hear; ministers have cried, Awake thou that sleepest, and arise from the dead; death has repeatedly come near and snatched away one and another of their acquaintance into darkness; yet still they are at ease. What then can rouse them? It is true, God can do it; for with him nothing is impossible. But have we any reason to hope that he will? We may indeed hope, but our hopes must be faint; for he has denounced many most awful threatenings against such characters; he threatens to give them up to their own hearts' lusts, to pour on them a spirit of slumber and of deep sleep; and it does not seem probable that he who denounces such threatenings, he who says, Wo to them that are at ease in Zion, will come to rouse them, till their false peace, and vain confidence shall be forever destroyed by the terrors of the last day. Then, we are told, sinners in Zion shall be afraid, and fearfulness will surprise the hypocrites in heart. Then they will begin to cry to the mountains, Fall on us; and to the hills, Cover us. Then the foolish virgins, the false and slumbering professors of Christianity, will awake, and cry in despair, Our lamps are gone out.

But however desperate the situation of such may appear, it is the duty of Christ's ministers to despair of none, so long as life remains. I must, therefore, improve the subject, by making one more attempt to rouse those among us, who are at ease in Zion. In making this attempt, I do not draw the bow at a venture. I do not speak feeling uncertain whether any of the characters whom I address are present. No, it is but too plain, that many, very many of you are at ease in Zion. Some such may be found probably in almost every pew. This house has become, with respect to many, like a great dormitory, where immortal souls are slumbering away their day of grace, and dreaming of peace, when there is no peace. From how few among you is the cry heard, What must I do to be saved? How few are seen flying from the wrath to come. How many luke-warm professors does the eye of Christ discover, who, though they have a name to live, are in reality dead. How few are the mourners in Zion. How few can say, Rivers of tears run down mine eyes, because men keep not God's law. How many of you never wept one hour in secret over your sins, or lost one hour's sleep in consequence of anxious concern for your salvation. Even whole families may yet be found among us, from which no prayer, no cry for mercy ascends to heaven. These, my friends, are awful symptoms. They indicate but too plainly a dreadful prevalence of spiritual insensibility among us. Like the inhabitants of the old world, you are eating and drinking, and planting and building, and marrying and giving in marriage, while death, like the flood, is constantly approaching and threatening to sweep you away with resistless violence to the judgment seat. God hearkens and hears, but you speak not aright. Almost no one repents of his wickedness, saying, What have I done? This insensibility must be removed, this fatal peace destroyed. In God's name, then, I must sound an alarm. In his name, and as his watchman,—who must answer for your souls, if they perish through my neglect,—I set the war-trumpet of Jehovah to my lips, and cry, Wo, wo, wo, to you that are at ease in Zion! Thus saith Jehovah, the great, the mighty, the terrible God, tremble ye that are at ease; rise up and be troubled, ye careless ones, and listen to my voice; for while ye say peace and safety, sudden destruction cometh upon you, and ye shall not escape. Your peace is delusive; your ease is full of danger; it is the stagnant calm which precedes the hurricane and the earthquake; it is the ease which the diseased patient feels when raging inflammation terminates in gangrene; the symptom, the immediate forerunner of death. No farther evidence of your guilt and danger is requisite; nothing more is necessary to secure your condemnation, than the very ease which you feel, and the false confidence which confirms it. It is your not fearing the wo, which brings the wo upon you. It is your very insensibility to your danger, which proves your danger to be great; it is your unconcern for your sins, which proves that they have never been pardoned. I ask not, then, whether you are guilty of great and notorious offences; I ask not, whether you are unbelievers, or impenitent, or apostates; I only ask, whether you are at ease in Zion? If you are, I, and yet not I, but Jehovah says, Wo, wo unto you! Nor is it every degree of concern, every slight momentary disturbance, every serious thought or check of conscience, which will prove that you are not exposed to this wo. No, it is your habitual feelings and state of mind, which decides your character; and if you are habitually at ease; if you are not working out your salvation, the wo still lies upon you. And remember, the longer it remains upon you, the more heavy and terrible does it become; for he who is not led to repentance by a consideration of the goodness and long-suffering of God, is treasuring up wrath against the day of wrath. Remember too, that the longer your false peace continues, so much the more improbable it is, that it will be effectually disturbed, till it is forever too late; for with respect to those who have long been at ease in Zion, God's commission to his ministers is, Go and say to this people, hear ye indeed, but understand not, and see ye indeed, but perceive not. Make the heart of this people gross, and make their ears heavy, and shut their eyes, lest they should hear with their ears, and see with their eyes, and understand with their hearts, and be converted, and I should heal them. The Lord called to weeping, and mourning, and girding with sackcloth, and behold joy and gladness, eating flesh and drinking wine, and it was revealed in mine ears by the

Lord of Hosts, Surely this iniquity shall not be purged from you till ye die, saith the Lord of Hosts.

And what will the end of these things be? Because I have called and ye refused, I have stretched out my hand and no man regarded; but ye set at nought my counsel and would none of my reprcof; I also will laugh at your calamity and mock when your fear cometh. My careless hearers, your ease must be disturbed, and come to an end. Yes, O yes; your fear will come as desolation, your destruction will come as a whirlwind; distress and anguish will come upon you; for the day of the Lord shall so come as a thief in the night, in which the heavens being on fire, shall be dissolved and pass away with a great noise, and the elements shall melt with fervent heat; and the earth with the works thereof shall be burnt up; for the mouth of the Lord hath spoken it. And he is not man, that he should lie, nor the son of man that he should repent. O, then, since your peace must be finally disturbed, is it not better, that it should be disturbed now, when true peace with God may be obtained, rather than hereafter, when it will avail nothing? Will you still cherish a serpent which is stinging you to the heart? Will you remain at ease, while your sins are unpardoned, while your souls lie in ruin, while God is daily angry, while the wrath to come is rushing on!

SERMON XXXIII.

A CLASS OF SINNERS EXCLUDED FROM MERCY.

It is a people of no understanding; therefore he that made them will not have mercy on them, and he that formed them will show them no favor.—Isaiah xxvii. 11.

My hearers, there is no error or mistake into which the wayward mind of man can fall, against which a warning or caution is not given us in the Bible. The passage which has just been read, is admirably adapted, if it was not expressly designed, to guard men against an error, which, though not often openly avowed, prevails, I suspect, very extensively. The error to which I allude is this: When sinners hear of the dangers to which they are exposed, and of the miseries which will be their portion hereafter, unless they repent, they often say in their hearts, we are God's creatures; he has brought us into existence without our consent; he is therefore bound in justice to take care of us, and to prevent our existence from becoming a curse. And even if he is not bound in justice to do this, yet he is merciful; and he will surely show mercy to his own creatures; he will not forsake forever the work of his own hands. We cannot therefore believe that he will make any of us miserable forever. We cannot doubt that, in some way or other, he will secure the final salvation, if not of all men, yet of all who are not more criminal than we have been. He will either save us without conversion, or, if conversion be necessary, he will cause us to be converted before we die. Such thoughts are, doubtless, entertained by hundreds and thousands who never avow them; and they serve to harden those by whom they are entertained in a false and fatal security, which scarcely any thing can disturb. Now it seems as if our text was uttered on purpose to sweep away all such thoughts, and to disturb the false peace which they produce. In this passage God adverts directly to the fact, that he is the Former, the Creator of those whom he, notwithstanding, threatens to destroy. He says, respecting at least one class of sinners, He that made them will not have mercy on them, and he that formed them will show them no favor. As if he had said, Though I am their Creator, and they are my creatures, though I am the Former of their bodies and the Father of their spirits; yet I will execute upon them all my threatenings, I will deal with them according to the rules of strict justice, and treat them as if there were no mercy in my nature. Let them not therefore hope to escape, because their Maker is their judge. Let them expect no more favor, than if they were to be judged by a stranger.

My hearers, if there are any among you who do not regard the threatenings of Jehovah as idle words, they will doubtless wish to know of what characters he speaks, what class of sinners he threatens to treat in this manner. They are clearly, though briefly described in our text. In discoursing upon it, I shall endeavor,

I. To illustrate this description:

II. To show the terribleness of the threatening here denounced; and,

III. To prove that it is just.

I. The characters here mentioned are described as persons of no understanding. But what is here meant by understanding? Certainly not what we commonly mean by that term. Certainly not reason, or intellectual abilities. No one can suppose that the persons here censured and threatened were idiots or madmen. Had this been their character, they would have been incapable of sin, and consequently undeserving of punishment. The word, understanding, is obviously used in this passage, as in very many others, to signify spiritual understanding, or a knowledge of religious truth. Thus we are told in one passage, that to depart from evil is understanding; in another, that the knowledge of God is understanding; in a third, that a good understanding have all they that keep his commandments; and in a fourth, that Christ's words are all plain to him that understandeth. Of course, to refuse to depart from evil, to be ignorant of God, and to disobey his commands, and to find Christ's words unintelligible, are proofs that, in the sense of the text, men are without understanding. In another passage we are told, that he who followeth vain persons, that is, he who imitates sinners, and walks in their ways, is void of understanding. Our Savior intimates that, to be ignorant of the defiling power of sin, and of the sinfulness of our hearts, is also a proof that we possess this character. And in another place he intimates, with equal clearness, that unbelief, or the absence of faith in him, is a proof that men are without understanding. In fine, we are told in general terms, that wicked men understand not judgment, but they who fear the Lord understand all things; and that the fear of the Lord is the beginning of wisdom. It is evident, then, that a man may possess great intellectual abilities, may be wise with respect to this world, may have acquired much knowledge of subjects not immediately connected with religion, and yet be without understanding in the sense of our text. They are so. The Lord looked down from heaven upon the children of men, to see if there were any that did understand. And what was the result of his examination? They are all gone out of the way, there is none that understandeth, no not one. We are also assured that madness is in the hearts of the children of men; and the prodigal son, whom all men naturally resemble, is represented as having been beside himself, till he resolved to return to his father. But some may ask, if all men are naturally without spiritual understanding, and if, as the text asserts, God will not have mercy on such as sustain this character, will it not follow that he can have mercy on none; that all must perish? I answer, it must be recollected, that the persons referred to in the text were God's ancient people; that they had been favored with religious instruction; that they had been clearly and repeatedly taught their duty, urged to perform it, and warned of the consequences of neglecting its performance. Of course, they had enjoyed many most favorable opportunities of acquiring spiritual understanding, of becoming wise unto salvation. They had the word of God in their hands; they had religious teachers to explain it and press upon them a compliance with its contents; and they had been the subjects of many providential dispensations, both merciful and afflictive, which were designed and well adapted to lead them to reflection. It was not till all these means of instruction had been long employed in vain; it was not till after repeated calls and warnings that the awful declaration in our text was made respecting them. It follows, that, though all men are naturally without spiritual understanding, this declaration does not refer to all. It refers to those only who, like the Jews, have long enjoyed, but have abused or neglected means of grace and opportunities of acquiring religious knowledge. Of such and such only God here says, He that made them will not have mercy on them, and he that formed them will show them no favor. Let us consider,

II. The terribleness of this threatening.

There is something terrible in its very sound. To hear the eternal, omnipotent Creator say respecting sinful, guilty, dependent creatures, I will show them no mercy, no favor, is enough to make the ears of every one that heareth to tingle. But terrible as is the sound of these words, their meaning is much more so. It includes every thing dreadful, every thing which man has reason to deprecate. It implies, as has already been observed, that God will deal with them according to the rules of strict justice; that he will treat them as they deserve; and as sinners deserve nothing, he will grant them nothing. But more particularly, this threatening implies,

1. That God will either deny them the common blessings of his providence, or grant them those blessings in anger, and send a curse with them. His language to such characters is, If ye will not lay it to heart, to give glory to my name, I will send a curse upon you, and I will curse your blessings. Yea, I have cursed them already, because ye laid it not to heart. The curse of the Lord is in the house of the wicked. Cursed shalt thou be in thy basket and store; cursed shalt thou be in thy children; cursed when thou goest out, and when thou comest in.

My hearers, it is a terrible thing to have the common blessings of providence given to us in anger, with a curse; for they will, in this case, be of no service to us; and we shall be called to render a strict account of them another day. Scarcely any thing can be more dreadful than to have talents, or knowledge, or wealth, or influence bestowed on us, without a heart to improve them; for they will terribly aggravate our final condemnation. A sinner, poor, ignorant, and without influence, is much less to be pitied, than one who possesses wealth, learning, or power; for he will have much less to answer for in the great day of account. The threatening implies,

2. That God will either deprive sinners of their religious privileges, means, and opportunities, or withhold his blessing, and thus render them useless. Thus he dealt with the Jews. He still sent them messengers, and instructions, and warnings; but did not send a blessing with them. Of course, they were entirely ineffectual, and answered no other purpose than to harden them in sin, and increase their condemnation. He said to them, Hear ye, indeed, but understand not, and see ye indeed, but perceive not. And he said this, because they had long refused to perceive and understand. In a similar manner he often treats similar characters at the present day. He still permits them to have the Bible in their hands, to hear the gospel, to enjoy the day and means of grace; but he permits this, not in mercy, but in anger; he withholds his blessing from these means, and in consequence they prove a savor of death unto death to those who possess them. This also is a most terrible evil. On this side of everlasting burnings, there can scarcely be a greater. Much less terrible would it be, to lose at once, and forever, religious privileges, means and opportunities, than to have them continued to us as a curse. This threatening implies,

3. That God will withhold from such characters the awakening, enlightening, and sanctifying influences of his Spirit. These influences are especially called his grace or favor. Of course he will withhold them from those to whom no favor is shown. And those from whom he withholds them will remain forever without understanding, without knowledge, without religion; and will, of course, perish in their sins. This is the evil which David deprecated so earnestly. O, take not thy Holy Spirit from me. This God himself represents as a most terrible evil. Wo unto them, he says, when I forsake them. Wo, indeed! for, my hearers, a sinner had much better be in the regions of despair, than in this world, after the Spirit of God has finally forsaken him; because he will do nothing but treasure up wrath against the day of wrath; and the longer he

lives, the more wrath will he accumulate. This threatening farther implies,

Lastly, that at the Judgment day God will condemn such characters to depart accursed into everlasting fire, and that he will grant them no mitigation of their miseries through eternity. There is no medium between mercy and condemnation. Those, therefore, on whom God has no mercy he must condemn. To shorten or mitigate their sufferings, would be a favor. But if he shows them no favor their sufferings can neither be shortened nor mitigated. To use the awful language of inspiration,—they must drink forever and ever of the fierceness of the wrath of Almighty God, which is poured out without mixture into the cup of his indignation.

And now, my hearers, put together all that has been said of the import of this threatening, and say, whether it is more than the words fairly and necessarily imply. Say, too, whether any threatening can be more terrible; whether any combination of words can be more deeply fraught with horror and despair than these, He that made them will not have mercy on them, and he that formed them will show them no favor. Alas, if he who made them, has no mercy on them, who will, who can? And what can be more deplorable than the situation of a sinner against whom this threatening is gone out! But is this terrible threatening just? Can the sin of which these characters are guilty deserve such a doom as this? This leads us to show, as was proposed,

III. That it is perfectly just. It is so,

1. Because the persons against whom this threatening is denounced never ask for mercy, never seek the favor of God. This is evident from their character. Being ignorant of God, of the sinfulness of their own hearts, and of the defiling power of sin, they feel not their need of mercy to pardon them, of grace to sanctify them, of God's favor to make them happy. Of course, they never ask or seek for these blessings. Not one among them ever said from his heart, God be merciful to me a sinner. And why should he give them what they never ask for; what they do not regard as worth seeking? We might as well say, that it is unjust for him not to give wealth to an indolent man, or learning to one who neglects study, as accuse him of injustice because he does not show mercy to those who

never seek it. If he shows them no favor, he shows them as much as they ask for, as much as they deserve. He had said to them, If thou cry after knowledge, and lift up thy voice for understanding; if thou seek for it as for silver and search for it as for hid treasures; thou shalt then understand the fear of the Lord, and find the knowledge of God. But they did not think the blessing worth all this trouble. They did not choose to have it on these reasonable terms. They chose rather to remain without understanding, though they were warned that, in consequence, they would lose forever the favor of God. How then can they complain, when they have what they chose?

2. The justice of this threatening will appear still more evident if we consider, that these persons have long rejected and abused the offered mercy and grace of God. We have already seen that our text refers, not to every one who is destitute of spiritual understanding, but to those only who, like the Jews, have been long favored with the means of acquiring it; those to whom God has spoken, whom he has offered to teach, whom he has tenderly invited and entreated to accept of mercy, and not to receive his grace in vain. Now such characters must, of course, have often sinned against the mercy and grace of God. Year after year, he has followed them, saying, Turn ye at my reproof, and I will pour out my Spirit upon you, I will make known my words to you. But they refused to turn. They set at nought all his counsels, they regarded none of his reproofs. They did not like to retain God in their knowledge, and practically said to him, Depart from us, for we desire not the knowledge of thy ways. How just is it then, that he should take them at their word; that he should never show them mercy, but give them up to walk in their own ways, and be filled with the fruit of their own devices! Mercy was offered to you, it was urged upon you; you were entreated to accept it, is a reply which will forever shut the mouth of all who perish under the threatening denounced in the passage.

3. This threatening is just because the characters to whom it refers must be guilty of many other aggravated offences. They must have been destitute of the fear of God; for to fear him is the beginning of wisdom. They must have refused to renounce their sins; for to depart from evil is understanding. They must have loved darkness rather than light; for they rejected

the latter and chose the former; and the reason was, their deeds were evil. They must have followed and imitated sinners; for this all do who are void of understanding. Finally, they must have disobeyed God's commands; for all who obey them have a good understanding. And who will venture to say, that men who disobey God's commands, who imitate sinners, whose deeds are evil, who love darkness rather than light, who refuse to renounce their sins, and who have no fear of God before their eyes, deserve that God should have mercy upon them, or show them any favor? If such characters can deserve mercy, who do not deserve it? If it is unjust to punish such characters, on whom can punishment be justly inflicted! Surely, if there are any on whom God ought not to have mercy, and to whom he ought to show no favor, they are such sinners as are described in our text.

And now, my hearers, what use shall we make of this subject? You have heard that there is a class of sinners on whom God will not have mercy, and to whom he will show no favor. Does it not then become us to inquire, whether there are any of this class among ourselves? Painful as is the thought, I cannot but fear that there are. I fear, greatly fear, that there are not a few in this assembly, of whom their Maker has said, I will not have mercy upon them. I have two reasons for fearing this, and I will tell you what they are. In the first place, it is but too certain that there are many among us, of whom it may be said in the sense of the text, they have no understanding. The proofs that many possess this character, are too plain to be denied or overlooked. Many of you, my hearers, cannot but know that you possess it. Many of you know that you are not influenced by the fear of God; and this is one proof that you have no understanding. Many of you know that you do not keep his commandments; this is another proof. Many of you know that you have never forsaken your sins; this is a third proof. Many of you know that you imitate the conduct of sinners; this is a fourth proof. Many of you know that the words of Christ, the doctrines of the gospel, do not, in your view, appear plain or intelligible; this is a fifth proof. Many of you know that you do not possess that spiritual knowledge of God which is described in the Scriptures; this is a sixth proof. And many of you know that you do not see the sinfulness of your own hearts, and the defiling nature of sin; this is a seventh proof. These, taken together, compose the principal characteristics of those who, in the sense of our text, have no understanding. And all these characteristics are certainly found in many persons now before me. And while, like the Jews, you possess these characteristics, you have like them long been favored, in a high degree, with religious privileges, means, and opportunities. I know of but few congregations, even in this highly favored land, that have enjoyed the means of grace, and of acquiring religious knowledge more amply than you have. You have had the Bible in your hands from your childhood. Its contents have been explained and urged upon you, Sabbath after Sabbath, and year after year. It has been the great aim of your minister to preach the gospel to you, in as plain and intelligible a manner as possible, and to hold up before every man his own character and situation in such a light that he could not, unless wilfully blind, avoid seeing it. He has endeavored to present the truth to your minds, and consciences, and hearts, in every way which he thought calculated to awaken, convince, alarm and melt you. You have also, in repeated instances, been addressed by some of the most able, faithful, and impressive ministers in New England. You have had opportunities of hearing the gospel not only in season, but out of season; not only on the sabbath but on other days; not only in the house of God, but in your own houses. Meetings for religious inquiry have been established; you have been invited to attend them; and those who felt unwilling to attend them have been often requested to visit their pastor at his own house, and converse with him in private. In short, the whole apparatus of religious means has been employed to make you wise unto salvation; and it is not perhaps too much to say, that the Jews themselves who are referred to in our text, were not warned more plainly or frequently than you have been. One thing at least is certain. They never heard of that Savior, and of that redeeming love which has been urged upon you again and again. And yet, as it respects many of you, all has proved in vain. Indeed, many of you have not diligently attended on these means. They have indeed attended public worship on the Sabbath, when no real or fancied difficulty prevented; for they had then nothing else to do. But all other opportunities of hearing the truth, have, by not a few, been entirely neglected. And now, unless a change for the better should soon be witnessed, our meetings for religious inquiry, and our weekly lecture must be given up, because so few think it worth their while to attend them. These facts prove conclusively, that the language of the text is no less applicable to many of this assembly, than it was to the Jews. They prove that there are many who do not seek after knowledge, who do not think it worth seeking for. Of course, they furnish one reason for fearing that God has said respecting them, he that made them will not have mercy on them, and he that formed them will show them no favor.

A *second* reason which I have for fearing this is, that, with respect to many of you, God appears to be already executing this threatening. He does not indeed take away your religious privileges and means of grace; but what is far more dreadful, he withholds his blessing from them. It is evident as facts can make it, that he does not have mercy upon you, that he does not show you favor; for he does not awaken you, he does not convince you of sin, he does not convert you, he does not pardon you. Of course, the means of grace do you no good. The language of God's dealings with hundreds in this assembly is, and for years has been, Make the heart of this people fat, and shut their eyes, and make their ears dull of hearing; lest they should hear with their ears, and see with their eyes, and understand with their hearts, and be converted, and I should heal them. And if he should continue to withhold his grace and mercy in the same way, for a few years longer, all who have passed the meridian of life, and many who have not reached it, will be in their graves, will have died without mercy, and will perish forever without mercy. And does not this look very much as if God had said respecting the impenitent part of this assembly, I will not have mercy on them? Does it not look as if the decree had gone forth against them? Does it not afford reason to fear that Christ has wept over them, as he did over Jerusalem, after her day of grace was ended, saying, O that thou hadst known, even thou, in this thy day, the things which belong to thy peace: but now they are hidden from thine eyes! My impenitent hearers, if Christ has said this of you, if God has in just displeasure determined to have no mercy upon you, your doom is as certain as if you were already shut up in the prison of despair, with an impassable gulf fixed between you and heaven. I do not assert that this is the case. I do not say that because God has not yet shown you mercy, he never will do it. But I do say, that there is reason, great reason to fear that such is the fact. And I do say, that if he determined not to have mercy upon you, and to show you no favor, this determination is perfectly just; for remember, I have often warned you to beware of grieving God's Holy Spirit, and turning away his love and mercy from you. Of no danger have I warned you more frequently, or more loudly than of this. I must then say, that if this danger has overtaken any of you, if the decree has gone out against you, it is most just. Were I certain that this is the case, I should scarcely think it worth while to address you again; but as it is possible that there are, at least, some among you, against whom the door of mercy is not yet shut, I would once more attempt to rouse them, hoping that it may not be too late. If any yield to the attempt, it will prove that, with respect to them, it is not too late. O then, be persuaded to yield to me, to believe me, while I once more remind you of the terribleness of this threatening, of the dreadful situation of those, on whom God will have no mercy; and while in his name I once more say to you, Turn ye at my reproof. I will pour out my Spirit upon you. If you can think of this threatening without being alarmed; if you can hear this invitation without being moved, it will be one more convincing proof that you are indeed without understanding. And if God does not in mercy bless this warning, it will be one more awful indication that he is determined to have no mercy upon you, to show you no favor. Tell me then, O, tell me, I beseech you, does this warning affect you? With the anguished solicitude of a parent inquiring whether the means just employed for the relief of an apparently expiring child are successful, I ask, does this warning affect you? Does the still small voice of God within you second the voice of his word? Does he say, Sinner, sinner! why will you die? And is there any thing within you which can yet hear and feel? If there is, blessed, O, blessed be a merciful God, that he has not yet in just anger shut up his tender mercies forever from you. Blessed be his name, that your consciences are not yet seared as with a hot iron, that you are not yet past feeling, that you are not yet given up to final hardness of heart. But if you are yet capable of feeling any thing, beware, O, beware! It may be the last time that the Spirit of God will ever cause the truth to affect you. If you should lose your present impressions he may depart, never to return; and God may say, I will not have mercy upon you. O then, cherish these impressions, as the apple of your eye. Cherish them as you would cherish your own souls. Watch the spark of conviction within you, as you would watch the dying lamp of life. Make it immediately your great business to become wise unto salvation. Cry after knowledge. Lift up your voice for understanding. Seek for it as for silver. Search for it as for hid treasure. Above all, depart from evil, and turn to him who giveth wisdom liberally, and upbraideth not. Let the wicked forsake his way, and the unrighteous man his thought, and let him turn unto the Lord. And are there any present to whom these directions will not apply, any who feel nothing? But why do I ask? If such there are, I can say nothing to them; I can do nothing for them. They are in the hands of God, and he must, and he will do with them, as seemeth good in his sight.

SERMON XXXIV.

PUNISHMENT OF THE IMPENITENT INEVITABLE AND JUSTIFIABLE.

As I live, saith the Lord, though Coniah the son of Jehoiakim king of Judah were the signet upon my right hand, yet would I pluck thee thence.—JEREMIAH. XXII. 24.

THIS chapter contains a message from God to the king of Judah. The first part of this message is composed of exhortations to repentance, and promises of pardon, if the fruits of repentance should appear. Then follow most awful threatenings: But if ye will not hear these words, I swear by myself, saith the Lord, that this house shall become a desolation. For thus saith the Lord unto the king's house of Judah, thou art Gilead unto me, and the head of Lebanon. Yet I will make thee a wilderness and cities not inhabited. Gilead, you will recollect, was the most pleasant and fertile part of Canaan, and Lebanon was its highest mountain. So the Jews were God's chosen people, his portion and, as we are elsewhere told, his heritage in the earth, in whom he delighted; and the kings of Judah were the head of this chosen people, and on many accounts peculiarly dear to God. They were the descendants of his servant David with whom he had made, a covenant, and Jeconiah the present king was the grandson of Josiah who, in zeal for God, nearly resembled his pious ancestor. Yet God here declares that, notwithstanding this, he would destroy Jeconiah and his kingdom, unless his judgments were averted by speedy repentance. In our text the same declaration is repeated in still more forcible language: As I live, saith the Lord, though Coniah king of Judah were the signet upon my right hand, yet would I pluck thee thence. The signet was a seal very anciently worn by nobles and monarchs upon the right hand, with which they were accustomed to seal their grants, legislative acts, and judicial sentences. Thus we read in Daniel that the king sealed the stone on the lion's den with his own seal. For this reason, as well as on account of its beauty and value, it was highly prized by the wearer; and, in consequence of its use in sealing royal grants and edicts, it was considered as a symbol of authority. Hence it appears that the declaration in our text is exceedingly strong. It is as if Jehovah said, Were the king of Judah dear to me, as the signet upon my right hand; dear to me as my sovereign power and authority over the universe, I would cast him from me for his sins, unless he repents.

That which immediately follows renders this passage still more interesting. After denouncing upon the sinful king the most awful judgments, God adds, O, earth, earth, earth, hear the word of the Lord. As if he had said, Let no one suppose that this declaration, confirmed by my oath, concerns Jeconiah only; but let all the inhabitants of the earth hear and know, that sooner than suffer impenitent sinners to go unpunished, I will give up all that I most prize, give up my sovereign power and authority. Let them hear and know that, however dear any of my creatures may be to me, I will cast them from me, if they sin and do not repent. I propose, in the present discourse,

I. To mention some awful instances in which God has verified this declaration;

II. To state so far as we can learn them from the Bible, the reasons which induce him to act in this manner.

The first instance which I shall mention, in which God has verified this declaration, is that of the apostate angels. These now fallen spirits were originally the most exalted of God's creatures, the noblest image of their Creator which his power ever stamped on the work of his hands. Like him they were perfectly holy; they loved him with perfect love, delighted in obeying his will, and for, we know not how long, a period, perhaps for thousands of ages, were employed in performing it.

In a word they were the immediate attendants on his throne, the inhabitants of that heaven which is the habitation of his holiness and glory. Hence if creatures can be dear to God and objects of his love, they were so. But they sinned, and what was the consequence? Let inspiration answer. God spared not the angels who sinned, but cast them down to hell, and reserves them under chains of darkness to the judgment of the great day. And our Savior teaches us, that hell itself and its torments were prepared for the devil and his angels. My hearers, look a moment attentively, and without prejudice, upon the awful display of God's justice and holy displeasure against sin. See how high these exalted intelligences once stood, how low they have fallen, how irremediable is their destruction. This one fact is worth ten thousand of those vain sophistical arguments with which sinners attempt to persuade themselves that God will not destroy them, though they persist in sin. Here are no human conjectures or human reasonings, but plain matter of fact.

And O, how awful, how alarming is the fact! What a death blow does it give to all the presumptuous hopes of impenitent sinners! How does it trample on all their vain reasonings! My hearers, were an angel from heaven to assure me that God is too merciful to cast any of his creatures into hell, I could not believe him, while the fact stands recorded in the Bible. Indeed, how could I, how could any man believe that God will not do what he has actually done? If with the fact staring him in the face, any impenitent sinner can hope that God will not destroy him, I would say to that sinner, are you of more consequence, or more dear to God, than were the angels of his presence? If not, why should he treat you more favorably, than he has treated them? You have transgressed the same law which they violated. The sentence which has been executed on them is already pronounced on you? How then can you hope that the same God who spared not them, will spare you? Let me prevail upon you to dismiss all such hopes at once; for as the Lord liveth, though you were the signet on his right hand; though you were dear to him as the angels of his presence, he would not save you, if you continue in sin. It is a much greater thing to cast down sinning angels from heaven to hell, than to cast sinful man out of the lower world into hell; and since God has done the greater, be assured he will not fail to do the less.

Another instance, in which God has verified the declaration in our text, is afforded by our first parents. That God loved them, there can be no doubt. That their happiness was dear to him, what he did to promote it, abundantly proves. He made them but little lower than the angels, stamped upon them his own image, crowned them with glory and honor, gave them a world with all that it contained; and as if this were not sufficient, planted for them a garden in that world, resembling heaven as nearly as any thing earthly can do it. Yet in the very day in which they first sinned, he pronounced on them sentence of death, banished them from paradise, and cursed the earth for their sake, to show his abhorrence of their sin. And can any of their descendants be more dear to him than they were? Can any of them hope to escape the curse which fell on the first sinful pair? Surely not. Know, sinful child of Adam, that, were you dear to God as were your first parents, he would not spare you in sin.

A third instance of a similar nature may be seen in the destruction of mankind by the flood. We have often read and heard of this event; but our conceptions of it are probably exceedingly inadequate. Indeed, they must be so; for who that has not witnessed such an event, can adequately conceive of it? We have good reason, let it be remembered, to believe, that the world was at least as populous then as it is now. Let your thoughts then run through the world; collect in imagination the many millions of its inhabitants into one vast assembly. See in this assembly all that is lovely in youth and beauty, all that is magnificent in rank and power, all that is admirable in intellect, all that is venerable in gray hairs. See the eternal Sovereign of the universe contemplating this vast assembly. He doubtless loves them; for they are the work of his own hands, and he hates nothing which he has made. Their happiness is doubtless dear to him, dear as the signet on his right hand; for we are assured, in language suited to our capacities, that it grieved him at the heart, when he saw them pursuing the road to misery. But though his love and mercy plead for them, their sins and his justice call for their destruction. Yet how much was there in such an assembly to move his pity; to forbid him to listen to the claims of strict justice. Surely, if he will ever relent, when the guilty stand before him, he would have relented then, when he saw how numerous were the victims which justice demanded. But he did not relent. He waited indeed one hundred and twenty years to give them an opportunity for repentance; and he sent Noah as a preacher of righteousness to warn them of their approaching fate; but he did not relent. No; the windows of heaven were opened to rain down destruction on the impenitent; and the fountains of the great deep were broken up, to whelm the guilty race in one common grave. And can you then hope, impenitent sinner, to escape the justice of a God who could do, who has done this? Can you hope that he, who did not relent when he saw a world ready to sink under the sword of justice, will relent when he sees you stand before his bar? No; were you the signet upon his right hand, could you unite in yourself all the beauty, the strength, the intellect, and the life, which now fills the world, he would not hesitate for a moment to doom you to destruction.

A fourth instance, similar in kind, though not equally awful, is presented to us in the history of God's ancient people, the children of Abraham, his friend. How greatly he loved them, how much he did for them, you need not be told. He chose them from among all the families of men to be his peculiar people. For their deliverance, protection, and support, miracles of the most wonderful kind were wrought so frequently, that they almost ceased to be considered as deviations from the established course of nature. For them God descended from heaven and spoke in an audible voice on Mount Sinai. Among them he dwelt almost two thousand years in a visible cloud of glory. To them he came and manifested himself in flesh. To them, says an apostle, pertained the adoption, and the glory, and the covenants, and the giving of the law and the promises. Theirs, he adds, are the fathers, and of them as concerning the flesh, Christ came, who is over all, God blessed forever. They were indeed, if any nation ever was, as the signet on God's right hand. Yet how terribly were they scourged! What is their history for some centuries, but a history of desolating judgments, inflicted on them by their offended God? And still his indignation follows them. For eighteen centuries, one generation of them after another has lived a wretched life; and then died without hope, under their Maker's curse. During all this time, God has been fulfilling the awful declaration which he made respecting them. It is a people that hath no understanding, therefore he that made them will not have mercy on them, and he that formed them will show them no favor. Behold, says an apostle, to the christian church, speaking of their sufferings, behold the severity of God. If he spared not them, take heed lest he spare not thee. And will he then, O impenitent sinner, spare thee? No; though thou wert the signet on his right hand, though thou wert dear to him as all the people whom he loved, and chose, he would not spare thee, unless thou shalt renounce thy sins.

We might easily refer you to multiplied instances of a similar character in the history of God's dealings with smaller communities, and with individuals. We might show you Moses, the highly favored and honored servant of God, shut out from Canaan, and doomed for one hasty, passionate word, to die with those whose carcasses fell in the wilderness. We might show you David, the man so beloved of his God, smarting with wounds, the anguish of which none but a parent's heart can conceive, and followed by an avenging sword, which God declared should never, while he lived, depart from his house. We might show you the mangled corse of an otherwise faithful prophet, who was for a single act of disobedience into which he was led by deceit, torn in pieces by a lion. But without insisting on these striking proofs of God's displeasure against sin, I shall mention only one instance more; but one which, above all that has been mentioned, displays God's inflexible adherence to the spirit of the declaration in our text. The instance to which I allude is that of our Lord and Savior Jesus Christ. He was indeed the signet on God's right hand in such a sense as no other being ever was; for he was his only begotten and well beloved Son. This object of his affection, though not himself a sinner, stood by his own consent in the place of sinners, to bear the punishment which their sins deserved. And was he treated more favorably than sinners are treated? Did God abate him one pang, take one drop from the bitter cup, or show him the least favor? No; it pleased the Lord to bruise him. He spared not his own Son. And will he then, O impenitent sinner, who by refusing to believe in Jesus Christ crucifiest him afresh, will God spare thee? No; though thou wert the signet on his right hand; though thou wert dear to him as the Son of his love, he would not spare thee, when his violated law and his insulted justice call for thy destruction. Such, my hearers, so terrible, so convincing are the proofs which God has exhibited, that he will sooner give up all that is dearest to him, than suffer sin to go unpunished, that he will sooner see heaven and earth pass away, than suffer one jot or one tittle to pass from his law, till all be fulfilled. Hear then, O earth, earth, earth! hear this word of Jehovah.

I am well aware, my hearers, that the light in which God has now been exhibited, will by no means be agreeable to the natural heart, that heart which, as inspiration assures us, is enmity against God, and not subject to his law. If any of you have such a heart in your bosoms, you will probably feel disposed to quarrel with what has been said. But remember, if you quarrel, you quarrel not with the speaker, but the Bible. If you strive, you strive not with man, but with that being who has said, Wo to him that striveth with his Maker. I have simply stated facts, as I find them recorded in God's word. I have only stated what he has declared he will do, and what he has actually done, to verify this declaration. Here I must leave it, and proceed, as was proposed,

II. To state some of the reasons why God has formed and enacted such a declaration; or, in other words, why he will sooner give up all that is dear to him, than suffer sin to go unpunished.

It is needless to remark that, among these reasons, a disposition to give pain has no place. As God has sworn by himself, that the wicked shall die, so he has sworn by himself, that he has no pleasure in their death. That he is not pleased to see them perish is abundantly evident from the means which he has employed to save them, and especially from the fact, that he has given his Son to open a way for their escape. We have already mentioned the sufferings of Christ, as a most striking proof of God's inflexible justice. We may add, that they afford an equally striking proof of his willingness to show mercy. Surely, no child of Adam can apply the epithet unmerciful to that God, who so loved the world that he gave his only begotten Son to die for its redemption.

Nor has a desire to revenge the insults and injuries which sinners have offered to himself, any place among the motives which induce God to punish sin; for he inflicts punishment, not as an injured individual, but as the Sovereign and Judge of the universe who is under the most sacred obligations to treat his subjects according to their deserts. This remark leads us directly to the grand reason why God is so inflexibly determined to punish sin, and to leave no impenitent sinner, however dear or highly exalted, to go unpunished. It is because the welfare of his great kingdom, the peace and happiness of the universe require it. It is because a relaxation of his law, a departure from the rules of strict justice, would occasion more misery than will result from a rigid execution of his law. If this can be made to appear, it will follow, that God's benevolence, his concern for the happiness of the universe, prompt him to punish sin, and to allow no impenitent sinner to go unpunished. With a view to make this appear, I remark,

That it is the nature and tendency of sin to produce universal misery. This is evident from the fact, that sin is a departure from God, the only source of happiness. God is the Father of lights, the Sun of the moral universe, the Giver of every good and perfect gift. To forsake him, then, is to lose every good and perfect gift. It is as if our world should fly off from the sun into the region of eternal darkness and frost. Besides sin inflames the appetites, enrages the passions, and, deposing reason from her throne, places them in her seat. Envy, hatred, malice, revenge, suspicion, avarice, pride, ambition and cruelty, are only different forms of sin. The breast, then, in which sin reigns uncontrolled must be the abode of misery. But this is not all. It is the tendency of sin to diffuse misery around, as far as its influence extends, as far as its power can reach. If you doubt this, consider for a moment what would be the consequence, should all the causes, which now operate to restrain the outbreakings of sin, be removed. There would then be no law but the will of the strongest. Systems of human legislation cannot exist, or, at least, cannot be carried into operation, without the assistance which they derive from oaths. But let God cease to punish sin, and oaths would become a mere nullity. They would have no binding influence on the conscience. Truth could not be discovered. The natural selfishness of the human heart, pressed on one side by most powerful temptations, and restrained by no countervailing force on the other, would continually break out in acts of injustice and violence. Neither reputation, nor liberty, nor property, nor life, would be safe for a single moment. Multitudes of tyrants would every where arise, who, after a brief reign of tumult and blood, would be assassinated, and succeeded by others. Their successors would pursue the same course, and share the same fate. In short, the earth would be, as it was before the flood, filled with violence. If you doubt this, look at the state of France, after her legislators had declared that there is no God, and caused the inscription, death is an eternal sleep, to be engraven where it should meet the notice of every passer-by; when the parent was betrayed by the son, and the son by the parent; no obligations were regarded; no man's liberty or life was secure for an hour. Yet even there all restraints were not removed; for a few years of disorder could not destroy all the effects of previous education, and obliterate all the salutary principles which had been previously imbibed. Where then would happiness find a dwelling on earth, were every restraint removed, were men suffered to go on from generation to generation in an unrestrained course of wickedness, neither fearing God nor regarding man?

Will any reply, if happiness could not be found on earth, during life, it might at least be enjoyed in heaven after death? Alas, my hearers, should God renounce his inflexible determination to punish sin, there would be no heaven. Inspiration teaches us, that the happiness of heaven consists in knowing, loving, serving, and praising God. It is his glory, we are told, which constitutes the light of the heavenly world above. But there would be no happiness in knowing, serving, or praising him, should he lose the perfections which compose and adorn his moral character. Take away his truth, his justice, his holiness, and all the glory which illuminates heaven would vanish into night. But should God renounce his determination to punish sin, he would stain all these perfections; nay, he would cease from that moment to possess them. He would no longer be true; for he has not only said but sworn, sworn by himself, that sinners shall not go unpunished. Where then would be his truth, should they escape? He would no longer be holy; for holiness implies hatred or opposition to sin. He would no longer be just; for justice consists in executing his law, and rewarding every one according to his works. In short, he would become altogether such an one as ourselves. Who then could find everlasting happiness in seeing, and praising through eternity, such a being as this? a being without truth, or holiness, or justice. Who could either respect or love him? How instantaneously would the praises of heaven cease! How would their golden harps drop from the hands of its now happy inhabitants; and how would angels be compelled to stop in the midst of their unfinished song, Just and true are all thy ways, O King of saints! The sun of the moral world would be forever eclipsed, and a black, endless night would shroud the universe. But this is not all. Were sin unrestrained, unpunished, it would soon scale heaven, as it has once done already in the case of the apostate angels; and there reign and rage with immortal strength through eternity, repeating in endless succession, and with increased aggravation, the enormities which it has already perpetrated on earth. We may add, that, after God had once surrendered his truth, his justice, and holiness; and laid aside the reins of government, he could never more resume them. Nor could he ever give laws, or make promises to any other world, or any other race of creatures, which would be worthy of the least regard. It would be instantly and properly said, He has once violated his word, and his oath, and he may do it again. He has once shown himself fickle, unjust, and unholy, and what security can we have that he will not do it again. Should he silence these clamors by an exertion of his Almighty power, he might indeed have slaves to cringe before him, but he could never have affectionate subjects who would serve him with cheerfulness and confidence; nor could he after once allowing sin to go unpunished, ever punish it again, without exposing himself to the charge of partiality and injustice.

Such, my hearers, would be the terrible consequences, or rather a part of the terrible consequences of God's renouncing his determination to punish sin. Can you then wonder or complain, that he so inflexibly adheres to this determination? Can you wonder that he will rather give up every thing most precious, than suffer any impenitent sinner, however dear or highly exalted, to escape? Do you not see that, by suffering any guilty individual to go unpunished, he would sacrifice the happiness of the universe to the selfish wishes of that individual? And is it not then most evident, that it is his benevolence, his love, his concern for the happiness of the universe, which prompts him to punish sin? Agreeably, we find the inspired writers ascribing the punishments which he inflicts to this cause. They tell us that he destroyed ancient sinners, because his mercy endureth forever; and God himself, when he said to Moses, I will cause all my goodness to pass before thee, mentioned as one proof of his goodness, that he will by no means clear the guilty. If this appears strange and incomprehensible to any of you, let me ask whether the concern of a just earthly monarch for the happiness of his subjects does not appear as clearly in the prison which he erects for the criminal and lawless, as in the rewards which he bestows on the obedient and faithful? If so, is it too much to say that the goodness of God shines as brightly in the flames of hell, as in the glories of heaven?

And now, my hearers, allow me to close by beseeching you to lay these things seriously to heart. I do not ask you to believe my opinions or reasonings; but I do ask you to believe plain matters of fact; I do ask you to consider attentively what God has actually done, that you may learn from it the character of the being with whom you have to do, in whose hands you are, and at whose bar you must stand. Remember inspiration has said, Why dost thou strive with him? for he giveth not an account of any of his matters. He will recompense it, whether thou choose or whether thou refuse. O, then, be persuaded to indulge no hopes of safety which rest on a belief that God will not execute all the threatenings recorded in his word. Be persuaded, instead of wasting your time and provoking him to anger by murmuring against his justice, to embrace at once the means which he has provided for the manifestation of his mercy. Of his mercy to those who repent and believe the gospel, we cannot say too much. We can only say, that it is equal to his justice; and that his determination to save all who repent, is as inflexible as his resolution to destroy all the impenitent. In consequence of the atonement which his Son has made, he can now be just, and yet justify and save all who believe in Jesus. O then, ye immortal spirits, ye probationers for eternity, hear, hear, hear, the words of your God! Hear and tremble, while the thunders of his fiery law burst out from Mount Sinai. Hear, believe, and rejoice, while his glad tidings of great joy are loudly proclaimed from Mount Zion. Let the wicked forsake his way, and the unrighteous man his thoughts; and let him turn to the Lord, for he will have mercy upon him, and to our God, for he will abundantly pardon.

SERMON XXXV.

THE GUILT OF INDIFFERENCE TO DIVINE THREATENINGS.

Yet they were not afraid, nor rent their garments, neither the king, nor any of his servants, that heard all these words.—JEREMIAH xxxvi, 24.

WHEN the events recorded in this chapter took place, Jeremiah had been employed for more than twenty years in discharging the duties of his prophetical office. During that period he had brought a great number of messages from God to his countrymen, in which their sins were enumerated, and the most terrible judgments denounced, both upon them and upon the neighboring nations, unless they should repent. But most of these messages had long since been forgotten; and a repetition of them seemed to produce no salutary effect. God therefore saw fit, instead of sending them new messages by the mouth of his prophet, to adopt another method of proceeding. A description of this method, and a statement of God's reasons for adopting it, are given in the first verses of the chapter before us: The word of the Lord came unto Jeremiah, saying, Take thee a roll of a book, and write therein all the words which I have spoken to thee against Israel, and against Judah, and against all the nations, from the day that I first spoke unto thee, even unto this day. It may be that the house of Judah will hear all the evil which I purpose to do unto them, and return every man from his evil way, that I may forgive their iniquity and their sin.

There did indeed seem reason to hope, that this method might produce the desired effect. Though the warnings, and threatenings, and revelations of God, when delivered separately, with perhaps long intervals intervening, had made no impression upon the hearers; yet it might be hoped that, when all these warnings and threatenings were collected, and presented to their minds at once, they would prove more efficacious. Accordingly, the experiment was tried, the record was made, and read, first to the people, and afterwards to the king and his princes; and we need only turn over the prophecy of Jeremiah to be convinced, that it was one of the most alarming, heart-affecting messages which was ever sent by God to men. It was, in effect, a letter written with his own hand, subscribed with his own name, sealed with his own seal, and dropped from heaven at their feet. And its contents were at once terrible and melting beyond description. It contained such denunciations of divine, Almighty vengeance, as, one would think, were sufficient to chill the blood and freeze the soul with horror; and, at the same time, such affectionate invitations to repentance, such tender and often repeated assurances of God's readiness to forgive the penitent offender, as must have melted any thing but a heart of adamant. Yet, says our text, yet they were not afraid, nor rent their garments, neither the king nor any of his princes when they heard these words. The mode of expression here made use of, plainly and forcibly intimates that there was sufficient reason why they should have been thus affected; and that their insensibility was exceedingly criminal. They ought to have been afraid, they ought to have rent their garments; that is, they ought both to have been alarmed, and to have felt in view of their sins, those strong emotions of grief, indignation and abhorrence, which the Jews were accustomed to express by rending their clothes.

And now, my hearers, judge, I pray you, between God and these incorrigible sinners. What other means could he employ to bring them to repentance, and thus render it possible to pardon their sins? And when these means proved ineffectual, what remained but to fulfil his word, manifest his truth and holiness, and satisfy the demands of justice, by executing upon them the destruction from which they refused to fly? If you judge righteous judgment, you will take part with God in his controversy with these obdurate rebels, and say that he and his throne are guiltless, that they richly deserved their fate. And yet, many of you cannot say this; many of you cannot, in the case before us, pronounce a righteous sentence, without at the same time condemning yourselves. God is pursuing, and for a long time has been pursuing, the same method with you, which he employed on this occasion with the Jews. He has caused all his awful denunciations against sin, all the terrible judgments which he has inflicted upon impenitent sinners, and all the far more terrible woes with which he will overwhelm them in the world to come, to be recorded in a book, in the volume of inspiration. The very roll, which Jeremiah wrote by God's command, in which he expresses so clearly his indignation against sin, and which it was so criminal in the king of Judah and his princes to disregard,—forms a part of this volume. Nor is this all. The same God, who spoke to them by his prophet, has, in these latter ages, spoken to you by his Son. By him he has revealed himself to us in the most interesting attitudes; he has addressed us in the most impressive language; he has addressed us as the God and Father of our Lord Jesus Christ; in the attitude of taking from his bosom his only begotten and well-beloved Son, that he might give him up for us all, to bear our sins on the cross. In the instructions, in the gospel of that Son, he has set before us denunciations of vengeance far more tremendous; invitations and offers of mercy far more tender; proofs of his goodness far more affecting; and motives to love and obedience far more powerful,—than were ever exhibited to his ancient people. He has brought life and immortality more clearly to light; he has rent asunder the veil which concealed the eternal world from the view of mortals; he has made the glories of heaven to blaze down upon our eyes; he has caused the unquenchable flames of hell to flash up before our faces; he has caused the groans of the latter, the songs of the former, the blast of the last trumpet, and the sentence which the final judge will pronounce upon the righteous and upon the wicked, to resound in our ears. In fine, all that he has done, all that he designs to do, he has recorded in the Scriptures. He has dictated them by his own Spirit; he has subscribed them with his own name; he has stamped upon them the broad seal of heaven; he has authenticated them by fulfilling many of the prophecies which they contain, and, addressing them to us as it were by name, has caused them to drop from heaven into our hands. And he has told us why all this is done. It is done with the same view with which the record of Jeremiah was made. It was done that we, and other sinners, to whom its contents relate, might read and hear them; and thus be induced to return unto our forsaken God, and receive, through the atonement and intercession of Jesus Christ, the forgiveness of all our iniquities. In part this design has been accomplished. The record has reached us. Its contents have been made known to us. You have all read them and heard them read. And some of you, we trust, have not heard them in vain. You have complied with the gracious design for which they were sent. You have been alarmed by their threatenings. You have felt grief and shame and self-abhorrence, in view of your sins; you have renounced them, and returned to your forsaken God, and he has freely forgiven you all your trespasses.

But many of you, my hearers, though you have heard and read the same truths, have not been thus affected by them. You have rather imitated the king of Judah and his princes. You have not been alarmed; you are not now alarmed, when you hear the threatenings of God's word; and some, who once were so, have ceased to feel alarm. Nor have you felt those emotions which the Jews were accustomed to express by rending their garments. You have not been grieved; you have not been ashamed; you have not felt self-abhorrence on account of your sins; nor have your hearts relented in view of God's mercies. No, as certainly as the charge in our text stands recorded against the king of Judah and his princes, so certainly does it stand recorded against you in the book of God's remembrance, that though you have heard all his words, yet you were not suitably alarmed, or affected by them; but listened to them, for the most part, with indifference and unconcern. This charge then we must as it were, extract from the records of heaven, and press it upon your attention. It is by far the heaviest charge which we have to bring against you, or indeed which can be brought against sinners. That you are moral, in the common acceptation of the term, we do not undertake to deny. That you are punctual in attending on the public worship of God, and treat the institutions of religion with apparent respect, I readily allow. That I am under great, very great obligations to your kindness and generosity, I acknowledge with gratitude. But still I must press upon you the charge of hearing the word of God with an almost total indifference, with a most criminal unconcern. I call you to witness against each other, that this charge is true. I call upon your own consciences to bear testimony to its truth. I call with reverence on the insulted majesty of heaven, to witness the manner in which his declarations are received in this house, and the little effect which they produce. What sinner is now led by them to fly from the wrath to come? What individual is now excited by them to ask, What shall I do to be saved? Where is the individual who is one half so much affected by all that God has said and recorded, as he would be by intelligence that some temporal calamity is impending? The charge is then fully substantiated. Heaven and earth, God and men, your own observation and your own consciousness, bear testimony to its truth.

And while it is thus proved in all its length and breadth to be true of impenitent sinners, it is also true, though we hope to a less extent, of many who have professed repentance. Yes, many who once trembled at the word of the Lord, have almost, if not entirely ceased to tremble at it. Many of the professed servants of God hear his declarations, his threatenings, his warnings, even those which are addressed to his church, with feelings very little removed from indifference. Nay they can see one of his most awful threatenings now executing, one of his most terrible judgments now inflicting upon us, without laying it seriously to heart. We allude to the almost total withdrawal of his gracious presence and of divine influences, a judgment, compared with which, pestilence, famine, and conflagration would be mercies. Yes, though we would fain not tell the disgraceful fact in Gath, nor publish it in the streets of Askelon, yet it must be told, that the words God, and Christ, and heaven, and hell, and judgment, and eternity, have almost become in this house idle words, without force or significancy; that the glorious glad tidings of the blessed God here excite no joy, and meet with no reception; that the things which many prophets and kings desired to see, and into which even angels desire to look, can scarcely command an hour's languid attention; and if God's threatenings are to excite fear, or his glad tidings to inspire joy, they must be proclaimed elsewhere; they must be addressed to hearts which have not acquired a more than adamantine hardness under the means of grace.

And is it indeed come to this? Is it indeed become a fact, that in this house, where God has so often displayed his power and grace, where the lighting down of his glorious arm has so often been seen, and where so many hearts once seemed to bow with reverence before his commands, and drink in with delight his promises, he is now become a cypher, and his word an idle tale? Is it true that he has, in this favored place, seen himself treated with such indignity, that even his patience and forbearance could no longer endure it, and he was constrained to depart? Yes, my hearers, it is indeed come to this. The glory is departed. The gracious presence of God, which once filled this house, and almost made itself visible, is withdrawn, and its departure will be final, it will never return, unless we become more suitably affected by the contents of his word, and by a recollection of the sins which have constrained him to forsake us; for his language respecting them who treat him as we have done, is, I will go and return to my place, until they acknowledge their offence and seek my face. But we shall never acknowledge our offence, till we are convinced of it; we shall never be convinced of it, till it is set clearly before us, in all its blackness and enormity, and with all its aggravations. This therefore I have of late frequently attempted to do; attempted it so often, that you are perhaps weary of the repetition and ready to wish that your attention might rather be called to some other subject. But, my hearers, what would it avail, in the present state of things, to call your attention to any other subject? What subject soever is chosen for a theme of discourse, it must be drawn from the word of God; and what can it avail to present subjects to you from his word, unless you pay some regard to its authority; unless you are, at least in some degree, affected by its contents, when they are pressed upon you?

On this often repeated subject I must therefore still insist. It must still be my first, my principal aim and endeavor, to make you sensible of the enormous, the heaven-provoking, heaven-daring wickedness of hearing without emotion the declarations of Jehovah. It is a sin which, however lightly any may regard it, involves in itself all the worst and most provoking sins of which men can be guilty. It involves, for instance, and expresses the utmost contempt of God. The man who hears God's threatenings without being afraid, and his kind invitations and promises without being melted, does in effect say to his face, I consider nothing which thou canst utter as of sufficient importance to excite the smallest emotion; neither thy favor nor thy displeasure is of the least consequence to me; I dread not thy threatenings, I regard not thy promises; after thou hast said all that thou canst say, I remain perfectly unmoved, and prepared to execute, not thy pleasure, but my own. And if this does not express the utmost contempt of God, what can express it? It is a well known fact, that our feelings toward any being may be estimated, with great exactness, by the regard which we pay to his words, and by the degree in which they affect us. If we feel any respect, or esteem, or affection for a person, we listen to his words with proportionable interest and attention; and if they relate to important subjects in which we are concerned, they will produce some effect upon our minds. On the contrary, if we thoroughly despise any one, all that he can say will be heard with indifference, and produce no effect upon us. This is so well known, that we cannot insult a man more grossly, we cannot wound his feelings more deeply, than by showing him that we pay no regard to any thing which he can say; that all his offers of friendship, all his threatened displeasure, all his arguments and entreaties, are heard by us with indifference and unconcern. No words which language affords could express contempt of him so effectually. Yet this insult, this greatest of insults, has been offered to the awful majesty of heaven and earth a thousand and ten thousand times, in this very house. And it is offered to him afresh as often as any individual hears his word read or spoken without being affected by it.

This sin also involves and indicates the highest degree of unbelief, of that unbelief which makes God a liar. When a man brings us intelligence of most important events, of events in which, if true, we are deeply interested, we cannot tell him more plainly that we disbelieve every thing which he has said, than by remaining perfectly unaffected. If we thus remain, he sees at once that we have no confidence at all in his veracity, or in other words, that we believe him to be a liar. Now the intelligence which God communicates to us in his word is, if true of the very highest, nay of infinite importance. Every man who believes it, feels that it is so, and is affected by it in exact proportion to the degree of his belief. He then who is but in a small degree affected by God's word, has but little faith in it, and he who is not at all affected by it, has no faith in it at all. He is as completely an infidel as any one who ever gloried in the name.

Again; those who hear or read the word of God without being affected, display extreme hardness of heart. They show that their hearts are absolutely unimpressible by any motives or considerations which infinite wisdom itself can suggest; that they are of so much more than flinty hardness, as to resist that word which God himself declares to be like a fire, and a hammer, that breaketh the rock in pieces. Such are some of the sins of which they are guilty, who hear without emotion the declarations of Jehovah. And we assert, with the utmost confidence and solemnity, that three worse sins never polluted the heart of fallen man, or fallen spirit. Three worse sins cannot be found in those regions of final abandonment and despair, where sin, in all its dreadful forms, rages uncontrolled. If any suppose that we exaggerate, that we portray the sinfulness of hearing God's word without regarding it in colors too dark, let them look into the Scriptures; and if any thing which is there recorded can produce conviction in their minds, they will find enough to convince them that we have not been, that on this subject we cannot be guilty of exaggerating. They will find multiplied proofs that, in God's estimation, no sin is so abominable as this; that no sin fills up so soon the sinner's measure of iniquity, or draws down such sure, and swift, and awful destruction upon his head. Look, for example, at the old world. It was corrupt, it was filled with violence, every imagination of the thoughts of man's heart was evil only, and that continually. Yet God still bore with it; for its inhabitants had not yet heard his messages with indifference. A day of grace, a space for repentance, was therefore afforded them. Noah, a preacher of righteousness, was sent to reprove them for their sins and to warn them of the destruction which was impending, and which would fall unless they repented. But they would not repent; they were not alarmed, they heard the warnings of Noah with indifference and unconcern; and this God could not bear; this sealed their doom, and the flood came and destroyed them all.

Look next at God's ancient people in the days of Jeremiah and his cotemporary prophets. They had for ages been guilty of every other sin which tended to provoke God to jealousy. They had forsaken him to worship idols; they had polluted his temple with their idolatrous abominations; they had offered their children in the fire to Moloch; and what their character and conduct were in other respects, we may learn from God's own description of it: Your hands are defiled with blood, and your fingers with iniquity; your lips have spoken lies, and your tongue muttered perverseness. None calleth for judgment, nor pleadeth for truth; they trust in vanity and speak lies, they conceive mischief and bring forth iniquity; their feet run to evil, and are swift to shed innocent blood; and judgment is turned away backward, and justice standeth afar off, for truth is fallen in the street and equity cannot enter. Now could any nation be in a worse moral and religious state than this? Yet all this God bore with, for years he bore with it. He sent them more highly gifted prophets, more faithful reprovers; and if they would have listened to these reprovers and turned from their iniquities, he would have forgiven all. But Jeremiah and other prophets had warned them in vain; when God had caused all his threatenings to be written in a book and read in their ears, and saw that they were not afraid, neither rent their clothes he could bear with them no longer, but gave them up to speedy and terrible destruction. Read the writings of Jeremiah and the other prophets of that age, and you will find that the unconcern with which they regarded God's reproofs and threatenings, are mentioned far more frequently than any of their other sins, as the immediate cause of their ruin.

Once more; look at the Jews in our Savior's time. From the testimony of their own historian, Josephus, as well as from the writings of the Evangelists, it is evident, that irreligion and every kind of immorality, every species of crime, prevailed among them in an almost unexampled degree. And yet our Savior says, If I had not come and spoken to them, they had not had sin. As if he had said, the sin of hearing, with unconcern and unbelief, the messages which I have brought them from heaven, so far transcends all other sins, that in comparison with it, they are as nothing, and not worthy even to come into the account. My hearers, this is decisive, this is sufficient. Nothing more need be said to prove that, in the judgment of God, there is no sin like that of making light of his declarations; that there is no sin which so certainly draws down the most terrible expressions of his indignation. My hearers, if any of you wonder at this, let me remind you that, in similar cases, we judge in a similar manner. Suppose a son to become idle, vicious, profligate; to be guilty of frequently and grossly disobeying his parents; to run into every kind of excess; yet they do not give him up as hopeless, do not disinherit or banish him on account of all this, so long as their expostulations, their entreaties, their tears appear to produce any effect upon his feelings. But when this ceases to be the case, when all which they can say is heard by him, and all their distress and their tears are seen by him, with perfect indifference, then they despair; then they say, he no longer regards us as his parents, we have lost all influence over his mind; there is no reason to hope that our endeavors to effect his reformation will avail any thing; let him go from us; let him follow his own course, since all attempts to restrain him are vain. Just so our Father in heaven bears and forbears, notwithstanding many gross provocations, so long as his word produces any effect upon us; so long as there seems to be the least reason to hope that we shall ever yield to its warnings and admonitions. But when he sees that they are all regarded with indifference; that we are neither alarmed by his threatenings, nor melted by his invitations, then he treats us as he treated Israel of old. Israel, says he, would not hearken to my voice, and my people would none of me: so I turned and gave them up to their own lusts, and they walked in their own counsels. Now, my careless hearers, this sin, this greatest of sins, this sin which has destroyed so many millions of immortal beings, we charge upon you; the truth of the charge has been sufficiently proved, and you yourselves cannot deny it. Even now many of you are, probably, exhibiting additional proofs of its truth. You have this day heard some of God's most terrible threatenings repeated; you have heard from his own word that he will execute them with infallible certainty, if you remain in your present state; and you have now heard how great, how provoking, how destructive a sin it is, not to be alarmed by these threatenings. Yet it is probable, it is, I fear, but too certain, that many of you are not alarmed; that many of you hear all this with as much unconcern, as the king of Judah and his princes heard the words of Jeremiah's roll. And if this is the case, what will it avail that your dispositions are amiable, that your morals are unimpeached, and that you treat the institutions of religion with some apparent respect? O, what can all these things avail, so long as your hearts are polluted, and your characters blackened in the sight of God, by the worst and most provoking of all sins? Were there any reason to hope that arguments or entreaties would induce you no longer to be guilty of it, gladly would I employ them. I would beseech you no more to tell Jehovah to his face that he cannot make you tremble, that he cannot make you weep, lest he should be provoked to make you tremble with evil spirits, and to cast you into outer darkness, where is weeping and wailing and gnashing of teeth. I would beseech you to comply with the purpose for which he has caused his declarations to be recorded and placed in your hands, by repenting of your sins, embracing the Savior, and receiving through him a full and gracious pardon. But in vain should I urge these and other considerations drawn from the word of God, so long as that word is regarded by you with indifference. I may go round and round, and assail you on every side, and seek every where for some avenue through which the truth may enter; but all will be vain, until you learn to revere and tremble at the words of Jehovah.

But shall our endeavors, my professing hearers, prove equally unsuccessful with you? If they do so, they will certainly continue to prove unsuccessful with impenitent sinners; for as Moses said to God; Lord, the children of Israel have not hearkened to me; how then should Pharaoh hear me? so we may say, If God's own professed servants do not tremble at his word, how can we hope that sinners will tremble? If it does not lead you to repentance, how shall it lead them to repent? My brethren, it is painfully affecting, it is in the highest degree alarming, to see how little apparent effect is now produced upon this church by appeals which would once have affected it like an electric shock. And it is still more affecting and alarming to see how little we are affected by the spiritual judgments under which we are perishing. Were a pestilence raging in this town, we should feel. Were half its habitations involved in one conflagration, we should feel. Nay, should trade and commerce suffer a stagnation, we should feel. But since we are suffering nothing more than the loss of God's gracious presence and its irreparable consequences, the decline of religion, the prevalence of a moral pestilence, which ends in the second death; and the spreading of a conflagration in which immortal souls are consumed, we seem to forget that we have any cause for sorrow and alarm. My brethren, these things ought not so to be; and let me add, so they must no longer be. If you ever did feel any thing, if you ever expect to feel any thing, now, now is the time to feel, and not to feel only, but to act. In Christ's name I say to you, Whosoever hath an ear, let him hear what the Spirit saith to the churches. In his name I say to you, Either cease to call me Master and Lord, or treat me as such by hearing and obeying my words. I charge every declining professor before God and the Lord Jesus Christ, and as he will answer it at the judgment day, to remember from whence he has fallen, and repent, and do his first works; and to recollect in a practical manner and with self-application, the declaration of Jehovah, To this man will I look, even to him that is poor, and of a contrite spirit, and that trembleth at my word.

And to all of every description I say, Hear ye, give ear; be not proud, for the Lord hath spoken; and what he hath spoken, he will assuredly perform. Hearken then to the voice of the Lord your God, before he cause darkness, and before your feet stumble upon the dark mountains, and while ye look for light, he turn it into the shadow of death, and make it gross darkness. But if ye will not hear it, my soul shall weep in secret places for your pride; and mine eye shall weep sore, and run down with tears, because of the destruction which is coming upon my people.

SERMON XXXVI.

THE SIN, DANGER, AND UNREASONABLENESS OF DESPAIR.

And they said, there is no hope; but we will walk after our own devices, and we will every one do the imagination of his evil heart.—JEREMIAH XVIII. 12.

THERE are two ways, my friends, in which the great enemy and deceiver of men endeavors, and alas! but too successfully, to effect their eternal ruin. In the first place, he labors, by a variety of artifices, to lull them asleep in false security and presumption. With this view, he leads them to pervert and abuse the gracious promises and invitations of the gospel; insinuates that God is too merciful to destroy his creatures; that his threatenings will never be executed, and that all will finally obtain salvation. If he finds any one who cannot be persuaded to believe these falsehoods, he suggests to them that religion is indeed important, but that it is unnecessary to think of it at present; that they have yet sufficient time for repentance, that they are less guilty than many others who have obtained mercy; and that it will be easy for them to become religious hereafter, and secure a title to heaven before death arrives. This method he pursues, principally with the young and thoughtless, and with those who abstain from gross vices, and pay some regard to the externals of religion. By these artifices he induces them to defer repentance to a more convenient season; robs them of their most precious opportunities, and leads them farther and farther from God and happiness.

In the second place, when these artifices begin to fail, he endeavors to drive men to despair. This method he pursues with the aged, with the openly vicious and abandoned, and with such also as have long enjoyed the means of grace, often experienced, but resisted, the influences of God's Spirit. To such he whispers, that it is too late; that their sins are too great to be forgiven; that their day of grace is past; that God has given them up to a reprobate mind, and that there is no mercy for them. Hence he infers that it is in vain for them now to think of religion, or use any means to obtain it; that, since they must perish, it is better for them to plunge into sin without restraint, and enjoy all the happiness which the world can afford. Thus he tempted Judas to destroy himself. Thus he tempted those who said, Let us eat and drink, for to-morrow we die; and thus also he tempted those whose language is recorded in our text. When the prophet, in the name of God, warned them of approaching judgment, and urged them to return from their evil ways; instead of complying, they despairingly exclaimed, There is no hope! we will, therefore, walk after our own devices, and we will every one do the imagination of his evil heart. This desperate resolution they executed, and destruction was the consequence.

In a similar manner, there is reason to fear, the tempter deceives and ruins some at the present day. It is probable, however, that the number thus ruined is comparatively small. So clearly does the Sun of Righteousness shine upon us; so encouraging are the precious promises of the gospel, and so numerous the instances in which even the vilest of sinners have obtained mercy, that probably very few finally perish in consequence of despondency. The opposite extreme is by far the most ruinous; for presumption and false hopes destroy, perhaps, hundreds, where despair of obtaining mercy proves fatal to one. Still it is possible that there may be some among us, whom the tempter has entangled in this snare. It is possible, though unknown to us, that there may be at least one person in this assembly, who is saying respecting himself, There is no hope; I have sinned so long, so often, and with so many aggravations, that I cannot be forgiven; my heart is so hard, that it cannot be softened; my mind so dark, that it cannot be enlightened; my sinful habits and propensities so deep-rooted that they cannot be eradicated; my attachment to sin and the world so strong, that it cannot be overcome. I fear that I am not one whom God intends to save; my day of grace is over; should I think of seeking religion, it would be now in vain; I will therefore think of it as little as possible, and devote myself to the pursuits and pleasures of the world, while I have opportunity to enjoy them.

Now, my friends, if there is only one person present, whom the great deceiver has entangled in this snare, it is our duty to attempt to deliver him from it; and could we succeed, we should be richly repaid for preaching, not only one, but ten thousand sermons. If there be one such person present, one who feels that what has been said describes his character, let him feel that this discourse is preached on purpose for him; that to him every word is addressed; and do you, my Christian friends, who have a hope of glory, pray that the spirit of God may single him out, and enable him to hear, to hope, and live; while we attempt to convince him, that it is at once sinful, dangerous and unreasonable, in the highest degree, to despair of God's mercy; to say that there is no hope.

I. To despair of God's mercy is sinful.

The ancient divines were accustomed to call despair one of the seven deadly sins. That it well deserves this character, is evident from its nature and effects. It is directly contrary to the will of God. He, we are told, taketh pleasure in them that fear him, and hope in his mercy. He must, therefore, be displeased with them that refuse to do this. It is also a great insult to the character of God. It calls in question the truth of his word; nay it gives him the lie; for he has told us that whosoever cometh to him, he will in no wise cast out. But the language of despair is, He will cast me out, though I should come to him. It calls in question, or rather denies the greatness of his mercy. He has told us that his mercy is infinite; that it is from everlasting to everlasting; but the language of despair is, My sins are beyond the reach of God's mercy, and therefore it is not infinite. It also limits the power of God. He has said, Is any thing too hard for me? With God nothing is impossible. But despair says, There are some things which are too hard for God; some things which it is impossible for him to perform. It is impossible that he should renew my heart, subdue my will, and make me fit for heaven. Thus despair limits or denies all

God's perfections, and, of consequence, greatly insults and provokes him. Despair is also contrary to the Spirit of God. The three principal graces of the Spirit are faith, hope and love. But despair is opposed to them all. That it is opposed to faith in God's promises, we have already seen; that it is opposed to hope, is evident from its very nature; and a little reflection will convince us, that it is equally inconsistent with love. To sum up all in one word, despair includes in itself the very essence both of impenitence and unbelief. It contains in itself the essence of impenitence; for it seals up the heart in a sullen, obstinate, unyielding frame, so that those who are under its influence cannot breathe one penitential sigh, or shed a single penitential tear. This effect it has on the devils. This effect it will produce in all the wicked at the judgment day. Hence it is directly opposed to that broken heart and contrite spirit, in which true repentance essentially consists. It also contains in itself the very essence of unbelief; for it shuts up the heart against all the promises of the gospel; against all the invitations of Christ; against all the revelations which God has made of his mercy, and represents him as a severe, inexorable, arbitrary tyrant, whom it is vain to endeavor to please. But unbelief and impenitence are every where represented as sins exceedingly great and provoking to God. How offensive, how provoking, then must be that despair, which includes in itself the essence of both these aggravated sins!

Again; despair is not only exceedingly sinful in itself, but the cause or parent of many other sins. As hope leads all who entertain it to endeavor to purify themselves, even as Christ is pure, so despair, the opposite of hope, leads all who are under its influence to wander farther and farther from God, and plunge without restraint into every kind of wickedness. This effect it had upon Cain. Instead of repenting and imploring pardon of God for the murder of his brother, he departed from the presence of the Lord, from all the religious privileges and instruction of his father's house, into the land of Nod; there by plunging into worldly and sinful pursuits, he endeavored to mitigate the anguish of his mind, and drive from it all thoughts of God and religion. A similar effect it had upon Saul. Despair of obtaining help from God led him to seek relief from witches and evil spirits, and finally to throw himself on his own sword. Equally awful were its effects upon Judas, whom it led to self-murder, as it probably has thousands since. The reason why despair should thus operate is evident. Take away from men all hope of obtaining any object, and they will never pursue it, but turn their attention to something else. So take away from men all hope of heaven; let them be fully convinced that it is not for them, that their day of grace is past, that their doom is fixed, and that repentance will avail nothing to alter it; and, of course, they will never repent; for they will feel no encouragement to do it; see no reason why they should attempt it. On the contrary, they will turn their attention to worldly and sinful pursuits, and endeavor by intemperance, or in some other equally dangerous way, to banish all thoughts of God and religion entirely from their minds. And when all their restraints are taken off; when they imagine that nothing will render their situation better, and that nothing which they may do can make it worse, the corruption of their hearts will have full room and liberty to operate, and will plunge them into every kind of wickedness.

II. Despair of God's mercy is dangerous. If it be sinful it must be so; for all sin is in its nature and tendency highly dangerous. But despair of God's mercy, is a sin which is dangerous in the highest degree. When a man gives himself up to this sin, he does, as it were, give himself up to the power and guidance of the devil; for he voluntarily throws away every thing which can protect or deliver him from the adversary. He throws away his Savior; he throws away God's mercy; he throws away the promises; he throws away the whole gospel of Christ; he throws away all hopes and thoughts of salvation, and consequently all endeavors to obtain it; for while he despairs of God's mercy, it is the same to him as if God had no mercy; while he despairs of Christ's ability or willingness to save, it is the same to him as if Christ had no power or disposition to save; and while he believes that the promises and invitations of the gospel are not for him to embrace, it is the same to him as if there were no gospel. All these things, therefore, the despairing sinner throws away; and when they are gone, what is there left? to what guide can he commit himself? Nothing remains, but a deceitful, malignant adversary, and a desperately wicked heart, both combined to mislead and destroy him. Yet to the guidance of these two fatal enemies every despairing sinner commits himself. Need any thing more be said, to prove that to despair of God's mercy, is dangerous in the highest degree.

III. Despair of God's mercy is no less groundless and unreasonable, than it is sinful and dangerous.

1. In the first place, it is unreasonable to despair of God's mercy, because he continues to you the enjoyment of life, and the means of grace. It is true that, with respect to some, the day of grace ends before the close of life, and their lives are preserved only that they may fill up the measure of their iniquities, and treasure up wrath against the day of wrath. But such persons are given over to a reprobate mind, and left to strong delusion, that they may believe a lie. God has said, Let them alone. His Spirit has forsaken them; conscience does not warn them; they seldom think of their danger, and are usually much more inclined to presumption than to despair. But we are now addressing those, who do think of their situation, whose consciences do warn and admonish them; and with respect to such we may generally say, that, while there is life, there is hope; for is not life a time of probation, a season of grace, an opportunity given us on purpose to make our peace with God? How unreasonable then is it to despair of mercy; while this season, this opportunity of obtaining mercy is afforded; unless you are determined not to improve it. The precious privileges which you enjoy, while this season continues, render despair still more unreasonable. What walls are these which surround you? Are they not the walls of God's house, a place where he has recorded his name, and respecting which he says, Wherever I record my name, there will I meet with you and bless you? What light is this which shines around you? Is it not the light of the Sabbath, of the day which the Lord has made, in which we have reason to rejoice and be glad? What volume is this before you? Is it not the word of God in which he reveals his grace and mercy to perishing sinners? What sound is this which now fills your ears? Is it not the sound of the gospel which brings life, and peace, and pardon, to all who believe and obey it? And will you then say, There is no hope, while the walls of God's house encircle you, while the light of the Sabbath shines upon you, while the word of God is before you, and

while the gospel of salvation sounds in your ears? Do they not all conspire to prove, that, though you are prisoners, you are prisoners of hope; and that there is still hope concerning you, if you will not neglect or put it from you in despair?

2. The character of God, as revealed in his word, shows that it is unreasonable for you to despair of his mercy. It is true that the description which the Scriptures give us of his character, is most perfectly suited to lead you to despair of obtaining his favor by your own works, or of tasting his mercy while you obstinately persist in sin. But it is also true, that it is no less perfectly suited to excite hope in the breasts of all who see the impossibility of saving themselves; who feel the burden and fetters of sin, and have the smallest desire to escape from its power. This the psalmist well knew: They that know God's name, says he, that is, they who are acquainted with his character, will put their trust in him. They cannot despair or despond; they cannot but hope in his mercy. The fact is, that despondency, as well as presumption, arises from ignorance of God. Ignorance of his justice, truth, and holiness, leads to presumption; and ignorance of his mercy, love, and grace, leads to despair. If we would be kept from both these dangerous extremes; if we would at the same time fear him, and hope in his mercy, we must contemplate the different perfections of his character together, and not view them separately, as we are prone to do. This the method pursued by the inspired writers naturally leads us to do. They very frequently set before us God's justice and mercy, his greatness and condescension, in the same passage. When to deter us from presumption they declare, that God will by no means clear the guilty, they tell us in the same verse, that he is merciful and gracious, that we may not despair. When they tell us that God is high, they immediately subjoin, Yet hath he respect unto the lowly. When they inform us that he is a God of vengeance, they are careful to assure us in the same chapter, that he is good to them that trust in him. When they describe him as the high and lofty One, who inhabiteth eternity, they add, He dwelleth with him who is of a humble and contrite spirit, to revive the spirit of the humble, and the heart of the contrite ones. While they declare that the soul that sinneth shall die, they encourage us to repent and turn from our sins by the assurance, that God has

no pleasure in the death of the wicked, but that the wicked turn from his evil way and live. Still farther to secure us from despair, they inform us, that God is love, that nothing is too hard for him, that his mercy endureth for ever, and that he is a sovereign God who can have mercy on whom he will have mercy. Surely then, the character of God renders it in the highest degree unreasonable to despair of salvation, unless we are determined to go on in sin, or to persist in seeking salvation by the works of the law.

3. The grand scheme of redemption revealed in the gospel, renders it still more unreasonable to indulge despair. This scheme God has devised and revealed, on purpose to glorify himself in displaying the unsearchable riches of his mercy and grace. Here he reveals himself as the God and Father of our Lord Jesus Christ, as the God of all grace and consolation, as a God who so loved the world as to give his only begotten Son to die for its redemption. By the sufferings and death of his Son he is reconciling the world to himself, not imputing to the penitent their trespasses. The mountains of guilt and transgression which interrupted the streams of his beneficence are removed, so that they can now flow and are flowing out to us in floods of enlightening, pardoning, and sanctifying grace. None of God's perfections now forbid him to pardon penitent sinners; for in the scheme of redemption, mercy and truth meet together, righteousness and peace embrace each other; God can now be just in justifying those who believe in Jesus. Nay, more, his justice, faithfulness, and truth, which once stood in the way of our salvation, now bind him to forgive and save all who confess, and repent of their sins. Surely then the gospel of Christ affords sufficient encouragement to animate the hopes of the most guilty, desponding sinner on earth, and render it in the highest degree unreasonable for any to despair of salvation who are not determined to reject it.

4. The person, character, and invitations of Christ, show in the most striking and conclusive manner, that despair of salvation is unreasonable. When God provided a Savior for us, he intended to provide one whose character should be a complete antidote to despair, as well as to all other evils. Accordingly, the person and character of his Son Christ Jesus are as perfectly calculated, as any thing possibly can be, to banish despair,

and excite confidence and hope. He is at once the Son of God, and the Son of Man. He is allied to heaven by his divinity, and to earth by humanity; and consequently unites in himself every thing that is amiable, admirable, or excellent, in the nature of God and in the nature of man. Though he is the Son of the Highest, he is not ashamed to be called the friend and brother of the lowest; nay, he glories in the title of the sinner's Friend. While his infinite wisdom, knowledge, and power, render him able to save even to the uttermost all that come unto God by him, his no less infinite compassion, condescension, and love, render him as willing, as he is able to save. To all who believe, he is made of God wisdom, and righteousness, and sanctification, and redemption. His blood, which speaks better things than the blood of Abel, cleanses from all sin. His Spirit can enlighten the most ignorant, subdue the most stubborn and sanctify the most polluted, and break the strongest fetter in which sin and the world ever bound the soul. The streams of his grace flow, free and uncircumscribed, as the light of the sun or the air of heaven. His language is, Let him that heareth come; and let him that thirsteth come; and whosoever will, let him come and take the water of life freely; and whosoever cometh, I will in no wise cast out. In short, it is a faithful saying, a true saying, and worthy of universal acceptation and belief, that Jesus Christ came into the world to save sinners, even the chief; and for any one who believes this saying, for any one who contemplates Christ's character, and listens to his invitation, to despair of salvation, is as impossible, as for a man to walk in darkness, who, with open eyes beholds the light of the meridian sun. One glimpse of his person and character is life to hope, and death to despondency. How unreasonable, then, is it, with such a Savior before us, for any to despair, unless they are determined to reject him.

Lastly. That it is unreasonable to despair of God's mercy, is evident from the characters of many to whom it has already been extended. Look at Manasseh. He sinned against God above all that were in Jerusalem before him, so that he seemed to have sold himself to commit iniquity. In addition to this, he was a murderer, a man stained with many murders; for we are told that he shed innocent blood very much, till he had filled Jerusalem from one end to the other. But in his affliction he humbled himself greatly before the God of his fathers, and besought him and prayed to him; and God was entreated of him, and heard his supplications. Look at St. Paul. He was a blasphemer, and bloody persecutor of the people of God; one who breathed nothing but threatenings and slaughter against his church, and compelled many of them to blaspheme. Yet he repented and obtained mercy; and he intimates that mercy was showed him for a pattern and encouragement to those who should come after him, to believe in Christ. Look at the Corinthian church. Some of you, says the apostle to them, were fornicators, and idolaters, and adulterers, and thieves, and covetous, and drunkards, and revilers, and extortioners; but, he adds, ye are washed, but ye are justified, but ye are sanctified, in the name of our Lord Jesus, and by the Spirit of our God. Such, my friends, are some of the instances recorded in the Bible, in which the greatest and vilest offenders obtained mercy on repentance. Who then will say, that it is not highly unreasonable for any to despair unless they are determined not to repent? Who can reasonably say, there is no hope for me, when such characters as these, through repentance, faith, and patience, are even now inheriting the promises?

Permit me now to ask, my friends, whether any of you are saying this? Are there any present, who are deterred from seeking salvation by nothing but discouragement and despondency; any who are saying in their hearts, We would attend seriously to religion, did we not fear that it will be to no purpose? If any such there are, they are the very persons whom we now address. You have heard, my irresolute, desponding friends, how sinful, how dangerous, and how unreasonable it is to say, There is no hope. Why then will you say it? why should you think that it will be vain for you to attend to religion? Will you say, I fear that, though God is merciful, there is no mercy for me? You have heard that there is mercy for the vilest, if they will repent. Will you say, I fear that I am not one of those whom God means to save? If you are determined to persevere in unbelief and despondency, you have reason to fear this; but if you begin sincerely to seek after God, you will have reason to hope that he means to save you; and if you repent and believe the gospel, you may be sure that he does. Will you say, I know not how to begin; if I study the Bible, it appears dark and difficult to understand; and when I listen to the preached word, it is the same? This is because you do not look to Christ for wisdom and instruction. He is able and willing to give us his Spirit to lead our minds into all truth. Will you say, I have often resolved and endeavored to be religious; but my resolutions have been broken; my endeavors have been vain; and I fear that, should I make another attempt, it would avail nothing. But your resolutions and attempts were made in dependance on your own strength. It was therefore to be expected that they would fail; for Christ says, Without me ye can do nothing. But make another attempt depending on his strength, and looking to him for assistance, and it will not be unsuccessful. Will you say, My will is so stubborn, my heart is so hard, and my mind so entangled by the love of the world and the fear of man, that I dare not hope for success? But did not Christ come to deliver us from this world, to preach deliverance to the captives, to set at liberty them that are bruised? Has he not done this for thousands already; and is he not equally able to do it for you? Will you say, I have difficulties and temptations to encounter, such as no other person ever had; and therefore I fear there is no hope? Even if this is the case, it affords no reason for despondency; for Christ is able to remove all difficulties, and overcome all temptations. Have you not heard that nothing is too hard for him? Will you say, I know Christ is able to save me; but I have so often grieved his Spirit, so long neglected his invitations, that I fear he will now afford me no assistance? But is he not even now bestowing upon you many blessings, notwithstanding this? Is he not preserving your life, permitting you to hear the gospel, and inviting you by his ministers, to come and receive salvation? If your unworthiness does not prevent him from bestowing these favors upon you, why should you fear that he will withhold his assistance in subduing your sins? Has he not said, Him that cometh unto me I will in no wise cast out?

And now, my desponding friends, what more will you say to justify your despondency? What more indeed can you say? What can you say of yourselves more discouraging than this, that you are entirely sinful, and guilty, and poor, and wretched, and blind, and naked? True, you are so, Christ knows that you are so; and his language is, I counsel thee to buy of me gold, tried in the fire, that thou mayest be rich, and white raiment that thou mayest be clothed. Will you say, I have nothing to buy with? Christ bestows them without money or price. Permit me to remind you of the value of what he thus bestows. Let me bring down from heaven that reward which he offers to those who embrace him. In this world, it is pardon of sins, peace of conscience, peace with God, the restoration of his image, joy unspeakable, support under trials, victory over all enemies including death and the grave; in a word, all good things. In the world to come, it is perfect holiness, full enjoyment, everlasting life, an eternal weight of glory, an immoveable throne, an unfading crown, a state of complete, never-ending, perpetually increasing glory and felicity. Such, my friends, are the rewards set before you. It is yet possible; nay, there is yet reason to hope, that you may obtain them. And are they not desirable? Are they not worth pursuing? Arise, then; we call upon you in the name of God, arise, and in the strength of Christ, pursue them. Lose no time in despondency. Say not, There is no hope. We have shown that you have no reason to say this. If you will persist in saying it, it is only an excuse; an excuse for neglecting that religion, which you are unwilling to embrace. It is not for want of encouragement, it is for want of a disposition, that you refuse to pursue the one thing needful. Let none then, after this, complain that there is nothing to encourage them. God has given them every thing necessary for their encouragement; every thing calculated to rouse them from despair. If then any persist in despair, and perish, God will be guiltless; their blood will be upon them.

But while we are attempting to justify God, and leave sinners without excuse; and while we would do every thing in our power to encourage the desponding and support the weak, it is also necessary to guard against the perversions of such as would derive from it encouragement to hope for heaven while they continue in sin. It is possible that some present may be hardened in their presumption by the very means which have been employed to keep others from despair. They may say, since there is so much reason to hope, and since it is so wrong to despair, we will hope for the best, and not despair of salvation, though we should continue a little longer in sin. If any are saying this, if any are thus poisoning themselves with the waters of life, I do most solemnly protest against this perversion, this abuse of the grace of God, and warn them of its danger. This is what the apostle calls making Christ the minister of sin, and turning the grace of God into wantonness; and the end of those who are guilty of it will be according to their works. They can derive no excuse for doing this from what has been said; for not a syllable has been uttered which tends, if rightly understood, to afford the smallest hope or consolation to those who persist in impenitence and unbelief. If any such still pretend, from what has been said, to hope in God's mercy, I would remind them of the words of the apostle; Whosoever hath this hope in him, purifieth himself, even as Christ is pure.

SERMON XXXVII.

THE STUBBORN SINNER SUBMITTING TO GOD.

I have surely heard Ephraim bemoaning himself thus; Thou hast chastised me, and I was chastised, as a bullock unaccustomed to the yoke; turn thou me, and I shall be turned; for thou art the Lord my God. Surely, after that I was turned, I repented; and after that I was instructed, I smote upon my thigh; I was ashamed, yea, even confounded, because I did bear the reproach of my youth. Is Ephraim my dear son? is he a pleasant child? for since I spoke against him, I do earnestly remember him still: therefore my bowels are troubled for him; I will surely have mercy upon him, saith the Lord.—JEREMIAH XXXI. 18, 19, 20.

THESE verses, my friends, may be considered as an epitome or abridgment of the book from which they are taken. The obstinate wickedness of the Israelites, the dreadful calamities which it brought upon them, and the happy effect of those calamities in leading some of them to repentance, and thus preparing them for pardon, are here briefly, but clearly and most affectingly described. In this description, my friends, we are deeply interested; for since the human heart, the nature and effects of repentance, the character of God and the methods of his proceedings, are ever essentially the same, it is evident that every thing which is recorded in Scripture respecting these subjects must be in a greater or less degree applicable to us. In our text each of these subjects is more or less distinctly brought into view. It describes three things, with which it is necessary that we should be acquainted, and which we propose particularly to consider in the following discourse.

I. We have here a description of the feelings and conduct of an obstinate impenitent sinner, while smarting under the rod of affliction. In this situation he is like a bullock unaccustomed to the yoke; wild, unmanageable, and perverse. Such, by his own confession, was Ephraim, when God began to correct him. For the iniquity of his covetousness was I wroth and smote him, and he went on frowardly in the way of his heart. Such were the inhabitants of Jerusalem. Thy sons, says the prophet to her, have fainted; they lie at the head of the streets, like a wild bull in a net,—that exhausts his strength in fruitless struggles to free himself. Such too was Paul, when first arrested by conviction. From the language in which Christ addressed him, it appears that he felt disposed to struggle and resist, like a stubborn bullock that kicks at the goad, and thus wounds himself, and not his master. And such, my friends, by nature are all mankind. Man, says an inspired writer, is born like a wild ass's colt. His proud, wayward temper, fond of liberty and unwilling to yield, renders it hard for him to submit, and exceedingly difficult to subdue him. Hence his heart is frequently represented by the inspired writers, as being froward and perverse. To describe him in one word, he is stout hearted. He not only possesses this temper, but glories in it,—as a proof of courage, independence, and nobleness of mind; while to confess a fault, solicit pardon, submit to correction, or yield to the will of another, are viewed by him as marks of disgraceful weakness and pusillanimity.

That such is the natural temper of man, must be evident to parents and all others, who are concerned in the education of children. How soon do they begin to discover a perverse and stubborn temper, a fondness for independence, and a desire to gratify their own will in every thing! and what severe punishments will they often bear, rather than submit to the authority of their parents and instructors! This disposition, so strong in us by nature, grows with our growth and strengthens with our strength; and to subdue it, is the principal design of all the calamities with which we are in this world afflicted by our heavenly Father. As the disease is constitutional, inveterate, and, unless removed, fatal, the afflictions which he makes use of as remedies are various, complicated and severe. Sometimes he afflicts sinners by taking away their property and sending poverty, as an armed man, to attack them. With this, among other punishments, he threatens the Israelites who in our text are spoken of as an individual: I will hedge up thy way, says he, with thorns, and make a wall that thou shalt not find thy paths; and I will take away my corn in the time thereof, and my wine in the season thereof, and will destroy her vines and fig-trees, and cause her mirth to cease. At other times he corrects us by depriving us of our relatives, who rendered life pleasant, by sharing with us its joys, or helping to bear its sorrows. To use the language of Scripture, he removes our friends into darkness, kills our children with death, or takes away the desire of our eyes with a stroke. If these afflictions do not avail, he brings the rod yet nearer, and touches our bone and our flesh. Then the sinner is chastened with pain upon his bed, and the multitude of his bones are filled with strong pain; so that his life abhorreth bread and his soul dainty meat. His flesh is consumed away, and his bones, that were not seen, stick out; yea, his soul draweth near to the grave, and his life unto the destroyer. All these outward afflictions are also frequently accompanied with inward trials and sorrows, still more severe. Conscience is awakened to perform its office, and fills the soul with terror, anxiety, and remorse. A load of guilt, a sense of God's anger, fears of death and judgment, and the tumultuous workings of passion, pride, enmity, and unbelief, torture and distract the mind and render it like the troubled sea which cannot rest, whose waters cast up mire and dirt. These are the arrows of the Almighty mentioned by Job, which enter the soul, the poison of which drinks up the spirits, as a fiery dart thrust through the body dries up the blood. To these terrible afflictions Solomon alludes, when he says, The spirit of a man may sustain his infirmity, but a wounded spirit who can bear?

Now when God visits impenitent sinners with these afflictions, they usually murmur, struggle, and reluctate, like a stubborn bullock unaccustomed to the yoke, or a wild bull entangled in a net. This indeed is not always the case. Sometimes they continue stupid, careless, and unconcerned, because they do not realize that it is God who afflicts them; but like the Philistines, when punished for detaining the ark, suppose that it is only a chance that has happened to them, with which God has nothing to do. At other times, they flatter themselves that God is correcting them for their good, as he does his children, not in anger but in mercy; and this groundless opinion, combined with a fear of provoking him to punish them still more severely, often produces a kind of selfish, slavish resignation to his afflictive dispensations. In addition to this, it may be observed, that, after a long series of very severe, and overwhelming calamities, sinners sometimes become so dejected and depressed, and their spirits are so much worn down by constant suffering, that they have no longer any strength to struggle or resist; but sink into a desponding, melancholy frame, and appear to submit to affliction because they cannot help it. But though their stony hearts are thus seemingly broken, yet they are not turned to flesh, but like the fragments of a broken stone remain hard and stony still. They feel something like sorrow for the sins which drew down afflictions upon them; but it is that worldly sorrow, mentioned by the apostle, which worketh death. But if we except these instances, which are rare, whenever an impenitent sinner realizes that it is God who afflicts him; that he does it in anger, and that he will perhaps never pardon him, he will invariably, like Ephraim, repine and struggle, and rebel, under afflictions, and will not unfrequently, like the persons mentioned in the Revelation, blaspheme God because of his plagues.

This perverse and rebellious temper manifests itself in a great variety of ways, as persons' circumstances, situation, and dispositions vary. Sometimes it displays itself merely in a refusal to submit, and a sullen, obstinate perseverance in those sins which caused the affliction. Thus it was with those of whom it is said, They cry not when God bindeth them; that is, they were like sullen, obstinate children, who scorn to reform, or weep, or cry for pardon, when their parents correct them. Of such too the prophet speaks, O Lord, says he, thou hast stricken them, but they have not grieved; thou hast consumed them, but they have refused to receive correction; they have made their faces harder than a flint, they have refused to return. At other times, impenitent sinners manifest their rebellious dispositions under the rod by flying to the world for comfort, and plunging with increased eagerness into its pleasures and pursuits, instead of calling upon God agreeably to his command, and repenting of their sins. Thus it was with those who when once they were corrected, said, Let us eat and drink, for to-morrow we die. With others this disposition displays itself in a settled formal endeavor to frustrate the will of God by sinning against him with a high hand, in open contempt of all his inflictions and threatenings. Of such the prophet Isaiah speaks: Ephraim and the inhabitants of Samaria say in the pride and stoutness of their hearts, The bricks are fallen down, but we will build with hewn stone; the sycamores are cut down, but we will replace them with cedars; as if they had said, God has taken away one idol, but we will set up another in its stead; he has punished us for one sin, and instead of renouncing it we will practice many. But the perverse unreconciled disposition of impenitent sinners most frequently appears in the increase of hard thoughts of God, and proud angry feelings towards him, as if he were severe, unmerciful, or unjust. What have I done? the unhumbled, corrected sinner often says in his heart, what have I done to deserve all these afflictions? Why must God needs punish me so much more than he does many others, who are as bad or worse than myself? Why did he take away that property which I had honestly acquired by so much care and labor, and which was necessary for the support of my family? What advantage can result from the death of the friend, the child, the wife, whom I have lost? Why can he not suffer me to enjoy at least a little peace, and not follow me with one affliction after another, as if he delighted in tormenting me? Or if I must be afflicted, why does he not sanctify my afflictions, and afford me those religious comforts and supports which I see many others enjoy? How can it be that he is either just or good, when his conduct appears so partial, and he suffers the world to be so full of misery! And, as if all this were not sufficient, I am told that, if I do not repent and believe, if I do not do something which I cannot do, I must not only be wretched here, but lie down in sorrow and be miserable forever. If this is true I will have nothing to do with such a being. Why did he create me? I did not wish him to do it, and all I ask of him now, is that he would take away my existence, and let me sink into nothing again, that I may at length find an end of suffering and sorrow. If this cannot be, if he must needs create me and keep me in being, why did he give me such a heart as I have? and if he dislikes it, why does he not take it away and give me a better?

Thus, my friends, does the proud, self-justifying heart of the afflicted, impenitent sinner, often rise against God, and quarrel with and condemn the Almighty; and when conscience is awakened to convince him of his guilt, alarm his fears, and lead him to think that there may possibly be a future state of endless punishment, and that he must submit and be reconciled to God, if he would avoid it, he endeavors in every conceivable way, to banish this salutary conviction from his mind, labors to persuade himself that there is no danger, that all will be saved; or that, if some perish, he shall not be among the number. If he cannot persuade himself to believe this, and his fears still follow him, he begins to look round for some other way of escape; one moment he wishes there was no God, that he was not such a God as he is, or that he could deceive, escape from, or get above him. But the next moment he sees that all these wishes are vain. Now he hopes that the Bible may not be true; but something whispers that it is, and his fears return. Thus perplexed, and distressed, like a bullock unaccustomed to the yoke, he struggles, wearies, and torments himself, and tries in every possible way to throw off his burden, escape from the heavy hand of God, and regain liberty and peace. A dreadful state of mind indeed; for woe to him that striveth with his Maker. My friends, do any of you know any thing of this state by experience? If so, you may perhaps listen with some interest to some observations on the second part of our text, in which we have a description of a penitent, humbled, broken-hearted sinner, confessing and lamenting his sins. What Ephraim was, when God began to correct him, we have already seen.

II. Let us contemplate the new views and feelings which, through divine grace, his afflictions were instrumental in producing. The person is the same; the character only is changed.

1. We here find the once stubborn and rebellious, but now awakened sinner deeply convinced of his guilt and sinfulness, and deploring his unhappy situation. It is good for man, says an inspired writer, to be afflicted, and to bear the yoke in his youth. He sitteth alone and keepeth silence, because he hath

borne it upon him; he putteth his mouth in the dust, if so be there may be hope. This happy effect affliction seems to have produced upon Ephraim. We no longer see him in the seat of the scorner, and setting his mouth against the heavens. No; he sits alone, and puts his mouth in the dust. His murmuring, repining tongue is silent, or is employed only in confessing and bewailing his sins. He still complains indeed, but it is of himself and not of God. He acknowledges the goodness, condescension, and justice of God in correcting him. Thou, O Lord, says he, hast chastised me. The word here rendered chastise, signifies to correct as a father. He next reflects with shame, grief, and self-abhorrence on the manner in which he had treated his fatherly correction. Thou hast chastised me, and I was like a bullock unaccustomed to the yoke. His obstinate perverseness and impiety in rebelling and murmuring against the correcting hand of God, seems to have been the first sin of which he was convinced. This is very frequently the case with other penitents. Perhaps more are convinced of sin, and brought to repentance, by reflecting on their impious unreconciled feelings under affliction than by reflecting on any other part of their sinful exercises. Such feelings have indeed a powerful tendency to show the sinner, what he is naturally very unwilling to believe, that his heart is enmity against God, and that reconciliation is indispensably necessary. Nothing can convince us of this truth, but our own experience of the enmity and opposition of our hearts. Let a man but be left to feel this for one hour, and he will never doubt again whether he is by nature an enemy to God. But though conviction of sin often begins, it never ends with this; but from this fountain the convinced sinner traces back the streams of depravity flowing through his whole life. Thus it was with Ephraim. From contemplating the enmity of his heart, while under the rod, he proceeds to look back to the sins of early life. Once he probably justified himself and gloried in them. But now he justly considers them as his shame and reproach. I was ashamed, says he, yea, even confounded, because I did bear the reproach of my youth. All the follies of his childhood, youth, and riper years, which had drawn down the judgments of God upon him, rush at once upon his mind, and overwhelm him with shame, confusion, and grief. Wretch that I am, we may consider him as exclaiming, what have I done? To what a wretched situation has my inexcusable folly and wickedness reduced me! How early did I begin to rebel against my Creator and Preserver; how soon begin to consider the Sabbath as a weariness, to neglect the word of God, to cast off fear and restrain prayer before him? How did I waste the season of childhood in vanity and folly! With what infatuated eagerness did I plunge into sinful pleasures and pursuits instead of remembering my Creator in the days of my youth! With what stupid idolatry have I worshipped creatures and the world, and feared their frowns and desired their smiles more than the anger or the favor of God. How have I wasted my time, abused my talents, misimproved opportunities, slighted divine calls and invitations and thus rendered the precious gift of existence a burden almost too heavy to bear. And when my indulgent heavenly Father, instead of cutting me off as I deserved, condescended to correct me for my good, how did my proud and stubborn heart rise and murmur against his dispensations. He has indeed nourished and brought me up and corrected me as a child, but, alas, in return I have only rebelled against him. What then do I not deserve? What punishment may I not expect? In all my afflictions he has punished me less than my iniquities deserve; and should he cut me off, and render me miserable forever, I must acknowledge the justice of his dispensations; for I have sinned; what shall I do, O thou Preserver of men? Such, my friends, were probably the reflections of Ephraim, and such will be the reflections of every afflicted sinner, when he is brought to contemplate his own character and conduct in their proper light.

2. In the second place, we find this awakened afflicted sinner praying. Convinced of his wretched situation and feeling his need of divine aid, he humbly seeks it from his offended God. Turn thou me, and I shall be turned, for thou art the Lord my God. This prayer nearly resembles those which we hear from the lips of other penitents in different parts of Scripture. O Lord, says the psalmist, open thou my lips, and my mouth shall show forth thy praise. Bring my soul out of prison, that I may praise thy name. Draw us, and we will run after thee. Enlarge our hearts, that we may run the way of thy commandments. These petitions plainly intimate that those who utter

them feel entangled, fettered, or imprisoned, and unable to get free. Like the apostle, they are brought into captivity by the law of sin, so that they cannot do the things that they would. Thus it was with penitent Ephraim. He felt the need of a thorough conversion; he longed to turn from sin and self and idols, to God with his whole heart; but guilty fears, unbelief, and remaining sin kept him back. He knew not that the great work was already performed; he considered himself as still a guilty, unconverted sinner; a body of death pressed him down, and filled him with desponding fears from which he could not escape. He felt that without divine assistance he could do nothing; and therefore, like a helpless captive, breathes a short, but fervent prayer for help. Turn thou me, says he, and I shall be turned. Observe, for what he prays; not that his afflictions may be removed, but that they might be sanctified; not that he might be delivered from punishment, but turned from sin to God. Observe also how he prays. He pleads nothing of his own as a reason why he should be heard. He does not, like the proud pharisee, thank God that he is not like other men. He mentions no good works, no worthiness, no resolution of amendment, in order to obtain the divine favor. His only plea is drawn from the character of the being whom he addressed, Turn thou me, for thou art the Lord my God. As if he had said, Thou art Jehovah, infinite in power, wisdom, and goodness, and art able to turn me; thou art also my God, my Creator, to whom I ought to turn. To thee I surrender myself; I would be in thy hands as clay in the hands of the potter. O thoroughly subdue my stubborn heart, and fashion me according to thy will. In a similar manner, and for similar blessings will every penitent sinner pray. Whatever his character may have been, as soon as he repents it will be said of him, Behold he prayeth. Though he once perhaps proudly fancied that he could help himself, and felt not the need of prayer, he now feels the truth of God's declaration, O sinner, thou hast destroyed thyself; but in me is thy help. He will also, like Ephraim, pray to be delivered from sin, rather than from punishment; and since the only way of access to God is through Christ, he will present all his petitions in his name, crying, Not for my sake, O Lord, but for thy Son's sake, pardon thou my iniquity, for it is great. Turn thou me, and I shall be turned; draw me, and I shall run after thee; Open thou my lips, and my mouth shall show forth thy praise.

3. In the third place, we find this corrected, mourning, praying sinner reflecting upon the effects of divine grace in his conversion. Surely, says he, after I was turned I repented, and after that I was instructed I smote upon my thigh; I was ashamed, yea, even confounded, because I did bear the reproach of my youth. It is worthy of remark, my friends, how soon the answer followed the prayer. In one verse, we find Ephraim calling God to turn or convert him. In the very next, we find him reflecting upon his conversion and rejoicing in it. And what were the effects of this change, thus suddenly produced by divine grace? The first was repentance. After I was turned, I repented. No man, my friends, truly repents, till he is converted or turned from sin to God; and every one who is really converted, will thus repent. He then begins to hate the sins which he formerly loved, and mourns over them with godly sorrow and brokenness of heart. And as no man can practise that which he hates, and for which he mourns, the real penitent will bring forth fruits meet for repentance, by confessing and renouncing his sins; making all the reparation in his power to those whom he may have injured, and diligently practising every good work. The second effect of conversion in this case was, self-loathing and abhorrence. He hated and abhorred, not only his sins, but himself for committing them. After I was instructed, says he, I smote upon my thigh. I was ashamed, yea, even confounded. The gesture, by which penitent Ephraim is here represented as expressing his self-abhorrence, is frequently mentioned in the Scriptures as indicating the strongest emotions of grief and holy indignation. Son of man, says Jehovah to the prophet Ezekiel, smite with thy hand, and stamp with thy foot, and cry, alas! for all the evil abominations of the house of Israel. In a similar manner penitent Ephraim expresses his abhorrence of his own former sins; and thus in the New Testament we find the humble publican smiting upon his breast in token of indignation against himself, while he cries, God be merciful to me a sinner. Still farther to express his grief and shame, the penitent adds to the most significant actions the most expressive words. I was ashamed, says he, yea, even confounded because I did bear the reproach of my youth. My

friends, should a man make use of such gestures, and employ such language at the present day to express his self-abhorrence for sin, he would by many be thought insane; and I doubt not that there are some present, who do not believe that any person, unless he has been guilty of the blackest crimes, can sincerely adopt such language, or entertain such feelings respecting himself. But every real penitent does entertain such feelings respecting himself—his past conduct, and can with the utmost sincerity adopt the strongest expressions of self-abhorrence which language affords. Not only so, but he finds all language far too weak to describe what he feels on account of his sins. Whatever men may think of him, and however exemplary his conduct toward them may have been, he does in fact consider himself as guilty of the blackest crimes; for in his view no crimes committed against a fellow creature can equal the rebellion, ingratitude and impiety which he has in his heart committed against God. Hence, like penitent Ephraim, he is ashamed and confounded when he reflects on his past conduct; and, like the repenting Jews, loathes himself for his iniquities and abominations.

And now, my friends, consider a moment what a change is here. He who was once like a bullock unaccustomed to the yoke, wild, sullen, unmanageable, and perverse, his mouth filled with murmuring complaints, and his heart with pride, unbelief, and opposition to God, now quiet, docile, and submissive, sits like a little child at the feet of his heavenly Father, which he bathes with penitential tears, while with a broken heart and a filial spirit he looks up and cries, Turn thou me, and I shall be turned, for thou art the Lord my God. Is Ephraim my dear son? Is he a pleasant child? My friends, is not this indeed a new creature? May not such a change be called being born again? What blessings are afflictions, when they are the means of producing it?

III. We proceed now to consider the third object here described, viz. a correcting, but compassionate and pardoning God, watching the result of his corrections and noticing the first symptoms of repentance, and expressing his gracious purposes of mercy respecting the chastened penitent sinner. In this description God represents himself,

First, as a tender father solicitously mindful of his penitent afflicted child. Is Ephraim my dear son? Is he a pleasant child? that is, according to a common mode of expression, is he not so? for since I spoke against him I do earnestly remember him. My friends, when God speaks against us, and seems to afflict us as an enemy, he does not forget us. On the contrary, he is then more mindful of us than at any other time. As a kind earthly father, after he has corrected a child for any fault carefully watches him to see what effect the correction produces; so our heavenly Father remembers and watches over us in seasons of adversity and affliction, to see if we show any disposition to return to him. He not only remembers, but earnestly and affectionately remembers us. How powerfully should this urge us constantly and affectionately to remember him at such seasons.

In the second place, God represents himself as listening to his complaints, confessions and petitions. I have surely, says he, heard Ephraim bemoaning himself. So he does still. As an affectionate parent, after confining a stubborn child to a solitary apartment, sometimes stands at the door without, secretly listening to his complaints, that he may release him on the first symptom of submission, so when God puts us into the prison of affliction, he invisibly, but attentively listens to catch the first penitential sigh, and hear the first breathings of prayer which escape us; and no music, not even the halleluias of angels, is more pleasing to his ears, than these cries and complaints of a broken heart; nor can any thing more quickly or more powerfully excite his compassion. Agreeably, he represents himself, as strongly affected by the complaints of Ephraim: My bowels, says he, are troubled for him. My friends, what astonishing compassion and love is this, that the infinite Eternal Jehovah should represent himself as troubled and grieved for the sufferings of penitent sinners under those afflictions which their sins had brought upon them! Certainly nothing in heaven or earth is so wonderful as this; and if this language does not affect us and break our hearts, nothing can do it.

Lastly. God declares his determination to pardon him: I will surely have mercy upon him. He calls me the Lord, his God, and I will be his God and Father, and freely forgive all his sins. In the same manner, my friends, will he deal with us, if we like Ephraim confess, repent of, and forsake our sins; for, says the apostle, if we confess our sins, he is faithful and just to forgive us, and to cleanse us from all unrighteousness; and then though our sins are of a crimson color and a scarlet die, they shall be as wool.

Thus, my friends, have we seen a contest between God and an obstinate, impenitent, afflicted sinner, issuing, through the submission and repentance of the latter, in a perfect, happy, and lasting reconciliation. In a similar manner must we all be reconciled to God, if we would not remain his enemies forever, and perish eternally as such. Permit me then to improve the subject by asking, are there not some present whose feelings and character resemble those of Ephraim, while he was struggling under the rod, like a bullock unaccustomed to the yoke? You have all, at some period of your lives, been called to drink more or less deeply of the cup of affliction. What then were your feelings, when it was put to your lips? What are they now, when God corrects you? When your earthly prospects are blasted, your desires crossed, your hopes disappointed, your friends or property taken away, your health impaired, and every thing seems to go wrong with you, how do you feel? Above all, how do you feel, when your fears are excited respecting death, and judgment, and you see no way of escape? Are your minds never like the troubled sea, which cannot rest? Do your hearts never feel disposed to rise against God, as a hard master? Do you not at times feel much of a murmuring, repining, discontented temper, and wish that it were in your power to order events differently? In a word, when afflictions or fears of future misery press hard upon you, do you sometimes feel like a wild beast entangled in a net, or a bullock unaccustomed to the yoke? If not, have you not continued hard and impenitent under your afflictions, instead of endeavoring that they might be sanctified? If so, you are certainly striving with your Maker, and your character resembles that of Ephraim before his conversion; and unless like him you become reconciled to God, you must perish; for wo to him that striveth with his Maker. If you ask, How are we to be reconciled? you may learn from his example. If like him you bemoan your wretched, lost condition, hate, and renounce, and mourn over your sins; feel ashamed and confounded before God, and sincerely pray for sanctifying, pardoning grace, you will most certainly like him be pardoned and accepted. In no other way can a reconciliation be effected. In no other way can you possibly escape from the wrath to come. You must be reconciled to God's holiness and justice; for never, never can he be reconciled to your sins. Sin is the only ground of contention. Do but renounce sin, and all will be well. To induce you to do this and be reconciled to God, consider the representation which he gives of himself in our text. Notwithstanding all your sins, he earnestly and affectionately remembers you still. He is now, as it were, listening and waiting to hear your complaints, petitions, and confessions; and if he can but hear from you one truly penitential sigh, or see one really penitential tear from your eyes, he will be grieved and troubled for your sorrows, and hasten to answer, comfort, adopt, and pardon you. O, then, let him not wait and listen in vain. If you feel desirous, but unable to return, cry unto him, Turn thou me, and I shall be turned; and when you retire from this house to your closets, let him have reason to say respecting each one of you by name, I have surely heard him bemoaning himself; therefore my bowels are troubled, and I will surely have mercy upon him. Thus there will be joy over you in heaven, as repenting sinners; you will feel in your own hearts those pure, refreshing joys which result from reconciliation with God.

SERMON XXXVIII.

CHRIST REJECTS NONE WHO COME UNTO HIM.

Him that cometh unto me, I will in no wise cast out.—JOHN VI. 37.

I NEED not tell you, my friends, that these are the words of Christ; for who but he would or could utter such words? Who but the compassionate Friend of sinners, the Shepherd, who came to seek and to save that which was lost, would say this? And who but he, in whom all fulness dwells, could say it? Who besides has compassion enough, and room enough, to receive and entertain all who will come to him without exception? But he has both. He can venture to say, If any man thirst, let him come unto me and drink; for he knows that there is in himself room for any, room for all; and that the waters of life, which flow from him, can never be exhausted. And he can also venture to say, Him that cometh unto me I will in no wise cast out; for he knows the worst who can come, and that his grace is sufficient for the worst. But why did he say this? Why give us such invitations and assurances? Because he knew they would be necessary. Because he knew that awakened and convinced sinners would be so much discouraged by their own ignorance, weakness, guilt, and unworthiness, as to need the most gracious and explicit assurances of his readiness to receive them. He knew that, if he made one exception, if he intimated that any one who came to him might be rejected, every convinced sinner would think himself to be that one, and would not dare to approach him. He was therefore pleased to express his invitations in the most general and encouraging terms which language could afford, exclaiming, Whosoever will, let him come, and him that cometh I will in no wise cast out. He had also a farther object in view. He intended to leave those who refused to come without excuse. He intended that, if sinners would perish, their destruction should evidently appear to be owing to themselves and not to him. He intended that no man, who heard the gospel, should have any cause to pretend that he was not invited to share in its benefits. He therefore made his invitations as general and comprehensive as possible, so as to exclude none who did not exclude themselves. And the same reason, which rendered it necessary that Christ should give us such invitations and assurances, make it necessary that his ministers should call your attention to them. This I shall now attempt to do. And I tell you frankly, my friends, what is my intention. It is to persuade you all, if possible, to come to Christ; and, if you will not, to leave you entirely without excuse in refusing to come.

With this view I shall endeavor to show,

1. What is meant by coming to Christ. Since Christ is now in heaven, whither our bodies cannot at present ascend, it is evident that by this expression cannot be meant a bodily approach to him. Agreeably, the apostle says, Say not in thy heart, who shall ascend into heaven, to bring down Christ from above; or who shall descend into the deep, to bring up Christ from the dead; for the word is nigh thee, even in thy mouth and in thy heart. It appears then that coming to Christ is an act, not of the body, but of the mind or heart, so that you may come to him without moving out of your places. When we come to a human friend who calls us, there are two actions performed. The first is an act of the soul, by which we choose or determine to come to that friend. The second is an act of the body, by which we execute the previous determination of the mind. But in coming to Christ there is only one act, an act of the soul; and this act consists in choosing and determining to forsake every thing else, and to comply with his invitations by repairing to him. In other words, coming to Christ is an act of choice, an act by which the soul freely chooses him in preference to every thing beside. Are there any who do not

understand this? I will endeavor to be more plain. Suppose that, while your attention is occupied by various interesting objects, you see the dearest friend you have on earth, approaching at a little distance. Your hearts immediately drop the objects which had previously engaged their attention; and, if I may so express it, spring forward to meet and welcome your friend before he arrives. So when persons come to Christ, their hearts leave the objects with which they had been occupied, fly to him with affectionate desire, and cling to him as the supreme object of their confidence and love. They see that he is just such a Savior as they need; they are sweetly, but powerfully drawn to him by the attractions of his moral glory and beauty, and feel bound to him by bonds which they have no wish to break. Hence coming to Christ is elsewhere called trusting in him, receiving him, believing in him, and loving him.

But it is necessary to observe farther, that all who thus come to Christ come to him in his official character, as the appointed Savior, and only Savior of sinners. They do not come to gratify their curiosity, or to quiet their consciences, but to be saved by him from sin and from its consequences. Of course, they come to him as sinners, feeling that they are so, that they are dead in sins, and justly exposed to everlasting wrath. Hence, coming to Christ is called fleeing from the wrath to come, and fleeing for refuge to lay hold on the hope set before us in the gospel. Those who thus come to Christ as a Savior, apply to him or receive him in all those characters which he sustains in consequence of being a Savior. They come to him, for instance, as a prophet or instructor, to be taught. Of course they feel that they need to be taught; that they are spiritually blind and ignorant, and that there is none who teacheth like him. Like Mary they sit at his feet and hear his word with the temper of little children; they wait upon him for farther communications of divine wisdom and knowledge, and consider his words as a sufficient proof of whatever he may assert. Hence, in the same passage in which he invites the weary and heavy laden to come to him, he also says to them, Learn of me. and ye shall find rest. Hence also, those who come to him are called his disciples, that is, his scholars or pupils.

Those who come to Christ come to him also as a priest. A

priest is one who, to use the language of the apostle, is ordained for men in things pertaining to God, to offer both gifts and sacrifices for sin; and at the same time to plead for those whose sacrifices he offers, that their sins may be pardoned, and their persons and services accepted. In other words, he is appointed to make an atonement for sin, and to intercede for sinners. Christ, as our high priest, does both. By once offering up himself as a sacrifice he has made atonement for sin; and he ever lives to intercede for all who come to God by him. Those then who come to him in his character of a priest, come as sinners, as those, who feel that they need an atonement which they are unable to make, that they are unworthy to approach a holy God, and that they need an advocate or intercessor to plead for them in the court of heaven, to present their petitions at the throne of grace, and to render their persons and their services acceptable to God. Hence they apply to Christ, believing that he is both able and willing to do all this for them.

Again; all who come to Christ come to him as a King. In this character he sits on the throne of his mediatorial kingdom, giving laws to his subjects, protecting and defending them, and subduing their enemies under their feet. Hence he requires all who come to him to take upon themselves his yoke; or, in other words, to submit cordially and cheerfully to his government. With this requisition all who really come to him readily comply. They joyfully give him the throne of their hearts, submit with delight to his law of love, follow him as their prince and captain, and confide in his power and grace to deliver them from the spiritual enemies by which they are enslaved and which they feel utterly unable to subdue. It appears then that coming to Christ, is a voluntary act of the soul, by which it freely chooses Christ, in preference to all other objects, and applies to him feeling ignorant, sinful, guilty, weak and helpless, to be taught, saved, and ruled by him alone.

We now proceed to show,

II. That those who thus come to Christ he will in no wise cast out. The terms, in no wise, are exceedingly strong and comprehensive. There is no case, character, or situation, to which they will not apply. But general expressions affect us much less, than those which are addressed to our own particular case. Let us then mention more particularly the cases which the general declaration includes.

1. We may consider our Savior as declaring that none who come to him shall be excluded on account of their age. On the one hand, none shall be excluded because they are too young. It was foretold of him that, when he should come as a shepherd, he should gather the lambs with his arms and carry them in his bosom. Agreeably to this prediction, he not only noticed the children who, in the temple, cried, Hosanna to the Son of David; but he took up young children in his arms and blessed them, and said expressly, Suffer little children to come unto me, and forbid them not. Surely then, he will cast out none because they are young. Hear this, ye children; hear it, little children. Jesus Christ says you may come to him, and that he will not cast you out, if you do come. Many as young as you have come to him, and he never cast out one of them. Come then, my children, to Christ, and cry, Hosanna to the Son of David. On the other hand, none who come to him shall be excluded because they are too old. It is true that there are peculiar difficulties attending the salvation of aged sinners, and that few of them probably are saved. But these difficulties are in themselves, not in Christ. They arise solely from their unwillingness to come. Those who come, though at the eleventh hour, are never rejected.

In the second place, we may consider Christ as here declaring that none, who come to him, shall be cast out on account of their situation in life. None shall be excluded because they are poor and despised of men; for Christ gathereth the outcasts of Israel; his gospel is preached particularly to the poor; and God has chosen the poor, who are rich in faith, to be heirs of his kingdom. Nor shall honors or riches exclude their possessors from the Savior, if they do not prevent them from coming to him; for though not many mighty or noble are called, yet some are, and though hard, it is not impossible for a rich man to be saved.

In the third place, we may understand Christ as declaring that none, who come to him, shall be cast out, on account of their ignorance and slowness to learn. He is one who can have compassion on the ignorant, and on them that are out of the way. While he hides himself from the wise and prudent he delights to reveal himself to babes in wisdom and knowledge. His first disciples were exceedingly foolish and slow of heart to understand his instructions. Yet he did not therefore reject them. Nor can ignorance present any obstacle to him who possesses all the treasures of wisdom and knowledge; who can give eyes to the blind, and hearing to the deaf. Indeed, it is the blind whom he especially promises to guide and instruct. Other instructors may dismiss those who have no capacity to receive instruction; but this Divine Teacher can impart a capacity, and give an understanding heart.

In the fourth place this declaration warrants us to assert that none, who come to Christ, shall be cast out on account of the number, magnitude, or aggravation of their sins. It is a doubt of this truth, which more than any thing else, discourages those, who are burdened with conscious guilt, from coming to the Savior for relief. They acknowledge that he is just such a Savior as they need; but their sins are so great that he will not be their Savior. They allow that his invitations and promises are as encouraging as possible; but doubt whether these invitations and promises are intended for them. It is therefore necessary to insist more particularly on the fact, that none, who come to Christ, will be excluded on account either of their past sins, or their present unworthiness. Permit me then to ask, do not the words, in no wise, include every conceivable case that can ever occur? I need not tell you that it is the same as if our Savior had said, I will on no account, on no pretence, for no cause whatever, cast out any one that comes to me. Now is there an individual in this house, who can with the least shadow of propriety pretend, that these expressions do not include him; that there is any thing in his case, to which this assurance does not extend? Is it not evident that, should our Savior exclude any one an account of the number or magnitude of his sins, the declaration in our text would, from that moment, be proved false? And would he utter such a declaration with a view to falsify it? He was under no obligation to utter it. He could have no inducement to do so, unless he intended to fulfil it. He knew what mankind were; he knew what length many of them would go in sin. Nay more, he foresaw all your sins; he knew that there would be such sinners as you are, and that you would hear of this declaration. Yet this knowledge did not deter him from making it. What then shall prevent him from fulfilling it? He is the Amen, the faithful and true Witness, nay the Truth itself, and he has declared that, though heaven and earth pass away, his word shall not pass away; no, not one jot or tittle of it, till all be fulfilled. Sooner then will the earth sink under your feet; sooner shall the heavens be wrapped together as a scroll and pass away, than you or any other sinner, who comes to Christ, will be excluded. And even if he were not truth, if he had no regard to his own word, his concern foi his reputation would secure you a favorable reception. You need not be told, that it is disgraceful to a person to undertake a work which he is not able to accomplish. Our Savior himself has taught us this truth. He advises those, who think of professing religion, to sit down first and count the cost, and not act like a man who should begin a work which he was unable to finish. And would he, think you, act contrary to his own advice? Would he undertake any work without counting the cost? But he has undertaken to save all that come to him. In the sight of all the holy angels he has pledged himself to do it. He has not only undertaken this work, but he has commenced it. He has laid the foundation of salvation to his church deep in his own blood; he has begun to raise the superstructure; and now, should he in any one instance fail, it would, with reverence be it spoken, be an eternal disgrace to his character,—a disgrace which all his creatures would witness. Nay more, it would bring a blot on the untarnished character of Jehovah, for he provided this Savior; he provided him on purpose for this work; and, should it be found that he has provided an insufficient Savior, one who was deficient either in power, in compassion, or in patience, his reputation for wisdom would suffer; and he would stand chargeable with providing inadequate means for the accomplishment of his purposes. And in fact, my friends, you charge him with this, whenever you plead the greatness of your guilt as a reason for doubting whether Christ be willing to receive you. But for this charge there is no foundation. It will be seen, to God's eternal glory, that he laid help on one that was mighty to save, able to save even to the uttermost. Surely then, you have all the evidence that can be given or desired, that, if you come to Christ, he will never cast you out.

But perhaps you will say, there must be some exceptions made to this assertion; for we are told that there is a sin unto death, a sin against the Holy Ghost, for which there is no forgiveness, either in this world or in the next. Those, therefore, who have committed this sin, Christ will not receive. Say rather, that those who have committed this sin will never come to Christ. Say rather, that there is no repentance, and, therefore, no forgiveness for it. Would they repent, would they come to Christ, even they might be pardoned. But the difficulty, and the only difficulty, is, that they will not. By committing this sin, they grieve away forever the Spirit of God, and of course, see no need of Christ, as a Savior, feel no desire for his salvation, and therefore will never come to him. Notwithstanding all that is said of the unpardonable sin, it still remains an eternal truth, that no one who comes to Christ, shall on any account be cast out.

III. What does this assertion imply? It is evident that more is implied than is expressed. I scarcely need tell you that it implies, not only that Christ will not exclude any, but that he will receive all that come to him; receive them into his arms, his heart, his church, his heaven; that he will do all that for them which he came to do for those who trust in him; that he will enlighten their minds, sanctify their hearts, wash away their sins, and save them with an everlasting salvation. This he will do for you, for every one of you, if you will come to him.

Permit me then to apply the subject by pressing every one present, who has not already embraced the Savior, to come to him without delay. As the mouth of God, and in my Master's name, I invite every one of you to do this. Our Creator, our God has made a great feast, a marriage feast for his Son; a feast for the entertainment of sinners; a feast in which all his inexhaustible stores, all the celestial dainties which infinite wisdom could devise, which Almighty power could create, are set forth. To this feast you are now invited. No tickets of admission are necessary. The Master of the feast stands at the door to receive you, declaring that not one, who comes, shall be cast out; and as his servant, sent forth for this very purpose, sent especially to you, I now invite you to come. I invite you, children; for there is a place for you. Leave your toys and follies then, and come to Christ. I invite you who are young; for your presence is especially desired. Leave your sinful amusements and companions then, and come to the Savior. I invite you who are in the meridian of life. To you, O men, I call, and my voice is to the sons of men. Particularly do I invite you, who are parents, to come and bring your children with you to the Savior's feast. I invite you, who are aged, to come and receive from Christ a crown of glory, which your gray hairs will be, if you are found in the way of righteousness. I invite you to come, ye poor, and Christ will make you rich in faith and heirs of his kingdom. I invite you to come who are rich, and bring your wealth to Christ, and he will give you durable riches and righteousness. I invite you, who are ignorant, to come and Christ will impart to you his treasures of wisdom and knowledge. I invite you, who possess human learning, to come, and Christ will baptize your knowledge, and teach you to employ it in the most advantageous manner. I invite you who are afflicted to come, for my God is the God of all consolation, and my Master can be touched with the feeling of your infirmities. I invite you, who feel yourselves to be the greatest of sinners, to come; for you will find many there, whose sins once equalled your own, now washed and made white in the blood of the Lamb. I invite you, who have long despised, and who still despise this invitation, to come; for Christ's language is, Hearken to me, ye stout-hearted, and far from righteousness. And if there be any one in this assembly, who thinks himself overlooked; if there be one who has not yet felt that this invitation is addressed to him, I now present it to that person, particularly, and invite him to come.

And now, my friends, I have done. My directions were to invite to the Savior's marriage feast as many as I should find. I have accordingly invited all and each of you. I take you to record, as witnesses against each other, that you have all received the invitation. I take each of your consciences to record, as witness against yourselves, that you have been invited, and as a witness for me, that I have discharged my commission. If then any of you do not come, you cannot ascribe it to the want of an invitation. If any of you perish, it will be, not because Christ did not offer to save you; nor because you did not hear the offer, but solely because you would not accept it. You are, therefore, left without excuse. I am aware, however, that you will fancy you have an excuse. You will pretend that you wish to come, but are unable. My friends, I know nothing of that. I am not directed to answer such objections. I have nothing to do with them. My business is simply to preach to you the gospel; to proclaim to you the glad tidings; to invite you to Christ, and to assure you, in his name, that, if you come, you shall most certainly be received. If you say that you cannot come; if you can make God believe it; if you dare go to the judgment seat with this excuse, and venture your eternal interests on its being accepted as sufficient, it is well. But before you determine on this course, permit me to remind you, that God's sentiments, as revealed in his word, differ very widely from yours, with respect to this excuse. He evidently considers your unwillingness, or inability, or whatever you choose to call it, to come to Christ, as your greatest sin. He, once and again, denounces upon you the most dreadful punishments for this very thing. He declares, not only that all who do not believe in Christ shall be condemned, but that they are condemned already. What you consider as your best excuse, he considers as your greatest sin. Beware then, my friends, how you make this excuse. If you are determined on making an excuse, say any thing rather than this.

I find in the Bible but one person who made this excuse; but one who attempted to justify himself by pretending that he was unable to do what his master required. And what answer did he receive? Out of thine own mouth will I judge thee, thou wicked and slothful servant. My friends, if any of you venture to make a similar excuse, be assured you will meet with a similar reply. Nor will any excuse be more successful; for Christ has taught us, that those who attempt to excuse themselves, as well as those who directly refuse to come, shall never taste of his supper.

Instead, therefore, of seeking for excuses, which will only prove your destruction, let me persuade you rather to comply with Christ's invitations. With this view permit me to call your attention to the moral sublimity, the grandeur, the magnificence, which characterize them. Look unto me, and be ye saved, all ye ends of the earth. If any man thirst, let him come unto me and drink. Whosoever will, let him come, and him that cometh I will in no wise cast out. And who is he that dares utter such language as this? Who dares thus stand in the midst of the world, of such a world as this, a thirsty, perishing world, and invite all, all its dying inhabitants without exception, to come to him and drink the waters of life and salvation? Can he have room sufficient for such an innumerable multitude? Has he not reason to fear that his treasures will be exhausted? Does he know what he says? Yes, my friends, he does know what he says; and he may well say it, for in him dwells all the fulness of the Godhead bodily. He has enough, and more than enough, for ten thousand such worlds as this. And, my hearers, this is saying much; for reflect a moment how much is necessary to supply the wants of a single immortal soul, through time and through eternity. Think how many souls there are, have been, and shall be, in the world. Think of the innumerable criminals, criminals of the most abandoned kind, of the murderers, the robbers, the conquerors, the blasphemers, the adulterers, the harlots, the impious, hardened wretches who neither fear God nor regard man, that have been, and still are, to be found among mankind. What an ocean of mercy is necessary to wash away their sins, to make the deep crimson white as snow. What an omnipotence of grace is requisite to fit such wretches for admission into a heaven of spotless purity, and make them holy as God. Yet all such Christ invites, all such he is able to save, all such he would save, would they come to him. Who then can describe, who can conceive the ten thousandth part of that grace and mercy which must be in Christ; or of the love which renders him thus willing to scatter that grace and mercy round him upon the worthless and undeserving. Is there not something inexpressibly grand, sublime and affecting in the idea of a being whose fulness enables him, whose generosity prompts to throw wide open the door of his heart, and invite a dying world to enter in and drink and be satisfied, and live forever;—of a being from whom flows light, holiness, and happiness sufficient to fill to overflowing all that come to him, be their numbers ever so many, their sins and wants and miseries ever so great; of a being, of whose fulness myriads of immortal beings may drink through a whole eternity without exhausting, or even diminishing it in the smallest degree. But perhaps, forgetting what has been said in a former part of this discourse, you will say, this fountain is fenced round with a barrier which we cannot pass. This being, who possesses such a fulness in himself, must from his very nature be so great, so glorious, so awful, that we cannot approach him, must be placed on a height which is to us inaccessible. But this conclusion, though apparently natural, is not just; for all this fulness dwells in a man. Yes, it is the Son of man, who thus brings all heaven down to earth. It is the Son of man, who thus has power on earth to forgive sins and to save sinners. Nor is it a man, like other men, tinctured with pride, or selfishness, or insensibility. No; it is a man all meekness and lowliness and gentleness and condescension; a man who is not ashamed to call us brethren; a man all made up of invitations, compassion and love; a man, whose every action, thought, and feeling combines with his lips to cry, Come unto me, all ye that are laboring and heavy laden, and I will give you rest; a man, who finds more pleasure in saving sinners, than they find in receiving salvation; and who uttered the very feelings of his heart, when he said, It is more blessed to give than to receive. Nor does he, while saying this, display a generosity which costs him nothing. Were this the case, we might the less wonder at the unbounded riches of his liberality. But it is not. The blessings which he offers and dispenses, inestimable as they are, cost him their full value. They cost thirty-three years' labor of him, who could create a world in six days. Nay more, they cost him his life. He paid the dreadful price in tears and groans and blood, in agonies unutterable. There is not a single blessing he offers you, O sinner, which did not cost him a pang. He purchased the privilege of offering you those very blessings which you have a thousand times rejected at the price of all that he possessed. Though he was rich, yet for our sakes he became poor. That he might offer you a mansion in heaven, he consented for years to be destitute of a place, where to lay his head. That he might wash you from those sins which made you unfit for heaven, he poured out his blood to the last drop. That you might be delivered from shame and everlasting contempt, he hid not his sacred face from shame and spitting. That you might escape the wrath of God, he bore it in his own person, though he fainted, sunk, and expired under the weight. That you, a malefactor, might live forever, the Lord of life and glory died as a malefactor on the cross. And now he offers you, without money and without price, all that cost him so dear. He even beseeches you as a favor to accept it, and will consider the joy arising from your acceptance and salvation as a sufficient recompense for all that he suffered in procuring it. Yet this is the being whom you complain that you cannot love. This the friend, to whom you think it hard to be grateful. O, astonishingly blinding, besotting, stupefying influence of sin! He, who has only to show his face to fill all heaven with rapture, and pour a flood of glory, light and joy through the new Jerusalem, cannot by all his bounties bribe, nor by all his entreaties induce you to love him; though heaven is the reward of loving, and hell the punishment of rejecting him. And can you indeed be content to remain ignorant of such a being, to remain a stranger, nay, an enemy to him forever? Can you consent to retain and cherish a heart, which feels no affection, no gratitude for such a benefactor as this? My friends, I would as soon possess the heart of a murderer, of a traitor, nay of a fiend, as a heart which turns cold and insensible from a crucified Redeemer—from bleeding, dying love—from the perfection of moral beauty and excellence. * * * *

SERMON XXXIX.

GOD HEARD IN THE STILL SMALL VOICE.

And behold the Lord passed by, and a great and strong wind rent the mountains, and brake in pieces the rocks before the Lord; but the Lord was not in the wind: and after the wind an earthquake; but the Lord was not in the earthquake: and after the earthquake a fire; but the Lord was not in the fire: and after the fire a still small voice. And it was so, when Elijah heard it that he wrapped his face in his mantle, and went out and stood in the entering in of the cave: and, behold, there came a voice unto him, and said, what dost thou here Elijah? —1 Kings xix. 12, 13.

In that part of Elijah's history, which is immediately connected with this passage, we have a striking exemplification of the great truth, that a good man, when God is with him, can do all things, and exhibit almost superhuman excellence; but that the same person, when God withdraws his secret influence, becomes weak like another man, and can do nothing. In the preceding chapter we see this prophet, unguarded and unassisted by any human power, fearlessly meeting an enraged monarch surrounded by his guards, reproving him for his sins, standing alone in the midst of thousands who thirsted for his blood, putting to death four hundred false prophets before the eyes of their idolatrous sovereign, and protector, and with a voice, like the voice of omnipotence, calling down, first fire, and then water from heaven. Thus he could act while God, by his secret influence, inspired him with faith and courage and zeal. But in this chapter we see the same prophet flying with trembling haste from the threatened vengeance of a woman, not venturing to think himself safe till he had fled a day's journey into the wilderness, and in a transport of peevishness and impatience wishing for death. Thus he acted when God, to humble him and show him his own weakness, left him to himself. The unbelief and pusillanimity which he exhibited on this occasion, deserved reproof; and in our text we have an account of the manner in which God reproved him. While he lay trembling and dispirited in a cave of Mount Horeb, he began to perceive the tokens of an approaching Deity. And, behold, the Lord passed by, and a great and strong wind rent the mountains and brake in pieces the rocks before the Lord; but the Lord was not in the wind: and after the wind, an earthquake; but the Lord was not in the earthquake: and after the earthquake, a fire; but the Lord was not in the fire: and after the fire a still small voice. And when Elijah heard it, he wrapped his face in his mantle, and went out and stood in the entrance of the cave. And, behold, there came a voice to him which said, What dost thou here Elijah?

My hearers, the manner in which God manifested himself to his prophet on this occasion, resembles, in many respects, the manner in which he now manifests himself to men, when he comes to reprove them for their sins, and thus prepare the way for their conversion and salvation. To trace this resemblance, is my design in the present discourse.

1. When God comes to reprove men for their sins, he usually manifests himself to them, or addresses them, not by his works, either of creation or providence, but by a still small voice. Thus it was in the instance before us. A tempestuous wind, an earthquake, and a fire were perceived by the prophet; but God was in neither of them. It is, however, necessary to explain this assertion, to show in what sense it is said that God was not in the wind, the earthquake, or the fire. It is certain that, in one sense, he was in each of them; for he is every where, working all in all. They were all the effect of his power; they were all proofs of his presence, and in all of them some of his natural perfections might be seen. But in another sense he was in none of them. He was in none of them as a reprover or instructor. He spoke from none of them. Neither the wind, the earthquake, nor the fire, said any thing to the prophet respecting his situation, his errors, or his duty. They might all have passed by, and left him as they found him, un-

instructed, unreproved. In none of them did he find God, in none of them did he hear his voice. They were rather the precursors, the heralds of the approaching Deity, than the Deity himself. And like heralds they proclaimed, though without a voice, the greatness, the majesty, and the power of him whose heralds they were. Or, like the trumpets which announce the approach of a monarch, they served to excite expectation, and awaken attention. But it was in the still small voice alone, that God manifested his presence to the prophet, as a reprover and instructor. In a similar manner does he still manifest himself to men when he comes to reprove and instruct them. His works continually pass before them, and in one sense he is in all his works. He shines upon us in the sun, he breathes upon us in the air, he supports us in the earth, he stands up before us in every thing which he has made, in every change and event produced by his providence. But in another sense, in the sense of our text, he is in none of these things. He is not in them in such a sense that men perceive his presence. He is not in them in such a sense that men find him there, or hear him speak to them. In a word, he is not in them as an instructor or reprover. For instance, the luminaries of heaven have a thousand times apparently passed over the face of the sky before your eyes; but with respect to you, God was not in them. You saw him not in the sun, you saw him not in the moon, in the stars. Again, you have all known something of the force of the winds; you have felt your habitations tremble before the fury of the blast. And not a few of you have witnessed more terrible proofs of its power on the ocean. You have seen the billows raised into mountains, and lashed into foam. You have felt the laboring vessel reel under you, while tossed by a tempest which seemed sufficient to rend the mountains, and break in pieces the rocks; and you have seen the tempest become a calm. But as it respected you, God was not in the wind, nor in the calm which succeeded. You saw his hand, you heard his voice in neither. If you then heard him in any thing, it was in a still small voice within you. Further, the globe which we inhabit, though not this particular part of it, has often been convulsed by the most terrible and desolating earthquakes. Even some parts of New England have been agitated in a degree sufficient to excite distressing apprehensions. But have the nations thus visited found God in the earthquake? Did our fathers find him there as an instructor and reprover? Far from it. Never have the survivors been reformed by such events. The earthquakes in New England did, indeed, occasion a kind of religious panic. A writer, who was then one of the ministers of Boston, informs us, that immediately after the great earthquake as it was called, a great number of his flock came and expressed a wish to unite themselves with the church. But on conversing with them he could find no evidence of improvement in their religious views or feelings, no convictions of their own sinfulness; nothing, in short, but a kind of superstitious fear, occasioned by a belief that the end of the world was at hand. All their replies proved that they had not found God in the earthquake.

Again, you have often heard the thunder bursting over your heads, and seen the fires of heaven flashing thick and dreadful around you. And more than once, or twice, or thrice, you have seen this town assailed by devouring flames, and in danger of a wide-wasting conflagration. But the succeeding conduct of our citizens sufficiently proves that they did not find God in the fire. If he was there to scourge us, he was not there to instruct us, or convince us of our sins. And the same remark may be applied to numberless other places which have suffered in a far greater degree than this town by the ravages of fire. Once more, you have all, in a greater or less degree, been afflicted by the dispensations of God's providence. Some of you have lost property; some of you children and friends; some of you have been visited by dangerous diseases, which brought death near; but in none of these afflictions did you find God. You saw not his hand, you heard not his voice. It was a chance that happened to you. I would not however be understood to mean, that the works of God and the dispensations of his providence are never made the occasion or means of leading men to serious reflection; for observation proves that they very often are so. Afflictions have led thousands to think of their ways; and, in consequence, they have turned their feet into God's testimonies. Still it is true that afflictions alone never produce this effect. So far as they produce any effect, it is not in a direct, but an indirect manner. As the tempest, the earthquake, and the fire roused the prophet, and prepared him to attend to what God would say to him; so the works and dispensations of providence are used to rouse thoughtless sinners, and awaken their attention to the still small voice of Jehovah. But they communicate no specific instruction or reproof. They do not tell the sinner in what respect he has done wrong, nor what it is to do right. They may amaze him, they may frighten him, they may plunge him into distress and despondency. But they leave him there. After they have done their utmost, the sinner is still left without God in the world, and without knowledge of the way in which God may be found. The same may be said of other means. Ministers may give voice and utterance to the Bible which is the word of God. Like James and John they may be sons of thunder to impenitent sinners. They may pour forth a tempest of impassioned, eloquent declamation. They may proclaim all the terrors of the Lord; represent the earth as quaking and trembling under the footsteps of Jehovah; flash around them the lightnings of Sinai; borrow, as it were, the trump of the archangel, and summon the living and the dead to the bar of God; kindle before their hearers the conflagration of the last day and the fires of eternity, and show them the Judge descending, the heavens departing as a scroll, the elements melting, the earth with its works consuming, and all nature struggling in the agonies of dissolution;—and still God may not be there; his voice may not be heard either in the tempest, the earthquake, or the fire; and if so, the preacher will have labored but in vain; his hearers, though they may for the moment be affected, will receive no permanent salutary impressions. Nothing effectual can be done unless God be there, unless he speaks with his still small voice. By this still, small voice we mean the voice of God's Spirit; the voice which speaks not only to man, but in man; the voice, which, in stillness and silence, whispers to the ear of the soul, and presses upon the conscience those great eternal truths, a knowledge and belief of which is connected with salvation. This voice almost every sinner sometimes hears. Most of you, my friends, have heard it. Some of you have heard it in this house, seconding the efforts of your minister, urging home upon you the truths which he exhibited, and enforcing his endeavors to convince you of sin, of righteousness, and of judgment. Some of you have heard it in the still and solitary hours of night while musing by your firesides, or lying awake upon your beds. There it has spoken to you, reminding you of the truths which you had formerly heard or read; and of the sins which you had forgotten; it has whispered, You are an accountable creature; the eye of God is upon you; he has noticed all your sins, he will bring you into judgment; you must repent or perish. Thus, while you alone could hear it, has the still silent voice admonished, warned, reproved and instructed you; and while you heard it God was there; there, as he was not in the tempest, the earthquake, or the fire; and you felt the truth of the apostle's assertion, God is not far from every one of us. Or perhaps you were constrained to say with the patriarch, Surely God is in this place and I knew it not. Such is the still small voice with which God speaks, probably to all sinners, certainly to all whom he convinces of sin, and brings to a knowledge of himself. We remark,

II. That when God speaks to men with this voice, he speaks to them personally, or does, as it were, call them by name. This he did in the case before us. He addressed the prophet by his name, Elijah. When he speaks to men in a general way only, by his written word, or by the voice of his ministers, he does not address them in this personal manner. He addresses characters and classes, not individuals. When this is the case no man hears for himself; no man feels that he is particularly addressed. Hence large congregations often sit and hear a message from God, while perhaps not a single individual among them feels that the message is addressed to himself, or that he has any personal concern in it. But it is not so when God speaks with his still small voice. Every one, to whom God thus speaks, whether he be alone, or in the midst of a large assembly, feels that he is spoken to, that he is called, as it were, by name. The message comes home to him, and says, as Nathan said to David, Thou art the man. Hence, while multitudes are around him, he sits as if he were alone. At him alone the preacher seems to aim. On him alone his eye seems to be fixed. To him alone every word seems to come. Absorbed in the truths thus presented, in reflecting on his own conduct, guilt, and danger, and on the character and commands of God, he is almost unconscious of the presence of his fellow worshippers; his attention is chained to the subject by bonds which he cannot break, and sentence after sentence, truth after truth, falls upon his ear, and is impressed on his conscience with a weight, an energy, and an efficacy, which omnipotence alone can give. And when God thus speaks to the whole or the greatest part of an assembly at once, as he sometimes does, when he comes to revive his work extensively, these effects are experienced, and these appearances exhibited by all. No scene, on this side the bar of God, can be more awfully, overpoweringly solemn, than the scene which such an assembly exhibits. Then the Father of spirits is present to the spirits he has made; present to each of them, and speaking to each. Each one feels that the eye of God is upon him, that the voice of God is speaking to him. Each one therefore, though surrounded by numbers, mourns solitary and apart. The powers of the world to come are felt. Eternity, with all its crushing realities, opens to view, and descends upon the mind. The final sentence, though uttered by human lips, comes with scarcely less weight, than if pronounced by the Judge himself. All countenances gather blackness, and a stillness, solemn, profound, and awful, pervades the place, interrupted only by a stifled sob, or a half repressed sigh. My hearers, such scenes have been witnessed. Within a very few years they have been witnessed in hundreds of places.

Nor need we wonder that the still small voice of God should produce such effects. Look at Elijah. While a tempestuous wind rent the mountains, and broke in pieces the rocks before his eyes; while the earth quaked under his feet, and consuming fires blazed around him, he stood with uncovered face, undismayed, unmoved. But no sooner was the still small voice heard, than he covered his face, and put himself in the posture of reverent, waiting attention. Look at Moses. When he saw miraculous tokens of God's presence in a burning, but unconsumed bush, he felt little other emotion than curiosity. But when a still small voice addressed him from that bush, he hid his face and was afraid. Look at Saul. When at midday a light suddenly shone around him, exceeding the brightness of the sun, it only surprised him. But when he heard a voice saying to him, Saul, Saul, why persecutest thou me? he trembled, he was confounded, he submitted. So at the present day, thousands who have witnessed tempests, and earthquakes, and fire; who have passed through floods of affliction, and who have been brought by sickness to the very gates of death, have returned from all these scenes unaffected, unmoved. Yet afterwards the same persons have, by the still small voice of God, not only been deeply impressed but permanently transformed. Is not my word, saith Jehovah, as a fire, and a hammer, which breaketh the rock in pieces? We remark,

III. That, when God speaks to men in this still small voice, he usually begins by turning their attention upon themselves, their conduct, and situation. He said to the prophet, What dost thou here, Elijah? a question which was most admirably adapted to convince, reprove, and humble him. It was as if God had said to him, Is this the proper place for thee, a prophet, a reprover, a reformer? Is this thy proper, thine appointed sphere of action? Are the people here whom I sent thee to warn? If not, why didst thou come here? what motive brought thee here? what art thou doing here? Similar questions in effect does God propose to men when he first speaks to them with his still small voice. Calling each one, as it were, by name, he says to him, What art thou doing in the world in which I have placed thee? what hast thou done? in what pursuits hast thou employed the time and the powers which I have given thee? And to these questions he constrains conscience to give a true, though reluctant answer. He makes her the sinner's accuser, makes her accuse him to his face, of his numberless sins of omission and commission, of time misspent, of faculties misemployed, of privileges misimproved, and mercies abused. At the same time he refutes all the sinner's objections and arguments; shows him, as he did Elijah, the fallacy of his excuses; strips him of all his vain pleas, and lays him speechless and self-condemned at the footstool of sovereign mercy. O what a long train of self-accusing thoughts and reflections is put in motion by the short questions, What art thou doing? what hast thou done? when they are pressed upon a sinner's conscience by the still small voice of God. And it is obvious to remark, that an attention to these questions is the first thing ncessary to a careless sinner. Until he considers what he has been doing in the world, he will see nothing of his sinfulness, guilt and danger; he will not know of what to repent, he will not feel his need of a Savior. Hence our Divine Teacher informs us that, when the Spirit of God comes, he will reprove the world of sin; that is, he will make men see what they have been doing, he will show them what they ought to have done, and thus convince them how widely their temper and conduct have differed from the rule of rectitude, the will of their Maker. And when they are brought to repentance, the same still small voice will whisper to them assurances of pardon and peace; for the Lord will speak peace to his people and his servants, and his Spirit shall witness with their spirits, that they are the children of God.

A few reflections and inferences will conclude the discourse.

1. We may learn from this subject, my Christian friends, to expect the conversion of sinners, not from any means or instruments however apparently powerful, but from the Spirit of God alone. I am indeed aware that your understandings are already perfectly convinced of this truth; but our feelings do not always correspond with it. We are sometimes ready to think that, if God would work miracles or send some extraordinary calamity, sinners would be converted, or at least convinced of their sins. But at such times we forget that God is not in the whirlwind, the earthquake, and the fire; that he usually speaks in a still small voice. At other times, after hearing a sermon which has appeared to them remarkably solemn and impressive, Christians will say, Certainly this sermon cannot fail of producing some salutary effects. But they forget that, unless the still small voice of God has also spoken, no salutary effect will follow. Whenever the work is done, it is effected not by might, nor by power, but by my Spirit, saith the Lord of Hosts. Let us then, above all things, desire and pray, that the Spirit and the still small voice of God may accompany the preaching of the gospel. This will prove far more efficacious than tempest, and earthquakes, and fire; and without this, not only all the apostles but all the angels, would preach in vain.

2. If the truth of the preceding remarks be allowed, it will follow, that what we call conversion and the other effects produced by the preaching of the gospel are not a mere excitement of the passions or animal feelings. Some seem to suppose that this is the case, and that those whom we call converts have been merely terrified or agitated by addresses to their passions. But were this the case, the tempest, the earthquake and the fire would be the most effectual means of producing conversion, and

the preacher, who could most eloquently and powerfully address the passions of his audience, would always be the most successful preacher. But this is by no means the fact. A plain simple exhibition of the truth by men of very moderate abilities and attainments has, in hundreds of instances, produced far greater effects, than the most impassioned and eloquent appeals which ever issued from mortal lips. The fact is, that when persons are converted, they are converted not because their passions have been addressed, not because they have been agitated or terrified, but because the still small voice of God has spoken to them, spoken within them, and taught them what they have been doing, what they are doing, and what they ought to have done. It is this alone which has given to the preachers of the gospel all the success which they have ever met with. It was this which made the preaching of the apostles successful. They went forth and preached every where that men should repent, the Lord working with them. It was this which rendered the preaching of their immediate disciples successful. They spoke the word, and the hand of the Lord was with them, and much people were turned to the Lord. And St. Paul declares that though he planted and Apollos watered the churches, it was God alone who gave the increase. Conversion then is, and always has been the work of God. It is not a delusion, a fancy, or an effect of human eloquence; but a necessary prerequisite to admission into heaven, and our Savior's declaration, Verily, verily, I say unto you, except ye be converted, ye shall in no wise enter the kingdom of God, is still as true as it is solemn and interesting.

To conclude. Permit me now, my hearers, in God's name to press upon each of you the question in our text. In doing this I would not, if I could, surround you with tempests, and earthquakes, and fires; for God would not be in them. Nor would I, were it in my power, pour forth a torrent of impassioned eloquence and tumultuously agitate your passions. On the contrary, I wish you to be cool, calm, collected, and self-possessed. I wish the voice of passion and every other voice to be hushed within you, that the still small voice of God may speak and be heard. And nothing but a faint hope that he will speak, at least to some present, encourages me to address you. Hoping and praying that, while I address his question to your ears, his own still small voice may address it to each of your hearts, I ask every individual present in his name, What dost thou here? What art thou doing, mortal and accountable creature, in the world wherever I have placed thee? Art thou performing the duty I have assigned thee? Art thou faithfully serving and glorifying me thy Creator? Art thou working out the salvation of thine immortal soul with fear and trembling? Or art thou living, hast thou lived only to gratify or enrich or exalt thyself, while me, the God in whose hand thy breath is, and whose are all thy ways, thou hast not glorified, art not glorifying? Again: what dost thou, mortal, accountable creature, here in this house of thy God? Hast thou come here to worship me in spirit and in truth; to confess thy sins and obtain pardon; to offer supplication and thanksgiving and praise to me, and to learn thy duty with a determination to perform it? Or hast thou come, thou canst scarcely tell why, come to provoke me by formal and heartless services, to assume the posture of devotion, but to offer no prayer, to sit and hear my words, but do them not, and to cover wandering thoughts and an insensible heart with a serious countenance? My hearers, the questions of your God and your Judge are before you. If you have heard my voice alone propose them, they will pass unheeded and soon be forgotten. But if the still small voice of God has pressed them upon your consciences, they cannot pass unheeded; they will be remembered, and they will be followed by effects which neither tempest, nor earthquake, nor fire could produce.

SERMON XL.

THE DAY OF SMALL THINGS NOT TO BE DESPISED.

Who hath despised the day of small things.—ZECHARIAH IV. 10.

THESE words were addressed by Jehovah to his ancient people, soon after their return from the Babylonish captivity. They were then few in number, poor, feeble, and on the point of being swallowed up by their enemies. But notwithstanding all these discouraging circumstances they proceeded, almost immediately after their return, to lay the foundations of a temple for the worship of God. It may well be supposed that, as it respects richness and magnificence, there would be a wide difference between such an edifice, as these poor captives could build, and that which had previously been erected by the wisest and wealthiest of monarchs. There was so; and those among them who had seen the temple of Solomon, wept aloud when they saw the foundations of the new temple laid, on account of its comparative meanness. Indeed, they seem to have felt as if such a temple were not worth finishing; and their unreasonable, ill-timed contempt of it, combined with other circumstances, so much discouraged their brethren, that for several years little was done towards its completion. It was with a view to reanimate them, and to encourage their exertions, that the message contained in this chapter was sent. In this message God reproved those who had regarded the new temple with contempt, and those also who thought that they were unable to finish it. He informed them that the work was his, that it was to be effected not by human might nor power but by his Spirit; that Zerubbabel, who had laid the foundations, should live to place the top stone, shouting, Grace, grace unto it; and that those who had despised the day of small things, or, in other words, the feeble commencement of the work, should witness its completion.

In farther discoursing on the passage before us, I shall endeavor to show,

I. That in all God's works, especially in his works of grace, which are effected not by might, nor by power, but by his Spirit, there is usually a day of small things;

II. That many often despise this day; and

III. That it ought not to be despised.

I. In all the works of God, and especially in his works of grace, which are effected not by might, nor by power, but by his Spirit, there is usually a day of small things; that is, in other words, there is a season in which his work makes but a very small and unpromising appearance. All that is necessary to convince you of the truth of this assertion is to refer you to some of God's works. Look at his works of creation. It was a day of small things with this world, when it lay a wild chaotic mass without form and void, and shrouded in darkness. Look at his works of providence. The oak was once an acorn; the mightiest rivers may be traced back to an insignificant rivulet or spring; the philosopher, the warrior, the statesman, the poet, was once an infant; the powerful civilized nation was once a horde of savages. But it is especially to God's works of grace, that the remark under consideration refers; and to them we must especially look for illustrations of its truth. It was a day of small things with the Old Testament church, when Abraham and his family were its only members. It was a day of small things with the New Testament church, when all its members could assemble in one small room, and sit down at one table. And every branch of this church, wherever planted, and however flourishing it may now be, has had its day of small things. It was such a day with the church of Christ in New England, when all its members disembarked from one vessel, and worshipped God on the barren shore, without a sanctuary, and without even a habitation to shelter them. And probably there is not a church in this country, which was not for a time small and feeble, and obliged to struggle with many difficulties. Similar remarks may be made respecting all the societies and institutions which have been formed for the promotion and diffusion of Christianity. Look, for instance, at the British and Foreign Bible Society, at the Baptist Missions in the East, at Sabbath Schools, and at all the National Societies which have been formed for the education of ministers, for sending missionaries to the heathen, and for the distribution of tracts. Compared with what they now [1824] are, they were originally but as the acorn compared to the oak.

Similar remarks may be made respecting God's work of grace in the hearts of individuals. Every Christian has his day, and almost all Christians, alas, much too long a day of small things; a day in which his love, faith, and hope, knowledge, usefulness, and comfort are small. Look at Nicodemus. It was such a time with him when he came to Jesus by night. Look at the twelve disciples. It was such a time with them until after the day of Pentecost. They were foolish, and slow of heart to believe; they were altogether in an error respecting the nature of that kingdom which Christ came to establish, and there were frequent strifes among them who should be the greatest. Look at the Corinthian Christians. I, brethren, says St. Paul, could not speak unto you as spiritual, but as carnal, even as unto babes in Christ. This language intimates, not only that the Corinthians had made little progress in religion, but that babes in Christ or young Christians generally, are in many respects carnal, and by no means distinguished for spirituality. Look too at the Hebrew Christians. Ye need, says an apostle, that one teach you what be the first principles of the oracles of God, and are become such as have need of milk, and not of strong meat. For every one that useth milk is unskilful in the word of righteousness, for he is a babe. If we turn from the primitive, to modern Christians, we shall find at least equally striking proofs that, generally speaking, they all have a day of small things. With many who, we hope, are Christians, this day continues through life. Indeed, in comparison with what Christians will be hereafter, in comparison with the spirits of just men made perfect, the attainments of the most eminent Christians in this world are but small things, and their whole life but a day of small things. It was St. John who said, It doth not yet appear what we shall be. It was St. Paul who said, I have not attained; I know but in part; we see through a glass darkly. In fine, the kingdom of God here below, whether we contemplate it as set up in the world, or in the hearts of individual Christians, is at first but as a grain of mustard seed, sown in the earth, or as a stone cut from a mountain.

II. Many persons despise the day of small things, which attends the commencement of God's works. His enemies do so. What do these feeble Jews? said some of his ancient enemies. Will they fortify themselves? will they make an end in a day? Will they revive the stones out of the heaps of rubbish that are burnt? If but a fox go up, he shall break down their wall. With at least equal contempt was Christianity regarded both by Jews and Gentiles, while its day of small things continued. And the same contempt is felt and expressed by multitudes of its enemies at the present day, with respect to the attempts which are making to evangelize the world. You need not be informed that ridicule is thrown with liberal hand upon the hopes and labors of missionaries among the heathen, and upon the expectation which Christians entertain of the conversion of the world. Because it is now a day of small things with respect to this work, because comparatively few of the heathen have as yet embraced Christianity, many of its avowed and secret enemies look with scorn upon all attempts to extend its influence, and gravely tell us, that the conversion of the heathen is impossible, and that even if it is to be desired, which they seem to doubt, it is not to be expected. With at least equal contempt do many of them look upon the commencement of God's work of grace in the hearts of individuals around them, and stigmatise it as the effect of weakness, superstition, or enthusiasm.

In the second place, not only the enemies, but even the friends of God, sometimes despise the day of small things, which attends his work during its infancy. They did so in the instance referred to in our text. They have done so in many instances since. We do not mean that, like his enemies, they regard his work with absolute contempt. But they think too little of it; they undervalue it, and they are by no means sufficiently thankful for it; and may therefore be said, comparatively speaking, to despise it. This for instance, is sometimes the case at the commencement of a revival of religion, especially when it commences and proceeds in a gentle and gradual manner, and is confined to individuals of little weight in society. In such circumstances, a considerable portion of the church, which is thus favored, are often guilty, in a greater or less degree, of despising the day of small things. They wish to see the wealthy, the learned, and the great brought to the foot of the cross; or, at least, to see great numbers converted; and because they do not see this, they will scarcely allow that there is any thing to encourage exertion, or call forth thankfulness. I leave it with your consciences, my professing friends, to decide whether a considerable part of this church has not more than once exemplified these remarks. Still more frequently, perhaps, are Christians guilty of despising, or too lightly esteeming the work of God in their own hearts. Forgetting that the Christian must be an infant, a child, and a youth before he can arrive at the stature of a perfect man in Christ Jesus, they wish, and seem to expect to become men at once; and when these unscriptural expectations are disappointed; when they find that with respect to their knowledge, faith, comfort, and usefulness, their day is a day of small things, they are too often ready to feel as if nothing had been done for them; and as if so small a portion of grace, as they possess, were scarcely worth cultivating. Hence, while looking for great things, they overlook small things; and neglect those means and exertions, by which alone small things can ever be made to become great. Others go still farther, and because they do not find in themselves so much religion as they wished and expected, will not allow that they possess a particle. Hence they will not unite with the friends of Christ, will not confess him before men, will not commemorate his dying love; as if these duties and privileges were reserved exclusively for mature and eminent Christians. In these and various other ways, which time will not allow me to particularize, Christians are often guilty of despising the day of small things.

I proceed now, as was proposed,

III. To state some reasons why it ought not to be despised.

1. We ought not to despise the day of small things, because such conduct tends to prevent its becoming a day of great

things. If all the Jews had despised the foundations of the temple, as some of them did, they would never have exerted themselves to finish it. So those who despise the day of small things, where missions are concerned, will do little to promote them. None who despise a small revival of religion will make the exertions which are necessary to render it great. And the Christian, who despises or overlooks the blessings which he has already received, will not seek and pray with proper earnestness for greater blessings. Besides, despising the day of small things always involves much ingratitude. It is practically saying, we have nothing to be thankful for. It leads us, instead of blessing God for what he has given, to murmur because he does not give more. And this directly tends to prevent him from giving more. It is a very trite but a very just remark, that the way to obtain much, is to be thankful for little. As it respects the attainment of blessings from heaven, this remark is especially true. Thanksgivings are at least as efficacious as prayers. And ingratitude will shut the ear of God against the most fervent prayers. Let none then despise the day of small things, unless they wish to prevent it from becoming a day of great things.

2. We ought not to despise the day of small things, because the inhabitants of heaven, whose judgment is according to truth, do not despise it. Angels do not. No, they rejoice over one sinner that repenteth. Though it be a poor sinner, an ignorant sinner, a despised individual, still they rejoice. They rejoice, though the work is just begun, and though its glory is obscured by many remaining defects, weaknesses and imperfections; evils which they see incomparably more clearly than we do. Now there is not, I believe, a single protestant missionary establishment in the world, which has not been the means of converting at least one individual. There is not then a protestant missionary establishment on earth, which has not occasioned joy in heaven. Of course, there is not one which is despised in heaven.

Again. Our Savior does not despise the day of small things. It was said of him, The bruised reed he will not break, and the smoking flax he will not quench; he will bring forth judgment unto victory. In this prediction young and feeble Christians, who have but little grace, are compared to the wick of an extinguished lamp, in which but a spark of fire remains. It does not burn brightly, it sends forth no flame; but it emits smoke, and that smoke mounts upward,—a fit emblem of the weakest Christian, whose desires, though faint and few, ascend to heaven. Yet even such a disciple as this, the compassionate Savior does not despise, and will not reject. No, he feeds his flock like a shepherd; he gathers the lambs with his arms and carries them in his bosom. See these remarks verified in his treatment of Nicodemus. Instead of despising him for his cowardice, ignorance, and slowness to learn, our Savior received him kindly, and gave up his own necessary rest, for the sake of communicating instruction to his mind. Look too at the manner in which Jesus treated his twelve disciples, and at his interview with Thomas, with Mary Magdalene, and with Cleophas after his resurrection; and you will be convinced that while on earth he did not despise the day of small things. Nor does he now despise it. Even so small a gift as a cup of cold water to the meanest of his disciples, if given for his sake, he does not despise. The feeble minded and the weak he commands his ministers to support and comfort. Them that are weak in faith he commands his churches to receive. Hear too what he says to one of his feeble churches; I have set before thee an open door, and no man can shut it; and I will make thine enemies to come and worship at thy feet, and to know that I have loved thee, for thou hast a little strength.

Once more. Our heavenly Father does not despise the day of small things. Hear what he said of a child, the son of Jeroboam: In him is found some good thing toward the Lord God of Israel; therefore he alone of the house of Jeroboam shall come to his grave in peace. Look also at the parable of the prodigal son. When he was yet a great way off, his father saw him, and had compassion, and ran and fell on his neck, and kissed him. In fine, as those of you who are parents do not despise, but are pleased with the first stammering accents of your children, especially when they lisp the words, father, mother, so our heavenly Father listens with pleasure to the first feeble, imperfect prayers of his children, when, guided by the Spirit of adoption, they come lisping, Abba, Father. Now if angels, if our Redeemer, and our heavenly Father, do not despise the day of small things, surely it does not become us, imperfect creatures, to despise it.

3. We ought not to despise the day of small things, because these things, though small, are of unspeakable value. Inspiration styles faith precious faith, and declares that it is more valuable than gold tried in the fire. Indeed it is so; for it is the gift of God, and who shall despise his gifts? It is the work of God, and there are no works like his works. The man, whose faith is but as a grain of mustard seed, is interested in all the promises of the gospel; he is a child of God, a joint-heir with Christ of the heavenly inheritance. In fine, grace, the least particle of grace, is glory begun; and all the figures which man ever made, were they placed in one line, with worlds for units, could not express the ten thousandth part of its value. How irrational then to despise what is so infinitely valuable.

Finally. We ought not to despise the day of small things, because it is the commencement of a day of great things. It will become so, because these small things are the work of God; and as for God, his work is perfect, and what he doth shall be forever. He never leaves his work unfinished; for his language is, I will work, and who shall let it? when I begin, I will make an end. These predictions will be verified in the future success of missionary exertions, and the final universal prevalence of Christianity. The stone cut from the mountain without hands, shall itself become a mountain, and fill the whole earth. The streams of divine knowledge, which now flow in scanty rivulets, shall become broad and deep rivers, and overflow the world; for the knowledge of the Lord shall fill the earth, even as the waters fill the seas. A little one shall become a thousand and a small one a strong nation. I the Lord will hasten it. These predictions will also be verified with respect to God's work of grace in the heart of every believer; for he who begins a good work in the heart, will perform it to the day of Christ Jesus; so that the weakest disciple may boldly say, with the psalmist, The Lord will perfect that which concerneth me; he will guide with his counsel and afterwards receive me to glory. Yes, that tender plant, that bruised reed, which trembles before every breeze, is the planting of the Lord, and shall become a tree of righteousness. That smoking wick shall burn bright. That poor, despised, ignorant, feeble Christian, who is now but a babe in grace, shall become a youth, a perfect man in Christ Jesus; for God will strengthen him, yea, he will help him; yea, he will uphold him with the right hand of his righteousness. In a word, the weakest Christian now on earth, shall one day be among the spirits of just men made perfect; shall be equal to the angels; shall shine forth like the sun in the kingdom of his Father; for the path of the just is as the rising light, which shineth more and more unto the perfect day. Permit me now to apply the subject,

1. By asking every individual present, is it with you, in a religious sense, even so much as a day of small things? In other words, have you any religion? have you faith, even as a grain of mustard seed? Has the light of heaven dawned within you? Unless you have been converted, regenerated, born of God, this is not the case; for if any man be in Christ, he is a new creature; he has been created anew in Christ Jesus unto good works; and if he be not in Christ, he is not a Christian, he has not a particle of faith, he is yet in his sins. If any ask, how may I ascertain whether I have become a subject of this new creation? I answer, every one who is a subject of it can say, Whereas I was once blind, I now see. Every subject of it loves and finds his happiness in those religious employments and pursuits, which he once hated or neglected; and has in a great measure lost his relish for those worldly, sinful pleasures in which he once delighted. Every Christian, though but a babe in grace, hungers and thirsts after righteousness, and desires the sincere milk of the word, that he may grow thereby. If this is the case with any of you, beware how you deny what God has done for you; beware how you despise the day of small things; beware how you ungratefully neglect to thank God for the inestimable blessings which he has bestowed upon you. I call them inestimable; for they strictly and literally are so. No man, no angel can estimate their worth, or the greatness of your obligation to him who bestowed them. O Christian, Christian, did you but know what God has done for you; could you see the end of the path into which he has guided you; could you behold the meridian brightness of that day which has dawned within you; how would you rejoice, and exult, and call upon your soul and all that is within you, to bless and extol your benefactor! How

would you watch over and cultivate and labor to increase the seeds of grace which he has sown within you? And how would this church exert itself, how would it bless God for every instance of conversion, for every token of his presence, did it duly estimate the day of small things! Seek and pray then, for this attainment; and if you would obtain greater blessings from heaven, send up more numerous and fervent thanksgivings for the blessings which it has already bestowed on us.

One caution, and I have done. There is an opposite error, or mistake, into which many professors fall. Instead of despising the day of small things, they trust too much to it, and are satisfied with it. They conclude too hastily, that the work of grace is begun in their hearts and flatter themselves that it will advance to perfection, without any additional exertion on their part. Nay more, they perhaps fancy that their attainments are great, and indulge in self-complacency and pride. This mistake is far more dangerous than the former. Better despise the day of small things, than be proud of it, or rest satisfied, or make it an excuse for sloth and presumption. That you may be guarded against this error, remember that the day of small things is a day of increase; that every one who has any grace, desires and labors to obtain more grace.

SERMON XLI.

GOD'S SPECIAL PRESENCE DISTINGUISHES HIS OWN PEOPLE.

If thy presence go not with me, carry us not up hence. For wherein shall it be known here, that I and thy people have found grace in thy sight? Is it not in that thou goest with us? So shall we be separated, I and thy people, from all the people that are upon the face of the earth.—Exodus xxxiii. 15, 16.

You doubtless recollect, my hearers, that the Israelites, while encamped in the wilderness at the foot of Mount Sinai, made and worshipped a golden calf. This sin would have been punished by their immediate and total destruction, had not the earnest intercession of Moses prevailed to obtain a pardon. But though, at his request, God forebore to destroy the offenders, he saw it necessary to manifest his displeasure, by withdrawing from them his sensible and gracious presence, and by commanding the tabernacle, which was its symbol, to be removed and pitched without the camp. At the same time, he intimated that he should no longer continue to go with them, as he had done; but should commit them to the guidance and protection of an angel. This intimation was not, however, expressed in such a manner, as to forbid all hope that it might be reversed; and therefore Moses felt encouraged to plead, that God would graciously condescend to accompany them as he had done. If thy presence, said he, go not with us, carry us not up hence. For wherein shall it be known here, that I and thy people have found grace in thy sight? Is it not in that thou goest with us? So shall we be separated from all people that are upon the face of the earth. That we may perceive the pertinency and force of this plea, we must recollect, that God had expressed a determination to make the Israelites a peculiar people unto himself, and, as such, to separate them and keep them separate from all other nations. Now this, Moses pleads, could not be effected, unless they continued to be favored with the manifested and gracious presence of their God. So long as they were favored with this blessing, it would separate them effectually from all other people; but should it be withdrawn, there would be nothing left to mark them out as the peculiar people of God; they would soon become like the other nations of the earth, and cease to be separated from them.

My hearers, the truth taught in this passage is one, in which we are all deeply interested, and with which it is highly important that we should all be acquainted. The Scriptures inform us, that the design, with which Christ gave himself for us, was, to purify unto himself a peculiar people; a people who should be different, and separate from, all other men. They teach us, that he requires all, who would be his disciples, to come out from among unbelievers and be separate, and that all who are his real disciples comply with this requisition. They inform us, that his disciples are not of the world, even as he is not of the world; and that, if any man be in Christ, in other words, if he be a real Christian, he is a new creature. He has new dispositions, new views, new feelings, new desires, and new objects of pursuit; in one word, a new character;—a character essentially different from that which he originally possessed, and from that of all other men. Thus a broad and well defined line of distinction is drawn between the true disciples of Christ, and the rest of mankind, analogous to that line which separated the Israelites from the heathen nations around them. Christ has redeemed them from their spiritual enemies, as God delivered Israel from Egyptian bondage, and he is leading them through this world to heaven, as God led the Israelites through the wilderness to the promised land, which was a type of the rest that remains for his people. And as he gave a promise to his ancient people, that his presence should go with them, so he has given his church many promises, that his manifested and gracious presence shall attend all the real disciples of Christ during their pilgrimage through this world. One of these promises, out of many which might be quoted, it may be proper to notice more particularly. He that hath my commandments and keepeth them, says our Savior, he it is that loveth me; and he that loveth me shall be loved of my Father, and I will love him, and will manifest myself to him. Judas saith unto him, not Iscariot, Lord, how is it that thou wilt manifest thyself unto us, and not unto the world? Jesus answered, If a man love me, he will keep my words, and my Father will love him, and we will come unto him, and make our abode with him. Hence it appears, that the Father and the Son come to every man who loves Christ and keeps his words; that is, to every real Christian, and dwell with him, and manifest themselves to him, as they do not to the world. Now the great truth to which we wish to lead your attention is this; nothing but this promised presence of God with his people can effectually separate them from other men; or, in other words, nothing else can preserve that broad line of distinction which separates real Christians from the unbelieving world. With a view to illustrate and establish this truth I shall attempt to show,

I. That the promised presence of God with his people, will, so long as they are favored with it, produce a wide difference and separation between them and all other men; and,

II. That in proportion as his presence is withdrawn from them, this difference and separation will diminish.

I. The promised presence of God with his people will, so long as they are favored with it, produce a wide difference and separation between them and all other men.

The remarks which I shall first make to prove the truth of this assertion may perhaps appear to some improper, and out of place; for they will relate, not so much to the peculiar presence of God with his people, as to the effects which a real belief of his universal presence must produce upon the mind of every one who entertains such a belief. That we may clearly perceive what these effects would be, let us take two persons as nearly alike in all respects, as is possible, who, in consequence of the similarity which exists between them, have become intimate and almost inseparable. Let us suppose that they both entertain that general, speculative, inoperative belief of the existence and universal presence of God, which is entertained probably by all who live in Christian lands. Now let us farther suppose, that to the mind of one of these persons, the constant presence of God, begins to appear like a reality. Suppose that he begins to believe it with that kind of faith which the Scriptures describe,—a faith which is the evidence of things not seen, and which causes its possessors to feel and act as if they saw him who is invisible. It is evident that a great change would immediately take place in this person's views and feelings. As soon as the existence and constant presence of such a being as Jehovah began to appear like realities, he could not fail to regard them as the most interesting and important of all realities. The objects which had previously engrossed his attention would sink into insignificance, when compared with the great and glorious object thus presented to his mind. The beings whose enmity he had feared, and whose friendship he had courted, would seem unworthy of regard compared with the infinite Being of beings, to whom they are indebted for their existence. In a word, all created objects would lose their value when the great Creator appeared, as stars disappear when the sun arises; and the mind would turn from them to contemplate him, as a child turns from its toys and amusements, when some more interesting object is presented to its view. This contemplation of God, as an ever present reality, would excite new reflections, feelings, and inquiries. Of these inquiries one of the first would be this, What have I to hope, or to fear, from this omnipotent, omnipresent Being, whose all-seeing eye constantly watches my conduct, and reads my heart? Does he regard me with approbation or with displeasure? The answers which the Scriptures give to these inquiries would soon convince him that God regards his character and conduct with decided disapprobation, and displeasure. Then the man's inquiry would be, How shall I avert the displeasure and secure the favor of this Almighty Being, who is ever with me, and on whom my happiness depends?

Now, let us farther suppose that, while the mind of one of these persons was occupied and engrossed by these new reflections, feelings, and inquiries, the other should remain as he was, without God in the world, without any realizing apprehension of his existence and presence. Would these two persons continue to be, as they had been, intimate and inseparable? Evidently not. Their views and feelings would no longer correspond. One would be thinking of the Creator, the other of creatures; one of this world, the other of the next; one of acquiring temporal objects, the other of averting the displeasure and securing the favor of God. And, as out of the abundance of the heart the mouth will speak, each of them would wish to converse respecting the objects which occupied his mind. The man who entertained new views of God's constant presence, regarding these views as highly important, would naturally feel a strong desire to impart them to his friend. His friend, on the other hand, would regard these views as unnecessary, perhaps as the effect of weakness, and wish to divert his attention from them. Thus, with respect to each other, they would be placed as it were in two different worlds. The society of each would gradually become less pleasing to the other; each would seek society more agreeable to his taste; and, though they might still regard each other with esteem and even with affection, a separation would be effected between them. It is evident, then, unless I am greatly deceived, that a realizing apprehension of the existence and constant presence of God, must produce a wide difference, and ultimately a separation, not always local indeed, but moral, between those who entertain such an apprehension, and those who do not.

But it may be easily made to appear still more evident, that such a difference and separation must be effected, when the Father and the Son come, agreeably to our Savior's promise, to reside in a man's heart, and favor him with the manifestations of their gracious presence. The occurrence of such an event, the entrance of such guests, into the heart must, it is obvious, be attended or followed by a great change in a man's views, feelings, and character. He then becomes, to use the expressive language of Scripture, a temple of the living God. Of those who are thus favored God himself says, I will dwell in them and walk with them, and they shall be my people and I will be their God. Now let but a man of taste come to occupy a house and garden, which had been long forsaken and neglected, and an alteration for the better will soon be perceived in them. Much more may we expect that a similar alteration will be effected in the soul, where the wonder-working God comes to reside in it, attended by all his enlightening and purifying and transforming energies. He is the Father of lights, the Sun of righteousness, and wherever he comes to dwell, he brings with him, and diffuses around him, a portion of his own celestial radiance. He causes the soul which he inhabits to see the light of the knowledge of his own glory in the face of Jesus Christ. The view, which is thus given to the soul, of God's ineffable glory and beauty, enables it to perceive the justice of his claims to the supreme love and undivided homage of all his intelligent creatures, and the infinite criminality of disregarding these claims. To withhold love, to disobey, to sin against, such a Being, now appears an exceedingly great evil. Thus, in the light of God's holiness and glory, the blackness and unspeakable malignity of sin are clearly seen, and the soul begins to perceive that it well deserves the terrible punishment which is denounced upon sinners in the word of God. At the same time, this divine light shines upon the man's past life, and enables him to see that it has been one continued course of sin and rebellion against God; it shines upon all the external, moral and religious duties, which he has ever attempted to perform, and shows him their insincerity, pollution, and worthlessness; it shines into all the hidden recesses of his heart, and discloses to him ten thousand lurking abominations, the existence of which he had never even suspected. In this respect the effects, produced by the entrance of God into the soul, resemble those which would result from admitting the light of the sun into a dark room, filled with every kind of filth and pollution. In fine, to every man in whom God takes up his residence he imparts, in a greater or less degree, his own views.

Now God's views of almost every object differ widely, as I need not inform you, from those of men. He himself says, My thoughts are not your thoughts; you judge according to the outward appearance, but my judgment is according to truth; the things which are highly esteemed among men are, in my sight, an abomination. Now if the views of God differ thus widely from those of men, and if he imparts his own views to every person whom he favors with his gracious presence, then it follows that the new views, with which such a person is favored must differ widely from those of all other men. And so far as he is influenced by these views, he will pursue a path different from that in which other men walk, and will of course be separated from them, for how can two walk together unless they be agreed? He will look at things unseen and eternal; but they look at things seen and temporal. He will wish and aim to walk with God; but they live without God in the world. He will seek and follow the narrow way to life; but they are following the broad road to destruction; and as these paths lead in opposite directions, those who follow one, must be separated from those who walk in the other.

Nor is this all. When God comes to dwell in the soul, he imparts to it a portion, not only of his own views, but of his own feelings. He not only illuminates the understanding with his own light, but, as an apostle expresses it, sheds abroad his love in the heart. Now consider a moment, my hearers, what a change must be produced in a selfish, sinful, polluted heart, a heart which inspiration declares to be full of evil and madness, deceitful above all things and desperately wicked, when that God, who is an infinitely pure, holy, and benevolent Spirit, and who hates sin with intense abhorrence, comes to reside in it. Can you suppose that he will dwell there in peace with those idols which he forbids us to worship, those sins which he abhors,—with his worst enemies? As well may we suppose that he would have allowed all the idols of the heathen to be set up and worshipped in his temple at Jerusalem. As well may we suppose that our Savior did not scourge out the buyers and sellers from the same temple when he entered it. As well may we suppose that Dagon did not fall before the ark of God, the symbol of Jehovah's presence, when it was brought into his temple. The Lord, we are assured, is a jealous God. He will not endure a rival. Behold, says a prophet, the Lord shall come into Egypt, and the idols of Egypt shall be moved at his presence. Much more may we suppose that, when he comes into the human heart, and makes it his temple, its former idols, its beloved sins, its domineering lusts, will be moved and overthrown, and a great moral purification be effected. Agreeably, an apostle informs us that, when God visited the Gentiles to take out from among them a people to his name, he purified the hearts of those who were thus taken; and, in passages too numerous to mention, he is represented as sanctifying all in whom he dwells, as teaching and disposing them to hate, repent of, and mortify their sinful propensities, to love and cultivate holiness, to be spiritually and heavenly minded, to be no longer conformed to this world, but to feel and live as pilgrims and strangers on earth, and to produce the fruits of the Spirit, which are love, joy, peace, long-suffering, goodness, meekness, temperance, and faith. In fine, he renews the soul after his own image in knowledge and true holiness; and thus, to use the language of inspiration, makes the man a new creature, a partaker of the divine nature. And must not this mighty change, produce a great difference, a wide moral separation between those who are the subjects of it, and all other men? Most evidently it must. And this difference and separation will be in exact proportion to the degree in which God manifests his gracious presence to the soul, and exerts upon it his sanctifying energies. Witness, for instance, the effects which a clear manifestation of God's presence produced upon Job: I have heard of thee by the hearing of the ear, but now mine eye seeth thee; wherefore I abhor myself and repent in dust and ashes.

I now proceed to show, as was proposed,

II. That, in proportion as God withdraws the manifestations of his presence from his people, this difference and separation between them and other men will diminish. Before exhibiting proofs of this truth, it may be proper to remark, that God never entirely withdraws his gracious presence from those who have once been favored with it. The promises which he has given them, the covenant which he has made with them, forbid this. His language to each of them is, I will never leave thee, nor forsake thee. And respecting all his people he says, I will make with them an everlasting covenant, that I will never turn away from them. But though these and many other similar promises render it certain that God's presence shall never be wholly withdrawn from his people; yet it is equally certain that he often suspends its sensible manifestations and effects, and, in the language of Scripture, hides himself from them. This is evident from the complaints of his people, recorded in the Scriptures. Job, David, and many others, complain that God had forsaken them, and hid himself from them; that he stood afar off, and that they could not find him; and they earnestly beseech him to return, to lift upon them the light of his countenance, and make them glad with his presence. This language all real

Christians understand; but it cannot easily be rendered intelligible to those who have never enjoyed God's presence, and who cannot therefore conceive how it is manifested. The following supposition may, perhaps, enable them to form some conception of its meaning.

Let us suppose, for a moment, that the sun was an intelligent being, and that by an act of his will he could withhold his enlightening and warming beams from one man, while he continued to shine upon others. It is evident that the man who was thus deprived of light and warmth, would soon complain of darkness and cold, and that he would earnestly desire to be again favored with those enlivening, cheering beams, which were so necessary to his happiness. And when the sun began once more to shine upon such a man, it might be said, figuratively speaking, to lift upon him the light of its countenance. Now God is the Sun of the soul. And he can shine into it, and render it luminous and happy. When he favors it with his presence and exerts upon it his influence, it is enlivened, and enlightened, and made to glow with love, and hope, and joy, and gratitude. But when he withdraws and suspends his influences, spiritual darkness and coldness are the consequence. Then it is night, it is winter with the soul. In proportion as he thus withdraws from his people, they cease to view him as a present reality. And in proportion as they cease to regard him as a present reality, they cease to have those views, and to exercise those affections, which constitute the grand essential difference between them and other men. Nor is this all. As holy affections decline, sinful affections revive. As the Creator sinks out of sight, creatures begin again to be regarded with an idolatrous attachment, just as the stars which are invisible, during the day, appear and sparkle when the sun is set. Hence the Christian becomes more and more worldly-minded, more and more conformed to the world, and, of course, the difference and separation, which existed between him and other men while he was favored with the presence of God, is less and less apparent, until at length he becomes, like Sampson after the Spirit of God had withdrawn from him, weak as any other man; nor will any thing raise him from this wretched state until he is again favored with the presence of God. It is then the peculiar presence of God with his people, and nothing else, which produces and maintains a difference and separation between them and other men. This truth St. Paul felt when he said, I can do all things through Christ strengthening me. I labored more abundantly than they all: yet not I, but the grace of God which was with me. I live; yet not I, but Christ liveth in me, and the life which I live in the flesh, I live by faith in the Son of God.

It remains only to make a suitable improvement of the subject. With this view, permit me, in the first place, to say to each individual in this assembly, Do you know experimentally the difference between the presence and the absence of God? If not, it is most certain that you never enjoyed his peculiar presence; and, of course, that you are not one of his people; for to be insensible of the difference between day and night, is not a more certain proof of physical or natural blindness, than it is of spiritual blindness, to be ignorant of the difference between the presence and the absence of God, the Sun of righteousness. If any one replies, I am not ignorant of this difference, for I trust that I have enjoyed the peculiar presence of God, I trust that the Father and the Son have taken up their residence in my heart;—let me ask that person farther, Has such a change been effected in your views and feelings as the entrance of such guests into your heart, might be expected to produce? Have you been led to see that the description, which inspiration gives of the human heart, is literally just and true with respect to your own heart? and have you, in consequence, been led, as was Job, to abhor yourself, and repent in dust and ashes? If not, be assured that your heart has never been God's residence.

Again. Have your views of God and of Jesus Christ been transforming? An apostle, speaking of himself and other Christians, says, We all, beholding as in a glass the glory of the Lord, are changed into the same image, from glory to glory. Are you thus transformed more and more into the image of the Lord? If not, he has never dwelt in your heart; for if any man have not the Spirit of Christ; if any man does not resemble Christ he is none of his.

Once more. Has what you call the presence of God led you to walk with God? Has it thus produced a moral difference and separation between you and the unbelieving world? Has it constrained you to obey the call which says, Come ye out from among them and be ye separate and touch not the unclean thing, and I will receive you, and will be a Father to you, and ye shall be my sons and daughters? If it has not, in some degree at least, produced these effects, be assured that what you call the presence of God is nothing but a delusion. It is an insult to the Father of lights, the High and Holy One, to pretend that you are his temple, that he dwells within you, unless you prove the justice of your pretensions by a corresponding temper and life. What! shall a man pretend to be the temple of the living God, the thrice Holy One of Israel, while his conduct evidently proves that his heart is filled with idols, and resembles a cage of unclean and hateful birds?

2. Let me improve this subject, by inquiring whether this church now enjoys the peculiar presence of God, as it once appeared to do? And yet why should I ask? It is, alas, but too evident that whatever exceptions we may make in favor of some individuals, this church, considered as a body, does not enjoy the peculiar presence of God, as it once apparently did. He seems to have withdrawn from us, at least for a time; and, if I may so express it, to have committed us, as he threatened to do his ancient people, to the care of an angel. Do any ask for proofs of this assertion? Where, I ask in reply, is the broad line of distinction which once separated between this church and an unbelieving world? Is it not become like a mere mathematical line? Nay, is it not, in many parts of it, become imperceptible? Should any of you come as strangers into the town, could you determine, simply by observing men's daily conduct, who do, and who do not profess to belong to the church of Christ? In some, in a very considerable number of cases, you might doubtless see a real difference between professors and other men; but in too many cases, no such difference could be discovered. And yet if God's people are a peculiar people, a people chosen out of the world, a people in whom he dwells, a wide difference ought ever to be seen between them and others. An apostle, writing to Christians, says, Ye are our epistle, known and read of all men. God himself says of his people, They shall be known among the nations; all that see them shall acknowledge them, that they are the seed which the Lord hath blessed. In fine, the children of God ought to carry, and while they enjoy his presence, they will carry, their

Father's name written as it were in their foreheads, where all may read it. Now if this is not the case with us, if we are become like the world around us, it is certain that God has, in a degree at least, if not entirely, withdrawn his peculiar and gracious presence from this church. And if he has withdrawn it, it is on account of our sins; for on no other account does he ever withdraw himself from a church. His own language is, I will go and return to my place, until they acknowledge their offence and seek my face. And this language, while it states the reasons of his absence informs us how long it will continue, and what we must do to procure his return. We must acknowledge, with unfeigned contrition, the sins which provoked him to forsake us, and with sincerity, earnestness, and perseverance seek his presence. As yet we have not done this. We have not been suitably affected by the loss of God's presence. We have been less affected by it than were the idolatrous Israelites themselves. We are informed in the context that, when they heard of God's determination to withdraw from them, and commit them to the guidance of an angel, they mourned, and none of them put on their usual ornaments. And shall we, who call ourselves Christians, be less affected by the loss of God's presence, than were these perverse, stiff-necked idolaters? Rather let us imitate Moses who pleaded importunately for this blessing and would take no denial. Let us all, as one man, cry with him, Lord let thy presence go with us; so shall it be known that we have found favor in thy sight; so shall thy church be separated as a people from the surrounding world, and adorn the doctrine of God her Savior in all things. My brethren, unless we do this, unless we once more obtain God's gracious presence in the midst of us, our state will become worse and worse; we shall become more and more conformed to a sinful world; iniquities, offences, and divisions will abound, till God shall come in anger to scourge us, and perhaps remove our candlestick out of its place. Our all, yes our all is at stake. O then, be persuaded to know in this your day the things which belong to the peace of this church, before they are hidden from your eyes. And let those of its members who are still favored with the presence of God, beware lest they lose it. Let them prize it above all other blessings, and walk circumspectly and humbly with their God; remembering that he is a jealous God, who will not bear a rival; and a holy God, who will not tolerate sin even in his own people.

To conclude. It is possible there may be some individuals in this assembly who, in consequence of not attending to the subject, have never been aware that such a blessing as the sensible, gracious presence of God may be enjoyed on earth. Let me beseech such persons, if any such there are present, to examine the Scriptures carefully, with special reference to this subject. Let them consider impartially the promises which have been quoted in this discourse, and the many inspired passages in which God's people are represented as either rejoicing in his presence, or mourning its loss. Let them remember that the High and Holy One, who inhabits eternity, has said, I dwell in the hearts of the humble and contrite. Should they be convinced after a careful examination, that such a blessing is attainable, that it is enjoyed by all real Christians, and that no man can dwell with God hereafter, unless God dwells in him here, they will surely need no additional inducement to seek it; for what can be so desirable, so honorable, as to enjoy the indwelling presence of the King of kings; as to be the temples of the living God; as to have our minds enlightened by the Father of lights, and our hearts filled with holy love by the God of holiness and love!

SERMON XLII.

HOW TO PROLONG THE GRACIOUS VISITS OF CHRIST.

And when it was day he departed, and went into a desert place; and the people sought him, and came unto him, and stayed him, that he should not depart from them. — LUKE IV. 42.

OUR blessed Savior, while on earth, met with a very different reception in different places. In one place we see all the inhabitants uniting in a request that he would depart out of their coasts. In another, they were so much provoked by his doctrine, that they thrust him out of their city, and led him to the brow of the hill on which it stood, with a design to cast him down headlong. Here, on the contrary, we see multitudes seeking him, and using every means in their power to prevent or retard his departure. The place where his presence was thus earnestly desired, was Capernaum. The inhabitants of this city heard him preach, and they were astonished at his doctrine. They saw him cast out a devil and were all amazed, and said one to another, What a word is this? Determined to improve the opportunity, which his presence afforded, they pressed upon him to hear the word of God, and brought to him all their sick to be healed. Having spent the day and the evening in these labors of love, our Savior rose early the next morning, and departed into a desert place, partly for the purpose of prayer, and partly, perhaps, to see whether they would follow him and request his longer stay. This temporary withdrawal only rendered them the more desirous of his presence. They sought him, and came unto him, and stayed him, that he should not depart from them.

My friends, the Savior is still, though invisibly, present in our world. Wherever his ministers are, there he is; for he has promised to be with them always, even to the end of the world. Wherever his people assemble in his name, there he is; for he has promised to be in the midst of them on such occasions. Sometimes, but not always, he chooses to manifest his presence by the production of visible effects. When this is the case, a revival of religion ensues. The spiritually sick are healed, and the spiritually dead raised to life. But it is often the case that, at such seasons, he seems to withdraw for a time, to see whether his presence is desired, whether his absence will be mourned, whether his people will be excited to greater diligence in seeking him. When this is the case, we may learn from our text what duty requires of us. We must seek him diligently, and, if possible, find him, and constrain him not to depart from us. In discoursing farther on this passage, I shall endeavor to show,

I. What means should be employed by a society that is favored with the gracious visits of Christ, to prolong their continuance, and prevent his departure; and,

II. To state some of the reasons which should induce us to employ these means.

I. What means should be employed to prolong the gracious visits of Christ? I answer, generally, we must endeavor to render his continuance with us agreeable to himself; and to avoid or banish from among us every thing which tends to render it otherwise. When we wish to induce an earthly friend to reside with us as long as possible, we naturally endeavor to render his residence with us agreeable; for no person will voluntarily continue long in a disagreeable place, or in unpleasant society. It is the same with respect to Christ. We must make his visits pleasant, or they will be few and of short continuance. Now nothing is so pleasant to him as holiness; nothing is so hateful to him as sin. Sin then, must be renounced and mortified, and holiness loved and practised, if we would induce him to stay long with us.

But more particularly; if we would prolong our Savior's gracious visits, either to ourselves, to our habitations, or to the place in which we reside, we must show him that we greatly desire, and highly value his presence. No person will consent to stay long with those, by whom his presence is not desired. Least of all will those consent to this, who are sensible of their own worth, and who know that there are other places, where they would be more welcome. Now our blessed Savior is perfectly sensible of his own worth. He knows that his favor is life, and his loving kindness better than life; and that, in comparison with himself, every thing is worthless. He knows that, great and powerful as he is, he can confer no favor upon a church or upon individuals more valuable than his gracious presence. He, therefore, justly expects that we should prize it accordingly, and consider every thing else as nothing in comparison with this. His language is, He that loveth father or mother, son or daughter, yea, his own life, more than me, is not worthy of me. If, therefore, he perceives that we love and desire any object whatever more than his presence, he will consider us unworthy of it and depart. Agreeably, we find him saying, respecting his ancient people, when they seemed to prefer other objects to himself, I will go and return to my place, till they acknowledge the offence and seek my face. The fact is, that, when we prefer any object to Christ, we make an idol of that object, and set up that idol in his presence. And can we expect that he will continue long with those who prefer an idol before him? Would he, while on earth, have gone into an idolatrous temple, and continued there, patiently witnessing his own disgrace, and choosing such a place as his residence? Certainly not; nor will he now long continue in a heart, in a house, or in a place, where he sees any idol preferred before him. The psalmist could say, If I forget thee, O Jerusalem, let my right hand forget her cunning; if I do not remember thee, let my tongue cleave to the roof of my mouth, if I prefer not Jerusalem above my chief joy. Similar must be our feelings with respect to Christ, if we would enjoy his presence. We must prefer it above our chief joy; and be able to exclaim with David, There be many that say, Who will show us any good? Lord, lift thou up the light of thy countenance upon me. Nor is it enough to feel these desires. We must express them to him in prayer; or they will be like the fruitless wishes of the sluggard, who desireth and hath nothing. Prayer is the offering up of our desires to God; and he will not seem to know our desires, much less gratify them, unless they are expressed and offered up to him in his appointed way. The more he seems to depart from us, the more earnestly must we follow him with our prayers and supplications, saying, with Jacob, We will not let thee go, except thou bless us; and, like the persons mentioned in our text, staying him that he may not forsake us.

2. With prayer we must unite penitence. Especially must we repent of those sins, which have been the probable cause of his beginning to withdraw. This is indispensably necessary; for we are told, that the Lord is near to them that have a broken heart, and saveth such as be of a contrite spirit. Without this, even prayer will not avail, as is evident from the case of Joshua, when his army was repulsed before Ai. Perplexed, grieved, and astonished at this unexpected repulse, which seemed so inconsistent with what God's promises taught him to expect, the Jewish captain rent his clothes, and, with the elders of Israel, put dust upon his head, and lay prostrate before God in earnest prayer, during the whole day. But God gave him to understand, that sin was the cause of this disaster; that no prayers could avail without repentance and reformation. And the Lord said unto Joshua, Get thee up; wherefore liest thou on thy face? Israel hath sinned, and hath transgressed my covenant; therefore they could not stand before their enemies, because they were accursed; neither will I be with you any more, except ye destroy the accursed from among you. Now sin is the accursed thing, which always provokes Christ to depart from those who entertain it; and no entreaties will prevent his departure, unless this accursed thing be repented of and renounced. Nay more, without this, he will not only withdraw his gracious presence, but will come out against us in anger; for his language to those who begin to decline from the way of truth is, I will come and fight against thee with the word of my mouth, except thou repent.

3. If we would prevent the Savior from depriving us of his gracious visits, we must receive them with profound humility, and a deep sense of our unworthiness of such a favor. His visits are always designed to humble us; and so long as they produce this effect, he will continue them; for the High and

Holy One, who inhabits eternity, dwells also with him who is of a humble and contrite heart. But if we begin to grow proud of his favors; if we imagine that he blesses us with his presence, on account of any worthiness or excellence of our own; if we begin to look down with contempt on others, who are less favored, he will quickly withdraw, and leave us to shame; for while he gives grace to the humble, he sets himself against the proud to abase them. A striking instance of this we have in the story of Hezekiah. He had enjoyed many favors, had been delivered from the Assyrian army, miraculously raised from sickness, and made instrumental of a great revival of religion. But, we are told, that Hezekiah rendered not again according to the benefit done unto him; but his heart was lifted up, therefore there was wrath upon Judah and Jerusalem.

4. If we would prevent the Savior from leaving us, we must assign sufficient reasons why he should prolong his stay. He always does what is right and reasonable. No entreaties can induce him to act in an unreasonable manner; for he is not like weak-minded man who can often be persuaded to act contrary to his judgment. But if we can assign any sufficient reasons for his continuance with us, he will infallibly prolong it, while those reasons continue to operate. We ought therefore, as Job expresses it, to fill our mouths with arguments, when we come to plead that he would not forsake us. The glory of his Father, the honor of his great name, the welfare of his people, the prosperity of his cause, are each of them reasons of sufficient weight to influence his conduct; and while either of these reasons requires his stay, we may be sure that he will not leave us.

5. If we would prevent Christ from leaving us, we must furnish him with employments, and with such kind of employments as are suited to his character. Every intelligent being has some ruling passion, and every such being will choose to reside where that passion can be most easily and effectually gratified. For instance, the ruling passion of a miser is the love of wealth; and therefore, he will ever choose to reside where he can most easily acquire it. Now the ruling passion of our Savior, is the love of doing good. My meat, says he, is to do the will of my Father and to finish his work. And again he says, It is more blessed to give than to receive. Agreeably, we find that, when on earth, he went about doing good, and,

where he found opportunities of doing the most good, there he always made the longest stay; nor do we find that, in a single instance, he left any place until he had done all the good they would allow him to do, and had healed all who either came or were brought to him for that purpose. If in any place he did not do many mighty works, it was because of their unbelief. It is the same still. Where he finds opportunities of doing the greatest good, there he ever best loves to stay.

If then we would prolong his gracious visits, we must furnish him with opportunities of doing good, and keep him constantly employed in this blessed work. We must bring to him ourselves, our children, our friends and acquaintances, to be pardoned, instructed, sanctified, and saved. We must not leave him without employment for a single day; and if he begins to withdraw, we must lay the sick, the dying, and the dead across his path; for nothing will stop his departure, like such an obstacle as this. Omnipotent as he is, he cannot step over a perishing soul, laid by faith across his way. As unbelief can paralize his arm, so faith can constrain him to work; and with gentle, but irresistible force, arrest his progress, even when he has begun to withdraw.

Such, in brief, are the means which must be employed by those who wish to prevent the Savior's departure. I proceed to notice, as was proposed,

II. Some of the reasons which should induce us to employ these means.

1. We ought to employ these means, because a neglect of them will infallibly grieve and offend our Redeemer. Every being who is capable of feeling affection, wishes to have his affection returned; to have his favors received with thankfulness, to have his presence desired, to be beloved by those whom he loves; and, on the contrary, every one feels grieved and offended, when those, whom he has loved, and loaded with benefits, treat him with ingratitude and neglect, and manifest no desire for his presence. Now Christ has loved his people with an infinite and everlasting love; he has given them most convincing proofs of his affection; he has bestowed upon them blessings unspeakably valuable, and purchased at an infinite expense; he rejoices in the prospect of enjoying their society forever in those mansions which he has prepared for their resi-

dence; and, therefore, he wishes them to desire and rejoice in his presence with them on earth; he wishes them to prefer it to every other object; and he therefore is, he must be grieved and displeased, when he sees that this is not the case; when he sees them neglect those means which have a tendency to prolong his gracious visits. And say, my hearers, shall we willingly grieve and offend this best of friends? Has he not suffered enough from us already? Did we not grieve him sufficiently by our impenitence, our unbelief, and hardness of heart, before our conversion? Is it not enough that he is despised and neglected by an unbelieving world? Shall we, his professed disciples, unite with them to treat him with neglect? When he says to us, Will ye also go away, or compel me by your coldness and indifference to forsake you? shall we not reply, as with one voice, No, Lord, we will not leave thee, nor willingly suffer any thing to compel thee to leave us!

2. The blessed effects which result from the gracious visits of Christ, furnish another reason why we should employ all proper means, and make every possible exertion to induce him to prolong them. Consider a moment, my friends, what Christ is, what he possesses, and what he does; and you will be convinced, at once, that nothing can be so beneficial, so desirable to any individual, place, or society, as his gracious presence. He is the brightness of the Father's glory. In him are hidden all the treasures of wisdom and knowledge; his riches are unsearchable; he possesses all power in heaven and on earth; power to forgive sins; power to heal the spiritually sick, and raise the spiritually dead; power to open and shut the gates of heaven; power to bring good out of evil, and transform afflictions to blessings; power to bestow every temporal and spiritual good. He is also fully disposed to exert this power; and, wherever he is, he must exert it, for he is too benevolent to be idle. His arm of everlasting strength is unceasingly prompted to beneficent exertion by a heart overflowing with boundless love. Say then, my friends, what blessing can be comparable to the gracious presence of such a being as this? It is indeed every blessing in one. It is an unspeakable gift. It is life, and light, and joy, and salvation. It is heaven, with all its treasures, poured out upon us at once in a boundless flood; for it is the presence of the Savior which constitutes heaven. And the

effects which it produces are such as might naturally be expected from such a source. It fills the hearts of believers with joy and peace, their minds with knowledge, their life with praise and thanksgiving, and their hands with every good work. It sweetens every temporal blessing; it gives power and efficacy to all the means of grace; it promotes the cause of God and religion; it builds up and beautifies the church of Christ: To say all in a word, it produces the salvation of immortal souls. But here the powers of language fail. No tongue can tell, no finite mind can conceive what is done, when only one immortal soul is rescued from eternal death, and made an heir of everlasting life. It is a truth, capable of mathematical demonstration, that the salvation of one such soul is of incomparably greater consequence, than the temporal happiness of the whole race of man. To say every thing that can be said, it is an event that causes joy in heaven, where there is fulness of joy; an event in which God, and Christ, and angels rejoice. But the gracious presence of Christ never fails to produce and to multiply this event; to bring, not one only, but many, to repentance and salvation. Surely, then, we ought to employ every possible means to secure the presence of a being whose presence produces such effects as these.

3. Another reason which should induce us to employ these means, may be found in the evils which result from the Savior's departure. These evils are in full proportion to the benefits which result from his presence. They respect, in the first place, the church of Christ. He is constituted head over all things to his church; and therefore the effects, which a church experiences on his departure from it, are similar to those which would result to a human body from the loss of its head. For instance, the head is the seat of intelligence, the palace, the presence-chamber of the soul, where she holds her court, and from whence she issues forth her counsels and commands to the members of the body. Take away the head, and the tongue loses its eloquence, the right hand its cunning, and the feet their director. It is the same in the body of which Christ is the head. It has no wisdom, nor knowledge, nor intelligence without him. Its members know not what to do; they have, in a spiritual sense, neither eyes, nor ears, without their head; and, therefore, infallibly wander, and stumble, and fall. We have no sufficiency of ourselves.

Again. The head is the bond of union. Take away the head from a human body, and the members soon separate and moulder into dust. So Christ is the only bond of union to his members. While he remains with them, they are firmly united; but when he departs, the connecting tie is broken; jealousies, dissensions, and divisions arise; the church becomes like a rope of sand; its members are easily separated and split into parties, and every one's heart, and hand, and tongue, is turned against his brother.

Farther. The head is necessary to the growth of the body. Without the head, the body can receive no nourishment, and consequently no strength; its growth is immediately suspended. It is the same with the body of Christ. His presence always causes its increase both in numbers and in graces. But when he departs, its growth ceases. Spiritual nourishment is no longer received, and the whole body declines.

Once more. The head is the seat of life and sensation. Take away the head, and death ensues. The body becomes insensible, as the clod of earth from which it was formed. It is the same with the church. Take away Christ, its head, its life, and it dies. Nothing remains, but a lifeless, insensible, putrefying carcass, fit only to produce and become food for worms. Well therefore might the Savior say to his disciples, Without me ye can do nothing; for as the body without the spirit is dead, so the church without Christ is also dead; and nothing but his return can restore it to life. Without his presence too, impenitent sinners must remain impenitent, and of course, inevitably perish; for if the living sicken and die, when he departs, it is evident that, without him, the dead will not arise to life. The means of grace may be employed, but they will have no effect; or rather, they will produce effects the most fatal. They will become a savor of death unto death. Ministers may still labor, but it will be in vain; for, without Christ, Paul may plant, and Apollos water to no purpose. Sinners will die, one after another, and fall into the hands of that God who is a consuming fire; while their posterity will grow up, ignorant and vicious, to walk in the steps of their sinful parents, and finally share their fate. To say all in a word, the situation of a place, which the Savior has finally forsaken, is such as the situation of the world would have been, if a Savior had never been provided; or rather, it is worse; since they will have to answer for the unbelief which compelled him to depart. Endeavor, my friends, to conceive, if you can, what would be the situation of our world without the sun. Every thing would speedily die; frost and darkness would seal up the earth, and nothing but sterility, and death, and eternal night, and endless winter would remain. Similar effects would result in the moral world from the final departure of Christ; for he is the Sun of Righteousness. There is no spiritual light, or warmth, or life, or fertility without him; every heart, every habitation, every place of which he takes his final leave, is given up to night without day; to a winter without a spring; and nothing remains for such, but a certain fearful looking for of judgment. The harvest being past, the summer ended, they will not, they cannot be saved. Now since such are the consequences of Christ's final departure, and since, whenever he departs, we know not that he will again return, ought we not, when we are favored with his gracious presence, to employ every possible means to induce him to continue it?

4. The conduct of impenitent sinners affords another reason why we should do this. They are continually doing every thing in their power to provoke the Savior to leave the place where they reside. Every day, and especially every Sabbath, they do in effect by their unbelief, by their neglect of his gracious invitations, and their other sins, put the Savior from them; and like the Gadarenes, urge him to depart. As often as he sees them in his house, he is constrained to look on them with grief, on account of the hardness of their hearts. Now since the enemies of Christ are thus constantly provoking him to leave us, it is evident that his friends ought to be proportionably diligent in endeavoring to prevent it, lest when he sees many wishing for his absence, and few or none earnestly desirous of his presence, he should withdraw, no more to return.

And now, my Christian friends, can any thing more be necessary to induce you to imitate the conduct of those mentioned in our text? We have as much reason to believe that the Savior has been with us, as if we had seen him. The works which he has done among us, bear witness of him. We have also reason to hope that he is still with us; or, at least, that he has only begun to withdraw, that he may see whether we suitably prize his presence; whether we will follow him and urge his longer stay. And can any who profess to love him be idle or unconcerned at such a time as this? Is it necessary to urge those who know the blessed effects of his presence better than we can describe them, to exert themselves for the purpose of preventing his departure? Will you not strive to banish from your hearts, from your houses, from the church, every thing which may provoke him to leave us? If he has not departed, we shall find him at his table. Let us then seek him there, and beseech him, and stay him, if possible, that he may not depart from us. I need not tell you, that we have great and unusual encouragement to do this. I need not tell you, that the present is a day of grace, of universal grace and bounty. It is confidently believed that never before, in the same space of time, were so many persons converted in this country, as within the last two years. Thousands, and perhaps ten thousands have been added to the church of Christ; and the number is rapidly augmenting. I have been informed by good authority that in one village in New England every person above the age of fifteen has become hopefully pious. My friends, what Christ has done in other places he may do for us. His hand is not shortened. Nothing but our iniquities can provoke him to leave us. We are not straitened in him, but in ourselves.

I am unwilling to dismiss this subject without saying something to my impenitent hearers; but what can I say to them? You do not realize the Savior's presence. You do not feel your need of the blessings he offers; you do not desire his presence; you rather wish for, than dread his absence. You will not accept his invitations, nor seek an interest in his favor. Even now you are about to depart from his table; and thus, in effect, you entreat him to depart from you. But pause, and reflect a moment. To what are the present religious appearances owing? What is it that excites hundreds and thousands, in all parts of our country, to turn their attention to religion? You can see no cause, but there must be a cause, and a powerful one, to produce such effects. And can you prove that God is not the cause? Do not effects which we witness strikingly correspond with our Savior's description of the operation of his Spirit? The wind bloweth where it listeth, and thou hearest the sound thereof, but canst not tell whence it cometh and whither it goeth?

so is every one who is born of the Spirit. Now, my friends, you hear the sound of this heavenly wind; you see its effects upon others; but feel little or nothing of them yourselves. And is it not important that you should feel them? If they are really the effects of God's Spirit, and if they are necessary to your salvation, it undoubtedly is so. And, my friends, can any of you prove that they are not? You must prove this; you must prove that all Christians are deceived, that there is no such thing as experimental religion, that all which is said of spiritual illumination is a delusion, or become the subjects of them yourselves; or, dreadful alternative! take your place with the unclean, and the abominable, in that lake which burneth with fire!

SERMON XLIII.

THE CHURCHES INCREASED.*

Then had the churches rest throughout all Judea, and Galilee, and Samaria, and were edified; and walking in the fear of the Lord, and in the comfort of the Holy Ghost, were multiplied.—ACTS IX. 31.

IN this passage, my friends, we have two things presented to our view, which it is at once pleasing and unusual to see. In the first place, we see the church of Christ enjoying an interval of rest. That this, though a very pleasing, should be an uncommon sight in a world like this, is not surprising. While passing through it the church of Christ is in an enemy's country; a country in which it is exposed to constant trials, temptations and assaults; and in which we are warned to expect tribulation. Like the first disciples it is embarked on a tempestuous sea, where the waves run high, and the winds are contrary; while the haven of eternal rest seems far distant, and a night black with stormy clouds conceals it from view. But when, as is sometimes the case, Jesus comes to visit his church walking upon the tempestuous sea, then for a short season the storms are hushed, the clouds scattered, and great calm succeeds. Then, as in the text, the churches enjoy rest. In the second place, we see in this passage, what is still more uncommon and pleasing, the church improving this season of rest in a suitable manner. Generally speaking, the churches of Christ are far from doing

* Preached at the first meeting of the Cumberland Conference of churches.

this. On the contrary, in the short intervals of outward peace and prosperity allotted them, they are prone to decline, to forsake their first love, and become formal, useless and conformed to the world; so that storms are often less dangerous and hurtful to them than a calm. But in the present instance, this was not the case. The churches improved this interval of rest in some measure as they ought. Hence they were edified or built up, and walking in the fear of God, and in the comfort of the Holy Ghost, were multiplied. In other words, their numbers, as well as their graces, were greatly increased.

The mode of expression here employed plainly intimates, that the great additions made to their churches were a consequence of their walking in the fear of God and in the comfort of the Holy Ghost. From the passage therefore, may be fairly deduced the following proposition:

When the members of churches walk in the fear of God and in the comfort of the Holy Ghost, great additions will probably be made to them of such as shall be saved.

To illustrate and establish this proposition, is my present design.

In the prosecution of this design I am led to inquire,

I. What is meant by walking in the fear of God? By the fear of God is here evidently meant, not that guilty, slavish fear, which impenitent sinners often feel, but the holy, filial fear, which is peculiar to real christians. This fear is every where represented by the inspired writers as one of the most essential parts of true religion, and is indeed not unfrequently used by them to denote religion itself. It is produced and maintained in the heart by the agency of the divine Spirit. It arises from a believing apprehension and an experimental knowledge of the existence, character, perfections, and constant presence of Jehovah; it is occasioned by a spiritual discovery, made to the soul, of his awful, adorable and infinite perfections; and its natural effects are, veneration for God, submission to his will, obedience to his commands, and a holy watchful care to avoid every thing which may grieve, displease, or provoke him to forsake us. From the brief description of the nature and effects of Godly fear, it appears, that walking in the fear of God implies,

1. A habitual and profound veneration for his character and institutions. This veneration is directly opposed to irreverence,

carelessness, and formality in the service of God. It extends to every thing of a religious nature with which he is connected. It leads those who are under its influence to worship him with humility and godly fear; to venerate his names and attributes; to treat his ordinances and institutions with reverential regard, to read and hear his word with humility and prostration of soul, to honor and sanctify his holy day, and to remember that holiness becometh his house forever. The profound veneration for God, and for every thing of a religious nature with which he is immediately connected, is required of us by the inspired writers in almost innumerable passages. Let us have grace, whereby we may serve God acceptably, with reverence and godly fear. Sanctify the Lord God in your hearts, and let him be your fear and your dread. Stand in awe and sin not. Keep thy foot when thou goest to the house of God. Serve the Lord with fear and rejoice with trembling. The Lord is in his holy temple, let all the earth keep silence before him. Remember the Sabbath day to keep it holy. Thou shalt not take the name of thy God in vain; for the Lord will not hold such guiltless. To this man will I look, who trembleth at my word. It requires but a very small acquaintance with the scriptures to convince us, that the most eminent saints, and those who were admitted to the greatest intimacy with their Maker, have ever been most distinguished for the reverence and godly fear which we are considering, and which these passages so expressly require. These dispositions are far more important than most christians are aware; for God is a jealous God, jealous for the honor of his great name, and he has given us many awful proofs that he will not suffer himself to he irreverently treated with impunity. On a most awful occasion he said, I will be sanctified in them that draw near to me. Churches, therefore, whose ministers do not feel and exhibit this veneration for God, who worship him in a formal, careless manner, and take little or no care to bring their hearts into a suitable frame, when they are about to enter his sanctuary, approach the throne of grace, or come to the table of Christ, have no claim to be considered as walking in the fear of God; nor any reason to hope for the tokens of his favor.

2. Walking in the fear of God implies humble and unreserved submission to his authority. That it is the natural tendency of fear to produce submission to the being feared, you need not be

told. This submission will correspond in nature and effect with the fear which occasions it. A servile fear will produce only a constrained, apparent submission; but the fear we are describing will produce a submission cordial and unreserved, such as the scriptures require. The influence of this fear will extend to all the powers and faculties of the soul. It will constrain the understanding to submit implicitly to the authority of God's revealed will; producing that meek, docile, child-like acquiescence in its decisions, without which our Savior assures us that none shall enter the kingdom of heaven. This disposition is directly opposed to that pride of human reason, that presumptuous, caviling, unyielding spirit, which leads men to set up their own vain fancies and prejudices in opposition to the word of God; to deny, pervert, or explain away those parts of it which they dislike; and to object against every thing which does not coincide with their own humors, or preconceived opinions. A person who is suitably influenced by this temper needs no arguments to convince him of the truth of any doctrine, however mysterious or contrary to his previous sentiments it may be, which comes supported by the authority of a plain *Thus saith the Lord.* This authority is to him, what oaths are said to be in another case, an end of all strife, and dissension, and he bows down before it with a ready and pleased submission.

The fear of God also influences the will, rendering it pliable and submissive; and conforming it to the will of God. Its language to God is, Not my will but thine be done. It is therefore directly opposed to that independent, rebellious, repining spirit, which leads men to set themselves up as the rivals of Jehovah, to question or disregard his authority, to oppose his sovereignty, to complain of the strictness of his law, and to murmur at the dispensations of his providence. It leads those who are under its influence to rejoice that the Lord reigns, and to feel pleased and satisfied with what he is, with all that he says, and with every thing he does. The indulgence of a discontented, unreconciled temper is therefore evidently incompatible with walking in the fear of God.

Farther. The fear of God controls and regulates the affections. It leads those who are under its influence to love and to hate, to hope and to fear, to rejoice and to mourn in conformity with the divine commands. It teaches us to love being, truth, and holiness; and to hate nothing but sin. It teaches us to hope for glory, honor, and immortality through the merits of Christ, and to fear nothing but the displeasure of God, and those sins which excite it. It teaches us to rejoice in God, and to mourn for our sins, and for the sins and miseries of others. These effects it produces in direct proportion to the degree in which its influence is felt.

Lastly. The fear of God controls, in some measure at least, the imagination. It is true that this lawless, and almost untameable power seems to be less influenced by the fear of God, than any other faculty of the soul. Still, wherever the fear of God exists, the imagination will be constrained, in some degree, to submit to it. Its sallies will be carefully watched, its excursive wanderings will be checked; it will be speedily recalled when it roams into forbidden ground, and be often compelled to assist the Christian in his meditations on death, judgment, and the realities of eternity. Knowing that the thought of foolishness is sin, he who fears God will at least strenuously endeavor to prevent vain thoughts from lodging within him, and his endeavors will gradually be crowned with success. Such is that submission of the soul to God, which walking in his fear implies.

3. Walking in the fear of God implies a holy jealousy of ourselves, and a watchful care to avoid every thing which may grieve, displease, or provoke him to forsake us. The kind of fear, which we are describing, proceeds from love. He who is under its influence fears God only because he loves him, and he fears him supremely because he loves him supremely. This supreme affection leads him to desire, above all things, God's favor and presence, and to dread nothing so much as their loss. He feels that God's favor is life, and that his loving kindness is far better than life. He feels that God is the health, the strength, the happiness, the life, the salvation of his soul. In one word, God is to him all in all. His language is, Whom have I in heaven but thee? and there is none on earth I desire besides thee. When God is present, difficulties vanish, burdens become light, afflictions are pleasant, sorrow is turned to joy, a new lustre is spread over the whole face of nature, temporal blessings are enjoyed with double relish, and spiritual

privileges become privileges indeed. But when God departs, strength, and hope, and happiness depart with him. The Christian finds that his sun is gone; his spirits droop; his graces languish; existence becomes a burden; the means of grace are insipid, and temporal friends and comforts become like pictures in the absence of light, which, however beautiful, can afford no pleasure. Since such are the consequences of God's absence, it is not surprising that the Christian should fear it above all things; and that this fear should lead him to guard with scrupulous watchfulness and care against every thing which may tend to expose him to such an affliction. Speaking of the covenant which he will make with his people, God says, I will put my fear in their hearts, that they shall not depart from me. Hence it appears, that it is the natural tendency of the fear of God to preserve those who feel its influence from apostacy and declension. It leads them like Enoch to walk with God; to keep near to him, to wait upon him in the diligent use of all the appointed means of grace, and to guard against the first symptoms of declension; and, when asked whether they will forsake him, to reply with Peter, Lord, to whom shall we go? thou hast the words of eternal life. Such, my friends, are the principal effects of the fear of God; and if we would walk in his fear, we must feel and exhibit these effects, not only occasionally, but habitually, and like David have respect to all God's commandments, and be in the fear of God all the day long.

In the preceding remarks I have attempted to show what effects the fear of God will produce upon the temper and conduct of an individual, who walks in it, or is habitually under its influence. Now, as churches are composed of individuals, it follows, that, when all, or nearly all the members of a church live under the habitual influence of this principle, the church itself, considered as a body, will walk in the fear of God; and all the duties which are incumbent on it as a body, will be diligently and faithfully performed. Of those duties, which are incumbent on the church itself, rather than on any member of it separately considered, the first is, to provide the means of grace and of religious instruction for itself, its children, and those who are immediately connected with it. It is the indispensable duty of every church to provide, if possible, a suitable place for the public worship of God, and a competent teacher to lead in his worship, and perform the other duties of the ministerial office. Every church ought to consider these things as the necessaries of life; for such they are in the strictest sense. Indeed, they have a much better claim to this title, than many things to which it is commonly applied. If, as our Savior informs us, one thing is needful, then the means of obtaining that one thing, are of the first, and most pressing necessity. It is indispensably necessary that a Christian should know and do the will of God; but it is not necessary that he should live. It is indispensably necessary that children should be instructed and converted, but it is not in the same sense necessary that they should live. It is better that he and his family should be without a shelter, and without food, than that they should be without the means of grace, of religious instruction and salvation. Every church which walks in the fear of God will feel this, and act upon this principle. They will say, we can do without everything else, better than we can do without the preaching of the gospel. They will say, If he who provideth not for the temporal wants of his own, and especially for those of his own house, has denied the faith, and is worse than an infidel, what is he who provides not for the far more pressing spiritual wants of his own soul, and of those who are dependent on him? Our fathers felt, and acted on this principle. As soon as a town contained sixteen families they felt able to support the gospel, and did support it. And every church which walks in the fear of God will feel and act in a similar manner. They will fear, that if they neglect it, they shall be found guilty of lightly esteeming those precious gifts which Christ purchased with his blood, that he might bestow them on the rebellious; for among these gifts, pastors and teachers for the work of the ministry, hold a conspicuous place; they will fear that by this neglect they shall offend God, and provoke him to forsake them; an evil, which as we have already seen, those who walk in his fear dread above all other evils. They will fear that, if, like the Jews, they run every man to take care of his own house, and suffer the house of God to lie waste, he will scourge them for it as he did his ancient church, by withholding his blessing, and blasting their labors. And they will fear when their children are suffered to grow up without enjoying the stated preaching of the gospel, and without forming habits of observing the Sabbath, and attending statedly on the public worship of God, they will acquire habits of neglecting all religious institutions, and perish in their sins. Surely no church, which does not dread these evils, and guard against them, so far as they are able, by providing a suitable place of worship, and a competent religious teacher, can be justly said to walk in the fear of God.

The second duty incumbent on churches, considered as such, consists in faithfully maintaining the discipline of Christ in his house. This duty a church which walks in the fear of God will, it is evident, carefully perform. They will not, by neglecting it, render themselves partakers of other men's sins. They will tolerate among themselves none of those sins which are expressly said to exclude such as are guilty of them from heaven. They will admit none but such as exhibit scriptural evidence that they are the disciples of Christ, and they will be induced by no worldly motives to retain such as he requires them to exclude. This they will do, lest God should forsake them, if he sees among them the accursed thing. A church which neglects this duty, which spares known offenders through fear of temporal inconvenience or loss, cannot be said to walk in the fear of God. They fear something else more than they fear him.

A third duty incumbent on churches, considered as such, consists in assembling at proper seasons for social worship. This duty an apostle expressly enjoins. Forsake not the assembling of yourselves together, as the manner of some is; but exhort one another daily. This last clause seems to intimate that he referred, not so much to assembling on the Sabbath, as to more private assemblies for the purpose of mutual exhortation and social prayer. Such meetings will be highly valued and carefully maintained by every church which walks in the fear of God.

A fourth duty incumbent on every church considered as such, is to take care of the religious education of its children. It is true that the religious education of children is a duty more immediately incumbent on their parents; but it is incumbent on churches to take care that such of their members as are parents perform this duty. The neglect of it ought to be regarded as a subject of church discipline. Addressing his ancient church as an individual, God says, Thou hast taken my sons and my daughters which thou hast borne unto me, and hast sacrificed them unto idols to be devoured. Is this a small matter, that thou hast slain my children? But it is evident that the Jewish church did not actually sacrifice children to idols in its collective capacity. This was the act of individual parents. Yet because the church did not interpose to prevent the sacrifice, it is charged upon it as the act of the whole. And so if children of the church are now sacrificed to Satan on the altar of the world by their parents, the church itself is answerable so far as their own neglect was the cause.

Lastly. It is the duty of churches, as such, to assist feeble and destitute sister churches with pecuniary aid according to their ability. The primitive churches considered it as a duty, nay it was often enjoined upon them as a duty, to assist other churches, when circumstances made it necessary, in supporting their poor. Much more then may we consider it as a duty to assist in furnishing them the means of grace, when without such assistance they cannot obtain the blessing. This is a duty which we owe, not only to them, but to the cause of Christ, which will thus be advanced, and to our fellow creatures, whose salvation may thus be effected. If the love of God does not dwell in him, who can see a brother or sister destitute of daily food without attempting to relieve them, how can the fear of God rule in a church, which can see sister churches destitute of the bread of life, without making an effort to supply them? I proceed to inquire,

II. What is meant by walking in the comforts of the Holy Ghost.

When our blessed Savior was about to be separated from his disciples he promised that he would not leave them comfortless, but that he would pray the Father, who would send them another Comforter, even the Spirit of truth, that he might abide with them forever. This gracious promise he has faithfully performed. The Holy Ghost has been sent from heaven to dwell in the hearts of believers, and all the comforts of a religious nature which they enjoy on earth, are communicated by him. These comforts are of various kinds, and it is impossible on the present occasion fully to describe them. We can only mention some of the principal. Among the consolations of the Spirit we might perhaps, without much impropriety, enumerate the graces which he bestows, and the temper which he produces. As the Spirit of grace, he is the author and the preserver of all those graces which constitute the Christian temper. As the Spirit of God, he makes the soul a partaker of the divine nature, and creates it anew in the image of God. As the Holy Spirit, he sanctifies us throughout, in spirit,and soul, and body, communicating to us that holiness without which no man can see the Lord. As the Holy Ghost sent down from heaven, he produces in us a heavenly temper, weans us from things below, and draws our affections to things above. The fruits of the Spirit, says an apostle, are love, joy, peace, long suffering, goodness, faith, meekness, temperance. Now if any happiness is connected with the exercise of these graces, if there is any pleasure in being holy, in resembling God, in possessing a heavenly temper, as there undoubtedly is the greatest, then the graces which the Spirit of God imparts and the temper which he produces, may justly be reckoned among the comforts of the Holy Ghost. But since these fruits of the Spirit are usually considered as something different from his consolations, we shall not farther insist upon them on the present occasion, though they are doubtless possessed by all, who walk in the comforts of the Holy Ghost. Of these comforts properly so called, I mention,

1. Peace of conscience, or, in other words, peace with God, arising from a persuasion wrought in the soul by the Holy Spirit, that we are pardoned and accepted in the Beloved. It is true that the pardon of sin is procured for us by the death and intercession of Christ; but it is also true that this blessing is applied to us only by the instrumentality of the Holy Spirit. It is his peculiar work, to subdue the enmity and unbelief of our hearts, and when this work is accomplished, to take the things which are Christ's, and show them to us. He opens the eyes of the guilty, desponding, and almost despairing sinner, and shows him that Christ is just such a Savior as he needs; that he has performed and suffered every thing necessary for the complete salvation of his people; that by him all who believe are justified from those things from which they could not be justified by the law of Moses; and that he is able to save, even

to the uttermost, all who come unto God by him, seeing he ever liveth to make intercession for them. These precious encouraging truths he persuades and enables the sinner to embrace; and the consequence is, that, being justified by faith, he has peace with God through our Lord Jesus Christ, and he feels that his sins are forgiven him for his name's sake. His conscience being purged from dead works, no longer condemns him, and therefore he has confidence towards God, and knows by experience the blessedness of him, whose iniquities are forgiven, and whose sins are covered. This blessedness, consisting in peace of conscience and peace with God, he continues to enjoy so long as he walks in the fear of God, and in the comforts of the Holy Ghost; being filled, as the apostle expresses it, with all joy and peace in believing.

With this state of pardon and acceptance is intimately connected,

2. A strong and well-grounded hope, arising at times to a full assurance, that we are adopted into God's family, and that consequently we have a title to all the privileges of his children. This hope, so productive of happiness to all who possess it, is produced and maintained in the souls of believers by the Spirit of God. Hence the apostle prays that the Christians at Rome might abound in hope, through the power of the Holy Ghost. This hope the Spirit produces and maintains by forming in the hearts of believers the image of their heavenly Father, giving them a filial temper towards him, and then shining in upon his work in their heart and enabling them to discern it. Agreeably, we find the apostle writing to believers, Ye have not received the Spirit of bondage again to fear, but ye have received the Spirit of adoption, whereby we cry, Abba Father; and the Spirit itself beareth witness with our spirits that we are the children of God; and if children, then heirs, heirs of God and joint heirs with Christ. Having thus convinced the believer that he is a child and an heir of God, the Holy Spirit enables him to claim and enjoy the privileges of a child, and the apostle informs us that, through Christ, Christians have access by one Spirit unto the Father. Agreeably, so long as Christians walk in the fear of God, the Holy Spirit enables them at all times to approach him as their Father in heaven, with holy boldness and filial confidence; to make known to

him all their wants, to cast upon him all their cares, and to claim his protection, guidance, assistance, and blessing. He also enables them to understand, believe, and apply to themselves the exceeding great and precious promises of his word; to feel a strong confidence that he will withhold from them no good thing, and that he will cause all things to work together for their good. Thus he comforts and supports them under their various trials, and enables them to discover, even in the severest, new proofs that they are the children of God. He teaches them that whom the Lord loveth he chasteneth, and scourgeth every son whom he receiveth; and that their present light afflictions which endure but for a moment, will work out for them a far more exceeding and an eternal weight of glory. Hence they are enabled to glory in tribulation, knowing that tribulation worketh patience and many other blessed effects.

3. Another branch of the comforts of the Holy Ghost consists in the foretastes, which he here gives believers, of the joys of heaven. The apostle, after informing us, that eye hath not seen, nor ear heard, nor the heart of man conceived of those things which God has prepared for them that love him, adds,— but God hath revealed them unto us by his Spirit. Of the truth of this assertion every Christian, who walks in the fear of God, is convinced by happy experience. Like the blessed inhabitants of heaven, such persons are enabled by the Holy Spirit, to enjoy fellowship with the Father, and with his Son Jesus Christ, to participate in the joy that is felt in heaven when sinners repent, and to unite with the spirits of the just made perfect in ascribing blessing and glory, and power unto God and the Lamb. At intervals, which return more or less frequently, in proportion to their diligence, zeal, and fidelity, God is pleased to grant them still greater consolation, to lift upon them the light of his countenance, and cause them to rejoice in his salvation. He sheds abroad his love in their hearts, makes them to know the great love wherewith he has loved them, shines in upon their souls with the pure, dazzling, transforming beams of celestial mercy, truth, and grace; displays to their enraptured view the ineffable beauties and glories of him who is the chief among ten thousand, and enables them in some measure to comprehend the lengths and breadths, the heights and depths of that love of Christ which passeth knowledge. While the

happy Christian, in these bright enraptured moments, sinks lower and lower in self-abasement and humility, the Spirit of God, stooping from his blest abode, raises him as it were on his celestial wings, and places him before the open door of heaven, and enables him to look in and contemplate the great I AM, the Ancient of days, enthroned with the Son of his love, the brightness of his glory. He contemplates, he wonders, he admires, he loves, he adores. Absorbed in the ravishing, the ecstatic contemplation of uncreated loveliness, glory, and beauty, he forgets the world, he forgets himself, he almost forgets that he exists. His whole soul goes forth in one intense flame of admiration, love and desire, and he longs to plunge into the boundless ocean of perfection which opens to his view, and to be wholly swallowed up and lost in God. With an energy and activity of soul unknown before, he roams and ranges through this infinite ocean of existence and happiness, of perfection and glory, of power and wisdom, of light and love, where he can find neither bottom nor shore. His soul dilates itself beyond its ordinary capacity, and expands to receive the tide of felicity which fills and overwhelms it. No language can do justice to his feelings, for his joys are unspeakable; but with an emphasis, a meaning, an energy, which God only could excite, and which God alone can comprehend, he exclaims in broken accents, My Father, and my God! Thus by the agency of the Spirit is he filled with all the fulness of God, and rejoices with joy unspeakable and full of glory, till his wise and compassionate Father, in condescension to the weakness of his almost expiring child, graciously draws a veil over glories too dazzling for mortal eyes long to sustain; leaving him still however in the enjoyment of that peace of God which passeth all understanding. Such, my friends, are the joys which the Spirit of God occasionally imparts to those who walk in his fear; or rather such is the exceedingly imperfect description of them which we are able to give.

Having thus attempted to show what is meant by walking in the fear of God and in the comforts of the Holy Ghost, I proceed to show,

III. That when the members of churches habitually walk in this manner, great additions will probably be made to them of such as shall be saved. That this will be the case appears probable,

1. From the consideration, that such a life and temper, displayed by professed christians, will naturally and most powerfully tend to convince all around them of the reality and happy effects of religion, to remove their prejudices against it, and to show them that its possession is highly desirable. No one who has attended to the subject can doubt, that, if we except the natural enmity of the heart to God, the manner in which professors generally live is the greatest of all obstacles to the success of the gospel. It is this which blunts the edge of the sword of the Spirit, and causes the arrows of conviction to rebound from the sinner's breast. It is in vain to press on our impenitent hearers the necessity of regeneration, while they see little or no difference between those who profess to have been the subjects of this change and themselves. It is vain to tell them that religion is productive of happiness, while professors appear gloomy, anxious, and dejected, instead of walking in the comforts of the Holy Ghost. But when professors live as they ought, when the fear of God rules in their hearts, and the peace of God beams forth in their countenances; when they cause their light to shine before men, and adorn the doctrine of God in all things; then sinners begin to tremble, their most plausible objection is wrested from them; their armor is taken away, and they are exposed, naked and defenceless to the arrows of conviction. The life of every christian then becomes a sermon more pungent and convincing than any which ministers can preach; and the church, while she thus appears fair as the moon, and clear as the sun, is more terrible than an army with banners to the enemies of religion.

2. That great additions will be made to churches which walk in this manner, is probable from the consideration, that walking in the fear of God and in the comfort of the Holy Ghost, is exceedingly pleasing to God, and naturally tends to draw down upon them his blessing. Indeed he has bound himself by many promises to bless and build up his church, when its members conduct in this manner; and in no instance, that can be adduced, has he failed to fulfil these promises. Them that honor him he will honor. But in no way can churches honor him more effectually than by living in the manner described above; and, therefore, when they thus honor him, they may expect that he will honor them by preserving them from division, and add-

ing abundantly to their numbers and graces. That this will probably be the case, appears,

Lastly, from the consideration that, when churches walk in this manner, it proves that God is pouring out his Spirit upon them, and that a revival of religion is already begun. That without the influences of the Holy Spirit a church cannot walk in his comforts, is too evident to require proof; and that without them no church will walk in the fear of God, is equally certain. Whenever we see a church walking in this manner, we may be confident that God has commenced a work of grace among them, and there is every reason to hope that this work will be carried on till many are added to the church.

The subject we have been considering, my friends, suggests several important reflections. And,

1. Permit me to ask all the professed disciples of Christ in this assembly, whether the churches which they represent, or with which they are connected, walk in the manner which has now been described. Have you reason to believe that all, or nearly all your members are walking in the fear of God, and in the comforts of the Holy Ghost? Are the churches to which you belong, diligent and faithful in the performance of these duties which are incumbent on them as a body, or in their collective capacity? Do they all consider the stated preaching of the gospel as the first necessary of life, and act accordingly? Is proper care taken to secure the religious education of children? Is discipline faithfully maintained, according to the rules of Christ's house? Is there no evil, no accursed thing tolerated among you? Are your members careful not to forsake the assembling of themselves together, as the manner of some is? and do they reprove, exhort, and admonish each other, agreeably to the commands of Christ and their own covenant obligations? If any of you are conscious that the churches which you represent, are not walking in this manner, permit me to ask,

2. How far is this melancholy and criminal deficiency owing tc yourselves? From the fact, that your churches have selected you to represent them on this occasion, we infer, that you have some reputation and influence among them. Now have you done every thing, which it is in your power to do, to persuade and induce your brethren to walk in this manner? Are you walking yourselves in this manner? If the Master, whom you

profess to serve, were visibly present, would he say of each of you, This man does walk in the fear of God, and in the comforts of the Holy Ghost? If not, can you say how far the declining state of the churches, which you represent, is imputable to yourselves, or how much, or how soon, their state might be improved by your example and exertions, were they such as they ought to be?

3. Permit me, with affectionate earnestness, to press upon every professed disciple of Christ here present, the importance, the indispensable necessity of walking himself, and of doing every thing in his power to induce his brethren to walk, in the manner which our text describes. To this the providence, as well as the word of God, now calls us. For a long time the churches in this vicinity, as well as through New England, have enjoyed rest; rest, probably, much more undisturbed, and privileges far greater, than were ever enjoyed by the primitive christians. Indeed, what they thought a calm, we should probably consider a storm. All they wished for was, to be exempted from the spoiling of their goods, from bonds and imprisonment, from the stake and the cross, and to have liberty to serve God in peace. They never thought of requesting an ungodly world to assist them in building places for worship, in supporting the gospel, or even in providing for their poor. All these things they regarded it as a privilege, as well as a duty, to perform. Could they have been placed in such a situation as we are, they would have thought it rest indeed. And shall we then abuse the goodness of God, and ungratefully requite him for the rest which he affords us by neglecting to walk in his fear, and practically regarding the consolations of his Spirit as a light thing? Shall we by misimproving a calm, provoke him to send us a storm? Shall we, by declining from our first love, and neglecting to repent, constrain him to remove our golden candlesticks out of their places? God forbid. Let us rather walk ourselves, and if possible, persuade the churches with which we are connected to walk in the fear of the Lord, and in the comforts of the Holy Ghost. And let us not confine our exertions to our own churches, but endeavor to make this county, at least, as a fruitful field, and a well watered garden. Let those who are of us build the old wastes, and repair the desolation of former generations, assured that, if we water others, we shall in turn be watered ourselves. And

O, that every member, every professor of religion present, may return with the spirit of a missionary, the spirit of primitive Christianity, glowing in his breast, and that his example and influence may work like leaven till all around him are leavened. And may God in mercy say to these churches, From this day forth I will bless you.

To conclude. From the subject before us, all present may learn much of the nature of true religion, and in what manner to distinguish it from its counterfeits. It consists in walking in the fear of God, and in the comfort of the Holy Ghost. These two things God has joined, and let no man attempt to put them asunder. He who does this, and teaches men to do it, shall be called least in the kingdom of heaven; that is, according to the Jewish idiom, shall never enter it. Beware then, my hearers, of making this separation yourselves; beware of all who attempt to make it. Wherever you hear a man speaking loudly of his religious joys and consolations, while he does not exhibit corresponding evidence that he fears God; while he is careless in his conduct, vain and trifling in his conversation, and irreverent in his manner of speaking of God and of religious subjects, be assured that his joy is only that of the hypocrite, or of the stony ground hearer which shall endure but for a moment; and be not surprised, if you should afterwards see such a man fall away. And on the other hand, when you hear a man profess to fear God, while he ridicules or denies the reality of the comforts of the Holy Ghost, be assured that he is one who, while he has the form of godliness, knows nothing of its power.

SERMON XLIV.

AN UNJUST IMPUTATION REPELLED BY JEHOVAH.

Have I been a wilderness to Israel? A land of darkness?—JEREMIAH II. 31.

TO AN ingenuous mind God never appears so irresistible, so overpowering, as when he addresses his creatures in the language of tender expostulation. He may speak in the loftiest accents of uncontrollable authority and almighty power; and such a mind, though awed, will too often hesitate to yield obedience. He may utter the language of severe rebuke, and terrible denunciation; his reproofs and threatenings may descend from heaven like a tempest of fire; but the heart, wrapped up in its own adamantine hardness, will brave the storm with sullen, unrelenting, and even apparently increasing obduracy. But when, laying aside the rightful claims of his authority, and the terrors of his wrath, God comes in the meek majesty of injured excellence, and unrequited kindness, to expostulate with his offending creatures, every heart, which has a particle of ingenuousness in its composition, relents, melts, and falls contrite at his feet, overcome by the omnipotence of love. Did all men possess such a disposition, he would seldom address them in any other language, and even now, destitute of it as they naturally are, he condescends occasionally to employ it. One instance of its use we have in our text, where, addressing his ancient people, God says, Have I been a wilderness to Israel? This language evidently intimates that they had regarded and treated him as such; and at the same time indirectly asks, whether they had any good reasons for regarding and treating him in this manner? Had he indeed been no better to them than a wilderness, a land of darkness? a question, this, which it was much more easy for him to ask, than for Israel to answer.

My hearers, we may, we should, consider our God and Redeemer, as still addressing, in similar language all who, while, like Israel, they are favored with his distinguishing blessings, like Israel treat him as if he had been to them only a wilderness, a land of darkness. Especially should we consider him as thus addressing those of his professing people, who have treated him in this manner. And are there none such among us? Should the symbols before us be transformed into the mangled body which they represent, and endowed with life and speech, should our crucified Redeemer appear standing upon that table, leaving the marks of the thorns, the scourge, and the cross; and look round upon this assembly with an omniscient eye, as he once looked upon Peter, would he find no professed disciples to whom he might justly say, Have I been a wilderness to you, a land of darkness? If not, why have you treated me as such? That every one may be able to answer these questions with respect to himself, it is necessary,

I. To show when professed Christians expose themselves to the charge which our text implies, or, in other words, when they treat their God and Redeemer as if he were to them a wilderness, a land of darkness.

The mention of a wilderness, especially of a wilderness, as it appears at night, when darkness prevails, suggests to us ideas of dreariness, solitude and gloom; of a place, where there is nothing to cheer, to nourish, or shelter us, where numberless obstacles impede the wanderer's progress, and through which is no discoverable path. In fine, we regard it as a place, which no one would choose to visit, unless impelled by necessity, and from which every one would wish to escape, as soon as circumstances should permit. And is it possible, perhaps some will ask, that any man, who professes to be a disciple of Christ, can regard his God and Redeemer in this light? Yes, my hearers, it is possible. Every declining professor of religion, every one who serves God with reluctance, who does not find pleasure in his service, regards him precisely in this light, and treats him as if he were a wilderness, a land of darkness. When a professor becomes slack and remiss in waiting upon God, careless in walking with him, and negligent in seeking communion with him, does he not practically say, God is, to me, a wilderness? The path in which he requires me to walk is adorned with no flowers, it furnishes no fruits. When he enters his closet with reluctance, enters it merely because conscience with her scourge impels; when he reads the Scriptures without interest, when he repeats prayers without feeling, when the minutes spent in these duties seem long, and he is eager to leave his closet, that he may engage in more pleasing worldly pursuits, does he not say as plainly as feelings and actions can say, God is a wilderness; the place to which I retire for the purpose of worshipping him, is a place of darkness, a place which has no attractions? We read of Doeg the Edomite, that he was on a certain occasion at the tabernacle detained before the Lord. The expression is remarkable. He was detained before the Lord. This language forcibly intimates, that he was there reluctantly; that he thought the time long, and would have preferred to be in some other place. Now he evidently regarded the place where God was worshipped as men regard a wilderness; that is as a place which he would not choose to visit, unless impelled by necessity, and from which he would wish to escape as soon as possible. In the same manner does every one regard it, who in any place of worship, whether private, social, or public, feels as if he were detained there, and as if he would prefer some other situation or employment.

Still more loudly does the professing Christian declare that he regards his God and Redeemer as a wilderness, when he repairs, in search of happiness, to the scenes of worldly pleasure, or to the society of worldly-minded men. He then says to them in effect, the ways of wisdom are not ways of pleasantness; a religious life is a life of constraint and melancholy; I should die with hunger and thirst, did I not occasionally forsake the wilderness in which I am doomed to live, and refresh myself with the fruits on which you are feasting. Suppose, my hearers, that while Adam resided in paradise the world had been filled, as it now is, with sinful inhabitants. Had he, in these circumstances, frequently, or occasionally, forsaken the garden of God, and wandered out into the world to seek happiness, in the society, or in the pursuits, of sinful men, would not his conduct have seemed to say, Paradise is a wilderness, a land of darkness, in which happiness is not to be found. I am weary of the presence of God, which is there manifested, and am constrained to come to you, in search of pleasures which my place of residence does not afford! Just so, when the professed friends of God wander from him, and from the path of duty, in search of happiness, they practically say, He is a wilderness, a land of darkness, in which I find nothing pleasant, nothing to allure, nothing which satisfies my desires.

Having thus shewn when we treat God as if he were a wilderness, a land of darkness, permit me,

II. To apply to all, who have treated him in this manner, the pathetic, melting expostulation in our text. Let me ask them, whether they have indeed found their God and Redeemer no better than a dark and dreary and desolate wilderness? With a view to assist you in answering this question, let me, in the first place, remind you of the temporal blessings which you enjoy. Look at your comforts, your possessions, your children, your friends, your liberty, your security? Did you find all these blessings in a wilderness, or did they come to you out of a land of darkness? Some of you have spent ten, some twenty, some forty, some sixty years, in the world. During all this time, you have had food to nourish you, garments to clothe you, and habitations to shelter you; and did you find all these things in a wilderness? If so, it must surely have been a most fruitful wilderness.

Let me in the second place, remind you of the religious privileges with which you have been favored. From your childhood you have had in your hands the Scriptures, the word of God, containing all things necessary to make you wise unto salvation, and have been taught to read them. From the same period, you have been permitted to enter the sanctuary of God, to present unto him your petitions, to listen to his instructions and invitations, to hear the gospel of salvation, and to see life and immortality brought to light. In fine, the full blaze of gospel day has shone around you. And did you find all this light in a land of darkness? Did you find the Bible, the sanctuary of God, and the gospel of salvation, in a wilderness? Surely, a wilderness, where such blessings are to be found, must be preferable to the most fertile spot on earth!

Thus far, the questions which we have asked are applicable to all alike. With those of you who are professors of religion, we may proceed further, and remind them of the spiritual blessings which they have, or profess to have, enjoyed. We may say to them, You have found the table of Christ spread for your refreshment. On that table Jesus Christ himself, his body, his blood, all the inestimable blessings which he dispenses, have been symbolically set before you, that you might eat, and drink, and live forever. When you entered the church of Christ, you professed to have found light to illuminate your minds, grace to sanctify your hearts, mercy to pardon all your sins, and divine consolations, which gave you joy and peace in believing. If you are what you profess to be, you really have found all these blessings. You have found that Christ's flesh is meat indeed, that his blood is drink indeed. You have enjoyed precious seasons of communion with him at his table, in his house, and in your closets. You have tasted the first fruits of the heavenly inheritance, celestial fruits, the food of angels, such as earth does not produce. And these fruits were the earnest, the pledge of better things to come, the proofs that God has adopted you as his children, and made you heirs of himself, and joint heirs with Jesus Christ. Look back, then, upon the years which have passed away, since you began to enjoy these blessings; review God's dealings with you, the favors which he has bestowed on you, during that period, and then say, what he has been to you. Will any of you say, can any of you say, He has been to me a wilderness, a land of darkness? Did you find all the inestimable blessings which have been mentioned in a wilderness? Was it a wilderness which produced the celestial fruits, on which you have feasted? Did a Savior, and salvation, and pardon, and peace, and everlasting life, come to you from a wilderness?

Once more. Has God been a wilderness, a land of darkness to this church, considered as a body? Look back, my brethren, and see what it was twenty years since. Consider how it has been preserved, blessed, increased, during the intervening period. Consider how much mercy, how much grace, how much divine interposition was daily necessary, to preserve it, and make it what it now is. Every day it has needed, and it has received, what no power on earth could give. O then, with how much propriety, with what irresistible force may God ask, Have I been a wilderness, a land of darkness to this branch of my church? From this enumeration of the blessings with which God has favored us, it must, I think, appear evident, that he has by no means been to us a wilderness, and that, if we have regarded and treated him as such, we have been guilty of great ingratitude, and injustice. And yet, notwithstanding all that has been said, there are probably some present, who feel as if, in one respect at least, God has been to them no better than a dark and dreary wilderness. We allude to those who, though they have professedly paid some attention to religious subjects, and have perhaps enrolled themselves among the visible followers of Christ, have found no happiness in religion. Such persons often say in their hearts, We have spent much time in religious pursuits, and have made many endeavors to find that rest and peace and consolation which Christ promises to his disciples, and of which many Christians talk so much. But all our endeavors have been in vain; and we must say, if we speak the truth, that our way has been like that of a man travelling through a wilderness, where he finds no path, no refreshment, but meets with thorns and briars and obstacles at every step. In reply to such complaints, we remark, that the persons who make them compose several different classes, and that the complaints of each of these classes are wholly unreasonable and without foundation. The first class which we shall mention, is composed of those who, to use the apostle's language, go about to establish their own righteousness, and do not submit to the righteousness of God. That such persons find no happiness in God, in religion, is not wonderful; for to God, and to religion, they are entire strangers. It is only by believing in Jesus Christ, that men are filled with joy and peace. But these persons never truly believed in Christ, never came to him for rest. Who then can wonder that they have not found it. They have indeed been wandering in a dark and thorny wilderness, but that wilderness is not God.

The second class which we shall mention, is composed of the slothful. That they should find no happiness in religion, is not surprising; for inspiration declares, that the way of the slothful man is a hedge of thorns. He finds no path, and at every effort which he makes to press forward, he feels the thorns piercing his flesh. But his difficulties and sufferings are the consequences of his own slothfulness, and he ought not therefore to ascribe them to religion. Would he lay aside his slothfulness, he would soon experience the truth of the assertion, The way of the righteous is made plain.

A third class of complainers is composed of such as an apostle calls double-minded men, who are unstable in all their ways. They are engaged in a vain attempt to reconcile, what our Savior has declared to be irreconcilable, the service of God, and that of mammon. In making this attempt they wander from God, and lose themselves in a wilderness; and then inconsistently complain, that wisdom's ways are not paths of peace, that God is to them a land of darkness. But their complaints are as unreasonable as those of a man, who should bury himself in a dungeon, and then complain that the sun gave no light. In fine, all who pretend that God is a wilderness, a land of darkness, prove only that they know him not. In opposition to them we may array the testimony of all who have ever known him. We may exhibit the testimony of the inspired writers, and of good men in former ages, who declare that God is light, and that in him is no darkness at all; that he is the Father of lights, from whom cometh down every good and perfect gift; that it is good to draw near to him; that it is not a vain thing to seek him; that in keeping his commandments there is great reward; that in his presence is fullness of joy, and at his right hand are pleasures forever more. Indeed, if there is any light, any happiness on earth, if there is any in heaven, if there is any in the universe, it is, it must be in God alone. If he is a wilderness, all is a wilderness; if he is a land of darkness, there is no land of light, and not only man, but all intelligent creatures, must be bewildered in darkness and wretchedness forever.

Permit me now to improve the subject,

1. By applying it to the members of this church, and to all the professed disciples of Christ before me. Let me say to each of them, Have you never treated your God and Redeemer as if he were a wilderness, a land of darkness? Have you never been negligent and remiss in waiting upon him in your closets, in attending upon his worship, in reading his word? Have

you never felt like Doeg the Edomite, when he was detained before the Lord? Have you never wandered from him and been slow to return? Have you never engaged in his service with reluctance, and with a disposition to leave it as soon as conscience would permit? If so, let me present to you, your God, your Redeemer, with the tender, affecting language of our text upon his lips. Hear him saying, Am I indeed a wilderness, a land of darkness, as your treatment of me would seem to imply? Have I been such to you? Have I deserved at your hands this neglect, this coldness and inconstancy of affection? Is there nothing in my character, nothing in all the blessings I have bestowed on you, that renders me worthy of different treatment? Surely, my brethren, no Christian's heart can resist this language. Surely, every Christian's heart will reply, with shame and sorrow, No, Lord, thou hast not deserved this treatment at my hands. Thou hast never been to me a wilderness, nor a land of darkness. So far as I have walked with thee humbly and faithfully, I have found thee, not a wilderness, but a paradise, not a land of darkness, but a region of light. I have found that the light of thy countenance, lifted upon me, gives more joy than sinners feel when their corn and their wine increase. It is folly the most inexcusable, it is madness the most unaccountable, which leads me to forsake thee, and to treat thee with a neglect, and a coldness, which thou art infinitely far from deserving. My brethren, is this the real language of your hearts? If so, God's expostulation has produced its proper, its designed effects. It has broken your hearts, it has led you to repentance. Come, then, and receive a free pardon, through that Savior, whose table you are about to approach. Come, and hear your offended, but pardoning God, say to you, I heal all thy backslidings, I freely forgive thee all thy trespasses; go in peace, and sin no more. Go and receive pledges of pardon and peace at the table of my Son. And while you hear God thus addressing you, let your heart reply, O Lord, I will praise thee; for though thou wast angry, justly angry with me, yet thine anger is turned away, and thou comfortest me. Who is a God like unto thee, that forgivest iniquity, transgression and sin?

2. In the second place, let me apply this subject to impenitent sinners, especially to those who, though they are convinced that

religion is important and even necessary, do not embrace it. To such persons let me say, You are guilty, in a far greater degree than those whom we have just been addressing, of treating God as if he were a wilderness, a land of darkness. You stand, with God on the one side, and the world on the other. When you look at the world, which is in reality a wilderness, it appears to you like a garden in which you love to walk, and whose flowery paths we cannot persuade you to quit. But when you turn to contemplate the service of God, a life of religion, it appears to you like a dark and dreary wilderness. On the borders of this wilderness you stand lingering, and though you are perhaps convinced that it contains in its bosom many valuable blessings, yet we cannot persuade you to enter it. Year after year you stand hesitating and lingering, often turning your eyes and your steps back to the world, which you are unwilling to leave. O then, how loudly do your feelings and your conduct say, God is a wilderness, a land of darkness. But can he indeed be so? Have good men in all ages been deceived? Are all the inhabitants of heaven deceived? Remember that, if there is any happiness in heaven, it consists in the service, the enjoyment of that very being whom you now regard as a wilderness. And if you continue to regard him as such in this world, you will regard him as such in the world to come. If you can find no happiness in serving him here, you cannot be happy in his service hereafter.

SERMON XLV.

DEMONSTRATION OF CHRIST'S LOVE.

Then said the Jews, Behold how he loved him!—JOHN XI. 36.

THIS exclamation was uttered at the tomb of Lazarus. It was occasioned by the tears which our Savior there shed. The unbelieving Jews, who, in consequence of the pointed manner in which he warned, reproved and threatened them, seem to have regarded him as unfeeling and morose, were surprised at seeing him exhibit such marks of sympathizing affection; and exclaimed with wonder, Behold how he loved him!

The use which I propose to make of this passage, has probably, already occurred to you. If the affection which Christ felt for Lazarus, and which was manifested by his tears only, appeared surprisingly great to the Jews; how great, how surprising, should the love which he has manifested for us appear in our eyes! If the Jews exclaimed, Behold how he loved Lazarus! merely because they saw him weeping at his tomb, with how much reason may we exclaim, Behold how he loved us! when we behold him in Bethlehem, in Gethsemane, and on Calvary! Indeed, an apostle tells us, that the love of Christ passeth knowledge; and at the same time intimates that it is exceedingly important to know as much of it as is possible, and that, in proportion as we know it, we shall be filled with the fulness of God. Let us then, before we approach the table of our Lord, spend a few moments in meditating upon his unsearchable, unconquerable love.

I need not inform you that love, like every other affection of the heart, is in its own nature invisible to every eye but that of omniscience. We cannot look into the heart, and see it glowing there. We can discern it only in the effects which it produces, in the external signs which constitute its language, and which manifest its existence. We see it as it exists, not in the fountain, but in the streams; and from the copiousness of the streams, we infer the fulness of the fountain. Where the genuine effects of love are most abundantly displayed, there, we conclude, love exists in the highest degree. It is by this rule that we are to estimate the greatness of our Savior's love. Let us then inquire what are the genuine effects, the external indications of love, and how far they appear in the conduct of our Redeemer.

1. One of the effects and indications of love, is a readiness to submit to privations and inconveniences for the sake of assisting or relieving the person beloved. It is by the degree in which our friends exhibit this effect of love, that we estimate the strength of their affection for us. The greater the inconveniences and privations, to which they are willing to submit for our sakes, so much the greater do we suppose their love for us to be. We infer that parents love their children, because we see them willing to make laborious exertions, and to deny themselves many comforts, for the sake of giving them an education, and of providing for their future wants. Should a servant readily consent, without the prospect of reward, to accompany his banished master into exile among savage nations, or in frozen inhospitable climes, we should consider his conduct as indicating a very high degree of disinterested affection. Should a person sell himself for a slave, in order to redeem his friend from slavery, we should form still more exalted ideas of the strength of his friendship. Now what proofs of this kind has our Savior exhibited of the greatness of his love for us! The scriptures fully answer this question; yet in consequence of our situation, and our ignorance of heaven, we can understand their answer but very imperfectly. They tell us that, when he was rich, he for our sakes became poor, that we, through his poverty, might be rich. They tell us that, when he was in the form of God,

he humbled and emptied himself and took upon him the form of a servant, and was made in the likeness of sinful flesh. They tell us that he had a glory with his Father before the world was; that he laid aside this glory and made himself of no reputation. In a word, they inform us that he left heaven, and lived a life of labor, poverty and contempt on earth. It appears from this account, then, that he submitted to be deprived for many years, of the glory, the society, and the felicity of heaven, of glory and felicity too great for us to conceive of; and that he voluntarily exchanged all this for the lowest state on earth, and cheerfully endured all the inconveniences, privations and wants, attendant on such a state. All this he submitted to because he loved us.

Now were I speaking to angels or to persons who had seen heaven, who know what it is, who know what glory and felicity our Savior enjoyed there, who know how widely it differs from earth, and how exquisitely painful it must be for one so holy, so averse to sin, as he was, to live in this sinful world, to witness the sins of its inhabitants, and to endure the contradiction of sinners; I say, were I speaking to persons who know all this, they would need nothing more to convince them, that our Savior's love was inconceivably great; nothing more to make them exclaim, Behold how he loved us! But, alas! I speak to those who know none of these things; or, at least, who know them but very imperfectly. Indeed I speak of what I know almost nothing myself. Little, however, as we know or conceive of what our Savior renounced, and of what he submitted to, for our sakes, does it not appear from the preceding remarks, that the love, which drew him down from heaven to earth, must have been without a parallel great? Is it not obvious that the love, which should lead a monarch to renounce his throne, a servant to follow his master into exile, or a man to sell himself into slavery for the redemption of his friend, would be weak in comparison with the love which Christ displayed for our sinful race, when he exchanged heaven for earth to save them?

2. Another effect and indication of love is a willingness to suffer pain for the beloved object. Other things being equal, we consider that love as the greatest which induces a willingness to suffer the greatest degree of pain. And this is just reason-

ing; for self-love makes us unwilling to suffer. Of course, when we are willing to suffer for the sake of another, it proves that we love him as we love ourselves; nay, that our love for him is sufficiently strong to counteract the influence of self-love. Let us then inquire what Christ's love for us led him to suffer for our sakes. But here we labor under the same difficulty which has been already mentioned; a difficulty arising from our ignorance. We know but little even of the bodily sufferings which he endured for our salvation. We know indeed that he was scourged till the naked bones appeared through his mangled flesh; that he was buffeted, or beaten upon the face; that his temples were pierced with thorns; that he was fastened to the cross by nails driven through his hands and feet, and that, with his whole weight thus suspended, he hung for six hours, bleeding, parched with thirst, and agonizing in the pangs of death. But though we know these facts, we know but little of his bodily sufferings. It is one thing to read or hear of what he suffered, and quite another thing to form a just conception of it. By what effort either of our understandings or of our imaginations are we to conceive of tortures which we never felt, to conceive of the pangs of crucifixion, to conceive of the agonies inflicted by hanging with the whole weight of the body suspended on nails driven through the hands and feet,—parts of the frame which are, perhaps above others, endowed with the most exquisite sensibility. One stroke of the scourge, one thorn piercing our temples, one of the many repeated blows by which the nails were urged home, would probably give us more lively ideas of what our Savior suffered than all our efforts can excite. And yet the tortures which his body endured were but a part, and incomparably the smaller part of his sufferings. They wrung from him no groan, no expression of anguish. But his mental sufferings did more. They wrung from him not only groans, but great drops of blood. Before he was arrested, and while his body was free from pain he was, we are told, in an agony; he exclaimed, My soul is exceedingly sorrowful, even unto death; and his sweat was as great drops of blood falling down to the ground. Is it asked, what occasioned this mental agony? I answer, it was the curse of the law which, we are told, he bore for us. It was the hand of his Father, the hand of omnipotence which, as the prophet informs us, bruised him and put him to grief. The burden of man's guilt which he bore, the weight of divine wrath which we deserved, was what crushed him down. He drank the cup which we were doomed to drink, that cup into which, an apostle tells us, was poured the fierceness of the wrath of Almighty God. It was of this he said, Father, if it be possible, let this cup pass from me. It was the agonies occasioned by drinking this cup which made him cry out, My God, my God, why hast thou forsaken me? Now if we cannot conceive the full extent of his bodily sufferings, how much less can we conceive of the nameless anguish of his soul? Who, on this side everlasting burnings, can conceive what it is to drink the fierceness of the wrath of Almighty God, poured out without mixture into the cup of his indignation. Yet under the united pressure of all these inconceivable corporeal and mental agonies, he consented to die, and it was love, love for us, which induced him to consent. Well then may we exclaim, while standing by his cross, Behold how he loved us! He himself says, Greater love hath no man than this, that he lay down his life for his friend. And the apostle, pursuing the same thought, intimates it to be possible that for a good man some would even dare to die. This greatest, strongest proof of love, our Savior has given by dying for us. And this proof was, in his case, peculiarly strong. Should *we* consent to die for a friend, we should only anticipate a death which we must sooner or later suffer, because we are mortal. But Christ was immortal. He was under no necessity of ever tasting the pangs of death. No man, says he, taketh my life from me, but I lay it down of myself. While we then, in dying for a friend, only give up a life which we must soon part with, he gave up for us a life which he might have retained forever. And not only so, but gave it up in the most painful manner possible, forsaken by his friends, insulted and mocked by his enemies, and agonizing under a complication of the most excruciating corporeal and mental tortures. Yet he had the same natural aversion to suffering which we feel. How great then must have been the strength of his love for us, since it could so far prevail over his love for himself, as to make him willing to bear all this for our sakes. Would either of you, were you able to do it, endure equal sufferings for the dearest object of your affections on earth? If any one replies, Yes, while the scourge, the thorns and the cross are out of sight, yet I cannot but suspect that when they came near, when he began to feel them, and above all, when the bitter cup of divine wrath was put to his lips, his courage and his love would fail. But our Savior's love for us,—blessed be his name,—did not fail. It was stronger than death.

3. Another proof and measure of love may be found in the number and value of the gifts which it bestows on the object beloved. We naturally conclude that a person, who, without any other motive than disinterested affection, gives us great and valuable gifts, loves us much; and the more numerous and costly his gifts are, so much the greater do we think his love to be. Tried by this, as by all other rules, our Savior's love for us will be found beyond all comparison great. His gifts cannot be numbered, nor can their value be computed. He gives us himself, and all that he possesses. He gives us the pardon of numberless sins, every one of which deserved death. He gives us divine light to illuminate our minds, divine grace to purify our hearts, and divine consolations to comfort us in our afflictions. Nay more, he gives us heaven, gives us everlasting life, felicity and glory; gives us kingdoms, crowns, and thrones; compared with which, the sceptre of the most powerful earthly monarch is a worthless bauble. Nor does he give what cost him nothing. No, he paid the full price of all that he gives us; and if we estimate the value of his gifts by the price they cost him, we shall be convinced that they are inestimable. It would have cost him infinitely less to give each of us a world, or many worlds; for to create a world, costs him but a word; but to purchase the gifts which he bestows on us cost him his blood, his life; cost him all the agonies which I have vainly attempted to describe. If then we measure his love by the gifts he bestows on us, we shall see that it is boundless, and we can only cry, What manner of love is this? Let no one reply, Where are the gifts of which you tell us? We have them not. I answer, Christ offers them freely to all of you, to each of you, even to the meanest and the worst; nay more, he urges and entreats you to accept of them. If you refuse or neglect to accept them, the fault is not his. The gift is not less real, nor the less a proof of his love, because you do not choose to accept it. All who do accept his offers find that they are not empty words.

They enter on the immediate enjoyment of many of his gifts, and receive an earnest which secures to them the final possession of all, so that they may say, Christ has loved us, and washed us from our sins in his own blood, and has made us kings and priests unto God, and we shall live and reign with him forever and ever

Lastly. Love may be measured by the provocations it overlooks, and by the degree of patience with which it bears unkindness and ingratitude. Of all the trials to which love can be exposed, this is the most severe. To love those who are kind, affectionate, and grateful for our love, to adhere to them in adversity, to suffer for them, and load them with favors, is comparatively easy; nor does it require a very high degree of affection to do this. But to persevere in doing good to the ungrateful and perverse, who are jealous and suspicious, and who render us evil for good; to bear with the most unreasonable and cruel provocations, continually repeated; to forgive again, and again, and again, and still find new acts of forgiveness called for; to see our very kindness turned against us, and yet to continue to be kind—this is indeed the victory, the triumph of love, strong, unconquerable love. Among all the effects of parental love, its strength is so clearly displayed in nothing as the manner in which it leads parents to bear with the multiplied follies, the ingratitude and disobedience of undutiful children. But in this, as in all other respects, the love which Christ has displayed for our race, rises far above a father's or a mother's love. For more than four thousand years before his coming, our race were employed, with very few exceptions, in disobeying and offending him. When he came, instead of being received by mankind as their friend and benefactor, he was hated, slandered, ridiculed, and persecuted with the utmost virulence and malignity. In a similar manner he has been treated by mankind ever since. Even his professed disciples often requite his love with the most cruel distrust, unkindness, and ingratitude. They show little concern for his honor. They are slow to believe, slow to learn, and quick to forget what he has taught them. Every day, and almost every hour, he has reason to say to them, O ye of little faith! Do ye thus requite my love, O ungrateful and unwise! All this he foresaw, when he consented to die for us; but the current of his love was too deep and strong to be checked or diverted from its course. And notwithstanding the innumerable slights and provocations which he has received, and is daily receiving, it still flows as deep and strong as ever. Sabbath after Sabbath, we make light of his invitations, and treat him with indifference and neglect; but he overlooks it all, and comes again with offers of mercy, again to be slighted. Year after year he stands knocking at the door of our hearts; and, though he finds them closed against him, waits and knocks still. Generation after generation of our ungrateful race, live and die rejecting him; yet his love does not become cold, and he still visits a thankless world with messages of mercy and offers of salvation. He endured, says an apostle, and he still endures, the contradiction of sinners against himself. Now was there ever love like this, love so perseveringly, I had almost said, obstinately, kind? love which could glow with undiminished fervor for so many centuries, with nothing amiable to excite it; no grateful returns to feed it, but, on the contrary, numberless provocations to extinguish it. Had not his love for our race been infinitely stronger than any thing which is called love among men, it would have wholly ceased some thousands of years since, and he would have desisted from making attempts to bless and save us. Well then may we lift up our hands in wonder and exclaim, Behold how he loves us! Well may we say of such love as this, many waters cannot quench it, neither can floods drown it.

We have now briefly noticed the principal ways in which love makes itself visible, and by which we may estimate its strength. From what has been said, it appears, I conceive, evident, that in all these ways, in submitting to privation, in enduring sufferings, in bestowing gifts, and in bearing with unkindness, ingratitude, and perverseness, our Savior has displayed a love for mankind which has no parallel, a love which is infinitely far from being equalled by any thing which the world has ever seen. In attempting to lead your minds to this conclusion, I have made no appeal to your passions. I have simply stated facts, and left them to speak for themselves. I am however ashamed to offer this to you as a description of our Savior's love for us. I feel, most painfully, that I have done no manner of justice to the subject. Had I the tongue of an angel, I could not do justice to it. God himself, speaking by the mouth of his inspired messengers, could only say that it is unsearchable, that it passeth knowledge. It is a theme which will employ the praises of saints and angels through a whole eternity. How then can a weak mortal set it before you in the space of a few minutes and in the compass of a few pages? I say not this to excuse the wretched manner in which the subject has been treated. But I am jealous for my Master's honor. I fear that this miserably imperfect attempt to display the greatness of his love, will only serve to lower it in your estimation. God forbid that this should be the case. Let me beseech you not to judge of his love by what has now been said of it. Rather go and learn it from the bible; and unite with me in the apostle's prayer, that the God of light, the Father of glory, would give us all, the spirit of wisdom and revelation in the knowledge of his Son, the eyes of our understanding being enlightened, that we may be enabled to comprehend what is the length, and breadth, and depth, and height, and to know the love of Christ which passeth knowledge. A few inferences will conclude the discourse.

1. Is the love of Christ for us so immeasurably great? Then surely we ought to return it. Our love to him ought to bear some proportion to his love for us. If his love for us is incomparably greater than that of any of our earthly friends, then we ought to love him more than we love any of our earthly friends. If he has done and suffered more for us than any earthly benefactor would or could do, we ought to feel more grateful to him than to any earthly benefactor. Ingratitude to him must be, of all ingratitude, the most base and inexcusable. A refusal to love him must involve more criminality than a refusal to love the nearest and kindest relative on earth. It is needless to prove these assertions. They bring with them their own evidence. They must come home with irresistible conviction to the bosom of every man who believes what is related of our Savior in the New Testament. There is something in our breasts which tells us, that such love deserves a return of affection, that such benefits justly claim our gratitude. The most savage nations on earth need no arguments to convince them that parental love ought to be returned, no motive to induce them to detest the character of an ungrateful, undutiful child. But every reason which can be assigned why a child should love and be grateful to his parents, may be urged with far great-

a force to prove, that the increase of love and gratitude to our Redeemer is an indispensable duty, and that the neglect of this duty is in the highest degree criminal and base. Would not the Jews have thought it strange, would not you think it strange, had Lazarus, after his resurrection, manifested no affection for the friend who wept over his grave, and raised him from the dead? But, O, how small were these favors, these proofs of love to Lazarus, in comparison with the favors, the proofs of love which the Savior has shown to us!

2. Let me further improve the subject by urging all who have hitherto neglected the Savior to return his love without longer delay. Are not your understandings convinced, do not your consciences testify that you ought to do this? And can your hearts then stand out in opposition, not only to the Savior's love, but to your own understandings and consciences? If they can you must surely cease to talk of the goodness of your hearts. You must surely cease to flatter yourselves that you are capable of real gratitude or affection, or that you possess any real sensibility; for where is the goodness, the gratitude, or the sensibility of that heart which can see what Christ has done and felt for it, without returning his affection? If then you would prove that you are not totally devoid of all these qualities, begin this day to return his love; or at least to reproach and condemn yourselves for having so long neglected to do it. And let all who feel consciously sinful and guilty, and who are deterred by conscious guilt and unworthiness from approaching the Savior, take encouragement from the wonderful love which he has displayed for our race, and approach him with full confidence and without the smallest delay. Trembling sinner, how can you fear to approach such love as this? What can you have to fear in approaching one, whose love for you has already led him to the cross? Will he, can he, who voluntarily suffered all this for your salvation, hurt you, or frown upon you when you come to him for mercy? O, then come to Christ. Whosoever will, let him come.

But whether I am, or am not successful, while pleading the Savior's cause with sinners, surely I cannot, my professing friends, be unsuccessful while I plead it with you. You profess to know something of his love. You know that all heaven wonders and is astonished while it sees what its Lord has done for you. And will not you then wonder and adore? Can you doubt the reality or the strength of that love which has been so strangely displayed? Can you any more distrust the Savior's love, because he sometimes afflicts you? Do you not perceive that he would much rather afflict himself, than afflict you, were not affliction necessary? Would he not rather wound the apple of his eye, than wound you, did not your own happiness require it? Most evidently he would; for all that he could suffer in your stead he has cheerfully suffered; and he would have cheerfully suffered all your afflictions, would it have answered the same purpose to you—it would have been adding one drop more to the bitter cup. He never afflicted you to shield himself. Whenever the question was, shall I suffer this, or shall my people suffer it? Shall I drink this cup, or shall my people drink it? he never hesitated a moment to take it all upon himself. And he would with equal cheerfulness suffer all your afflictions for you, and allow you to live in uninterrupted peace and prosperity, did not your own good require that you should fometimes suffer in your own persons. And he still sympathizes with you in all that you necessarily suffer. His word teaches you that, in all your afflictions, he is afflicted, and he assures his people that whosoever touches them touches the apple of his eye. How can you doubt whether he who says this, he who gave himself, his life, his blood for you, will deny you any thing which he sees to be really necessary to your happiness; whether he would hesitate to give you a world or many worlds, if your happiness would be increased by the gift? How can you doubt that he would as soon cut off his right hand, as take away from you a partner, a child, a relative, or give you the smallest pain, unless he saw it to be necessary? O, then, what reason have we for sorrow, shame, and self-reproach, if we have even been tempted by affliction, to doubt his love: and still more, if we have been led by it to murmur or repine! Let us, then, never more be guilty of this conduct. Let us not stab to the heart our already deeply wounded Savior, by distrusting that love of which he has given us such infallible proofs; or murmuring at those afflictions which he sends in love, and for our good. Let us rather say with the apostle, the love of Christ constraineth us, to live not to ourselves, but to him who died for us.

SERMON XLVI.

CHRIST'S SPECIAL TENDERNESS TOWARDS PENITENT DISCIPLES.

Go your way, tell his disciples, and Peter, that he goeth before you into Galilee; there shall ye see him, as he said unto you.—MARK XVI. 7.

THESE words were spoken by an extraordinary messenger, in a most interesting place, on a memorable occasion. They were spoken by an angel, in the sepulchre of Christ, just after his resurrection. They were addressed to a company of women who, with a strange mixture of love to Christ, and disbelief, or forgetfulness of his prediction that he should rise from the dead, had come to embalm his remains. But instead of a dead Savior, they found in his tomb an angel, who soon removed the fears which his appearance occasioned by saying, Fear not, for I know that ye seek Jesus who was crucified. He is not here, he is risen. Go, tell his disciples, and Peter, that he goeth before you into Galilee; there shall ye see him, as he said unto you.

It must be recollected, that this angel was a messenger of Christ, and that from him he had doubtless received the message. A question naturally suggests itself, why our Lord, in giving him this message, directed him to make this particular mention of Peter. The angel had said, Go tell his disciples; and did not the general term include Peter? Was not he one of the disciples? He was; but he was, at this time, a fallen disciple. Three days before, he had denied his Master in the most shameful and criminal manner. And as he had then disowned his Master, he might well fear; he probably did fear, that his Master would disown him; and no longer consider or treat him as a disciple. But though Peter had fallen, he had also repented of his fall. No sooner was his sin committed, than, melted by a look from his much injured Master, he went out and wept bitterly. And by making an early visit to his Master's tomb on the morning of the third day, he showed that he still loved him; that his fall was the effect of sudden and powerful temptation, rather than of deliberate wickedness. But though penitent, he could not be certain of pardon; and had the message in our text been addressed to the disciples only, he would probably have doubted, whether he might consider it as including himself. Such doubts, however, his kind and forgiving Master took care to banish by directing his messsenger to mention Peter particularly by name; and to inform him that his Master was ready to admit him into his presence, and fulfil the promise which he had made before his death.

My hearers, our blessed Savior is, yesterday, to-day, and forever, the same. He is governed by principles and measures which are, like himself, unchangeable; and we may therefore conclude that, as he has acted once, he will always act in similar circumstances. If he formerly had a special regard for fallen disciples, who had been overtaken in a fault, and who, though truly penitent, were doubtful whether he would forgive them, he has the same regard for such characters still; and if he then directed his messenger, to remind them of his promises in a particular manner, he still directs his ministers to do the same. His instructions are, Comfort ye, comfort ye, my mourning people; strengthen the weak hands, and say to them who are of a fearful heart, Be strong, fear not, your God will save you.

In discoursing further on this subject, I propose to show why Christ has such a special regard to his mourning, penitent disciples, who, in consequence of their sins, doubt whether he will acknowledge or forgive them.

I. That Christ should pay a special regard, and send particular invitations, to persons of this description, is perfectly agreeable to his character. It is so, whether we view him as man, or as God, or as God and man united in the person of the Mediator. It is agreeable to his character considered as a man.

Viewed in this light he possesses all the innocent dispositions and characteristics of our nature. Now I need not inform you, that men are disposed, almost perhaps without exception, to regard with peculiar favor, and to treat with special kindness, those who appear humble, modest and diffident. Were you about to invite a number of persons to visit you; and were there one among them, who you had reason to believe would, in consequence of diffidence or conscious unworthiness, be scarcely persuaded to think himself welcome, you would send that person a peculiarly pressing invitation, and treat him on his arrival with perhaps more than ordinary kindness. In a similar manner you would treat an offending but penitent child, who, broken hearted on account of his fault, could scarcely think it possible that you would ever again love him as you had formerly done. Now this disposition our Savior, viewed as man, possesses in the highest degree; and this alone, were there no other reason, would induce him to treat mourning, penitent offenders with peculiar kindness.

Nor is this mode of conduct less agreeable to his character considered as God. As such he says, I dwell with him who is of a humble and contrite heart, to revive the spirit of the humble, and to revive the heart of the contrite ones. To this man will I look, even to him that is of a contrite spirit and that trembleth at my word. Though the Lord be high, he hath respect unto the lowly, and giveth grace unto the humble.

Still more agreeable, if possible, is this mode of proceeding to the character of Christ, viewed as God and Man united in the person of the Mediator. In this character he combines all the disposition of man and all the readiness of God to treat with peculiar kindness the mourning penitent. In this character he said, Blessed are the poor in spirit, for theirs is the kingdom of heaven. Blessed are they that mourn, for they shall be comforted; and he is sufficiently disposed to fulfil his own declaration. This too is the character in which it was said of him, The bruised reed he will not break, and the smoking flax he will not quench; expressions, in which a weak, a penitent sinner, borne down with a weight of conscious guilt, is figuratively but very beautifully and strikingly described.

This leads us to observe,

II. That to regard mourning, desponding penitents with peculiar favor perfectly corresponds with the offices which Christ sustains, and with the object for which he came into the world. He came to proclaim glad tidings to the meek, to comfort all that mourn, to give them beauty for ashes, the oil of joy for mourning, and the garments of praise for the spirit of heaviness. He came as a shepherd to bring back those who had been driven away, to bind up those who are bruised, and to heal those who are sick; in a word, he came to seek and to save the lost, those who without him feel lost and undone. He must therefore, in accomplishing the object for which he came, comfort all who mourn for sin and regard them with peculiar kindness. With such characters indeed his business principally is; for whom should the physician visit, but the sick; and whom should he visit first and most frequently, for whom should he feel most tenderly concerned, but those whose moral diseases are most painful, who view themselves as sick unto death?

III. A third reason why our Savior treats such characters with peculiar tenderness is, that they are prepared to receive forgiveness and consolation in a proper manner. He pities all. He is ready and disposed to impart his blessings to all. But he can impart his blessings only in a certain way, in a way consistent with the glory of God, and the honor of his law. Now in this way he can bestow pardon and consolation on those only, who truly repent and mourn for sin. Were he to pardon and save the impenitent, who feel no sorrow for sin, who scarcely perceive that they are sinners, who still persist in pursuing a sinful course, and even justify themselves in it, he would dishonor his Father, prostrate his authority and law, and become in effect the patron of rebels, the minister of sin. In fact, he cannot pardon such characters; for they will not accept ot pardon; they feel no need of it. Nor can he impart to them spiritual consolation; for they have no spiritual troubles to be removed. However much disposed you might be, my hearers, to pardon and befriend one who had injured you, yet if he refused to acknowledge that he had done you any injury; if he rejected every offer of pardon, if he still persisted in his injurious conduct, you evidently could not force him to receive your forgiveness; nor could you compel him to be your friend. How then can Christ pardon those who will not accept of pardon; how comfort those who are not distressed? Or, to allude to the case mentioned in our text, what would it have availed to send Peter the message under consideration, to inform him that Christ was ready to meet him in Galilee, if he had felt no love to Christ, no sorrow for having offended him, no wish to see him? As little would it now avail, to offer pardon and salvation through Christ, or to send messages and invitations of mercy to those who do not mourn for sin, nor even feel that they are sinners. But when a man feels that this is his character, when he cordially acknowledges that he has violated the divine law, and the precepts of the gospel, and that in consequence he deserves God's everlasting displeasure; when, like Peter, he weeps bitterly over his offences, and is ready to fear that one so vile and unworthy as himself can never be pardoned, or received as a disciple, then he is prepared to receive pardon and consolation in a proper manner; then Christ can impart to him these blessings; then he will receive them with humble, admiring gratitude; and, like pardoned Peter, will consecrate the remainder of his life to the service of his kind, condescending Savior, loving much, because much has been forgiven.

IV. Another reason why Christ treats persons whose character and situation resemble those of Peter with peculiar kindness, is, that they peculiarly need such treatment. St. Paul, after directing the Corinthian church to restore an offending, but penitent brother, adds as a reason why they should do it speedily, lest he be swallowed up with overmuch sorrow. Of this there is always danger in the case of persons whose situation resembles that of Peter. Their case will admit of no delay. Their doubts and anxieties must be speedily removed, or despondency, if not complete despair, will be the consequence. Had Christ, after his resurrection, treated Peter with harshness, or even with neglect, he might like Judas, have destroyed himself in sullen despair. And while it is thus necessary that such persons should be speedily comforted, it is by no means easy to comfort them. They seem to themselves so vile, so utterly undeserving of pardon, so worthy of everlasting punishment, that no general promises, no common invitations, are sufficient to remove their guilty fears, and give them confidence and peace. Messages of kindness, addressed to Christ's disciples at large, afford them no consolation; for they doubt whether they are his disciples. Christ must therefore send them a particular assurance of pardon; he must address them as it were by name, and with an aspect of peculiar graciousness, before they will believe his readiness to receive and forgive them. All this our wise and compassionate Redeemer well knows; and he acts accordingly; displaying his kindness most clearly to those who feel most unworthy of it; and most speedily to those who immediately need it.

Lastly. Christ regards mourning penitents with peculiar favor, because he is himself the author of their repentance. He is exalted, we are told, as a Prince and a Savior, to give repentance and remission of sins to his people. Whenever they repent, it is because he has given them repentance. He had given it to Peter. He had given him a look which broke his heart, and caused him to go out and weep bitterly. In a similar manner he has looked at all who mourn for sin with godly sorrow. He has fulfilled to them the promise which says, I will pour upon my people the spirit of grace and supplication, and they shall look on me whom they have pierced, and mourn, as one that mourneth for a first-born. Having thus begun a good work in them, he must finish it. Having given them repentance, he must give them pardon; for when he bestows the former, it is on purpose to prepare them for the latter.

Such, my hearers, are some of the principal reasons why Christ regards mourning, penitent sinners with peculiar favor, and treats them with peculiar kindness. A brief improvement of the subject will now conclude the discourse.

1. If all men possessed the character of Peter; if all, like him, saw and lamented their sins, how inexpressibly delightful would be the employment of the ministers of Christ! Then our message would indeed be glad tidings; we should have nothing to do but to proclaim glad tidings to all. No more should we be constrained to perform the painful duty of setting your sins before you, and of proclaiming the terrors of the Lord; no more accusations, no more threatenings, no mention of wrath to come, would you then hear from our lips. We might sit as messengers of peace in our Savior's forsaken tomb, and say to all, Peace be unto you; be not afraid,—ye seek Jesus of Nazareth, and ye shall soon see him in heaven. O, it would be too much, happiness too great, too transporting, thus to proclaim pardon and salvation to all, and to see all joyfully receive these

blessings; to address precious promises to every one by name, and to know that every one hears and believes these promises; to pour the water of life into the lips of the dying and of the dead, and see them start up to life and holy activity; to see tears of repentance mingled with smiles of heaven-descended joy, and hear the expressions of doubt, and fear, and anxiety, exchanged for the rapturous accents of wonder, and thankfulness, and peace, and love. And why may we not see and hear all this? Why may we not always proclaim only glad tidings, and see them produce universal gladness? Why must our pained lips still give utterance to messages of divine wrath; and speak of a death without hope; of a judgment without mercy; of a hell without end; of a despairing eternity? Only, I answer, only because you will not all repent of, and mourn for sin. Only do this, and you will never more hear of your sins, except as having been fully pardoned; of death, except as a messenger, who is to convey you to heaven; nor of the judgment day, except as of the day which is to witness your open acknowledgment by the Judge as his friend; nor of hell, except as a place, the danger of which you have forever escaped; nor of eternity, except as it measures the duration of your happiness. O then, my hearers, why will you not all repent of sin, all mourn for sin, all renounce your sins? Will it not most terribly aggravate your remorse, and your wretchedness in the future world, to reflect, that the pardon of your sins, the special regard and favor of Christ, and everlasting happiness might once have been secured, by renouncing and mourning for your sins; sins which only serve to render you unhappy even in the present life! Do any reply, we know not what are the sins which we must renounce, or for which we must mourn? We have not, like Peter, denied Christ, and need not, therefore, repent as he did. Alas, my hearers, we have all denied Christ. I have done it; you have done it. He considers all as denying him, who do not confess him before men. He considers all, who do verbally confess him, as denying him, when they do not act agreeably to their professions. In one, or in both of these ways, we have all denied him, and crucified him afresh. We have denied him in a manner even more criminal than that of which Peter was guilty. He denied him on a sudden surprise, when he saw him in the hands of his enemies, when to confess relation to him was to incur contempt, abuse, punishment, perhaps death itself. We have no dangers of this kind to tempt us to deny Christ, our Savior; nor have we denied him once only, or on a sudden surprisal, but we have denied him deliberately, repeatedly; have persisted in our denial of him for years. Even now many of you are about to go from his table, and thus to say, by your conduct, I am not a servant of Christ; I do not acknowledge him as my Master; I do not wish to remember him. And you, my friends, who will remain and approach his table,—have not you formerly done this? and are not some of you still in various ways denying, offending, and grieving him, when you profess to come, in a manner no less criminal than the conduct of Peter? Now these are the sins which you are required to mourn over and confess. For these sins every one has reason to mourn apart. And will you, can you, do you mourn for these sins? Are any of you looking to him, whom you have pierced by your neglect, unkindness, and ingratitude; looking to him on the cross, where lifted up he draws the hearts of sinners to himself? Do you there see him as it were looking at you with a reproving, expostulating, yet mild and forgiving look, and hear him saying, Did I suffer all this for thee, O sinner? and is this thy return? Dost thou not know thy Savior? Dost thou deny him who dies here for thee? and wilt thou, by persisting in thy denial, compel me to deny thee hereafter before my Father and the holy angels? My hearers, if this dying love leads any of you to repentance; if any of you are, like Peter, seeking a place where to weep; if your past treatment of the Savior appears most ungrateful, cruel, and monstrous; if in consequence you feel worthy of his everlasting displeasure; then, in his name I say, peace be unto you; your sins are forgiven, be not afraid. Are there any whose guilt seems to them so great, who feel so unworthy, that they cannot be satisfied with general assurances of pardon, cannot yet believe that Christ acknowledges and loves them as his disciples? To such Christ directs us to speak as it were by name, to say to each of them, Christ loves thee, and gave himself for thee. He was delivered for thy sins, and raised again for thy justification. Come, see the place, where thy Lord, thy surety lay. See, he is released; thy surety is discharged, a sufficient proof that the debt is paid, that thy creditor is satisfied. Christ is gone before thee into heaven, to appear for thee in the presence of God, as thy advocate and representative. There shalt thou see him, as he has said. There shalt thou be like him, there shalt thou behold his glory forever and ever.

My professing friends, what encouragement does this subject afford all penitent, yet doubting, trembling characters to approach the table of our Lord. If any of you cannot take this encouragement, it is because you are not in a penitent frame. Remember the message in our text was sent, not to Peter falling, but to Peter mourning. Remember then from whence you are fallen, and repent, and this message shall be your consolation.

SERMON XLVII.

THE END OF TIME.

And the angel whom I saw stand upon the sea and upon the earth, lifted up his hand to heaven; and sware by him that liveth forever and ever, who created heaven and the things that therein are, and the earth and the things that therein are, and the sea and the things which are therein, that there should be time no longer: but in the days of the voice of the seventh angel, when he shall begin to sound, the mystery of God should be finished, as he hath declared to his servants the prophets.—REVELATION x. 5, 6, 7.

IN the commencement of this chapter St. John informs us, that he saw in vision a mighty angel descend from heaven, clothed with a cloud, and having a rainbow upon his head, while his countenance shone resplendent as the sun, and his feet were like pillars of fire. This angel, placing one foot upon the land and the other upon the sea, lifted his hand to heaven, and swore by the everlasting God, who created the heavens, the earth, and the sea, with all which they contain, and who therefore possesses both the right and the power to prescribe limits to their duration, that there should be time no longer; but that in the days of the voice of the seventh angel, when he shall begin to sound, the mystery of God shall be finished, as he hath declared to his servants the prophets.

My hearers, we have witnessed, and perhaps reflected and moralized on the lapse of time. In this passage we are called to contemplate its termination. We are called to see that current, on whose bosom we have been borne ever since our existence commenced, swallowed up in the ocean of eternity. This forms a most interesting object of contemplation; but it is too vast, and embraces too many particulars, to be seen by us at once as a whole. Let us, then, divide it into parts, and consider them separately. The several particulars which it is necessary to consider may be included in an answer to the three following questions:

What is meant by the end of time?

When will the event denoted by this phrase arrive?

What will be the attending circumstances and consequences of this event?

I. What is meant by the end of time? or, in other words, by the declaration, There shall be time no longer?

Time, so far as man has any concern with it, is that portion of duration which is commensurate with the existence of our world, and which is measured by its diurnal and annual revolutions. It began when this world began to exist. Agreeably we are informed that, in the beginning, that is the beginning of time, God created the heavens and the earth. Previous to this event there was, properly speaking, no such thing as time. There was duration, there was eternity, but time there was none. So long as this world continues to exist, time will continue; and when it shall cease to exist, the end of time will have arrived; or, in the language of our text, there will be time no longer. The end of time, and the end of the world, are, then, expressions of the same import.

II. When will the event denoted by these expressions arrive? We learn from our text that it will arrive when the mystery of God shall be finished. To that period the oath of the angel refers; and when that period arrives there shall be time no longer. By the mystery of God is intended the design, or object, for which he created the world, and toward the accomplishment of which he has ever since been advancing. This design is here called a mystery, that is, something secret or concealed; because, until God revealed it, it was entirely hidden from mortals; and because it is still but partially revealed. So far as was necessary for the information of mankind, God has communicated it to his servants the prophets, and the other inspired writers of the sacred volume, that through their instrumentality it might be made known to others. From them we learn, that God's great object in creating this world and its inhabitants was to gratify, and glorify himself. Their language is, The Lord hath made all things for himself; Thou Lord hast made all things; and for thy pleasure they are, and were created; and they represent God, as saying, respecting every one who is called by his name, I have created him for mine own glory. Now God at once glorifies and gratifies himself, when he displays his perfections in his works. Some of his perfections, as, for instance, his power, wisdom and goodness, he displayed in the creation of the world; and they, as well as some other perfections of his nature are still displayed in its providential government. But the principal display of his perfections is made in the work of redemption by Jesus Christ, the great object to which all his works of creation and providence ultimately refer. Agreeably, inspiration informs us, that for Jesus Christ all things were created; that all power in heaven and earth is given to him; that to him all judgment is committed, that he is made head over all things to his church; and that to him there is given dominion and glory and a kingdom that all people, nations, and languages, should serve him. This kingdom here mentioned is usually called Christ's mediatorial kingdom; and over this kingdom he is to reign so long as the sun and moon endure; that is, in other words, till time shall be no more. When the purposes for which this kingdom was given to Christ, and set up in the world, are accomplished, the mystery of God, mentioned in our text, will be finished. Now the purposes, for which this kingdom was given to Christ, include two things. The first is, the complete salvation of all who are given to him by the Father. We are informed that by him, as the Captain of their salvation, God is bringing many sons to glory. He must then reign, his mediatorial kingdom must continue, till all the chosen sons of God are brought home to glory, or to mansions prepared for them in heaven, their Father's house. Hence our Savior declares that, before the end shall come, the gospel of his kingdom must be preached to all nations. The reason is obvious. The destined subjects of this kingdom, the chosen sons of God and heirs of salvation, are to be gathered, we read, out of every kindred and nation and tongue and people. Of course, the gospel, by which they are to be called and gathered into the kingdom of Christ, must be preached to all nations before the mystery of God can be finished, before the end of time and of the world can arrive.

The second thing, included in these purposes, is the complete and final subjugation of all Christ's enemies. Agreeably, an apostle informs us, that he must reign till all enemies are put under his feet; and that, when this is done, when he shall have put down all opposing rule, and power, and authority, then the end shall come. This event synchronizes, as our text informs us, with the sounding of the trumpet of the seventh angel. Accordingly, we read in a succeeding chapter that when the seventh angel sounded, great voices were heard in heaven, saying, the kingdoms of this world are become the kingdoms of our Lord and Savior. Thus when all Christ's chosen people are brought home to glory, and all his incorrigible enemies are placed under his feet, the mystery of God which he is now accomplishing will be finished, and then will the end come and there will be time no longer. Time, then, may be considered as an island, raised out of the ocean of eternity by the Creator for specific purposes, and destined, when these purposes shall be accomplished, to sink again and be lost in the ocean from which it rose, and whose waves on every side bound its shores. The appointed day and hour when this shall take place is known, we are informed, neither to man nor to angel, but to God only. It must however be obvious to all, who can discern the signs of the times, that though it is still at a considerable distance, the course of events betokens its approach. We have already remarked that, before the end can come, the gospel must be preached to all nations. And how much has been recently done, how much is now doing and with increasing success, to accomplish this work! God's ancient people, the Jews, must also be called into the fold of Christ, and with them the fulness of the Gentiles. And present appearances indicate, as I need not inform you, that these events are not very far distant.

The downfall of Papal superstition, of Mohammedanism, and of the Turkish empire, are predicted events, which must take place before the end of time can arrive. And that these events are not very distant, who can doubt? The great mystery of God is then evidently approaching its consummation, the end of all things is comparatively at hand. And it becomes us to remember that, with respect to ourselves, the end of time is still more near. To each individual the hour of death is the end of time. When that hour arrives to any one, God does in effect say to him, there shall be time no longer. Let us now inquire,

III. What will be the attending circumstances and consequences of this event? That this question may receive a proper answer it must be considered with reference to ourselves, our race, and the world which we inhabit.

1. With respect to ourselves, considered as individuals, the end of time, or, which is the same thing to us, the end of our lives will be attended by circumstances, and followed by consequences, most important and interesting.

In the first place, we shall then be separated at once from all temporal and earthly objects. The relations which we now sustain to such objects, and the connexions which now bind us to them, will be entirely and forever dissolved. The world will no longer be our habitation; this country will no longer be our country; our houses, lands, and other temporal possessions, for which we have labored, will no longer be our property. One moment after our death they will no more be our's than if we had never possessed them. The richest and the poorest of us will then be reduced in this respect to a perfect equality. The places which now know us will know us no more forever. Of all our possessions nothing will remain to us but the necessity of accounting for them to our Judge, and the consequences of the manner in which we have employed them. Then too, the ties which now bind us to our fellow creatures will be dissolved. We may now have numerous relations and connections; we may surround ourselves by a large circle of admiring, affectionate friends; but death will separate us from them all, and in one moment after its arrival we shall be as friendless as the beggar who dies unknown in a foreign land. Our surviving friends may indeed weep over our remains; they may honor them with sumptuous funeral rites; they may say much in our praise, and give us a place in their memories; but we shall know nothing of all this, nor, if we could, would it afford us the smallest gratification. In fine, the world with all which it contains will be no more to us than if it ceased to exist, at the very moment of our dissolution. To these remarks there may be one exception. If we are real Christians, if we have become united to Christ as our Head, and to his people as fellow members, we have formed a union which death itself cannot dissolve. The truly pious will meet all their pious friends again, meet and know them as friends, and be separated from them no more forever.

In the second place, with the end of time our state of probation, and our day of grace will end. We shall be removed from our present religious privileges and means of spiritual improvement. Not another petition can we ever offer, not another sentence can we ever read in the word of God; not another offer of pardon and salvation can we ever hear; not another opportunity of warning, or of doing good to our fellow mortals can we enjoy. Prepared or unprepared we must go. Our accounts, whether ready or not ready for the inspection of our Judge, must be sealed up to the judgment of the great day; our plans, our begun enterprises, our works, whether finished or unfinished, must all be left just as they are. No part of the work which God has required to be performed in time, can be done in eternity; for there is in this sense no work nor device.

In the third place, when time ends, eternity will begin. The moment in which we leave this temporary and mutable state, we shall enter a state which is eternal, and, of course, unchangeable. Sound philosophy unites with revelation in declaring, that no essential change can take place in eternity. The moment in which we leave the body and enter the future world, eternity will set its stamp upon us, exclaiming, Such as I find you, you shall continue to be while I endure. He that is righteous, let him be righteous still, and he that is sinful, let him be sinful still. It is necessary, however, to recollect that, when the good man leaves the body, he leaves all his remaining sins and imperfections behind, and enters eternity a pure and spotless spirit; while on the other hand, the wicked leave all their apparent goodness behind, and enter eternity with the character and feelings of a fiend; for, says our Savior, To him that hath, more shall be given, and he shall have abundance; but from him that hath not, shall be taken away even that which he seemeth to have.

Let us next consider the circumstances and consequences which will attend and follow the end of time with respect to the human race. Considering them separately, as individuals, these circumstances and consequences will be the same to each of them, as have already been mentioned. But we now speak of them collectively, including ourselves, of course, in the number.

And first, when the end of time shall arrive, the general

resurrection will take place. Then all that are in the graves shall hear the voice of the Son of man and come forth; they that have done good to the resurrection of life, and they that have done evil to the resurrection of damnation; for there shall be a resurrection not of the just only but also of the unjust.

In the second place, at the end of time, the day of judgment, the great day for which all other days were made, will arrive The Judge will be seen by every human eye, coming in the clouds of heaven with power and great glory; the whole human family, small and great, shall be placed before his tribunal to be judged and rewarded according to their works; the righteous and the wicked shall be separated from each other; the former shall be called to inherit the kingdom prepared for them from the foundation of the world, while the latter will be doomed to depart accursed into everlasting fire prepared for the devil and his angels. These sentences will be no sooner pronounced than executed. The righteous will ascend triumphantly with their Savior to heaven, there to live and reign with him forever; while the wicked will be thrust down to their destined prison, between which and the abodes of the blessed a great and impassable gulf will be fixed.

It remains only to consider what will then be the fate of the globe which we inhabit. It has already been seen that the end of time, and the end of this world must take place at the same moment. While the world continues, time must continue, and when the world ends, time ends. Agreeably, we are informed that, when the period referred to shall arrive, the earth with all its works shall be burnt up; for then the design for which it was created will have been accomplished, and its longer existence would be useless. Then the gold, the silver, the jewels, and all the glittering but delusive objects, for which so many thousands have bartered their souls, shall be destroyed; then the monuments, the palaces, the cities, which their vain builders fondly hoped would render their names imperishable, shall be whelmed in one common ruin; then the exploits and achievements, the civil and political systems, from which their authors hoped to derive a deathless fame, shall all be blotted out and forgotten; then those literary works on which the impious pride of man had inscribed the epithet, immortal, will be consumed like a worthless scrap of paper. In fine, all the works of men will pass away with the world which contained them, and it will be clearly seen, that they 'built too low, who built beneath the skies;' and that all who did not labor for the glory and honor and immortality beyond the grave, labored in vain, and spent their strength for nought.

It will have already occurred to you, my hearers, that we have led your attention to the subject before us with special reference to the circumstances in which we meet. We have just passed the line which separates two of those divisions of time, by which our short span is measured out. We have bid an eternal farewell to one year, and entered on another, which to some of us must, and to any of us may, prove the last. Yes, to some of us, the end of time, with its attending circumstances and consequences, will arrive before the close of the present year. There are some present who have reason to say, My breath is corrupt, my days are extinct, the graves are ready for me. Whether I shall preach, whether you will hear, another new-year's sermon, God only knows. During the past year, twenty-eight individuals of this society, nineteen adults and nine children, have passed the bounds of time, and entered on eternity. This number does not include those who have died while absent from us. To an equal number the end of time will probably arrive during the present year. As no one of us can say that he shall not be among this number, let us pause, and, with the end of time full in our view, indulge those reflections which it is suited to excite, and for which the occasion calls.

1. In view of this subject, how insignificant, how unworthy of an immortal being, do all merely temporal and earthly pursuits appear! Look at these pursuits, ye who are engaged in them, and then at the scene before us, and methinks you can scarcely fail to be convinced of the irrationality of your conduct. You have spent many years in these pursuits, and what is all that you have really acquired worth? What will all the connections you have formed, and all the friends you have acquired, be worth to you, when the hour of separation, which may come tomorrow, shall arrive? What will all the applause you ever have obtained, or ever can obtain, be worth to you, when your ear, closed in death, can no longer hear it? What will a portion in this world be worth to you, when the world itself,

with all which it contains, is burnt up? What is it worth to those who died the last year? The answer to all these questions is short,—just nothing. You have spent many years then, the most valuable years of life, years which if spent aright would have secured eternal salvation, in acquiring nothing. Nor is this all. By thus laboring for temporal, when you ought to have been pursuing spiritual and eternal objects, you have incurred the just displeasure of your Creator; you have been treasuring up wrath against the day of wrath. Yes, sinner, the only treasure you have accumulated is a treasure of wrath. Of all that you have acquired this, this alone, can you carry with you when you leave this world. Can you then deny that your conduct has been irrational in the extreme? If you do deny it let me ask, whether you really believe that your souls are immortal? If so, you believe that they will exist after death, that they will be in existence a hundred or a thousand years hence, and that, when that period arrives, happiness will appear to them as desirable, and misery as dreadful, as it does now. Have you then secured any thing which will promote your happiness a hundred years after death? Have not all your cares and labors had respect to the present life? And if this be not folly what is? Surely the folly of him who wastes his childhood and youth in idleness and play, is wisdom itself compared with the folly of him who lays up his treasure on earth, and makes no provision but for the present life.

That you may be still farther convinced of this, contrast your conduct with that of the real Christian, who has diligently sought, in God's appointed way, for glory and honor and immortality beyond the grave. He has laid up something for eternity, something which will render him completely happy when time shall be no more. And the portion which he has secured is not only valuable but safe; for it is laid up in heaven. This world, with all which it contains, may be burnt up, without diminishing his treasure in the smallest degree. Death may come, the end of time may come, and his happiness, instead of being diminished, will be immeasurably increased; for at death he goes to his portion; while you, at death, will go from yours forever. Is not his conduct then wisdom and yours folly? Would it not be folly to invest all your property in a bank which you knew would fail, or embark it without insurance on board a vessel which you knew would founder? If any of you are convinced that it would be, remember that it is not yet too late to be wise. The end of time is not yet arrived to you; and until that arrives, you will enjoy the day of grace and the means of salvation. O, then, improve them while you may. Whatever you do must be done quickly, for your time is short, and there is no work nor device nor knowledge in the grave whither you are hastening.

2. In full view of the end of time let me ask, are you all, my hearers, prepared for it? Are you prepared to part with your friends, to leave all your temporal possessions, to be removed from the means of grace, to enter the world of spirits, the eternal world, to have the stamp of eternity placed upon your characters? In a word, are you prepared to meet your God, to stand before him in judgment and see the earth sink from under your feet in the flames of one wide-wasting, all-devouring conflagration? If you are not prepared, nay, if you have the smallest doubt of your own preparedness, give yourselves no rest till all scriptural cause of doubt is removed.

3. Proper views of the subject before us will be useful to us, my Christian friends, in approaching the table of our Lord. In approaching that table, we shall act a part in the great work which God is carrying on, and commemorate an event which constitutes its corner stone. We shall scarcely assert more than the Scriptures will warrant, if we assert, that the world was created to serve as a spot on which the cross of Christ might be erected. In approaching this table we shall also observe an institution which forms a connecting chain between the first and second coming of Christ, or between his crucifixion and the end of the world. The return of each communion season adds a new link to this chain; and though we shall all be laid in the grave long before its completion, yet the work will be carried on by successive generations of believers, and the Lord's supper will be observed for the last time on earth but a few days before his second coming. But for an eternity of ages after that event, the blessings which are here symbolically represented and received by faith, will continue to be enjoyed by all who ever worthily partook of the Lord's supper. My brethren, are you prepared to come and observe in a proper manner an institution so sacred, so interesting, so intimately connected with the most

important event of time, and taking hold in its consequences of the remotest ages of eternity? Can you come and by faith look back along this chain to the cross of Christ, as the foundation of your hopes, and then look forward to the end of time and see him coming in the clouds of heaven to fulfil, and more than fulfil all your hopes? Surely if you can do this, you will be ready to say with Paul, I am crucified to the world and the world to me. What have I any more to do with its idols or its perishing objects? What indeed have I to do with it, or in it, but to perform the appointed duties of my station and finish the work for which I was placed here? Too long have I run in the race with men of this world, who have their portion in this life. Too long have I been a competitor for the worthless prize which they are pursuing. But I will be so no longer. I forsake the race, I stand aside, and say, Let others pursue and obtain, if they can, the pleasures, the applause, the possessions, which this world offers to her votaries. I resign them all. I have another race to run, I have nobler objects to pursue; and to this race, to these objects, to the service of my Savior, and to the pleasures, the honors, the possessions of eternity, I now, in the presence of God, consecrate my future life and all my powers. My brethren, can you hesitate to adopt and carry into effect this language? Do not those of our number, who died the past year, now wish that they had adopted it? Could you be assured that to you the end of time will arrive before the conclusion of the present year, would you not aim to adopt it? Why not then adopt it now? He whom you call your Master requires you to be always ready, and waiting for his coming, because you know not when he will come, and because he will come at an hour when he is not expected. Is he then really your Master, or is he not? You can prove that he is, only by obeying him. Before you approach his table, then, and seal your covenant engagements afresh, inquire whether it is your present fixed purpose, to obey this command. Inquire whether you are proving that you truly repent of the sins of the past year, by sincerely resolving that you will endeavor not to bring them into the year on which you have entered.

To conclude. On the last new year's day, many, who are now gone from us, were in your situation. They sat in your seats; they heard such truths as you are now hearing; they saw the Lord's table spread before them. And now, after the lapse of one year only, one short year, they are in eternity; some of them, we hope, in heaven; others, we fear, not. Such a change, such a mighty change can one year make. And as one year since they were in your situation, so before this year closes, some of you will probably be in their's. Yes, some of you have heard the last new-year's sermon.

SERMON XLVII.

THE FEELINGS AND EMPLOYMENT OF SAINTS IN HEAVEN.

And cast their crowns before the throne.—REVELATION IV. 10.

SAINT JOHN, in this chapter, describes a vision, with which he was favored, of the heavenly world. After presenting to our view the throne of God, in the midst of which Jesus Christ appeared, as a lamb that had been slain, he proceeds to inform us by whom this throne was surrounded. Among those who surrounded it, he saw four and twenty elders, clothed in white robes, and having on their heads crowns of gold. These elders represented the whole church of Christ in its perfect and glorified state, as it will appear in heaven, after the consummation of all things. Their white robes were an emblem of the spotless purity with which it will then be adorned; while their golden crowns represent the regal dignity, the glory, honor, and immortality, with which, agreeably to the often repeated promise of our Savior, all his real disciples shall be invested in heaven. In our text the apostle informs us what use they made of these crowns. They cast them before the throne, or at the foot of the throne, on which sat the Father and the Son. This action, like every other part of the apostle's vision, was symbolical, or figurative. It is not however on that account less full of instruction. It illustrates in a very clear and striking manner, some of the principal traits in that character, which all the redeemed will possess in heaven. Let us then, endeavor to ascertain its import, together with the feelings which prompted it, and of which it was an expression.

In attempting this, it is necessary to recollect, that all the rewards, which await the righteous in heaven, are often summed up in the comprehensive expression of a kingdom. I appoint unto you a kingdom, said our Savior to his disciples, as my Father hath appointed unto me. To him that overcometh will I grant to sit with me in my throne, even as I overcame, and am seated with my Father on his throne. In allusion to these and other similar promises, St. Paul says, there is laid up for me a crown of righteousness, which the Lord, the righteous Judge, shall give me at that day; and not to me only, but to all them also which love his appearing. And in the same spirit all the redeemed in heaven are represented as saying to Christ, Thou hast made us kings unto God, and we shall reign forever and ever.* As the rewards of heaven are thus called a kingdom, and as a crown is the distinguishing badge or ornament of royalty which is worn by kings alone, it follows that, as has already been intimated, the crown mentioned in the text represented every thing which the righteous had received as a reward. Casting these crowns at the foot of the throne, was, therefore, the same as casting their kingdom, with all its dignity, glory and honor, at the feet of God and the Lamb. Hence it is easy to perceive the import of this action and the feelings which prompted it. In the first place, it was an acknowledgment of what God is, and of what he deserves from his creatures. The Scriptures inform us that he is one, of whom, and through whom, and to whom are all things. All things are of him, as their Creator, and First Cause; all things are through him, as they are preserved, sustained and affected by his constant agency; and all things are to him, as they are designed for his pleasure and glory. Of all these truths the action, which we are contemplating, was an acknowledgment. They who performed it, declared by its performance, a full, heart-felt conviction, that all which they were, and all which they possessed, was from God, and that therefore all ought to be rendered to him alone; that all the streams which issued from this fountain ought to flow back to it again. Were there any doubt that such was in fact the import of this action, the language with which it was accompanied must remove it. While they cast their crowns before the throne, they exclaimed, Thou art worthy, O Lord, to receive glory, and honor, and power; for thou hast made all things, and for thy pleasure they are, and were created. And as they uttered this ascription, they cast themselves also before the throne; thus in effect saying, From thee, O Lord, we derived all that we are, and all that we possess; and to thee, therefore, we bring it back. To thee belongs all glory, and honor, and power, and to thee therefore we ascribe it. And while this action expressed a general acknowledgment, that all glory is due to God, it implied a more particular acknowledgment, that to him all the glory of their salvation belonged. It was as if they had said, From thee, O Lord, we have received these crowns; but we are wholly unworthy of them; to thee alone they belong; for by thy sovereign grace alone were we prepared for them; by thy grace alone were we enabled to perform the good work which thou hast been pleased thus to reward; and by thy grace were we brought to the enjoyment of these rewards. Grace prompted the plan of our salvation, and grace carried it into execution. Grace prepared for us a Savior, and chose us in him before the foundation of the world; grace inclined us to choose, and to follow the Savior thus provided; and grace has finally crowned us with eternal glories. To thy grace then, O our God, thy free, rich, sovereign, distinguishing grace, belongs all the glory of our salvation, and to that grace we ascribe it. In all that we offer, or can offer, we do but present thee with that which is thine own. Not one gem in these celestial crowns belongs to us; not one will we retain. Thou art all in all, and we are nothing; nothing but shadows painted by thy beams, nothing but sinful dust and ashes, deserving of everlasting destruction, whom thou hast rescued, pardoned, sanctified, preserved, and raised to glory.

Having thus considered the import of this action, let us attend, in the second place, to the feelings which prompted it, and of which it was an expression.

In the first place, it was prompted by, it was an expression of, perfect humility. This quality has never existed on earth in perfection, except while our Savior resided here, since the fall. Ever since the fall, man has been a proud creature. Indeed the exercise of pride was one essential part of his fall. Not content with the honor and immortality with which he was crowned, he proudly desired to become as a god, knowing good and evil. The same proud disposition has ever since constituted a principal feature in the character of fallen man. It essentially consists in a disposition to exalt and arrogate glory to ourselves, and thus withhold it from him to whom alone it is due. Hence the constant struggle which has ever existed among fallen men for pre-eminence. Hence the love and desire for the chief room, and the uppermost seats. Hence, too, the little success which attends the preaching of the gospel. Pride forms the principal obstacle which exists in the heart of man to the reception of its humbling doctrines. And even after the pride of the heart is so far subdued as to admit these doctrines, it still maintains its existence, and occasions the Christian more trouble than all other sinful propensities united. It is the very last of his internal enemies, over which he obtains any victory; and many, many victories does it previously obtain over him. In his breast it usually assumes the form of spiritual pride, the most absurd and detestable form which it can assume. An exemplification of it in this form we see in our Savior's first disciples. It prompted their frequent disputes respecting the question who should be the greatest in the kingdom of heaven. It prompted the request made by two of them, that they might sit, one on the right hand, and the other on the left of our Savior, in his kingdom. In a thousand similar ways it has operated in the hearts of Christians ever since. If their Savior is graciously pleased to grant them any peculiar, though yet wholly undeserved manifestations of his love; to favor them with any unusual consolation, to furnish them with more than ordinary gifts for the benefit of the church, or to crown their endeavors to do good with success, immediately this busy sin begins to operate; self-complacent thoughts and feelings begin to rise; and a vain, wicked elation of mind ensues, which obliges their generous benefactor either to withdraw his gifts, or embitter them with some attendant infirmity or affliction. Thus even St. Paul himself, after being favored with a rapture into the third heaven, was obliged to have a thorn in the flesh, a messenger of Satan to buffet him, lest he should be exalted above measure. In Christians of smaller attainments, favors incomparably less than he enjoyed, are sufficient to exalt them above measure, and to make a thorn in the flesh necessary for their humiliation. The exercise of more than ordinary generosity, or a little more than usual fluency and fervency in prayer, or one instance of conversion effected by their instrumentality, may produce such consequences. Nay, they may be proud even of their humility, proud of the manner in which they confess, and of the earnestness with which they pray against the operations of pride. To this fruitful, accursed source of mischief must be also ascribed, all the discontent and mournings of which they are guilty; for a man free from pride would be always contented and thankful; all the censorious remarks which they make respecting others, for a perfectly humble man can never be censorious; all the dissensions which prevail among Christians; for only by pride cometh contention. This evil farther leads them to overrate their own attainments, conceals from them their deficiencies, and thus in various ways retards their progress. Nothing is a greater obstacle to prayer than pride; nothing more effectually prevents us from receiving answers to prayer; for why should God bestow further favor upon one who is proud of those which he has already received? Should any of you my hearers, employ a servant to carry your alms to the poor, and should you find that he appropriated part of the money designed for this purpose to his own use, or that he gave it to your pensioners in his own name, and thus diverted their gratitude from you to himself, would you not cease to employ him? And can we then wonder that God should withhold his gifts from those who make use of them to nourish pride, and who take part of the glory of them, to themselves? Indeed this is the grand reason why we receive so little. God is abundantly able to give, willing to give, disposed to give his people far more than they receive; but he is obliged to withhold from them his gifts, to hide his face from them, to turn his smiles into frowns, lest their pride should be increased. But this pride must all be left behind forever, when they leave the body. No particle of it will ascend with them to heaven. There they will have no wish for the chief places, no desire for admiration and applause. There they will keep back no part of the glory which belongs to their Creator and Redeemer; but, like their representatives seen by John in the vision before us, will cast their crowns and tnemselves, without the least reserve, before the throne of God and the Lamb. Nothing within them will say, I was saved because I deserved salvation. Nothing in them will say, we were in part the authors of our own salvation; but the language of every heart will be, My salvation was wholly of the Lord. Jesus is the author, the finisher, and rewarder of my faith.

In the second place, the action which we are contemplating, expressed, and was prompted by perfect love to God and the Redeemer. Not the understandings only but the hearts of those who performed it, said, God is infinitely lovely, infinitely worthy of all the affection which we can feel, of every proof of affection which we can offer. Now I need not inform you that every man will choose to crown or adorn that object which he best loves. Naturally the object which every man best loves is himself. Hence he wishes to crown, adorn, exalt himself. Thus pride springs from selfishness, and the one is always in exact proportion to the other. But every Christian begins, when he becomes such, to love God supremely. Of course he begins to wish that God may be glorified and exalted. But in the present life, this love, and, of course, its effects are not perfect. As there is some pride, so there is some selfishness, in the heart of the most holy Christian on earth. But in heaven there is none. There the redeemed love God perfectly, love him with all their heart, and soul, and mind, and strength; love him far better than they love themselves. Of course their whole desire is to glorify and exalt him. They are far better pleased to see their crowns at his feet than upon their own heads. At his feet, therefore, they cast them, and in performing this action express, in the most striking manner, perfect love.

In the third place, this action was prompted by, and expressed perfect gratitude. The natural effect of gratitude for favors received, is a wish to make some return for those favors; and to make such return is, of course, its natural expression. The more numerous and valuable these returns are, the greater is the gratitude which prompted them presumed to be. Look then, at the return which these redeemed spirits make to God for his goodness. They bring themselves, their crowns, all that they are, and all that they have, and cast it at his feet. The language of this action is, Lord, we would fain make some return for all thy goodness to us. But we have nothing except what thou hast given us. All this we bring to thee, and consecrate it without reserve to thy service. Did we possess more, we would consecrate it to the same use. It is enough for us to see and promote thy glory, to be instruments of thy pleasure, and to have thee accept our worthless services, our inadequate returns.

Lastly. This action expresses the most profound reverence. Had they felt nothing more than love and gratitude, they might have attempted to place their crowns on the head, or at least in the hands of him who was the object of these affections. But they regarded him also with the most awful veneration. This they expressed by casting their crowns at his feet. It was as if they had said, that which is the brightest ornament of our heads, is barely worthy to lie at the feet of Jehovah. At his feet we ourselves are scarcely worthy to be. But since he permits us to be there, we esteem that place as the highest honor we can enjoy, and prefer it to all earthly thrones, prefer it even to a throne in heaven without our God.

Reflections.—1. From this subject it may easily be made to appear that the views and feelings of Christians in this world resemble those of the redeemed in heaven, and differ from them not at all in kind, but only in degree. They resemble them just as the opening blossoms and immature fruit of a tree, resemble the perfectly ripe fruit of the same tree. Every Christian, who has listened to these remarks, can scarcely fail to have felt a consciousness, that he possesses in some degree the views and feelings which have now been described. He feels something of the same love to his God and Redeemer, of the same gratitude for his goodness, the same reverence for his character, which are manifested by his brethren made perfect in heaven; and he is so far possessed of humility, as to be sensible and ashamed of his pride, and to hate and pray and struggle against it. He also expresses these feelings in a similar manner. He ascribes, he loves to ascribe glory to God, and the Lamb, and he wishes to ascribe it to them more perfectly. He wishes to cast himself, and all that he possesses, without reserve, at their feet; and he is ashamed, he feels self-abhorrence, he repents, when he finds himself withholding any part of their due. Never is he so happy, as in those favored moments when he can make the nearest approaches to the temper, and engage most earnestly in the employments of the heavenly world. How plain, how undeniably evident then is it, that he is preparing for that world and destined to enjoy it. He is here in the school of Christ, going through a course of education to fit him for it. This course will be completed, and as soon as it is completed he shall be raised to join those who have passed before him through the Christian seminary, and whose education for heaven is finished. Hence,

2. Every one present may easily learn whether he belongs to this happy, highly favored number. In order to ascertain this, you have only to inquire whether you are conscious of possessing views and feelings similar to those which have now been described; whether you possess a kindred spirit with those celestial beings who are now casting themselves and their crowns before the throne of the Eternal; whether, while you contemplate them, your hearts say, Were I among them, and possessed of a crown like them, I well know what use I should choose and rejoice to make of it; and especially whether you prove the sincerity, the reality of these feelings by aiming to glorify God on earth, and cast yourselves and all that you possess at his feet. If so, you do indeed belong to the family, a branch of which we have been contemplating, and ere long you shall be among them, wear a robe and crown like them, and with them exultingly cast it before the throne. And remember the more you do for God in this world, the brighter will your celestial crown be. And will you not wish it to be bright, when you cast it at the feet of the Redeemer? Will you not wish to be able to make large returns for all his favors? Can you be contented that your crown should be the least glorious of all which will be cast before him? If not, daily strive to brighten it now. Every good work which you perform, every acceptable prayer which you offer, every right feeling which you exercise, every sincere attempt to grow in grace and knowledge, will add one to the gems which adorn it, and help to render it less unworthy of being cast at your Redeemer's feet.

3. How evident does it appear from this subject, that no self-righteous character, no one who trusts in himself, or in his own merits for salvation is preparing for heaven, or possesses any thing of its spirit, or without a change in his disposition can be admitted there. Such a man, instead of casting the crown at the feet of Christ, places it on his own head, and wears it there; and there he would wear it even could he enter heaven. He

has none of the views, none of the feelings, which animate its humble inhabitants in performing the action before us. Indeed, according to his views, it would be perfectly proper that he should wear it; for if he gains it by his own wisdom, strength and goodness, why should he not retain it? who, besides himself, has any right to it? He has fairly won and therefore ought to wear it. But no such self-won crowns will ever be seen in heaven. All the crowns which will ever be seen there, are crowns which Christ merited, and which his grace assisted his people to obtain. All the white robes ever seen there, will be robes which were washed and made white, not by our tears, nor in any fountain which human wisdom ever opened but in the blood of Christ; the fountain in which all may wash and be clean.

Finally. Let us now, my professing friends, while we come around the table of our Lord, endeavor to render this place, as much as possible, like heaven, by imitating the temper of heaven. This table is an earthly representation of the rainbow-encircled throne, which John saw in vision. Here our God and Saviour sits on a mercy seat to accept our vows and offerings. Bring yourselves then, and all that you possess, as an offering, and with love, gratitude, humility, and reverence, cast it down at his feet. Thus by anticipating the employments of heaven, you will be increasingly prepared to join in them; you will carry away more of a heavenly spirit, and will obtain fresh courage to maintain your Christain warfare, animated by the assurance, that neither selfishness, nor pride, nor any other enemy, which now assails you and defiles your services, shall be able to follow you to heaven.

www.ingramcontent.com/pod-product-compliance
Lightning Source LLC
LaVergne TN
LVHW021106110826
845150LV00001B/181

* 9 7 8 1 4 2 5 5 6 5 1 0 7 *